DIETERLY

Motivation
and Work Behavior

McGRAW-HILL SERIES IN MANAGEMENT

KEITH DAVIS, CONSULTING EDITOR

Motivation
and Work Behavior

Richard M. Steers
University of Oregon

Lyman W. Porter
University of California, Irvine

McGraw-Hill Book Company

New York
St. Louis
San Francisco
Auckland
Düsseldorf
Johannesburg
Kuala Lumpur
London
Mexico
Montreal
New Delhi
Panama
Paris
São Paulo
Singapore
Sydney
Tokyo
Toronto

Motivation and Work Behavior

1 2 3 4 5 6 7 8 9 0 K P K P 7 9 8 7 6 5

This book was set in Times Roman by National ShareGraphics, Inc.
The editors were Thomas H. Kothman and Michael Weber;
the cover was designed by Anne Canevari Green;
the production supervisor was Charles Hess.
The drawings were done by J & R Services, Inc.
Kingsport Press, Inc., was printer and binder.

Library of Congress Cataloging in Publication Data

Steers, Richard M   comp.
    Motivation and work behavior.

    (McGraw-Hill series in management)
    Includes indexes.
    1. Motivation (Psychology) 2. Psychology, Industrial. I. Porter, Lyman W., joint comp. II. Title.
HF5548.8.S719   658.31'4   74–31413
ISBN 0–07–060940–3

Contents

Preface

The interest in and study of motivation in work organizations has escalated dramatically in recent years. If we consider the level of knowledge and research in the area just twenty years ago, we can see that it largely consisted of classic, though singular, efforts to set forth some basic theoretical generalizations based on only fragmentary research data. Beginning in the early 1960s, however, interest in motivational problems of organizations increased significantly, and this trend has continued into the 1970s. It is difficult to pick up a current research journal in organizational behavior, industrial psychology, or the general area of management without finding at least one selection dealing with motivational problems at work.

Such intense interest in the field is a healthy sign that increased knowledge will be gained on this important topic. Simultaneously, however, a potential problem exists in ensuring that the various research efforts are somehow integrated and synthesized so that we can maximize our understanding of the main issues involved. This book is largely the result of our concern for this potential problem. Several major theories of motivation have been "floating around" over the past decade, but few attempts have been made to study them in a comparative fashion. Moreover, while a great deal has been written concerning the relation of motivational processes to various other important organizational factors (such as leadership, group dynamics, and so on), this literature has also been largely fragmentary. Our hope in organizing this book, then, is to bring together in one volume the major contemporary theories, research, and applications in the area of motivation and work behavior.

It is our belief that a thorough knowledge of motivation as it affects organizational processes requires at least three important inputs. First, the reader must gain a general knowledge of what is meant by the concept of motivation, as well as of historical approaches to the study of motivation. Moreover, the reader needs a fairly comprehensive framework for analyzing the various theories and applications that exist. We have attempted to deal with these matters in Part One of the book. Second, it is our contention that the serious student of motivation must be conversant with the major theories that exist in the field today. These theories—and the research associated with them—are described in Part Two. Finally, we feel that theories alone are of little value unless the student can understand how motivational processes relate to other organizational variables. Such interrelationships are covered in detail in Parts Three and Four. In addition, Part Four attempts to review and synthesize what has been learned concerning the role of motivation in organizational settings.

The approach taken here is to integrate text materials with selections authored by some of the foremost scholars in the field. The major focus in the text and readings is on a blend of theoretical formulations with practical applications. Thus, chapters generally contain some major theoretical propositions, some research evidence relevant to the theories, and some examples of how such models have been or could be applied in existing organizations. Futhermore, each chapter contains suggested additional readings for students desiring a greater in-depth study of a particular topic, as well as questions to stimulate discussion and analysis of the major issues.

This book is designed primarily for students of organizational behavior, industrial psychology, and general management. It should also be useful for managers who wish to gain an increased understanding of problems of work motivation. It is assumed that the reader has had some previous exposure to organizational behavior, perhaps through an introductory course. This book attempts to build upon such knowledge and to analyze general organizational processes, using the concept of motivation as the basic unit of analysis.

We wish to express our sincere appreciation to all those who have contributed to the realization of this project. In particular, our thanks go to Daniel N. Braunstein, Richard T. Mowday, and Eugene F. Stone for their helpful comments and suggestions on earlier drafts of the manuscript. We are also indebted to Rita Edwards and Dan Centurione for their valuable assistance in preparing the manuscript for publication. In addition, we are grateful to our respective schools for providing stimulating motivational environments in which to work. Finally, a special note of appreciation is due our wives, Sheila and Meredith, for their support and encouragement throughout the project.

Richard M. Steers
Lyman W. Porter

Motivation
and Work Behavior

Part One

Initial Considerations

Chapter 1

The Role of Motivation in Organizations

The topic of motivation at work has received considerably increased attention in recent years among both practicing managers and organizational researchers. One has only to ask first-level supervisors what their most taxing work problems are for evidence of the importance of the concept to management, and one can observe the greater preponderance of empirical articles relating to the topic in recent psychological and management journals for evidence of its importance to researchers. Several factors appear to account for the emergence of this topic as a focal point of interest.

To begin with, managers and organizational researchers have recently begun to direct more attention toward the *behavioral* requirements of an organization. In addition to the need for financial and physical resources, every organization requires people in order to function. More specifically, Katz and Kahn (1966) have posited that organizations have three behavioral requirements in this regard: (1) people must be attracted not only to join the organization but also to remain in it; (2) people must perform the tasks for which they are hired, and must do so in a dependable manner; and (3) people must go beyond this dependable role performance and engage in some form of creative, spontaneous, and innovative behavior at work (Katz, 1964; Katz & Kahn, 1966). In other words, for an organization to be effective, according to this reasoning, it must come to grips with the motivational problems of stimulating both the decision to participate and the decision to produce at work (March & Simon, 1958).

A second and related reason behind the increased attention being directed toward motivation centers around the pervasive nature of the concept itself. Motivation as a concept represents a highly complex phenomenon that affects, and is affected by, a multitude of factors in the organizational milieu. A comprehensive understanding of the way in which organizations function requires that at least some attention be directed toward the question of why people behave as they do on the job (that is, the determinants of employee work behavior *and* the ramifications of such behavior for an organization). An understanding of the topic of motivation is thus essential in order to comprehend more fully the effects of variations in other factors (such as leadership style, job redesign, and salary systems) as they relate to performance, satisfaction, and so forth.

Third, given the ever-tightening constraints placed on organizations by unions, governmental agencies, increased foreign and domestic competition, citizens' lobbies, and the like, management has had to look for new mechanisms to increase—and in some cases just to maintain—its level of organizational effectiveness and efficiency. Much of the "slack" that organizations could depend upon in the past is rapidly disappearing in the face of these new environmental type of constraints. Because of this, management must ensure that it is deriving full potential benefit from those resources—including human resources—that it does have at its disposal. Thus, organizational effectiveness becomes to some degree a question of management's ability to motivate its employees to direct at least a reasonable effort toward the goals of the organization.

A fourth reason can be found in the nature of present and future technology required for production. As technology increases in complexity, machines tend to become necessary *yet insufficient* vehicles of effective and efficient operations. Modern technology can no longer be considered synonomous with the term "automation." Consider the example of the highly technologically based space program in the United States. While mastery of the technological and mechanical aspects of aerospace engineering was requisite for placing a man on the moon or for developing Skylab, a second and equally important ingredient was the ability of an organization (in this case NASA) to bring together thousands of employees who would work at peak capacity to *apply* the technology required for success. In other words, it becomes necessary for an organization to ensure that it has employees who are both capable of using—*and willing to use*—the advanced technology to achieve organizational objectives.

Finally, while organizations have for some time viewed their financial and physical resources from a long-term perspective, only recently have they begun seriously to apply this same perspective to their human resources. Many organizations are now beginning to pay increasing attention to developing their employees as future resources (a "talent bank") upon which they can draw as they grow and develop. Evidence for such concern can be seen in the recent growth of management and organization development programs, in the increased popularity of "assessment center" appraisals, in recent attention to manpower planning, and in the emergence of "human resource accounting" systems. More concern is being directed, in addition, toward stimulating employees to enlarge their job skills (through training, job design, job rotation, and so on) at both the blue-collar and the white-collar levels in an effort to ensure a continual reservoir of well-trained and highly motivated people.

In summary, then, there appear to be several reasons why the topic of motivation is receiving greater attention by both those who study organizations and those who manage them. The old simplistic, prescriptive guidelines concerning "economic man" are simply no longer sufficient as a basis for understanding human behavior at work. New approaches and greater understanding are called for to deal with the complexities of contemporary organizations.

Toward this end, this book will attempt to assist the serious student of motivation to obtain a more comprehensive and empirically based knowledge of motivation at work. This will be done through a combination of explanatory text and readings on current theories, research, and applications in the field. Before discussing some of the more current approaches to motivation, however, some consideration is in order concerning the nature of basic motivational processes. This consideration is followed by a brief history of early psychological and managerial approaches to the topic. Finally, a conceptual framework is presented to aid in the comprehension and evaluation of the various theories and models that follow. Throughout this book, emphasis is placed on the comparative approach; that is, we are primarily concerned with similarities among—and differences between—the various theories and models rather than with the presentation and defense of one particular theory. Such an approach should allow readers to draw their own conclusions as to which theory they feel is most suitable for their needs. Moreover, because of the pervasive nature of the topic, we feel that the concept of motivation can best be understood only by considering its role as it affects—and is affected by—other important variables which constitute the work environment. Thus, special emphasis is placed throughout on the study of *relationships* between major variables (for example, motivation as it relates to leadership and productivity) rather than on the simple enumeration of facts or theories.

THE NATURE OF MOTIVATION

The term "motivation" was originally derived from the Latin word *movere,* which means "to move." However, this one word is obviously an inadequate definition for our purposes here. What is needed is a description which sufficiently covers the various aspects inherent in the process by which human behavior is activated. A brief selection of representative definitions indicates how the term has been used:

. . . the contemporary (immediate) influences on the direction, vigor, and persistence of action. (Atkinson, 1964)

. . . how behavior gets started, is energized, is sustained, is directed, is stopped, and what kind of subjective reaction is present in the organism while all this is going on. (Jones, 1955)

. . . a process governing choices made by persons or lower organisms among alternative forms of voluntary activity. (Vroom, 1964)

A motive is an inner state that energizes, activates, or moves (hence, "motivation"), and that directs or channels behavior toward goals. (Berelson & Steiner, 1964)

. . . to steer one's actions toward certain goals and to commit a certain part of one's energies to reaching them. (Gellerman, 1968)

A motive is a restlessness, a lack, a yen, a force. Once in the grip of a motive, the organism does something. It most generally does something to reduce the restlessness, to remedy the lack, to alleviate the yen, to mitigate the force. (Sanford & Wrightsman, 1970)

These definitions appear generally to have three common denominators which may be said to characterize the phenomenon of motivation. That is, when we discuss motivation, we are primarily concerned with: (1) what energizes human behavior; (2) what directs or channels such behavior; and (3) how this behavior is maintained or sustained. Each of these three components represents an important factor in our understanding of human behavior at work. First, this conceptualization points to an energetic force within individuals that "drives" them to behave in certain ways. Second, there is the notion of goal orientation on the part of individuals; their behavior is directed *toward* something. Third, this way of viewing motivation contains a *systems orientation*; that is, it considers those forces in the individuals and in their surrounding environments that feed back into the individuals either to reinforce the intensity of their drive and the direction of their energy or to dissuade them from their course of action and redirect their efforts. These three components of motivation appear again and again in the theories and research that follow.

THE MOTIVATIONAL PROCESS: BASIC CONSIDERATIONS

Building upon this definition, we can now diagram a *general* model of the motivational process. While such a model is an oversimplification of far more complex relationships, it should serve here to represent schematically the major sets of variables involved in the process. Later, we can add to this model to depict how additional factors may affect human behavior at work.

The basic building blocks of a generalized model of motivation are: (1) needs or expectations; (2) behavior; (3) goals; and (4) some form of feedback. The interaction of these variables is shown in Exhibit 1. Basically, this model posits that individuals possess in varying strengths a multitude of needs, desires, and expectations. For example, they may have a high need for affiliation, a

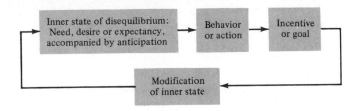

Exhibit 1 A generalized model of the basic motivation process. (*After Dunnette & Kirchner, 1965.*)

strong desire for additional income, or an expectation that increased effort on the job would lead to a promotion. These "activators" are generally characterized by two phenomena. First, the emergence of such a need, desire, or expectation generally creates a state of disequilibrium within the individuals which they will try to reduce; hence, the energetic component of our definition above. Second, the presence of such needs, desires, or expectations is generally associated with an anticipation or belief that certain actions will lead to the reduction of this disequilibrium; hence, the goal-orientation component of our definition.

In theory, the following is presumed to be the chain of events: Based on some combination of this desire to reduce the internal state of disequilibrium and the anticipation or belief that certain actions should serve this purpose, individuals act or behave in a certain manner that they believe will lead to the desired goal. The initiation of this action then sets up a series of cues, either within the individuals or from their external environment, which feeds information back to the individuals concerning the impact of their behavior. Such cues may lead them to modify (or cease) their present behavior or they may reassure them that their present course of action is correct.

An example should clarify this process. Individuals who have a strong desire to be with others (that is, have a high "need for affiliation") may attempt to increase their interactions with those around them (behavior) in the hope of gaining their friendship and support (goal). Based on these interactions, they may eventually reach a point where they feel they have enough friends and may then direct their energies toward other goals. Or, conversely, they may receive consistent negative feedback that informs them that their behavior is not successful for goal attainment and they may then decide to modify such behavior. In either case, we can see the important moderating function of feedback on subsequent behavior and goals.

At least two types of human behavior can be identified as they relate to motivational processes: instrumental and consummatory (Birch & Veroff, 1966). Instrumental behavior concerns acts that are directed toward the *means* to certain ends, while consummatory behavior concerns acts that are directed toward the *ends* themselves. Take the example of a thirsty person seeking a drink of water. The pursuit of the water represents instrumental behavior (that is, it is not an end in itself), while the act of drinking the water, once found, represents a consummatory act (that is, an end in itself). However, it should be noted that, in some instances, it is difficult to distinguish which type of behavior a given act represents. For example, a person who works hard and puts in a considerable amount of overtime on the job may do so either because he or she wants the added income to buy a new car (an instrumental act) or simply because he or she enjoys working (a consummatory act). Birch and Veroff (1966) point out a further distinction between these two forms of behavior: the intensity of instrumental behavior generally persists or even increases as such behavior occurs, while the intensity of consummatory behavior tends to diminish as it occurs, at least until the need prompting such behavior again becomes manifest. That is, to use the above example, a person *seeking* water (instrumental behavior) will continue to seek it until it is found, while a person *drinking* the water (consummatory behavior) will eventually feel a lessening desire for the water, at least until he or she is thirsty again.

The general model of the motivational process appears fairly simple and straightforward. Such is not the case, however. Several complexities exist which tend to complicate the theoretical simplicity. Dunnette and Kirchner (1965) and others have identified four such complications. First, motives can really only be *inferred;* they cannot be seen. Thus, when we observe individuals putting in a great deal of overtime, we really do not know whether they are doing it because of the extra income they receive or simply because they enjoy their work. In fact, at least five reasons have been identified for why it is difficult to infer motives from observed behavior: (1) any single act may express several motives; (2) motives may appear in disguised forms; (3) several motives may be expressed through similar or identical acts; (4) similar motives may be expressed in different behavior; and (5) cultural and personal variations may significantly moderate the modes of expression of certain motives (Hilgard & Atkinson, 1967).

A second complication of the model centers around the dynamic nature of motives. Any individual at any one time usually has a host of needs, desires, and expectations. Not only do these motives change but they may also be in conflict with each other. A desire to put in extra hours at the office to "get ahead" may be in direct conflict with a desire to spend more time with one's family. Thus, given the changing nature of an individual's particular set of motives, and given their often conflicting nature, it becomes exceedingly difficult to observe or measure them with much certainty.

Third, considerable differences can exist among individuals concerning the manner in which they select certain motives over others and the intensity with which they pursue such motives. A salesperson who has a strong need for achievement may in large measure satisfy this need by one big sale and then turn his or her attention to other needs or desires. A second salesperson, however, may be spurred on by such a sale to increase his or her achievement motive and to try for an even bigger sale in the near future. Or, as found by Atkinson and Reitman (1956), a high need for achievement may be related to performance only when certain other needs (such as need for affiliation) were not aroused. In other words, it is important to realize that individual differences exist among employees which can significantly affect what they desire and how they pursue such desires.

A final complication of the model is the impact of goal attainment on subsequent motives and behavior. The intensity of certain motives (such as hunger, thirst, sex) is generally considerably reduced upon gratification. When this happens, other motives come to the forefront as primary motivating factors. However, the attainment of certain other goals may also lead to an *increase* in the intensity of some motives. For example, as Herzberg, Mausner, and Snyderman (1959) and others have argued, giving a person a pay raise does not long "satisfy" the desire for more money: in fact, it may even heighten this desire. Similarly, promoting an employee to a new and more challenging job may intensify the drive to work harder in anticipation of the *next* promotion. Thus, while the gratification of certain needs, desires, and expectations may at times lead individuals to shift their focus of attention toward different motives, at other times such gratification can serve to increase the strength of the motive.

In conclusion, it must be remembered that the above description of motivational processes represents a very general model of human behavior. As will be seen in the following chapters, considerable research has been done in an attempt to more rigorously define the nature of the relationships between the major variables in this process, particularly as they relate to behavior in the work situation. We have reviewed this general model in an effort to provide a basic framework for the understanding and analysis of the more specific theories that follow. However, before proceeding with these theories, we shall first review very briefly some early psychological approaches to motivation, and then follow our review with a discussion of some traditional management approaches to motivating employees.

EARLY PSYCHOLOGICAL APPROACHES TO MOTIVATION

Most psychological theories of motivation, both early and contemporary, have their roots—at least to some extent—in the principle of *hedonism*.[1] This principle, briefly defined, states that individuals tend to seek pleasure and avoid pain. Hedonism assumes a certain degree of conscious behavior on the part of individuals whereby they make intentional decisions or choices concerning future actions. In theory, people rationally consider the behavioral alternatives available to them and act to maximize positive results and to minimize negative results. The concept of hedonism dates back to the early Greek philosophers; it later reemerged as a popular explanation of behavior in the eighteenth and nineteenth centuries, as seen in the works of such philosophers as Locke, Bentham, Mill, and Helvetius. Bentham even went so far as to coin the term "hedonic calculus" in 1789 to describe the process by which individuals calculate the pros and cons of various acts of behavior.

Toward the end of the nineteenth century, motivation theory began moving

---

[1] For a more detailed discussion of early psychological models of motivation, see Cofer & Appley (1964) and Atkinson (1964).

from the realm of philosophy toward the more empirically based science of psychology. As consideration of this important topic grew, it became apparent to those who attempted to use the philosophically based concept of hedonism that several serious problems existed. Vroom explained this dilemma as follows:

> There was in the doctrine no clear-cut specification of the types of events which were pleasurable or painful, or even how these events could be determined for a particular individual; nor did it make clear how persons acquired their conceptions of ways of attaining pleasure and pain, or how the source of pleasure and pain might be modified by experience. In short the hedonistic assumption has no empirical content and was untestable. Any form of behavior could be explained, after the fact, by postulating particular sources of pleasure or pain, but no form of behavior could be predicted in advance [1964, p. 10]

In an effort to fill in this void, several theories of motivation began evolving which attempted to formulate empirically verifiable relationships among sets of variables which could be used to predict behavior. The earliest such theory centered around the concept of instinct.

Instinct Theories

While not rejecting the notion of hedonism, psychologists like James, Freud, and McDougall argued that a more comprehensive explanation of behavior was necessary than simply assuming a rational person pursuing his or her own best interest. In short, they posited that two additional variables were crucial to our understanding of behavior: instinct and unconscious motivation.

Instead of seeing behavior as being highly rational, these theorists saw much of it as resulting from instinct. McDougall, writing in 1908, defined an instinct as "an inherited or innate psychophysical disposition which determines its possessor to perceive, or pay attention to, objects of a certain class, to experience an emotional excitement of a particular quality upon perceiving such an object, and to act in regard to it in a particular manner, or at least, to experience an impulse to such an action." However, while McDougall saw instinct as purposive and goal directed, other instinct theorists, like James, defined the concept more in terms of blind and mechanical action. James (1890) included in his list of instincts the following: locomotion, curiosity, sociability, love, fear, jealousy, and sympathy. Each person was thought by James and McDougall to have such instincts in greater or lesser degree and these instincts were thought to be the prime determinants of behavior. In other words, individuals were seen as possessing automatic *predispositions* to behave in certain ways, depending on internal and external cues.

The second major concept associated with instinct theories is that of unconscious motivation. While the notion of unconscious motivation is implicit in the writings of James, it was Freud (1915) who most ardently advocated the existence of such a phenomenon. Based upon his clinical observations, Freud argued that the most potent behavioral tendencies were not necessarily those that individuals *consciously* determined would be in their best interests. Individuals were not always aware of all of their desires and needs. Rather, such unconscious phenomena as dreams, slips of the tongue ("Freudian slips"), and neurotic symptoms were seen by Freud as manifestations of the hedonistic principle on an *unconscious* level. Thus, a major factor in human motivation was seen here as resulting from forces unknown even to the individual himself.

The instinct theory of motivation was fairly widely accepted during the first quarter of this century. Then, beginning in the early 1920s, it came under increasing attack on several grounds (Hilgard & Atkinson, 1967; Morgan & King, 1966). First, there was the disturbing fact that the list of instincts continued to grow, reaching nearly six thousand in number. The sheer length of such a list seriously jeopardized any attempt at parsimony in the explanation of motivation. Second, the contention that individuals varied greatly in the strengths or intensities of their motivational dispositions was becoming increasingly accepted among psychologists, adding a further complication to the ability of instinct theory to fully explain behavior. Third, some researchers found that at times there may be little relation between the strengths of certain motives and subsequent behavior. Fourth, some psychologists came to question whether the unconscious motives as described by Freud were really instinctive or whether they were *learned* behavior. In fact, this fourth criticism formed the basis of the second "school" of motivation theorists who later became known as "drive" theorists.

Drive Theories

Researchers who have been associated with drive theory typically base their work on the influence that learning has on subsequent behavior. Thus, such theories have a historical component which led Allport (1954) to refer to them as "hedonism of the past"; that is, drive theories generally assume that decisions concerning present behavior are based in large part on the consequences or rewards of past behavior. Where past actions led to positive consequences, individuals would tend to repeat such actions; where past actions led to negative consequences or punishment, individuals would tend to avoid repeating them. This position was first elaborated by Thorndike in his "law of effect." Basing his "law" on experimental observations of animal behavior, Thorndike posited:

> Of several responses made to the same situation, those which are accompanied or closely followed by satisfaction to the animal will, other things being equal, be more firmly connected with the situation, so that when it recurs, they will be more likely to occur; those which are accompanied or closely followed by discomfort to the animal will, other things being equal, have their connections with that situation weakened, so that when it recurs, they will be less likely to occur. The greater the satisfaction or discomfort, the greater is the strengthening or weakening of the bond [1911, p. 244].

While this law of effect did not explain why some actions were pleasurable or satisfying and others were not, it did go a long way toward setting forth an empirically verifiable theory of motivation. Past learning and previous "stimulus-response" connections were viewed as the major causal variables of behavior.

The term "drive" was first introduced by Woodworth (1918) to describe the reservoir of energy that impels an organism to behave in certain ways. While Woodworth intended the term to mean a general supply of energy within organism, others soon modified this definition to refer to a host of specific energizers (such as hunger, thirst, sex) toward or away from certain goals. With the introduction of the concept of drive, it now became possible for psychologists to predict in advance—at least in theory—not only what goals an individual would strive toward but also the strength of the motivation toward such goals. Thus, it became feasible for researchers to attempt to test the theory in a fairly rigorous fashion, a task that was virtually impossible for the earlier theories of hedonism and instinct.

A major theoretical advance in drive theory came from the work of Cannon in the early 1930s. Cannon (1939) introduced the concept of "homeostasis" to describe a state of disequilibrium within an organism which existed whenever internal conditions deviated from their normal state. When such disequilibrium occurred (as when an organism felt hunger), the organism was motivated by internal drives to reduce the disequilibrium and to return to its normal state. Inherent in Cannon's notion was the idea that organisms exist in a dynamic environment and that the determining motives for behavior constantly change, depending upon where the disequilibrium exists within the system. Thus, certain drives, or motives, may move to the forefront and then, one satisfied, retreat while other drives become paramount. This concept can be seen to a large extent in the later works of Maslow and Murray (see Chapters 2 and 3).

The first comprehensive—and experimentally specific—elaboration of drive theory was put forth by Hull. In his major work *Principles of Behavior,* published in 1943, Hull set down a specific equation to explain an organism's "impetus to respond": Effort = Drive × Habit. "Drive" was defined by Hull as an energizing influence which determined the intensity of behavior, and which theoretically increased along with the level of deprivation. "Habit" was seen as the strength of relationship between past stimulus and response (S-R). Hull hypothesized that habit strength depended not only upon the closeness of the S-R event to reinforcement but also upon the magnitude and number of such reinforcements. Thus, Hull's concept of habit draws very heavily upon Thorndike's law of effect. Hull argued that resulting effort, or motivational force, was a *multiplicative* function of these two central variables.

If we apply Hull's theory to an organization setting, we can use the following example to clarify how drive theory would be used to predict behavior. A person who has been out of work for some time (high deprivation level) would generally have a strong need or desire to seek some means to support himself or herself (goal). If, based upon *previous* experience, this person draws a close association between the securing of income and the act of taking a job, we would expect him or her to search ardently for employment. Thus, the motivation to seek employment would be seen, according to this theory, as a multiplicative function of the intensity of the need for money (drive) and the strength of the feeling that work has been associated with the receipt of money in the past (habit).

Later, in response to empirical evidence which was inconsistent with the theory, Hull (1952) modified his position somewhat. Instead of positing that behavior was wholly a function of antecedent conditions (such as past experiences), he added an incentive variable to his equation. His later formulation thus read: Effort = Drive × Habit × Incentive. This incentive factor, added in large measure in response to the attack by the cognitive theorists (see below), was defined in terms of anticipatory reactions to future goals. It was thus hypothesized that one factor in the motivation equation was the size of, or attraction to, future potential rewards. As the size of the reward varied, so too would the motivation to seek such a reward. This major revision by Hull (as amplified by Spence, 1956) brought drive theory into fairly close agreement with the third major category of motivational theories, the cognitive theories. However, while cognitive theories have generally been applied to humans, including humans at work, drive theory research has continued by and large to study animal behavior in the laboratory. Because of this distinction, and because of the increasing popularity of cognitive theories in the study of work behavior, we will concentrate in much of the remainder of this book on this third theoretical formulation.

Cognitive Theories

The third major line of development in psychological approaches to motivation is the cognitive theories. Whereas drive theories viewed motivation largely as a function of past satisfactions (habits), cognitive theories saw it as a sort of "hedonism of the future." The basic tenet of this theory is that a major determinant of human behavior is the beliefs, expectations, and anticipations individuals have concerning future events. Behavior is thus seen as purposeful and goal directed, and based on conscious intentions.

Two of the most prominent early researchers in this field were Edward Tolman and Kurt Lewin. While Tolman studied animal behavior and Lewin human behavior, both took the position that organisms make conscious decisions concerning future behavior based on cues from their environment. Such a theory is largely *ahistorical* in nature, as opposed to the historical notion inherent in drive theory. Tolman (1932) argued, for example, that learning resulted more from changes in beliefs about the environment than from changes in the strengths of past habits. Cognitive theorists did not entirely reject the concept that past events may be important for present behavior, however. Lewin (1938), whose work is characterized by an ahistorical approach, noted that the historical and ahistorical approaches were in some ways complementary. Past occurrences could have an impact on present behavior to the extent that they modified present conditions. For example, the past experience of a child who burned a finger on a hot stove may very likely carry over into the present to influence behavior. In general, however, the cognitive theorists posit that it is the "events of the day" that largely influence behavior; past events are important only to the extent that they affect present and future beliefs and expectations.

In general, cognitive theories, or expectancy/valence theories as they later became known (see Chapter 6), view motivational force as a multiplicative function of two key variables: expectancies and valences. "Expectancies" were seen by Lewin (1938) and Tolman (1959) as beliefs individuals had that particular actions on their part would lead to certain outcomes. "Valence" denoted the amount of positive or negative value placed on the outcomes by an individual. Individuals were viewed as engaging in some form of choice behavior where they first determined the potential outcomes of various acts of behavior and the value they attached to each of these outcomes. Tolman (1959) refers to this as a "belief-value matrix." Next, individuals selected that mode of behavior which maximized their potential benefits. When put into equation form, such a formulation reads: Effort = Expectancy × Valence.

This conceptualization of the motivational process differs from drive theory in several respects. First, as has already been mentioned, while drive theory emphasizes past stimulus-response connections in the determination of present behavior, expectancy/valence theory stresses anticipation of response-outcome connections.

Second, as pointed out by Atkinson (1964), a difference exists between the two theories with regard to what is activated by a drive (in drive theory) or expectation (in expectancy/valence theory). In drive theory, the magnitude of the goal is seen as a source of *general* excitement; that is, it represents a nonselective influence on performance. In expectancy/valence theory, on the other hand, *positively* valent outcomes are seen as acting *selectively* to stimulate particular forms of behavior that should lead to these outcomes.

Third, a subtle difference exists concerning the nature in which outcomes and rewards acquire their positive or negative connotations. This difference has been described by Porter and Lawler as follows:

> For drive theory, this has traditionally come about through their ability to reduce the tension associated with the deprivation of certain physiologically based drives. It also states that some outcomes acquire their rewarding or adverse properties through their association with primary reinforcers. Outcomes that gain their values this way are typically referred to as secondary reinforcers. Expectancy theory has been much less explicit on this point. However, expectancy theorists seem typically to have included more than just physiological factors as determinants of valence. For example, needs for esteem, recognition, and self-actualization have been talked about by expectancy theory with explaining performance. Drive theory, on the other hand, has focused largely on learning rather than performance and has not found it necessary to deal with motives like self-actualization in order to explain this learning [1968, p. 11].

However, while several differences can thus be found between drive theories and cognitive theories, Atkinson (1964) has emphasized that the two approaches actually share many of the same concepts. Both stress the importance of some form of goal orientation; that is, both posit the existence of some reward or outcome that is desired and sought. Moreover, both theories include the notion of a learned connection between central variables; drive theory posits a learned stimulus-response association, while cognitive theories see a learned association between behavior and outcome.

Just as there has been an evolutionary process in psychological theories of motivation, so too have there been major developments and trends in the way managers in work organizations approach motivation in the work situation. With these general psychological theories in mind, we shall now shift our attention to the workplace and review some of these early managerial approaches to motivating employees. It will be noted in the discussion below that, although psychological and managerial models of motivation developed, roughly, during the same period, there are few signs of any cross-fertilization of ideas until very recently.

EARLY MANAGERIAL APPROACHES TO MOTIVATION AT WORK

Despite the fact that large-scale, complex organizations have existed for several hundreds of years, managerial attention to the role of motivation in such organizations is a most recent phenomenon. Before the industrial revolution, the major form of "motivation" took the form of fear of punishment—physical, financial, or social. However, as manufacturing processes became more complex, large-scale factories emerged which destroyed many of the social and exchange relationships which had existed under the "home industries," or "putting-out," system of small manufacturing. These traditional patterns of behavior between workers and their "patron" were replaced by the more sterile and tenuous relationship between employees and their company. Thus, the industrial revolution was not only a revolution in a production sense but also in a social sense.

The genesis of this *social* revolution can be traced to several factors. First, the increased capital investment necessary for factory operation required a high degree of efficiency in order to maintain an adequate return on investment. This meant that an organization had to have an efficient work force. Second, and somewhat relatedly, the sheer size of these new operations increased the degree of impersonalization in superior-subordinate relationships, necessitating new forms of supervising people. Third, and partly as a justification of the new depersonalized factory system, the concept of social Darwinism came into vogue. In brief, this philosophy argued that no person held responsibility for other people and that naturally superior people were destined to rise in society, while naturally inferior ones would eventually be selected out of it. In other words, it was "every man for himself" in the workplace.

These new social forces brought about the need for a fairly well-defined *philosophy* of management. Many of the more intrinsic motivational factors of the home industry system were replaced by more extrinsic factors. Workers—or, more specifically, "good" workers—were seen as pursuing their own best economic self-interests. The end result of this new approach in management was what has been termed the "traditional" model of motivation.

Traditional Model

This model is best characterized by the writings of Frederick W. Taylor (1911) and his associates in the scientific management school. Far from being exploitative in intent, these writers viewed scientific management as an economic boon to the worker as well as to management. Taylor saw the problem of inefficient production as a problem primarily with management, not workers. It was management's responsibility to find suitable people for a job and then to train them in the most efficient methods for their work. Having been thus well trained, management's next responsibility was to install a wage incentive system whereby workers could maximize their income by doing exactly what management told them to do and doing it as rapidly as possible. Thus, in theory, scientific management represented a joint venture of management and workers to the mutual benefit of both. If production problems arose, they could be solved either by altering the technology of the job or by modifying the wage incentive program.

This approach to motivation rested on several very basic contemporary assumptions about the nature of human beings. Specifically, workers were viewed as being typically lazy, often dishonest, aimless, dull, and, most of all, mercenary. To get them into the factories and to keep them there, an organization had to pay a "decent" wage, thus outbidding alternative forms of livelihood (e.g., farming). To get workers to produce, tasks were to be simple and repetitive, output controls were to be externally set, and workers were to be paid bonuses for beating their quotas. The manager's major task was thus seen as closely supervising workers to ensure that they met their production quotas and adhered to company rules. In short, the underlying motivational assumption of the traditional model was that, for a price, workers would tolerate the routinized, highly fractionated jobs of the factory. These assumptions and expectations, along with their implied managerial strategies, are summarized in Exhibit 2.

As this model became increasingly applied in organizations, several problems began to arise. To begin with, managers, in their quest for profits, began modifying the basic system. While jobs were made more and more routine and specialized (and "efficient" from a mass-production standpoint), management began putting severe constraints on the incentive system, thereby limiting worker income. Soon, workers discovered that, although their output was increasing, their wages were not (at least not proportionately). Simultaneously, fear of job security arose. As factories became more "efficient," fewer workers were needed to do the job and layoffs and terminations became commonplace. Workers responded to the situation through elaborate and covert methods of restriction of output in an attempt to optimize their incomes, while at the same time protecting their jobs. Unionism began to rise, and the unparalleled growth and efficiency that had occurred under scientific management began to subside.

In an effort to overcome such problems, some organizations began to reexamine the simplicity of their motivational assumptions about employees and to look for new methods to increase production and maintain a steady work force. It should be pointed out, however, that the primary economic assumption of the traditional model was not eliminated in the newer approaches and that it remains a central concept of many motivational approaches today. Recent studies among both managers and workers indicate that money is a primary motivational force and that many workers will, in fact, select jobs based more upon salary prospects

Exhibit 2   General Patterns of Managerial Approaches to Motivation (After Miles, Porter, & Craft, 1966)

Traditional model	Human relations model	Human resources model
Assumptions 1. Work is inherently distasteful to most people. 2. What they do is less important than what they earn for doing it. 3. Few want or can handle work which requires creativity, self-direction, or self-control.	**Assumptions** 1. People want to feel useful and important. 2. People desire to belong and to be recognized as individuals. 3. These needs are more important than money in motivating people to work.	**Assumptions** 1. Work is not inherently distasteful. People want to contribute to meaningful goals which they have helped establish. 2. Most people can exercise far more creative, responsible self-direction and self-control than their present jobs demand.
Policies 1. The manager's basic task is to closely supervise and control his subordinates. 2. He must break tasks down into simple, repetitive, easily learned operations. 3. He must establish detailed work routines and procedures, and enforce these firmly but fairly.	**Policies** 1. The manager's basic task is to make each worker feel useful and important. 2. He should keep his subordinates informed and listen to their objections to his plans. 3. The manager should allow his subordinates to exercise some self-direction and self-control on routine matters.	**Policies** 1. The manager's basic task is to make use of his "untapped" human resources. 2. He must create an environment in which all members may contribute to the limits of their ability. 3. He must encourage full participation on important matters, continually broadening subordinate self-direction and control.
Expectations 1. People can tolerate work if the pay is decent and the boss is fair. 2. If tasks are simple enough and people are closely controlled, they will produce up to standard.	**Expectations** 1. Sharing information with subordinates and involving them in routine decisions will satisfy their basic needs to belong and to feel important. 2. Satisfying these needs will improve morale and reduce resistance to formal authority—subordinates will "willingly cooperate."	**Expectations** 1. Expanding subordinate influence, self-direction, and self-control will lead to direct improvements in operating efficiency. 2. Work satisfaction may improve as a "by-product" of subordinates making full use of their resources.

than job content (Mahoney, 1964; Opinion Research Corporation, 1947; Opsahl & Dunnette, 1966). (See Chapter 15.) However, newer approaches have tended to view the role of money in more complex terms as it affects motivational force. Moreover, these newer theories argue that additional factors are also important inputs into the decision to produce. One such revisionist approach to motivation at work is the "human relations" model.

Human Relations Model

Beginning in the late 1920s, initial efforts were begun to discover why the traditional model was inadequate for motivating people. The earliest such work, carried out by Mayo (1933, 1945) and Roethlisberger and Dickson (1939), pointed the way to what was to become the human relations school of management by arguing that it was necessary to consider the "whole person" on the job. These researchers posited that the increased routinization of tasks brought about by the industrial revolution had served to drastically reduce the possibilities of finding satisfaction in the task itself. It was believed that, because of this change, workers began seeking satisfaction elsewhere (such as from their fellow workers). Based on this early research, some managers began replacing many of the traditional assumptions with a new set of propositions concerning the nature of human beings (see Exhibit 2). Bendix (1956, p. 294) best summarized this evolution in managerial thinking by noting that the "failure to treat workers as human beings came to be regarded as the cause of low morale, poor craftsmanship, unresponsiveness, and confusion."

The new assumptions concerning the "best" method of motivating workers were characterized by a strong social emphasis. It was argued here that management had a responsibility to make employees *feel* useful and important on the job, to provide recognition, and generally to facilitate the satisfaction of workers' social needs. Attention was shifted away from the study of man-machine relations and toward a more thorough understanding of interpersonal and group relations at work. Behavioral research into factors affecting motivation began in earnest, and morale surveys came into vogue in an attempt to measure and maintain job satisfaction. The basic ingredient that typically was *not* changed was the nature of the required tasks on the job.

The motivational strategies which emerged from such assumptions were several. First, as noted above, management felt it had a new responsibility to make workers feel important. Second, many organizations attempted to open up vertical communication channels so employees would know more about the organization and would have greater opportunity to have their opinions heard by management. Company newsletters emerged as one source of downward communication; employee "gripe sessions" were begun as one source of upward communication. Third, workers were increasingly allowed to make routine decisions concerning their own jobs. Finally, as managers began to realize the existence of informal groups with their own norms and role prescriptions, greater attention was paid to employing *group* incentive systems. Underlying all four of these developments was the presumed necessity of viewing motivation as largely a social process. Supervisory training programs began emphasizing that a supervisor's role was no longer simply that of a taskmaster. In addition, supervisors had to be understanding and sympathetic to the needs and desires of their subordinates. However, as pointed out by Miles (1965), the basic goal of management under this strategy remained much the same as it had been under the traditional model; that is, both strategies aimed at securing employee compliance with managerial authority.

Human Resources Models

More recently, the assumptions of the human relations model have been challenged, not only for being an oversimplified and incomplete statement of human behavior at work, but also for being as manipulative as the traditional model. These newest models have been proposed under various titles, including McGregor's (1960) "Theory Y," Likert's (1967) "System 4," Schein's (1972) "Complex Man," and Miles' (1965) "Human Resources model." We shall adopt the latter term here as being more descriptive of the underlying philosophy inherent in these newer approaches.

Human resources models generally view humans being motivated by a complex set in interrelated factors (such as money, need for affiliation, need for achievement, desire for meaningful work). It is assumed that different employees often seek quite different goals in a job and have a diversity of talent to offer. Under this conceptualization, employees are looked upon as reservoirs of potential talent and management's responsibility is to learn how best to tap such resources.

Inherent in such a philosophy are several fairly basic assumptions about the nature of people. First, it is assumed that people want to contribute on the job. In this sense, employees are viewed as being somewhat "premotivated" to perform. In fact, the more people become involved in their work, the more meaningful the job can often become. Second, it is assumed that work does not necessarily have to be distasteful. Many of the current efforts at job enrichment and job redesign are aimed at increasing the potential meaningfulness of work by adding greater amounts of task variety, autonomy, responsibility, and so on. Third, it is argued that employees are quite capable of making significant and rational decisions affecting their work and that allowing greater latitude in employee decision making is actually in the best interests of the organization. Finally, it is assumed that this increased self-control and direction allowed on the job, plus the completion of more meaningful tasks, can in large measure determine the level of satisfaction on the job. In other words, it is generally assumed that good and meaningful performance leads to job satisfaction and not the reverse, as is assumed in the human relations model.

Certain implied managerial strategies follow naturally from this set of assumptions. In general, this approach would hold that it is management's responsibility to first understand the complex nature of motivational patterns. Based upon such knowledge, management should attempt to determine how best to use the potential resources available to it through its work force. It should assist employees in meeting some of their own *personal* goals within the organizational context. Moreover, such a philosophy implies a greater degree of participation by employees in relevant decision-making activities, as well as increased autonomy over task accomplishment. Thus, in contrast to the traditional and human relations models, management's task is seen not so much as one of manipulating employees to accept managerial authority as it is of developing a "partnership" or "family" of employees, with each member contributing according to his or her abilities and interests toward the organization's goals.

In conclusion, it should be pointed out that the human resources approach to motivation has only recently begun to be adopted. Many organizations have attempted to implement such models piecemeal; for example, several organizations have ongoing experiments in enriching the nature of the job (Ford, 1969; Maher, 1971; Myers, 1970; Special Task Force, HEW, 1973). However, full-scale adoptions of such models, including the multitude of strategic implications for managers, are rare at present. In fact, when one looks across organizations it becomes readily apparent that all three models have their staunch advocates, and empirical evidence supportive of each approach can be offered in defense of one's preferred strategy (Schein, 1972). It may be that further research will demonstrate that each has its rightful place, depending upon the nature of the organization, its technology, its people, and, most of all, its goals and priorities for the future.

A FRAMEWORK FOR ANALYSIS

Before proceeding to a consideration of some of the more highly developed or widely accepted contemporary theories of motivation, we should place this complex topic within some meaningful conceptual framework. Such a framework would serve as a vehicle not only for organizing our thoughts concerning human behavior at work but also for evaluating the ability of each of the theories that follows to deal adequately with all the factors in the work situation. In other words, it should provide a useful beginning for later analyses by pointing to several important factors to look for in the theoretical approaches that follow.

The conceptual model we wish to pose here (after Porter & Miles, 1974) consists of two parts. First, it assumes that motivation is a complex phenomenon that can best be understood within a multivariate framework; that is *several* important—and often quite distinct—factors must be taken into account when explaining motivational processes. Second, the model proposed here argues that these motivationally relevant factors must be viewed within a systems framework; we must concern ourselves with interrelationships and interactive effects among the various factors. It is our belief, then, that a full comprehension of the intricacies of human behavior at work requires the student of motivation to consider both parts of this equation: a multivariate conceptual approach and an integrating systems framework. Let us briefly examine each part of this proposed framework for analysis.

Multivariate Conceptual Approach

If motivation is concerned with those factors which energize, direct, and sustain human behavior, it would appear that a comprehensive theory of motivation at work must address itself to at least three important sets of variables which constitute the work situation. First, some consideration must be given to the characteristics of the individual; second, some thought should be directed toward the behavioral implications of the required job tasks; and third, some concern should be shown for the impact of the larger organizational environment. These three sets of variables, along with examples of each, are depicted in Exhibit 3.

Characteristics of the Individual   The natural starting point for any theory of motivation is the nature of the individual himself. We are concerned here with what the employee *brings to* the work situation. Considerable research (see, for example, Atkinson, 1964; Vroom, 1964) has demonstrated that differences in individuals can at times account for a good deal of the variance in effort and performance on a job. Thus, when we examine the factors comprising the motivational force equation, we must ask how large an input is made by these variations within people themselves. At least three major categories of individual difference characteristics have been shown to affect the motivational process: interests, attitudes, and needs.

"Interests" refers to the direction of one's attention. It appears likely that the nature of an employee's interests would affect both the manner and the extent to which external stimuli (like money) would affect his behavior. Consider the example of two people working side by side on the same job and earning identical salaries. Person A is highly interested in the work; person B is not. In this example, person A can be seen as "self-motivated" to some degree because he or she is pursuing a central interest (his or her work), and we would expect this person to derive considerable satisfaction from the activity. If person A were offered a pay raise to take a less interesting job, he or she would be faced with making a decision of whether to keep the more interesting job or to earn more money, and it is not inconceivable that the intrinsic rewards of the present job would be motivation enough *not* to accept the transfer. Person B, however, who is not interested in the work, has no such conflict of choice in our simplified example; there is no motivation to stay on the present job and the added income of the new job could be a strong incentive for change. Some empirical research exists (reviewed in Porter & Steers, 1973; see Chapter 8) in support of our hypothetical example. Several studies have shown that an employee's motivation to participate (stay on the job) is to a large extent determined by the degree of fit between his or her vocational interests and the realities of the job. Thus, interests may be considered one factor that individuals generally bring to the organization that, at least to some extent, can affect how they behave at work.

Exhibit 3   Variable Affecting the Motivational Process in Organizational Settings (After Porter & Miles, 1974)

I. Individual characteristics	II. Job characteristics (examples):	III. Work environment characteristics
1. Interests	Types of intrinsic rewards	1. Immediate work Environment
2. Attitudes (examples)	Degree of autonomy	• Peers
• Toward self	Amount of direct performance feedback	• Supervisor(s)
• Toward job		2. Organizational actions
• Toward aspects of the work situation	Degree of variety in tasks	• Reward practices
3. Needs (examples)		System-wide rewards
• Security		Individual rewards
• Social		• Organizational climate
• Achievement		

Note: These lists are not intended to be exhaustive; they are meant to indicate some of the more important variables influencing employee motivation.

In addition to interests, an employees' attitudes or beliefs may also play an important role in their motivation to perform. Individuals who are very dissatisfied with their jobs, or with their supervisor, or any number of other things, may have little desire to put forth much effort. Several theories of motivation have encompassed the notion of attitudes as they relate to performance behavior at work. For example, Korman (1970, 1971) has proposed a theory of motivation centering around one's attitudes about oneself (that is, one's self-image). This theory posits that individuals attempt to behave in a fashion consistent with their own self-image. If employees see themselves as failures on the job, they will not put forth much effort and their resulting performance will probably be poor. Such action will then reinforce the negative self-image. Two important points can be made here. First, various attitudes (in this case, attitudes about oneself) can play an important role in motivational force to perform. Second, in this example, there is a specific implied managerial strategy to improve employee effort: The manager should attempt to modify the employees' self-image. If the employees in our example were proud to work for the XYZ Company and if they saw themselves as effective contributors to the company's goals, they would, in theory, be more likely to perform at a higher level.

The individual characteristic that has received the most widespread attention in terms of motivation theory and research is the concept of "needs." A need may be defined as an internal state of disequilibrium which causes individuals to pursue certain courses of action in an effort to regain internal equilibrium. For example, individuals who have a high need for achievement might be motivated to engage in competitive acts with others so they can "win," thereby satisfying this need. The theories of Maslow and of McClelland and Atkinson use this concept of need as the basic unit of analysis. While further discussion of these types of theories is reserved for the following two chapters, suffice it to say that variations in human needs can be significant factors in the determination of effort and performance.

Characteristics of the Job   A second set of variables to be considered when viewing the motivational process involves those factors relating to the attributes of an individual's job. We are concerned here with *what an employee does* at work. How much feedback is provided? Does the work offer intrinsic rewards (for example, is it personally satisfying)? Such factors have been shown in many studies to be strongly related to an individual's desire to perform well on a task. In Chapter 12, we shall review some of the research aimed at uncovering relationships between variations in the nature of the task, on the one hand, and resulting performance and job satisfaction, on the other. Moreover, Chapter 8 will review many of these job attributes as they relate to subsequent turnover and absenteeism.

Herzberg's (Herzberg et al., 1959; Herzberg, 1966, 1968) "dual factor" theory of motivation, which is reviewed in Chapter 4, also has its roots in the nature of the task as it affects performance. In fact, Herzberg was one of the first theorists to argue in favor of "job enrichment" as a mechanism for increasing both performance and job satisfaction. In summary, then, our conceptual framework points to the nature of job attributes or characteristics as a major concern that must be taken into account when developing a comprehensive theory of motivation at work.

Characteristics of the Work Environment   The final set of variables under our analytical framework that appears to be relevant to the motivational process is concerned with the nature of the organizational, or work, environment. Work environment factors can be divided for our purposes into two major categories: those associated with the immediate work environment (the work group), and those associated with the larger problem of organizationwide actions. Both categories, however, focus primarily on *what happens to* the employee at work.

As indicated in Exhibit 3, there are at least two major factors in the immediate work environment which can affect work behavior. The first is the quality of peer-group interactions. Research dating from the Hawthorne studies (Roethlisberger & Dickson, 1939) indicates that peer-group influence can significantly influence an employee's effort. Such influence can occur at both ends of the productivity continuum: peers can exert pressure on "laggards" to contribute their fair share of output, or they can act to curb the high productivity of the "rate-buster." These considerations are discussed in Chapter 10. Similarly, super-visory or leadership style can influence effort and performance under certain circumstances (see Chapter 11). Immediate supervisors can play an important role in motivation because of their control over desired rewards (such as bonuses, raises, feedback) and because of their central role in the structuring of work activities. In other words, supervisors have considerable influence over the ability or freedom of employees to pursue their own personal goals on the job.

The second major category of work environment variables—organiza-tionwide actions—are concerned with several factors which are common throughout the organization and are largely determined by the organization it-self. Such factors would include both systemwide rewards (like fringe benefits) and individual rewards (such as overall salary system and allocation of status). These topics are discussed in Chapter 15. Moreover, the emergent organizational climate that pervades the work environment would also fall into this category (see Chapter 9). Factors such as openness of communication, perceived relative emphasis on rewards versus punishment, degree of interdepartmental coopera-tion, and so forth, may at times influence individuals' decisions to produce on the job.

Interactive Effects

Based on the foregoing discussion, it becomes apparent that a multitude of varia-bles throughout the organizational mileiu can be important inputs into the moti-vational force equation. Such a conclusion forces us to take a broad perspective when we attempt to understand or explain why employees behave as they do at work. However, this simple enumeration of motivationally relevant factors fails to recognize how these variables may interact with one another within a systems type of framework to determine work behavior. In other words, the second half of our conceptual framework stresses the fact that we must consider motivational models from a dynamic perspective. For example, an individual may have a strong desire to perform well on the job, but he or she may lack a clear under-standing of his or her proper role. The employee may thus waste or misdirect effort and thereby fail to receive expected rewards. Similarly, an employee may truly want to perform at a high level, but simply lack the necessary ability for good performance on his or her particular job. The important point here is that, when viewing various approaches to motivation, it becomes clear that one must be aware of the interactive dynamics between major sets of variables that may influence resulting effort and performance.

While most theories of motivation look to some extent at the relationships between certain variables, two theories have recently emerged which incorporate a systems framework and use the concept of interactive effects as the basic unit of analysis. The first of these is the equity, or social comparison, theory (see Chapter 5). Equity theory is primarily concerned with the dynamic relationship between individuals (such as their attitudes about the fairness of the work situa-tion) and the particular actions (such as rewards) taken by the organization. Equity theory thus includes at least two of the three major sets of variables discussed above as being relevant to an understanding of motivation. The second systems type of theory is expectancy/valence theory, which is discussed in Chapter 6. This theory, based on the work of the early cognitive theorists like Lewin, Tolman, and Peak, argues that a major factor in motivation is the anticipation, or expectation, that individuals have concerning future states of affairs. Thus, it is concerned not only with such organizational environment factors as reward systems and climate but also with the nature of the required job tasks *and* how the individuals themselves view their jobs and work environment. Emphasis is placed on how these three sets of variables interact to determine level of effort on the job.

Each of the five theories of work motivation that will be considered in the following chapters has focused on *at least* one of these three major factors: the individual, the job, or the organizational environment. Several of the theories have included more than one factor. Moreover, some of the more highly developed models have placed such variables within a systems framework and have studied the interactive effects between the major sets of variables. Hopefully, the framework for analysis presented here will aid in understanding the pervasive nature of motivation and in evaluating the adequacy of each of the major theories to explain human behavior at work.

A note of caution is in order first, however. When evaluating the theories and research that follow, the student of motivation must determine whether he or she seeks to find the "one best way" to motivate workers or whether different approaches may be more relevant, depending on the needs for which the theory is employed. That is, both practicing managers and organizational researchers must decide whether they want to find an ultimate *universal* theory of motivation which can be used to analyze all relevant problems or whether they want to adopt a situational, or *contingency,* approach and select that theory which appears most pertinent to the specific problem at hand. The answer to this question will in large measure determine not only how one attempts to understand the role of motivation at work, but also how one attempts to implement organizational changes designed to increase the desire of employees to perform.

PLAN OF BOOK

The remainder of this book consists of three parts. Part Two introduces the student to five major contemporary theories of motivation as they relate to the work situation. Each chapter includes an introductory section, or overview, which lays the foundation for an understanding of the articles that follow. This overview includes suggested additional readings for the student who wishes to study the subject in greater detail. The particular articles within each chapter have been selected so as to cover not only the theoretical propositions of each model but also to review some of the research associated with each theory. The articles, when taken together, will, it is hoped, present both the strengths and weaknesses of the various theories.

Part Three concentrates on the study of the relationship of motivation to various other important phenomena found in the work situation. Emphasis is placed on interrelationships among various factors (e.g., the relation between job design and motivation), and each chapter presents a broad survey of the relevant theories and research on the topic. Again, overviews, suggested additional readings, and several theoretical or empirical articles accompany each chapter.

Finally, in Part Four we summarize and integrate what has, hopefully, been learned here. Consideration is given not only to how the various issues in motivation relate to one another, but also how they relate to the broader concerns of organizational behavior. The implications of such information for managerial practice is also discussed.

REFERENCES

Allport, G. W. The historical background of modern social psychology. In G. Lindzey (Ed.), *Handbook of social psychology.* Cambridge, Mass.: Addison-Wesley, 1954.

Atkinson, J. W. *An introduction to motivation.* Princeton, N.J.: Van Nostrand, 1964.

Atkinson, J. W., & Reitman, W. R. Performance as a function of motive strength and expectancy of goal attainment. *Journal of Abnormal Social Psychology,* 1956, **53,** 361–366.

Bendix, R. *Work and authority in industry.* New York: Wiley, 1956.

Berelson, B., & Steiner, G. A. *Human behavior.* New York: Harcourt, Brace & World, 1964.

Birch, D., & Veroff, J. *Motivation: A study of action.* Belmont, Calif.: Brooks/Cole, 1966.

Cannon, W. B. *The wisdom of the body.* New York: Norton, 1939.

Cofer, C. N., & Appley, M. H. *Motivation: Theory and research.* New York: Wiley, 1964.

Dunnette, M. D., & Kirchner, W. K. *Psychology applied to industry.* New York: Appleton-Century-Crofts, 1965.

Ford, R. *Motivation through the work itself.* New York: American Management Association, 1969.

Freud, S. The unconscious. In *Collected papers of Sigmund Freud,* Vol. IV (Riviere, J., trans.) London: Hogarth Press, 1949. (Original edition, 1915.)

Gellerman, S. W. *Motivation and productivity.* New York: American Management Association, 1963.

Herzberg, F. *Work and the nature of man.* Cleveland: World, 1966.

Herzberg, F. One more time: How do you motivate employees? *Harvard Business Review,* 1968, **46,** 53–62.

Herzberg, F., Mausner, B., & Snyderman, B. B. *The motivation to work.* New York: Wiley, 1959.

Hilgard, E. R., & Atkinson, R. C. *Introduction to psychology.* New York: Harcourt, Brace & World, 1967.

Hull, C. L. *Principles of behavior.* New York: Appleton-Century-Crofts, 1943.

Hull, C. L. *A behavior system: An introduction to behavior theory concerning the individual organism.* New Haven: Yale University Press, 1952.

James, W. *The principles of psychology.* Vols. I and II. New York; Henry Holt, 1890.

Jones, M. R. (Ed.) *Nebraska symposium on motivation.* Lincoln: University of Nebraska Press, 1955.

Katz, D. The motivational basis of organizational behavior. *Behavioral Science,* 1964, **9,** 131–146.

Katz, D., & Kahn, R. *The social psychology of organizations.* New York: Wiley, 1966.

Korman, A. K. Toward an hypothesis of work behavior. *Journal of Applied Psychology,* 1970, **54,** 31–41.

Korman, A. K. Expectancies as determinants of performance. *Journal of Applied Psychology,* 1971, **55,** 218–222.

Lewin, K. *A dynamic theory of personality.* New York: McGraw-Hill, 1935.

Lewin, K. *The conceptual representation and the measurement of psychological forces.* Durham, N.C.: Duke University Press, 1938.

Likert, R. *The human organization.* New York: McGraw-Hill, 1967.

Maher, J. R. *New perspectives in job enrichment.* New York: Van Nostrand Reinhold Co., 1971.

Mahoney, T. A. Compensation preference of managers. *Industrial Relations,* 1964, **3,** 135–144.

March, J. G., & Simon, H. A. *Organizations.* New York: Wiley, 1958.

Mayo, E. *The human problems of an industrial civilization.* New York: Macmillan, 1933.

Mayo, E. *The social problems of an industrial civilization.* Boston: Harvard University Press, 1945.

McDougall, W. *An introduction to social psychology.* London: Methuen, 1908.

McGregor, D. *The human side of enterprise.* New York: McGraw-Hill, 1960.

Miles, R. E. Human relations or human resources? *Harvard Business Review,* 1965, **43**(4), 148–163.

Miles, R. E., Porter, L. W., & Craft, J. A. Leadership attitudes among public health officials. *American Journal of Public Health,* 1966, **56,** 1990–2005.

Morgan, C. T., & King, R. A. *Introduction to psychology.* New York: McGraw-Hill, 1966.

Myers, M. S. *Every employee a manager.* New York: McGraw-Hill, 1970.

Opinion Research Corporation. *Public opinion index for industry,* 1947.

Opsahl, R. L., & Dunnette, M. D. The role of financial compensation in industrial motivation. *Psychological Bulletin,* 1966, **66,** 94–118.

Porter, L. W., & Lawler, E. E., III. *Managerial attitudes and performance.* Homewood, Ill.: Irwin, 1968.

Porter, L. W., & Miles, R. E. Motivation and management. In J.W. McGuire (Ed.), *Contemporary management: Issues and viewpoints.* Englewood Cliffs, N.J.: Prentice-Hall, 1974.

Porter, L. W., & Steers, R. M. Organizational, work and personal factors in employee turnover and absenteeism. *Psychological Bulletin,* 1973, **80,** 151–176.

Roethlisberger, F., & Dickson, W. J. *Management and the worker.* Cambridge, Mass.: Harvard University Press, 1939.

Sanford, R. H., & Wrightsman, L. S., Jr. *Psychology.* Belmont, Calif.: Brooks/Cole, 1970.

Schein, E. *Organizational psychology.* Englewood Cliffs, N.J.: Prentice-Hall, 1972.

Special Task Force to the Secretary of Health, Education, and Welfare. *Work in America.* Cambridge, Mass.: The M.I.T. Press, 1973.

Spence, K. W. *Behavior theory and conditioning.* New Haven: Yale University Press, 1956.

Taylor, F. W. *Scientific management.* New York: Harper and Brothers, 1911.

Thorndike, E. L. *Animal intelligence: Experimental studies.* New York: Macmillan, 1911.

Tolman, E. C. *Purposive behavior in animals and men.* New York: Appleton-Century-Crofts, 1932.

Tolman, E. C. Principles of purposive behavior. In S. Koch (Ed.), *Psychology: A study of a science.* Vol. 2. New York: McGraw-Hill, 1959.

Vroom, V. H. *Work and motivation.* New York: Wiley, 1964.

Woodworth, R. S. *Dynamic psychology.* New York: Columbia University Press, 1918.

Part Two

Contemporary Theories and Research

Chapter 2

Need Hierarchy Theory

OVERVIEW

Certainly one of the most popular theories of motivation today is Maslow's need hierarchy theory. From the time of its introduction in the mid-1940s until the late 1950s, this theory remained primarily in the realm of clinical psychology. As more attention began to be focused on the role of motivation at work, however, the need hierarchy theory emerged in the early 1960s as an appealing model of human behavior. Due largely to the popularization of the model by D. McGregor (1960, 1967), this theory became widely discussed and used by both organizational theorists and practicing managers.

Maslow's model consists of two fundamental premises. To begin with, the human being is viewed largely as a "wanting" animal, motivated by a desire to satisfy certain specific types of needs. Based on his clinical observations, Maslow (1943, 1954) posited that most individuals pursue with varying intensities the following needs: (1) physiological; (2) safety; (3) belongingness; (4) esteem; and (5) self-actualization. Those needs which are largely unsatisfied tend to produce tensions within individuals which lead them to behave in a certain fashion in the hope of reducing the tension and restoring internal equilibrium. Once a need becomes satisfied it loses its potency as a motivating force until it again becomes manifest. For example, when a person's physiological needs (say, for food) have been met, they will no longer motivate behavior until the person again becomes hungry. Until such time, according to Maslow, the individual would be motivated by other needs. In other words, many of these needs are cyclical. In this regard, the model is similar to other "need" theories of motivation and personality (such as Murray's theory; see Chapter 3).

Unique with Maslow, however, is his second fundamental premise. Specifically, Maslow argues that the needs which individuals pursue are universal across most populations and that they are arranged sequentially in hierarchical form. That is, once the lower needs are satisfied, the individual moves up the hierarchy one level at a time and attempts to satisfy the next higher-order needs.

Parenthetically, it is of interest to note that Maslow (1954) discussed two additional needs in his earlier work: the cognitive and the aesthetic. Cognitive needs are the needs to know and understand. Examples of cognitive needs include the need to satisfy one's curiosity and the desire to learn. Aesthetic needs include the desire to move toward beauty and away from ugliness. These two needs were not included in Maslow's hierarchical arrangement, however, and have generally been omitted from discussions of his concepts as they relate to organizational settings.

Although Maslow's original concern centered around the development of a model which was generally descriptive of the relation between motivation and personality, he later focused his attention specifically on the motivational problems of employees in work settings (Maslow, 1965). When the need hierarchy concept was applied to work organizations, the implications for managerial actions became obvious. Managers had the responsibility, according to this line of reasoning, to create a "proper climate" in which employees could develop to their fullest potential. This proper climate might include increasing the opportunities for greater autonomy, variety, responsibility, and so forth, so that employees could work toward higher-order need satisfaction. Failure to provide such a climate would theoretically increase employee frustration and could result in poorer performance, lower job satisfaction, and increased withdrawal from the organization. (See Chapter 9 for a discussion of organizational environment factors as they affect motivation and performance.)

The first selection that follows presents the early developmental work on the theory as advanced by Maslow. Following this, Lawler and Suttle review much of the research aimed at verifying the original model. While Maslow's theory has received widespread attention over the years and has appeared to many to be "intuitively obvious," it has only been quite recently that empirical verification attempts have been made.

REFERENCES AND SUGGESTED ADDITIONAL READINGS

Alderfer, C. P. A new theory of human needs. *Organizational Behavior and Human Performance*, 1969, **4**, 142–175.

Alderfer, C. P. *Existence, relatedness, and growth.* New York: Free Press, 1972.

Clark, J. W. Motivation in work groups: A tentative view. *Human Organization,* 1960, **19,** 199–208.

Ghiselli, E. E., & Johnson, D. A. Need satisfaction, managerial success, and organizational structure. *Personnel Psychology,* 1970, **23,** 569–576.

Hall, D. T., & Nougaim, K. E. An examination of Maslow's need hierarchy in an organizational setting. *Organizational Behavior and Human Performance,* 1968, **3,** 12–35.

Maslow, A. H. A theory of human motivation. *Psychological Review,* 1943, **50,** 370–396.

Maslow, A. H. *Motivation and personality.* New York: Harper, 1954.

Maslow, A. H. *Eupsychian management.* Homewood, Ill.: Irwin, 1965.

Maslow, A. H. *Toward a psychology of being.* New York: Van Nostrand Reinhold, 1968.

McGregor, D. *The human side of enterprise.* New York: McGraw-Hill, 1960.

McGregor D. *The professional manager.* New York: McGraw-Hill, 1967.

Miner, J. B., & Dachler, H. P. Personnel attitudes and motivation. In P. H. Mussen and M. R. Rosenzweig (Eds.), *Annual review of psychology.* Palo Alto, Calif.: Annual Reviews, Inc., 1973.

Mitchell, V. F. Need satisfactions of military commanders and staff. *Journal of Applied Psychology,* 1970, **54,** 282–287.

Payne, R. Factor analysis of a Maslow-type need satisfaction questionnaire. *Personnel Psychology,* 1970, **23,** 251–268.

Porter, L. W. A study of perceived need satisfaction in bottom and middle management jobs. *Journal of Applied Psychology,* 1961, **45,** 1–10.

Porter, L. W. Job attitudes in management: I. Perceived deficiencies in need fulfillment as a function of job level. *Journal of Applied Psychology,* 1962, **46,** 375–384.

Porter, L. W. Job attitudes in management: II. Perceived importance of needs as a function of job level. *Journal of Applied Psychology,* 1963, **47,** 141–148.

Schneider, B., & Alderfer, C. P. Three studies of measures of need satisfaction in organizations. *Administrative Science Quarterly,* 1973, **18,** 489–505.

Wofford, J. C. The motivational bases of job satisfaction and job performance. *Personnel Psychology,* 1971, **24,** 501–518.

Wolf, M. G. Need gratification theory: A theoretical reformulation of job satisfaction/dissatisfaction and job motivation. *Journal of Applied Psychology,* 1970, **54,** 87–94.

A Theory of Human Motivation

A. H. Maslow

DYNAMICS OF THE BASIC NEEDS

The "Physiological" Needs

The needs that are usually taken as the starting point for motivation theory are the so-called physiological drives . . .

Undoubtedly these physiological needs are the most prepotent of all needs. What this means specifically is that, in the human being who is missing everything in life in an extreme fashion, it is most likely that the major motivation would be the physiological needs rather than any others. A person who is lacking food, safety, love, and esteem would most probably hunger for food more strongly than for anything else.

If all the needs are unsatisfied, and the organism is then dominated by the physiological needs, all other needs may become simply non-existent or be pushed into the background. It is then fair to characterize the whole organism by saying simply that it is hungry, for consciousness is almost completely pre-empted by hunger. All capacities are put into the service of hunger-satisfaction, and the organization of these capacities is almost entirely determined by the one purpose of satisfying hunger. The receptors and effectors, the intelligence, memory, habits, all may now be defined simply as hunger-gratifying tools. Capacities that are not useful for this purpose lie dormant or are pushed into the background . . .

Obviously a good way to obscure the "higher" motivations, and to get a lopsided view of human capacities and human nature, is to make the organism extremely and chronically hungry or thirsty. Anyone who attempts to make an emergency picture into a typical one and who will measure all of man's goals and desires by his behavior during extreme physiological deprivation is certainly being blind to many things. It is quite true that man lives by bread alone—when there is no bread. But what happens to man's desires when there *is* plenty of bread and when his belly is chronically filled?

At once other (and "higher") needs emerge and these, rather than physiological hungers, dominate the organism. And when these in turn are satisfied, again new (and still "higher") needs emerge and so on. This is what we mean by saying that the basic human needs are organized into a hierarchy of relative prepotency.

One main implication of this phrasing is that gratification becomes as important a concept as deprivation in motivation theory, for it releases the organism from the domination of a relatively more physiological need, permitting thereby the emergence of other more social goals. The physiological needs, along with their partial goals, when chronically gratified cease to exist as active determinants

Abridged from the *Psychological Review*, I (1943) 370–96, by permission of the American Psychological Association.

or organizers of behavior. They now exist only in a potential fashion in the sense that they may emerge again to dominate the organism if they are thwarted. But a want that is satisfied is no longer a want. The organism is dominated and its behavior organized only by unsatisfied needs. If hunger is satisfied, it becomes unimportant in the current dynamics of the individual.

This statement is somewhat qualified by a hypothesis to be discussed more fully later, namely, that it is precisely those individuals in whom a certain need has always been satisfied who are best equipped to tolerate deprivation of that need in the future; furthermore, those who have been deprived in the past will react to current satisfactions differently from the one who has never been deprived.

The Safety Needs

If the physiological needs are relatively well gratified, there then emerges a new set of needs, which we may categorize roughly as the safety needs. All that has been said of the physiological needs is equally true, although in lesser degree, of these desires. The organism may equally well be wholly dominated by them. They may serve as the almost exclusive organizers of behavior, recruiting all the capacities that they are primarily safety-seeking tools. Again, as in the hungry man, we find that the dominating goal is a strong determinant not only of his current world-outlook and philosophy but also of his philosophy of the future. Practically everything looks less important than safety (even sometimes the physiological needs which being satisfied, are now underestimated). A man, in this state, if it is extreme enough and chronic enough, may be characterized as living almost for safety alone. . . .

The healthy, normal, fortunate adult in our culture is largely satisfied in his safety needs. The peaceful, smoothly running, "good" society ordinarily makes its members feel safe enough from wild animals, extremes of temperature, criminals, assault and murder, tyranny, etc. Therefore, in a very real sense, they no longer have any safety needs as active motivators. Just as a sated man no longer feels hungry, a safe man no longer feels endangered. If we wish to see these needs directly and clearly we must turn to neurotic or near-neurotic individuals, and to the economic and social underdogs. In between these extremes, we can perceive the expressions of safety needs only in such phenomena as, for instance, the common preference for a job with tenure and protection, the desire for a savings account, and for insurance of various kinds (medical, dental, unemployment, disability, old age). . . .

The Love Needs

If both the physiological and the safety needs are fairly well gratified, then there will emerge the love and affection and belongingness needs, and the whole cycle already described will repeat itself with this new center. Now the person will feel keenly, as never before, the absence of friends or a sweetheart or a wife or children. He will hunger for affectionate relations with people in general, namely, for a place in his group, and he will strive with great intensity to achieve this goal.

He will want to attain such a place more than anything else in the world and may even forget that once, when he was hungry, he sneered at love.

In our society the thwarting of these needs is the most commonly found core in cases of maladjustment and more severe psychopathology. Love and affection, as well as their possible expression in sexuality, are generally looked upon with ambivalence and are customarily hedged about with many restrictions and inhibitions. Practically all theorists of psychopathology have stressed thwarting of the love needs as basic in the picture of maladjustment. Many clinical studies have therefore been made of this need and we know more about it perhaps than any of the other needs except the physiological ones.

One thing that must be stressed at this point is that love is not synonymous with sex. Sex may be studied as a purely physiological need. Ordinarily sexual behavior is multi-determined, that is to say, determined not only by sexual but also by other needs, chief among which are the love and affection needs. Also not to be overlooked is the fact that the love needs involve both giving *and* receiving love.

The Esteem Needs

All people in our society (with a few pathological exceptions) have a need or desire for a stable, firmly based, (usually) high evaluation of themselves, for self-respect, or self-esteem, and for the esteem of others. By firmly based self-esteem, we mean that which is soundly based upon real capacity, achievement, and respect from others. These needs may be classified into two subsidiary sets. These are, first, the desire for strength, for achievement, for adequacy, for confidence in the face of the world, and for independence and freedom. Second, we have what we may call the desire for reputation or prestige (defining it as respect or esteem from other people), recognition, attention, importance, or appreciation. These needs have been relatively stressed by Alfred Adler and his followers, and have been relatively neglected by Freud and the psychoanalysts. More and more today, however, there is appearing widespread appreciation of their central importance.

Satisfaction of the self-esteem need leads to feelings of self-confidence, worth, strength, capability, and adequacy, of being useful and necessary in the world. But thwarting of these needs produces feelings of inferiority, of weakness, and of helplessness. These feelings in turn give rise to either basic discouragement or else compensatory or neurotic trends. An appreciation of the necessity of basic self-confidence and an understanding of how helpless people are without it, can be easily gained from a study of severe traumatic neurosis.

The Need for Self-Actualization

Even if all these needs are satisfied, we may still often (if not always) expect that a new discontent and restlessness will soon develop, unless the individual is doing what he is fitted for. A musician must make music, an artist must paint, a poet must write, if he is to be ultimately happy. What a man *can* be, he *must* be. This need we may call self-actualization.

This term, first coined by Kurt Goldstein, is being used in this paper in a much more specific and limited fashion. It refers to the desire for self-fulfilment, namely, to the tendency for one to become actualized in what one is potentially. This tendency might be phrased as the desire to become more and more what one is, to become everything that one is capable of becoming.

The specific form that these needs take will of course vary greatly from person to person. In one individual it may be expressed maternally, as the desire to be an ideal mother, in another athletically, in still another aesthetically, in the painting of pictures, and in another inventively in the creation of new contrivances. It is not necessarily a creative urge although in people who have any capabilities for creation it will take this form.

The clear emergence of these needs rests upon prior satisfaction of the physiological, safety, love and esteem needs. We shall call people who are satisfied in these needs, basically satisfied people, and it is from these that we may expect the fullest (and healthiest) creativeness. Since, in our society, basically satisfied people are the exception, we do not know much about self-actualization, either experimentally or clinically. It remains a challenging problem for research . . . .

Degrees of Relative Satisfaction

So far, our theoretical discussion may have given the impression that these five sets of needs are somehow in a stepwise, all-or-none relationship to one another. We have spoken in such terms as the following: "If one need is satisfied, then another emerges." This statement might give the false impression that a need must be satisfied 100 per cent before the next need emerges. In actual fact, most members of our society who are normal are partially satisfied in all their basic needs and partially unsatisfied in all their basic needs at the same time. A more realistic description of the hierarchy would be in terms of decreasing percentages of satisfaction as we go up the hierarchy of prepotency. For instance, if I may assign arbitrary figures for the sake of illustration, it is as if the average citizen is satisfied perhaps 85 per cent in his physiological needs, 70 per cent in his safety needs, 50 per cent in his love needs, 40 per cent in his self-esteem needs, and 10 per cent in his self-actualization needs.

As for the concept of emergence of a new need after satisfaction of the prepotent need, this emergence is not a sudden, saltatory phenomenon but rather a gradual emergence by slow degrees from nothingness. For instance, if prepotent need A is satisfied only 10 per cent then need B may not be visible at all. However, as this need A becomes satisfied 25 per cent, need B may emerge 5 per cent; as need A becomes satisfied 75 per cent, need B may emerge 90 per cent; and so on.

Unconscious Character of Needs

These needs are neither necessarily conscious nor unconscious. On the whole, however, in the average person, they are more often unconscious. It is not necessary at this point to overhaul the tremendous mass of evidence which indicates the crucial importance of unconscious motivation. It would by now be expected, on a priori grounds alone, that unconscious motivations would on the whole be rather more important than the conscious motivations. What we have called the basic needs are very often largely unconscious although they may, with suitable techniques and with sophisticated people, become conscious . . .

SUMMARY

1. There are at least five sets of goals which we may call basic needs. These are briefly physiological, safety, love, esteem, and self-actualization. In addition, we are motivated by the desire to achieve or maintain the various conditions on which these basic satisfactions rest and by certain more intellectual desires.

2. These basic goals are related to one another, being arranged in a hierarchy of prepotency. This means that the most prepotent goal will monopolize consciousness and will tend of itself to organize the recruitment of the various capacities of the organism. The less prepotent needs are minimized, even forgotten or denied. But when a need is fairly well satisfied, the next prepotent ("higher") need emerges, in turn to dominate the conscious life and to serve as the center of organization of behavior, since gratified needs are not active motivators.

Thus man is a perpetually wanting animal. Ordinarily the satisfaction of these wants is not altogether mutually exclusive but only tends to be. The average member of our society is most often partially satisfied and partially unsatisfied in all of his wants. The hierarchy principle is usually empirically observed in terms of increasing percentages of non-satisfaction as we go up the hierarchy. Reversals of the average order of the hierarchy are sometimes observed. Also it has been observed that an individual may permanently lose the higher wants in the hierarchy under special conditions. There are not only ordinarily multiple motivations for usual behavior but, in addition, many determinants other than motives.

3. Any thwarting or possibility of thwarting of these basic human goals, or danger to the defenses which protect them or to the conditions upon which they rest, is considered to be a psychological threat. With a few exceptions, all psychopathology may be partially traced to such threats. A basically thwarted man may actually be defined as a "sick" man.

4. It is such basic threats which bring about the general emergency reactions.

5. Certain other basic problems have not been dealt with because of limitations of space. Among these are *(a)* the problem of values in any definitive motivation theory, *(b)* the relation between appetites, desires, needs and what is "good" for the organism, *(c)* the etiology of the basic needs and their possible derivation in early childhood, *(d)* redefinition of motivational concepts, i.e., drive, desire, wish, need, goal, *(e)* implication of our theory for hedonistic theory, *(f)* the nature of the uncompleted act, of success and failure, and of aspiration-level, *(g)* the role of association, habit, and conditioning, *(h)* relation to the theory of interpersonal relations, *(i)* implications for psychotherapy, *(j)* implication for theory of society, *(k)* the theory of selfishness, *(l)* the relation between needs and cultural patterns, *(m)* the relation between this theory and Allport's theory of

functional autonomy. These as well as certain other less important questions must be considered as motivation theory attempts to become definitive.

A Causal Correlational Test of the
Need Hierarchy Concept
Edward E. Lawler III and J. Lloyd Suttle [1]

Basic to much of the current thinking on motivation in organizations is the idea that needs are arranged in a hierarchy. Maslow's (1943, 1954, 1968, 1970) theory of human motivation is clearly the best known of the need hierarchy theories, although prior to Maslow, Langer (1937) had already stated a need hierarchy theory. More recently, several writers have offered modifications of and alternatives to Maslow's theory (e.g., Alderfer, 1969, in press). Maslow's need hierarchy theory has enjoyed widespread acceptance, particularly in the writings of many prominent organizational theorists (e.g., Argyris, 1964; Haire, 1956; McGregor, 1960; Schein, 1965). It has been used to explain such diverse issues as why pay can become unimportant and why self-actualization seems to be very important to people today.

Maslow's (1943, 1954, 1970) hierarchical model is composed of a five-level classification of human needs, and a set of hypotheses about how the satisfaction of these needs affects their importance.

The five need categories are as follows:

1 *Physiological* needs, including the need for food, water, air, etc.
2 *Safety* needs or the need for security, stability, and the absence from pain, threat, or illness.
3 *Belongingness* and *Love* needs.
4 *Esteem* needs, including both a need for personal feelings of achievement or self-esteem and also a need for recognition or respect from others.
5 The need for *Self-Actualization,* a feeling of self-fulfillment or the realization of one's potential.

More important than the definition of these five need groups, however, is the *process* through which each class of needs becomes important or active. According to Maslow, the five need categories exist in a hierarchy of prepotency, such that the lower or more basic needs are inherently more important (prepotent) than the higher or less basic needs. This means that before any of the higher level

Abridged from *Organizational behavior and human performance,* 1972, **7**, 265–287. Copyright 1972 by Academic Press. Reprinted by permission.
[1]The authors would like to thank Frank Smith, Bruce Ward and Edward Fitzgerald for their cooperation.

needs will become important, a person's physiological needs must be satisfied. Once these physiological needs have been satisfied, however, their strength or importance decreases, and the next higher level of need (safety) becomes the strongest motivator of behavior. This process of "increased satisfaction—decreased importance—increased importance of the next higher need" repeats itself until the highest level of the hierarchy is reached. At that level, Maslow has proposed in later revisions of his theory (1968, 1970) that a reversal occurs in the satisfaction-importance relationship. He states that for self-actualization needs, increased satisfaction leads to *increased* need strength. ". . . When we examine people who are predominantly growth-motivated . . . gratification breeds increased rather than decreased motivation, heightened rather than lessened excitement" (Maslow, 1968, p. 30).

In short, individual behavior is motivated by an attempt to satisfy the need which is *most important* at any particular point in time. Further, the strength of any need is determined by its position in the hierarchy, and by the degree to which it and all lower needs have been satisfied. Maslow's theory predicts a dynamic, step-by-step, causal process of human motivation, such that behavior is governed by a continuously changing (though predictable) set of "important" needs. An increase (change) in the satisfaction of the needs in one category *causes* the strength of these needs to decrease, and as a result the importance of the needs at the next-higher level increases.

Alderfer's (1969, in press) model, like Maslow's, sees needs as being arranged in a hierarchy. However, his model argues for three levels of needs (existence, relatedness and growth). He like Maslow, argues that the satisfaction of a need influences its own importance and the importance of higher level needs. However, while he supports Maslow's hypothesis that the satisfaction of growth needs may lead to their being more, rather than less important, Alderfer differs from Maslow in his hypothesis that the lack of satisfaction of higher order needs can lead to lower order needs becoming more important. He also assumes that all needs are simultaneously active and thus, prepotency does not play as major a role in his theory as it does in Maslow's.

Despite the great deal of attention that need hierarchy theory has received in the literature during the last ten years, very few attempts have been made to test the predictions that are derivable from it. An adequate test of it is possible only if the effects of changes in satisfaction and importance and the causal bases for these changes are fully considered. This would seem to require that longitudinal or experimental data be collected. The obvious difficulty in collecting such data may partially account for the fact that so few studies have been done.

With the exception of a recent study by Hall and Nougaim (1968) and some early studies on the effects of starvation and thirst (e.g., Keys et al., 1950; Wolf, 1958), most tests of the hierarchical need model have relied exclusively on cross-sectional data (e.g., Alderfer, 1969; Goodman, 1968). The results of these studies have generally shown that lowerlevel workers tend to be less satisfied and/or more concerned with lowerlevel (safety) needs, while managers or higher-level workers express concern for higher-level (achievement, esteem, self-actualization) needs. Although such results might be predicted from Maslow's theory, they do not in themselves provide a test of the model. The original model offers no predictions about absolute or relative degrees of need satisfaction and strength, and consequently, any conclusions drawn from such data about the validity of the model must be discounted.

Research on the effects of starvation and thirst shows that when people are hungry or thirsty they often can think of little else and their social relationships deteriorate (Keys *et al.*, 1950; Wolf, 1958). This would seem to provide some support for the hierarchical need concept but only for lower level needs. Furthermore, there is a great deal of data on animals and humans which show that as lower level needs become more satisfied, they become less important (Cofer & Appley, 1964). This provides considerable support for the satisfaction-importance view where lower level needs are concerned. However, it says nothing about higher order needs which often are said to be the most important determinants of behavior in organizations (e.g., Argyris, 1964; Haire, 1956).

Alderfer (1969) has been able to partially test the need hierarchy concept by using cross-sectional data. His approach was to correlate individual need satisfaction with need strength both within and across need levels. In terms of cross-sectional data, Maslow's model would predict a negative correlation between the satisfaction and importance of the same need and a positive correlation between the satisfaction and the importance of the need at the next higher level. Alderfer found little data to support the Maslow need hierarchy concept. He did find some tendency for the satisfaction of lower level needs to be negatively associated with their importance and concluded that the frustration hypothesis—i.e., need frustration generates increased need strength, while satisfaction causes decreased importance—may be valid at lower need levels. Dachler and Hulin (1969) have also presented some data to support the view that for lower level needs, increased satisfaction leads to decreased importance.

As was the case with the other cross-sectional studies mentioned above, however, it is difficult to conclusively prove or disprove a dynamic or causal hypothesis through the analysis of data such as Alderfer's, which was collected at only one point in time. Hall and Nougaim (1968) recognized this limitation of cross sectional data, and they have used longitudinal data in order to test Maslow's theory. In a study at American Telephone & Telegraph Co. (AT&T) in which individual attitudes (need satisfactions and strengths) were measured through annual unstructured interviews over a five-year time span, Hall and Nougaim found little data to support Maslow's model. Although their analysis included both static and dynamic correlations (the correlation of changes in variables), they found little evidence that the increasing satisfaction of a need results in either the decreased strength of the need itself, or an increased strength of the next higher need. Their results differ from Alderfer's in that they did not find a tendency for lower level needs to decrease in importance as they became better satisfied.

Although in some ways the Hall and Nougaim study does represent the most direct test of the Maslow model to date, it suffers from a number of problems. The sample was small (49) and consisted only of managers who had been in AT&T for five years. In addition, the data used in the study were based on the post hoc coding of unstructured interviews that were not designed to produce data relevant to Maslow's theory. Further, the agreement among the coders was on the low side (.55–.59) as might be expected because of the unstructured nature of the interviews. Thus, although the study represents the first use of longitudinal data to test the need hierarchy view, the results cannot be considered conclusive as the authors themselves point out.

Recently Alderfer (in press) has collected longitudinal data in two settings to test his theory. These data offer some support for his view that the satisfaction of relatedness needs should influence the importance of growth needs but they do not test Maslow's theory.

In summary, this review of research relevant to Maslow's theory shows that there is relatively little existing research which supports the theory. The Alderfer (1969) and Hall and Nougaim (1968) studies would indicate, for example, that the satisfaction-importance relationships that are valid for one level of the need hierarchy might not be valid for other levels. Furthermore, attempts by Hall and Nougaim to test the specifics of the theory have pointed out the need for a more exact specification of the time lag which exists between changes in satisfaction and changes in importance. Alderfer (in press) has hypothesized, for example, that the causal effects of the satisfaction-importance relationship occur almost instantaneously, while Hall and Nougaim have proposed that changes in the bases of motivation might follow a pattern of career stage changes. Maslow, in the latest revision of his theory (1970, p. 20), has speculated that the hierarchy may take an entire life time to unfold, ". . . self-actualization does not occur in young people . . ." In short, a close examination of Maslow's model and of the research which supports it points out the need for much more empirical work before it can be accepted as valid . . . .[a]

The results of the present study like those of several previous studies offer little support for the view that the needs of managers in organizations are arranged in a multilevel hierarchy. Does this mean it is safe to reject the Maslow need hierarchy view as invalid? Probably not. Such a conclusion would be premature since the theory has still only been tested in a few situations. The present study certainly does not provide conclusive evidence against the theory. It sampled only a small number of people and these did not represent a random sample of the population. Before the theory can be rejected it should be tested in many more situations on a much broader range of people . . . .

A particularly surprising aspect of the present study was the lack of support it provided for the view that as the satisfaction of a need increases its importance

---

[a] *Editors' note:* Due to space limitations, the presentation of results has been omitted from this book. The interested reader is advised to see the original article for a more detailed presentation.

should decrease. This was expected not only on the basis of Maslow's theory but also on the basis of Alderfer's (1969) work. It is, however, congruent with Mobley and Locke's (1970) view that satisfaction does not determine importance. Dachler and Hulin (1969), citing the work of Friedlander (1965), suggest that when certain item formats are used, a spurious curvilinear relation may appear between satisfaction and importance. If this occurred in the present study it would account for the low satisfaction-importance correlations that were found. In order to determine if a curvilinear relationship existed between satisfaction and importance in the present data, eta coefficients were computed for each of the thirteen items and frequency distributions were plotted. There was no evidence of curvilinear relationships existing between need satisfaction and need importance. To the extent that any relationship existed, it was a slight linear one as was shown by the tendency of satisfaction and importance to correlate positively in the case of the lower level needs.

It could be argued that the failure of the present study to find data that are supportive of the need hierarchy concept is due to the fact that too short a time span was used. The only way to finally answer this point is, of course, to collect additional data using different time spans. This should be done and represents a logical next step. The present study used two different time lag intervals in order to increase the likelihood that the proper time lag would be covered. The fact that this step was taken and still no support was found for the need hierarchy concept suggests that even with different time intervals support might not be found for the theory.

Future research would seem to be well advised to use time intervals of greater than one year. Maslow at times says that needs may have to be chronically satisfied before people will move on to the next higher need. If this is true then one year may be too short an interval. It may also be that different time intervals operate for different needs. Perhaps lower order needs have to be satisfied for only a short period before the person moves on to the next level, while at the higher levels needs have to be satisfied for longer periods of time. Finally, at the highest level no amount of satisfaction may lead the person to decrease the importance of those needs. This possibility cannot be rejected on the basis of the present data. If it is true, it will be extremely difficult to develop data to substantiate the need hierarchy theory.

It may be, as has been suggested by Hall and Nougaim (1968), that people progress up the hierarchy gradually through their entire life. Hall and Nougaim's view is more oriented to a career stage model. They argue that as people mature different needs become important to them. Particular needs become important to them not because their lower level needs are satisfied, but in response to problems they have to face at a given moment—for example, where they stand in terms of their own maturity. As Hall and Nougaim observe, "If these career stages are, in fact, universal, it is not difficult to see how an observer might 'read in' a hierarchical mechanism to aid in explaining the need changes which accompany them. If Maslow observed people at various stages in their careers–and he indicates clinical and observational data were important inputs in his model—he might see needs emerge in the order he describes. And he might also see people express more satisfaction in the lower need areas. However, he could be incorrect in his inferences that lowerlevel gratification causes higher needs to emerge" (p. 29).

It is impossible to test the Hall and Nougaim view with the present data. All that can be said is that the present data are not in conflict with it. In order to test the career stage view, data covering a much longer time period would be needed.

Despite the lack of empirical support for the idea of a multilevel hierarchy of needs, it is far too early to give up on the idea that some kind of hierarchy exists. There is the evidence from the studies on starvation and thirst which strongly suggests that when the basic biological existence needs are not satisfied, higher order needs do not come into play. This relationship has not been tested by any of the later studies, since none of them studied people whose basic needs were not satisfied. In addition, there is the evidence from the Alderfer study which shows that as lower level needs become more satisfied some higher level needs become more important. Finally, there is an abundance of evidence which suggests that as certain lower level needs become satisfied they become less important. This evidence provides some support for the view that needs exist in a two-level hierarchy rather than a three-, four-, or five-level hierarchy. A number of different two-level theories could be stated. Maslow (1968) has himself suggested the rudiments of a two-level hierarchy in his concept of deficiency motivation and growth motivation. The lower level of this revised model includes the physiological, safety, belongingness, love, respect, and self-esteem needs. "It is these needs which are essentially deficits in the organism, empty holes, so to speak, which must be filled up for health's sake, and furthermore, must be filled from without by human beings *other* than the subject, that I shall call deficits or deficiency needs" (Maslow, 1968 pp. 22–23). Once these more basic needs have been sufficiently gratified, the healthy person then becomes conscious of and motivated by the needs in the second or higher level, i.e., the growth needs, or the need for self-actualization.

Maslow implies that this two-level hierarchy is biologically based, in that being deprived of the satisfaction of *any* of the lower-level needs (safety, belongingness, esteem) results in illness, just as the deprivation of the need for food, water, air, etc. produces sickness. However, at this point the following slightly different two-level hierarchy seems to best fit the available evidence.

On the lowest level of the hierarchy are the basic biological needs (hunger, thirst, reproduction, oxygen, and physical safety), while all other needs are on the second level. The lower level needs are clearly distinguished from the higher level ones in that they are biologically based, the base can be specified with some confidence. It is not clear what the biological bases for the higher level needs are. Further, all the lower level needs show a linear inverse relationship between satisfaction and importance; higher satisfaction leads to lower importance. No such clearcut relationship exists for the needs that are classifed as higher level.

In this two-level system, all the lower level needs would have to be sufficiently satisfied before the higher level ones would come into play. Further, once the lower level needs were satisfied, no prediction could be made about which higher level need would come into play or about what the sequence would be in which the various needs would come into play. For some people self-actualization needs might become active immediately after the basic needs are satisfied, while for others, social needs might come into play. Presumably, the prepotency of the higher level needs for an individual would be determind by such things as his childhood experience, his age, and his career stage. Only if these were known and their impact on need strength known could any predictions be made. The fact that people experience widely differing socialization experiences or may be at different points in their careers leads to large individual differences in the relative prepotence and the overall ordering of the higher order needs. Because of this, it is misleading to state any generalizations about which needs are usually the most prepotent. In fact, it may be that many of the higher level needs are not and cannot be present in many people. Such needs as the need for self-actualization may be strong motivating forces for some but not for others. Further, no matter how satisfied some people become in other need areas it is likely that they will never experience a strong need for self-actualization.

Unfortunately the two-level theory presented here cannot be adequately tested by the data collected in the present study. A large part of the reason for this is that the present study collected no data on the satisfaction of lower level needs. The data collected in the present study are not in disagreement with this view but they do not test the key propositions in it. Thus, before this or any other need hierarchy theory is accepted as valid, considerably more research needs to be done.

REFERENCES

Alderfer, C. P. A new theory of human needs. *Organizational Behavior and Human Performance*, 1969, **4**, 142–175.

Alderfer, C. P. *Existence, relatedness, and growth: Human needs in organizational settings.* Glencoe, Ill.: Free Press, in press.

Argyris, C. *Integrating the individual and the organization.* New York: Wiley, 1964.

Cofer, C. N., & Appley, M. H. *Motivation: Theory and research.* New York: Wiley, 1964.

Dachler, H. P., & Hulin, C. L. A reconsideration of the relationship between satisfaction and judged importance of environmental and job characteristics. *Organization Behavior and Human Performance*, 1969, **4**, 252–266.

Friedlander, F. Relationships between the importance and the satisfaction of various environmental factors. *Journal of Applied Psychology*, 1965, **49**, 160–164.

Goodman, R. A. On the operationality of the Maslow Need Hierarchy. *British Journal of Industrial Relations*, 1968, **6**, 51–57.

Hackman, J. R., & Lawler, E. E. Employee reactions to job characteristics. *Journal of Applied Psychology Monograph*, 1971, **55**, 259–286.

Haire, M. *Psychology in management.* New York: McGraw-Hill, 1956.

Hall, D. T., & Nougaim, K. E. An examination of Maslow's need hierarchy in an organizational setting. *Organizational Behavior and Human Performance,* 1968, **3,** 12–35.

Keys, A., Brozek, J., Henschel, A., Mickelsen, O., & Taylor, H. *The biology of human starvation.* (Vol. II). Minneapolis: University of Minnesota Press, 1950.

Langer, W. C. *Psychology and human living.* New York: Appleton-Century Crofts, 1937.

Maslow, A. H. A theory of human motivation. *Psychological Review,* 1943, **50,** 370–396.

Maslow, A. H. *Motivation and personality.* New York: Harper, 1954.

Maslow, A. H. *Toward a psychology of being.* (2nd ed.) New York: Van Nostrand Reinhold, 1968.

Maslow, A. H. *Motivation and personality.* (2nd ed.) New York: Harper and Row, 1970.

McGregor, D. *The human side of enterprise.* New York: McGraw-Hill, 1960.

Mobley, W. H., & Locke, E. A. The relationship of value importance to satisfaction. *Organizational Behavior and Human Performance,* 1970, **5,** 463–483.

Schein, E. H. *Organizational psychology.* Englewood Cliffs, N. J.: Prentice-Hall, 1965.

Wolf, A. V. *Thirst: Psysiology of the urge to drink and problems of lack of water.* Springfield, Ill.: Charles C. Thomas, 1958.

QUESTIONS FOR DISCUSSION

1 Why do you think Maslow's theory of motivation has been so popular among both managers and organizational researchers?

2 What research evidence is offered by Maslow in support of his theory?

3 Critically evaluate the research findings and conclusions of Lawler and Suttle.

4 How useful a concept is Maslow's basic theory as it applies to work settings?

5 Is Maslow's need hierarchy model a theory of motivation or a theory of personality? Explain.

6 Specifically, how could you redesign a typical blue-collar job so as to assist employees in meeting their higher-order needs? What about white-collar workers' jobs?

7 Do you think it is generally easier for managers to self-actualize than workers? Why or why not?

8 If a person's job failed to facilitate his pursuit of self-actualization, what courses of action might he or she take?

Chapter 3

Achievement Motivation Theory

OVERVIEW

In addition to Maslow's need-based theory of motivation, there is a second theory which uses the concept of human needs as the basic unit of analysis. This theory, which has alternatively been termed "need achievement theory" and "achievement motivation theory," posits that a major portion of an individual's will to perform can be explained or predicted by the intensity of his or her need for achievement.

This model has its origin in the early work of Henry A. Murray and his associates at the Harvard Psychological Clinic during the 1930s. Based on several years of clinical observations, Murray (1938) wrote his classic *Explorations in Personality* in which he argued that individuals could be classified according to the strengths of various personality-need variables. These needs were believed to represent a central motivating force, both in terms of the intensity and the direction of goal-directed behavior. A need was defined as "a construct . . . which stands for a force . . . in the brain region, a force which organizes perception, apperception, intellection, conation and action in such a way as to transform in a certain direction an existing, unsatisfying situation [1938, p. 123]." A somewhat briefer definition has been offered by McClelland [1971, p. 13]: "a recurrent concern for a goal state." Needs were not something that could be observed by the researcher. On the contrary, Murray [1938, p. 54] stated that the analysis of such needs was "a hypothetical process, the occurrence of which is imagined in order to account for certain objective and subjective facts." In other words, one could only *infer* needs from observed behavior.

Moreover, needs were viewed as largely learned behavior—rather than innate tendencies—which were activated by cues from the external environment. This conception closely resembles the concepts of "motive" and "drive" and can be likened to a state of disequilibrium. According to Murray, each need was composed of two factors: (1) a qualitative or directional component which represents the object toward which the motive is directed; and (2) a quantitative or energetic component which represents the strength or intensity of the motive toward the object.

Murray and his associates viewed an individual's personality as being composed of many divergent, and often conflicting, needs which had the potential of motivating human behavior. This list of needs included the needs for achievement, affiliation, power, autonomy, nurturance, and deference. Thus, for example, individuals with a strongly aroused need for achievement would typically attempt to engage in activities where they could excel and accomplish something important to them. According to this model, needs may be manifest (or "objectified") or latent. A latent need does not imply that the need is not strong, only that it has been inhibited and has found no overt form of expression. Thus, a person may have a high need for achievement but such a need may not be strongly aroused because of impediments in the environment (such as the lack of a challenging task). The result would theoretically be poor performance. If sufficient arousal of the need were attained (by providing a challenging job), we would expect the resulting drive to energize achievement-oriented behavior.

This conceptualization, based on multiple needs, bears a strong resemblance to Maslow's theory in that: (1) both posit the existence of a set of goals toward which behavior is directed; and (2) both are hypothetical constructs designed to describe behavior and are based on clinical observations, not empirical research. Murray does not, however, suggest a hierarchy of such needs as Maslow has.

While Murray was concerned with an entire set of needs, most current research in this area has focused on the specific need for achievement, particularly as it relates to performance in organizational settings. (Some recent research has also been carried out on the needs for power and affiliation.) One of the most prominent contemporary investigators in the area of need for achievement (abbreviated "*n* Ach") research is David C. McClelland. McClelland and his associates view the achievement motive as a relatively stable predisposition to strive for success. More specifically, *n* Ach is defined as "behavior toward competition with a standard of excellence" (McClelland, Atkinson, Clark, & Lowell, 1953). The basis or reward for such a motive is posited to be the positive affect associated with successful performance. McClelland, Atkinson, and their associates present a series of primarily laboratory studies indicative of a strong positive relation between high need for achievement and high levels of performance and executive success (Atkinson, 1958; Atkinson & Feather, 1966; McClelland, 1951; McClelland et al., 1953). More recent studies both in the field and in the laboratory have tended to support such a conclusion (Cummin, 1967; Hundal, 1971; Steers, 1973; Wainer & Rubin, 1969; Weiner & Kukla, 1970). However, Cofer and Appley [1964, p. 374] caution that "the theory McClelland and his co-workers have developed is neither compelled by nor directly derived from their data, but is presumably consistent with the data."

In the selections that follow, Litwin and Stringer review in detail a fairly sophisticated version of the achievement motivation model which has been proposed by Atkinson. In addition, they discuss the measurement techniques used to determine the level of *n* Ach, followed by a review of some of the more prominent research in support of the theory. A specific, albeit brief, example of this type of research is provided in the Cummin selection. Cummin discusses not only methodological issues but also compares *n* Ach scores with other need scores as each is associated with executive success.

Finally, on a more theoretical plane, McClelland proposes a formalized theory of motive acquisition. A central concern of this article is the nature by which needs and motives are learned or aquired. Relevant research is discussed. In all, we have tried in these selections to provide a fairly broad examination of achievement motivation, including theoretical propositions, available research, and several applications as they relate to situations in ongoing organizations.

REFERENCES AND SUGGESTED ADDITIONAL READINGS

Atkinson, J. W. Motivational determinants of risk-taking behavior. *Psychological Review*, 1957, **64**, 359–372.

Atkinson, J. W. *An introduction to motivation*. Princeton, N.J.: Van Nostrand, 1964.

Atkinson, J. W., & Feather, N. T. *A theory of achievement motivation*. New York: Wiley, 1966

Cofer, C. N., & Appley, M. H. *Motivation: Theory and research*. New York: Wiley, 1964.

Cummin, P. C. TAT correlates of executive performance. *Journal of Applied Psychology*, 1967, **51**, 78–81.

Gellerman, S. W. *Motivation and productivity*. New York: American Management Association, 1963.

Heckhausen, H. *The anatomy of achievement motivation*. New York: Academic Press, 1967.

Hundal, P. S. A study of entrepreneurial motivation: Comparison of fast- and slow-progressing small-scale industrial entrepreneurs in Punjab, India. *Journal of Applied Psychology*, 1971, **55**, 317–323.

Litwin, G., & Stringer, R. A. *Motivation and organizational climate*. Boston: Graduate School of Business Administration, Harvard University, 1968.

McClelland, D. C. *Personality*. New York: Dryden Press, 1951.

McClelland, D. C. *The achieving society*. Princeton, N.J.: Van Nostrand, 1961.

McClelland, D. C. Business drive and national achievement. *Harvard Business Review*, 1962, **40(4)**, 99–112.

McClelland, D. C. *Assessing human motivation*. New York: General Learning Press, 1971.

McClelland, D. C., Atkinson, J. W., Clark, R. A., & Lowell, E. L. *The achievement motive.*

McClelland, D. C., & Winter, D. G. *Motivating economic achievement.* New York: Free Press, 1971.

Murray, H. A. *Explorations in personality.* New York: Oxford University Press, 1938.

Steers, R. M. Task goals, individual need strengths, and supervisory performance. Unpublished doctoral dissertation, Graduate School of Administration, University of California, Irvine, 1973.

Wainer, H. A., & Rubin, I. M. Motivation of research and development enterpreneurs. *Journal of Applied Psychology,* 1969, **53,** 178–184.

Weiner, B., & Kukla, A. An attributional analysis of achievement motivation. *Journal of Personality and Social Psychology,* 1970, **15,** 1–20.

Motivation and Behavior
George H. Litwin and Robert A. Stringer, Jr.

THE ATKINSON MODEL

In his *Introduction to Motivation* (1964), Atkinson presents a formal theory or model of motivated behavior, utilizing a number of principles of motivation which have emerged from the research in this field. We will state the principles embodied in this theory or model, using a simple mechanistic analogy, and then proceed to examine some technical details of the Atkinson model. The basic principles are summarized below:[1]

1 All reasonably healthy adults have a considerable *reservoir of potential energy*. Studies thus far have not indicated that differences in the total amount of potential energy are important determinants of motivation.

2 All adults have a number of basic "motives" or "needs" which can be thought of as valves or outlets that channel and regulate the flow of potential energy from this reservoir.

3 Although most adults within a given culture may have the same set of motives or energy outlets, they will differ greatly in the relative strength or "readiness" of various motives. A strong motive may be thought of as a valve or energy outlet that opens easily and has a larger aperture for energy flow (due, usually, to frequent use). A weak motive can be thought of as a tight, sticky valve that, even when open, allows only limited energy flow.

4 Whether or not a motive is "actualized," that is, whether energy flows through *this* outlet into behavior and useful work, depends on the specific situation in which the person finds himself.

5 Certain characteristics of the situation arouse or trigger different motives, opening different valves or energy outlets. Each motive or energy outlet is responsive to a different set of situational characteristics.

6 Since various motives are directed toward different kinds of satisfaction, the pattern of behavior that results from arousal of a motive (and the opening of that energy outlet) is quite distinct for each motive. That is, each motive leads to a different pattern of behavior.

7 By changing the nature of the situational characteristics or stimuli, different motives are aroused or actualized, resulting in the energizing of distinct and different patterns of behavior.

In other words, all adults carry around with them the potential energy to behave in a variety of ways. Whether they behave in these ways depends on: (a) the relative strength or readiness of the various motives a person has; and (b) the situational characteristics or stimuli presented by the situation determine, in large

From *Motivation and organizational climate,* Boston: Division of Research, Graduate School of Business Administration, Harvard University, 1968, 10–27. Reprinted by permission.

[1] The mechanical analogy and the language are our own. Neither David McClelland nor John Atkinson should bear any responsibility for this oversimplified description.

part, which motives will be aroused and what kind of behavior will be generated.

For example, an employee may be used to working in small informal work groups. He is dependent on the group for much of his work satisfaction. We might say that this employee is motivated by a *need for affiliation.* His affiliation energy outlet seems to be wide open when he is allowed to do his job around other people. If the situation was changed, and the worker had to work alone, or if talking was prohibited, or if fellow workers were unfriendly, there would be little opportunity for social interaction. In this new environment, this worker's affiliation energy outlet would not be used. Other motives may be stimulated by the new situation, but we can see how the worker's overall pattern of motivation and behavior would be changed.

Specifically, the Atkinson model holds that *aroused motivation* (to strive for a particular kind of satisfaction or goal) is a joint multiplicative function of (a) the *strength of the basic motive* [M], (b) the *expectancy* of attaining the goal [E], and (c) the *perceived incentive value* of the particular goal [I]. In other words, a person's aroused motivation to behave in a particular way is said to depend on the strength or readiness of his motives, and on two kinds of perceptions of the situation: his expectancies of goal-attainment and the incentive values he attaches to the goals presented. The model can be summarized as follows:

$$\text{Aroused Motivation} = \text{M} \times \text{E} \times \text{I}$$

Motives are conceived here as dispositions to strive for general and often internalized goals. They are presumably acquired in childhood and are relatively enduring and stable over periods of time. Expectancies and incentive values depend on the person's experience in specific situations like the one he now confronts, and they change as the person moves about from one situation to another or as the situation itself is altered.

This theory or model of motivation is closely related to the field theory of behavior proposed by Kurt Lewin (1938) and to several other prominent theories of motivation and behavior (see Feather, 1959; Atkinson, 1964, pp. 274–275). These theories all state that the tendency to act in a certain way depends on the strength of the expentancy or belief that the act will lead to a particular outcome or goal and on the value of that outcome or goal to the person.

The Atkinson model was developed to explain behavior and performance related to the *need for achievement* (*n* Achievement), which is defined as a need to excel in relation to competitive or internalized standards. More recently the model has been extended to explain behavior related to the *need for power* (*n* Power), defined as a need for control and influence over others, and the *need for affiliation* (*n* Affiliation), defined as a need for warm, friendly relationships. All these qualities of motivation have been shown to be important determinants of performance and success in business and government organizations (see McClelland, 1961; Vroom, 1964; and Andrews, 1967).

MEASUREMENT OF MOTIVE STRENGTH

The presence and strength of these motives are assessed through thematic apperceptive methods. This basic method, called the TAT (Thematic Apperception Test), was developed by Murray (1938). Present methods are derivations of the original TAT, aimed at the study of particular motives and suited to particular populations (e.g., college students, business men, Negro Americans). The subject is shown a series of pictures, usually of people in fairly ambiguous social and work situations, and he is asked to make up an imaginative story suggested by each picture of the series. These stories are written (by the subject) or recorded (by the experimenter) and analyzed in detail for evidence of the different kinds of imagery associated with various motives.

Such tests are often referred to as projective tests because the subject "projects" into his story his own thoughts, feelings, and attitudes. What the tests actually do is provide us with samples of the kinds of things a person spends his time thinking and daydreaming about when he is not under pressure to think about anything in particular. What do his thoughts turn to when he is by himself and not engaged in a special job? Does he think about his family and friends, about relaxing and watching the Rose Bowl on TV, about getting a particular customer or colleague off his back? Or does he spend his time thinking and planning how he will sell a customer on a new product, cut production costs, or invent a better steam trap, toothpaste tube, or guidance system?

NEED FOR ACHIEVEMENT[2]

If a man spends his time thinking about doing his job better, accomplishing something unusual and important, or advancing his career, the psychologist says he has a high *need for achievement,* often written n Achievement—he is concerned with achievement and derives considerable satisfaction from striving for achievement. A man with a strong *need for achievement* thinks not only about the achievement goals, but about how he can attain them, what obstacles or blocks he might encounter, and how he will feel if he succeeds or fails.

What are people with a strong *need for achievement* good for? Evidence indicates that they seek out, enjoy, and do well at jobs that are entrepreneurial in character. They make good business executives, particularly in challenging or developing industries. They enjoy activity and often become salesmen, sales managers, consultants, or fund raisers. Years of careful empirical research have made possible and understanding of why a man with a strong *need for achievement* exhibits such characteristics in his behavior.

1. *He likes situations in which he takes personal responsibility for finding solutions to problems.* The reason is obvious. Otherwise, he could get little personal achievement satisfaction from the successful outcome. Not a gambler, he does not prefer situations the outcome of which depends on chance or other factors beyond his control, rather than on his abilities and efforts. For example:

[2]The material in this section is adapted from "Business Drive and National Achievement" by David C. McClelland (1962).

Some business school students in one study played a game in which they had to choose between two options, each of which afforded only one chance in three of succeeding. For one option they rolled a die, and if it came up at either of two of the six possibilities, they won. For the other option they had to work on a difficult business problem which they knew that only one out of three people on the average had been able to solve in the time allotted.

Under these conditions, the men with high *n* Achievement consistently chose to work on the buiness problem, even though they knew the odds of success were statistically the same for rolling the die.

To men strong in achievement concern, the idea of winning by chance simply does not produce the same achievement satisfaction as winning by their own personal efforts. Obviously, such a concern for taking personal responsibility is useful in a business executive. He may not be faced very often with the alternative of rolling dice to determine the outcome of a decision, but there are many other ways by which he could avoid taking personal responsibility, such as passing the buck or trying to get someone else (or a committee) to take the responsibility for getting something done.

The famed self-confidence of good executive (which, actually, is related to high achievement motivation) is also involved here. He thinks it can be done if he takes responsibility, and very often he is right because he has spent so much time thinking about how to do it that he does it better.

2. *Another characteristic of a man with a strong achievement concern is his tendency to set moderate achievement goals and to take calculated risks.* Again his strategy is well suited to his needs. Only by taking on moderately difficult tasks is he likely to get the achievement satisfaction he wants. If he takes on an easy or routine problem, he will succeed but will get very little satisfaction out of his success, the mere simplicity of the task not affording adequate opportunity to prove his ability and achievement. If he takes on an extremely difficult problem, he is unlikely to get any satisfaction because he may not succeed. Such an eventuality might disprove his ability and frustrate rather than satisfy his need to achieve. In between these two extremes, he stands the best chance of maximizing both his sense of personal achievement and his likelihood of succeeding.

Applying Atkinson's model, it is only the moderate risk situation which simultaneously maximizes his expectancy of success and the incentive value associated with that success, thereby allowing maximal satisfaction of the need. The point can be made with the children's game of ring toss, a variant of which we have used with individuals of all ages, to discover how a person with *high need for achievement* approaches it. To illustrate:

The child is told that he scores when he succeeds in throwing a ring over a peg on the floor and that he can choose to stand anywhere he pleases. Obviously, if he stands next to the peg, he can score a ringer every time, but if he stands a long distance away, he will hardly ever get a ringer. The curious fact is that children with high concern for achievement quite consistently stand at moderate distances from the peg where they are most apt to get achievement satisfaction (or, to be more precise, where the decreasing probability-of-success curve crosses the increasing satisfaction-from-sucess curve). The ones with low concern for achievement, on the other hand, distribute their choices of where to stand quite randomly over the entire distance. In other words, people with high *need for achievement* prefer a situation where there is a challenge, where there is some real risk of not succeeding, but where that risk is not so great that they might not overcome it by their own efforts.

We waste our time feeling sorry for the entrepreneur whose constant complaints are that he is overworking, that he has more problems than he knows how to deal with, that he is doomed to ulcers because of overwork, and so on. The bald truth is that he has high *need for achievement*—that he lives the very challenges he complains about. In fact, a careful study might well show that he creates most of them for himself. He may talk about quitting business and living on his investments, but if he did, he might then really get ulcers. The state of mind of being a little overextended is precisely the one he seeks, since overcoming difficulties gives him achievement satisfaction. His real problem is that of keeping the difficulties from getting too big for him, which explains in part why he talks so much about them—it is a nagging problem for him to keep them at a level he can handle.

3. *The man who has a strong concern for achievement also wants concrete* ✓ *feedback as to how well he is doing.* Otherwise how could he get any satisfaction out of what he had done? Business is almost unique in the amount of feedback it provides in the form of sales, cost, production, and profit figures. It is no accident that the symbol of the businessman in popular cartoons is a wall chart with a line on it going up or down. The businessman, sooner or later, knows how well he is doing; salesmen will often know their success from day to day. There is a concreteness in this knowledge of results which is by and large missing from the kind of feedback professionals get.

The teacher will serve as a representative example of such a professional. His job is to transmit certain attitudes and certain kinds of information to his students. He does get some degree of feedback as to how well he has done his job, but results are fairly imprecise and hardly concrete. His students, colleagues, and even his institution's administration may indicate that they like his teaching, but he still has no real objective or precise evidence that his students have learned anything from him. Many of his students do well on examinations, but he knows from past experience that they will forget much of what they have written in a year or two. If he has high *need for achievement* and is really concerned about whether he has done his job well, he must be satisfied with sketchy, occasional evidence that his former pupils did absorb some of his ideas and attitudes. Most likely, however, he is *not* a person with high *need for achievement* and is quite satisfied with the affection and recognition that he gets for his work. These feedback measures will gratify needs other than his *need for achievement*.

Obviously not everyone likes to work in situations where the feedback is concrete. It can prove him right, but it also can prove him wrong. The person with high *n* Achievement has a compelling interest to know whether he was right or wrong. He thrives and is happier when this condition is satisfied by the situation than when it is not, as is usually the case in the professional situation. When an individual with a high *need for achievement* does involve himself in a professional situation, furthermore, he usually seeks out a role where more concrete feedback on performance is provided, such as that of a trial lawyer, a doctor who establishes a clinic, or a professor who becomes a fund raiser.

NEED FOR POWER

If a man spends his time thinking about the influences and control he has over others, and how he can use this influence, say, to win an argument, to change other people's behavior, or to gain a position of authority and status, then the psychologist says he has a high *need for power,* often written *n* Power. He derives satisfaction from controlling the means of influence over others.

Men with a strong need for power will usually attempt to influence others directly—by making suggestions, by giving their opinions and evaluations, and by trying to talk others into things. They seek positions of leadership in group activities; whether they become leaders or are seen only as "dominating individuals" depends on other attributes such as ability and sociability. They are usually verbally fluent, often talkative, sometimes argumentative. Men with a strong *need for power* are seen by others as forceful and outspoken, but also as hard-headed and demanding.

As should be expected, men with a strong concern for power prefer positions which allow the exercise of power. They enjoy roles requiring persuasion, such as teaching and public speaking. In addition, a man with a high concern for power will seek out positions which involve control of the means of influencing others, such as political office or top management slots. Studies of the motivation of managers have shown that although strong achievement motivation distinguishes the successful manager or entrepreneur from other people, the men in top management, and particularly organization presidents, are strongly motivated by the *need for power.*

For the past 20 years, social scientists have been involved in the study of influence and power. Much of this research deals with topics such as "Authoritarian Personality" and "Fascism," and represents largely a kind of social criticism regarding the use of power rather than a genuine scientific exploration of power motivation. In a democracy, matters relating to the accumulation of personal power are inevitably treated with suspicion and dread, and some scientists have been quick to interpret the natural concerns with influence, control, and power which develop in society as a dangerous threat to our democratic institutions and way of life.

What research has been done indicates clearly that men with strong *need for power* do not always gain power and that even when they do, what use they make of this power is determined by *other needs and values.* A man with a strong *n*

Power, little concern for warm, affiliative relationships, and strong authoritarian values would certainly tend toward autocratic and dictatorial action. On the other hand, a man with strong *n* Power, considerable sensitivity to other's feelings, and a desire to give service to others would probably make an excellent Peace Corps worker or missionary. This polarity in the use of power is illustrated in a study by Andrews (1967) of two Mexican companies. One of these was a dynamic and rapidly growing organization whose employees were enthusiastic about their work; the other organization, despite a large initial investment and favorable market, had shown almost no growth and had serious problems of dissatisfaction and turnover, particularly in the management ranks. Assessment of personnel motivation in both these companies showed that those in the upper management of the more dynamic organization were much higher in *n* Achievement than either their own subordinates or those in the upper management of the static organization. The presidents of both of these companies were *very high* in the *need for power*. In the case of the dynamic organization, the president's *need for power*, combined with a moderate *need for achievement* and a strong commitment to achievement values, had helped create a thriving, successful business. In the other case, the president's *need for power* and rather authoritarian values led him to dominate every other person in the organization, make all the decisions himself, and leave almost no room for individual responsibility.

Politics as an activity represents one of the clearest theaters for expression of the *need for power*, and men who run for political office characteristically demonstrate very strong power motivation. Here the explicit goal is control of the means of influencing others (e.g., law enforcement, executive position), and this goal can only be reached by influencing many others (e.g., the voters). The various writings on the American Presidency may be the richest literature available on the phenomenology of power, how power is gained, and how it affects men who have it. The following two passages, from Theodore H. White's *The Making of the President 1960*, are very vivid description of the phenomenology of power—how power is experienced by the man who seeks and gains it:

> Shortly before he died in 1950, the great Henry L. Stimson was asked which of the many Presidents of his acquaintance had been the best. Stimson, according to the man from whom I heard the tale, reflected a minute or two, for his career stretched over half a century of American history. He had known intimately or served importantly more Presidents, Democratic and Republican, than any other citizen of his age—from Theodore Roosevelt through Taft, Wilson, Coolidge and Hoover to Franklin D. Roosevelt and Harry S. Truman. After reflection, Stimson replied to his friend:
>
> If, by the phrase "best President," the friend meant who had been the most efficient President—why, of course, the answer would be William Howard Taft. Under Taft, the Cabinet met in order, affairs marched to the agenda of the meeting, responsibility was clearly deputized, and when each man rose from the Cabinet table he knew exactly what he was to do and to whom he was to report. Yes, Taft certainly

was the most efficient. If, however, continued Stimson, by the "best President" one meant the "greatest President," then the answer must be different. The name would, without doubt, be Roosevelt—but he was not sure whether the first name was Theodore or Franklin. For both of these gentlemen, you see, not only understood the *use* of power; they knew the *enjoyment* of power, too. And that was the important thing.

Whether a man is burdened by power or enjoys power; whether he is trapped by responsibility or made free by it; whether he is moved by other people and outer forces or moves them—this is of the essence of leadership.

. . . . .

A one-time personal aide of President Truman once put the matter to me in this way: "The most startling thing a new President discovers is that his world is *not* monolithic. In the world of the Presidency, giving an order does *not* end the matter. You can pound your fist on the table or you can get mad or you can blow it all and go out to the golf course. But nothing gets done except by endless follow-up, endless kissing and coaxing, endless threatening and compelling. There are all those thousands of people in Washington working for you in the government—and every one is watching you, waiting, trying to guess what you mean, trying to get your number. Can they fool you? Can they outwait you? Will you be mad when you hear it isn't done yet? And Congress keeps shoving more and more power into the President's lap—the Formosa resolution gives the President power to declare war all by himself; and Congress keeps setting up new regulatory agencies, and you have to hire and fire the men who run them. And they're all testing you. How much can they get away with? How much authority can they take? How much authority do *you* want them to have? And once you choose your men—you have to keep them; which means the endless attrition of *your* will against *their* will, because some of them will be damned good men . . . (White, 1965, pp. 366–367).

NEED FOR AFFILIATION

If a man spends his time thinking about the warm, friendly, companionate relationships he has, or would like to have, the psychologist says he has a *need for affiliation*, often written *n* Affiliation. Thoughts about restoring close relationships that have been disrupted, consoling or helping someone, or participating in friendly, companionate activities such as bull sessions, reunions, and parties are regarded as evidence of affiliation motivation.

Since they want other to like them, men with a strong *need for affiliation* are likely to pay attention to the feelings of others. In group meetings they make efforts to establish friendly relationships, often by agreeing or giving emotional support. Men with strong *need for affiliation* seek out jobs which offer opportunities for friendly interaction. In business, these men often take supervisory jobs where maintaining good relationships is more important than decision making. People who have institutionalized helping roles, such as teachers, nurses, and counselors, also demonstrate strong *need for affiliation*.

While strong *n* Affiliation does not seem to be important for effective managerial performance, and might well be detrimental, recent research has suggested that some minimal concern with the feelings of others and with the companionate quality of relationships is necessary for superior managerial and executive capability. It is reasonable to assume that such basic affiliative concern is critical in understanding others and in building good working relationships with both superiors and subordinates—this affiliative concern is a means to attain other, broader kinds of satisfaction and might well be labeled *interpersonal competence*. Moment and Zaleznik give a graphic description of this kind of behavior:

> People need each other to get work done and to live full lives. The fullness of life is measured by achievements. Communicating with people is the ultimate achievement process. Something new is created through talking and working with people. The ultimate achievement is the creation of new and better resolutions of social and technical problems.
>
> Although there are standards of excellence for individuals' contributions, real resolutions of problems are tested in the communication process. . . .
>
> . . . his behavior clearly communicates his feelings. He also communicates his confidence in himself; he will unapologetically defend his positions, but he will also change his position in accordance with what he is learning in the process. He acknowledges in his behavior that he is communicating with specific people, rather than thinking out loud about ideas separated from people. His behavior says that the other persons as individuals, as well as sources of ideas, are bound up in the problemsolving process (Moment and Zaleznik, 1963, pp. 120–121).

Compare this with Moment and Zaleznik's description of the "social specialists," which we would characterize as men with strong *need for affiliation*:

> People need each other for support. Feeling lonely, disliked, and disrespected by people is the worst thing that could happen to a person. Living together in harmony is the ultimate value. One must work hard and do a good job in order to be accepted by others. But work should not be allowed to interfere with harmony, respect, and affection.
>
> One learns from experience that being close and friendly with people is more important than career success. Having friends and being friendly are necessary to support and encourage a person through periods of disappointment and hardship.
>
> Satisfaction is derived from being liked and accepted in the group. Argument and conflict are frustrating and make for an unhappy experience (Moment and Zaleznik, 1963, pp. 123–124).

SUMMARY

In this chapter a theory of motivation developed out of more than 20 years of laboratory and field research has been presented. Some emphasis was placed on a recent formal model, the Atkinson model, which states that aroused motivation (to strive for a particular goal) is a function of the strength of the basic need and two situationally determined factors, the expectancy of goal-attainment and the perceived incentive value of the goal.

We have tried to describe the three kinds of motivation that we will focus on in this monograph—achievement motivation, power motivation, and affiliation motivation. There are at least three ways of describing these motivational tendencies, all of which we have employed. First, we have tried to define the nature of the basic need or goal, particularly in terms of the kind of satisfaction that is desired. Second, we have described the quality of aroused motivation, in terms of the thoughts and feelings of the motivated person. Third, we have identified patterns of behavior which stem from arousal of the *need for achievement,* the *need for power,* and the *need for affiliation.* It is not always possible to distinguish among these levels of description without being overly tedious. However, the reader should try to keep in mind the very important difference between *motive,* which is a relatively stable personality characteristic, and *aroused motivation,* which is a situationally influenced action tendency. The reader should also keep in mind that aroused motivation can be described in terms of a *pattern of thoughts and feelings,* which is a situationally influenced action tendency. The reader should also keep in mind that aroused motivation can be described in terms of a *pattern of thoughts and feelings,* such as would be revealed in thematic apperceptive stories, or in terms of a *pattern of behavior* which is likely to result from motive arousal.

The specific scoring procedures which are used to analyze thematic apperceptive stories, and which allow us to measure the relative strength of *n* Achievement, *n* Power, and *n* Affiliation have not been dealt with. These scoring procedures are described in detail in Atkinson's *Motives in Fantasy, Action, and Society* (1958). Nonprofessional scorers can use these procedures to derive specific scores which provide objective measures of the strength of aroused motivation. The objectivity of these measures is demonstrated by the high agreement that is possible among scorers working independently. Recent attempts to develop computer programs to do this scoring have been quite successful, providing definite evidence of the objectivity of these scoring procedures (see Litwin, 1965).

The *n* Achievement, *n* Power and *n* Affiliation scores derived from thematic apperceptive tests through application of the scoring procedures described by Atkinson (1958) are assumed to represent the strength of aroused motivation. That is, they are products of motive strength *and* of situational factors. Under certain circumstances, these scores can also provide a useful index of the strength of the basic motives. When a group of people with similar backgrounds and experiences (and, presumably, perceptions) are in the same constant situation, differences in motivation scores can be assumed to represent differences in the strength of basic motives—the subjective or idiosyncratic elements are assumed to cancel each other out. That is, the situational influences are held constant and relative differences in score represent differences in motive strength.

The administrative implications of the kind of motivation theory we have described are quite dramatic. By identifying and learning to influence particular expectancies and incentives associated with a motive network, it is possible to strengthen the aroused motivation or behavior tendency. Though the role of reinforcement in the Atkinson model has not been clearly specified, the effects of reinforcement on aroused motivation are well established. Using our oversimplified, hydraulic model of the Atkinson theory, reinforcement can be represented as an enlargement of the valve capacity associated with any particular motive. Just as water enlarged the proverbial hole through which the little Dutch boy stuck his finger, so the repeated passage of energy through these motivational valves tends to wear away at their edges, making them larger and more easily opened, increasing their total capacity for energy flow. By tying the expectancies and incentives to as many consistent cues as possible in the business environment, the likelihood of a particular pattern of behavior can be increased.

Since different motives lead to different behavior patterns, it is important that the manager learn to identify, at least in a rough way, different kinds of basic motives or needs. He must also be able to "fit" the demands of a job to a pattern of behavior that will result from and provide satisfaction for the arousal of a given motive. He can create this fit by the selection and appropriate placement of people with different motives, by altering somewhat the demands of a given job, or by *selectively* arousing, satisfying, and thereby reinforcing the kind of motivation that will lead to the most appropriate job behavior. Once he has obtained what he considers a reasonable fit, he can proceed to build into the work situation the kinds of expentancies and incentives that will arouse the desired motivation and assure persistent patterns of behavior.

REFERENCES

Andrews, J.(1967) "The Achievement Motive in Two Types of Orgainzations," *Journal of Personality and Social Psychology,* **6**: 163–168.

Atkinson, J. W.,ed. (1958) *Motives in Fantasy, action, and Society.* Princeton: D. Van Nostrand Company.

Atkinson, J. W. (1964) *An Introduction to Motivation.* Princeton: D. Van Nostrand Company.

Feather, N. T.(1950) "Subjective Probability and Decision under Uncertainty," *Psychological Review,* **66**: 150–164.

Herzberg, F. (1966) *Work and the Nature of Man.* Cleveland: World Publishing Company.

Lewin, K.(1938) *The Conceptual Representation and the Measurement of Psychological Forces.* Durham: Duke University Press.

Litwin, G. H.(1965) "The Language of Achievement: An Analysis of Achievement-Related Themes in Fantasy Using Mechanical Methods," unpublished doctoral dissertation, Harvard University.

McClelland, D. C.(1961) *The Achieving Society.* Princeton: D. Van Nostrand Company.

McClelland, D. C.(1962) "Business Drive and National Achievement," *Harvard Business Review,* **40**: July-August, 99–112.

Moment, D., and A. Zaleznik (1963) *Role Development and Interpersonal Competence.* Boston: Division of Research, Harvard Business School.

Murray, H. A.(1938) *Exploration in Personality.* New York: Oxford University Press.

Myers, M. S.(1966) "Conditions for Manager Motivation," *Harvard Business Review,* **44**: January-February, 58–71.

Vroom, V. H. (1964) *Work and Motivation.* New York: John Wiley and Sons.
White, T. H. (1965) *The Making of the President 1960.* New York: Atheneum Publishers.

TAT Correlates of Executive Performance
Pearson C. Cummin

The most comprehensive delineation of the executive personality to date has been achieved by William Henry (1949). Although the individual personality is shaped to some extent by the internalization of the executive role, Henry maintains that the process of executive selection tends to favor those individuals "whose personality structure is most readily adaptable to this particular role [p. 286]." Although Henry's meticulous description of the executive personality afforded no empirical evidence, it suggested a pattern of needs which seemed to motivate the executive and which would lend themselves to empirical validation.

In *The Achieving Society,* McClelland (1961) found that high n Achievement scores (as measured by the TAT) were significantly related to "entrepreneurial" success in several different countries. McClelland defines an entrepreneurial occupation as one in which the individual has *(a)* "more responsibility for *initiating* decisions," *(b)* "more *individual responsibility* for decisions and their effects,"*(c)* "more *objective feedback* of accurate data indicating the success of his decisions," and *(d)* "a job which *entails more risk* and challenge in that there is more chance of a serious wrong decision being observed [pp. 2–3]." He concludes that n Achievement and entrepreneurial success are strongly associated and that when an association is not found between these variables, then one or more of the conditions defining the enterpreneurial role have not been met.

The present study proposed to extend McClelland's findings relating n Achievement to "entrepreneurial" success. Executives who were rated as more or less successful were compared in six motives. n Affiliation, n Power, n Autonomy, n Agression, and n Deference, as well as n Achievement, were examined. These additional motives were selected from Murray's (1943) list of needs as those which best fitted Henry's description of the executive personality.

The hypotheisis tested in this study was that more successful executives would score high in n Achievement, n Power, and n Autonomy, whereas less successful executives would have high scores in n Affiliation, n Agression, and n Deference.

From *Journal of Applied Psychology*, 1967, **51**, 78–81. Copyright by the American Psychological Association. Reprinted by permission.

The choice of the Achievement motive as one of the factors to be used in differentiating successful from less successful executives was based primarily on three considerations. First, much of McClelland's (1953, 1963) research has been centered around this motive, and he has shown that there is a strong association between n Achievement and entreprenurial success. Second, one of Henry's major characterizations of the successful business executive was "achievement desires." Third, n Achievement had already been adapted into a scoring manual by McClelland, which made the question of its reliability far less doubtful.

One of Henry's characterizations of the successful business executive involved the nature of his interpersonal relations. Successful executives were described as being detached and impersonal toward their subordinates, and as having broken all emotional ties with their parents. Whyte (1956) also describes the successful executive as a man who is concerned with "getting ahead" and not just "fitting in." It was on the basis of these two considerations that the hypotheisis concerning the relationship of n Affiliation to success was formulated.

The Power motive was chosen primarily because of Henry's findings that successful executives are constantly struggling for increased responsibility. Whyte refers to this mobility drive as the "executive neurosis"; but whether the successful executive enjoys moving steadily up the power hierarchy of the organization or whether he does it out of fear of being replaced from below, the result is the same.

There has been no published research that has studied the relationship of the three remaining motives to business success. With respect to Autonomy, Whyte suggested that, while unsuccessful executives have a feeling of personal attachment toward the organization and its policies, successful executives tend to be more "out for themselves." They are not tied to the organization and will not hesitate to go elsewhere if they feel their prospects of advancement are too restricted with their current firm. This theory was generally supported by Hagen's (1959) findings that major executives tend to have achieved their success by moving diagonally from one firm to another, or even from one occupational field to another; while minor executives, who will never rise above a certain level, have tended to progress slowly and vertically up through the organization.

Henry states that a successful executive is an "active, striving, *agressive* person," but that his aggressions are "channeled into work or struggles for status and prestige [p. 289]." Primarily on the basis of this statement, it was hypothesized that the successful executives would be low in n Agression, whereas the unsuccessful executives would be high.

The theory on which the choice of the Deference motive was based is largely the result of an intuitive deduction on the part of the author, although there is some basis for it in Whyte's study. Whyte states that one of the major drives of the potentially unsuccessful executive is to become a part of the organization, whereas the potentially successful executive, with his well-defined self-identity, chooses to remain emotionally disconnected with his firm.

METHOD

Sample

The subject (*S*) sample and the experimental conditions are described in detail in Moment and Zaleznik's (1963) *Role Development and Interpersonal Competence*. Fifty-two business men from Boston and the surrounding area were divided into four groups. The first group consisted of engineers and technical supervisors and represented the middle level of organization hierarchy. The second group was more heterogeneous and was made up of top executives as well as men in middle management.

The *S*s in the third and fourth groups were secured a year later. The members of Group 3 were selected so as to fall in a relatively narrow age range, whereas Group 4 comprised a wide range of ages and two women. In general, however, all four groups may be said to fall within Roe's (1956) "organization-type" occupational grouping. The median age of the sample was 35. Median salary ranged from $7,500 to $11,000; and the median educational level was "some graduate work." These data were obtained through a detailed questionnaire which each *S* was required to complete.

Each *S* was also administered a written form of a specially constructed Thematic Apperception Test (TAT). These consisted of four pictures showing situations in which business men are obviously involved. The instructions given on this test were similar to ones employed in the TAT.

Experimental Procedure

A modified version of McClelland's scoring manuals for n Achievement, n Affiliation, and n Power was used to test the presence or absence and strength of each of these three motives. The description and scoring manual for n Autonomy, n Agression, and n Deference were divised by the present author.

Both Imagery and Need received a $+1$ as they do in McClelland's scoring system. The rationale behind this was that Imagery indicated the presence of a motive while Imagery and Need (Need was not scored without scoring Imagery) indicated an active concern over that motive. Contrary to McClelland's system, *S*s were not given a -1 for Unrelated Imagery, and the distinction between Doubtful and Definite Imagery was not made. Because of the small number of TAT pictures ($N = 4$) and the relatively large number of motives under consideration, it was considered impractical to score a -1 for the lack of related Imagery in any one motive. All motives not scored recived an automatic 0.

The third category into which each of the six motives was subdivided was created by the author. Before devising the scoring manuals, 20 of the 48 protocols were read in order to obtain a general idea of the nature of some of the stories. It was discovered at this time that a significant number of the stories apparently adopted a somewhat ambivalent attitude toward the motive Imagery and Need which they expressed. This ambivalence often took the form of punishment, either by guilt or by other external forces, for the expression of a particular motive. Ambivalence was scored with a -1.

Each of the 48 TAT protocols was then scored independently by the author and another rater. The reliability percentages for four cards with six motives per card which were scored for each S ranged from 78% to 97% agreement. The reliability percentages for each motive on all 192 cards (4 per S) ranged from 82% to 98%. The scores of the two raters were only considered in agreement when identical for each motive on each card, and the above degree of reliability was thus considered adequate for the present study. Having scored each protocol independently, the two raters then met to discuss scoring disagreements and arrived at a consensus.

Classification of the Raw Data

The sample was divided into two groups of more and less successful executives. The distinction was made by dividing Ss into six age groups. The annual income of each individual was listed under the appropriate age group. The median salary was then taken for each of the six groups. All Ss at, or above, the median salary in their group were labeled as more successful. Those below the median were considered to be less successful.

Next, the total score of each S was computed for each need. The Ss were then divided again into their respective age groups, and the mean score of each need was computed. All scores at, or above, the mean were considered high for that particular motive; all scores below the mean were considered low.

Testing the Hypothesis

Because the hypothesis predicts the direction of influence of each motive on greater or lesser success in business, a one-tailed test of significance was employed in most cases. The chi-square technique in 2×2 contingency tables was used to test each specific hypothesis.

RESULTS

The results are shown in Table 1. The first hypothesis was that more successful executives would have high scores in n Achievement, whereas less successful executives would have low scores on this motive. The p value was significant beyond the .01 level of confidence.

The second hypotheisis was that more successful executives would have low

Table 1   Relationship of Career Success to TAT Motive

Motive	x^2	p	Hi motive Hi success	Hi motive Lo success	Lo motive Hi success	Lo motive Lo success
n Achievement	5.58	.01	19	5	10	14
n Affiliation	1.26	.30[a]	15	6	14	13
n Power	6.21	.01	18	4	11	15
n Autonomy	0.51	.25	15	7	14	12
n Aggression	0.11	.80[a]	7	3	22	16
n Deference	0.01	.50	11	8	18	11

[a] p value is two-tailed because results were in the opposite direction from that which was predicted.

scores in n Affiliation, whereas less successful executives would have high scores. The direction of the results was opposite from that which was predicted. It is interesting to note that had the hypothesis predicted that successful executives would have *high* scores instead of low for n Affiliation, the value of p would have been .15.

The third hypothesis was that more successful executives would have high scores in n Power, whereas less successful executives would have low scores. The p value was significant beyond the .01 level of confidence.

The final three hypotheses relating success in business to n Autonomy, n Agression, and n Deference were not supported.

DISCUSSION

On the two motives (n Achievement and n Power) which differentiated more successful from less successful business executives, the findings concerning n Achievement are probably the most significant in that they support previous research.

McClelland's research indicated a strong association between n Achievement and entrepreneurial success. The term "entrepreneurial," however, may not be specific to the business community at large. It takes into account only a small portion of businessmen. The significance of the results of the present study is that n Achievement was shown to be related to success in much more diversified sample of the business population. The results also gave empirical validation to Henry's characterization of successful business executives as men with "achievement desires." They indicated, however, the limited extent to which Henry's characterization of successful business executives bears up under rigorous empirical validation.

The successful validation of the hypothesis concerning the power motive was considered significant because of the lack of any previous research connecting it with success in business. A chi-square showed no significant correlation between n Power and n Achievement. The findings provide empirical support for the observations of Henry and Whyte that successful executives are constantly struggling for increased responsibility. The positive findings related to power suggest that achievement striving alone is not the sole criteria for differentiating more from less successful executives. There is also a definite desire, on the part of successful executives, for increased responsibility and control within the organizational hierarchy.

The overall picture, then, of the successful executive is one of an individual who is determined to maintain a high standard of excellence in his work, and to assume greater responsibilities and more control over his environment as he advances within the organization.

These findings suggest that the analysis of motives by means of the TAT has promise for executive selection. However, at this stage, the practical use of this technique is limited. Further research supporting these findings on different populations is needed before these methods can be validly employed in industry.

REFERENCES

Hagen, D. H. Family atmosphere and other childhood patterns as precursors of career interests. Unpublished doctoral dissertation, Harvard University, 1959.

Henry, W. E. The business executive: The psychodynamics of a social role. *American Journal of Sociology,* 1949, **54,** 286–291.

McClelland, D. C. *The achieving society.* New York: Van Nostrand, 1961.

McClelland, D. C. n Achievement and entrepreneurship: A longitudinal study. Harvard University, 1963. (Mimeo)

McClelland, D. C., Atkinson, J. W., Clark, R., & Lowell, E. *The achievement motive.* New York: Appleton-Century-Crofts, 1953.

Moment, D., & Zaleznick, A. Role development and interpersonal competence. Boston: Harvard University Press, 1963.

Murray, H. A. *Thematic apperception test manual.* Cambridge: Harvard University Press, 1943.

Roe, A. *The psychology of occupations.* New York: Wiley, 1956.

Whyte, W. H. *The organization man.* New York: Anchor, 1956.

Toward a Theory of Motive Acquisition
David C. McClelland[1]

Too little is known about the processes of personality change at relatively complex levels. The empirical study of the problem has been hampered by both practical and theoretical difficulties. On the practical side it is very expensive both in time and effort to set up systematically controlled educational programs designed to develop some complex personality characteristic like a motive, and to follow the effects of the education over a number of years. It also presents ethical problems since it is not always clear that it is as proper to teach a person a new

From *American Psychologist,* 1965, **20,** 321–333. Copyright by the American Psychological Association. Reprinted by permission.

[1] I am greatly indebted to the Carnegie Corporation of New York for its financial support of the research on which this paper is based, and to my collaborators who have helped plan and run the courses designed to develop the achievement motive—chiefly George Litwin, Elliott Danzig, David Kolb, Winthrop Adkins, David Winter, and John Andrews. The statements made and views expressed are solely the responsibility of the author.

motive as it is a new skill like learning to play the piano. For both reasons, most of what we know about personality change has come from studying psychotherapy where both ethical and practical difficulties are overcome by the pressing need to help someone in real trouble. Yet, this source of information leaves much to be desired: It has so far proven difficult to identify and systematically vary the "inputs" in psychotherapy and to measure their specific effects on subsequent behavior, except in very general ways (cf. Rogers & Dymond, 1954).

On the theoretical side, the dominant views of personality formation suggest anyway that acquisition or change of any complex characteristic like a motive in adulthood would be extremely difficult. Both behavior theory and psychoanalysis agree that stable personality characteristics like motives are laid down in childhood. Behavior theory arrives at this conclusion by arguing that social motives are learned by close association with reduction in certain basic biological drives like hunger, thirst, and physical discomfort which loom much larger in childhood than adulthood. Psychoanalysis, for its part, pictures adult motives as stable resolutions of basic conflicts occurring in early childhood. Neither theory would provide much support for the notion that motives could be developed in adulthood without somehow recreating the childhood conditions under which they were originally formed. Furthermore, psychologists have been hard put to it to find objective evidence that even prolonged, serious, and expensive attempts to introduce personality change through psychotherapy have really proven successful (Eysenck, 1952). What hope is there that a program to introduce personality change would end up producing a big enough effect to study?

Despite these difficulties a program of research has been under way for some time which is attempting to develop the achievement motive in adults. It was undertaken in an attempt to fill some of the gaps in our knowledge about personality change or the acquisition of complex human characteristics. Working with n Achievement has proved to have some important advantages for this type of research: The practical and ethical problems do not loom especially large because previous research (McClelland, 1961) has demonstrated the importance of high n Achievement for entrepreneurial behavior and it is easy to find businessmen, particularly in underdeveloped countries, who are interested in trying any means of improving their entrepreneurial performance. Furthermore, a great deal is known about the origins of n Achievement in childhood and its specific effects on behavior so that educational programs can be systematically planned and their effects evaluated in terms of this knowledge. Pilot attempts to develop n Achievement have gradually led to the formulation of some theoretical notions of what motive acquisition involves and how it can be effectively promoted in adults. These notions have been summarized in the form of 12 propositions which it is the ultimate purpose of the research program to test. The propositions are anchored so far as possible in experiences with pilot courses, in supporting research findings from other studies, and in theory.

Before the propositions are presented, it is necessary to explain more of the theoretical and practical background on which they are based. To begin with, some basis for believing that motives could be acquired in adulthood had to be found in view of the widespread pessimism on the subject among theoretically oriented psychologists. Oddly enough we were encouraged by the successful efforts of two quite different groups of "change agents"—operant conditioners and missionaries. Both groups have been "naive" in the sense of being unimpressed by or ignorant of the state of psychological knowledge in the field. The operant conditioners have not been encumbered by any elaborate theoretical apparatus; they do not believe motives exist anyway, and continue demonstrating vigorously that if you want a person to make a response, all you have to do is elicit it and reward it (cf. Bandura & Walters, 1963, pp. 238 ff.). They retain a simple faith in the infinite plasticity of human behavior in which one response is just like any other and any one can be "shaped up" (strengthened by regard)—presumably even an "achievement" response as produced by a subject in a fantasy test. In fact, it was the naive optimism of one such researcher (Burris, 1958) that had a lot to do with getting the present research under way. He undertook a counseling program in which an attempt to elicit and reinforce achievement-related fantasies proved to be successful in motivating college students to get better grades. Like operant conditioners, the missionaries have gone ahead changing people because they have believed it possible. While the evidence is not scientifically impeccable, common-sense observation yields dozens of cases of adults whose motivational structure has seemed to be quite radically and permanently altered by the educational efforts of Communist Party, Mormon, or other devout missionaries.

A man from Mars might be led to observe that personality change appears to be very difficult for those who think it is very difficult, if not impossible, and much easier for those who think it can be done. He would certainly be oversimplifying the picture, but at the very least his observation suggests that some theoretical revision is desirable in the prevailing views of social motives which link them so decisively to early childhood. Such a revision has been attempted in connection with the research on n Achievement (McClelland, Atkinson, Clark, & Lowell, 1953) and while it has not been widely accepted (cf. Berelson & Steiner, 1964), it needs to be briefly summarized here to provide a theoretical underpinning for the attempts at motive change to be described. It starts with the proposition that all motives are learned, that not even biological discomforts (as from hunger) or pleasures (as from sexual stimulation) are "urges" or "drives" until they are linked to cues that can signify their presence or absence. In time, clusters of expectancies or associations grow up around affective experiences, not all of which are connected by any means with biological needs (McClelland et al., 1953, ch. 2), which we label motives. More formally, motives are "affectively toned associative networks" arranged in a hierarchy of strength or importance within a given individual. Obviously, the definition fits closely the operations used to measure a motive: "an affectively toned associative cluster" is exactly what is coded in a subject's fantasies to obtain an n Achievement score. The strength of the motive (its position in the individual's hierarchy of motives) is measured essentially by counting the number of associations belonging to this cluster as compared to others that an individual produces in a given number of opportunities. If one thinks of a motive as an associative network, it is easier to imagine how one might go about changing it: The problem becomes one of moving its position up on the hierarchy by increasing its salience compared to other clusters. It should be possible to accomplish this end by such tactics as: *(a)* setting up the network—discovering what associations, for example, exists in the achievement area and then extending, strengthening, or otherwise "improving" the network they form; *(b)* conceptualizing the network—forming a clear and conscious construct that labels the network; *(c)* tying the network to as many ones as possible in everyday life, especially those preceding and following action, to insure that the network will be regularly rearoused once formed; and *(d)* working out the relation of the network to superordinate associative clusters, like the self-concept, so that these dominant schemata do not block the train of achievement thoughts—for example, through a chain of interfering associations (i.e., "I am not really the achieving type").

This very brief summary is not intended as a full exposition of the theoretical viewpoint underlying the research, but it should suffice to give a rough idea of how the motive was conceived that we set out to change. This concept helped define the goals of the techniques of change, such as reducing the effects of associative interference from superordinate associate clusters. But what about the techniques themselves? What could we do that would produce effective learning of this sort? Broadly speaking, there are four types of empirical information to draw on. From the animal learning experiments, we know that such factors as repetition, optimal time intervals between stimulus, response, and reward, and the schedule of rewards are very important for effective learning. From human learning experiments, we know that such factors as distribution of practice, repetitions, meaningfulness, and recitation are important. From experiences with psychotherapy (cf. Rogers, 1961), we learn that warmth, honesty, nondirectiveness, and the ability to recode associations in line with psychoanalytic or other personality theories are important. And, from the attitude-change research literature, we learn that such variables as presenting one side or two, using reason or prestige to support an argument, or affiliating with a new reference group are crucial for developing new attitudes (cf. Hovland, Janis, & Kelley, 1953). Despite the fact that many of these variables seem limited in application to the learning situation in which they were studied, we have tried to make use of information from all these sources in designing our "motive acquisition" program and in finding support for the general propositions that have emerged from our study so far. For our purpose has been above all to produce an effect large enough to be measured. Thus we have tried to profit by all that is known about how to facilitate learning or produce personality or attitude change. For, if we could not obtain a substantial effect with all factors working to produce it, there would be no point to studying the effects of each factor taken one at a time. Such a strategy also has the practical advantage that we are in the position of doing our best to "deliver the goods" to our course participants since they were giving us their time and attention to take part in a largely untried educational experience. [2]

Our overall research strategy, therefore is "subtractive" rather than "additive." After we have demonstrated a substantial effect with some 10–12 factors working to produce it, our plan is to subtract that part of the program that deals with each of the factors to discover if there is a significant decline in the effects. This will obviously require giving a fairly large number of courses in a standard institutional setting for the same kinds of businessmen with follow-up evaluation of their performance extending over a number of years. So obviously it will be some time before each of the factors incorporated into the propositions which follow can be properly evaluated so far as its effect on producing motive change is concerned.

The overall research strategy also determined the way the attemts to develop the achievement motive have been organized. That is to say, in order to process enough subjects to permit testing the effectiveness of various "inputs" in a reasonable number of years, the training had to be both of *short duration* (lasting one the three weeks) and *designed for groups* rather than for individuals as in person-to-person counseling. Fortunately these requirements coincide with normal practice in providing short courses for business executives. To conform further with that practice, the training has usually also been *residential* and *voluntary*. The design problems introduced by the last characteristic we have tried to handle in the usual ways by putting half the volunteers on a waiting list or giving them a different, technique-oriented course, etc. So far we have given the course to develop n Achievement in some form or another some eight times to over 140 managers or teachers of management in groups of 9–25 in the United States, Mexico, and India. For the most part the course has been offered by a group of two to four consultant psychologists either to executives in a single company as a company training program, or to executives from several different companies as a self-improvement program, or as part of the program of an institute or school devoted to training managers. The theoretical propositions which follow have evolved gradually from these pilot attempts to be effective in developing n Achievement among businessmen of various cultural backgrounds.

The first step in a motive development program is to create confidence that it will work. Our initial efforts in this area were dictated by the simple practical consideration that we had to "sell" our course or nobody would take it. We were not in the position of an animal psychologist who can order a dozen rats, or an academic psychologist who has captive subjects in his classes, or even a psychotherapist who has sick people knocking at his door every day. So we explained to all who would listen that we had every reason to believe from previous re-

---

[2]Parenthetically, we have found several times that our stated desire to evaluate the effectiveness of our course created doubts in the minds of our sponsors that they did not feel about many popular courses for managers that no one has ever evaluated or plans to evaluate. An attitude of inquiry is not always an asset in education. It suggests one is not sure of his ground.

search that high n Achievement is related to effective entrepreneurship and that therefore business executives could expect to profit from taking a course designed to understand and develop this important human characteristic. What started as a necessity led to the first proposition dealing with how to bring about motive change.

   Proposition 1. The more reasons an individual has in advance to believe that he can, will, or should develop a motive, the more educational attempts designed to develop that motive are likely to succeed. The empirical support for this proposition from other studies is quite impressive. It consists of *(a)* the prestige-suggestion studies showing that people will believe or do what prestigeful sources suggest (cf. Hovland et al., 1953); *(b)* the so-called "Hawthorne effect" showing that people who feel they are especially selected to show an effect will tend to show it (Roethlisberger & Dickson, 1947); *(c)* the "Hello-Goodbye" effect in psychotherapy showing that patients who merely have contact with a prestigeful medical authority improve significantly over waiting list controls and almost as much as those who get prolonged therapy (Frank, 1961); *(d)* the "experimenter bias" studies which show that subjects will often do what an experimenter wants them to do, even though neither he nor they know he is trying to influence them (Rosenthal, 1963); *(e)* the goalsetting studies which show that setting goals for a person particularly in the name of prestigeful authorities like "science" or "research" improves performance (Kausler, 1959; Mierke, 1955); *(f)* the parent-child interaction studies which show that parents who set higher standards of excellence for their sons ar more likely to have sons with high n Achievement (Rosen & D'Andrade, 1959). The common factor in all these studies seems to be that goals are being set for the individual by sources he respects—goals which imply that his behavior should change for a variety of reasons and that it *can* change. In common-sense terms, belief in the possibility and desirability of change are tremendously influential in changing a person.

   So we have used a variety of means to create this belief: the authority of research findings on the relationship of n Achievement to entrepreneurial success, the suggestive power of membership in an experimental group designed to show an effect, the prestige of a great university, our own genuine enthusiasm for the course and our conviction that it would work, as expressed privately and in public speeches. In short, we were trying to make every use possible of what is sometimes regarded as an "error" in such research—namely, the Hawthorne effect, experimenter bias, etc., because we believe it to be one of the most powerful sources of change.

   Why? What is the effect on the person, theoretically speaking, of all this goal setting for him? Its primary function is probably to arouse what exists of an associative network in the achievement area for each person affected. That is, many studies have shown that talk of achievement or affiliation or power tends to increase the frequency with which individuals think about achievement or affiliation or power (cf. Atkinson, 1958). Such an arousal has several possible effects which would facilitate learning:*(a)* It elicits what exists in the person of a "response" thus making it easier to strengthen that response in subsequent learning. *(b)* It creates a discrepancy between a goal (a "Soll-lage" in Heckhausen's—1963—theory of motivation) and a present state ("Ist-lage") which represents a cognitive dissonance the person tries to reduce (cf. Festinger, 1957); in common-sense terms he has an image clearly presented to him of something he is not but should be. *(c)* It tends to block out by simple interference other associations which would inhibit change—such as, "I'm too old to learn," "I never learned much from going to school anyway," "What do these academics know about everyday life?" or "I hope they don't get personal about all this."

After the course has been "sold" sufficiently to get a group together for training, the first step in the course itself is to present the research findings in some detail on exactly how n Achievement is related to certain types of successful entrepreneurial performance. That is, the argument of *The Achieving Society* (McClelland, 1961) is presented carefully with tables, charts and diagrams, usually in lecture form at the outset and with the help of an educational TV film entitled the *Need to Achieve*. This is followed by discussion to clear up any ambiguities that remain in their minds as far as the central argument is concerned. It is especially necessary to stress that not all high achievement is caused by high n Achievement—that we have no evidence that high n Achievement is an essential ingredient in success as a research scientist, professional, accountant, office or personnel manager, etc.; that, on the contrary, it seems rather narrowly related to entrepreneurial, sales, or promotional success, and therefore should be of particular interest to them because they hold jobs which either have or could have an entrepreneurial component. We rationalize this activity in terms of the following proposition.

Proposition 2. The more an individual perceives that developing a motive is consistent with the demands of reality (and reason), the more educational attempts designed to develop that motive are likely to succeed. In a century in which psychologists and social theorists have been impressed by the power of unreason, it is well to remember that research has shown that rational arguments do sway opinions, particularly among the doubtful or the uncommitted (cf. Hovland et al., 1953). Reality in the form of legal, military, or housing rules does modify white prejudice against Negroes (cf. Berelson & Steiner, 1964, p. 512). In being surprised at Asch's discovery that many people will go along with a group in calling a shorter line longer than it is, we sometimes forget that under most conditions their judgments conform with reality. The associative network which organizes "reality"—which places the person correctly in time, place, space, family, job, etc.—is one of the most dominant in the personality. It is the last to go in psychosis. It should be of great assistance to tie any proposed change in an associative network in with this dominant schema in such a way as to make the change consistent with reality demands or *"reasonable"* extensions of them. The word "reasonable" here simply means extensions arrived at by the thought processes of proof, logic, etc. which in adults have achieved a certain dominance of their own.

The next step in the course is to teach the participants the n Achievement coding system. By this time, they are a little confused anyway as to exactly what we mean by the term. So we tell them they can find out for themselves by learning to code stories written by others or by themselves. They take the test for n Achievement before this session and then find out what their own score is by scoring this record. However, we point out that if they think their score is too low, that can be easily remedied, since we teach them how to code and how to write stories saturated with n Achievement; in fact, that is one of the basic purposes of the course: to teach them to think constantly in n Achievement terms. Another aspect of the learning is discriminating achievement thinking from thinking in terms of power or affiliation. So usually the elements of these other two coding schemes are also taught.

Proposition 3. The more thoroughly an individual develops and clearly conceptualizes the associative network defining the motive, the more likely he is to develop the motive. The original empirical support for this proposition came from the radical behaviorist Skinnerian viewpoint: If the associative responses are the motive (by definition), to strengthen them one should elicit them and reinforce them, as one would shape up any response by reinforcement (cf. Skinner, 1953). But, support for this proposition also derives from other sources, particularly the "set" experiments. For decades laboratory psychologists have known that one of the easiest and most effective ways to change behavior is to change the subject's set. If he is responding to stimulus words with the names of animals, tell him to respond with the names of vegetables, or with words meaning the opposite, and he changes his behavior immediately and efficiently without a mistake. At a more complex level Orne (1962) had pointed out how powerful a set like "This is an experiment" can be. He points out that if you were to go up to a stranger and say something like "Lie down!" he would in all probability either laugh or escape as soon as possible. But, if you say "This is an experiment. Lie down!" more often than not, if there are other supporting cues, the person will do so. Orne has demonstrated how subjects will perform nonsensical and fatiguing tasks for very long periods of time under the set that "This is an experiment ." At an even more complex level, sociologists have demonstrated often how quickly a person will change his behavior as he adopts a new role set (as a parent, a teacher, a public official, etc.). In all these cases an associative network exists usually with a label conveniently attached which we call set and which, when it is aroused or becomes salient, proceeds to control behavior very effectively. The purpose of this part of our course is to give the subjects a set or a carefully worked out associative network with appropriate words or labels to describe all its various aspects (the coding labels for parts of the n Achievement scoring system like Ga^+, I^+, etc; cf. Atkinson, 1958). The power of words on controlling behavior has also been well documented (cf. Brown, 1958).

It is important to stress that it is not just the label (n Achievement) which is taught. The person must be able to produce easily and often the new associative network itself. It is here that our research comes closest to traditional therapy which could be understood as the prolonged and laborious formation of new associative networks to replace anxiety-laden ones. That is, the person over time comes to form a new associative network covering his relations, for example, to his father and mother, which still later he may label an "unresolved Oedipus complex." When cues arise that formerly would have produced anxiety-laden associations, they now evoke this new complex instead, blocking out the "bad" associations by associative interference. But all therapists, whether Freudian or Rogerian, insist that the person must learn to produce these associations in their new form, that teaching the label is not enough. In fact, this is probably why so-called directive therapy is ineffective: It tries to substitute new constructs ("You should become an achiever") for old neurotic or ineffective ones ("rather than being such a slob") without changing the associative networks which underlie these surface labels. A change in set such as "Respond with names of vegetables" will not work unless the person has a whole associative network which defines the meaning of the set. The relation of the argument is obvious both to Kelley's (1955) insistence on the importance of personal constructs and to the general semanticists' complaints about the neurotic effects of mislabeling or overabstraction (Korzybski, 1941).

But, theoretically speaking, why should a change in set as an associative network be so influential in controlling thought and action? The explanation lies in part in its symbolic character. Learned acts have limited influence because they often depend on reality supports (as in typewriting), but learned thoughts (symbolic acts) can occur any time, any place, in any connection, and be applied to whatever the person is doing. They are more generalizable. Acts can also be inhibited more easily than thoughts. Isak Dinesen tells the story of the oracle who told the king he would get his wish so long as he never thought of the left eye of a camel. Needless to say, the king did not get his wish, but he could easily have obeyed her prohibition if it had been to avoid *looking* at the left eye of a camel. Thoughts once acquired gain more control over thoughts and actions than acquired acts do because they are harder to inhibit. But why do they gain control over actions? Are not thoughts substitutes for actions? Cannot a man learn to think achievement thoughts and still not act like an achiever in any way? The question is taken up again under the next proposition, but it is well to remember here that thoughts are symbolic acts and that practice of symbolic acts facilitates performing the real acts (cf. Hovland, 1951, p. 644).

The next step in the course is to tie thought to action. Research has shown that individuals high in n Achievement tend to act in certain ways. For example: they prefer work situations where there is a challenge (moderate risk), concrete feedback on how well they are doing, and opportunity to take personal responsibility for achieving the work goals. The participants in the course are therefore introduced to a "work" situation in the form of a business game in which they will have an opportunity to show these characteristics in action or more specifically to develop them through practice and through observing others play it. The game is designed to mimic real life: They must order parts to make certain objects (e.g. a Tinker Toy model bridge) after having estimated how many they think they can construct in the time allotted. They have a real chance to take over, plan the whole game, learn from how well they are doing (use of feedback), and show a paper profit or loss at the end. While they are surprised often that they should have to display their real action characteristics in this way in public, they usually get emotionally involved in observing how they behave under pressure of more or less "real" work situation.

Proposition 4. The more an individual can link the newly developed network to related actions, the more the change in both thought and action is likely to occur and endure. The evidence for the importance of action for producing change consists of such diverse findings as *(a)* the importance of recitation for human learning, *(b)* the repeated finding that overt commitment and participation in action changes attitudes effectively (cf. Berelson & Steiner, 1964, p. 576), and *(c)* early studies by Carr (cf. McGeoch & Irion, 1952) showing that simply to expose an organism to what is to be learned (e.g., trundling a rat through a maze) is nowhere near as effective as letting him explore it for himself in action.

Theoretically. the action is represented in the associative network by what associations precede, accompany, and follow it. So including the acts in what is learned *enlarges* the associative network or the achievement construct to include action. Thus, the number of cues likely to trip off the n Achievement network is increased. In common-sense terms, whenever he works he now evaluates what he is doing in achievement terms, and whenever he thinks about achievement he tends to think of its action consequences.

So far the course instruction has remained fairly abstract and removed from the everyday experiences of businessmen. So, the next step is to apply what has been learned to everyday business activities through the medium of the well-known case-study method popularized by the Harvard Business School. Actual examples of the development of the careers or fims of business leaders or entrepreneurs are written up in disguised form and assigned for discussion to the participants. Ordinarily, the instructor is not interested in illustrating "good" or "bad" managerial behavior—that is left to participants to discuss—but in our use of the material, we do try to label the various types of behavior as illustrating either n Achievement and various aspects of the achievement sequence (instrumental activity, blocks, etc.), or n Power, n Affiliation, etc. The participants are also encouraged to bring in examples of managerial behavior from their own experience to evaluate in motivational terms.

Proposition 5. The more an individual can link the newly conceptualized association-action complex (or motive) to events in his everyday life, the more likely the motive complex is to influence his thoughts and actions in situations outside the training experience. The transfer-of-training research literature is not very explicit on this point, though it seems self-evident. Certainly, this is the proposition that underlies the practice of most therapy when it involves working through or clarifying, usually in terms of a new, partially formed construct system, old memories, events from the last 24 hours, dreams, and hopes of the future. Again, theoretically, this should serve to enlarge and clarify the associative network and increase the number of cues in everyday life which will rearouse it. The principle of symbolic practice can also be invoked to support its effectiveness in promoting transfer outside the learning experience.

For some time most course participants have been wondering what all this has to do with them personally. That is to say, the material is introduced originally on a "take it or leave it" objective basis as something that ought to be of interest to them. But sooner or later, they must confront the issue as to what meaning n Achievement has in their own personal lives. We do not force this choice on them nor do we think we are brainwashing them to believe in n Achievement. We believe and we tell them we believe in the "obstinate audience" (cf. Bauer, 1964), in the ultimate capacity of people to resist persuasion or to do in the end what they really want to do. In fact, we had one case in an early session of a man who at this point decided he was not an achievement-minded person and did not want to become one. He subsequently retired and became a chicken farmer to the relief of the business in which he had been an ineffective manager. We respected that decision and mention it in the course as a good example of honest self-evaluation. Nevertheless, we do provide them with all kinds of information as to their own achievement-related behavior in the fantasy tests, in the business game, in occasional group dynamics sessions—and ample opportunity and encouragement to think through what this information implies so far as their self-concept is concerned and their responsibilities to their jobs. Various devices such as the "Who am I" test, silent group meditation, or individual counseling have been introduced to facilitate this self-confrontation.

Proposition 6. The more an individual can perceive and experience the newly conceptualized motive as an improvement in the self-image, the more the motive is likely to influence his future thoughts and actions. Evidence on the importance of the ego or the self-image on controlling behavior has been summarized by Allport (1943). In recent years, Rogers and his group (Rogers, 1961; Rogers & Dymond, 1954) have measured improvement in psychotherapy largely in terms of improvement of the self-concept in relation to the ideal self. Indirect evidence of the importance of the self-schema comes from the the discussion over whether a person can be made to do things under hypnosis that are inconsistent with his self-concept or values. All investigators agree that the hypnotist can be most successful in getting the subject to do what might normally be a disapproved action if he makes the subject perceive the action as consistent with his self-image or values (cf. Berelson & Steiner, 1964, p. 124).

The same logic supports this proposition. It seems unlikely that a newly formed associative network like n Achievement could persist and influence behavior much unless it had somehow "come to terms" with the pervasive superordinate network of associations defining the self. The logic is the same as for Proposition 2 dealing with the reality construct system. The n Achievement associations must come to be experienced as related to or consistent with the ideal self-image; otherwise associations from the self-system will constantly block thoughts of achievement. The person might be thinking, for example: "I am not that kind of person; achievement means judging people in terms of how well they perform and I don't like to hurt people's feelings."

Closely allied to the self-system is a whole series of networks only half conscious (i.e., correctly labeled) summarizing the values by which the person lives which derive from his culture and social milieu. These values can also interfere if they are inconsistent with n Achievement as a newly acquired way of thinking. Therefore, it has been customary at this point in the course to introduce a value analysis of the participants' culture based on an analysis of children's stories, myths, popular religion, comparative attitude surveys, customs, etc., more or less in line with traditional, cultural anthropological practice (cf. Benedict, 1946; McClelland, 1946). For example, in America we have to work through the problem of how being achievement oriented seems to interfere with being popular or liked by others which is highly valued by Americans. In Mexico a central issue is the highly valued "male dominance" pattern reflected in the patriarchal family and in the *macho* complex (being extremely masculine). Since data shows that dominant fathers have sons with low n Achievement and authoritarian bosses do not encourage n Achievement in their top executives (Andrews, 1965), there is obviously a problem here to be worked through if n Achievement is to survive among thoughts centered on dominance. The problem is not only rationally discussed. It is acted out in role-playing sessions where Mexicans try, and often to their own surprise fail, to act like the democratic father with high standards in the classic Rosen and D'Andrade (1959) study on parental behavior which develops high n Achievement. Any technique is used which will serve to draw attention to possible conflicts between n Achievement and popular or traditional cultural values. In the end it may come to discussings parts of the *Bhagavad Gita* in India, or the *Koran* in Arab countries, and seem to oppose achievement striving or entrepreneurial behavior.

Proposition 7. The more an individual can perceive and experience the newly conceptualized motives as an improvement on prevailing cultural values, the more the motive is likely to influence his future thoughts and actions. The cultural anthropologists for years have argued how important it is to understand one's own cultural values to overcome prejudices, adopt more flexible attitudes, etc., but there is little hard evidence that doing so changes a person's behavior. What exists comes indirectly from studies that show prejudice can be decreased a little by information about ethnic groups (Berelson & Steiner, 1964, p. 517), or that repeatedly show an unconscious link between attitudes and the reference group (or subculture to which one belongs—a link which presumably can be broken more easily by full information about it, especially when coupled with role-playing new attitudes (cf. Berelson & Steiner, 1964, pp. 566 ff.).

The theoretical explanation of this presumed effect is the same as for Propositions 2 and 6. The newly learned associative complex to influence thought and action effectively must somehow be adjusted to three superordinate networks that may set off regularly interfering associations—namely, the networks associated with reality, the self, and the social reference group or subculture.

The course normally ends with each participant preparing a written document outlining his goals and life plans for the next two years. These plans may or may not include references to the achievement motive; they can be very tentative, but they are supposed to be quite specific and realistic; that is to say, they should represent moderate levels of aspiration following the practice established in learning about n Achievement of choosing the moderately risky or challenging alternative. The purpose of this document is in part to formulate for oneself the practical implications of the course before leaving it, but even more to provide a basis for the evaluation of their progress in the months after the course. For it is explained to the participants that they are to regard themselves as "in training" for the next two years, that 10–14 days is obviously too short a time to do more than conceive a new way of life: it represents the residential portion of the training only. Our role over the next two years will be to remind them every six months of the tasks they have set themselves by sending them a questionnaire to fill out which will serve to rearouse many of the issues discussed in the course and to give them information on how far they have progressed towards achieving their goals.

Proposition 8. The more an individual commits himself to achieving concrete goals in life related to the newly formed motive, the more the motive is likely to influence his future thoughts and actions.

Proposition 9. The more an individual keeps a record of his progress toward achieving goals to which he is committed, the more the newly formed motive is likely to influence his future thoughts and actions. These propositions are both related to what was called "pacing" in early studies of the psychology of work. That is, committing oneself to a specific goal and then comparing one's performance to that goal has been found to facilitate learning (cf. Kausler, 1959), though most studies of levels of aspiration have dealt with goal setting as a result rather than as a "cause" of performance. At any rate, the beneficial effect of concrete feedback on learning has been amply demonstrated by psychologists from Thorndike to Skinner. Among humans the feedback on performance is especially effective if they have high n Achievement (French, 1958), a fact which makes the relevance of our request for feedback obvious to the course participants.

The theoretical justification for these propositions is that in this way we are managing to keep the newly acquired associative network salient over the next two years. We are providing cues that will regularly rearouse it since he knows he is still part of an experimental training group which is supposed to show a certain type of behavior (Proposition 1 again). If the complex is rearoused sufficiently often back in the real world, we believe it is more likely to influence thought and action that if it is not aroused.

As described so far the course appears to be devoted almost wholly to cognitive learning. Yet this is only part of the story. The "teachers" are all clinically oriented psychologists who also try to practice whatever has been learned about the type of human relationship that most facilitates emotional learning. Both for practical and theoretical reasons this relationship is structured as warm, honest, and nonevaluative, somewhat in the manner described by Rogers (1961) and recommended by distinguished therapists from St. Ignatius[3] to Freud. That is to say, we insist that the only kind of change that can last or mean anything is what the person decides on and works out by himself, that we are there not to criticize his past behavior or direct his future choices, but to provide him with all sorts of information and emotional support that will help him in his self-confrontation. Since we recoginze that self-study may be quite difficult and unsettling, we try to create an optimistic relaxed atmosphere in which the person is warmly encouraged in his efforts and given the opportunity for personal counseling if he asks for it.

Proposition 10. Changes in motives are more likely to occur in an interpersonal atmosphere in which the individual feels warmly but honestly supported and respected by others as a person capable of guiding and directing his own future behavior. Despite the widespread belief in this proposition among therapists (except for operant conditioners), one of the few studies that directly supports it has been conducted by Ends and Page (1957) who found that an objective learning-theory approach was less successful in treating chronic alcoholics than a person-oriented, client-centered approach. Rogers (1961) also summarizes other evidence that therapists who are warmer, more emphatic, and genuine are more successful in their work. Hovland et al. (1953) report that the less manipulative the intent of a communicator, the greater the tendency to accept his conclusions. There is also the direct evidence that parents of boys with high n Achievement are warmer, more encouraging and less directive (fathers only) than parents of boys with low n Achievement (Rosen & D'Andrade, 1959). We tried to model ourselves after those parents on the theory that what is associated with high n Achievement in children might be most likely to encourage its development in adulthood. This does not mean permissiveness or promiscuous reinforcement of all kinds of behavior; it also means setting high standards as the parents of the boys with high n Achievement did but having the relaxed faith that the participants can achieve them.

The theoretical justification for this proposition can take two lines: Either one argues that this degree of challenge to the self-schema produces anxiety which needs to be reduced by warm support of the person for effective learning to take place, or one interprets the warmth as a form of direct reinforcement for change following the operant-conditioning model. Perhaps both factors are operating. Certainly ther is ample evidence to support the view that anxiety interferes with learning (cf. Sarason, 1960) and that reward shapes behavior (cf. Bandura & Walters, 1963, pp. 283 ff.).

---

[3]In his famous spiritual exercises which have played a key role in producing and sustaining personality change in the Jusuit Order, St. Ignatius states: "The director of the Exercizes ought not to urge the exercitant more to poverty or any promise than to the contrary, not to one state of life or way of living more than another . . .[while it is proper to urge people outside the Exercizes] the director of the Exercizes . . . without leaning to one side or the other, should permit the Creator to deal directly with the creature, and the creature directly with his Creator and Lord."

One other characteristic of the course leads to two further propositions. Efforts are made so far as possible to define it as an "experience apart," "an opportunity for self-study," or even a "spiritual retreat" (though the term can be used more acceptably in India than in the United States). So far as possible it is held in an isolated resort hotel or a hostel where there will be few distractions from the outside world and few other guests. This permits an atmosphere of total concentration on the objectives of the course including much informal talk out- side the sessions about Ga^+, Ga^-, I^+, and other categories in the coding defini- tion. It still comes as a surprise to us to hear these terms suddenly in an informal group of participants talking away in Spanish or Telugu. The effect of this retreat from everyday life into a special and specially labeled experience appears to be twofold: It dramatizes or increases to salience of the new associative network, and it tends to create a new reference group.

Proposition 11. Changes in motives are more likely to occur the more the setting dramatizes the importance of self-study and lifts it out of the routine of everyday life. So far as we know there is no scientific evidence to support this proposition, though again if one regards Jesuits as successful examples of personality change, the Order has frequently followed the advice of St. Ignatius to the effect that "the progress made in the Exercizes will be greater, the more the exercitant withdrAws from all friends and acquaintances, and from all worldly cares." Theory supports the proposition in two respects: Removing the person from everyday routine *(a)* should decrease interfering associations (to say nothing of interfering appoint- ments and social obligations), and *(b)* should heighten the salience of the experi- ence by contrast with everyday life and make it harder to handle with the usual defenses ("just one more course," etc.) That is to say, the network of achievement-related associations can be more strongly and distinctly aroused in contrast to everyday life, making cognitive dissonance greater and therefore more in need of reduction by new learning. By the same token we have found that the dramatic quality of the experience cannot be sustained very long in a 12–18 hour-a-day schedule without a new routine attitude developing. Thus, we have found that a period somewhere between 6 to 14 days is optimal for this kind of "spiritual retreat." St Ignatius sets an outside limit of 30 days, but this is when the schedule is less intensive (as ours has sometimes been), consisting of only a few hours a day over a longer period.

Proposition 12. Changes in motives are more likely to occur and persist if the new motive is a sign of membership in a new reference group. No principle of change has stronger empirical or historical support than this one. Endless studies have shown that people's opinions, attitudes, and beliefs are a function of their refer- ence group and that different attitudes are likely to arise and be sustained pri- marily when the person moves into or affiliates with a new reference group (cf. Berelson & Steiner, 1964, pp. 580 ff.). Many theorists argue that the success of groups like Alcoholics Anonymous depends on the effectiveness with which the group is organized so that each person demonstrates his membership in it by "saving" another alcoholic. Political experience has demonstrated that membership in small groups like Communist or Nazi Party Cells is one of the most effective ways to sustain changed attitudes and behavior.

Our course attempts to achieve the result *(a)* by the group experience in isolation—creating the feeling of alumni who all went through it together; *(b)* by certain signs of identification with the group, particularly the language of the coding system, but also including a certificate of membership; and *(c)* by arranging where possible to have participants come from the same community so that they can form a "cell" when they return that will serve as an immediate reference group to prevent gradual undermining of the new network by other pressures.

In theoretical terms a reference group should be effective because its members constantly provide cues to each other to rearouse the associative network, because they will also reward each other for achievement-related thoughts and acts, and because this constant mutual stimulation, and reinforcement, plus the labeling of the group, will prevent assimilation of the network to bigger, older, and stronger networks (such as those associated with traditional cultural values).

In summary, we have described an influence process which may be conceived in terms of "input," "intervening," and "output" variables as in Table 1. The propositions relate variables in Column A via their effect on the intervening variables in Column B to as yet loosely specified behavior in Column C, which may be taken as evidence that "development" of n Achievement has "really" taken place. The problems involved in evaluation of effects are as great and as complicated as those involved in designing the treatment, but they cannot be spelled out here, partly for lack of space, partly because we are in an even earlier stage of examining and classifying the effects of our training one and two years

Table 1   Variables Conceived as Entering into the Motive Change Process

A Input or independent variables	B Intervening variables	C Output or dependent variables
1. Goal setting for the person (P1, P11)	Arousal of associative network (salience)	Duration and/or extensiveness of changes in:
2. Acquisition of n Achievement associative network (P2, P3, P4, P5)	Experiencing and labeling the associative network	1. n Achievement associative network
3. Relating new network to superordinate networks	Variety of cues to which network is linked	2. Related actions: use of feedback, moderate risk taking, etc.
reality (P2)	Interfering associations	3. Innovations (job improvements)
the self (P6)	assimilated or by-	
cultural values (P7)	passed by reproductive interference	4. Use of time and money
4. Personal goal setting (P8)		5. Entrepreneurial success as defined by nature of job held and its rewards
5. Knowledge of progress (P3, P4, P9)		
6. Personal warmth and support (P10)	Positive effect associated with network	
7. Support of reference group (P11, P12)		

Note. P1, P11, etc., refer to the numbered propositions in the text.

later preparatory to conceptualizing more clearly what happens. It will have to suffice to point out that we plan extensive comparisons over a two-year period of the behaviors of our trained subjects compared with matched controls along the lines suggested in Column C.

What the table does is to give a brief overall view of how we conceptualize the educational or treatment process. What is particularly important is that the propositions refer to *operationally defined* and *separable* treatment variables. Thus, after having demonstrated hopefully a large effect of the total program, we can subtract a variable and see how much that decreases the impact of the course. That is to say, the course is designed so that it could go ahead perfectly reasonably with very little advanced goal setting (P1), with an objective rather than a warm personal atmosphere (P11), without the business game tying thought to action (P9), without learning to code n Achievement and write achievement-related stories (P3), without cultural value analysis (P7), or an isolated residential setting (P1, P11, P12). The study units are designed in a way that they can be omitted without destroying the viability of the treatment which has never been true of ther studies of the psychotherapeutic process (cf. Rogers & Dymond, 1954).

But is there any basis for thinking the program works in practice? As yet, not enough time has elapsed to enable us to collect much data on longterm changes in personality and business activity. However, we do know that businessmen can learn to write stories scoring high in n Achievement, that they retain this skill over one year or two, and that they like the course—but the same kinds of things can be said about many unevaluated management training courses. In two instances we have more objective data. Three courses were given to some 34 men from the Bombay area in early 1963. It proved possible to develop a crude but objective and reliable coding system to record whether each one had shown *unusual* entrepreneurial activity in the two years prior to the course or in the two years after the course. "Unusual" here means essentially an unusual promotion or salary raise or starting a new business venture of some kind. Of the 30 on whom information was available in 1965, 27 percent had been unusually active before the course, 67 percent after the course ($x^2 = 11.2$, $p. < 0.01$). In a control group chosen at random from those who applied for the course in 1963, out of 11 on whom information has so far been obtained, 18 percent were active before 1963, 27 percent since 1963.

In a second case, four courses were given throughout 1964 to a total of 52 small businessmen from the small city of Kakinada in Andhra Predesh, India. Of these men, 25 percent had been unusually active in the two-year period before the course, and 65 percent were unusually active immediately afterwards ($x^2 = 17.1$, $p < 0.01$). More control data and more refined measures are needed, but it looks very much as if, in India at least, we will be dealing with a spontaneous "activation" rate of only 25 percent—35 percent among entrepreneurs. Thus we have a distinct advantage over psychotherapists who are trying to demonstrate an improvement over a two-thirds spontaneous recovery rate. Our own data suggest that we will be unlikely to get an improvement or "activation" rate much above the two-thirds level commonly reported in therapy studies. That is, about one-third of the people in our courses have remained relatively unaffected. Nevertheless the two-thirds activated after the course represent a doubling of the normal rate of unusual entrepreneurial activity—no mean achievement in the light of the current pessimism amoung psychologists as to their ability to induce lasting personality change among adults.

One case will illustrate how the course seems to affect people in practice. A short time after participating in one of our courses in India, a 47-year-old businessman rather suddenly and dramatically decided to quit his excellent job and go into the construction business on his own in a big way. A man with some means of his own, he had had a very sucessful career as employee-relations manager for a large oil firm. His job involved adjusting management-employee difficulties, negotiating union contracts, etc. He was well-to-do, well thought of in his company, and admired in the community, but he was restless because he found his job increasingly boring. At the time of the course his original n Achievement score was not very high and he was thinking of retiring and living in England where his son was studying. In an interview, eight months later, he said the course had served not so much to "motivate" him but to "crystallize" a lot of ideas he had vaguely or half consciously picked up about work and achievement all through his life. It provided him with a new language (he still talked in terms of standards of excellence, blocks, moderate risk, goal anticipation, etc.), a new construct which served to organize those ideas and explain to him why he was bored with his job, despite his obvious success. He decided he wanted to be an n-Achievement-oriented person, that he would be unhappy in retirement, and that he should take a risk, quit his job, and start in business on his own. He acted on his decision and in six months had drawn plans and raised over £1,000,000 to build the tallest building in his large city to be called the "Everest Apartments." He is extremely happy in his new activity because it means selling, promoting, trying to wangle scarce materials, etc. His first building is partway up and he is planning two more.

Even a case as dramatic as this one does not prove that the course produced the effect, despite his repeated use of the constructs he had learned, but what is especially interesting about it is that he described what had happened to him in exactly the terms the theory requires. He spoke not about a new motive force but about how existing ideas had been crystallized into a new associative network, and it is this new network which *is* the new "motivating" force according to the theory.

How generalizable are the propositions? They have purposely been stated generally so that some term like "attitude" or "personality characteristic" could be substituted for the term "motive" throughout, because we believe the propositions will hold for other personality variables. In fact, most of the supporting experimental evidence cited comes from attempts to change other characteristics. Nevertheless, the propositions should hold best more narrowly for motives and especially the achievement motive. One of the biggest difficulties in the way of testing them more generally is that not nearly as much is known about other human characteristics or their specific relevance for success in a certain type of work. For example, next to nothing is known about the need for power, its relation to success, let us say, in politics or bargaining situations, and its origins and course of development in the life history of individuals. It is precisely the knowledge we have about such matters for the achievement motive that puts us in a position to shape it for limited, socially and individually desirable ends. In the future, it seems to us, research in psychotherapy ought to follow a similar course. That is to say, rather than developing "all purpose" treatments, good for any person and any purpose, it should aim to develop specific treatments or educational programs built on laboriously accumulated detailed knowledge of the characteristic to be changed. It is in this spirit that the present research program in motive acquisition has been designed and is being tested out.

REFERENCES

Allport G. W. The ego in contemporary psychology. *Psychological Review,* 1943, **50,** 451–78.

Andrews J. D. W. The achievement motive in two types of organizations. *Journal of Personality and Social Psychology,* 1965, in press.

Atkinson, J. W. (ed.) *Motives in fantasy action and society.* Princeton, N.J.: Van Nostrand, 1958.

Bandura, A. and Walters, R. H. *Social learning and personality development.* New York: Holt, Rinehart &Winston. 1963.

Bauer, R. A. The obstinate audience: the influence process from the point of view of social communication. *American Psychologist, 1964,* **19,** 319–29.

Benedict, Ruth. *The chrysanthemum and the sword.* Boston: Houghton Mifflin, 1946.

Berelson, B., and Steiner, G. A. *Human behavior: An inventory of scientific findings.* Harcourt, Brace, 1964.

Brown, R. W. *Words and things.* Glencoe, Ill.: Free Press, 1958.

Burris, R. W. The effect of counseling on achievement motivation. Unpublished doctoral dissertation, Indiana University, 1958.

Ends, E. J., and Page, C. W. A study of three types of group psychotherapy with hospitalized male inebriantes. *Quarterly Journal on Alcohol, 1957,* **18,** 319–24.

Eynsenck, H. J. The effects of psychotherapy: An evaluation. *Journal of Consulting Psychology,* 1952, **16,** 319–24.

Festinger, L. *A theory of cognitive dissonance.* New York: Harper & Row. 1957.

Frank, J. *Persuasion and healing.* Baltimore: Johns Hopkins Press, 1961.

French, E. G. Effects of the interaction of motivation and feedback on task performance. In J. W. Atkinson (ed.), *Motives in fantasy, action and society.* Princeton, N. J.: Van Nostrand, 1958, pp. 400–408.

Heckhausen, H. Eine Rehmentheorie der Motivation in zehn Thesen. *Zeitschrift fur experimentelle und angewandte Psychologie,* 1963, **X/4,** 604–26.

Hovland, C. I. Human learning and retention. In S. S. Stevens (ed.), *Handbook of experimental psychology.* New York: Wiley, 1951.

Hovland, C. I., Janis, I. L., and Kelley, H. H. *Communication and persuasion: Psychological studies of opinion change.* New Haven: Yale University Press, 1953.

Kausler, D. H. Aspiration level as a determinant of performance. *Journal of Personality,* 1959, **27,** 346–51.

Kelley, G. A. *The psychology of personal constructs.* New York: Norton, 1955.

Korzybski, A. *Science and sanity.* Lancaster, Pa.: Science Press, 1941.

McClelland, D. C. *The achieving society.* Princeton, N. J.: Van Nostrand, 1961.

McClelland, D. C. *The roots of consciousness.* Princeton, N. J.: Van Nostrand, 1964.

McClelland, D. C., Atkinson, J. W., Clark, R. A. and Lowell, E. L. *The achievement motive.* New York: Appleton-Century, 1953.

McGeoch, J. A., and Irion, A. L. *The psychology of human learning.* (2d ed.). New York: Longmans, Green, 1952.

Mierke, K. *Wille und Leistung.* Gottingen: Verlag fur Psychologie, 1955.

Orne, M. On the social psychology of the psychological experiment: With particular reference to demand characteristics and their implications. *American Psychologist,* 1962, **17,** 776–83.

Roethlisberger, F. J., and Dickson, W. J. *Management and the worker.* Cambridge: Harvard University Press, 1947.

Rogers, C. R. *On becoming a person.* Boston: Houghton Mifflin, 1961.

Rogers. C. R., and Dymond, R. F. (eds.). *Psychotherapy and personality change.* Chicago: University of Chicago Press, 1954.

Rosen, B. C., and D'Andrade, R. G. The psychosocial origins of achievement motivation. *Sociometry.* 1959, **22,** 185–218.

Rosenthal, R. On the social psychology of the psychological experiment. The experimenter's hypothesis as unintended determinant of experimental results. *American Scientist,* 1963, **51,** 268–83.

Sarason, I. Empirical findings and theoretical problems in the use of anxiety scales. *Psychological Bulletin,* 1960, **57,** 403–15.

Skinner, B. F. *Science and human behavior.* New York: Macmillan, 1953.

QUESTIONS FOR DISCUSSION

1. Would you classify Murray's basic model of motivation as an instinct theory, a drive theory, or a cognitive theory? Why?
2. In what ways have Atkinson and McClelland modified and extended Murray's original formulation of the model?
3. Researchers have often found that persons with high needs for achievement simultaneously have low needs for affiliation. What factors might explain such findings?
4. What basic differences exist between achievement motivation theory and Maslow's need hierarchy theory? What importance would you attach to such differences?
5. How would you go about improving the performance of an employee who has a low need for achievement?
6. If high need achievement people tend to be superior performers, why could a manager not increase organizational performance simply by hiring only high *n* Ach employees?
7. What uses might a line manager make of achievement motivation theory?
8. What can managers learn from McClelland's theory of motive acquisition that could be applied in their relations with subordinates and peers?

Chapter 4

Motivation-Hygiene Theory

OVERVIEW

Another very popular theory of motivation is that proposed by Frederick Herzberg. This model, which is variously termed the two-factor theory, the dual-factor theory, and the motivation-hygiene theory, has been widely received among managers concerned with the problems of human behavior at work. It appears, however, to be somewhat less popular among organizational researchers for reasons to be discussed below.

There are, in reality, two distinct aspects of the motivation-hygiene theory. The first and more basic part of the model represents a formally stated theory of work behavior. It is this formalized two-factor theory of motivation which is considered in this chapter. The second aspect of Herzberg's work has focused upon the behavioral consequences of job enrichment and work redesign programs. This second part of the theory—the benefits and drawbacks of job redesign—will be discussed in Chapter 12.

Herzberg and his associates began their initial work on factors affecting work motivation in the mid-1950s. Their first effort entailed a thorough review of existing research to that date on the subject (Herzberg, Mausner, Peterson, & Capwell, 1957). Based on this review, Herzberg carried out his now famous survey of 200 accountants and engineers from which he derived the initial framework for his theory of motivation. The theory, as well as the supporting data, was first published in 1959 (Herzberg, Mausner, & Snyderman) and was subsequently amplified and developed in a later book (Herzberg, 1966). This latter work, written largely in response to criticisms of his earlier work, contained the results of several additional research investigations carried out among various types of employees. The findings were interpreted by Herzberg as being largely supportive of the theory.

One of the most significant contributions of Herzberg's work was the tremendous impact it had on stimulating thought, research, and experimentation on the topic of motivation at work. This contribution should not be overlooked. Before 1959, little research had been carried out in the area of *work* motivation (with the notable exception Viteles [1953] and Maier [1955]), and the research that did exist was largely fragmentary. Maslow's work on the need hierarchy theory and Murray, McClelland, and Atkinson's work on achievement motivation theory were largely concerned with laboratory-based findings or clinical observations, and neither had seriously addressed the problems of the workplace at that time. Herzberg filled this void by specifically calling attention to the need for increased understanding of the role of motivation in organizations.

Moreover, he did so in a systematic manner and in language that was easily understood by a large body of managers. He advanced a theory that was simple to grasp, based on some empirical data, and—equally important—offered specific action recommendations for managers to improve employee motivational levels. In doing so, he forced organizations to examine closely a number of possible misconceptions concerning motivation. For example, Herzberg argued that money should not necessarily be viewed as the most potent force on the job. Moreover, he stated that other "context" factors in addition to money which surround an employee's job (such as fringe benefits and supervisory style) should not be expected to markedly affect motivation either. He advanced a strong case that managers must instead give considerable attention to a series of "content" factors (such as opportunities for achievement, recognition, and advancement) that have an important bearing on behavior. According to Herzberg, it is these content factors, and not money or other context factors, that are primarily related to work motivation. These contributions are often overlooked in the heated debates over the validity of the empirical data behind the theoretical formulations.

Herzberg, in addition, probably deserves a good deal of credit for acting as a stimulus to other researchers who have advocated alternative theories of work motivation. A multitude of research articles have been generated as a result of the so-called "Herzberg controversy." Some of these articles strongly support Herzberg's position (e. g., Bockman, 1971; Whitset & Winslow, 1967), while others seriously question the research methodology underlying the theory (e. g., House & Wigdor, 1967; Vroom, 1964). Such debate is healthy for any science. The serious student of motivation should consider Herzberg's theory—just as any other theory—to be one attempt at modeling work behavior. As such, the theory should be dissected and/or modified in a continuing effort to develop comprehensive and accurate predictors of human behavior on the job. In other words, it appears that a fruitful approach to this "controversial" theory would be to learn from it that which can help us to develop more improved models, rather than to accept or reject the model totally.

Herzberg's theory has been revised and built upon (sometimes substantially) in later works. The interested reader should consult the references at the end of this introduction. In particular, consideration should be given to the articles by: Evans and McKee; Hackman; Paine; Pennings; Saleh and Hyde; Soliman; Wernimont; and Williamson and Karras.

Three selections relating to the motivation-hygiene theory follow. First, Herzberg describes the basic tenets of the model and reviews some of his own research in support of the model. Next, House and Wigdor attempt to summarize much of the reasearch relating to the theory and draw some general conclusions concerning its strengths and weaknesses. Finally, King, while also reviewing much of the research, takes a critical look at the basic theoretical formulations of the model that should be taken into account when evaluating the theory. It is suggested that, when reading this material, one should attempt to compare Herzberg's model to the models proposed by Maslow and Murray (Chapters 2 and 3). Certain similarities can be found as well as some very specific differences. Again, reference may be made to the analytical framework suggested in Chapter 1.

REFERENCES AND SUGGESTED ADDITIONAL READINGS

Bobbitt, H. R., Jr., & Behling, O. Defense mechanisms as an alternate explanation of Herzberg's Motivator-Hygiene results. *Journal of Applied Psychology*, 1972, **56**, 24–27.

Bockman, V. M. The Herzberg controversy. *Personnel Psychology*, 1971, **24**, 155–189.

Burke, R. J. Are Herzberg's motivators and hygienes unidimensional? *Journal of Applied Psychology*, 1966, **50**, 317–321.

Dunnette, M. D., Campbell, J. P., & Hakel, M. D. Factors contributing to job satisfaction and job dissatisfaction in six occupational groups. *Organizational Behavior and Human Performance*, 1967, **2**, 143–174.

Evans, M. G., & McKee, D. Some effects of internal versus external orientations upon the relationships between various aspects of job satisfaction. *Journal of Business Administration*, 1970, **2**, 17–24.

Ford, R. *Motivation through the work itself*. New York: American Management Association, 1969.

Grigaliunas, B. S., & Herzberg, F. Relevance in the test of motivator-hygiene theory. *Journal of Applied Psychology*, 1971, **55**, 73–79.

Hackman, R. C. *The motivated working adult*. New York: American Management Association, 1969.

Herzberg, F. The motivation-hygiene concept and problems of manpower. *Personnel Administration*, 1964, **27(1)**, 3–7.

Herzberg, F. *Work and the nature of man*. Cleveland: World Publishing, 1966.

Herzberg, F., Mausner, B., Peterson, R. O., & Capwell, D. F. *Job attitudes: Review of research and opinion.* Pittsburgh: Psychological Services of Pittsburgh, 1957.

Herzberg, F., Mausner, B., & Snyderman, B. *The motivation to work.* New York: Wiley, 1959.

House, R. J., & Wigdor, L. A. Herzberg's dual-factor theory of job satisfaction and motivation. *Personnel Psychology,* 1967, **20,** 369–390.

Lindsay, C. A., Marks, E., & Gorlow, L. The Herzberg theory: A critique and reformulation. *Journal of Applied Psychology,* 1967, **20,** 330–339.

Locke, E. A. In defense of defense mechanisms: Some comments on Bobbitt and Behling. *Journal of Applied Psychology,* 1972, **56,** 297–298.

Maier, N. R. F. *Psychology in industry.* (2nd ed.) Boston: Houghton-Mifflin, 1955.

Miner, J. B., & Dachler, H. P. Personnel attitudes and motivation. In P. H. Mussen & M. R. Rosenzweig (Eds.), *Annual Review of Psychology.* Palo Alto, Ca.: Annual Reviews, Inc., 1973.

Paine, F. T. What do better college students want from their jobs? *Personnel Administration,* 1969, **32(2),** 26–29.

Pennings, J. M. Work value systems of white-collar workers. *Administrative Science Quarterly,* 1970, **15,** 397–405.

Saleh, S. D., & Hyde, J. Intrinsic vs. extrinsic orientation and job satisfaction. *Occupational Psychology,* 1969, **43,** 47–53.

Schneider, J., & Locke, E. A. A critique of Herzberg's incident classification system and a suggested revision. *Organizational Behavior and Human Performance,* 1971, **6,** 441–457.

Schwab, D. P., DeVitt, H. W., & Cummings, L. L. A test of the adequacy of the two-factor theory as a predictor of self-report performance effects. *Personnel Psychology,* 1971, **24,** 293–303.

Schwab, D. P., & Heneman, H. G., III. Aggregate and individual predictability of the two-factor theory of job satisfaction. *Personnel Psychology,* 1970, **23,** 55–66.

Soliman, H. M. Motivation-hygiene theory of job attitudes: An empirical investigation and an attempt to reconcile both the one- and the two-factor theories of job attitudes. *Journal of Applied Psychology,* 1970, **54,** 452–461.

Viteles, M. S. *Motivation and morale in industry.* New York: Norton, 1953.

Vroom, V. H. *Work and motivation.* New York: Wiley, 1964.

Waters, L. K., & Roach, D. The two-factor theories of job satisfaction: Empirical tests for four samples of insurance company employees. *Personnel Psychology,* 1971, **24,** 697–705.

Waters, L. K., & Waters, C. W. An empirical test of five versions of the two-factor theory of job satisfaction. *Organizational Behavior and Human Performance,* 1972.

Wernimont, P. F. A systems view of job satisfaction. *Journal of Applied Psychology,* 1972, **56,** 173–176.

Whitsett, D. A., & Winslow, E. K. An analysis of studies critical of the motivation-hygiene theory. *Personnel Psychology,* 1967, **20,** 391–416.

Williamson, T. R., & Karras, E. J. Job satisfaction variables among female clerical workers. *Journal of Applied Psychology,* 1970, **54,** 343–346.

One More Time: How Do You Motivate Employees?
Frederick Herzberg

How many articles, books, speeches, and workshops have pleaded plaintively, "How do I get an employee to do what I want him to do?"

The psychology of motivation is tremendously complex, and what has been unraveled with any degree of assurance is small indeed. But the dismal ratio of knowledge to speculation has not dampened the enthusiasm for new forms of snake oil that are constantly coming on the market, many of them with academic testimonials. Doubtless this article will have no depressing impact on the market for smoke oil, but since the ideas expressed in it have been tested in many corporations and other organizations, it will help—I hope—to redress the imbalance in the aforementioned ratio.

'MOTIVATING' WITH KITA

In lectures to industry on the problem, I have found that the audiences are anxious for quick and practical answers, so I will begin with a straightforward, practical formula for moving people.

What is the simplest, surest, and most direct way of getting someone to do something? Ask him? But if he responds that he does not want to do it, then that calls for a psychological consultation to determine the reason for his obstinacy. Tell him? His response shows that he does not understand you, and now an expert in communication methods has to be brought in to show you how to get **through to him**. Give him a monetary incentive? I do not need to remind the reader of the complexity and difficulty involved in setting up and administering an incentive system. Show him? This means a costly training program. We need a simple way.

Every audience contains the "direct action" manager who shouts, "Kick him!" And this type of manager is right. The surest and least circumlocuted way of getting someone to do something is to kick him in the pants—give him what might be called the KITA.

There are various forms of KITA, and here are some of them:

●*Negative physical KITA*. This is a literal application of the term and was frequently used in the past. It has, however, three major drawbacks: (1) It is inelegant; (2) it contradicts the precious image of benevolence that most organi-

From *Harvard Business Review*, 1968, **46**(1), 53–62. Copyright 1968 by the President and Fellows of Harvard College; all rights reserved.

Author's note: I should like to acknowledge the contributions that Robert Ford of the American Telephone and Telegraph Company has made to the ideas expressed in this paper, and in particular to the successful application of these ideas in improving work performance and the job satisfaction of employees.

zations cherish; and (3) since it is a physical attack, it directly stimulates the autonomic nervous system, and this often results in negative feedback—the employee may just kick you in return. These factors give rise to certain taboos against negative physical KITA.

The psychologist has come to the rescue of those who are no longer permitted to use negative physical KITA. He has uncovered infinite sources of psychological vulnerabilities and the appropriate methods to play tunes on them. "He took my rug away"; "I wonder what he meant by that"; "The boss is always going around me"—these symptomatic expressions of ego sores that have been rubbed raw are the result of application of:

●*Negative Psychological KITA.* This has several advantages over negative physical KITA. First, the cruelty is not visible; the bleeding is internal and comes much later. Second, since it affects the higher cortical centers of the brain with its inhibitory powers, it reduces the possibility of physical backlash. Third, since the number of psychological pains that a person can feel is almost infinite, the direction and site possibilities of the KITA are increased many times. Fourth, the person administering the kick can manage to be above it all and let the system accomplish the dirty work. Fifth, those who practice it receive some ego satisfaction (oneupmanship), whereas they would find drawing blood abhorrent. Finally, if the employee does complain, he can always be accused of being paranoid, since there is no tangible evidence of actual attack.

Now, what does negative KITA accomplish? If I kick you in the rear (physically or psychologically), who is motivated? *I* am motivated; you move! Negative KITA does not lead to motivation, but to movement. So:

●*Positive KITA.* Let us consider motivation. If I say to you, "Do this for me or the company, and in return I will give you a reward, an incentive, more status, a promotion, all the quid pro quos that exist in the industrial organization," am I motivating you? The overwhelming opinion I receive from management people is, "Yes, this is motivation."

I have a year-old Schnauzer. When it was a small puppy and I wanted it to move, I kicked it in the rear and it moved. Now that I have finished its obedience training, I hold up a dog biscuit when I want the Schnauzer to move. In this instance, who is motivated—I or the dog? The dog wants the biscuit, but it is I who want it to move. Again, I am the one who moves. In this instance all I did was apply KITA frontally; I exerted a pull instead of a push. When industry wishes to use such positive KITAs, it has available an incredible number and variety of dog biscuits (jelly beans for humans) to wave in front of the employee to get him to jump.

Why is it that managerial audiences are quick to see that negative KITA is *not* motivation, while they are almost unanimous to their judgment that positive KITA *is* motivation? It is because negative KITA is rape, and positive KITA is seduction. But it is infinitely worse to the seduced than to be raped; the latter is an unfortunate occurrence, while the former signifies that you were a party to your own downfall. This is why positive KITA is so popular: it is a tradition; it is in the American way. The organization does not have to kick you; you kick yourself.

Myths about Motivation

Why is KITA not motivation? If I kick my dog (from the front or the back), he will move. And when I want him to move again, what must I do? I must kick him again. Similarly, I can charge a man's battery, and then recharge it, and recharge it again. But it is only when he has his own generator that we can talk about motivation. He then needs no outside stimulation. He *wants* to do it.

With this in mind, we can review some positive KITA personnel practices that were developed as attempts to instill "motivation":

1 *Reducing time spent at work*—This represents a marvelous way of motivating people to work—getting them off the job! We have reduced (formally and informally) the time spent on the job over the last 50 or 60 years until we are finally on the way to the "6 ½-day weekend." An interesting variant of this approach is the development of off-hour recreation programs. The philosophy here seems to be that those who play together, work together. The fact is that motivated people seek more hours of work, not fewer.

2 *Spiraling wages*—Have these motivated people? Yes, to seek the next wage increase. Some medievalists still can be heard to say that a good depression will get employees moving. They feel that if rising wages don't or won't do the job, perhaps reducing them will.

3 *Fringe benefits*—Industry has outdone the most welfare-minded of welfare states in dispensing cradle-to-the-grave succor. One company I know of had an informal "fringe benefit of the month club" going for a while. The cost of fringe benefits in this country has reached approximately 25% of the wage dollar, and we still cry for motivation.

People spend less time working for more money and more security than ever before, and the trend cannot be reversed. These benefits are no longer rewards; they are rights. A 6-day week is inhuman, a 10-hour day is exploitation, extended medical coverage is a basic decency, and stock options are the salvation of American initiative. Unless the ante is continuously raised, the psychological reaction of employees is that the company is turning back the clock.

When industry began to realize that both the economic nerve and the lazy nerve of their employees had insatiable appetites, it started to listen the the behavioral scientists who, more out of a humanist tradition than from scientific study, criticized management for not knowing how to deal with people. The next KITA easily followed.

4 *Human relations training*—Over 30 years of teaching and, in many instances, of practicing psychological approaches to handling people have resulted in costly human relations programs and, in the end, the same question: How do you motivate workers? Here, too, escalations have taken place. Thirty years ago it was

necessary to request, "Please don't spit on the floor." Today the same admonition requires three "please"s before the employee feels that his superior has demonstrated the psychologically proper attitudes toward him.

The failure of human relations training to produce motivation led to the conclusion that the supervisor or manager himself was not psychologically true to himself in his practice of interpersonal decency. So an advanced form of human relations KITA, sensitivity training, was unfolded.

5 *Sensitivity training*—Do you really, really understand yourself? Do you really, really, really trust the other man? Do you really, really, really, really, cooperate? The failure of sensitivity training is now being explained, by those who have become opportunistic exploiters of the technique, as a failure to really (five times) conduct proper sensitivity training courses.

With the realization that there are only temporary gains from comfort and economic and interpersonal KITA, personnel managers concluded that the fault lay not in what they were doing, but in the employee's failure to appreciate what they were doing. This opened up the field of communications, a whole new area of "scientifically" sanctioned KITA.

6 *Communications*—The professor of communications was invited to join the faculty of management training programs and help in making employees understand what management was doing for them. House organs, briefing sessions, supervisory instruction on the importance of communication, and all sorts of propaganda have proliferated until today there is even an International Council of Industrial Editors. But no motivation resulted, and the obvious thought occurred that perhaps management was not hearing what the employees were saying. That let to the next KITA.

7 *Two-way communication*—Management ordered morale surveys, suggestion plans, and group participation programs. Then both employees and management were communicating and listening to each other more than ever, but without much improvement in motivation.

The behavioral scientists began to take another look at their conceptions and their data, and they took human relations one step further. A glimmer of truth was beginning to show through in the writings of so-called higher-order-need psychologists. People, so they said, want to actualize themselves. Unfortunately, the "actualizing" psychologists got mixed up with the human relations psychologists, and a new KITA emerged.

8 *Job participation*—Though it may not have been the theoretical intention, job participation often became a "give them the big picture" approach. For example, if a man is tightening 10,000 nuts a day on an assembly line with a torque wrench, tell him he is building a Chevrolet. Another approach had the goal of giving the employee a *feeling* that he is determining, in some measure, what he does on his job. The goal was to provide a *sense* of achievement rather than a substantive achievement in his task. Real achievement, of course, requires a task that makes it possible.

9 *Employee counseling*—The initial use of this form of KITA in a systemat-

ic fashion can be credited to the Hawthorne experiment of the Western Electric Company during the early 1930's. At that time, it was found that the employees harbored irrational feelings that were interfering with the rational operation of the factory. Counseling in this instance was a means of letting the employees unburden themselves by talking to someone about their problems. Although the counseling techniques were primitive, the program was large indeed.

The counseling approach suffered as a result of experiences during World War II, when the programs themselves were found to be interfering with the operation of the organizations; the counselors had forgotten their role of benevolent listeners and were attempting to do something about the problems that they heard about. Psychological counseling, however, has managed to survive the negative impact of World War II experiences and today is beginning to flourish with renewed sophistication. But, alas, many of these programs, like all the others, do not seem to have lessened the pressure of demands to find out how to motivate workers.

Since KITA results only in short-term movement, it is safe to predict that the cost of these programs will increase steadily and new varieties will be developed as old positive KITAs reach their satiation points.

HYGIENE VS. MOTIVATORS

Let me rephrase the perennial question this way: How do you install a generator in an employee? A brief review of my motivation-hygiene theory of job attitudes is required before theoretical and practical suggestions can be offered. The theory was first drawn from an examination of events in the lives of engineers and accountants. At least 16 other investigations, using a wide variety of populations (including some in the Communist countries), have since been completed, making the original research one of the most replicated studies in the field of job attitudes.

The findings of these studies, along with corroboration from many other investigations using different procedures, suggest that the factors involved in producing job satisfaction (and motivation) are separate and distinct from the factors that lead to job dissatisfaction. Since separate factors need to be considered, depending on whether job satisfaction or job dissatisfaction is being examined, it follows that these two feelings are not opposites of each other. The opposite of job satisfaction is not job dissatisfaction but, rather, *no* job satisfaction; and, similarly, the opposite of job dissatisfaction is not job satisfaction, but *no* dissatisfaction.

Stating the concept presents a problem in semantics, for we normally think of satisfaction and dissatisfaction as opposites—i. e., what is not satisfying must be dissatisfying, and vice versa. But when it comes to understanding the behavior of people in their jobs, more than a play on words is involved.

Two different needs of man are involved here. One set of needs can be thought of as stemming from his animal nature—the built-in drive to avoid pain from the environment, plus all the learned drives which become conditioned to the basic biological needs. For example, hunger, a basic biological drive, makes it necessary to earn money, and then money becomes a specific drive. The other set of needs relates to that unique human characteristic, the ability to achieve and, through achievement, to experience psychological growth. The stimuli for the growth needs are tasks that induce growth; in the industrial setting, they are the *job content*. Contrariwise, the stimuli inducing pain-avoidance behavior are found in the *job environment*.

The growth or *motivator* factors that are intrinsic to the job are: achievement, recognition for achievement, the work itself, responsibility, and growth or advancement. The dissatisfaction-avoidance or *hygiene* (KITA) factors that are extrinsic to the job include: company policy and administration, supervision, interpersonal relationships, working conditions, salary, status, and security.

A composite of the factors that are involved in causing job satisfaction and job dissatisfaction, drawn from samples of 1,685 employees, is shown in Exhibit 1. The results indicate that motivators were the primary cause of satisfaction, and

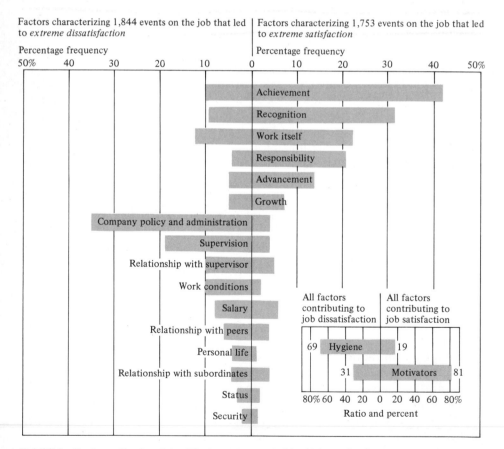

Exhibit I Factors affecting job attitudes, as reported in 12 investigations.

hygiene factors the primary cause of unhappiness on the job. The employees, studied in 12 different investigations, included lower-level supervisors, professional women, agricultural administrators, men about to retire from management positions, hospital maintenance personnel, manufacturing supervisors, nurses, food handlers, military officers, engineers, scientists, housekeepers, teachers, technicians, female assemblers, accountants, Finnish foremen, and Hungarian engineers.

They were asked what job events had occurred in their work that had let to extreme satisfaction or extreme dissatisfaction on their part. Their responses are broken down in the exhibit into percentages of total "positive" job events and of total "negative" job events. (The figures total more than 100% on both the "hygiene" and "motivators" sides because often at least two factors can be attributed to a single event; advancement, for instance, often accompanies assumption of responsibility.)

To illustrate, a typical response involving achievement that had a negative effect for the employee was, "I was unhappy because I didn't do the job successfully." A typical response in the small number of positive job events in the Company Policy and Administration grouping was, "I was happy because the company reorganized the section so that I didn't report any longer to the guy I didn't get along with."

As the lower right-hand part of the exhibit shows, of all the factors contributing to job satisfaction, 81% were motivators. And of all the factors contributing to the employees' dissatisfaction over their work, 69% involved hygiene elements.

Eternal Triangle

There are three general philosophies of personnel management. The first is based on organizational theory, the second on industrial engineering, and the third on behavioral science.

The industrial engineer holds that man is mechanistically oriented and economically motivated and his needs are best met by attuning the individual to the most efficient work process. The goal of personnel management therefore should be to concoct the most appropriate incentive system and to design the specific working conditions in a way that facilitates the most efficient use of the human machine. By structuring jobs in a manner that leads to the most efficient operation, the engineer believes that he can obtain the optimal organization of work and the proper work attitudes.

The behavioral scientist focuses on group sentiments, attitudes of individual employees, and the organization's social and psychological climate. According to his persuasion, he emphasizes one or more of the various hygiene and motivator needs. His approach to personnel management generally emphasizes some form of human relations education, in the hope of instilling healthy employee attitudes and an organizational climate which he considers to be felicitous to human values. He believes that proper attitudes will lead to efficient job and organizational structure.

There is always a lively debate as to the overall effectiveness of the ap-

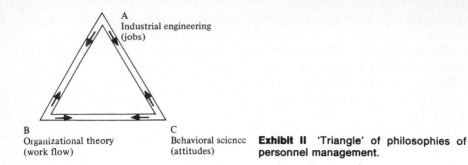

Exhibit II 'Triangle' of philosophies of personnel management.

proaches of the organizational theorist and the industrial engineer. Manifestly they have achieved much. But the nagging question for the behavioral scientist has been: What is the cost in human problems that eventually cause more expense to the organization—for instance, turnover, absenteeism, errors, violation of safety rules, strikes, restriction of output, higher wages, and greater fringe benefits? On the other hand, the behavioral scientist is hard put to document much manifest improvement in personnel management, using his approach.

The three philosophies can be depicted as a triangle, as is done in Exhibit 2, with each persuasion claiming the apex angle. The motivation-hygiene theory claims the same angle as industrial engineering, but for opposite goals. Rather than rationalizing the work to increase efficiency, the theory suggests that work be *enriched* to bring about effective utilization of personnel. Such a systematic attempt to motivate employees by manipulating the motivator factors is just beginning.

The term *job encrichment* describes this embryonic movement. An older term, job enlargement, should be avoided because it is associated with past failures stemming from a misunderstanding of the problem. Job enrichment provides the opportunity for the employee's psychological growth, while job enlargement merely makes a job structurally bigger. Since scientific job enrichment is very new, this article only suggests the principles and practical steps that have recently emerged from several successful experiments in industry.

Job Loading

In attempting to enrich an employee's job, management often succeeds in reducing the man's personal contribution, rather than giving him an opportunity for growth in his accustomed job. Such an endeavor, which I shall call horizontal job loading (as opposed to vertical loading, or providing motivator factors), has been the problem of earlier job enlargement programs. This activity merely enlarges the meaninglessness of the job. Some examples of this approach, and their effect, are:

● Challenging the employee by increasing the amount of production expected of him. If he tightens 10,000 bolts a day, see if he can tighten 20,000 bolts a day. The arithmetic involved shows that multiplying zero by zero still equals zero.

- Adding another meaningless task to the existing one, usually some routine clerical activity. The arithmetic here is adding zero to zero.
- Rotating the assignments of a number of jobs that need to be enriched. This means washing dishes for a while, then washing silverware. The arithmetic is substituting one zero for another zero.
- Removing the most difficult parts of the assignment in order to free the worker to accomplish more of the less challenging assignments. This traditional industrial engineering approach amounts to subtraction in the hope of accomplishing addition.

These are common forms of horizontal loading that frequently come up in preliminary brainstorming sessions on job enrichment. The principles of vertical loading have not all been worked out as yet, and they remain rather general, but I have furnished seven useful starting points for consideration in Exhibit 3.

A Successful Application

An example from a highly successful job enrichment experiment can illustrate the distinction between horizontal and vertical loading of a job. The subjects of this study were the stockholder correspondents employed by a very large corporation. Seemingly, the task required of these carefully selected and highly trained correspondents was quite complex and challenging. But almost all indexes of performance and job attitudes were low, and exit interviewing confirmed that the challenge of the job existed merely as words.

A job enrichment project was initiated in the form of an experiment with one group, designated as an achieving unit, having its job enriched by the principles described in Exhibit 3. A control group continued to do its job in the traditional way. (There were also two "uncommitted" groups of correspondents

Exhibit III   Principles of vertical job loading

Principle	Motivators involved
A. Removing some controls while retaining accountability	Responsibility and personal achievement
B. Increasing the accountability of individuals for own work	Responsibility and recognition
C. Giving a person a complete natural unit of work (module, division, area, and so on)	Responsibility, achievement, and recognition
D. Granting additional authority to an employee in his activity; job freedom	Responsibility, achievement, and recognition
E. Making periodic reports directly available to the worker himself rather than to the supervisor	Internal recognition
F. Introducing new and more difficult tasks not previously handled	Growth and learning
G. Assigning individuals specific or specialized tasks, enabling them to become experts	Responsibility, growth, and advancement

formed to measure the so-called Hawthorne Effect—that is, to gauge whether productivity and attitudes toward the job changed artificially merely because employees sensed that the company was paying more attention to them in doing something different or novel. The results for these groups were substantially the same as for the control group, and for the sake of simplicity I do not deal with them in this summary.) No changes in hygiene were introduced for either group other than those that would have been made anyway, such as normal pay increases.

The changes for the achieving unit were introduced in the first two months, averaging one per week of the seven motivators listed in Exhibit 3. At the end of six months the members of the achieving unit were found to be outperforming their counterparts in the control group, and in addition indicated a marked increase in their liking for their jobs. Other results showed that the achieving group had lower absenteeism and, subsequently, a much higher rate of promotion.

Exhibit 4 illustrates the changes in performance, measured in February and March, before the study period began, and at the end of each month of the study period. The shareholder service index represents quality of letters, including ac-

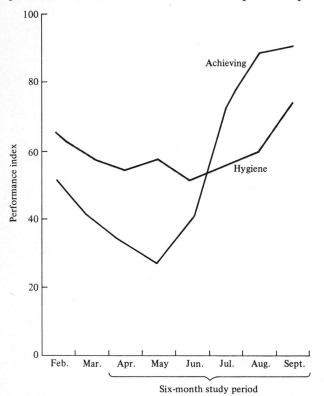

Exhibit IV   Shareholder service index in company experiment. [Three-month cumulative average]

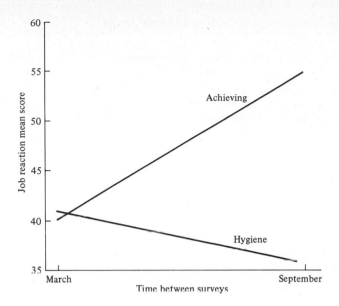

Exhibit V Changes in attitudes toward tasks in company experiment. [Changes in mean scores over six-month period]

curacy of information, and speed of response to stockholders' letters of inquiry. The index of a current month was averaged into the average of the two prior months, which means that improvement was harder to obtain if the indexes of the previous months were low. The "achievers" were performing less well before the six-month period started, and their performance service index continued to decline after the introduction of the motivators, evidently because of uncertainty over their newly granted responsibilities. In the third month, however, performance improved, and soon the members of this group had reached a high level of accomplishment.

Exhibit 5 shows the two groups' attitudes toward their job, measured at the end of March, just before the first motivator was introduced, and again at the end of September. The correspondents were asked 16 questions, all involving motivation. A typical one was, "As you see it, how many opportunities do you feel that you have in your job for making worthwhile contributions?" The answers were scaled from 1 to 5, with 80 as the maximum possible score. The achievers became much more positive about their job, while the attitude of the control unit remained about the same (the drop is not statistically significant).

How was the job of these correspondents restructured? Exhibit 6 lists the suggestions made that were deemed to be horizontal loading, and the actural vertical loading changes that were incorporated in the job of the achieving unit. The capital letters under "Principle" after "vertical loading" refer to the corresponding letters in Exhibit 3. The reader will note that the rejected forms of

Exhibit VI   Enlargement vs. Enrichment of Correspondents' Tasks in Company Experiment

Horizontal loading suggestions (rejected)	Vertical loading suggestions (adopted)	Principle
Firm quotas could be set for letters to be answered each day, using a rate which would be hard to reach.	Subject matter experts were appointed within each unit for other members of the unit to consult with before seeking supervisory help. (The supervisor had been answering all specialized and difficult questions.)	G
The women could type the letters themselves, as well as compose them, or take on any other clerical functions.	Correspondents signed their own names on letters. (The supervisor had been signing all letters.)	B
All difficult or complex inquiries could be channeled to a few women so that the remainder could achieve high rates of output. These jobs could be exchanged from time to time.	The work of the more experienced correspondents was proofread less frequently by supervisors and was done at the correspondents' desks, dropping verification from 100% to 10%. (Previously, all correspondents' letters had been checked by the supervisor.)	A
The women could be rotated through units handling different customers, and then sent back to their own units.	Production was discussed, but only in terms such as "a full day's work is expected." As time went on, this was no longer mentioned. (Before, the group had been constantly reminded of the number of letters that needed to be answered.)	D
	Outgoing mail went directly to the mailroom without going over supervisors' desks. (The letters had always been routed through the supervisors.)	A
	Correspondents were encouraged to answer letters in a more personalized way. (Reliance on the form-letter approach had been standard practice.)	C
	Each correspondent was held personally responsible for the quality and accuracy of letters. (This responsibility had been the province of the supervisor and the verifier.)	B, E

horizontal loading correspond closely to the list of common manifestations of the phenomenon in Exhibit III, left column.

STEPS TO JOB ENRICHMENT

Now that the motivator idea has been described in practice, here are the steps that managers should take in instituting the principle with their employees:

1   Select those jobs in which (a) the investment in industrial engineering does not make changes too costly, (b) attitudes are poor, (c) hygiene is becoming very costly, and (d) motivation will make a difference in performance.

2   Approach these jobs with the conviction that they can be changed. Years of tradition have led managers to believe that the content of the jobs is

sacrosanct and the only scope of action that they have is in ways of stimulating people.

3 Brainstorm a list of changes that may enrich the jobs, without concern for their practicality.

4 Screen the list to eliminate suggestions that involve hygiene, rather than actual motivation.

5 Screen the list for generalities, such as "give them more responsibility," that are rarely followed in practice. This might seem obvious, but the motivator words have never left industry; the substance has just been rationalized and organized out. Words like "responsibility," "growth," "achievement," and "challenge," for example, have been elevated to the lyrics of the patriotic anthem for all organizations. It is the old problem typified by the pledge of allegiance to the flag being more important than contributions to the country—of following the form, rather than the substance.

6 Screen the list to eliminate any *horizontal* loading suggestions.

7 Avoid direct participation by the employees whose jobs are to be enriched. Ideas they have expressed previously certainly constitute a valuable source of recommended changes, but their direct involvement contaminates the process with human relations *hygiene* and, more specifically, gives them only a *sense* of making a contribution. The job is to be changed, and it is the content that will produce the motivation, not attitudes about being involved or the challenge inherent in setting up a job. That process will be over shortly, and it is what the employees will be doing from then on that will determine their motivation. A sense of participation will result only in short-term movement

8 In the initial attempts at job enrichment, set up a controlled experiment. At least two equivalent groups should be chosen, one an experimental unit in which the motivators are systematically introduced over a period of time, and the other one a control group in which no changes are made. For both groups, hygiene should be allowed to follow its natural course for the duration of the experiment. Pre- and post-installation tests of performance and job attitudes are necessary to evaluate the effectiveness of the job enrichment program. The attitude test must be limited to motivator items in order to divorce the employee's view of the job he is given from all the surrounding hygiene feelings that he might have.

9 Be prepared for a drop in performance in the experimental group the first few weeks. The changeover to a new job may lead to a temporary reduction in efficiency.

10 Expect your first-line supervisors to experience some anxiety and hostility over the changes you are making. The anxiety comes from their fear that the changes will result in poorer performance for their unit. Hostility will arise when the employees start assuming what the supervisors regard as their own responsibility for performance. The supervisor without checking duties to perform may then be left with little to do.

After a successful experiment, however, the supervisor usually discovers the supervisory and managerial functions he has neglected, or which were never his because all his time was given over to checking the work of his subordinates. For example, in the R&D division of one large chemical company I know of, the supervisors of the laboratory assistants were theoretically responsible for their training and evaluation. These functions, however, had come to be performed in a routine, unsubstantial fashion. After the job enrichment program, during which the supervisors were not merely passive observers of the assistants' performance, the supervisors actually were devoting their time to reviewing performance and administering thorough training.

What has been called an employee-centered style of supervision will come about not through education of supervisors, but by changing the jobs that they do.

CONCLUDING NOTE

Job enrichment will not be a one-time proposition, but a continuous management function. The initial changes, however, shold last for a very long period of time. There are a number of reasons for this:

- The changes should bring the job up to the level of challenge commensurate with the skill that was hired.
- Those who have still more ability eventually will be able to demonstrate it better and win promotion to higher-level jobs.
- The very nature of motivators, as opposed to hygiene factors, is that they have a much longer-term effect on employees' attitudes. Perhaps the job will have to be enriched again, but this will not occur as frequently as the need for hygiene.

Not all jobs can be enriched, nor do all jobs need to be enriched. If only a small percentage of the time and money that is now devoted to hygiene, however, were given to job enrichment efforts, the return in human satisfaction and economic gain would be one of the largest dividends that industry and society have ever reaped through their efforts at better personnel management.

The argument for job enrichment can be summed up quite simply: If you have someone on a job, use him. If you can't use him on the job, get rid of him, either via automation or by selecting someone with lesser ability. If you can't use him and you can't get rid of him, you will have a motivation problem.

Herzberg's Dual-Factor Theory of Job Satisfaction and Motivation: A Review of the Evidence and a Criticism

Robert J. House
Lawrence A. Wigdor

In 1959, Herzberg, Mausner and Snyderman reported research findings that suggested that man has two sets of needs: his need as an animal to avoid pain, and his need as a human to grow psychologically. These findings led them to advance

From *Personnel Psychology*, 1967, **20**, 369–389. Reprinted by permission.

a "dual factor" theory of motivation. Since that time, the theory has caught the attention of both industrial managers and psychologists. Management training and work-motivation programs have been installed on the basis of the dual-factor theory. Psychologists have both advanced criticisms and conducted substantial research relevant to the dual-factor theory. The purpose of this paper is to review the theory, the criticisms, and the empiric investigations reported to date, in an effort to assess the validity of the theory.

Whereas previous theories of motivation were based on causal inferences of the theorists and deduction from their own insights and experience, the dual-factor theory of motivation was inferred from a study of need satisfactions and the reported motivational effects of these satisfactions on 200 engineers and accountants.

The subjects were first requested to recall a time when they had felt exceptionally good about their jobs. The investigators sought by further questioning to determine the reasons for their feelings of satisfaction, and whether their feelings of satisfaction had affected their performance, their personal relationships, and their well-being. Finally, the sequence of events that served to return the workers' attitudes to "normal" was elicited.

In a second set of interviews, the same subjects were asked to describe incidents in which their feelings about their jobs were exceptionally negative— cases in which their negative feelings were related to some event on the job.

Herzberg and his associates concluded from their interview findings that job satisfaction consisted of two separate independent dimensions: the first dimension was related to job satisfaction, and the second dimension to job dissatisfaction. These dimensions are not opposite ends of the same continuum, but instead represent two distinct continua. High satisfaction is not in the main brought about by the absence of factors that cause dissatisfaction. Those job characteristics that are important for, and lead to, job satisfaction but not to job dissatisfaction are classified as "satisfiers," while those that are important for, and lead to, job dissatisfaction but not to job satisfaction are classified as "dissatisfiers." A few job characteristics functioned in both directions.

According to the theory, the satisfiers are related to the nature of the work itself and the rewards that flow directly from the performance of that work. The most potent of these are those characteristics that foster the individual's needs for self-actualization and self-realization in his work. These work-related or intrinsic factors are achievement, recognition, work itself, responsibility, and advancement.

A sense of performing interesting and important work (work itself), job responsibility, and advancement are the most important factors for a lasting attitude change. Achievement, more so than recognition, was frequently associated with the long-range factors of responsibility and the nature of the work itself. Recognition that produces good feelings about the job does not necessarily have to come from superiors; it might come from peers, customers, or subordinates. Where recognition is based on achievement, it provides more intense satisfaction.

The dissatisfaction factors are associated with the individual's relationship to the context or environment in which he does his work. The most important of these is company policy and administration that promotes ineffectiveness or inefficiency within the organization. The second most important is incompetent technical supervision—supervision that lacks knowledge of the job or ability to delegate responsibility and teach. Working conditions, interpersonal relations with supervisors, salary, and lack of recognition and achievement can also cause dissatisfaction.

The second major hypothesis of the dual-factor theory of motivation is that the satisfiers are effective in motivating the individual to superior performance and effort, but the dissatisfiers are not. In his most recent book, Herzberg (1966, p. 75) advances the following analogy to explain why the satisfier factors or "motivators" affect motivation in the positive direction.

> When a child learns to ride a bicycle, he is becoming more competent, increasing the repertory of his behavior, expanding his skills—psychologically growing. In the process of the child's learning to master the bicycle, the parents can love him with all the zeal and compassion of the most devoted mother and father. They can safeguard the child from injury by providing the safest and most hygienic area in which to practice; they can offer all kinds of incentives and rewards; and they can provide the most expert instructors. But the child will never, never learn to ride the bicycle—unless he is given a bicycle! The hygiene factors are not a valid contributor to psychological growth. The substance of the tasks is required to achieve growth goals. Similarly, you cannot love an engineer into creativity, although by this approach you can avoid his dissatisfactions with the way you treat him. Creativity will require a potentially creative task to do.

CRITICISMS OF THE TWO-FACTOR THEORY

The theory has been criticized on several grounds: first, that it is methodologically bound; second, that it is based on faulty research; and third, that it is inconsistent with past evidence concerning satisfaction and motivation. Each of these criticisms will be reviewed here.

Methodological Bounds of the Theory

Vroom (1964) has argued that the storytelling critical-incident method, in which the interviewee recounts extremely satisfying and dissatisfying job events, accounts for the associations found by Herzberg *et al.* and that other methods are required to adequately test the theory.

> It is . . . possible that obtained differences between stated sources of satisfaction and dissatisfaction stem from defensive processes within the individual respondent. Persons may be more likely to attribute the causes of satisfaction to their own achievements and accomplishments on the job. On the other hand, they may be more likely to attribute their dissatisfaction not to personal inadequacies or deficiencies,

but to factors in the work environment; i. e., obstacles presented by company policies or supervision. (Vroom, 1964, p. 129)

"People tend to take the credit when things go well, and enhance their own feelings of self-worth, but protect their self-concept when things go poorly by blaming their failure on the environment" (Vroom, 1966, pp. 7, 8). He further states, "If you grant the assumption about the way in which biases operate, it follows that the storytelling methods may have very little bearing on the actual consequence of managerial practice." (Vroom, 1966, p. 10).

Faulty Research Foundation

Not only has it been argued that the theory is method bound, but it is also argued that the research from which it was inferred is fraught with procedural deficiencies.

The most important criticism involves the utilization of Herzberg's categorization procedure to measure job dimensions, the satisfiers and "hygiene factors." The coding is not completely determined by the rating system and the data, but requires, in addition, interpretation by the rater. For example, the dimension of supervision encompasses, among others, the categories: (a) "supervisor competent," (b) "supervisor incompetent," and (c) "supervisor showed favoritism." The three classifications all require an interpretation of the supervisor's behavior. If the respondent offers the evaluation, no interpretation by the rater is required. However, if the subject merely describes the supervisor's behavior, an evaluation by the rater is necessary.

The necessity for interpretations of the data by a rater may lead to contamination of the dimensions so derived. Employing one of Herzberg's own incidents to illustrate the dimension of recognition, Vroom (1964) pointed out the way in which the dual-factor theory may contaminate the coding procedure. The dimensions in the situation can quite possibly reflect more the rater's hypothesis concerning the compositions and interrelations of dimensions than the respondent's own perceptions. A more objective approach, to minimize the possibility of learning more about the perceptions of raters than those of interviewees, would be to have the respondents do the rating and perform the necessary evaluations (Graen, 1966).

Second, and closely related to the first methodological problem, is the inadequate operational definitions utilized by Herzberg and associates to identify satisfiers and dissatisfiers. Numerous critics (Malinovsky & Barry, 1965; Burke, 1966; Ewen, 1964; Dunnette, 1965) have questioned the mutual exclusiveness of these dimensions. Malinovsky and Barry (1965) reported that it is possible that correlations between motivator items and between hygiene items in the evaluations of factors resulted from response-set effects—the tendency of the workers to respond in the same manner to like-worded statements.

Table 1 Summary of Factors which Showed Significant Differences between Positive and Negative Incidents of Job Feelings Representing 10 Studies of 17 Populations

Investigator → Population factor	Herzberg et al. Accnts.	Herzberg et al. Eng.	Clegg Agri. ext. wkrs.	Walt Prof. women	Schwartz Util. supv.	Anderson Unsk. hosp.	Anderson Sk. hosp.	Anderson Nurs.	Myers Eng.	Myers Sci.	Myers Mfg. supr.	Myers Hrly. tech.	Myers Fem. assem.	Saleh Pre-retiree	Herzberg Finn supr.	Gendel Hskp. wkrs.	Perczel Hung. eng.	Totals
Achievement	X	X	X	X	X	X	X	X	X	X	X	X	X	X	X		X	15
Recognition	X	X	X	X	X	X	X		X	X	X	X	X		X	X	X	14
Work itself	X	X	X	X							X			X	X		X	5
Responsibility	X	X		X	X	X			X	X		X		X	X	X		10
Advancement	X	X		X	X		X							X	X	X		5
Possibility of growth					X	X	X											2
																		51-0
Co. pol. & adm.	X	X	X	X	X	X	X	X	X	X	X	X	X	X	X	X	X	16
Supervision—technical	X	X	X	—	X	X	X	X	X	X	X	X		X	X	X	X	13
Interpersonal relat.—sup.	X	X	X			X		X						X	X			5
Interpersonal relat.—peers		X		—		X								X	X	X		5-1
Interpersonal relat.—sub.			X	—	—									X				2-2
Working conditions			X	X	X	X		X							X	X		8
Status				X														1
Personal life	X		X	X														3
Security					X													1
Salary																X		1
																		54-3
TOTALS	9	9	7	8-2	9-1	5	5	5	3	3	3	5	2	9	9	8	6	105 + 3 = 108

X Correct prediction
– Incorrect prediction
X Correct prediction—sample too small for Statistical Significance test
Reproduced by permission of The World Publishing Company from *Work and the nature of man* by Frederick Herzberg. Copyright © 1966 by Frederick Herzberg.

Table 2 Frequency of Reports for Satisfiers and Dissatisfiers Out of Total Number of 1,220 People in Six Studies Reported by Herzberg (1966)

Factor	Satisfier	Dissatisfier	Total number of people
Achievement	440	122	1,220
Recognition	309	110	1,220
Advancement	126	48	1,220
Responsibility	168	35	1,220
Work itself	175	75	1,220
Policy and administration	55	337	1,220
Supervision	22	182	1,220
Work conditions	20	108	1,220
Relations with superior	15	59	1,220
Relations with peers	9	57	1,220

Reproduced by permission of The World Publishing Company from *Work and the nature of man* by Frederick Herzberg. Copyright © 1966 by Frederick Herzberg.

The original study has also been criticized because it contains no measure of overall satisfaction (Ewen, 1964). However, such a measure is important if a factor is to be called a satisfier or dissatisfier. There is no basis for assuming that the factors described as hygiene or motivators contribute to respondent overall satisfaction or dissatisfaction.

Smith and Kendall (1963) have shown that a worker may dislike some aspects of his job, yet still think it is acceptable. Similarly, workers may dislike the job despite many desirable characteristics. Smith and Kendall (1963) propose that job satisfaction is a function of the perceived characteristic of a job in relation to an individual's frame of reference. A particular job condition can be a satisfier or dissatisfier.

Other procedural criticisms concern the lack of reliability data for the critical-incident method, and the fact that the research was not based solely on current satisfaction with a presently existing job situation. As a result, there is no control over the sampling time for the data, and no basis for drawing inferences about the relative contribution of various job factors to overall job satisfaction.

Inconsistency with Previous Evidence

If the dual-factor theory were correct, we should expect highly satisfied people to be highly motivated and to produce more. Based on a rather exhaustive review of the empiric research up to 1955, Brayfield and Crockett (1955) concluded that one's position in a network of relationships need not imply strong motivation for outstanding performance within the system, and that productivity may only be peripherally related to many of the goals toward which the industrial worker is striving. Herzberg *et al.* (1959) cited 27 studies in which there was a quantitative relationship between job attitude and productivity. Of these, only 14 revealed a positive relationship. In the remaining 13, job attitudes and productivity were not related. In 1964, Vroom examined 20 studies dealing with strength between job satisfaction and job performance. Seventeen studies revealed a positive relationship with a medium correlation of .14, while 3 studies revealed a negative relationship. At the present time, there seems to be general agreement among most researchers that the effect of satisfaction on worker motivation and productivity depends on situational variables yet to be explicated by future research. Furthermore, as Friedlander (1966a, p. 143) reported, no data are presented by Herzberg to indicate a direct relationship between incidents involving intrinsic job characteristics and incidents containing self-reports of increased job performance. According to the Protestant ethic, it is conceivable that self-reports of increased job performance may be nothing more than moral justification for increased job employment.

Vroom (1966, p. 11) summarizes these arguments succinctly:

> In discussing the administrative implication of his findings, Herzberg loses sight of the distinction between recall of satisfying events and actual observation of motivated behavior. He appears to be arguing that the satisfiers are also motivators; i. e., that those job content conditions which produce a high level of satisfaction also motivate the person to perform effectively on his job.

If one reflects on the kinds of conditions necessary for productive work, it becomes quite clear that motivation is only one of them. Clearly, when working conditions, the quality of leadership, the suitability of supplies and equipment, the efficiency of scheduling and coordinating procedures, or the abilities of members of the work force are found deficient, highly motivated behavior may have either little effect on productivity or even possibly the effect of causing frustration which interfers with productivity.

EMPIRIC RESEARCH BASED
ON CRITICAL-INCIDENT METHODOLOGY

In *Work and the Nature of Man,* Herzberg (1966) reports the results of 10 critical-incident studies on 17 different populations. He asserts that these studies support the dual-factor theory in 97 percent of the cases. Table 1 is taken from Herzberg's 1966 book and summarizes the results of these studies. Each x in the table represents a correct prediction. The blank spaces suggest no significant evidence either way because of (a) failure of an investigator to include the factor in the analysis, (b) the scoring of only major factors in the events, (c) the general rarity of a factor occuring, or (d) occasional moderate frequency of a factor to be associated with both satisfaction and dissatisfaction.

The chart shows that theoretical predictions, when made for each seperate study, were valid in 97 percent of the cases.

However, compilation of the *number of people* mentioning one of Herzberg's ten factors as a satisfier or dissatisfier yields Table 2. (This analysis is restricted to those factors mentioned more than four times. By restricting this analysis to those factors, several factors are excluded. The excluded factors are Opportunity for growth, Interpersonal relations with subordinates, Status, Personal life, Security and Salary. With the exception of Opportunity for growth, these excluded factors are peripheral to the Two-Factor theory, and their inclusion in this analysis would not change the major conclusion suggested by the analysis.)

From this table it can be observed that achievement is seen by *most respondents* as more of a dissatisfier than Relations with supervisors or Working conditions. In fact, Achievement can be considered the third major dissatisfier. Recognition is also found to be more of a dissatisfier than both Working conditions and Relations with superiors. Using these data from Table 2, one can rank dissatisfiers as follows:

Company policy and administration
Supervision
Achievement
Recognition
Working conditions
Work itself
Relations with superior
Advancement
Responsibility

This ranking can be partially explained by considering the fact that every factor did not appear in every study reported by Herzberg. However, in all studies, each factor had an equal chance of occurring and did not because of failure of respondents to mention incidents relating to all factors . . . .

CONCLUSIONS

Our secondary analysis of the data presented by Herzberg (1966) in his most recent book yields conclusions contradictory to the proposition of the Two-Factor theory that satisfiers and dissatisfiers are unidimensional and independent. Although many of the intrinsic aspects of jobs are shown to be more frequently identified by respondents as satisfiers, achievement and recognition are also shown to be very frequently identified as dissatisfiers. In fact, achievement and recognition are far more frequently identified as dissatisfiers than working conditions and relations with the superior.

Since the data do not support the satisfier-dissatisfier dichotomy, the second proposition of the Two-Factor theory, that satisfiers have more motivational force than dissatisfiers, appears highly suspect. This is true for two reasons. First, any attempt to separate the two requires an arbitrary definition of the classifications satisfier and dissatisfier. Second, unless such an arbitrary separation is employed, the proposition is untestable.

Turning to our review of previous studies based on methods other than the storytelling method, four important conclusions emerge concerning the operation of, and variables associated with, the various job characteristics pertinent to satisfaction or dissatisfaction. These four conclusions are:

1 A given factor can cause job satisfaction for one person and job dissatisfaction for another person, and vice versa.

Job satisfaction is a function of the perceived characteristics of a job in relation to an individual frame of reference. A particular job condition on the basis of this theoretical, can be a satisfier, dissatisfier or irrelevant depending on conditions in comparable jobs, conditions of other people, of the qualifications and past experience of the individual as well as on numerous situational variables of the present job. Thus, job satisfaction is not an absolute phenomena but is relative to the alternatives available to the individual. (Smith & Kendall, 1963, p. 14.)

Variables that partially determine whether a given factor will be a source of satisfaction or dissatisfaction on the job were shown to be:

Job or occupational level: Centers and Bugental (1966), Myers (1964), Rosen (1963), Friedlander (1966b), Dunnette (1965).
Age of respondents: Singh and Baumgartel (1966), Saleh (1964), Friedlander (1966b), Wernimont (1966).
Sex of respondents: Centers and Bugental (1966), Gibson (1961), Myers (1964).
Formal education: Singh and Baumgartel (1966).
Culture: Turner and Lawrence (1965), Ott (1965).
Time-dimension variable: Ewen (1964), Wernimont (1966).
Respondent's standing in his group: Eran (1966).

2   A given factor can cause job satisfaction and dissatisfaction in the same sample (Dunnette, 1965; Ewen, 1964; Gordon, 1965; Burke, 1966; Ewen, Smith, Hulin & Locke, 1966; Friedlander, 1963; Wernimont, 1966; Halpern, 1966; Ott, 1965; Hinrichs & Mischkind, 1967; Graen, 1966; Malinovsky & Barry, 1965).
3   Intrinsic job factors are more important to both satisfying dissatisfying job events (Dunnette *et al.,* 1967; Wernimont, 1966; Ewen, Smith, Hulin & Locke, 1966; Graen, 1966; Friedlander, 1964).
4   These conclusions lead us to agree with the criticism advanced by Dunnette, Campbell and Hakel (1967) that the Two-Factor theory is an oversimplification of the relationships between motivation and satisfaction, and the sources of job satisfaction and dissatisfaction.

REFERENCES

Brayfield, A. H., and Crockett, W. H. "Employee Attitudes and Employee Performance." *Psychological Bulletin,* LII(1955), 396–424.
Burke, R. "Are Herzberg's Motivators and Hygienes Unidimensional?" *Journal of Applied Psychology,* L(1966), 317–321.
Centers, R., and Bugental, D. E. "Intrinsic and Extrinsic Job Motivations among Different Segments of the Working Population." *Journal of Applied Psychology.* L(1966), 193–197.
Dunnette, M. D. "Factor Structure of Unusually Satisfying and Unusually Dissatisfying Job Situations for Six Occupational Groups." Paper read at Midwestern Psychological Association. Chicago, April 29—May 1, 1965.
Dunnette, M. D., Campbell, J. P., and Hakel, M. D. "Factors Contributing to Job Satisfaction and Job Dissatisfaction in Six Occupational Groups." *Orgainzational Behavior and Human Performance,* II(1967), 143–174.

Eran, M. "Relationship Between Self-Perceived Personality Traits and Job Attitudes in Middle Management." *Journal of Applied Psychology,* XLIX(1966), 424–430.

Ewen, R. B. "Some Determinants of Job Satisfaction: A Study of the Generality of Herzberg's Theory." *Journal of Applied Psychology,*XLVIII(1964), 161–163.

Ewen, R. B., Smith, P. C., Hulin, C. L., and Locke, E. A. "An Empirical Test of the Herzberg Two-Factor Theory," *Journal of Applied Psychology,*L(1966), 544–550.

Fantz, R. "Motivational Factors in Rehabilitation." Unpublished PH.D. Thesis, Western Reserve University, 1962.

Fine, S., and Dickman, R. "Satisfaction and Productivity." Paper presented at the American Psychological Association Convention, St. Louis, Missouri, September, 1962.

Fournet, G. P., Distefano, M. K., Jr., and Pryer, M. "Job Satisfaction: Issues and Problems." *Personnel Psychology,*XIX(1966), 165–183.

Friedlander, F. "Underlying Sources of Job Satisfaction." *Journal of Applied Psychology,* XLVII(1963), 246–250.

Friedlander, F. "Job Characteristics as Satisfiers and Dissatisfiers," *Journal of Applied Psychology,* L(1966), 143–152.(a)

Friedlander, F. "Importance of Work Versus Nonwork among Socially and Occupationally Stratified Groups." *Journal of Applied Psychology,*L(1966), 437–441.(b)

Friedlander, F., and Walton, E. "Positive and Negative Motivations Toward Work." *Administrative Science Quarterly,*IX(1964), 194–207.

Gibson, J. W. "Sources of Job Satisfaction and Job Dissatisfaction as Interpreted from Analysis of Write-in Responses." Unpublished PH.D. thesis, Western Reserve University, 1961.

Gordon, G. G. "The Relationship of Satisfiers and Dissatisfiers to Productivity, Turnover, and Morale." Paper presented at the American Psychological Association Convention, Chicago, Illinois, September 1965.

Graen, G. "Motivator and Hygiene Dimensions for Research and Development Engineers." *Journal of Applied Psychology,*L(1966), 563–566.

Graglia, A., and Hamlin, R. "Effect of Effort and Task Orientation on Activity Preference." Paper presented at Eastern Psychological Association Meeting, Philadelphia, 1964.

Hahn, C. "Dimensions of Job Satisfaction and Career Motivation." Unpublished manuscript, 1959.

Halpern, G. "Relative Contributions of Motivator and Hygiene Factors to Overall Job Satisfaction." *Journal of Applied Psychology,*L(1966), 198–200.

Hamlin, R. M., and Nemo, R. S. "Self-Actualization in Choice Scores of Improved Schizophrenics." *Journal of Clinical Psychology,*XVIII(1962), 51–54.

Haywood, H. C., and Dobbs, V. "Motivation and Anxiety in High School Boys." *Journal of Personality,* XXXII(1964), 371–379.

Herzberg, F. *Work and the Nature of Man.* Cleveland: World Publishing Company, 1966.

Herzberg, F., Mausner, B., Peterson, R., and Capwell, D. F. *Job Attitudes: Review of Research and Opinion.* Pittsburgh: Psychological Services of Pittsburgh, 1957.

Herzberg, F., Mausner, B., and Snyderman, B. *The Motivation to Work*(Second Edition). New York: John Wiley and Sons, 1959.

Hinrichs, J. R., and Mischkind, L. A. "Empirical and Theoretical Limitations of the Two-Factor Hypothesis of Job Satisfaction." *Journal of Applied Psychology,* LI(1967), 191–200.

Kuhlen, R. G. "Needs, Perceived Need Satisfaction Opportunities, and Satisfaction with

Occupation." *Journal of Applied Psychology,*XLVII(1963), 56–64.

Malinovsky, M. R., and Barry, J. R. "Determinants of Work Attitude." *Journal of Applied Psychology,* XLIX(1965), 446–451.

Myers, M. S. "Who Are Your Motivated Workers?" *Harvard Business Review,*XLII(1964), 73–88.

Ott, D. C. "The Generality of Herzberg's Two-Factor Theory of Motivation." Unpublished PH.D. thesis, The Ohio State University, 1965.

Porter, L. W. "Job Attitudes in Management:I. Perceived Deficiencies in Need Fulfillment as a Function of Job Level." *Journal of Applied Psychology,* XLVI(1962), 375–384.

Rosen, H. "Occupational Motivation of Research and Development Personnel." *Personnel Administration,* XXVI(1963), 37–43.

Saleh, S. "A Study of Attitude Change in the Pre-Retirement Period." *Journal of Applied Psychology,* XLVIII(1964), 310–312.

Sandvold, K. "The Effect of Effort and Task Orientation on the Motivator Orientation and Verbal Responsivity of Chronic Schizophrenic Patients and Normals." Unpublished PH.D. thesis, University of Illinois, 1962.

Schwartz, P. *Attitudes of Middle Management Personnel,* Pittsburgh: American Institute for Research, 1959.

Singh, T. M., and Baumgartel, H. "Background Factors in Airline Mechanics' Work Motivations." *Journal of Applied Psychology,*L(1966), 337–339.

Smith, P. C., and Kendall, L. M. "Cornell Studies of Job Satisfaction." Unpublished manuscript, 1963.

Turner, A. N., and Lawrence, P. R. *Industrial Jobs and the Worker.* Cambridge: Harvard University Graduate School of Business Administration, 1965.

Vroom, V. H. *Work and Motivation.* New York: John Wiley and Sons, 1964.

Vroom, V. H. "Some Observations Regarding Herzberg's Two-Factor Theory." Paper presented at the American Psychological Association Convention, New York, September, 1966.

Wernimont, P. F. "Intrinsic and Extrinsic Factors in Job Satisfaction." *Journal of Applied Psychology,* L(1966), 41–50.

Yadov, V. A. "The Soviet and American Worker: Job Attitudes." *Soviet Life* January, 1965.

Clarification and Evaluation of The Two-Factor Theory of Job Satisfaction

Nathan King [1]

According to the two-factor theory of job satisfaction, the primary determinants of job satisfaction are intrinsic aspects of the job, called motivators (e. g., achievement, recognition, the work itself, responsibility, and advancement), whereas the primary determinants of job dissatisfaction are extrinsic factors, called hygienes (e. g., company policy and administration, supervision, salary, interpersonal relations with co-workers, and working conditions).

The two-factor theory originated from a study by Herzberg, Mausner, and Snyderman (1959). These investigators interviewed 203 accountants and engineers and asked them to describe specific instances when they felt exceptionally good or exceptionally bad about their jobs. Upon analyzing the content of these

Table 1   Percentage of Good and Bad Critical Incidents in Which Each Job Factor Appeared (Herzberg et al., 1959)

Factor	Percentage[a]	
	Good	Bad
Achievement (M)	41*	7
Recognition (M)	33*	18
Work itself (M)	26*	14
Responsibility (M)	23*	6
Advancement (M)	20*	11
Salary (H)	15	17
Possibility of growth (M)	6	8
Interpersonal relations — subordinate (H)	6	3
Status (H)	4	4
Interpersonal relations — superior (H)	4	15*
Interpersonal relations — peers (H)	3	8*
Supervision — technical (H)	3	20*
Company policy & administration (H)	3	31*
Working conditions (H)	1	11*
Personal life (H)	1	6*
Job security (H)	1	1
Percentage of total contributed by Ms	78	36
Percentage of total contributed by Hs	22	64

Note. — Abbreviations are: M = motivator; H = hygiene.

[a] The percentages total more than 100% since more than one job factor can be mentioned in a single critical incident.

* The difference between the percentage of good and bad critical incidents is significant at the .01 level.

From *Psychological Bulletin*, 1970, **74**, 18–31. Copyright by the American Psychological Association. Reprinted by permission.

[1] The author is especially grateful to Charles L. Hulin and Milton R. Blood for reading earlier versions of this paper and providing helpful comments.

Table 2   Five Versions of the Two-Factor Theory of Job Satisfaction

Theory	Supporting data	
	Critical incident data	Correlational data
I. All motivators (Ms) combined contribute more to job satisfaction (S) than to job dissatisfaction (D), and all hygienes (Hs) combined contribute more to D than to S.	All Ms combined are mentioned proportionately more often in good critical incidents (Gs) than in bad critical incidents (Bs), and all Hs combined are mentioned proportionately more often in Bs than in Gs.	The multiple correlation (R) between the Ms and S is greater than the R between the Ms and D, and the R between the Hs and D is greater than the R between the Hs and S.
II. All Ms combined contribute more to S than do all Hs combined, and all Hs combined contribute more to D than do all Ms combined.	All Ms combined are mentioned in Gs more frequently than are all Hs combined, and all Hs combined are mentioned in Bs more frequently than are all Ms combined.	The R between the Ms and S is greater than the R between the Hs and S, and the R between the Hs and D is greater than the R between the Ms and D.
III. Each M contributes more to S than to D, and each H contributes more to D than to S.	Each M is mentioned proportionately more often in Gs than in Bs, and each H is mentioned proportionately more often in Bs than in Gs.	Each M correlates more with S than with D, and each H correlates more with D than with S.
IV. Theory III holds, and in addition, each principal M contributes more to S than does any H, and each principal H contributes more to D than does any M.	The data support Theory III, and in addition, each principal M is mentioned in Gs more frequently than is any H, and each principal H is mentioned in Bs more frequently than is any M.	The data support Theory III, and in addition, each principal M correlates with S more than does any H, and each principal H correlates with D more than does any M.
V. Only Ms determine S, and only Hs determine D.	Only Ms are mentioned in Gs, and only Hs are are mentioned in Bs.	Only Ms correlate with S, and only Hs correlate with D.

critical incidents, it was found that the good critical incidents were dominated by reference to intrinsic aspects of the job (motivators), while the bad critical incidents were dominated by reference to extrinsic factors (hygienes). As indicated in Table 1, this tendency was quite marked; in the reports of good critical incidents, motivators were alluded to almost four times as frequently as hygienes (78% vs. 22%), whereas in bad critical incidents, hygienes were mentioned about twice as frequently as motivators (64% vs. 36%).

Subsequent to the orginal study (Herzberg et al., 1959), a considerable number of empirical studies designed to test the validity of the two-factor theory were published, and a heated controversy has developed between supporters and critics of the theory.

It is the opinion of this writer that a major portion of the controversy stems from the lack of an explicit statement of the theory. At least five distict versions of the two-factor theory have been stated or implied by various researchers. It is the purpose of this paper to explicate and to evaluate these various forms of the theory.

FIVE VERSIONS OF THE TWO-FACTOR THEORY

Table 2 lists five versions of the two-factor theory and an example of two types of data which might be used to support each of the different versions. The critical incident data (second column of Table 2) refer to data of the same type as is illustrated in Table 1; whereas correlational data (third column of Table 2) might be obtained, for example, by simultaneously measuring satisfaction with each of a group of job factors, overall job satisfaction, and overall job dissatisfaction. As almost all of the relevant empirical investigations have made use of the critical incident technique, the different versions of the two-factor theory are discussed in terms of critical incident data.

Theory I

Theory I states that all motivators combined contribute more to job satisfaction than to job dissatisfaction and that all hygienes combined contribute more to job dissatisfaction than to job satisfaction. Critical incident data support Theory I if (a) all motivators combined are mentioned proportionately more often in good critical incidents than in bad critical incidents, and (b) all hygienes combined are mentioned proportionately more often in bad than in good incidents. Clearly the data of Table I meet these two requirements; motivators composed 78% of the job factors mentioned in good critical incidents compared to only 36% mentioned in bad incidents, whereas the hygienes favored the bad incidents (64% compared to 22%).

Actually, Theory I requires that critical incident data meet only one condition, as conditions a and b (see the preceding paragraph) are redundant. That is, a implies b, and b implies a. This redundancy follows from the necessity that the proportion of motivators plus the proportion of hygienes mentioned in either type of critical incident must equal one.

Let M_g denote the proportion of factors mentioned in good critical incidents which are motivators, and let H_g be the proportion which are hygienes. Similarly, define M_b and H_b, where the subscript b denotes bad critical incidents. In this notation, a states that $M_g > M_b$, and b states that $H_b > H_g$.

$$\text{Since } M_g + H_g = 1, \text{ and } M_b + H_b = 1,$$
$$M_g > M_b \rightarrow 1 - H_g > 1 - H_b \rightarrow H_b > H_g.$$

That is, a implies b. The proof that b implies a is analogous.

Theory I appears to be the version of the two-factor theory adopted by Whitsett and Winslow (1967) in their review of a study by Dunnette, Campbell, and Hakel (1967). In the Dunnette et al. study, subjects used a Q-sort technique in order to assign to each of 12 job factors, a score which represented the extent

Table 3   Mean Scores of Motivators and Hygienes in Good and Bad Critical Incidents (Dunnette et al., 1967)

Occupational group	Motivators		Hygienes	
	Good	Bad	Good	Bad
Store managers	4.59	4.22	3.43	3.84
Sales clerks	4.37	4.17	3.63	3.68
Secretaries	4.61	4.23	3.45	3.75
Engineers & scientists	4.71	4.22	3.34	3.74
Machine equipment				
salesmen	4.76	4.17	3.16	3.79
Army reservists & students	4.54	4.20	3.51	3.77

to which the factor determined a good and bad critical incident. The mean scores of the motivator and hygiene factors in the good and bad critical incidents of workers in six different occupational groups are given in Table 3. As indicated in this table, the mean motivator score was greater in good than in bad critical incidents in all six occupational groups. Also, in each occupational group, the mean hygiene score was greater in bad than in good incidents. Although this critical incident data is not of the same type as that illustrated in Table 1, the results clearly support Theory I. In their review of the Dunnette et al. (1967) experiment, Whitsett and Winslow concluded:

> We feel that the direct data of this study are supportive of the M-H theory and what the author feels in nonsupportive is a misinterpretation of the underlying structure of the M-H theory [p. 404]

The M-H theory to which Whitsett and Winslow here referred appears to be Theory I, whereas Dunnette et al. must have been considering a "stronger" version of the two-factor theory.

Theory II

Theory II states that all motivators combined contribute more to job satisfaction than do all hygienes combined, and conversely, that the hygienes contribute more to job dissatisfaction than do the motivators. Critical incident data support Theory II if (a) all motivators combined are mentioned in good critical incidents more frequently than are all hygienes combined, and (b) all hygienes combined appear more frequently in bad incidents than do all motivators combined. The data of Table 1 exemplify these conditions; in good critical incidents, motivators were mentioned more frequently than hygienes (78% vs. 22%), whereas in bad incidents, hygienes appeared more frequently (64% vs. 36%).

Unlike the critical incident data used to support Theory I, conditions a and b are here not redundant. For example, it is possible for all motivators combined to be mentioned more frequently than all hygienes combined in both good and bad incidents.

Herzberg (1966) implied, in a review of a replication of the original study, that the "basic" two-factor theory is Theory II. In commenting on two arrows in a chart, which illustrated the relative frequencies of motivators and hygienes in the reports of good and bad critical incidents and which indicated that the data supported Theory II, Herzberg stated:

> Once again, the two arrows shown at the bottom of the chart, indicating the divergent trends for motivators and hygiene factors, serve to verify the basic theory as these factors are involved in positive and negative job-attitude sequences [p. 101].

Apparently the "basic theory" is here Theory II; however, it is puzzling to this writer why Herzberg (1966), in a review of nine replications of the original study, failed to mention the fact that Theory II was supported in every one of the 15 different occupational groups studied.

In terms of critical incident data, Theory II is a stronger theory than Theory I. That is, if specific critical incident data meet the requirements of Theory II, then the data also support Theory I; however, critical incident data which support Theory I do not necessarily meet the conditions of Theory II. The proof of the first statement follows from the necessity that the proportion of motivators plus the proportion of hygienes mentioned in either type of critical incident must equal one.

Using the notation of the proof given in the section on Theory I, the requirements of Theory II are denoted as $M_g > H_g$ and $H_b > M_b$, and Theory I is supported if $M_g > M_b$ and $H_b > H_g$.

Since $M_g + H_g = 1$, and $M_b + H_b = 1$,

$M_g > H_g$ and $H_b > M_b \rightarrow M_g > .5, H_g < .5, H_b > .5$, and $M_b < .5 \rightarrow M_g > M_b$ and $H_b > H_g$.

The proof of the second statement is accomplished by producing a counterexample of its negation:

Let $M_g = .8, H_g = .2, M_b = .6$, and $H_b = .4$.

This example is admissible, for the conditions $M_g + H_g = 1$ and $M_b + H_b = 1$ are satisfied. Clearly Theory I is supported, as $M_g > M_b$ and $H_b > H_g$; however, Theory II is not supported because $M_b > H_b$.

Theory III

Theory II is essentially a strong version of Theory I. Instead of requiring that all motivators *combined* contribute more to job satisfaction than to job dissatisfaction, Theory III states that *each* motivator contributes more to satisfaction than to dissatisfaction (and conversely, that each hygiene contributes more to dissatisfaction than to satisfaction).

In the case of Theories I and II, where only one or two conditions are specified, it seems reasonable to conclude that a single critical incident study either supports or contradicts the particular theory depending upon whether or not the data meet the specifications indicated in Table 2. However, in the case of Theory III, where many more conditions are specified, sampling errors must be given more serious consideration. That is, one would not claim that a single critical incident study contradicted Theory III if it did not quite meet all the conditions specified in Table 2. For example, one would not claim that the data of Table 1 exemplify a contradiction of Theory III merely because the most infrequently mentioned motivator (possibility of growth) appeared in 8% of the bad incidents and in only 6% of the good incidents. It may thus be necessary to restrict a statement of the confirmation of Theory III to collections of similar studies rather than to individual studies. It should be noted, however, that a single study might be said to contradict Theory III if, for example, a frequently mentioned motivator appeared significantly more often in bad than in good critical incidents.

On at least one occasion Herzberg implied that the basic two-factor theory is Theory II; however, in summarizing the results of nine replications of the original study, Herzberg (1966) suggested that *the* theory is Theory III:

> The chart shows that of the 51 significant differences reported for the six motivator factors, *every one* was in the predicted direction. For the 57 significant hygiene factors, 54 were in the predicted direction. In sum, then, the predictions from the theory were wrong in less than 3 percent of the cases [p. 125].

Evidently "the theory" is a theory which predicts that each motivator will appear proportionately more often in good than in bad critical incidents and that each hygiene will appear proportionately more often in bad than in good incidents— namely, Theory III.

Table 4   Number of Individuals Mentioning Each of Ten Job Factors in the Bad Critical Incidents of Six Studies Reported by Herzberg (1966) (House & Wigdor, 1967)

Factor	Frequency
Company policy & administration (H)	337
Supervision (H)	182
Achievement (M)	122
Recognition (M)	110
Working conditions (H)	108
Work itself (M)	75
Relations with superior (H)	59
Relations with peers (H)	57
Advancement (M)	48
Responsibility (M)	35

Note. — Abbreviations are: M = motivator; H = hygiene

Theory IV

Critical incident data support Theory IV if, in addition to supporting Theory III, each principal motivator is mentioned in good critical incidents more frequently than is any hygiene, and each principal hygiene is mentioned in bad critical incidents more frequently than is any motivator. The data illustrated in Table 1, for example, do not meet these conditions; recognition was mentioned in considerably more bad incidents than were working conditions and interpersonal relations with peers.

House and Wigdor (1967) apparently acknowledged that replications of the original experiment supported Theory III; however, in a secondary analysis of this data they criticized the two-factor theory for failing to meet the requirements of Theory IV. These investigators ranked 10 job factors according to the total number of individuals mentioning the factor in the bad critical incidents of six studies reported by Herzberg (1966). As indicated in Table 4, achievement and recognition were mentioned by more individuals than were three hygienes. House and Wigdor concluded:

> Our secondary analysis of the data presented by Herzberg (1966) in his most recent book yields conclusions contradictory to the proposition of the Two-Factor theory that satisfiers [factors appearing in good incidents] and dissatisfiers [factors appearing in bad incidents] are unidimensional and independent. Although many of the intrinsic aspects of jobs are shown to be more frequently identified by respondents as satisfiers, achievement and recognition are also shown to be very frequently identified as dissatisfiers. In fact, achievement and recognition are more frequently identified as dissatisfiers than working conditions and relations with the superior [p. 385].

Apparently "the Two-Factor theory" is here a theory which requires that each principal hygiene contributes more to job dissatisfaction than does any motivator, and conversely, that each principal motivator contributes more job satisfaction than does any hygiene—namely, Theory IV.

Theory V

According to Theory V, only motivators determine job satisfaction, and only hygienes determine job dissatisfaction.

Herzberg (1964) suggested Theory V in a discussion of the events leading up to the original investigation:

> From a review and an analysis of previous publications in the general area of job attitudes, a two-factor hypothesis was formulated to guide the original investigation. This hypothesis suggested that the factors involved in producing job satisfaction were separate and distinct from the factors that let to job dissatisfaction [p. 3].

This "two-factor hypothesis," which states that the factors involved in producing job satisfaction are *separate* and *distinct* from the factors leading to job dissatisfaction, clearly appears to be Theory V.

However, it is questionable whether Herzberg intended to suggest Theory V; for in referring to the results of the original experiment, Herzberg (1964) stated, "The proposed hypothesis appears verified [p. 4]." Certainly these results (see Table 1) do not serve as verification of Theory V. The results of the original study might possibly be interpreted as supporting Theory V if evidence indicated that the measurement errors were considerably biased in opposition to Theory V; however, evidence presented in the evaluation section indicates that the Herzberg-type experiments were biased in *favor* of Theory V.

Regardless of Herzberg's intensions, other investigators have evidently interpreted the "two-factor hypothesis" as Theory V. For example, Lindsay, Marks, and Gorlow (1967) quoted Herzberg's statement of the hypothesis and then restated it in the following manner:

> Satisfaction(s) is a function or motivators (M) and other potential factors and/or error of measurement . . .; dissatisfaction (DS) is a function of hygienes (H) plus other potential factors and/or error of measurement [p. 331].

EVALUATION

Irrelevant Empirical Studies

Many of the empirical studies which have been considered relevant to the two-factor theory are not directly relevant to the validity of the theories of Table 2.

Extensions beyond the Domain of Job Satisfaction   The two-factor theories have been extended beyond the domain of job satisfaction. For example, Hamlin and Nemo (1962) attempted to explain differences between improved and unimproved schizophrenics in terms of a two-factor theory. Such an extension is beyond the scope of this paper.

Studies by Hinton (1968) and Levine and Weitz (1968) are ostensibly within the domain of job satisfaction. However, the job investigated in these studies was the "job" of student, which appears to this writer to be sufficiently unlike other jobs as to warrant exclusion from consideration in this paper.

Predictions on a Job Satisfaction-Dissatisfaction Continuum   Several investigators (Ewen, Smith, Hulin, & Locke, 1966; Graen, 1968; Hinrichs & Mischkind, 1967) adopted a version of the two-factor theory which makes statements about an overall job satisfaction-dissatisfaction (S-D) continuum. More specifically, these investigators adopted a two-factor theory which states that motivations account primarily for variance on the satisfaction portion of the S-D continuum and that hygienes account primarily for variance on the dissatisfaction end of the continuum. For example, Ewen et al. (1966) grouped subjects according to their degree of satisfaction with three job factors, and then assumed that the two-factor theory predicts differences between certain groups in terms of scores on an

S-D continuum. This particular version of the two-factor theory, although possibly worthy of consideration in its own right, is considerably unlike the theories of Table 2; the theories of Table 2 make statements about a job satisfaction continuum and a job dissatisfaction continuum—*not* about an S-D continuum. These studies might be relevant to some of the theories of Table 2 if additional assumptions concerning the relationships among satisfaction, dissatisfaction, and S-D were made. However, the evaluation of such assumptions is beyond the scope of this paper.

Likewise, an experiment by Lindsay et al. (1967) is here irrelevant. Lindsay et al. created descriptions of hypothetical job situations and had subjects indicate the degree of S-D inherent in each situation, thus attempting to discover how motivators and hygienes interact in determining S-D.

Studies concerning Aspects of the Job other than Satisfaction or Dissatisfaction   Several empirical studies investigated the extent to which individual job factors contributed to aspects of the job other than satisfaction or dissatisfaction. Friedlander and Walton (1964) had respondents indicate which factors operated to *keep* them with their present employer and which factors might cause them to *leave*. Similarly, Centers and Bugental (1966) had respondents indicate which three of six job factors were most important in *keeping* them on their present job. Friedlander (1966) measured the perceived importance of job factors to feelings of satisfaction *or* dissatisfaction—that is, contributions to job satisfaction and to job dissatisfaction were not measured separately; and similarly, Singh and Baumgartel (1966) had subjects rate job factors on a scale of importance *in general*—importance for job satisfaction and for job dissatisfaction were not measured separately. Although these four studies may be relevant to particular extensions of the two-factor theory, they are not directly relevant to the theories of Table 2.

Studies in Which Only Satisfaction with Individual Job Factors Were Measured   The theories of Table 2 are concerned with the relative contributions of individual contributions of individual job factors to overall job dissatisfaction. Any study which measures only satisfaction with individual job factors is not relevant, for without measures of overall job satisfaction and dissatisfaction, the relative contributions of individual factors to the overall measures cannot be determined. Such studies simply indicate what the most-liked characteristics of a specific job happen to be. Thus, studies by Friedlander (1965) and Wolf (1967) are irrelevant. Friedlander measured only the degree of satisfaction with individual job factors, and Wolf simply had respondents indicate which aspects of a job were the most liked and which were the least liked.

Factor Analytic and Scaling Studies   Although it may be desirable for the job factors to be factors in some factor analytic sense, the theories of Table 2 place no such restrictions on the motivators and hygienes. Thus, studies which merely consist of a factor analysis of characteristics of a job or of a job situation (Graen, 1966; Lodahl, 1964) are here considered irrelevant.

Likewise, a study by Burke (1966) is irrelevant. Burke used the unfolding technique in one dimension (Coombs, 1964) in order to determine whether or not subjects, along with Herzberg's principal job factors, could be placed on a latent unidimensional continuum so as to account for individual differences in relative preferences for job factors.

Studies lacking Adequate Descriptions of Measures Used Four studies (Friedlander, 1963; Halpern, 1966; Malinovsky & Barry, 1965; Weissenberg & Gruenfeld, 1968) in which overall job satisfaction was purportedly measured did not clarify whether the measure used was a measure of job satisfaction or overall satisfaction-dissatisfaction (S-D). In either case, however, little information is lost by the omission of these studies. If it was S-D that was measured, the study is not directly relevant to the theories of Table 2; and if it was job satisfaction that was measured, the study is irrelevant to Theories I and III and, at most, relevant to only parts of Theories II, IV, and V, as overall job dissatisfaction was measured in none of the four studies.

Relevant Empirical Studies

As there appear to be no relevant empirical studies which support either Theory IV or Theory V, this evaluation is restricted to Theories I, II, and III.

Table 5 indicates whether or not each relevant empirical study supports Theories I, II, and III.

Table 5   Empirical Studies Relevant to the Validity of Theories I, II, or III

Study	Theoretical support		
	Theory I	Theory II	Theory III
Replications of the original study			
Saleh (1964)	yes	yes	
Myers (1964); 5 different occupational groups (Gps)	yes in all 5	yes in all 5	
Herzberg's (1966) review of 5 other studies; 7 Gps	yes in all 7	yes in all 7	yes[a]
Replications using a questionnaire			
Schwartz et al. (1963)	yes	yes	
Herzberg (1965)	yes	yes	
Subjects coded the perceived determinants of their critical incidents			
Friedlander (1964)	no	irrelevant	
Lahiri and Srivastva (1967)			
Present job	yes	irrelevant	
Imaginary job	yes	irrelevant	no[a]
Dunnette el al. (1967); 6 Gps	yes in all 6	irrelevant	
Wernimont (1966); 2 Gps			
Forced choice	yes in both	irrelevant	
Free choice	yes in both	irrelevant	no data[b]
Correlational studies			
Hulin and Smith (1967); 2 Gps	irrelevant	irrelevant	no

[a]Considered collectively.
[b]Relevant data were evidently collected but not published.

Replications of the Original Study   Herzberg (1966) reviewed nine studies (e. g., Herzberg, 1965; Myers, 1964; Saleh, 1964; Schwartz, Jenusaitis, & Stark, 1963) which, in toto, consist of replications of the original study in 15 different occupational groups. In two of the studies (Herzberg, 1965; Schwartz et al., 1963) an open-ended questionnaire patterened after the original interview, rather than an interview, was used. Theories I and II were supported in every one of the 15 occupational groups studied. That is (using the notation of the proof given in the section on Theory I), in each group studied, $M_g > M_b$, $H_b > H_g$, $M_g > H_g$, and $H_b > M_b$. These data, considered in toto, also support Theory III; in all replications combined, 42 hygienes and 36 motivators appeared significantly more ($p < .01$, according to Herzberg, 1966) in one type of critical incident than in the other, and of these, all the motivators and all but 3 hygienes were significant in the predicted direction.

Studies in Which Subjects Coded the Perceived Determinants of Their Critical Incidents   In the original study and in its replications, the experimenters coded the indormation given in the reports of critical incidents. Several critics (Ewen, 1964; Graen, 1966; House & Wigdor, 1967) pointed out that the coding system is not completely determined by the data and a preestablished rating system, but requires additional interpretation by the experimenter. Before one can rule out the possibility of experimenter coding biases, it is necessary to consider studies in which the subjects themselves coded the perceived determinants of their reported critical incidents (subject-coded studies). Four relevant studies (Dunnette et al., 1967; Friedlander, 1964; Lahiri & Srivastva, 1967; Wernimont, 1966) fall into this category.

Friedlander (1964) had respondents indicate, on a 4-point scale, the degree to which each of 18 job factors contributed toward producing the feeling of satisfaction inherent in a good critical incident and the feeling of dissatisfaction inherent in a bad critical incident. The mean scores of each job factor in good and bad incidents are given in the first two columns of Table 6. In analyzing the data Friedlander used these mean scores; however, an alternative analysis seems more appropriate. Since the satisfaction scores were scaled independently of the dissatisfaction scores (i. e., the satisfaction scores were first determined in response to a good critical incident, and then the dissatisfaction scores were determined in response to a bad incident), the two scales are not necessarily comparable. Assuming that the mean dissatisfaction scores represent scale values on a scale which is no stronger than an interval scale, it is admissible to transform these scores by any linear transformation. For purposes of comparison with the satisfaction scores, it thus seems most appropriate to transform the dissatisfaction scores by the unique linear transformation which yields mean scores having the same mean and variance as the satisfaction mean scores. The last column of Table 6 contains the mean dissatisfaction scores, and the data are here analyzed by comparing the original satisfaction scores to the *rescaled* dissatisfaction scores.

Table 6   A Reanalysis of Friedlander's (1964) Data

	Mean scores		
Job factor	Satis- faction	Dissatis- faction	Rescaled dissatis- faction
Motivators			
Promotion	2.10	1.99	2.54
Challenging assignments	3.10	2.67	3.42
Recognition	3.23	2.61	3.35
Merit increases	1.80	1.60	2.03
Achievement	3.38	2.80	3.59
Responsibility	2.84	2.01	2.57
Growth	3.38	2.19	2.80
Work itself	3.46	2.39	3.06
Use of best abilities	2.99	2.89	3.71
Hygienes			
Relations with supervisor	3.06	2.09	2.67
Relations with co-workers	2.73	1.46	1.85
Technical supervision	2.56	1.75	2.23
Working conditions	2.31	1.60	2.03
Security	2.56	1.64	2.08
Employee benefits	1.46	1.30	1.64
Home life	1.63	1.16	2.04
Work group	2.19	1.77	2.25
Management policies	2.01	2.28	2.92
Mean score of motivators	2.92	2.35	3.01
Mean score of hygienes	2.28	1.72	2.19

As indicated in Table 6, the data do not support Theory I; the mean motivator score was greater in bad than in good incidents (3.01 vs. 2.92), and the mean hygiene score was greater in good than in bad incidents (2.28 vs. 2.19).

The data of Table 6 are irrelevant to Theory II. That is, it is inappropriate, for example, to claim that all motivators combined contributed more to good incidents than did all hygienes combined on the basis that the mean motivator score was greater than the mean hygiene score in good critical incidents (2.92 vs. 2.28), for the amount of overlap among the job factors was not taken into consideration. If the set of motivators represented broad overlapping categories relative to the set of hygienes, the contribution of all motivators combined would be over-represented by the mean motivator score. Comparing the mean motivator score to the mean hygiene score in either type of critical incident is, in terms of correlational data, analogous to comparing the means of sets of correlation coefficients rather than multiple correlation coefficients. Correlational data (third column of Table 2), however, *are* relevant to Theory II, because the multiple correlation coefficient takes into consideration the intercorrelations (or overlap) among the factors. And the Herzberg-type critical incident studies are also relevant to Theory II, for in these studies there is no overlap among the job factors (i. e., the factors represent mutually exclusive categories).

Table 7 A Reanalysis of Lahiri and Srivastva's (1967) Data

	Mean scores			
	Present job		Imaginary job	
Job factor	Satis- faction	Rescaled dissatis- faction	Satis- faction	Rescaled dissatis- faction
Motivators				
Recognition	6.32	6.68	7.97	8.33
Challenging assignments	6.59	6.06	7.73	7.38
Growth	6.09	6.98	7.88	8.44
Achievement	7.03	6.47	8.68	7.74
Liking for the work	7.00	6.30	8.76	7.78
Accomplishment	7.65	6.02	8.21	7.96
Use of best abilities	7.18	5.96	8.53	8.11
Responsibility	8.00	5.79	8.68	7.45
Autonomy	6.35	6.10	7.29	8.68
Promotion	4.59	8.05	7.53	8.52
Prestige	6.91	6.82	8.18	8.64
Work itself	6.35	6.22	8.53	8.00
Status	6.73	6.88	8.26	8.15
Hygienes				
Relations with co-workers	6.82	5.30	8.09	7.20
Superior's help	6.12	7.36	7.41	7.96
Friendliness of superior	7.16	6.98	7.12	7.70
Technical competence of superior	5.44	6.82	7.47	7.65
Salary	4.94	7.91	7.38	8.56
Security	7.29	6.13	8.29	7.34
Working conditions	6.53	4.63	7.62	7.26
Benefits	6.47	5.69	7.53	7.57
Fairness of authority	6.12	6.33	7.91	8.58
Freedom of expression	5.79	6.47	7.78	8.42
Work group	6.12	5.90	7.00	7.90
Managerial policies	5.12	8.69	6.59	8.27
Home life	8.00	5.11	8.82	6.16
Mean score of motivators	6.68	6.40	8.17	8.09
Mean score of hygienes	6.22	6.41	7.62	7.70

Lahiri and Srivastva (1967) had respondents indicate, on a 10-point scale, the degree to which each of 26 job factors contributed toward satisfaction and dissatisfaction in both actual and imaginary good and actual and imaginary bad critical incidents. (in the imaginary critical incidents, subjects were asked to think of a "best" and a "worst" job they could imagine themselves doing.) The general methodology of this study was the same as that of Friedlander's (1964) study; and thus, Lahiri and Srivastva's data were reanalyzed in the same way as Friedlander's data. Table 7 contains the mean satisfaction and rescaled dissatisfaction scores of each job factor in the two different situations.

As indicated in Table 7, the data supported Theory I in both the present and imaginary job situations. That is, for both situations, the mean motivator score was greater in good than in bad incidents, and the mean hygiene score was greater in bad than in good incidents.

The data of Lahiri and Srivastva (and also Dunnette et al., 1967; Wernimont, 1966) are irrelevant to Theory II on the same grounds that Friedlander's (1964) data are irrelevant to Theory II.

The experiment by Dunnette et al., (1967), which is discussed in the section on Theory I, is also a subject-coded study. In describing both a good and a bad critical incident, the Q-sort items representing job factors were sorted into a 7-point quasi-normal distribution. Thus, the scores representing contributions of job factors to good incidents are comparable to the scores derived from the reports of bad incidents, and unlike the studies of Friedlander (1964) and Lahiri and Srivastva (1967), it is unnecessary to rescale the mean scores. As indicated in Table 3, Theory I was supported in all six occupational groups studied.

Wernimont (1966) constructed 50 pairs of positive items describing good critical incidents and 50 pairs of negative items describing bad incidents. One member of each pair represented a motivator, the other represented a hygiene, and the members of each pair were equated in terms of social desirability. The respondents were first required to indicate which member of each pair most closely described a good or a bad critical incident (forced choice situation), and they were then asked to go back over the items and indicate the 10 items which were the most descriptive of each type of critical incident (free choice situation).

Table 8   **Success of Predictions Based on Theory III in Studies Where Subjects Coded the Perceived Determinants of Their Critical Incidents**

Job factor	Friedlander (1964)	Lahiri and Srivastva (1967) Present	Lahiri and Srivastva (1967) Imaginary	Dunnette et al. (1967) (6 groups)	Wernimont (1966), forced choice (2 groups)	Total
Motivators						
Achievement	−	+	+	6+	2+	10+, 1−
Recognition	−	−	−	5−, 1+	2−	10−, 1+
Work itself	+	+	+	6+	2+	11+
Responsibility	+	+	+	6+	2+	11+
Advancement	−	−	−	6−	2−	11−
Hygienes						
Company policy & administration	+	+	+	5+, 1−	2+	10+, 1−
Supervision	−	+	+	5+, 1−	2+	9+, 2−
Working conditions	−	−	−	6+	2−	6+, 5−
Relations with superior	−	−	+	5+, 1−	no data[a]	6+, 3−
Relations with peers	−	−	−	6−	no data[a]	9−

Note. — A plus sign signifies a correct prediction, and a minus sign an incorrect prediction.
   [a]Relations with superior and relations with peers were grouped into a single category — interpersonal relations.

The data were analyzed separately for two different occupational groups—engineers and accountants. Theory I was supported in both occupational groups in both the forced choice and free choice situation. That is, in all four situations, motivator items were selected more often in good than in bad incidents, and hygiene items were selected more often in bad than in good incidents.

If Theory III is valid, one would not expect to find incorrect predictions made for the *same* job factors in all occupational groups. (Definition of an incorrect prediction for a job factor: if a motivator, the mean score in bad incidents is greater than the mean score in good incidents; and if a hygiene, the mean score in good incidents is greater than the mean score in bad incidents.) That is, if incorrect predictions are due entirely to sampling errors, one would expect the errors to be randomly distributed among the different job factors. However, as indicated in Table 8, recognition, advancement, and relations with peers were *consistently* linked to incorrect predictions. Thus, the results of the subject-coded studies contradict Theory III, indicating that the support given Theory III by the Herzberg-type studies merely reflects experimenter coding biases.

Correlational Studies   In both the Herzberg-type studies and the subject-coded studies, the determinants of satisfaction and dissatisfaction were measured by direct self-report. While the very nature of satisfaction and dissatisfaction may require that these constructs be measured by a self-report technique, it is neither necessary nor desirable that the *determinants* of satisfaction and dissatisfaction be measured by direct self-report. As emphasized by several critics (Dunnette et al., 1967; House & Wigdor, 1967; Vroom, 1964), the use of these self-report measures permits an explanation of the results solely in terms of defensive biases inherent in such measures. For example, even though the subjects accurately report the determinants of critical incidents, the recall of the incidents may be selective so that those good incidents which happen to be recalled tend to be biased toward those incidents which were due to one's own efforts (motivators) as opposed to those incidents which were due to the efforts of others (hygienes).

In correlational studies, the extent to which job factors contribute toward satisfaction and dissatisfaction is not determined by self-report but is inferred from the correlations between measures of satisfaction with individual job factors and measures of overall satisfaction and dissatisfaction. Thus, in order to eliminate the possible defensive biases of the measures used in critical incident studies, the correlational studies should be considered.[2] Although correlational data may not be sufficient to permit a determination of the causal relationships stated in the theories of Table 2, certainly correlational support is a necessary requirement.

[2]It should be noted that in correlational studies, not only are defensive biases eliminated, but also, the assumption (implicit in the critical incident studies) that the determinants of critical incidents are identical to the determinants of less-than-critical incidents is not made. However, it is the opinion of the writer that this second distinction between correlational and critical incident studies is much less crucial than the defensive bias distinction.

Table 9 Correlations between Satisfaction with Each of Five Job Factors and Measures of Overall Job Satisfaction and Overall Job Dissatisfaction (Hulin & Smith, 1967)

Job factor	Males		Females	
	Satisfaction	Dissatisfaction	Satisfaction	Dissatisfaction
Motivators				
Work itself	.68*	.44	.45	.43
Promotion	.40	.38	.46	.14
Hygienes				
Pay	.39	.24	.12	.18
Supervision	.53*	.25	.31	−.03
Co-workers	.48*	.13	.20	−.08

*The difference between the correlation with satisfaction and with dissatisfaction is significant at the .05 level.

One correlational study (Hulin & Smith, 1967) is relevant. Hulin and Smith measured satisfaction with each of the five job factors of the Job Description Index (JDI); (Smith, 1967). In addition, overall job satisfaction was measured on one-fourth of the subjects, overall job dissatisfaction was measured on another one-fourth of the subjects, and a measure of overall satisfaction-dissatisfaction (S-D) was obtained on the remaining half of the subjects, where the overall measures consisted of variations of the General Motors Faces Scale (Kunin, 1955).[3] Since the theories of Table 2 do not make statements about an S-D continuum, data from only half the respondents are directly relevant.

The correlations between satisfaction with each of the five job factors and the two relevant overall measures are given in Table 9. In the male group, the two hygienes, supervision and co-workers, correlated significantly more with overall satisfaction than with overall dissatisfaction. However, these differences may be partially explained by possible differences in the reliabilities of the satisfaction and dissatisfaction measures. That is, if the dissatisfaction measure is much less reliable than the satisfaction measure, the hygienes might be expected to correlate more with satisfaction than with dissatisfaction, even though Theory III is valid. Certainly this possibility should be considered, especially since Hulin and Smith mentioned that the variability of scores on the dissatisfaction measure was considerably less than the variability on the satisfaction measure. As the reliabilities of the overall satisfaction and dissatisfaction measures are not known, it is not possible to obtain a reasonable estimate of the "true" correlations. However, as shown in Table 10, if the largest conceivable discrepancy between the reliabilities of the overall measures was assumed, the two hygienes, supervision and co-workers, would still correlate considerably higher with satisfaction than with dissatisfaction. It is thus concluded that the results of this study contradict Theory III.

[3]This description of the Hulin and Smith study is actually incomplete. However, the omitted portion of the study is not directly relevant, for it is essentially concerned with predictions on an S-D continuum.

Table 10 Correlations of Table 9 "Corrected" for Attenuation so as to Support Theory III as Much as Possible

	Males	
Job factor	Satisfaction	Dissatisfaction
Motivators		
Work itself	.68	.66
Promotion	.40	.57
Hygienes		
Pay	.39	.36
Supervision	.53	.38
Co-workers	.48	.20

Note.—The correlations are "corrected" for the attenuation of one variable under the assumption that the reliability of the overall satisfaction measure was 1 and that the reliability of the overall dissatisfaction measure was .44—the highest observed correlation between overall dissatisfaction and any other variable (work itself).

Since Hulin and Smith considered only five of Herzberg's principal job factors, this study is irrelevant to Theories I and II; Theories I and II contain statements about the effects of all motivators combined and all hygienes combined.

CONCLUSION

In considering all relevant empirical studies, the following conclusions seem justified:

1. Theory III, being supported by the Herzberg-type studies but not by the subject-coded studies, merely reflects experimenter coding biases.

2. Theory I, although being supported by both the Herzberg-type studies and the subject-coded studies, has not been adequately tested in studies where the determinants of satisfaction and dissatisfaction were measured by techniques other than direct self-report. It is thus possible that Theory I merely reflects defensive biases inherent in such self-report measures.

3. Theory II has not been adequately tested in studies other than the Herzberg-type critical incident studies. It is thus possible that Theory II merely reflects experimenter coding biases or defensive biases inherent in self-report measures.

The relationship between these conclusions and the principle of multiple operationalism (Garner, Hake, & Eriksen, 1956; Webb, Campbell, Schwartz, & Sechrest, 1966) should be noted. According to the principle of multiple operationalism, a hypothesis is validated only if it is supported by two or more different methods of testing, where each method contains specific idiosyncratic weaknesses, but where the entire collection of methods permits the elimination of all alternative hypotheses. The application of this principle to Theories I, II, and III indicates that none of these theories have been validated. In the case of Theory III, three distinct methods, each containing different weaknesses, were used: Herzberg-type studies, subject-coded studies, and a correlational study. And two alternative hypotheses were considered: (a) the support given Theory III by the Herzberg-type studies is due not to the validity of Theory III but to experimenter coding biases; and *(b)* this support is due to defensive biases inherent in the self-report measures used. Neither did all three types of studies support Theory III nor were the two alternative hypotheses eliminated. In the case of Theory I, only the Herzberg-type studies and the subject-coded studies were used. Although both types of studies supported Theory I and although the alternative hypothesis analogous to hypothesis *a* was eliminated, these studies did not eliminate the alternative hypotheses analogous to hypothesis *b*. Likewise, Theory II was not validated, for neither of the two alternative hypotheses were eliminated.

SUGGESTIONS FOR FUTURE RESEARCH

The preceding section indicates a major gap in the relevant empirical studies—namely, studies which are relevant to Theories I and II and in which the determinants of satisfaction and dissatisfaction are measured by techniques other than direct self-report. It is thus suggested that correlational studies patterned after the study by Hulin and Smith (1967) be performed. However, three exceptions to the Hulin and Smith design should be made: *(a)* Satisfaction with each of Herzberg's principal motivators and hygienes, rather than with only the five JDI factors, are measured, *(b)* the use of a measure of overall dissatisfaction which is possibly more reliable than the measure used by Hulin and Smith, and *(c)* the calculation of the multiple correlation coefficients indicated in Table 2.

In both types of critical incident studies (Herzberg-type studies and subject-coded studies) there appeared to be no differences among different occupational groups in terms of the support given Theories I, II, and III; however, this similarity may merely reflect a similarity of defense mechanisms rather than a similarity of determinants of job satisfaction. It is thus desirable that subsequent correlational studies consider relatively homogeneous occupational groups separately, for it may be found that Theory I or II is valid for specific occupational groups.

REFERENCES

Burke, R. J. Are Herzberg's motivators and hygienes unidimensional? *Journal of Applied Psychology,* 1966, **50,** 317–321.

Centers, R., and Bugental, D. E. Intrinsic and extrinsic job motivations among different segments of the working population. *Journal of Applied Psychology,* 1966, **50,** 193–197.

Coombs, C. H. *A theory of data.* New York: Wiley, 1964.

Dunnette, M. D., Campbell, J. P., & Hakel, M. D. Dissatisfaction in six occupational groups. *Organizational Behavior and Human Performance,* 1967, **2,** 143–174.

Ewen, R. B. Some determinants of job satisfaction: A study of the generability of Herzberg's theory. *Journal of Applied Psychology,* 1964, **48,** 161–163.

Ewen, R. B., Smith, P. C., Hulin, C. L., & Locke, E. A. An empirical test of the Herzberg two-factor theory. *Journal of Applied Psychology,* 1966, **50,** 544–550.

Friedlander, F. Underlying sources of job satisfaction. *Journal of Applied Psychology,* 1963, **47,** 246–250.

Friedlander, F. Job characteristics as satisfiers and dissatisfiers. *Journal of Applied Psychology,* 1964, **48,** 388–392.

Friedlander, F. Relationships between the importance and the satisfaction of various environmental factors. *Journal of Applied Psychology,* 1965, **49,** 160–164.

Friedlander, F. Importance of work versus nonwork among socially and occupationally stratified groups. *Journal of Applied Psychology,* 1966, **50,** 437–441.

Friedlander, F., & Walton, E. Positive and negative motivations toward work. *Administrative Science Quarterly,* 1964, **9,** 194–207.

Garner, W. R., Hake, H. W., & Eriksen, C. W. Operationism and the concept of perception. *Psychological Review,* 1956, **63,** 149–159.

Graen, G. B. Motivator and hygiene dimensions for research and development engineers. *Journal of Applied Psychology,* 1966, **50,** 563–566.

Graen, G. B. Testing traditional and two-factor hypotheses concerning job satisfaction. *Journal of Applied Psychology,* 1968, **52,** 366–371.

Halpern, G. Relative contributions of motivator and hygiene factors to overall job satisfaction. *Journal of Applied Psychology,* 1966, **50,** 198–200.

Hamlin, R. M., & Nemo, R. S. Self-actualization in choice scores of improved schizophrenics. *Journal of Clinical Psychology,* 1962, **18,** 51–54.

Herzberg, F. The motivation-hygiene concept and problems of manpower. *Personnel Administration,* 1964, **27(1),** 3–7.

Herzberg, F. The motivation to work among Finnish supervisors. *Personnel Psychology,* 1965, **18,** 393–402.

Herzberg, F., Mausner, B., & Snyderman, B. *The motivation to work.* (2nd ed.) New York: Wiley, 1959.

Hinrichs, J. R., & Mischkind, L. A. Empirical and theoretical limitations of the two-factor hypothesis of job satisfaction. *Journal of Applied Psychology,* 1967, **51,** 191–200.

Hinton, B. L. An empirical investigation of the Herzberg methodology and two-factor theory. *Organizational Behavior and Human Performance,* 1968, **3,** 217–238.

House, R. J., & Wigdor, L. A. Herzberg's dual-factor theory of job satisfaction and motivation: A review of the evidence and a criticism. *Personnel Psychology,* 1967, **20,** 369–389.

Hulin, C. L., & Smith, P. A. An empirical investigation of two implications of the two-factor theory of job satisfaction. *Journal of Applied Psychology,* 1967, **51,** 396–402.

Kunin, T. The construction of a new type of attitude measure. *Personnel Psychology,* 1955, **8,** 65–77.

Lahiri, D. K., & Srivastva, S. Determinants of satisfaction in middle-management personnel. *Journal of Applied Psychology,* 1967, **51,** 254–265.

Levine, E. L., & Weitz, J. Job satisfaction among graduate students: Intrinsic versus extrinsic variables. *Journal of Applied Psychology,* 1968, **52,** 263–271.

Lindsay, C. A., Marks, E., & Gorlow, L. The Herzberg theory: A critique and reformulation. *Journal of Applied Psychology,* 1967, **51,** 330–339.

Lodahl, T. M. Patterns of job attitudes in two assembly technologies. *Administrative Science Quarterly,* 1964, **8,** 482–519.

Malinovsky, M. R., & Barry, J. R. Determinants of work attitudes. *Journal of Applied Psychology,* 1965, **49,** 446–451.

Myers, M. S. Who are your motivated workers? *Harvard Business Review,* 1964, **42(1),** 73–88.

Saleh, S. D. A study of attitude change in the preretirement period. *Journal of Applied Psychology,* 1964, **48,** 310–312.

Schwartz, M. M., Jenusaitis, E., & Stark, H. Motivational factors among supervisors in the utility industry. *Personnel Psychology,* 1963, **16,** 45–53.

Singh, T. N., & Baumgartel, H. Background factors in ariline mechanics' work motivations: A research note. *Journal of Applied Psychology,* 1966, **50,** 337–359.

Smith, P. C. The development of a method of measuring job satisfaction: The Cornell studies. In E. A. Fleishman (Ed.), *Studies in personnel and industrial psychology.* Homewood, Illinois: Dorsey Press, 1967.

Vroom, V. H. *Work and motivation.* New York: Wiley, 1964.

Weissenberg, P., & Gruenfeld, L. W. Relationship between job satisfaction and job involvement. *Journal of Applied Psychology,* 1968, **52,** 469–473.

Wernimont, P. F. Intrinsic and extrinsic factors in job satisfaction. *Journal of Applied Psychology,* 1966, **50,** 41–50.

Whitsett, D. A., & Winslow, E. K. An analysis of studies critical of the motivator-hygiene theory. *Personnel Psychology,* 1967, **20,** 391–415.

Webb, E. J., Campbell, D. T., Schwartz, R. D., & Sechrest, L. *Unobtrusive measures: Nonreactive research in the social sciences.* Chicago: Rand McNally, 1966.

Wolf, M. G. The relationship of content and context factors to attitudes toward company and job. *Personnel Psychology,* 1967, **20,** 121–132.

QUESTIONS FOR DISCUSSION

1. Why do you feel Herzberg's theory has been so readily accepted by practicing managers?
2. Why have some organizational researchers taken issue with the basic formulations and the research evidence of Herzberg's theory?
3. How might you defend Herzberg's two-factor theory against its critics?
4. How would you compare and contrast Herzberg's theory of work motivation with the theories proposed by Maslow and Murray?
5. What role does money play in motivation under Herzberg's theory?
6. What is the basic difference between "motivators" and "hygiene" factors? Which are more important in work motivation? Why?
7. What could a manager learn from the two-factor theory that would be of use in motivating a poor performer?

Chapter 5

Equity Theory

OVERVIEW

We now come to the consideration of a relatively recent model of work motivation: equity theory. This theory represents a significant departure from the three previous models discussed. In fact, perhaps the best way to introduce equity theory is by way of contrast with these previous models of motivation.

To begin with, while each of the previous models represents a single line of theoretical development—indeed, is often associated with one individual—the development of equity theory can be traced to several prominent theorists working somewhat independently within the same general parameters. These variations on the theme are variously termed "cognitive dissonance" theory (Festinger, 1957; Heider, 1958), "distributive justice" or "exchange" theory (Homans, 1961; Jacques, 1961; Patchen, 1961), and "equity" or "inequity" theory (Adams, 1963, 1965; Weick, 1964). While each of these models differs in some respects from the others, the general thrust of all of them is toward one basic unit of analysis. Specifically, such theories argue that a major determinant of job performance and satisfaction is the degree of equity, or inequity, that an individual perceives in a work situation.The degree of equity is defined in terms of a ratio of an individual's inputs (such as effort) to outcomes (such as pay) *as compared to* a similar ratio for a relevant "other." Because of this comparative aspect, the theory has also been called "social comparison" theory. In our discussions below, we shall concentrate on Adams's formulation of equity theory as an example. This variation of the general model appears to be the most highly developed and heavily researched statement on the topic.

There is also a second important distinction between equity theory and the three earlier models. While the earlier theories focused on the identification of specific factors in the individual or his environment which determined behavior, equity theory (as well as expectancy/valence theory, to be discussed later) concentrates on an understanding of the *processes* by which behavior is energized and sustained. It is thus a more dynamic approach to the study of motivationally relevant variables in a work situation. Because of this, equity theory has been called a "process" theory by Campbell et al. (1970), while the theories of Maslow, Murray, and Herzberg have been termed "content" theories.

A third major distinction that differentiates equity theory from the models discussed earlier is that this theory posits that a major share of motivated behavior is based on the *perceived* situation and not necessarily on the actual set of circumstances. Where Maslow and Murray saw behavior largely as a result of personality-need variables, and where Herzberg saw behavior as the result of objective job content and job context factors, equity theory generally argues that is is the perceived equity of the situation that stimulates behavior and satisfaction. In other words, if an employee "thinks" he is being paid less than his coworkers for the same amount and quality of work, he would, according to this model, be dissatisfied and would move to reduce the inequity through various means. Such a hypothesis is particularly interesting in view of several findings which indicate that workers generally tend to overestimate the salaries of others (Lawler, 1971).

Two articles on equity theory are presented below. The first, by Adams, includes both a fairly well-developed statement of the theory and a discussion of how the theory works in a variety of situations. Adams also reviews several studies which either support or are consistent with the model as formulated. In a second and more recent article, Goodman and Friedman review the current research on the theory and discuss how these findings relate to the model. Methodological issues are also discussed. As will be noted in both articles, the vast majority of evidence supportive of equity theory is laboratory-based. (A notable exception to this trend is the recent field study by Telly, French, & Scott [1971].) The interested reader is specifically referred to Lawler (1968) and Pritchard (1969) for two additional excellent reviews of research and theoretical issues issues relating to this model.

REFERENCES AND SUGGESTED ADDITIONAL READINGS

Adams, J. S. Toward an understanding of inequity. *Journal of Abnormal and Social Psychology,* 1963, **67,** 422–436.

Adams, J. S. Injustice in social exchange. In L. Berkowitz (Ed.), *Advances in experimental social psychology.* Vol. 2. New York: Academic Press, 1965.

Campbell, J. P., Dunnette, M. D., Lawler, E. E., III, & Weick, K. E., Jr. *Managerial behavior, performance, and effectiveness.* New York: McGraw-Hill, 1970.

Festinger, L. *A theory of cognitive dissonance.* Evanston, Ill.: Row, Peterson, 1957.

Heider, F. *The psychology of interpersonal relations.* New York: Wiley, 1958.

Homans, G. *Social behavior.* New York: Harcourt, Brace & World, 1961.

Jacques, E. *Equitable payment.* New York: Wiley, 1961.

Lawler, E. E., III. *Pay and organizational effectiveness: A psychological view.* New York: McGraw-Hill, 1971.

Lawler, E. E., III, & O'Gara, P. W. Effects of inequity produced by underpayment on work output, work quality, and attitudes toward the work. *Journal of Applied Psychology,* 1967, **51**, 403–410.

Patchen, M. The choice of wage comparisons. Englewood Cliffs, N. J.: Prentice-Hall, 1961.

Pritchard, R. D. Equity theory: A review and critique. *Organizational Behavior and Human Performance,* 1969, **4**, 176–211.

Pritchard, R. D., Dunnette, M. D., & Jorgenson, D. O. Effects of perceptions of equity and inequity on worker performance and satisfaction. *Journal of Applied Psychology,* 1972, **56**, 75–94.

Telly, C. S., French, W. L., & Scott, W. G. The relationship of inequity to turnover among hourly workers. *Administrative Science Quarterly,* 1971, **16**, 164–172.

Tornow, W. W. The development and application of an input-outcome moderator test on the perception and reduction of inequity. *Organizational Behavior and Human Performance,* 1971, **6**, 614–638.

Weick, K. E., Jr. Reduction of cognitive dissonance through task enhancement and effort expenditure. *Journal of Abnormal and Social Psychology,* 1964, **68**, 533–539.

Weick, K. E., Jr. The concept of equity in the perception of pay. *Administrative Science Quarterly,* 1966, **11**, 414–439.

Wiener, Y. The effects of task and ego-oriented performance on two kinds of overcompensation inequity. *Organizational Behavior and Human Performance,* 1970, **5**, 191–208.

Inequity in Social Exchange
J. Stacy Adams

In what follows it is hoped that a fairly comprehensive theory of inequity will be elaborated. The term *inequity* is used instead of *injustice* first, because the author has used this term before (Adams and Rosenbaum, 1962; Adams, 1963a,b, 1965; Adams and Jacobsen, 1964), second, to avoid the confusion of the many connotative meanings associated with the term *justice,* and third, to emphasize that the primary concern is with the causes and consequences of the absence of equity in human exchange relationships. In developing the theory, major variables affecting perceptions of inequity in an exchange will be described. A formal definition of inequity will then be proposed. From this point the effects of inequity upon behavior and cognitive processes will be discussed and research giving evidence of the effects will be presented. For heuristic purposes employee-employer exchanges will be a focus because such relations are within the experience of almost everyone and constitute a significant aspect of human intercourse. Moreover, much empirical research relating to inequity has been undertaken in business and industrial spheres or in simulated employment situations. It should be evident, however, that the theoretical notions offered are quite as relevant to any social situation in which an exchange takes place, explicitly or implicitly, whether between teammates, teacher and student, lovers, child and parent, patient and therapist, or opponents or even enemies, for between all there are expectations of what is fair exchange.

A. ANTECEDENTS OF INEQUITY

Whenever two individuals exchange anything, there is the possibility that one or both of them will feel that the exchange was inequitable. Such is frequently the case when a man exchanges his services for pay. On the man's side of the exchange are his education, intelligence, experience, training, skill, seniority, age, sex, ethnic background, social status, and, of course, the effort he expends on the job. Under special circumstances other attributes will be relevant. These may be personal appearance or attractiveness, health, possession of certain tools, the characteristics of one's spouse, and so on. They are what a man perceives as his contributions to the exchange, for which he expects a just return. As noted earlier, these are the same as Homans' (1961) investments. A man brings them into an exchange, and henceforth they will be referred to as his *inputs.* These inputs, let us emphasize, are *as perceived by their contributor* and are not necessarily isomorphic with those perceived by the other party to the exchange. This suggests two conceptually distinct characteristics of inputs, *recognition* and *relevance.*

The possessor of an attribute, or the other party to the exchange, or both, may recognize the existence of the attribute in the possessor. If either the possessor or both members of the exchange recognizes its existence, the attribute has the potentiality of being an input. If only the nonpossessor recognizes its existence, it cannot be considered psychologically an input so far as the possessor is concerned. Whether or not an attribute having the potential of being an input is in fact an input is contingent upon the possessor's perception of its relevance to the exchange. If he perceives it to be relevant, if he expects a just return for it, it is an input. Problems of inequity arise if only the possessor of the attribute considers it relevant to the exchange, or if the other party to the exchange considers it irrelevant and acts accordingly. Thus, unless prohibited from doing so by contract terms, an employer may consider seniority irrelevant in granting promotions, thinking it wiser to consider merit alone, whereas the employee may believe that seniority is highly relevant. In consequence, the employee may feel that injustice has been done. Conversely, the employer who is compelled to use seniority rather than merit as a promotion criterion may well feel that he has been forced into an inequitable exchange. In a personal communication Crozier (1960) made a relevant observation. Paris-born bank clerks worked side by side with clerks who did identical work and earned identical wages but who were born in the provinces. The Parisians were dissatisfied with their wages, for they considered that a Parisian upbringing was an input deserving recognition. The bank management, although recognizing that place of birth distinguished the two groups, did not, of course, consider birthplace relevant in the exchange of services for pay.

The principal inputs that have been listed vary in type and in their degree of relationship to one another. Some variables such as age are clearly continuous; others, such as sex and ethnicity, are not. Some are intercorrelated: seniority and age, for example. Sex, on the other hand, is largely independent of the other variables, with the possible exception of education and some kinds of effort. Although these intercorrelations, or the lack of them, exist in a state of nature, it is probable that the individual cognitively treats all input variables as independent. Thus, for example, if he were assessing the sum of his inputs, he might well "score" age and seniority separately. It is as if he thought, "I am older and have been with Acme longer than Joe," without taking account of the fact that the two attributes are correlated. This excursion into the "black box" should not imply, as Homans (1961) seems to imply, that men assess various components of an exchange on an ordinal scale. If the work of Jaques on equitable payment (1956, 1961a) is taken at face value, there is reason to believe in this respect that men employ interval and ratio scales, or that, at the very least, they are capable of making quite fine ordinal discriminations.

On the other side of an exchange are an individual's receipts. These *outcomes,* as they will be termed, include in an employee-employer exchange pay, rewards intrinsic to the job, satisfying supervision, seniority benefits, fringe benefits, job status and status symbols, and a variety of formally and informally sanctioned perquisites, such as the right of a higher-status person to park his car in a privileged location. These are examples of positively valent outcomes. But outcomes may have negative valence. Poor working conditions, monotony, fate uncertainty, and the many "dissatisfiers" listed by Herzberg *et al.* (1959) are no less "received" than, say, wages and are negatively valent. They would be avoided, rather than approached, if it were possible. As in the case of job inputs, job outcomes are often intercorrelated. For example, greater pay and higher job status are likely to go hand-in-hand.

In other than employee-employer exchanges, though they are not precluded from these exchanges, relevant positive outcomes for one or both parties may consist of affection, love, formal courtesies, expressions of friendship, fair value (as in merchandise), and reliability (as part of the purchase of a service).Insult, rudeness, and rejection are the other side of the coin. It may be noted that in a vast array of social relations reciprocity is a functional element of the relation. What is in fact referred to by reciprocity is equality of exchange. The infinitive "to reciprocate" is commonly used to denote an obligation to give someone equal, positively valent outcomes in return for outcomes received. When a housewife says "John, we must have the Browns over, to reciprocate," she means to maintain a social relationship by reestablishing a parity in the outcomes of the two families. In this connection, it can be observed that reciprocation is usually "in kind." That is, there is a deliberate effort to match outcomes, to give equal value for value received. People who undershoot or overshoot the mark are called "cheapskates" or "uppish" and pretentious, respectively.

In a manner analogous to inputs, outcomes are *as perceived,* and, again, they should be characterized in terms of recognition and relevance. If the recipient or both the recipient and giver of an outcome in an exchange recognize its existence, it has the potentiality of being an outcome psychologically. If the recipient considers it relevant to the exchange and it has some marginal utility for him, it *is* an outcome. Not infrequently the giver may give or yield something which, though of some cost ot him, is either irrelevant or of no marginal utility to the recipient. An employer may give an employee a carpet for his office in lieu, say, of a salary increment and find that the employee is dissatisfied, perhaps because in the subculture of that office a rug has no meaning, no psychological utility. Conversely, a salary increment may be inadequate, if formalized status recognition was what was wanted and what had greater utility. Or, in another context, the gift of a toy to a child may be effectively irrelevant as reciprocation for a demonstration of affection on his part if he seeks affection. Fortunately, in the process of socialization, through the reinforcing behavior of others and of the "verbal community" (Skinner, 1957), the human organism learns not only what is appropriate reciprocation, but he learns also to assess the marginal utility of a variety of outcomes to others. In the absence of this ability, interpersonal relations would be chaotic, if not impossible. An idea of the problems that would exist may be had by observing travelers in a foreign culture. Appropriate or relevant reciprocation of outcomes is difficult, even in such mundane exchanges as tipping for services.

In classifying some variables as inputs and others as outcomes, it is not implied that they are independent, except conceptually. Inputs and outcomes are, in fact, intercorrelated, but imperfectly so. Indeed, it is because they are imperfectly correlated that there need be concern with inequity. There exist normative expectations of what constitute "fair" correlations between inputs and outcomes. The expectations are formed—learned—during the process of socialization, at home, at school, at work. They are based by observation of the correlations obtaining for a reference person or group—a co-worker or a colleague, a relative or neighbor, a group of co-workers, a craft group, an industry-wide pattern. A bank clerk, for example, may determine whether her outcomes and inputs are fairly correlated, in balance so to speak, by comparing them with the ratio of the outcomes to the inputs of other female clerks in her section. The sole punch-press operator in a manufacturing plant may base his judgment on what he believes are the inputs and outcomes of other operators in the community or region. For a particular professor the relevant reference group may be professors in the same discipline and of the same academic "vintage." While it is clearly important to be able to specify theoretically the appropriate reference person or group, this will not be done here, as the task is beyond the scope of the paper and is discussed by others (e.g., Festinger, 1954; Hyman, 1942; Merton and Kitt, 1950; Patchen, 1961). For present purposes, it will be assumed that the reference person or group will be one comparable to the comparer on one or more attributes. This is usually a co-worker in industrial situations, according to Livernash (1953), but, as Sayles (1958) points out, this generalization requires verification, as plausible as it may appear.

When the normative expectations of the person making social comparisons are violated, when he finds that his outcomes and inputs are not in balance in relation to those of others, feelings of inequity result. But before a formal definition of inequity is offered, two terms of reference will be introduced to facilitate later discussion, *Person* and *Other*. *Person* is any individual for whom equity or inequity exists. *Other* is any individual with whom Person is in an exchange relationship, or with whom Person compares himself when both he and Other are in an exchange relationship with a third party, such as an employer, or with third parties who are considered by Person as being comparable, such as employers in a particular industry or geographic location. Other is usually a different individual, but may be Person in another job or in another social role. Thus, Other might be Person in a job he held previously, in which case he might compare his present and past outcomes and inputs and determine whether or not the exchange with his employer, present or past, was equitable. The terms Person and Other may also refer to groups rather than to individuals, as when a class of jobs (e.g., toolmakers) is out of line with another class (e.g., lathe operators), or when the circumstances of one ethnic group are incongruous with those of another. In such cases, it is convenient to deal with the class as a whole rather than with individual members of the class.

B. DEFINITION OF INEQUITY

Inequity exists for Person whenever he perceives that the ratio of his outcomes to inputs and the ratio of Other's outcomes to Other's inputs are unequal. This may happen either (a) when he and Other are in a direct exchange relationship or (b) when both are in an exchange relationship with a third party and Person compares himself to Other. The values of outcomes and inputs are, of course, as perceived by Person. Schematically, inequality is experienced when either

$$\frac{O_\mathrm{p}}{I_\mathrm{p}} < \frac{O_\mathrm{a}}{I_\mathrm{a}}$$

or

$$\frac{O_\mathrm{p}}{I_\mathrm{p}} > \frac{O_\mathrm{a}}{I_\mathrm{a}}$$

where $O = \Sigma_{oi}$, $I = \Sigma_{oi}$ and p and a are subscripts denoting Person and Other, respectively. A condition of equity exists when

$$\frac{O_\mathrm{p}}{I_\mathrm{p}} = \frac{O_\mathrm{a}}{I_\mathrm{a}}$$

The outcomes and inputs in each of the ratios are conceived as being the sum of such outcomes and inputs as are perceived to be relevant to a particular exchange. Furthermore, each sum is conceived of as a weighted sum, on the assumption that individuals probably do not weight elemental outcomes or inputs equally. The work of Herzberg et al. (1959) on job "satisfiers" and "dissatisfiers" implies strongly that different outcomes, as they are labeled here, have widely varying utilities, negative as well as positive. It also appears reasonable to assume that inputs as diverse as seniority, skill, effort, and sex are not weighted equally. Zaleznik et al. (1958), in attempting to test some predictions from distributive justice theory in an industrial corporation, gave equal weight to five factors which correspond to inputs as defined here—age, seniority, education, ethnicity, and sex—but were unable to sustain their hypotheses. In retrospect, they believe (Zaleznik et al., 1958) that weighting these inputs equally may have represented an inadequate assumption of the manner in which their respondents summed their inputs.

From the definition of inequity it follows that inequity results for Person not only when he is, so to speak, relatively underpaid, but also when he is relatively overpaid. Person, will, for example, feel inequity exists not only when his effort is high and his pay low, while Other's effort and pay are high, but also when his effort is low and his pay high, while Other's effort and pay are low. This proposition receives direct support from experiments by Adams and Rosenbaum (1962), Adams (1963a), and Adams and Jacobsen (1964) in which subjects were inequitably overpaid. It receives some support also from an observation by Thibaut (1950) that subjects in whose favor the experimenter discriminated displayed "guilty smirks" and "sheepishness." The magnitude of the inequity experienced will be a monotomically increasing function of the size of the discrepancy between the ratios of outcomes to inputs. The discrepancy will be zero, and equity will exist, under two circumstances: first, when Person's and Other's outcomes are equal and their inputs are equal. This would be the case, for example, when

Person perceived that Other's wages, job, and working conditions were the same as his and that Other was equal to him on such relevant dimensions as sex, skill, seniority, education, age, effort expended, physical fitness, and risk incurred (risk of personal injury, of being fired for errors committed, for instance). Secondly, the ratios will be equal when Person perceives that Other's outcomes are higher (or lower) than his and that Other's inputs are correspondingly higher (or lower). A subordinate who compares himself to his supervisor or work group leader typically does not feel that he is unjustly treated by the company that employs them both, because the supervisor's greater monetary compensation, better working conditions, and more interesting, more varied job are matched on the input side of the ratio by more education, wider range of skills, greater responsibility and personal risk, more maturity and experience, and longer service.

Although there is no direct, reliable, evidence on this point, it is probable, as Homans (1961) conjectured, that the threshholds for inequity are different (in absolute terms from a base of equity) in cases of under- and overreward. The threshold would be higher presumably in cases of overreward, for a certain amount of incongruity in these cases can be acceptably rationalized as "good fortune" without attendant discomfort. In his work on pay differentials, Jaques (1961b) notes that in instances of undercompensation, British workers paid 10% less than the equitable level show "an active sense of grievance, complaints or the desire to complain, and, if no redress is given, an active desire to change jobs, or to take action . . ." (p. 26). He states further, "The results suggest that it is not necessarily the case that each one is simply out to get as much as he can for his work. There appear to be equally strong desires that each one should earn the right amount—a fair and reasonable amount relative to others" (p. 26).

In the preceding discussion, Person has been the focus of attention. It should be clear, however, that when Person and Other are in an exchange interaction, Other will suffer inequity if Person does, but the nature of his experience will be opposite to that of Person. If the outcome-input ratio discrepancy is unfavorable to Person, it will be favorable to Other, and vice versa. This will hold provided Person's and Other's perceptions of outcomes and inputs are equivalent and provided that the outcome-input ratio discrepancy attains threshold level. When Person and Other are not engaged in an exchange with one another but stand in an exchange relationship with a third party, Other may or may not experience inequity when Person does. Given the prerequisites mentioned above, he will experience inequity if he compares himself to Person with respect to the same question as induces Person to use Other as a referent (e.g., "Am I being paid fairly?").

C. CONSEQUENCES OF INEQUITY

Although there can be little doubt that inequity results in dissatisfaction, in an unpleasant emotional state, be it anger or guilt, there will be other effects. A major purpose of this paper is to specify these in terms that permit specific predictions to be made. Before turning to this task, two general postulates are presented, closely following propositions from cognitive dissonance theory (Festinger, 1957). First, the presence of inequity in Person creates tension in him. The tension is proportional to the magnitude of inequity present. Second, the tension created in Person will motivate him to eliminate or reduce it. The strength of the motivation is proportional to the tension created. In short, the presence of inequity will motivate Person to achieve equity or to reduce inequity, and the strength of motivation to do so will vary directly with the magnitude of inequity experienced. From these postulates and from the theory of cognitive dissonance (Festinger, 1957; Brehm and Cohen, 1962), means of reducing inequity will be derived and presented. As each method of reduction is discussed, evidence demonstrating usage of the method will be presented. Some of the evidence is experimental; some of it is the result of field studies, either of a survey or observational character.

1. Person Altering His Inputs

Person may vary his inputs, either increasing them or decreasing them, depending on whether the inequity is advantageous or disadvantageous. Increasing inputs will reduce felt inequity, if

$$\frac{O_p}{I_p} > \frac{O_a}{I_a}$$

conversely, decreasing inputs will be effective, if

$$\frac{O_p}{I_p} < \frac{O_a}{I_a}$$

In the former instance, Person might increase either his productivity or the quality of his work, provided that it is possible, which is not always the case. In the second instance, Person might engage in "production restriction," for example. Whether Person does, or can, reduce inequity by altering his inputs is partially contingent upon whether relevant inputs are susceptible to change. Sex, age, seniority, and ethnicity are not modifiable. Education and skill are more easily altered, but changing these requires time. Varying inputs will also be a function of Person's perception of the principal "cause" of the inequity. If the discrepancy between outcome-input ratios is primarily a function of his inputs being at variance with those of Other, Person is more likely to alter them than if the discrepancy is largely a result of differences in outcomes. Additionally, it is postulated that given equal opportunity to alter inputs and outcomes, Person will be more likely to lower his inputs when

$$\frac{O_p}{I_p} < \frac{O_a}{I_a}$$

than he is to increase his inputs when

$$\frac{O_p}{I_p} > \frac{O_a}{I_a}$$

This is derived from two assumptions: first, the assumption stated earlier that the threshold for the perception of inequity is higher when Person is overrewarded than when he is underrewarded; secondly, the assumption that Person is motivated to minimize his costs and to maximize his gains. By the second assumption, Person will reduce inequity, insofar as possible, in a manner that will yield him the largest outcomes.

Altering certain inputs has the corollary effect of altering the outcomes of Other. A change in the quality and amount of work performed, for instance, will usually affect the outcomes of Other. When this is the case, the effect of both changes will operate in the same direction in the service of inequity reduction. It follows, therefore, that *less* a change in inputs is required to eliminate inequity than if the change had no effect on Other's outcomes. Inputs, a change in which would have no or very little impact on Other's outcomes, are attributes such as education, age, and seniority—at least to the extent that they are uncorrelated with performance.

Several experiments have been conducted specifically to test the hypothesis that Person will reduce inequity by altering his inputs (Adams and Rosenbaum, 1962; Adams, 1963a; Adams and Jacobsen, 1964).

2. Person Altering His Outcomes

Person may vary his outcomes, either decreasing or increasing them, depending on whether the inequity is advantageous or disadvantageous to him. Increasing outcomes will reduce inequity, if

$$\frac{O_p}{I_p} < \frac{O_a}{I_a}$$

conversely, decreasing outcomes will serve the same function, if

$$\frac{O_p}{I_p} > \frac{O_a}{I_a}$$

Of these two possibilities, the second is far less likely, and there is no good evidence of the use of this means of reducing inequity, though some may be available in the clinical literature. There are, however, data bearing on attempts to increase outcomes, data other than those related to wage increase demands in union-management negotiations, probably only a part of which are directly traceable to wage inequities.

In the experiment by Thibaut (1950), to which reference was made earlier, teams of 5 or 6 boys made up of approximately equal numbers of popular and unpopular boys were assigned either high- or low-status roles in playing a series of four games. The low-status teams were unfairly treated in that, although they were comparable in their characteristics (i.e., their inputs) to the high-status teams, they were forced to adopt an inferior, unpleasant role vis-a-vis the other team. For example, in one game they formed a human chain against which the other team bucked; in another, they held the target and retrieved thrown bean bags. Thus, since their inputs were equal to, and their outcomes lower than, those of the high-status teams, they were clearly suffering the disadvantages of inequity. From Thibaut's report of the behavior of the low-status teams, it is evident that at least four means of reducing the inequity were used by them: lowering the high-status team members' outcomes by fighting with them and displaying other forms of hostility; lowering their inputs by not playing the games as required, which would also have had the effect of lowering the outcomes of the high-status team members; by leaving the field, that is, withdrawing and crying; and by trying to interchange roles with the high-status teams. The latter is the relevant one for purposes of discussion here.

Thibaut (1950) reports that about halfway through the second game the participants had come to understand the experimenter's intention, i.e., that the status differentiation was to be permanent. At this stage of the experiment low-status subjects began to express mobility aspirations, asking the experimenter that the roles of the two teams be reversed. This may be interpreted as an attempt to establish equity by increasing outcomes, since assumption of high status would have been accompanied by pleasurable activities. Interestingly, though the report is not entirely clear on this point, there is the suggestion that, when the attempt of low-status subjects to increase their outcomes was rejected by the experimenter, they desisted and, instead, engaged more in withdrawal.

Also giving evidence that increasing outcomes will serve to reduce inequity is a study of unfair wages among clerical workers by Homans (1953). Two groups of female clerical workers in a utilities company, cash posters and ledger clerks, worked in the same, large room. Cash posting consisted of recording daily the amounts customers paid on their bills, and management insisted that posting be precisely up to date. It required that cash posters pull customer cards from the many files and make appropriate entries on them. The job was highly repetitive and comparatively monotonous, and required little thought but a good deal of walking about. Ledger clerks, in contrast, performed a variety of tasks on customer accounts, such as recording address changes, making breakdowns of over- and underpayments, and supplying information on accounts to customers and others on the telephone. In addition, toward the end of the day, they were required by their supervisor to assist with "cleaning up" cash posting in order that it be current. Compared to the cash posters, ledger clerks performed a number of nonrepetitive clerical jobs requiring some thought; they had a more *responsible* job; they were considered to be of higher status, since promotion took place from cash poster to ledger clerk; and they were older and had more seniority and experience. Their weekly pay, however, was identical.

Summarizing in the terms of the inequity model, cash posters had distinctly lower inputs than ledger clerks (i.e., they were younger, and had less experience, less seniority, and less responsibility). With respect to outcomes they received equal wages, but their jobs were somewhat more monotonous and less interesting. On the other hand, the ledger clerks' inputs were superior with respect to age, experience, seniority, skill, responsibility, and versatility (they were required to know and do cash posting in addition to their own jobs). Their earnings were equal to the cash posters', but they were required to "clean up" (note connotation) posting each day, an activity that would deflate self-esteem and would, therefore, be a negative outcome. In the balance, then, the net outcomes of ledger clerks and cash posters were approximately of the same magnitude, but the inputs of the clerks were definitely greater. From this it would be predicted that the ledger clerks felt unfairly treated and that they would try to increase their outcomes.

The evidence reported by Homans (1953) is that the ledger clerks felt the inequity and that they felt they ought to get a few dollars more per week to show that their jobs were more important—that their greater inputs ought to be matched by greater outcomes. On the whole, these clerks seemed not to have done much to reduce inequity, though a few complained to the union representative, with, apparently, little effect. However, the workers in this division voted to abandon their independent union for the CIO, and Homans intimates that the reason may have been the independent union's inability to force a resolution of the inequity.

The field studies of dissatisfaction with status and promotions by Stouffer *et al.* (1949) and the experiments by Spector (1956), in which expectation of promotion and morale, which were described in Section II, may also be interpreted as cases of inequity in which dissatisfactions were expressions of attempts by Persons to increase their outcomes.

3. Person Distorting His Inputs and Outcomes Cognitively

Person may cognitively distort his inputs and outcomes, the direction of the distortion being the same as if he had actually altered his inputs and outcomes, as discussed above. Since most individuals are heavily influenced by reality, substantial distortion is generally difficult. It is pretty difficult to distort to oneself, to change one's cognitions about the fact, for example, that one has a BA degree, that one has been an accountant for seven years, and that one's salary is $700 per month. However, it is possible, within limits, to alter the utility of these. For example, State College is a small, backwoods school with no reputation, or, alternatively, State College has one of the best business schools in the state and the dean is an adviser to the Bureau of the Budget. Or, one can consider the fact that $700 per month will buy all of the essential things of life and a few luxuries, or, conversely, that it will never permit one to purchase a Wyeth oil painting or an Aston Martin DB5. There is ample evidence in the psychological literature, especially that related to cognitive dissonance theory, that individuals do modify or rearrange their cognitions in an effort to reduce perceived incongruities (for a review, see Brehm and Cohen, 1962). Since it has been postulated that the experience of inequity is equivalent to the experience of dissonance, it is reasonable to believe that cognitive distortion may be adopted as a means of reducing inequity.

In a variety of work situations, for example in paced production line jobs, actually altering one's inputs and outcomes may be difficult; as a consequence these may be cognitively change in relatively subtle ways.

Although not a cognitive change in inputs and outcomes per se, related methods of reducing inequity are for Person to alter the *importance* and the *relevance* of his inputs and outcomes. If, for example, age were a relevant input, its relative importance could be changed to bring about less perceived inequity. Person could convince himself that age was either more or less important than he thought originally. In terms of the statement made earlier that net inputs (and outcomes) were a weighted sum of inputs, changing the importance of inputs would be equivalent to changing the weights associated with them. Altering the relevance of inputs and outcomes is conceived of as more of an all-or-none process: Present ones are made irrelevant or new ones are made relevant. For instance, if Person perceived that the discrepancy between his and Other's outcome-input ratios were principally a result of his outcomes being too low, he might become "aware" of one or more outcomes he had not recognized as being relevant before, perhaps that his job had variety absent from Other's job. Obviously, importance and relevance of inputs and outcomes are not completely independent. An outcome suddenly perceived as being relevant automatically assumes some importance; conversely, one that is made irrelevant in the service of inequity reduction assumes an importance of zero. Nevertheless, the psychological processes appear to be different and it is useful, therefore, to keep them conceptually distinct. . . .

4. Person Leaving the Field

Leaving the field may take any of several ways of severing social relationships. Quitting a job, obtaining a transfer, and absenteeism are common forms of leaving the field in an employment situation. These are fairly radical means of coping with inequity. The probability of using them is assumed to increase with magnitude of inequity and to decrease with the availability of other means.

Data substantiating the occurrence of leaving the field as a mode of reducing inequity is sparse. In the aforementioned study by Thibaut (1950), it was observed that low-status team members withdrew from the games as it became increasingly clear what their fate was and as, it must be presumed, the felt injustice mounted. In a study by Patchen (1959) it was observed that men who said their pay should be higher had more absences than men who said the pay for jobs was fair. This relationship between perceived fairness of pay and absenteeism was independent of actual wage level. That absenteeism in this study was a form of withdrawal is strongly supported by the fact that men with high absence rates were significantly more likely than men with low rates to say that they would not go on working at their job, if they should chance to inherit enough money to live comfortably without working.

5. Person Acting on Other

In the face of injustice, Person may attempt to alter or cognitively distort Other's inputs and outcomes, or try to force Other to leave the field. These means of reducing inequity vary in the ease of their use. Getting Other to accept greater outcomes, which was a possible interpretation of some of the findings by Leventhal *et al.* 1964,,, would obviously be easier than the opposite. Similarly, inducing Other to lower his inputs may be easier than the reverse. For example, all other things being equal, such as work group cohesiveness and the needs and ability of an individual worker, it is probably easier to induce a "rate buster" to lower his inputs than to get a laggard to increase them. The direction of the change attempted in the inputs and outcomes of Other is the reverse of the change that Person would make in his own inputs and outcomes, whether the change be actual or cognitive. By way of illustration, if Person experienced feelings of inequity because he lacked job experience compared to Other, he could try to induce Other to decrease a relevant input instead of increasing his own inputs.

Cognitive distortion of Other's inputs and outcomes may be somewhat less difficult than distortion of one's own, since cognitions about Other are probably less well anchored than are those concerning oneself. This assumption is consistent with the finding that "where alternatives to change in central attitudes are possible, they will be selected" (Pilisuk, 1962, p. 102). Acceptable evidence that inequity, as such, is reduced by cognitive distortion of Other's inputs or outcomes is nonexistent, although there is ample evidence that cognitive dissonance may be reduced by perceptual distortion (e.g., Bramel, 1962; Brehm and Cohen, 1962; Steiner and Peters, 1958). An observation made while pretesting procedures for an unpublished study by Adams (1961) is little better than anecdotal. To test some hypotheses from inequity theory, he paired a subject and a stooge at a "partner's desk." Each performed sequentially one part of the preparation of a personnel payroll. In one condition the subject was paid $1.40 per hour and performed the relatively complex task of looking in various tables for standard and overtime rates, looking up in other tables the products of pay rates and hours worked, and recording the products on a payroll form. The stooge, whose pay was announced as being $2.10 per hour, performed the presumably much easier task of summing products on a machine and recording the totals on the form the subject passed to him across the desk. In addition, the stooge was programmed to be slightly ahead of the subject in his work, so that his task appeared fairly easy. It was hoped that these conditions would lead the subject to perceive that, compared to the stooge, he had higher inputs and lower outcomes. Nothing of the sort happened. Most subjects pretested felt that the relationship was equitable, and this appeared to result from the fact that they distorted cognitively the stooge's inputs in an upward direction. Specifically, they convinced themselves that the stooge was performing a "mathematical task." Simple *adding* on a machine became *mathematics*.

Forcing Other to leave the field, while theoretically possible, is probably difficult of realization and would, no doubt, be accompanied by anxiety about potential consequences or simply by the discomfort of having done something socially unpleasant. This aspect makes it costly to Person; it lowers his outcomes to some extent. Firing an individual in an employer-employee exchange and some divorces and separations are common examples of this means put to use.

Somewhat though barely more subtle is the practice of creating an inequity by withholding expected outcomes (e.g., salary increases, promotions) to the point where an individual leaves the field "voluntarily."

6. Person Changing the Object of His Comparison

Person may change Other with whom he compares himself when he experiences inequity and he and Other stand in an exchange relationship with a third party. This mode is limited to the relationship specified; it is not applicable when Person and Other are in a direct exchange. Changing the object of comparison in the latter situation would reduce to severing the relationship.

The resolution of inequity by changing comparison object is undoubtedly difficult of accomplishment, particularly if Person has been comparing himself to Other for some time. Person would need to be able to make himself noncomparable to Other on one or more dimensions. For instance, if Other, whose outcome input ratio was previously equal to Person's received a salary increase without any apparent increment in inputs, Person could try to reduce the resulting feeling of inequity by conceiving of Other as belonging now to a different organizational level. But this would likely meet with little success, at least in this culture. A cognitive change of this sort would be extremely unstable, unless it were accompanied by changes in the perception of Other's inputs: for instance, that Other had assumed greater responsibility when his salary was increased. But this involves a process of inequity reduction already referred to.

In the initial stages of comparison processes, as when a man first comes on the job, it probably is relatively easy to choose as comparison Others individuals who provide the most equitable comparisons. This does not necessarily entail making comparisons with men whose outcomes and inputs are the same as one's own; it is sufficient that their outcome input ratio be equal to one's own. In a study of the choice of wage comparison, Patchen (1961) asked oil refinery workers to name someone whose yearly earnings were *different* from theirs and then proceeded to ask them questions about the resulting wage comparisons and about their satisfaction with them. Of the workers who named someone earning *more* than they, 60% indicated satisfaction with the comparison and only 17.6% reported dissatisfaction. Among those who were satisfied, 44.6% stated they were satisfied because they had financial or other advantages, i.e., compensating outcomes, and 55.8% indicated satisfaction with the upward comparison because the person with higher earnings had more education, skill, experience, seniority and the like, i.e., higher inputs. Patchen's data may be recast and reanalyzed to make a different point, Among the men who chose comparison persons whose outcome-input ratios seemingly were equal to theirs, approximately 85% were satisfied with the comparison and only about 4% were dissatisfied. While Patchen's study does not bear directly either on what wage comparisons men actually make in their day-to-day relations with other or on changes in comparison persons when inequity arises, it gives clear evidence that comparisons are made on the basis of the equality of the outcome-input ratios of the comparer and comparison person and that such comparisons prove satisfying, i.e., are, at least, judged to be not inequitable.

7. Choice among Modes of Inequity Reduction

Although reference has been made previously to conditions that may affect the use of one or another method of reducing inequity, there is need for a general statement of conditions that will govern the adoption of one method over another. Given the existence of inequity, any of the means of reduction described earlier are potentially available to Person. He may alter or attempt to alter any of the four terms in the inequality formula or change his cognitions about any of them, or he may leave the field and change his comparison Other, but it is improbable that each of the methods are equally available to him *psychologically* (no reference is made to environmental constraints that may affect the availability of methods), as the work of Steiner and his colleagues on alternative methods of dissonance reduction suggests (Steiner, 1960; Steiner and Johnson, 1964; Steiner and Peters, 1958; Steiner and Rogers, 1963).

Set forth below are some propositions about conditions determining the choice of modes by person. As will be noted, the propositions are not all independent of one another, and each should be prefaced by the condition, *ceteris paribus*.

a   Person will maximize positively valent outcomes and the valence of outcomes.

b   He will minimize increasing inputs that are effortful and costly to change.

c   He will resist real and cognitive changes in inputs that are central to his self-concept and to his self-esteem. To the extent that any of Person's outcomes are related to his self-concept and to his self-esteem, this proposition is extended to cover his outcomes.

d   He will be more resistant to changing cognitions about his own outcomes and inputs than to changing his cognitions about Other's outcomes and inputs.

e   Leaving the field will be resorted to only when the magnitude of inequity experienced is high and other means of reducing it are unavailable. Partial withdrawal, such as absenteeism, will occur more frequently and under conditions of lower inequity.

f   Person will be highly resistant to changing the object of his comparisons, Other, once it has stabilized over time and, in effect, has become an anchor.

These propositions are, admittedly, fairly crude, but they permit, nevertheless, a degree of prediction not available otherwise. In the resolution of a particular injustice, two or more of the processes proposed may be pitted one against the other. To propose which would be dominant is not possible at this stage of the development of the theory. One might propose that protection of self-esteem would dominate maximization of outcomes, but it would be conjecture in the absence of evidence.

CONCLUSION

Dissatisfaction is both so commonplace and such an irritant, particularly in industrial and other large organizations, that it has been the subject of widespread research (see Vroom, 1964, for a recent, thorough review). Despite prima facie evidence that feelings of injustice underlay a significant proportion of cases of dissatisfaction, thorough behavioral analyses of injustice were not made until recently. In the classic Hawthorne studies (Roethlisberger and Dickson, 1939), there was ample evidence that much of the dissatisfaction observed among Western Electric Company employees was precipitated by felt injustice. Describing complaints, the authors referred frequently to reports by workers that wages were not in keeping with seniority, that rates were too low, that ability was not rewarded, and the like, as distinguished from reports that, for example, equipment was not working and that the workshop was hot. They stated that "no physical or logical operations exist which can be agreed upon as defining them" (p. 259), and they sought "personal or social situations" (p. 269) that would explain the complaints parsimoniously. Yet, the notion of injustice was not advanced as an explanatory concept.

It is not contended here, of course, that all dissatisfaction and low morale are related to a person's suffering injustice in social exchanges. But it should be clear from the research described that a significant portion of cases can be usefully explained by invoking injustice as an explanatory concept. More importantly, much more than dissatisfaction may be predicted once the concept of injustice is analyzed theoretically.

In the theory of inequity that has been developed in this chapter, both the antecedents and consequences of perceived injustice have been stated in terms that permit quite specific predictions to be made about the behavior of persons entering social exchanges. On the whole, empirical support for the theory is gratifying, but it falls short of what is desirable. More research is required. This is particularly so because some of the support comes from data leading to the formulation of parts of the theory. Needed are direct tests of propositions made in the theory, as well as empirical tests of novel derivations from the theory. Some research filling these needs is under way. Being tested, for example, is the hypothesis that overpaid workers for whom an increase in inputs is impossible will reduce inequity by decreasing their outcomes, specifically by developing unfavorable attitudes toward their employer, their working conditions, the pay rates, and so on.

In order for more refined predictions to be made from the theory, theoretical, methodological, and empirical work are also required in at least two areas related to it. First, additional thought must be given to social comparison processes. The works of Festinger (1954), Hyman (1942), Merton and Kitt (1950), Newcomb (1943), and Patchen (1961) are signal contributions but still do not allow sufficiently fine predictions to be made about whom Person will choose as a comparison Other when both are in an exchange relationship with a third party.

For example, as a function of what variables will one man compare himself to a person on the basis of age similarities and another man compare himself on the basis of attitude similarities? Second, psychometric research is needed to determine how individuals aggregate there own outcomes and inputs and those of others. Is the assumptive model that net outcomes are the algebraic sum of elemental outcomes weighted by their importance a valid one?

The need for much additional research notwithstanding, the theoretical analyses that have been made of injustice in social exchanges should result not only in a better general understanding of the phenomenon, but should lead to to degree of social control not previously possible. The experience of injustice need not be an accepted fact of life.

REFERENCES

Adams, J. S. (1961). Wage inequities in a clerical task. Unpublished study. General Electric Company, New York.

Adams, J. S. (1963a). Toward an understanding of inequity. *J. abnorm. soc. Psychol.* **67,** 422–436.

Adams, J. S. (1963b). Wage inequities, productivity, and work quality. *Industr. Relat.* **3,** 9–16.

Adams, J. S. (1965). Etudes expérimentales en matière d'inégalités de salaires, de productivité et de qualité du travail. *Synopsis,* **7,** 25–34.

Adams, J. S., and Jacobsen, Patricia R. (1964). Effects of wage inequities on work quality. *J. abnorm. soc. Psychol.* **69,** 19–25.

Adams, J. S., and Rosenbaum, W. B. (1962). The relationship of worker productivity to cognitive dissonance about wage inequities. *J. appl. Psychol.* **46,** 161–164.

Bramel, D. (1962). A dissonance theory approach to defensive projection. *J. abnorm. soc. Psychol.* **64,** 121–129.

Brehm, J. W., and Cohen, A. R. (1962). *Explorations in cognitive dissonance.* New York: Wiley.

Clark, J. V. (1958). A preliminary investigation of some unconscious assumptions affecting labor efficiency in eight supermarkets. Unpublished doctoral dissertation (Grad. Sch. Business Admin.). Harvard Univer.

Crozier, M. (1960). Personal communication to the author.

Festinger, L. (1954). A theory of social comparison processes. Hum. Relat. **7** 117–140.

Festinger, L. (1957). *A theory of cognitive dissonance.* Evanston, Ill.: Row, Peterson.

Herzberg, F., Mausner, B., and Snyderman, Barbara B. (1959). *The motivation to work.* New York: Wiley.

Homans, G. C. (1950). *The human group.* New York: Harcourt, Brace.

Homans, G. C. (1963). Status among clerical workers. *Hum. Organiz.* **12,** 5–10.

Homans, G. C. (1961). *Social behavior: its elementary forms.* New York: Harcourt, Brace.

Hyman, H. (1942). The psychology of status. *Arch. Psychol.* **38,** No. 269.

Jaques, E. (1956). *Measurement of responsibility.* London: Tavistock.

Jaques, E. (1961a). *Equitable payment.* New York: Wiley.

Jaques, E. (1961b). An objective approach to pay differentials. *Time Motion Study* **10,** 25–28.

Leventhal, G., Reilly, Ellen, and Lehrer, P. (1964). Change in reward as a determinant of satisfaction and reward expectancy. Paper read at West. Psychol. Assoc. Portland, Ore.

Livernash, E. R. (1953). Job evaluation. In W. S. Woytinsky *et al.* (Eds.), *Employment and wages in the United States.* New York: Twentieth Century Fund, pp. 427–435.

Merton, R. K., and Kitt, Alice S. (1950). Contributions to the theory of reference group behavior. In *Continuities in social research.* R. K. Merton and P. F. Lazarsfeld (Eds.), Glencoe, Ill.: Free Press, pp. 40–105.

Newcomb, T. M. (1943). *Personality and social change: attitude formation in a student community.* New York: Dryden.

Patchen, M. (1959). Study of work and life satisfaction, Report No. II: absences and attitudes toward work experience. Inst. for Social Res., Ann Arbor, Mich.

Patchen, M. (1961). *The choice of wage comparisons.* Englewood Cliffs, N. J.: Prentice-Hall.

Roethlisberger, F. J., and Dickson, W. J. (1939). *Management and the worker.* Cambridge, Mass.: Harvard Univer. Press.

Sayles, L. R. (1958). *Behavior of industrial work groups: prediction and control.* New York: Wiley.

Skinner, B. F. (1957). *Verbal behavior.* New York: Appleton.

Spector, A. J. (1956). Expectations, fulfillment, and morale. *J. abnor. soc. Psychol.* **52,** 51–56.

Steiner, I. D. (1960). Sex differences in the resolution of A-B-X conflicts. *J. Pers.* **28,** 118–128.

Steiner, I. D., and Johnson, H. H. (1964). Relationships among dissonance reducing responses. *J. abnorm. soc. Psychol.* **68,** 38–44.

Steiner, I. D., and Peters, S. C. (1958). Conformity and the A-B-X model. *J. Pers.* **26,** 229–242.

Steiner, I. D., and Rogers, E. D. (1963). Alternative responses to dissonance. *J. abnorm. soc. Psychol.* **66,** 128–136.

Stouffer, S. A., Suchman, E. A., DeVinney, L. C., Starr, Shirley A., and Williams R. M., Jr. (1949). *The American soldier: adjustment during army life.* Vol. 1. Princeton, N. J.: Princeton Univer. Press.

Thibaut, J. (1950). An experimental study of the cohesiveness of underprivileged groups. *Hum. Relat.* **3,** 251–278.

Vroom, V. H. (1964). *Work and motivation.* New York:Wiley.

Weick, K. E.(1964). Reduction of cognitive dissonance through task enhancement and effort expenditure. *J. abnor. soc. Psychol.* **66,** 533–539.

Zaleznik, A., Christensen, C. R., and Roethlisberger, F. J. (1958). The motivation, productivity, and satisfaction of workers. A prediction study (Grad. Sch. Business Admin.) Harvard Univer.

An Examination of Adams'
Theory of Inequity
Paul S. Goodman and Abraham Friedman

This paper examines the empirical evidence directly testing Adams' (1963a, 1965) theory of inequity.[1] Adams' theoretical statement and initial experimental design have stimulated considerable interest among researchers interested in motivation, organizational performance, and compensation systems. Although others (Homans, 1961; Jaques, 1961) have presented similar concepts of inequity, Adams' formulation has generated more systematic empirical evidence. Given this growing body of data, it is useful to assess critically the validity of the theory in order to determine possible directions for future research and possible implications of the theory for practice. This type of review is particularly important now because a number of researchers have recently questioned the utility of the theory (Lawler, 1968a; Pritchard, 1969; Wiener, 1970).

ADAMS' THEORY OF INEQUITY

Adams (1965: 280) defined inequity as follows: Inequity exists for Person whenever he perceives that the ratio of his outcomes to inputs and the ratio of Other's outcomes to Other's inputs are unequal. This may happen either *(a)* when Person and Other are in a direct exchange relationship or *(b)* when both are in an exchange relationship with a third party and Person compares himself to Other. Outcomes refer to rewards such as pay or job status which Person receives for performing his job. Inputs represent the contributions Person brings to the job, such as age, education, and physical effort. Outputs, a term not used in the definition, refer to products of Person's work, such as the number of interviews completed or pages proofed.

The basic assumptions, propositions, and derivations of the theory (Adams, 1965: 280–296) can be divided into two general classes: those dealing with the conditions of inequity and those dealing with the resolution of inequity. Propositions concerning conditions of inequity include: inequity is a source of tension; the greater the feeling of inequity, the greater drive to reduce this tension; inequity results from input-outcome discrepancies relative to Other versus absolute input-outcome discrepancies; the threshold for underpayment is lower than for overpayment; inputs and outcomes are additive. Sample propositions dealing with resolution of inequity include: Person will allocate rewards in a dyad proportionate to each member's contributions; Person will resist changing input-outcome cognitions about self more than about Other; Person who is overpaid in an hourly pay system will produce more than an equitably paid Other; Person

From *Administrative Science Quarterly*, 1971, **16,** 271–288. Reprinted by permission.
[1]This paper was supported in part by Grant USPHS 5-ROI MH-18 512-02 to the senior author and Dr. L. Richard Hoffman.

who is overpaid in a piece-rate system will produce higher quality but fewer units than an equitably paid Other.

Listing these propositions serves two functions. (1) It indicates the range of the theory requiring empirical assessment. Previous reviewers (Lawler, 1968a; Pritchard, 1969) have considered propositions dealing mainly with the effect of inequity on performance. (2) It provides a logical basis for organizing the paper. The evidence relevant to propositions concerning resolution of inequity are analyzed first, because there are more studies in this area and because the evidence for these propositions bears on propositions concerning conditions of inequity. Empirical evidence about conditions of inequity are analyzed second.

RESOLUTION OF INEQUITY AND PERFORMANCE

Inequity-Performance

These studies examine how resolution of inequity affects job performance. The basic design is as follows: The experimenter, posing as an employer, advertises for individuals interested in part-time work—for example, interviewing for attitude survey. A contact is made, and the subject comes to the prospective employer. The experimenter creates the inequity induction by paying the subject more or less than the going rate, or by paying more or less than the going rate and also telling the subject that his qualifications for the job are lower than a comparison Other receiving the same pay. The pay is either on an hourly or piece-rate basis. After some initial job training, the subject performs the task over a stated period of time, returns to the employer, completes a postjob experimental questionnaire, and is paid. The number of units—for example, interviews—completed, quality of work, and attitudinal responses from the questionnaire represent the major dependent variables.

There are four types of studies in this area: overpaid-hourly, overpaid-piece rate, underpaid hourly, and underpaid-piece rate.

Overpaid-Hourly   The basic hypothesis is that overpaid subjects will raise their inputs by producing more as a means of reducing inequity. Four studies (Adams & Rosenbaum, 1962; Arrowood, 1961; Goodman & Friedman, 1969; Pritchard et al., 1970) have generally supported this hypothesis. Kalt (1969) provided nominal support for the hypothesis, but the induction in this study was not particularly effective. Studies by Valenzi and Andrews (1969), Evan and Simmons (1969), and Anderson and Shelly (1970) indicated no differences in productivity between over and equitably paid groups. Three studies (Friedman & Goodman, 1967; Lawler, 1968b; Wiener, 1970) have obtained findings which support and some which reject the hypotheses.

The studies which did not support the hypothesis had two distinguishing characteristics: their hourly rate of pay was lower and their induction of overpayment differed from the supporting studies. The lower rate of pay was a limitation because it undermined the notion of overpayment. The supporting studies, on the other hand, paid an hourly rate higher than the modal rate for most of the subjects, and, therefore, produced a more powerful induction.

The second distinguishing characteristic of the nonsupporting studies was the use of an induction which overpays by circumstances. Subjects were told their pay exceeded the modal rate for the job because of a special circumstance—for example, a private foundation was subsidizing the work, or there was a mistake in the advertisement for the job. If subjects in these studies selected the most similar comparison Others—those working on the same job—their outcomes would be high relative to their inputs, but the same as their comparison Others and, therefore, although they may have reported their pay as high, they should not have experienced inequity. In Evan and Simmons' (1969: 234) study, using an overpaid-by-circumstance design, only 53 percent of their overpaid subjects reported they were overpaid. Also, in their second experiment they (1969: 234) concluded: "Although acknowledging the discrepancy between their authority and salary (it was higher) the overpaid subjects did not translate this awareness into a psychological feeling of being inequitable paid." Therefore, this evidence indicates that the overpaid-by-circumstance induction is not very successful in creating feelings of inequity, and studies using this induction, and the lower hourly rate are not suitable tests of the overpaid hypothesis (Adams, 1968). A similar induction is used in selected experimental groups in Lawler (1968b) and Pritchard et al. (1970); the results also do not support the hypothesis.

The main criticism against the supporting studies is that the results are attributed to devalued self-esteem rather than to feelings of inequity (Lawler, 1968a; Pritchard, 1969). The inductions in these studies (Adams & Rosenbaum, 1962; Arrowood, 1961) provided similar pay to equitably and overpaid subjects, but told the overpaid subjects his qualifications were lower—devalued—and thus he was overpaid relative to the equitably paid Other. If the subject's increased productivity was an attempt to demonstrate valued abilities that had been devalued by the induction, then the results cannot be interpreted in equity terms even though the data appear in the predicted direction.

A number of studies (Friedman & Goodman, 1967; Andrews & Valenzi, 1970; Wiener, 1970) demonstrated that feelings of self-qualification can affect performance variation in equity experiments. However, it is difficult to extrapolate from these studies to those supporting the main hypothesis. For example, Wiener (1970) showed that overpaid subjects—those whose inputs were devalued—produced significantly more than equitably paid subjects in an ego-involved task, but not more in a less ego-involved task. Since these subjects only produced more in a condition where task abilities were central to one's self-concept, Wiener argued that their behavior represented a reaction to devalued self-esteem rather than to feelings of overpayment. Even is this interpretation is accepted, it is difficult to extrapolate from this study to those supporting the equity hourly hypothesis for two reasons. First, the induced ego orientation in this study far exceeded that in any other inequity study. Second, subjects in the overpaid-unqualified group did not report significantly greater feelings of over-payment than those in the equitably paid group; a relationship which does appear in the supporting studies. Empirically we know that reaction to devalued self-esteem can affect performance in inequity experiments. What has not been empirically demonstrated is that reaction to devalued self-esteem accounts for more production variance than feelings of inequity in studies supporting hypothesis.

An analysis of supporting studies indicates that the inequity explanation is more tenable than the devalued self-esteem explanation. Some studies have minimized conditions likely to evoke feelings of devalued self-esteem by: (1) not hiring qualified subjects (Adams & Rosenbaum, 1962); (2) distinguishing in the analysis between qualified subjects and those who felt overpaid (Arrowood, 1961); (3) using a psuedotest to pretend to validate the subjects' lower qualifications (Goodman & Friedman, 1968); (4) not selecting an ego-involved task; and (5) using a reduced dissonance control group. In these studies inputs were devalued and pay was also reduced, commensurate with the lower qualifications. Since subjects in both the overpaid and reduced dissonance groups were devalued, then no differences should have appeared between these groups if reaction to devalued self-esteem was more salient than to wage inequity; however, the differences did appear (Goodman & Friedman, 1968).

A study by Pritchard et al. (1970) employed an induction which did not rely on devaluation of self or on overpaid-by-circumstance, and successfully supported the hourly hypothesis. In their induction the payment system was changed after several days' work so that subjects were getting more or less money for the same amount of work; that is, the relationship between past and present input and outcome ratios was modified to create feelings of inequity. Since their design used a relatively unambiguous method to create feelings of inequity, did not rely on devaluation of self nor on overpaid-by-circumstance (Wiener, 1970), and it embraced a longer experimental time period—greater than 30 hours—than in most experiments (for example, Valenzi & Andrews, 1969—2 hours), its supporting data provides one of the most powerful tests of the hourly hypothesis.

Another major criticism (Lawler, 1968a) of the supporting studies is that feelings of job insecurity evoked by the experimental induction reduce the efficacy of the equity explanation. That is, if the subject feels that subsequent employment is based on initial high job performance, and if this feeling is more salient in the overpaid-unqualified condition, then differential performance represents a way of buying job security rather than reducing inequity.

In a study on the possible effects of job insecurity, Arrowood (1961) found overpaid subjects produced more than control subjects in both high and low job-security conditions. Perhaps more important, however, is the likelihood of job-insecurity feelings being evoked by the inductions in the studies under consideration. Only the Adams and Rosenbaum (1962) study leaves the length of future employment ambiguous, and therefore, likely to evoke feelings of insecurity. The other studies seem quite clear in stating the employment period, and the employment period is relatively short—2 hours to part-time for 7 days. The authors' own experience indicates that presenting a clear, short work period with a statement that no future work is available substantially reduces the contamination from feelings of job insecurity.

Summary   There is some evidence to support the hypothesis that overpaid subjects increase their productivity as a way of bringing their inputs and outcomes in balance and thus of reducing feelings of inequity. Studies which used the overpay-by-circumstance induction and paid a lower rate were not considered adequate tests of the hypothesis. Although the effects of devalued self-esteem and job insecurity can affect performance variation in the equity studies, there is no compelling evidence that they represent the major source of production variance in the supporting studies. The Pritchard et al. (1970) study, which supports the hypothesis, offers a more useful way to test the hypothesis.

Overpaid-Piece Rate   The basic hypothesis is that overpaid subjects will produce higher quality and lower quantity than equitably paid subjects. The assumption for this hypothesis is: Overpaid subjects will increase their inputs as a means of achieving equity. These inputs can lead to greater quantity or quality. However, increases in quantity can only increase inequity because every unit is overpaid. Therefore, inputs are invested in increased quality and inputs and outcomes per unit achieve a balanced relationship.

The design for the piece-rate studies is the same as that described for the hourly system except that the job is advertised and paid by the piece.

The empirical support for this hypothesis seems relatively straightforward. Adams and Rosenbaum (1962), Adams (1963b), Adams and Jacobsen (1964), and Goodman and Friedman (1969) reported lower quantity and higher quality for the overpaid group. Lawler et al. (1968) supported this relationship for the initial work session but not over subsequent experimental sessions. Wood and Lawler (1970) reported lower quantity for the overpaid piece-rate subjects. Andrews (1967) reported lower quantity and higher quality for the overpaid subjects as compared to equitably paid subjects, but the differences were not statistically significant. Moore (1968) presented data contrary to the equity prediction; however, she used the overpaid-by-circumstance induction, which is not particularly effective. Moore (1968: 101) indicated that the connection between inputs and outcomes was not successfully created, hence the divergence between this and other piece-rate studies.

Although there seems to be support for the piece-rate hypothesis, alternative explanations should be considered. First, the piece-rate system probably does not initially evoke feelings of overpayment. Most of the subjects had never worked piece-rate and no referent in these studies was available to translate the piece-rate into some effective wage. Therefore, at the time of employment the subjects probably did not feel overpaid, which is in contrast to a basic assumption of the piece-rate hypothesis.

A second dimension of the induction is whether it evokes perception of pay on a global or a unit basis. The hypothesis assumes perception of pay on a unit basis; that is, to reduce inequity one cannot increase production since each unit is overpaid. Therefore, by increasing quality, balance per unit can be achieved. However, it is not clear that subjects perceived pay on a unit basis. Most of the subjects were unfamiliar with a piece-rate system. Their work time was limited and specified in hours. Also, the fact that overpaid subjects reduced the number of units produced, and thus their pay over time (Andrews, 1967), suggests that they evaluated in a global sense the amount earned, the amount they could earn in the next time period, and how much they thought they should earn as a function of the induction or past wages. This conclusion does not mean the subject did not feel overpaid. The process of overpayment could have worked as follows: The subject was hired and told his qualifications were low in comparison to some Other who received the same rate. At that time, feelings of inequity would not have been salient because the 30-cent rate was not translatable into a common referent. After a period of work, a global or dollar amount would have been calculated and compared to some minimal acceptable rate. If the amount earned seemed reasonable, the induction should have taken effect. That is, the subject knew he could earn an acceptable wage and he knew that his qualifications were less than those of Other receiving the same potential wage, therefore, it was congruent to reduce quantity and to invest more time in improving the quality of his inputs. Andrews (1967) reported overpaid piece-rate workers did produce fewer pieces in their second hour of production than in the first hour.

The implication of asserting that the individual adopts a global versus unit assessment is that this assertion rejects the assumption that differences in quality and quantity from the overpaid group are a function of intrinsic characteristics of the payment scheme, as Adams has hypothesized. The differential emphasis between quality and quantity can be traced to the nature of the induction and characteristics of the task. Most of the overpaid inductions (Adams & Jacobsen, 1964; Lawler, 1968b) emphasized the importance of quality, and thus focused on one salient way to achieve equity; that is, the induction provided the subjects with an instrumental way to reduce inequity. The task became an added dimension in this explanation for two reasons. First, in both proofreading and interviewing tasks quality is an important component; it is difficult for someone proofreading not to recognize quality as an intrinsic part of task performance. Second, in both tasks quality and quantity are inversely related; and if the induction and task focus on quality, it is not surprising that while quality increases as a means of dissonance reduction for the overpaid subjects, quantity decreases. Goodman and Friedman (1969) examined the effect of differential emphasis on quantity or quality in a piece-rate induction, indicating that the perceived instrumentality of quality in resolving overpayment led to the amount of quantity or quality produced. That is, overpaid subjects increased quality or quantity if it was perceived as instrumental to reducing inequity, not because of some characteristic of the payment scheme.

There are two other studies relevant to the quantity-quality issue. A study by

Andrews (1967) used a task similar to most of the other studies but omitted statements emphasizing quality over quantity. Inequity was induced by varying the level of pay. The results seemed to suggest that overpaid piece-rate workers produce better quality and lower quantity. However, the quantity and quality differences between the experimental and control subjects were not statistically examined and were not very substantial. Therefore, this study does not provide strong support for Adams' basic hypothesis.

The second study, by Wood and Lawler (1970), also focused on whether subjects in an overpaid situation first reduce their outcomes to avoid inequity and as a consequence increase quality or first increase quality and as a consequence reduce quantity and their outcomes. A task was designed in which quantity was not dependent on quality. Wood and Lawler (1970) reported that overpaid subjects produced less than equitably paid subjects and that low productivity was not dependent on striving for increased quality. This study is not in conflict with the present paper's interpretation of the quality-quantity issue. It merely stated that given a task where quantity was not dependent on quality, and quantity was the focal output measure, then lower quantity in the overpaid situation was selected as a means of avoiding increased dissonance.

A third dimension of the induction which may reduce the internal validity of the piece-rate studies is the problem of devalued self-esteem. That is, as with the hourly studies, production differences may be a reaction to devalued self-esteem rather than to feelings of inequity. There are several studies which provide additional information on this problem. Lawler et al. (1968) used the unqualified induction in a piece-rate study but designed the study to cover several work periods rather than the single two-hour session found in most inequity experiments. He (1968) reported the modal finding—lower quantity-higher quality for overpaid subjects—in the initial session but no differences between overpay and controls in subsequent sessions, and also that feelings of self-qualification to perform the job increased over the three work sessions for the overpaid subjects. One interpretation of these finds is that subjects reduced productivity in the initial session as a reaction to devalued self-qualification, learned that they could perform the task, and then increased their feelings of confidence and produced more. Another interpretation, consistent with inequity theory, is that increasing quality and lowering the quantity in the initial work situation followed the hypothesized resolution strategy, but that the piece-rate system, which rewarded for increasing rather than reducing outputs, and the failure to repeat the inequity induction, caused the hypothesized differences not to reappear in the latter work sessions. The increase in feelings of self-qualification could reflect both a desire to increase inputs and a successful work experience. Therefore, either interpretation is tenable, and additional information is necessary to indicate a preferred choice.

On the self-qualification issue, Andrews (1967) used the same task and procedures as the other studies, but varied pay to induce inequity rather than to devaluate qualifications. His data supported Adams' hypothesis but the differences were not strong and did not provide definitive support to the inequity versus self-qualification argument. Because neither of these two studies demonstrated the importance of devalued self-esteem in explaining production variance in inequity studies, and because the supporting piece-rate studies tried to minimize the effect of reactions to devalued self-esteem, this alternative explanation of the piece-rate findings is not accepted.

Job security represents the last dimension which can affect internal validity of the piece-rate studies. The problem is exactly the same as in the hourly studies. The unqualified induction can increase feelings of job insecurity which can lead to higher quality productivity as a way of protecting the job. Adams and Jacobsen (1964) designed a study to deal with the job security issue by creating high and low job security conditions as well as the inequity experimental conditions. Because the high and low prospect condition did not contribute significantly to production variation, nor did it interact with the inequity conditions, job security was not considered a major confounding variable. Evans and Molinari (1970), employing a similar design, reported that for quality of work produced there was a weak inequity main effect $p > .10$) and no significant inequity-security interaction effect; for quantity of work produced there was a significant inequity-security interaction. They (1970) suggested that in their secure condition the inequity effect paralleled Adams' hypothesis, but did not hold in the insecure condition. Although the present experiment indicated that feelings of insecurity could affect performance in inequity experiments, it did not indicate that this dimension is important in evaluating the internal validity of the supporting piece-rate studies. First, the insecurity induction was quite strong in the Evans and Molinari (1970) study and it had no parallel in the studies supporting the hypothesis. Second, the secure condition in their experiment paralleled the studies under consideration and provided data supporting the piece-rate hypothesis. Also, most researchers in the piece-rate studies had been quite clear in advertising that the job was for a limited time to minimize any insecurity effect.

Summary   The data from the overpaid piece-rate studies supported Adams' hypothesis more consistently than that from the hourly studies. However, it is less clear that the data supported some of the assumptions underlying the hypothesis. It is unlikely that piece-rate subjects initially felt overpaid or conceptualized overpayment on a unit basis—two assumptions necessary to explain the differential emphasis on quantity verus quality for overpaid subjects.

Although the data did not support some of the mechanisms underlying the piece-rate hypothesis, the findings could be interpreted in the inequity framework. That is, overpaid subjects did experience inequity after an initial performance period and differentially emphasized quanity or quality outputs—whichever seemed more successful in resolving inequity. The problem with most piece-rate studies is that the perceived instrumentality of quantity or quality outputs was a function of artifacts in the induction and task rather than intrinsic characteristics of the payment system as suggested by Adams.

Underpaid-Hourly   The basic hypothesis is that underpaid subjects decrease their inputs to achieve an input-outcome balance. Masters (1968) showed that increasing outcomes is also a relevant resolution strategy in the underpaid hourly condition. Since his population—young children—and design differ greatly from the studies under consideration, Masters' study is not included.

The change in inputs can affect the quantity or quality of outputs; Adams does not specify which output dimension would change. The emphasis on quality or quantity seems a function of the instrumental task characteristics and the relationship between quantity and quality. If quality is an instrumental task requirement, as in proofreading, then decreased inputs will lead to lower quality. If quality and quantity are inversely related, then quantity will increase as quality decreases. On the other hand, if quantity and quality are positively related, decreased inputs will decrease quantity.

Four underpaid-hourly studies, using the same general design of the other studies, tested Adams' hypothesis. An experiment by Evan and Simmons (1969) and one by Pritchard et al. (1970) supported the underpaid hourly hypothesis. Another experiment by Evan and Simmons (1969) and one by Valenzi and Andrews (1969) did not support the underpaid hypothesis.

In the Evan and Simmons (1969: 234) experiment which did not support the hypothesis, the induction probably did not create strong feelings of inequity. It was thus not an effective test of the hypothesis. The differences in results between the Valenzi and Andrews (1969) and the supporting studies are more difficult to reconcile because many factors—populations, rates of pay, tasks, length of employment—were different.

While it is difficult to delineate why there were no differences among underpaid and equitably paid groups in the Valenzi and Andrews (1969) study, the following factors seem relatively clear for the Evan and Simmons (1969) and Pritchard et al. (1970) studies. First, underpaid subjects did express feelings of underpayment. Second, the time periods for both studies were short and clearly stated, thus minimizing feelings of insecurity. In the Valenzi and Andrews (1969) study subjects were to work for at least six weeks, a more ambiguous recruitment procedure. Third, the Pritchard et al. (1970) study used an unambiguous referent for creating feelings of underpayment—past work and wages to present work and wages. Thus it created a powerful induction. From these three factors it seemed reasonable to conclude that the Evan and Simmons (1969) and Pritchard et al. (1970) studies did provide some positive evidence for the underpaid-hourly hypothesis.

Summary There were not enough studies to adequately test the validity of the hourly underpaid hypothesis, but from the few existing studies there appears to be some preliminary support for the hypothesis.

Underpaid-Piece Rate The basic hypothesis is that underpaid subjects will produce a large number of low quality outputs because the production of low quality outputs permits increasing outcomes without substantially increasing inputs.

Two studies (Andrews, 1967; Lawler & O'Gara, 1967) successfully tested this hypothesis. Both reported greater quantity and lower quality from the underpaid subjects. Lawler and O'Gara (1967) also reported that the underpaid subjects perceived the job as interesting—an outcome—and at the same time simpler and less challenging—inputs—than the equitably paid subjects. The attitudinal differences were congruent with Adams' hypothesis that inequity resolution would occur by increasing outcomes and decreasing inputs. Although Moore (1968) examined the underpaid condition, the induction in that study did not provide a satisfactory test of the hypothesis.

Many problems in interpreting the other inequity-performance studies have been avoided in this payment condition. In addition, by introducing new measures to capture additional forms of the resolution process these studies tested the hypothesis better. Because these studies specifically demonstrated that underpaid subjects cognitively devalued their inputs and raised their outcomes, one is more certain that the underpaid subjects were attempting to resolve inequity.

Summary   The data from these studies supported Adams' hypothesis. Although more studies are needed to provide full confirmation of the hypothesis, the two cited studies were probably freer of alternative explanations than the other inequity-performance studies.

Other Inequity Resolution Studies

The majority of studies testing Adams' theory focused on the effect of inequity on performance. Recently other studies have been designed to test resolution strategies unrelated to job performance. These studies were distinguished from the inequity-performance studies in one or more of the following ways: (1) The inequity resolution process between Person and Other was examined. Inequity-performance studies have focused on the employer-Person relationship, with Other's identity generally ambiguous. (2) The dependent variable in these studies concerned the allocation of rewards rather than changes in performance to achieve equity. (3) The studies occurred in either a laboratory setting or in an on-going organization. The inequity-performance studies were experiments in a simulated work situation in the field.

Leventhal and his associates (see Leventhal et al., 1969a) have conducted most of the laboratory experiments in this area. Typically, subjects participated in an experiment to fulfill a class requirement. The subject was led to believe he was performing with a partner on a task for monetary rewards. The experimenter varied the inputs contributed by each member, and Other initially allocated the rewards after the task performance on an overpaid, equitably paid or underpaid basis. The subject could then reallocate the rewards, thus providing a test of inequity theory.

Findings from these studies supported the general proposition from Adams' model that Person will allocate rewards earned by the dyad in accordance with each member's contributions. Each study by Leventhal attempted to test some theoretical elaboration of this general proposition: for example, Leventhal et al. (1969a) showed that when Person could not change his inputs he was likely to reduce inequity by reallocating available rewards. Overpaid subjects reduced their share of outcomes; underpaid subjects increased their share. Leventhal et al. (1969b) indicated that alternative theoretical explanations were not as useful as the inequity model in explaining this reallocation behavior. Leventhal and Bergman (1969) examined conditions in which the general proposition did not hold, and found that under extreme conditions of underpayment, Person would reduce rather than try to increase his outcomes. Leventhal and Lane (1970), using a different strategy to refine the hypothesis, indicated that sex was a moderator of the inequity resolution process.

Lane and Messé (1969), using a similar design, reported some parallel findings. Given a task where inputs were equal, outcomes were most frequently allocated on an equal basis. Other variables which related to the selection of equal distribution of outcomes included:(1) the sex composition of the dyad—heterogeneity was associated with role symmetric choices, or, equal allocation of outcomes; (2) sex of chooser—females made more role symmetric choices; (3) whether choices were made publicly or privately—the former was more associated with role symmetric choices; and (4) personality—the greater the concern for others the more role symmetric choices. In a second experiment Lane and Messé (1969) varied the inputs of the chooser and receiver in the dyad and analyzed the allocation of rewards. The inputs of the receiver—high or low—seemed more important in affecting allocation of rewards than those of the chooser. That is, when the receiver's inputs were low the chooser allocated in his own favor, regradless of whether his own inputs were high or low. Also, there was some evidence that the chooser would distort the levels of his inputs as a way of alleviating feelings of dissonance. When choosers worked one-third as long as receivers, about 40 percent said they worked about the same as receivers and preferred a more equal distribution of outcomes.

These findings are directed to hypotheses not previously tested and deal with critical dimensions in the theory. For example, the definition of relevant inputs affects the resolution of inequity. Leventhal extended theoretically and empirically some aspects of this definition process, arguing that the locus of control for Other's behavior affects Person's assessment of Other's inputs. If Person believes Other operates under involuntary constraints, Person is more likely to attribute higher inputs to him. This hypothesis is based on the assumptions that Person's perception of inputs is affected by the difference between actual and expected performance and that Person expects lower performance when constraints on Other are high. Leventhal and Michaels (1970) varied the external constraints by telling Person that Other had useful or nonuseful training for a particular task. As predicted, with performance held constant, individuals with nonuseful training were considered more deserving of rewards than those with useful training.

These laboratory studies do represent a new direction in inequity research, but they have several limitations which should be noted. First, pay, the main outcome in the experiments, does not seem very relevant (Leventhal & Michaels, 1969). Subjects were recruited to participate in the study and course credits were the initial payments. At the conclusion of the experiment subjects returned the money they subsequently received. These conditions are not conducive to making pay a relevant outcome.

Second, the mechanism for reallocating rewards, a critical dimension in testing for inequity resolution strategies, lack credibility. For example, in Leventhal et al. (1969b), subjects were told that the high-scoring member of their dyad would divide the money after the task was finished, but that the low-scoring member could modify the initial allocation. The subjects were then told that the two members of the dyad tied in their scores and a coin was flipped to determine who would allocate the money. The other member of the dyad, who really was nonexistent, won and then the subject was told that the winner had decided on the allocation himself or randomly selected the basis of allocation. Allocation occurred and then the subject reallocated. The low relevance of the pay, and the low credibility of this reallocation induction as further evidenced by the fact that some subjects recognized the deception (Leventhal & Michaels, 1969) increased the salience of experimental demand characteristics and thus chances for experimental error.

A third problem concerns how well the induction creates perceptions that one's inputs are related to outcomes. This relationship is basic to testing Adams' hypotheses. Because the subject had little time in these studies to test how his inputs were related to outcomes and because prior to task performance the subject knew that the other member of the dyad could determine his rewards, it was likely that his outcomes would not be perceived as directly dependent on his inputs (Leventhal et al., 1969b).

Weick and Nesset (1968) in using a different design to examine the inequity resolution process, developed a force choice format which contains 10 pairs of hypothetical work situations, the situations varying in degrees of inequity. Subjects have to select the preferred work situation and then to indicate preferred resolution strategies to make the least preferred choice in the pair more comfortable. Analysis of the resolution strategies indicated subjects were more likely to change individual circumstances by increasing effort than interpersonal circumstances by finding a new comparison Other. This was consistent with Adams' (1965: 294) hypothesis. Seeking higher wages was the most preferred strategy for underpaid subjects. It is interesting that this alternative had not been examined in the inequity resolution studies. Subjects did select quitting as an alternative, which seems contrary to Adams' hypothesis that leaving the field would occur only when other strategies were blocked. However, because the instrument permitted responding to more than one resolution strategy, it is not surprising to see that leaving the field was selected as an option, and therefore, Adams' hypothesis about withdrawal was not adequately tested.

Weick and Nesset's (1968) force choice instrument represents a new approach in testing inequity theory hypotheses. Refinements of this methodology would be important for assessing the validity of inequity theory because the use of different methods to test similar hypotheses is a very powerful validation strategy. Some of the limitations of this force choice instrument were discussed by Weick and Nesset (1968: 414). Other additions, such as assessing the instrument's reliability and using an independent criterion, would improve the instrument's validity.

In a correlational study in an organization, Penner (1967), directly testing dimensions of Adams' hypothesis, indicated that propensity to leave the company was twice as likely for those individuals who perceived their salary as inequitable. Although there has been other research on the satisfaction, absenteeism, and turnover relationships (Hulin, 1968), these studies were not direct tests of Adams' theory. Therefore more work is needed to test preferences for alternative resolution strategies in the field.

Summary   Studies in this section focused on inequity resolution between Person and Other, considered resolution strategies other than changing performance, and used designs different from the inequity-performance studies. The basic proposition tested is that Person allocates outcomes to himself and Other proportional to their respective inputs. The effects of the source of inequity, of how much control Other had over his inputs, and of Person's sex on the distribution of outcomes between Person and Other were investigated. Redefinition of Other's inputs and anticipation of future behavior from Other were other processes mediating the distribution of outcomes. These findings seemed congruent with Adams' theory, and in some cases (Weick & Nesset, 1968; Leventhal & Michaels, 1970) offered extensions to the theory. Additional studies are needed, however, to provide a more critical analysis.

CONDITIONS OF INEQUITY

Other studies which bear on Adams' theory concern determinants of feelings of inequity and the psychological state of inequity. The role of the comparison Other as a determinant of inequity has received surprisingly little attention. There have been field studies which indicated that an imbalance between Person and Other led to feelings of inequity (Penner, 1967; Lawler, 1965); these provided a confirmation of a basic assumption in the theory. An experiment by Wicker and Bushweiler (1970) indicated that the degree of liking between Person and Other could moderate perceptions of inequity during an exchange in this dyad. However, the complex processes leading to the selection of a comparison Other had not been pursued. Weick and Nesset (1968) made the most significant advance in this area, distinguishing between three comparison conditions of equity: own equity—Person had a balanced input-outcome ratio (L/L, low inputs-low outcomes) but it is unbalanced in regard to Other (H/L, high inputs-low outcomes); comparison equity—Person had an equal input-outcome ratio with Other but both were unbalanced (H/L, H/L); own comparison equity—Person had a balanced input-outcome ratio which equaled Other's (L/L, H/H). Weick and Nesset's (1968) findings indicated that subjects chose equitable conditions interms of Other's input-outcome ratio (H/L, H/L) rather than in terms of their own input-outcome ratio. Subjects also chose situations where their own input-outcome ratio was in balance and equal to Other's ratio rather than a situation of own equity (L/L, H/L). Other analyses indicated that overpayment relative to one's own inputs (L/H, L/H) was preferred to overpayment in terms of Other's inputs

(L/L, H/L). This study was especially important as the first that empirically examined some of the alternative comparison models, and focused on Person's input-outcome ratio as a source of inequity without reference to Other.

There are some very preliminary findings on the effect of past and future input-outcome ratios on the evaluation of present feelings of inequity, for example, Pritchard et al. (1970) indicated that past input-outcome ratio could induce present feelings of inequity. Although there is some data indicating that optimism about future outcomes is associated with present feelings of satisfaction (Goodman, 1966), the evidence supporting the effect of future input-outcome ratios on inducing present feelings of inequity is not yet clear (Lawler, 1970).

Other factors, such as characteristics of the individual and the organization providing the outcomes, can affect feelings of inequity. Penner (1967) indicated that high performers were more likely to feel dissatisfied with their pay; high inputs were more likely to lead to feelings of inequity. Klein and Maher (1966), using education as an input, indicated that college educated respondents were more likely to feel dissatisfied with their pay than noncollege respondents.

Organizational factors also seem to affect feelings of inequity. Penner (1967) reported that when pay and performance were not perceived as related, feelings of dissatisfaction with pay would more likely occur. In equity terms this reward system did not reward increased inputs for performance, and therefore, inequity resulted. A corollary finding was that when pay was determined by budgetary constraints rather than by inputs, dissatisfaction with pay resulted. Probably the most provocative finding from Penner's study was that increasing one organizational reward, like amount of freedom, could affect feelings of inequity about other rewards, like pay. Implicit in this finding was a hypothesis from Adams' theory which asserts that outcomes are additive. Although Penner's (1967) study represented an important test in the field of Adams' work, it lacked some important control procedures. For example, variables such as amount of pay, organizational level, and type of job should have been controlled in an analysis of the relationship between amount of freedom and feelings about pay. Since these controls were absent in Penner's (1967) analysis, the findings must be considered tentative.

The last set of studies to be reviewed concerns the psychological state of inequity. Adams argued that inequity is a source of tension which an individual is motivated to reduce. To some extent, all the studies confirming any inequity hypotheses are testing this assumption. Some studies, however, directly measured the affective state associated with inequity, and confirmed Adams' basic contention (Leventhal et al., 1969a; Pritchard et al., 1970). Pritchard et al.'s (1970) research went beyond confirming the inequity and dissatisfaction relationship to indicate that inequity with one input-outcome ratio may generalize to other outcomes. For example, their data indicated that subjects in a condition of pay inequity exhibited lower job satisfaction than equitably paid subjects.

Another hypothesis in inequity theory—that the threshold for underpayment is lower than for overpayment—received fairly consistent support from different investigators (Andrews, 1967; Weick & Nesset, 1968).

Summary   Studies in this section extended our understanding of inequity theory by examining how the comparison process affected feelings of inequity, individual and organizational factors which affected feelings of inequity, as well as some aspects of the state of inequity. Although none of the findings presented seriously challenged Adams' theory, more, better controlled studies are needed to adequately test the validity of the hypotheses discussed in this section.

METHODOLOGICAL ISSUES

Recruitment-Selection

There are a number of important moderators—ability (Bass, 1968; Moore, 1968); past work experience (Friedman & Goodman, 1967); past wages (Andrews, 1967); need preferences (Lawler & O'Gara, 1967)—which can affect interpretation of inequity studies. Some moderators, like need for money represent an alternative explanation for variation in the dependent variables, and therefore must be controlled to assess the role of the inequity explanation. For example individuals high in need for money may work hard in a piece-rate experiment not as a means of reducing inequity but to satisfy a need for more money. Although it can be argued that these moderators should be equally distributed across experimental conditions, given the relatively small sample size in most studies and the fact that despite random assignment the moderators often are not equally distributed (Goodman & Friedman, 1968), it seems desirable to measure and analyze the effects of the relevant moderators. The fact that few investigations (Lawler et al., 1968, is an exception) have done this casts doubt on the internal validity of the studies we have examined.

A recruitment-selection bias is also relevant for interpreting the external validity or generalizability of some inequity studies. For example, since the method of payment is often advertised during recruitment, there is probably a differential selection process for hourly and piece-rate studies, with the latter selecting out more subjects because of the ambiguity of how much they can make (Evans & Molinari, 1970). Although this differential selection does not limit the internal validity of a particular study, it does limit one's ability to compare hourly and piece-rate studies (Adams, 1936b). One solution to this problem would be to examine the differences between people who respond and do not respond to the simulated advertisements about either hourly or piece-rate jobs.

Induction

The induction is an important experimental event for explaining differences among studies. Inequity theory postulates an imbalance between Person's outcomes and inputs in comparison to Other as a condition of inequity. To successfully operationalize this concept, however, one must deal with the following cognitions (Vroom, 1964):

1   Person's evaluation of his inputs.
2   Person's perception of the relevance of his inputs for task performance.
3   Person's perception of E's perception of his inputs.

4 Person's perception of Other's outcome-input ratio.

5 Person's perception of future outcomes.

6 Person's perception of the outcomes relative to alternative outcomes—his past outcomes—the outcomes for this class of tasks, and so forth.

7 The relative importance Person attaches to using 4, 5, and 6 as comparison points.

These conditions are basic to assessing the internal validity of any inequity experiment. If, for example, the subject selects comparison Others different from those intended by the experimenter, then the substantive interpretation of an experiment is limited, and since the comparison Other in most experiments is ambiguously specified, this particular problem is likely to occur. Or subjects could define relevant outcomes differently from the experimenter. Because many of the studies are advertised as part of some research and because helping in research has been identified as an additional outcome which affects performance differences in inequity studies (Heslin & Blake, 1969), failure to control on definition of outcomes introduces a source of experimental error.

None of the studies reviewed recognized most of these conditions in specifying their experimental design; therefore, another source of error has not been controlled. These conditions could be controlled either by directly building them into the induction or measuring these cognitions and including them in the analysis.

Developing an adequate control group, a problem relevant to inequity resolution studies, is another aspect of the induction which deserves attention. The equitable condition, characterized by an absence of tension, has been the modal control group. At issue is the source and degree of motivation exhibited by subjects in this group. One equity study (Friedman & Goodman, 1967) showed that equitably paid control subjects, as a way of confirming their valued abilities, were actually highly motivated to produce. Although this problem has been identified by others (Weick, 1967b), it has not captured the attention of researchers, concerned with inequity. The Pritchard et al. (1970) study illustrated how the subject's own performance could provide a baseline for assessing subsequent feelings of inequity. Also, by introducing various levels of inequity—high, medium, and low overpayment—more refined contrasts could be made and assumptions about the similarity between an overpaid and equitable induction could be avoided.

Task

The experimental task represents another source of error which should be controlled. The design of future studies, especially when performance is a major dependent variable, must reflect the following problems found in past inequity studies. First, if the hypothesis indicates a differential emphasis on quality or quantity, tasks in which these two are relatively independent should be developed. This issue is particularly important in studies where one wants to know if the subject is reducing quantity or increasing quality. Some recent studies (Wood

& Lawler, 1970; Wiener, 1970) have reported tasks where quantity and quality are independent.

Second, if the subject modifies the task in a way unintended by the experimenter (Weick, 1967a), internal validity can be reduced. Although there are no data available to assess the effect of task modifiability in these studies, it does represent a problem in interpreting inequity studies. For example, it is possible for the subject to modify some of the scoring procedures in the questionnaire or proofreading tasks used in inequity-performance studies. The problem is how to evaluate the modification. On one hand, it might represent a new input and it should then be measured. However, it would be difficult to add this input to other measures of outputs such as the number of units produced and form some common index of contributions to the job. On the other hand, if this modification increases productivity, counting this additional productivity may not reflect an increase in inputs; the subject may merely have found a more efficient way to increase outputs without additional effort.

A third and related problem concerns the need for an independent assessment of the relationship between inputs and outputs for different tasks. Basic to the inequity-resolution studies in the strategy of modifying inputs to reduce inequity. Outputs are taken to be measures of inputs. The problem is to what extent do the number of outputs—questionnaires for example—reflect the amount of inputs—effort—expended. If the amount of effort per unit varies with the level of performance and type of task, then evaluation of inputs from outputs becomes a less desirable measure. Unfortunately, there is no evidence on this particular point, and therefore, the issue can only be raised for consideration in future studies.

The fourth task-related problem concerns the amount of time allocated for task performance. There has been considerable variation in the studies reviewed; some took less than 10 minutes (Leventhal et al., 1969b), others took more than 30 hours (Pritchard et al., 1970). Although there do not seem to be any clear differences between studies which support or do not support the inequity hypotheses on the time dimension, there is evidence that the time dimension is relevant in assessing the validity of inequity studies. For example, change over time in subject behavior within an experimental session (Andrews, 1967) was important in assessing whether subjects were overpaid in piece-rate studies. The fact that some studies (Lawler et al., 1968; Pritchard et al., 1970) have not supported the inequity hypotheses over several experimental sessions raises questions about the effectiveness of the theory or the induction over time. In any case, it would seem desirable to use multiple sessions over time in future studies—most studies have been single sessions—and to systematically assess behavior over time both within and between sessions and to identify factors like differential task success which affect performance over time.

Measurement and Data Analysis

There are a number of problems of measurement and analysis which confound the interpretation of the reviewed studies and should be eliminated in future studies. First, measures of the effectiveness of the induction must be introduced immediately after the induction. This would require one experimental group that would be tested after the induction but would not complete the experimental session. In many of the reviewed studies this measurement was taken after the experiment and thus was contaminated by the experimental experience. Second, and most important, inequity theory focuses on the complex interrelationship among multiple cognitions. Most of the research reviewed has dealt with only a few cognitions. One contribution to research would be to develop additional measures using different methods to capture the multiple cognitions used to define inequity (Zedeck & Smith, 1968) and to resolve it.

Problems in working with a small sample size, with subject mortality, and with weak statistical techniques which characterized some of the earlier studies (Arrowood, 1961; Goodman & Friedman, 1968), seem to have been avoided in the most recent studies (Pritchard et al., 1970). Thus it seems that data analysis issues have been recognized and probably will receive continued attention in future studies.

THEORETICAL OVERVIEW

The purpose of this paper is to examine the empirical evidence testing Adams' theory of inequity. It is important in making this assessment to review all the varied propositions in the theory, not just inequity-performance; for this alone does not permit an adequate evaluation of the theory.

Three general conclusions about the relative validity can be offered. First, some assumptions and hypotheses derived from the theory have relatively clear empirical support; they are: inequity is a source of tension (Pritchard et al., 1970); the greater the inequity the greater the drive to reduce it—all supporting studies; input-outcome discrepancies relative to Other are a source of inequity (Weick & Nesset, 1968); the threshold for underpayment is lower than for overpayment (Leventhal et al., 1969b); Person maximizes positive outcomes in inequity resolution (Leventhal & Michaels, 1979); Person allocates rewards in a dyad in porportion to each member's contributions (Leventhal et al., 1969a); underpaid piece-rate subjects produce more than equitably paid subjects (Lawler & O'Gara, 1967).

Second, there are a set of assumptions and hypotheses which have tentative empirical support. The tentative label is applied to these hypotheses either because there have not been enough tests of the hypothesis or because the evidence is mixed. In this latter category, we have argued that the supporting evidence is greater than the nonsupporting evidence. Hypotheses in this second set include: Person will resist changing input-outcome cognitions central to his self-concept (Levanthal & Lane, 1970); Person will resist changing his comparison Other once Other has become a referent (Weick & Nesset, 1968); overpaid-hourly subjects produce more than equitably paid subjects (Pritchard et al., 1970); overpaid piece-rate subjects produce less quantity and higher quality than equitably paid subjects (Adams & Jacobsen, 1964); underpaid-hourly subjects will invest lower inputs than equitably paid subjects (Evan & Simmons, 1969).

Third, the following are a set of hypotheses which either have not been tested, or have been tested in a single study with poor controls; if input-outcome discrepancies are the same for Person and Other no inequity results; inequity is greater when both inputs and outcomes are discrepant for Other; inputs and outcomes are additive; within certain limits of inequity Person manipulates inputs and outcomes to reduce inequity; Person will resist changing cognitions about his own inputs and outcomes more than about Other's inputs and outcomes; Person will leave the field when inequity is high and other reduction strategies are unavailable.

The evidence seems to provide initial support for some of Adams' propositions, but the critical test of the theory will depend on: (1) empirical support for the propositions listed above that are not fully tested; (2) elaboration of conceptual areas not fully specified by Adams to generate new propositions for testing; and (3) contrasting of inequity theory with other theories to evaluate its comparative advantages in prediction.

Although the general concept of inequity has been well stated by Adams, the components of perceived inequity have not been theoretically specified in sufficient detail. One important problem concerns the process by which inputs and outcomes are defined as relevant. Advancing our knowledge in this area would permit identification of determinants of inequity and prediction of inequity. Weick (1966) and Leventhal and Michaels (1970) have provided some provocative thinking about the input-outcome specification problem which should stimulate further theorizing and research.

A related problem concerns how information is combined when Person evaluates his input-outcome ratio. Person must deal with information not only about his own multiple inputs and outcomes, but also about input-outcome ratios of Others. How is this information combined? Einhorn (1970a, 1970b) has developed a conceptual and operational procedure for testing whether people use linear or nonlinear models when combining information. This type of research could be applied to inequity studies to provide a better understanding of how different methods of combining information lead to feelings of inequity.

Another problem subsumed in the inequity concept is the selection and use of a referent in evaluating one's inputs and outcomes. The major theoretical focus has been derived from social comparison theory and Other has been critical in the determination of inequity. There are, however, other relevant referents in inequity evaluation such as Person's concept of his own self-worth, past input-outcome ratios, and future input-outcome ratios. The critical issue, then, is specifying a theoretical framework to permit the identification and weighting of multiple referents used in evaluating the input-outcome ratio.

The inequity resolution process requires further elaboration and testing before the utility of the theory can be assessed. The basic issues for both cognitive and behavioral resolution modes are how are salient resolution strategies defined and which strategies are most likely to be evoked. Expectancy theory (Lawler, 1970) might provide a general framework for predicting resolution processes. The expectancy and valence components could be defined for each resolution strategy and the expected force associated with each strategy assessed.

Testing competing hypotheses from inequity theory and other theoretical perspectives provides another way to assess its comparative validity. For example, expectancy theory (Porter & Lawler, 1968), which focuses primarily on the perceived relationship between behavior and valued rewards, would not predict increased performance for overpaid subjects in the hourly condition since performance is not related to pay; inequity theory does predict increased performance, Lawler (1968a) has argued that the reported performance differences in the hourly study are attributed to the characteristics of the induction, and that expectancy theory represents a preferred theoretical perspective. We would argue that there is an inequity effect in those studies, although expectancy theory probably is a more powerful long-run predictor. Pritchard et al.'s (1970) study suggests a future model for comparing both theories; it examines different levels of inequity in payment systems with different expectancies that pay and performance are related.

The concept of insufficient rewards (Weick, 1967b) represents another theoretical position which contrasts with inequity theory predictions. Inequity theory predicts no increase in effort from underpaid subjects in the hourly condition; the insufficient rewards concept predicts increased effort. A design incorporating different levels of underpayment would permit a test of these contrasting hypotheses. We would expect inequity theory predictions to be supported at moderate levels of underpayment, and insufficient reward predictions at greater levels.

Research on the norm of reciprocity (Pruit, 1968), the norm of social responsibility (Goranson & Berkowitz, 1966; Berscheid et al., 1968; Greenglass, 1969), or the belief in a just world (Simmons & Lerner, 1968) poses an interesting challenge to the development of inequity theory. To what extent, for example, is there a norm of equity? How would such a norm differ from the reciprocity or social responsibility norms? Levanthal et al (1969b) have made some preliminary attempts to empirically separate these concepts; however, there seems to be little interchange in the development of these three perspectives. Messé et al. (1970) examined the effect of inequity in the resolution of interpersonal conflict; another potentially useful area to expand inequity theory.

Until research in the above areas is well developed, it will be difficult to delimit with certainty the relevance of Adams' theory for organizational processes. However, there are some indications of directions in which the theory may contribute. First, and its most general contribution, inequity theory offers a relatively simple model to explain and to predict an individual's feelings about various organizational rewards. Although the experimental studies have focused primarily on feelings of inequity about pay, the model seems generalizable to other types of rewards such as promotion, supervisor support, status (Stephenson

& White, 1968), and to other types of relationships such as that of buyer-seller (Leventhal et al., 1970). The primary contribution of the model will certainly not be in explaining performance. The data at the present time only indicate a very short term effect of inequity on performance. Also, it is important to remember that variations in performance represent only one inequity resolution made. Neither the theory nor present research indicates it is the dominant resolution strategy. Unfortunately, the large number of studies in the inequity-performance area have led some people to think of Adams' theory as primarily a motivation-performance model.

Second, the delineation of the comparison model an individual uses in evaluating his input-outcome ratio should be relevant for organizational decision makers involved in determining appropriate levels of rewards. For example, identifying Others Person considers in evaluating his pay should indicate what groups of individuals should be included in a salary survey, one mechanism for setting levels of pay.

Another contribution of the inequity model to administration may be in the area of the interchangeability of rewards. A topic that needs further empirical analysis concerns how an individual combines his outcomes and inputs. This type of research should aid organizational decision makers by identifying what kind of rewards like freedom have an additive effect of other rewards like pay, and which rewards can be substituted for others (Penner, 1967).

Finally, research on allocation of rewards suggests that achieving balance between input and outcome is an important decision rule. However, there may be alternative forces or competing decision rules in organizations that conflict with an equitable allocation. For example, an experiment by Rothbart (1968) indicated supervisors consider competing models of inequity and of the relative effectiveness of different reward-punishment schedules in allocation of possible outcomes. Identifying individual or structural factors which evoke these competing decision rules and their consequences would represent another contribution of the theory.

REFERENCES

Adams, J. Stacy. Toward an understanding of inequity. *Journal of Abnormal and Social Psychology,* 1963, **67,** 422–36. (a)

Adams, J. Stacy. Wage inequities, productivity and work quality, *Industrial Relations,* 1963, **3,** 9–16. (b)

Adams, J. Stacy. Inequity in social exchange. In L. Berkowitz (ed.), *Advances in Experimental Social Psychology,* vol. 2. New York: Academic Press, 1965, 267–300.

Adams, J. Stacy. Effects of overpayment: Two comments on Lawler's paper. *Journal of Personality and Social Psychology,* 1968, **10,** 315–16.

Adams, J. Stacy, and Jacobsen, Patricia R. Effects of wage inequities on work quality. *Journal of Abnormal and Social Psychology,* 1964, **69,** 19–25.

Adams, J. Stacy, and Rosenbaum, William B. The relationship of worker productivity to cognitive dissonance about wage inequities. *Journal of Applied Psychology,* 1962, **46,** 161–64.

Anderson, Bo, and Shelly, Robert. A replication of Adams' experiment and a theoretical formulation. *Acta Sociologica,* 1970, **13,** 1–10.

Andrews, I. R. Wage inequity and job performance: An experimental study. *Journal of Applied Psychology,* 1967, **51,** 39–45.

Andrews, I. R., and Valenzi, E. Overpay inequity or self-image as a worker: A critical examination of an experimental induction procedure. *Organizational Behavior and Human Performance,* 1970, **53,** 22–27.

Arrowood, Arthur J. Some effects on productivity of justified and unjustified levels of reward under public and private conditions. Doctoral dissertation. University of Minnesota, 1961.

Bass, Bernard M. Ability, values, and concepts of equitable salary increases in exercise compensation. *Journal of Applied Psychology,* 1968, **52,** 299–303.

Berscheid, Ellen, Boye, David, and Walster, Elaine. Retaliation as a means of restoring equity. *Journal of Personality and Social Psychology,* 1968, **10,** 370–76.

Einhorn, Hillel J. The use of nonlinear, noncompensatory models in decision making. *Psychological Bulletin,* 1970, **73,** 221–30 (a)

Einhorn, Hillel J. Use of nonlinear, noncompensatory models as a function of task and amount of information. *Organizational Behavior and Human Performance,* 1970, **6,** 1–27. (b)

Evan, William M., and Simmons, Roberta G. Organizational effects of inequitable rewards: Two experiments in status inconsistency. *Administrative Science Quarterly,* 1969, **14,** 224–237.

Evans, Martin G., and Molinari, Larry. Equity piece-rate overpayment, and job-security: Some effects on performance. *Journal of Applied Psychology,* 1970, **54,** 105–14.

Friedman, Abraham, and Goodman, Paul S. Wage inequity, self-qualifications, and productivity. *Organizational Behavior and Human Performance,* 1967, **2,** 406–17.

Goodman, Paul S. A study of time perspective: Measurement and correlates. Doctoral dissertation, Cornell University, 1966.

Goodman, Paul S., and Friedman, Abraham. An examination of the effect of wage inequity in the hourly condition. *Organizational Behavior and Human Performance,* 1968, **3,** 340–52.

Goodman, Paul S., and Friedman, Abraham. An examination of quantity and quality of performance under conditions of overpayment in piece rate. *Organizational Behavior and Human Performance,* 1969, **4,** 365–74.

Goranson, Richard E., and Berkowitz, Leonard. Reciporcity and responsibility reactions to prior help. *Journal of Personality and Social Psychology,* 1966, **3,** 227–32.

Greenglass, Esther R. Effects of prior help and hindrance on willingness to help another: Reciprocity or social responsibility, *Journal of Personality and Social Psychology,* 1969, **11,** 224–31.

Heslin, Richard, and Blake, Brian. Performance as a function of payment, commitment and task interest. *Psychonomic Science,* 1969, **15,** 323–24.

Homans, George. *Social behavior.* New York: Harcourt, Brace & World, 1961.

Hulin, Charles L. Effects of changes in job-satisfaction levels on employee turnover. *Journal of Applied Psychology, 1968,* **52,** 122–26.

Jacques, E. *Equitable payment.* New York: Wiley, 1961.

Kalt, Neil C. Temporal resolution of inequity: An exploratory investigation. Doctoral dissertation. University of Illinois, 1969.

Klein, S. M., and Maher, J. R. Education level and satisfaction with pay. *Personnel Psychology*, 1966, **19**, 195–208.

Lane, Irving M., and Messé, Lawrence A. Equity and distribution of rewards. Working paper, Michigan State University, 1969.

Lawler, Edward E. Manager's perceptions of their subordinates' pay and their superiors' pay. *Personnel Psychology*, 1965, **18**, 413–22.

Lawler, Edward E. Equity theory as a predictor of productivity and work quality. *Psychological Bulletin*, 1968, **70**, 596–610. (a)

Lawler, Edward E. Effects of hourly overpayment on productivity and work quality. *Journal of Personality and Social Psychology*, 1968, **10**, 306–13. (b)

Lawler, Edward E. *Pay and organizational effectiveness*, New York: McGraw-Hill, 1970.

Lawler, Edward E., and O'Gara, Paul W. Effects of inequity produced by underpayment on work output, work quality, and attitudes toward work. *Journal of Applied Psychology*, 1967, **51**, 403–10.

Lawler, Edward E., Koplin, Cary A., Young, Terence F., and Fadem, Joel A. Inequity reduction over time in an induced overpayment situation. *Organizational Behavior and Human Performance*, 1968, **3**, 253–68.

Leventhal, Gerald S., and Anderson, David. Self-interest and the maintenance of equity. *Journal of Personality and Social Psychology*, 1970, **15**, 57–62.

Leventhal, Gerald S., and Bergman, James T. Self-depriving behavior as a response to unprofitable inequity. *Journal of Experimental and Social Psychology*, 1969, **5**, 153–71.

Leventhal, Gerald S., and Lane, Douglas W. Sex, age, and equity behavior. *Journal of Personality and Social Psychology*, 1970, **15**, 312–16.

Leventhal, Gerald S., and Michaels, James W. Extending the equity model: Perception of inputs and allocation of reward as a function of duration and quantity of performance. *Journal of Personality and Social Psychology*, 1969, **12**, 303–09.

Leventhal, Gerald S., and Michaels, James W. Locus of cause and equity motivation as determinants of reward allocation. Working paper, North Carolina State University, 1970.

Leventhal, Gerald S., Allen, John, and Kemelgor, Bruce. Reducing inequity by reallocating rewards. *Psychonomic Science*, 1969, **14**, 295–96. (a)

Leventhal, Gerald S., Weiss, Thomas, and Long, Gary. Equity, reciprocity, and reallocating rewards in the dyad. *Journal of Personality and Social Psychology*, 1969, **13**: 300–05. (b)

Leventhal, Gerald S., Younts, Charles M., and Lund, Adrian K. Tolerance for inequity in buyer-seller relationships. Working paper, North Carolina State University, 1970.

Masters, John C. Effects of social comparison upon subsequent self-reinforcement behavior in children. *Journal of Personality and Social Psychology*, 1968, **10**, 391–401.

Messé, Lawrence, Dawson, Jack, and Lane, Irving. Equity as a mediator of the effect of reward level on behavior in the prisoner's dilemma game. Working paper, Michigan State University, 1970.

Moore, Loretta M. Effects of wage inequities on work attitudes and performance. Masters thesis, Wayne State University, 1968.

Penner, Donald. *A study of causes and consequences of salary satisfaction*. Crotonville, N.Y.: General Electric Behavioral Research Service, 1967.

Porter, Lyman, and Lawler, Edward E. *Managerial attitudes and performance.* Homewood, Ill.: Irwin, 1968.

Pritchard, Robert D. Equity theory: A review and critique. *Organizational Behavior and Human Performance,* 1969, **4**, 176–211.

Pritchard, Robert D., Jorgenson, Dale O., & Dunnette, Marvin D. The effects of perceptions of equity and inequity on worker performance and satisfaction. Working paper, Purdue University, 1970.

Pruit, Dean. Reciprocity and credit building in a laboratory dyad. *Journal of Personality and Social Psychology,* 1968, **8**, 143–47.

Rothbart, Myron. Effects of motivation, equity and compliance on the use of reward and punishment. *Journal of Personality and Social Psychology, 1968,* **9**, 353–62.

Simmons, Carolyn, and Lerner, Melvin. Altruism as a search for justice. *Journal of Personality and Social Psychology,* 1968, **9**, 216–25.

Stephenson, G. M., and White, J. H. An experimental study of some effects of injustice on children's moral behavior. *Journal of Experimental Social Psychology,* 1968, **4**, 367–83.

Valenzi, E. R., and Andrews, I. R. Effect of underpay and overpay inequity when tested with a new induction procedure. In *Proceedings,* 77th Annual Convention. Washington, D. C.: American Psychological Association, 1969, 593–94.

Vroom, Victor. *Work and motivation.* New York: Wiley, 1964.

Weick, Karl E. The concept of equity in the perception of pay. *Administrative Science Quarterly,* 1966, **11**, 414–39.

Weick, Karl E. Organizations in the laboratory. In Victor Vroom (ed.), *Methods of organization research.* Pittsburgh: University of Pittsburgh, 1967. Pp. 1–56 (a).

Weick, Karl E. Dissonance and task enhancement: A problem for compensation theory, *Organizational Behavior and Human Performance,* 1967, **2**, 189–207. (b)

Weick, Karl E., and Nesset, Bonna. Preferences among forms of equity. *Organizational Behavior and Human Performance,* 1968, **3**, 400–16.

Wicker, Allan W., and Bushweiler, Gary. Perceived fairness and pleasantness of social exchange situations: Two factorial studies of inequity. *Journal of Personality and Social Psychology,* 1970, **15**, 63–75.

Wiener, J. The effect of task and ego oriented performance on two kinds of overcompensation inequity. *Organizational Behavior and Human Performance,* 1970, **5**, 191–208.

Wood, Ian, and Lawler, Edward E. Effects of piece-rate overpayment on productivity. *Journal of Applied Psychology,* 1970, **54**, 234–38.

Zedeck, Sheldon, and Smith, Patricia Cain. A psychophysical determination of equitable payment: A methodological study. *Journal of Applied Psychology,* 1968, **52**, 343–47.

QUESTIONS FOR DISCUSSION

1 Using the analytical framework proposed in Chapter 1, how would you evaluate Adams's theory of inequity?

2 How would you compare equity theory to Herzberg's dual-factor theory?

3 How would you evaluate the research evidence in support of equity theory?

4 Under this theoretical formulation, why would one's peers be so important in determining individual job satisfaction?

5 What major factors differentiate equity theory from the three theories covered earlier?

6 Why has equity theory been largely ignored by many managers and writers in organizational behavior?
7 What can line managers learn from equity theory that could help them to improve their supervisory abilities?

Chapter 6

Expectancy/Valence Theory

OVERVIEW

We now come to the fifth and final major theory of motivation and work behavior to be reviewed here. This theory also goes under several names, including expectancy theory, instrumentality theory, path-goal theory, and valence-instrumentality-expectancy (VIE) theory. We shall use the term "expectancy/valence theory" as being more descriptive of the two major variables of the formulation.

Expectancy/valence theory is the second "process" theory to be considered in this book (after equity theory). It can be classified as a process theory—in contrast to a content theory—primarily because it attempts to identify relationships among variables in a dynamic state as they affect individual behavior. This systems orientation is in direct contrast to the content theories which have attempted largely to specify correlates of motivated behavior. In expectancy/valence theory, like equity theory, it is the relationship among inputs that is the basic focal point rather than the inputs themselves.

The expectancy/valence model is also a cognitive theory of motivation (see Chapter 1). Individuals are viewed as thinking, reasoning beings who have beliefs and anticipations concerning future events in their lives. Drawing heavily on the earlier works of Lewin, Tolman, and Peak, this theory posits that human behavior is to a considerable extent a function of the interactive processes between the characteristics of an individual (such as personality traits, attitudes, needs, and values) and his or her perceived environment (such as supervisor's style, job or task requirements, and organization climate). In fact, it is the assumed existence of these anticipations, based on the individual-environment interaction, that differentiates expectancy/valence theory most markedly from other theories of work motivation.

Let us begin our discussion of this theory by considering on a general level the major hypothesized determinants of performance (Cummings & Schwab, 1973; Porter & Lawler, 1968; Vroom, 1960). Performance in organization settings appears to be a function of at least three important variables: motivational levels, abilities and traits, and role perceptions. First, an individual must *want* to perform. Otherwise, he or she will, at best, carry out a task only halfheartedly and, at worst, may refuse to do anything at all. We are speaking here of intentional behavior; that is, behavior directed toward specific tasks or outcomes. Thus, a basic prerequisite to task performance on most jobs becomes the desire—or motivation—of the employee to do the assigned tasks.

But motivation alone will not ensure task performance. A person must also have the necessary abilities and skills. Such is the purpose of education and training both before the person begins the job and while he or she holds it. Similarly, it is important to have personality traits that are at least somewhat compatible with the job requirements. For example, it is usually thought that a salesperson must be something of an extrovert. More introverted persons, it is assumed, are not "aggressive" enough to get the sales. Organizations have for decades used various personality and vocational interest tests in an effort to improve the match between individual and job, thereby hoping to affect resulting performance.

Finally, a third important factor in performance is role clarity. A person must usually have an accurate understanding of what the job requirements are if he or she is to be expected to devote full and efficient energy to them. A misunderstanding can lead to a considerable waste of effort—and poor performance— even if the person is highly motivated and has the required abilities. Thus, there appear to be at least three factors that significantly influence performance: one must be motivated, one must have the necessary abilities and traits, and one must have fairly clear role prescriptions.

The majority of the theoretical and empirical work by expectancy/valence theorists has focused on the "motivation" variable of the above equation. Put most simply, this theory argues that motivational force to perform—or effort—is a multiplicative function of the expectancies, or beliefs, that individuals have concerning future outcomes *times* the value they place on those outcomes. Vroom (1964, p. 18) defines "expectancy" as "an action-outcome association." It is a statement of the extent to which an individual believes that a certain action will result in a particular outcome. Theoretically, an expectancy can take on a mathematical value of from 0 (absolutely no belief that an outcome will follow a particular action) to 1 (complete certainty that an outcome will follow a particular action). Usually, however, an expectancy would take on a probability value somewhere between these two extremes.

More recently, the generalized concept of expectancy has been divided into two specific types: "$E \rightarrow P$ expectancy" and "$P \rightarrow O$ expectancies" (Campbell et al., 1970; Lawler, 1973). An $E \rightarrow P$ expectancy represents a belief that effort, such as a salesperson's increasing the number of calls made per day, will lead to desired performance, namely, increased sales. That is, the closer the *perceived* relationship between effort and resulting job performance, the greater the $E \rightarrow P$ expectancy. $P \rightarrow O$ expectancies, on the other hand, are beliefs or anticipations that an individual has concerning the likelihood that performance will, in fact, lead to particular outcomes. A salesperson, for example, may be almost certain of receiving a raise or a bonus if he or she succeeds in increasing sales (that is, high $P \rightarrow O$ expectancy); or, conversely, he or she may feel that such success would probably go unrewarded (low $P \rightarrow O$ expectancy). The multiplicative combination of these two types of expectancies, then, determines the "expectancy" part of the expectancy/valence equation.

Valence, the second major component of the theory, can be defined as the value, or preference, which an individual places on a particular outcome. Valences may take on theoretical values of from $+1.0$ to -1.0. That is, a person may be very strongly attracted to a particular outcome, such as a pay raise, and may assign the outcome a high positive value, or the person may very strongly want to avoid the outcome, such as being fired, and may assign a negative valence to it.

Under the expectancy/valence model, then, we would determine an individual's motivational force to perform (effort) by multiplying his $E \rightarrow P$ expectancy *times* his $P \rightarrow O$ expectancies *times* his outcome valences. Perhaps a very simple example will clarify this relationship. If the salesperson of our previous example places a high probability (let us say 8 out of 10) on increased sales resulting from increased effort, we would say he or she has a high $E \rightarrow P$ expectancy. Moreover, if this person strongly believes (at the same probability) that such a sales increase would lead to a bonus or a pay raise, we would say he or she has a high $P \rightarrow O$ expectancy. Finally, if our salesperson truly values the receipt of this bonus or pay raise, he or she would be described as placing a high valence, such as .9, on such a reward. When these three factors are combined in a multiplicative fashion (.8 $\times$ .8 $\times$ .9 = .58), we can see that under this theory our person would have a strong motivational force to perform. If ability as a salesperson is also high, and if role prescription is clear, we would then expect to see success in job performance. On the other hand, if expectancies were high (.8 and .8, respectively), but there was little genuine desire for the pay raise (for whatever reasons), the valence would be fairly low (let us say .1 instead of .9). Again computing the motivational force (.8 $\times$ .8 $\times$ .1 = .06), we can see that in this latter case our salesperson would have little desire to perform.

This example should give a general idea of how the three major components of the motivational force equation interact. The model is discussed in greater detail in the four selections that follow. First, Vroom sets forth the initial formulations of the model. This important, early developmental effort is then extended by Lawler, who updates the model in the light of later research. Lawler gives particular attention to the determinants of $E \rightarrow P$ and $P \rightarrow O$ expectancies. Third, Hackman and Porter provide an example of expectancy/valence research, discussing such topics as how expectancies and valences are actually measured in field settings. Finally, Mitchell and Biglan review a good portion of the research literature on the model, summarizing existing knowledge and pointing directions for future research needs. Taken together, these selections give a comprehensive review of expectancy/valence theory. A key factor, present in all the selections, is the developmental nature of the theory itself—which has, over the past decade, evolved into a fairly well-developed theory of work motivation. However, as is evident, a good deal more testing and modeling work is necessary, for the theory, although it shows definite promise, still requires a firmer empirical-analytical base that can come only from further thought and investigation.

REFERENCES AND SUGGESTED ADDITIONAL READINGS

Campbell, J. P., Dunnette, M. D., Lawler, E. E., III, & Weick, K. E. *Managerial behavior, performance, and effectiveness.* New York: McGraw-Hill, 1970.

Cummings, L. L., & Schwab, D. P. *Performance in organizations.* Glenview, Ill.: Scott, Foresman, 1973.

Evans, M. G. The effects of supervisory behavior on the path-goal relationship. *Organizational Behavior and Human Performance,* 1970, **5**, 277–298.

Galbraith, J., & Cummings, L. L. An empirical investigation of the motivational determinants of task performance: Interactive effects between valence-instrumentality and motivation-ability. *Organizational Behavior and Human Performance,* 1967, **2**, 237–258.

Georgopoulos, B. S., Mahoney, G. M., & Jones, N. W., Jr. A path-goal approach to productivity. *Journal of Applied Psychology,* 1957, **41**, 345–353.

Graen, G. Instrumentality theory of work motivation: Some experimental results and suggested modifications. *Journal of Applied Psychology Monograph,* 1969, **53**, (2, Part 2).

Heneman, H. G., III, & Schwab, D. P. Evaluation of research on expectancy theory predictions of employee performance. *Psychological Bulletin,* 1972, **78**, 1–9.

Lawler, E. E., III. A correlational-causal analysis of the relationship between expectancy attitudes and job performance. *Journal of Applied Psychology,* 1968, **52**, 462–468.

Lawler, E. E., III. *Motivation in work organizations.* Monterey, Calif.: Brooks/Cole, 1973.

Lawler, E. E., III, & Porter, L. W. Antecedent attitudes of effective managerial performance. *Organizational Behavior and Human Performance,* 1967, **2**, 122–142.

Lawler, E. E., III, & Porter, L. W. The effects of performance on job satisfaction. *Industrial Relations,* 1967, **7(1)**, 20–28.

Mitchell, T. R. Expectancy models of job satisfaction, occupational preference and effort: A theoretical, methodological and empirical appraisal. *Psychological Bulletin,* 1974, **81**, 1096–1112.

Mitchell, T. R., & Nebeker, D. M. Expectancy theory predictions of academic effort and performance. *Journal of Applied Psychology,* 1973, **57,** 61–67.

Porter, L. W., & Lawler, E. E., III. *Managerial attitudes and performance.* Homewood, Ill.: Irwin, 1968.

Porter, L. W., & Lawler, E. E., III. What job attitudes tell us about motivation. *Harvard Business Review,* 1968, **46**(1), 118–126.

Pritchard, R. D., & Sanders, M. S. The influence of valence, instrumentality, and expectancy on effort and performance. *Journal of Applied Psychology,* 1973, **57,** 55–60.

Vroom, V. H. *Some personality determinants of the effects of participation.* Englewood Cliffs, N.J.: Prentice-Hall, 1960.

Vroom, V. H. *Work and motivation.* New York: Wiley, 1964.

An Outline of a Cognitive Model
Victor H. Vroom

The model to be described is similar to those developed by other investigators including Lewin (1938), Rotter (1955), Peak (1955), Davidson, Suppes, and Siegel (1957), Atkinson 1958), and Tolman (1959). It is basically ahistorical in form. We assume that the choices made by a person among alternative courses of action are lawfully related to psychological events occurring contemporaneously with the behavior. We turn now to consider the concepts in the model and their interrelations.

THE CONCEPT OF VALENCE

We shall begin with the simple assumption that, at any given point in time, a person has preferences among outcomes or states of nature. For any pair of outcomes, x and y, a person prefers x to y, prefers y to x, or is indifferent to whether he receives x or y. Preference, then, refers to a relationship between the strength of a person's desire for, or attraction toward, two outcomes.

Psychologists have used many different terms to refer to preferences. The terms, valence (Lewin, 1938; Tolman, 1959), incentive (Atkinson, 1958), attitude (Peak, 1955), and expected utility (Edwards, 1954; Thrall, Coombs, and Davis, 1954; Davidson, Suppes and Siegel, 1957) all refer to affective orientations toward outcomes. Other concepts like need (Maslow, 1954), motive (Atkinson, 1958), value (Allport, Vernon, and Lindzey, 1951), and interest (Strong, 1958) are broader in nature and refer to the strength of desires or aversions for large classes of outcomes.

For the sake of consistency, we use the term valence throughout this book in referring to affective orientations toward particular outcomes. In our system, an outcome is positively valent when the person prefers attaining it to not attaining it (i. e., he prefers x to not x). An outcome has a valence of zero when the person is indifferent to attaining or not attaining it (i. e., he is indifferent to x or not x), and it is negatively valent when he prefers not attaining it (i. e., he prefers not x to x). It is assumed that valence can take a wide range of both positive and negative values.

We use the term motive whenever the referent is a preference for a class of outcomes. A positive (or approach) motive signifies that outcomes which are members of the class have positive valence, and a negative (or avoidance) motive signifies that outcomes in the class have negative valence.

It is important to distinguish between the valence of an outcome to a person and its value to that person. An individual may desire an object but derive little satisfaction from its attainment—or he may strive to avoid an object which he later finds to be quite satisfying. At any given time there may be substantial discrepancy between the anticipated satisfaction from an outcome (i. e., its valence) and the actual satisfaction that it provides (i. e., its value).

There are many outcomes which are positively or negatively valent to persons, but are not in themselves anticipated to be satisfying or dissatisfying. The strength of a person's desire or aversion for them is based not on their intrinsic properties but on the anticipated satisfaction or dissatisfaction associated with outcomes to which they are expected to lead. People may desire to join groups because they believe that membership will enhance their status in the community, and they may desire to perform their jobs effectively because they expect that it will lead to a promotion.

In effect, we are suggesting that means acquire valence as a consequence of their expected relationship to ends. Peak (1955) has discussed this relationship in some detail. She hypothesizes that attitudes, i. e., affective orientations toward objects, are "related to the ends which the object serves" (p. 153). From this general hypothesis it is possible for Peak to distinguish two types of determinants of attitudes: (1) The cognized instrumentality of the object of the attitude for the attainment of various consequences; and (2) the intensity and the nature of the affect expected from these consequences. If an object is believed by a person to lead to desired consequences or to prevent undesired consequences, the person is predicted to have a positive attitude toward it. If, on the other hand, it is believed by the person to lead to undesired consequences or to prevent desired consequences, the person is predicted to have a negative attitude toward it.

General support for these predictions is provided by a number of studies and experiments conducted by Peak and her associates. Rosenberg (1956) showed that it is possible to predict subjects' attitudes toward free speech for communists and desegregation in housing from their reported goals and their judgments of the probability that free speech and segregation will aid or block attainment of these goals. In a follow-up experiment, Carlson (1956) changed subjects' attitudes toward desegregation by modifying their beliefs regarding the consequences of desegregation for the attainment of their goals. Peak (1960) has also shown that students' attitudes toward conditions believed to hinder the attainment of good grades are more negative on the day of the quiz, when their motivation for attaining good grades was presumably strongest.

We do not mean to imply that all the variance in the valence of outcomes can be explained by their expected consequences. We must assume that some things are desired and abhorred "for their own sake." Desegregation may be opposed "on principle" not because it leads to other events which are disliked, and people may seek to do well on their jobs even though no externally mediated rewards are believed to be at stake.

Without pretending to have solved all of the knotty theoretical problems involved in the determinants of valence, we can specify the expected functional relationship between the valence of outcomes and their expected consequences in the following proposition.

Proposition 1. *The valence of an outcome to a person is a monotonically increasing function of the algebraic sum of the products of the valences of all other outcomes and his conceptions of its instrumentality for the attainment of these other outcomes.*

In equation form the same proposition reads as follows:

$$V_j = f_j \left[\sum_{k=1}^{n} (V_k I_{jk}) \right] (j = 1 \ldots n)$$

$$f_j' > O; i\, I_{jj} = O$$

where V_j = the valence of outcome j

I_{jk} = the cognized instrumentality ($-1 \leqslant I_{jk} \leqslant 1$) of outcome j for the attainment of outcome k

THE CONCEPT OF EXPECTANCY

The specific outcomes attained by a person are dependent not only on the choices that he makes but also on events which are beyond his control. For example, a person who elects to buy a ticket in a lottery is not certain of winning the desired prize. Whether or not he does so is a function of many chance events. Similarly, the student who enrolls in medical school is seldom certain that he will successfully complete the program of study; the person who seeks political office is seldom certain that he will win the election; and the worker who strives for a promotion is seldom certain that he will triumph over other candidates. Most decision-making situations involve some element of risk, and theories of choice behavior must come to grips with the role of these risks in determining the choices that people do make.

Whenever an individual chooses between alternatives which involve uncertain outcomes, it seems clear that his behavior is affected not only by his preferences among these outcomes but also by the degree to which he believes these outcomes to be probable. Psychologists have referred to these beliefs as expectancies (Tolman, 1959; Rotter, 1955; Atkinson, 1958) or subjective probabilities (Edwards, 1954; Davidson, Suppes, and Siegel, 1957). We use the former term throughout this book. An expectancy is defined as a momentary belief concerning the likelihood that a particular act will be followed by a particular outcome. Expectancies may be described in terms of their strength. Maximal strength is indicated by subjective certainty that the act *will* be followed by the outcome while minimal (or zero) strength is indicated by subjective certainty that the act *will not* be followed by the outcome. . . .

Expectancy is an action-outcome association. It takes values ranging from zero, indicating no subjective probability that an act will be followed by an outcome, to 1, indicating certainty that the act will be followed by the outcome. Instrumentality, on the other hand, is an outcome-outcome association. It can take values ranging from -1, indicating a belief that attainment of the second outcome is certain without the first outcome and impossible with it, to $+1$, indicating that the first outcome is believed to be a necessary and sufficient condition for the attainment of the second outcome.

THE CONCEPT OF FORCE

It remains to be specified how valences and expectancies combine in determining choices. The directional concept in our model is the Lewinian concept of force. Behavior on the part of a person is assumed to be the result of a field of forces each of which has direction and magnitude. The concept of force as used here is similar to Tolman's performance vector (1959), Atkinson's aroused motivation (1958), Luce's subjective expected utility (1962), and Rotter's behavior potential (1955).

There are many possible ways of combining valences and expectancies mathematically to yield these hypothetical forces. On the assumption that choices made by people are subjectively rational, we would predict the strength of forces to be a monotonically increasing function of the *product* of valences and expectancies. Proposition 2 expresses this functional relationship.

Proposition 2. *The force on a person to perform an act is a monotonically increasing function of the alebraic sum of the products of the valences of all outcomes and the strength of his expectancies that the act will be followed by the attainment of these outcomes.*

We can express this proposition in the form of the following equation:

$$F_i = f_i \left[\sum_{f=1}^{n} (E_{ij} V_j) \right] (i = n+1 \ldots m)$$

$$f_i' > O; \, i \cap j = \Phi, \, \Phi \text{ is the null set}$$

where F_i = the force to perform act i

F_{ij} = the strength of the expectancy ($O \leqslant E_{ij} \leqslant 1$) that act i will be followed by outcome j

V_j = the valence of outcome j

It is also assumed that people choose from among alternative acts the one corresponding to the strongest positive (or weakest negative) force. This formulation is similar to the notion in decision theory that people choose in a way that maximizes subjective expected utility.

Expressing force as a monotonically increasing function of the product of valence and expectancy has a number of implications which should be noted. An outcome with high positive or negative valence will have no effect on the generation of a force unless there is some expectancy (i. e., some subjective probability greater than zero) that the outcome will be attained by some act. As the strength of an expectancy that an act will lead to an outcome increases, the effect of variations in the valence of the outcome on the force to perform the act will also increase. Similarly, if the valence of an outcome is zero (i. e., the person is indifferent to the outcome), neither the absolute value nor variations in the strength of expectancies of attaining it will have any effect on forces.

Our two propositions have been stated in separate terms, but are in fact highly related to one another. Insofar as the acts and outcomes are described in different terms the separation is a useful one. We have in the first proposition a basis for predicting the valence of outcomes, and in the second proposition a basis for predicting the actions that a person will take with regard to the outcome. The distinction between acts and outcomes is not, however, an absolute one. Actions are frequently described in terms of the particular outcomes which they effect. For example, a person may be described as having chosen a particular occupation only when he successfully attains it, or he may be described as having chosen to perform effectively in that occupation only when he succeeds in doing so. In such cases the derivations from the two propositions become identical. The conditions predicted to affect the valence of the occupation or of effective performance in it are identical to those predicted to affect the relative strength of forces toward and away from these outcomes.

REFERENCES

Allport, G. W., Vernon, P. E., & Lindzey, G. *Study of values.* (rev. ed.) Boston: Houghton Mifflin, 1951.

Atkinson, J. W. Towards experimental analysis of human motivation in terms of motives, expectancies, and incentives. In Atkinson, J. W. (Ed.), *Motives in fantasy, action, and society.* Princeton: Van Nostrand, 1958, pp. 288–305.

Carlson, E. R. Attitude change through modification of attitude structure. *Journal of Abnormal and Social Psychology,* 1956, **52,** 256–261.

Davidson, D., Suppes, P., & Siegel, S. *Decision making: An experimental approach.* Stanford: Stanford University Press, 1957.

Edwards, W. The theory of decision making. *Psychological Bulletin,* 1954, **51,** 380–417.

Lewin, K. The conceptual representation and the measurement of psychological forces. *Contributions to Psychological Theory.* Durham, N.C.: Duke University Press, 1938, **1,** No. 4.

Luce, R. D. Psychological studies of risky decision making. In Strother, G. B. (Ed.), *Social science approaches to business behavior.* Homewood: Dorsey, 1962, 141–161.

Maslow, A. H. *Motivation and personality.* New York: Harper, 1954.

Peak, Helen. Attitude and motivation. In Jones, M. R. (Ed.), *Nebraska symposium on motivation.* Lincoln: University of Nebraska Press, 1955, pp. 149–188.

Rosenberg, M. J. Cognitive structure and attitudinal affect. *Journal of Abnormal and Social Psychology,* 1956, **53,** 367–372.

Rotter, J. B. The role of the psychological situation in determining the direction of human behavior. In Jones, M. R. (Ed.), *Nebraska symposium on motivation.* Lincoln: University of Nebraska Press, 1955, pp. 245–268.

Strong, E. K., Jr. Satisfactions and interests. *American Psychologist,* 1958, **13,** 449–456.

Thrall, R. M., Coombs, C. H., & Davis, R. L. (Eds.), *Decision processes.* New York: Wiley, 1954.

Tolman, E. C. Principles of purposive behavior. In Koch, S. (Ed.), *Psychology: A study of a science.* Vol. 2. New York: McGraw-Hill, 1959, pp. 92–157.

Expectancy Theory

Edward E. Lawler, III

Like drive theory, expectancy theory can be traced back to hedonism and the work of the English utilitarians. In the 1930s, however, expectancy theory began to develop a different thrust. At this point, Tolman (1932) began to talk about expectations and to argue for an approach that was more cognitively oriented, and Kurt Lewin (1935) presented a cognitively oriented theory of behavior that contained terms such as "valence" and "force." Out of this early work by Tolman and Lewin, a number of very similar motivation theories have developed. All of these theories include a concept of valence—that is, the attractiveness of an outcome—and a concept of expectancy—that is, the likelihood that an action will lead to a certain outcome or goal. The theories also converge in that they see valence and expectancy combining multiplicatively to determine behavior, hence, these theories can be referred to as expectancy × valence theories of motivation.

A number of theorists have picked up the main points of the early work of Tolman and Lewin and have built their own motivation theories within the ex-

Table 1   Expectancy Theories of Motivation

Theorist	Determinants of impulse to action
Tolman	Expectancy of goal, demand for goal
Lewin	Potency × valence
Edwards	Subjective probability × utility
Atkinson	Expectancy × (motive × incentive)
Rotter	Expectancy, reinforcement value
Vroom	Expectancy × valence, where valence is (instrumentality × valence)
Peak	Instrumentality × attitude (affect)

(From *Pay and Organizational Effectiveness: A Psychological View* by E. E. Lawler. Copyright 1971 by McGraw Hill Book Company. Used by permission of the publisher.)

pectancy × valence framework. The more prominent of these theorists are listed in Table 1. All of the theorists maintain that the strength of a tendency to act in a certain way depends on the strength of an expectancy that the act will be followed by a given consequence (or outcome) and on the value or attractiveness of that consequence (or outcome) to the actor.

Vroom's theory (1964) is the only one listed in Table 1 that was stated specifically for the purpose of dealing with motivation in the work environment. Thus, his theory is the logical one to examine to see how expectancy theory can be applied to work motivation. For Vroom, valence *(V)* refers to affective orientations toward particular outcomes. An outcome is positive if a person prefers attaining it to not attaining it, neutral if the person is indifferent to it, and negative if the person prefers not attaining it. Valence can vary from $+1$ to -1: maximally positive outcomes are $+1$; maximally negative outcomes are -1; neutral outcomes are 0. Vroom emphasizes that valence refers to an outcome's anticipated reward value rather than an outcome's actual reward value when obtained.

Vroom defines expectancy *(E)* as a momentary belief about the likelihood that a particular act will be followed by a particular outcome. Hence, like other expectancy theorists, Vroom sees an expectancy as a response outcome association. Expectancies can be described in terms of their strength: maximal strength, designated by the number 1, is subjective certainty that the act will be followed by the outcome; minimal strength, designated by the number 0, is subjective certainty that the act will not be followed by this outcome.

Like other expectancy theorists, Vroom argues that expectancy and valence combine multiplicatively to determine motivation or force. The multiplicative aspect of the theory is important; it means that unless both valence and expectancy are present to some degree, there will be no force. When either or both are 0, the product will be 0 and motivation will be 0. If, for example, a person wants to perform well but does not feel that his effort will result in good performance, he will have no motivation to perform well.

Any action may be interpreted as leading to a number of outcomes; hence, one must consider how the combination of the various outcomes influences behavior. Vroom's theory argues for multiplying the valence of each outcome times the strength of the expectancy that the act will lead to the attainment of the outcome and then taking the algebraic sum of all the resulting products. Thus, he writes his theory as follows: Force $= \Sigma \ (E \times V)$, where Σ means that the products for all outcomes are added to determine force. This is a key point in the theory, since it means that tying a valent reward, such as pay, to a desired behavior, such as good performance, will not be enough to motivate the desired behavior. Pay can be highly valued and can be seen as closely related to performance, but if negative consequences, such as feeling tired or being rejected by a work group, are also perceived as related to good performance, there may be no motivation to perform. Finally, according to Vroom, a person will be motivated to perform well in a situation only if performing well has the highest $E \times V$ force in that particular situation. Performing well can have a strong force, but if performing poorly has a stronger force, the person will not be motivated to perform well.

There is one area in which Vroom's theory—and indeed all the expectancy theories—gets into muddy water. This difficulty involves the distinction between acts and outcomes. As Vroom states, "the distinction . . . is not, however, an absolute one. Actions are frequently described in terms of particular outcomes which they affect" (p. 19). Vroom uses the term "action" to refer to behavior that is within the person's repertoire—for example, trying to perform well or seeking a job. Thus, the belief that an act (trying to perform well) will lead to an outcome (performing well) is an expectancy; the relationship between an outcome (performing well) and another outcome (a reward such as pay) is an instrumentality that affects the valence of the original outcome. Many expectancy theorists are even less clear than Vroom is about the distinction between actions and outcomes. Some have tended to ignore the fact that trying to perform an act does not always lead to performing it. In some situations, trying to perform an act is equivalent to performing it; in these situations, it is reasonable to argue that motivation is determined by the kind of outcomes to which performing the act leads, since expectancies are likely to be 1. In many other situations, trying to perform an act does not always lead to performing it. For instance, good job performance does not automatically result from trying to perform well; hence, beliefs—the person's subjective probability—about whether good performance will result must be taken into account to explain behavior. . . .

A number of developments in motivation theory have taken place since Vroom stated his expectancy theory in 1964. The expectancy model presented here draws on these developments to provide the best available model for understanding motivations in organizations. This model is based on four points that research on human motivation suggests are valid.

1   People have preferences among the various outcomes that are potentially available to them.

2   People have expectancies about the likelihood that an action (effort) on their part will lead to the intended behavior or performance.

3   People have expectancies (instrumentalities) about the likelihood that certain outcomes will follow their behavior.

4   In any situation, the actions a person chooses to take are determined by the expectancies and the preferences that person has at the time.

Figure 1 presents an illustration of the expectancy model in diagrammatic form. It shows the major factors that influence the strength of a person's motivation to perform in a given manner. First, motivation is shown to be influenced by the expectancy that effort or action on the part of the person will lead to the intended behavior. Thus, expectancy is simply the person's estimate of the probability that he will accomplish his intended performance, given the situation in which he finds himself. This can be labeled an $E \rightarrow P$ (effort $\rightarrow$ performance)

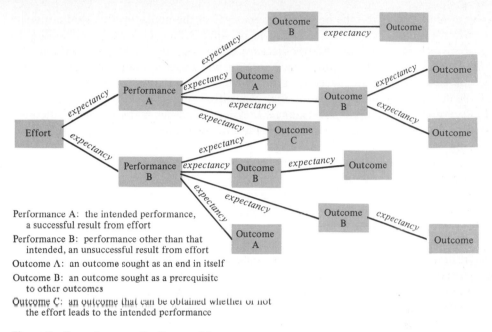

Performance A: the intended performance,
   a successful result from effort

Performance B: performance other than that
   intended, an unsuccessful result from effort

Outcome A: an outcome sought as an end in itself

Outcome B: an outcome sought as a prerequisite
   to other outcomes

Outcome C: an outcome that can be obtained whether or not
   the effort leads to the intended performance

Figure 1 Expectancy motivation model.

expectancy. For example, a manager may think that he has a 50 percent chance of producing 2000 cars a week in his plant if he tries. If we consider this kind of expectancy as varying from 0 to 1, the manager's $E \rightarrow P$ expectancy could be represented as .5. This kind of expectancy is typically more salient for complex and higher-level tasks than for simple tasks where little ability or skill is required.

Figure 1 also shows that expectancies about the consequences of task performance influence motivation. The model shows a number of expectancies, since successful task performance typically leads to a number of outcomes (as does unsuccessful performance). These expectations, which can be labeled $P \rightarrow O$ expectancies (performance $\rightarrow$ outcomes), are subjective probability estimates and can vary from 0 to 1 in the same manner as the $E \rightarrow P$ expectancies. To return to the manufacturing manager example, he may be sure that if his plant does produce 2000 cars a week he will receive a pay increase (his $P \rightarrow O$ expectancy equals 1). At the same time, he may also believe that there is a 50 percent probability that he will receive a promotion if he succeeds in producing 2000 cars. In addition, he may see a number of other outcomes associated with producing 2000 cars, and he may see still other outcomes associated with trying but failing to produce 2000 cars.

In many instances where the $E \rightarrow P$ expectancy is less than 1, it is important to consider what outcomes a person connects with trying to perform in a given way and failing. In other words, where success cannot be assured, it is necessary to consider the person's perceived probability that performance other than the intended one will be the outcome. In the case of the manager, this would involve considering the possibility of trying to produce 2000 cars a week and failing. In some situations, people obtain outcomes simply because they try to perform at a certain level. In these situations, a person will observe many of the same outcomes resulting from successful and unsuccessful performance, and he will realize that he will still receive a number of positive outcomes even though he fails to accomplish the desired performance. In some situations, many negative outcomes may be tied to failing to perform at the intended level, which may make trying very unattractive if failure is likely.

The model in Figure 1 also shows that only some of the outcomes are seen as leading to other outcomes. This factor is included to stress the point that some outcomes are sought as ends in themselves (for example, personal growth is sought as an end in itself), while others are sought because they lead to other outcomes (for example, money is sought because of what it will buy, not as an end in inself). The attractiveness of any outcome can be thought of as varying from very desirable $(+1)$ to very undesirable (-1). As has been repeatedly stressed, there are two reasons why outcomes that are associated with performance may be valent: (1) they directly satisfy a person's needs, or (2) they lead to an outcome or set of outcomes that satisfy a particular need or set of needs.

Overall, then, the model illustrated in Figure 1 suggests that a person's motivation to perform in a particular way will be influenced by his expectancies about trying to perform in that way, his expectancies about the outcomes associated with performing at that level $(P \rightarrow O)$, and the attractiveness of the outcomes involved. These factors combine to produce a motivational force to perform in the specified manner. For our hypothetical manager, this means that his $E \rightarrow P$ expectancy for producing 2000 cars, his $P \rightarrow O$ expectancies for producing 2000 cars, and the perceived attractiveness of the outcomes combine to determine his motivation to produce 2000 cars.

Figure 1 does not show how the various expectancy factors combine to determine motivation. Most expectancy theories have operated on the assumption that the higher the $E \rightarrow P$ expectancy and the more closely performance is seen to be related to positively valent outcomes, the greater will be the motivation. Based on past research, this assumption seems generally valid. Motivation does seem to be greatest when $E \rightarrow P$ is high for successful performance and low for unsuccessful performance and when $P \rightarrow O$ is high for positive outcomes and low for negative outcomes. Some theorists have argued for multiplying the various terms in the expectancy model together in order to obtain a single motivation score. In the case of our model, this approach would involve multiplying all $P \rightarrow O$ expectancies by the valence of the outcomes and then adding the products. This sum would then be multiplied by the $E \rightarrow P$ expectancy for successful performance. In terms of a formula such as Vroom's this gives $(E \rightarrow P) \times \Sigma [(P \rightarrow O) (V)]$. This formula can be expanded further to indicate that people often consider both the possibility of attaining their intended level of performance and the possibility of their failing in the following manner: $\Sigma [(E \rightarrow P) \times \Sigma [(P \rightarrow O) (V)]]$.

Some writers have suggested that it is premature to hypothesize multiplicative relationships among these expectancy factors because such relationships go beyond what can be measured (Campbell et al., 1970), and the writers undoubtedly are right. However, it is still important to think of these terms as combining in a basically multiplicative manner for several reasons, probably the most important of which has to do with what happens when either $E \to P$ or $P \to O$ is 0. When $E \to P$ is 0, the prediction is that no motivation will be present; if an additive relationship were hypotheized, the prediction would be that some motivation will be present. The no motivation prediction would seem to fit with the finding that people are not motivated to initiate actions that they have no chance of completing successfully. Similarly, the multiplicative model predicts that if $P \to Os$ are 0, there will be no motivation, even if $E \to P$ is high. This statement is illustrated by the observation that people do not perform many tasks, even though it is obvious that they are able to perform these tasks. The multiplicative combination also allows negative valences to accumulate in such a way that motivation can be negative; negative motivation can be seen in the desires of people to avoid many kinds of activities. Thus it seems logical to assume that the factors in our expectancy motivation model combine multiplicatively, even though this relationship has not been firmly established.

In organizations, people are often forced to choose among a number of behaviors that are relatively attractive. Simply stated, the expectancy model predicts that people will choose to behave in whatever way has the highest motiva tional force. That is, people will choose to behave in whatever way has the highest $\Sigma[(E \to P) \times \Sigma[(P \to O)(V)]]$ score for them. In the case of productivity, this means people will be motivated to be highly productive if they feel they can be highly productive and if they see a number of positive outcomes associated with being a high producer. However, if for some reason they will receive approximately the same outcomes for being less highly productive, they probably will be low producers.

Managers often ask why their subordinates are not more productive. They seem to feel that people should be productive almost as if it is a question of morality or of instinct. The expectancy approach suggests asking a rather different question: productive in a given situation? People are not naturally productive (or nonproductive). Thus, managers who wonder why their people are not more productive should start by comparing the rewards given to good performers with the rewards given to poor performers. Time after time, no real difference is found when this comparison is made. Thus, the workers' perception of the situation is that the good and the poor performers receive the same treatment, and this view is crucial in determining motivation. The example of an automobile assembly-line worker highlights this point. His pay is typically not affected by his performance, and his job is so simple that he receives no satisfaction from doing it well. Being highly productive does nothing more for him than to make him tired. Why should he be productive?

In summary, the expectancy model answers the two questions that were raised at the beginning of this chapter. It argues that both the attractiveness of the outcomes and the person's $E \rightarrow P$ and $P \rightarrow O$ expectancies influence which outcomes a person will try to obtain and how these outcomes will be sought. In order to answer one of these questions, it is necessary to answer the other, since they are so closely related. The choice of a behavior also implies a choice of which outcome will be sought, and the choice of an outcome partially determines what behavior will be attempted . . . .

DETERMINANTS OF $E \rightarrow P$ EXPECTATIONS

The single most important determinant of a person's $E \rightarrow P$ expectancies is the objective situation. Sometimes, of course, a person's perception of the situation is not accurate, and as a result the objective situation may not completely determine a person's $E \rightarrow P$ expectancies. However, it seems safe to assume that over time most people's $E \rightarrow P$ perceptions begin to fit reality reasonably well. Several of the other factors that influence $E \rightarrow P$ expectancies tend to encourage this. One of the most influential of these factors is the communication of other people's perceptions of the person's situation. Other people's perceptions are not necessarily accurate, but more often than not they can be a corrective force when a person badly misperceives reality. This communication is most likely to be influential when the person communicating his or her perception is very experienced in the situation and is less emotionally involved in the situation. For example, the ski instructor can often effectively correct the new skier's misperceptions about the likelihood that the new skier can successfully negotiate a particular turn, since the ski instructor is a more objective and experienced observer. In many situations an older employee can effectively counsel a new employee about the difficulty of doing a job. Often a job looks much more difficult to the new employee than it in fact is, and the result is turnover or low performance.

Learning plays an important role in determining $E \rightarrow P$ expectancies, as well as helping to make these expectancies more accurate. As people gain more experience in a situation, they typically are able to develop more accurate $E \rightarrow P$ expectancies. After a number of trials at doing something, a person knows from his own experience what his ratio of successful to unsuccessful efforts is. From a straight statistical-sampling perspective, once a large number of trials have occurred, it is possible to estimate the likelihood of a particular event with great accuracy.

There is some evidence that personality factors can cause people's $E \rightarrow P$ probabilities to diverge from reality. Psychologists who have written about personality have emphasized that individuals have a self-image. Some time during infancy, human beings learn to distinguish themselves from their environment. They learn that they can influence the environment or act on it, and they get feedback about the effectiveness of these actions. Some things that people try to make happen do happen, while others do not happen. From this interaction with their environment, people develop a concept of themselves and of their competence in dealing with the environment. They learn what they can do and what they cannot do. They receive feedback from others about how they are perceived.

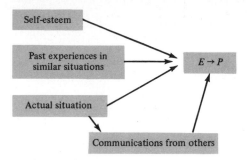

Figure 2   Determinants of $E \rightarrow P$ expectancies.

Out of these experiences people develop a knowledge of their existence and a self-image—that is, a view of what they are like. A crucial component of people's self-image is the beliefs they have concerning their response capabilities and their value and effectiveness. These beliefs are at the core of what is frequently referred to as self-esteem and are important for understanding the kinds of $E \rightarrow P$ expectancies people have.

Self-esteem can be influenced either positively or negatively depending on a person's effectiveness in dealing with his environment; but once a person has reached maturity, self-esteem—like a person's needs—appears to become relatively stable. There are large individual differences in self-esteem. Low-self-esteem people are generally poor estimators of their own ability to successfully carry out certain behaviors. They generally tend to underestimate the likelihood that they will be successful, although sometimes they are unrealistically high in their estimates. Not surprisingly, people's self-esteem tends to be related to their $E \rightarrow P$ expectancies; as a result, motivating low-self-esteem people to perform well is difficult, since they are predisposed to believing that they cannot perform well. On the other hand, high-self-esteem people tend to have realistic $E \rightarrow P$ expectancies; thus, they respond more predictably and realistically to their environment. One way an organization can deal with this effect of self-esteem on motivation is by selecting only people who have high self-esteem, and another way is by trying to raise the self-esteem of the people already in the organization. The latter solution presumably can be accomplished by providing the right kinds of jobs and leadership; however, the solution does not come easily, given the relative stability of people's self-esteem.

Figure 2 summarizes what has been said about the determinants of $E \rightarrow P$ expectancies, which are shown as being directly influenced by four factors: the person's self-esteem, his past experiences, the actual situation, and communications received from others. The figure also shows that the actual situation, in addition to directly influencing the person's $E \rightarrow P$ expectancies, influences what is communicated to the person, making it the crucial determinant of $E \rightarrow P$ expectancies. Because $E \rightarrow P$ expectancies are reality based, by changing the situation in which employees find themselves, organizations can influence employees' $E \rightarrow P$ expectancies—thus influencing motivation. As we shall see, job design has a strong influence on $E \rightarrow P$ expectancies and thus can influence motivation.

DETERMINANTS OF $P \rightarrow O$ EXPECTANCIES

Like $E \rightarrow P$ expectancies, $P \rightarrow O$ expectancies are strongly influenced by the objective situation, by people's past experiences in similar situations, and by what other people say about the situation. For example, one study has shown that people's perceptions of the probability that pay is related to performance are in accord with reality (Lawler, 1967). In this study, pay was clearly related to performance in one group of organizations where managers reported a strong relationship; managers reported a weak relationship in another group of organizations, and evidence supported their perception.

There is a great deal of evidence that verbal reports by co-workers can strongly influence a worker's $P \rightarrow O$ expectancies. Whyte (1955), in his work on incentive plans, has shown how workers are influenced by other workers' reports on the consequences of performing well. For example, workers can be convinced that if they are highly productive, the pay rate will be reduced, even though they have never seen it happen, and even though the company says it won't happen. Workers believe the event will happen because the event has been predicted by their fellow workers, who represent a high credibility source. Whyte also shows that workers develop other beliefs about the consequences of high productivity (for example, that high productivity will lead to rejection by other workers) even though they have never experienced such consequences.

Like $E \rightarrow P$ expectancies, $P \rightarrow O$ expectancies tend to be accurate, although there is evidence that under certain conditions $P \rightarrow O$ expectancies may be distorted. Raiffa (1968) has shown that people's subjective probabilities are generally related to actual mathematical probabilities. However, it has also been found that subjective probabilities tend to be larger than actual probabilities at low values and smaller than the actual probabilities at higher values. Thus, it seems that people tend to underestimate the possibility of a "sure thing" and to overestimate the possibility of a "long shot." Some sources have commented that evidence of the latter is present in the betting and gambling habits of most Americans.

Some research suggests that $P \rightarrow O$ probabilities are influenced by the nature of the outcomes. One group of studies has shown that, to most people positive outcomes seem more likely to occur than negative ones. Other studies have suggested that people see very positive outcomes as less likely to be obtained than less positive ones. Thus, people exhibit a general tendency to downgrade the possibility that very positive things will happen to them; people also downgrade the possibility that negative things will happen to them.

Some of the research on achievement motivation has suggested that $E \rightarrow P$ probabilities can influence certain $P \rightarrow O$ probabilities. Specifically, when the $E \rightarrow P$ probability is around .5, the achievement motive is aroused, and $P \rightarrow O$

expectancies having to do with achievement-type outcomes are affected. Apparently, when $E \rightarrow P$ is very high or very low, people do not see successful performance on their part as leading to feelings of achievement or competence, as they do when $E \rightarrow P$ is around .5.

Like $E \rightarrow P$ probabilities, there is reason to believe that $P \rightarrow O$ probabilities are influenced by people's personalities. Rotter (1966) has developed a measure of the degree to which people believe in internal versus external control of rewards. A person who is high on internal control believes that he can influence what happens to him and what outcomes he obtains. A person who is high on external control believes that fate and forces beyond his control influence what happens to him and what outcomes he receives. Rotter suggests that consistent individual differences appear on this dimension such that some people consistently feel they can influence what happens to themselves, while others consistently tend to believe that things are beyond their control.

Research data suggest that internal-control people are generally better motivated to perform well, presumably since they see a stronger connection between their behavior and the goals they seek. In other words, people who are oriented toward internal control are more likely to feel that performance on their part will lead to rewards than are people who believe in external control. Because of this, internal-control people are easier to motivate by the use of rewards that are contingent on their performance.

Rotter's data show fairly large differences between various segments of American society in the degree to which people believe in internal versus external control. Businessmen and college students tend to be high on internal control, while convicts and ghetto youths tend toward external control.

Overall, despite the research on internal versus external control, people's perception of a particular situation is most strongly influenced by the actual situation. One of the reasons that $P \rightarrow O$ beliefs are so important is that they can be greatly influenced by the policies and practices of organizations. Since $P \rightarrow O$ beliefs are based on the actual work situations and organizations control some important parts of the work situation, organizations can influence $P \rightarrow O$ expectancies by changing the situation. A leader's behavior, the design of jobs, and the pay and promotion systems all influence important $P \rightarrow O$ beliefs and are under the control of organizations. Organizations can also influence $P \rightarrow O$ beliefs by selecting people for membership on the basis of their beliefs in internal versus external control. For example, if the organization wanted (as well it might) to have people with high $P \rightarrow O$ beliefs, it could select people who are high on internal control.

Figure 3 summarizes what has been said so far about the determinants of $P \rightarrow O$ beliefs. It shows that $P \rightarrow O$ expectancies are influenced by past experience, communicated probabilities, $E \rightarrow P$ expectancies, the attractiveness of outcomes, and belief in internal versus external control. It also shows that the actual situation influences what is communicated as well as directly influencing the person's $P \rightarrow O$ expectancies.

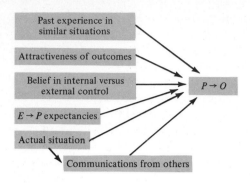

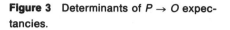

Figure 3   Determinants of $P \rightarrow O$ expectancies.

REFERENCES

Campbell, J. P., Dunnette, M. D., Lawler, E. E., & Weick, K. E. *Managerial behavior, performance, and effectiveness.* New York: McGraw-Hill, 1970.

Lawler, E. E. The multitrait-multirater approach to measuring managerial job performance. *Journal of Applied Psychology,* 1967, **51**, 369–381.

Lawler, E. E. *Pay and organizational effectiveness: A psychological view.* New York: McGrawHill, 1971.

Lewin, K. *A dynamic theory of personality.* New York: McGraw-Hill, 1935.

Raiffa, H. Decision analysis: Introductory lectures on choices under uncertainty. Reading, Mass.: Addison-Wesley, 1968.

Rotter, J. B. Generalized expectancies for internal versus external control of reinforcement. *Psychological Monographs,* 1966, **80**(1), 1–28.

Tolman, E. C. *Purposive behavior in animals and men.* New York: Century Co., 1932.

Vroom, V. H. *Work and motivation.* New York: Wiley, 1964.

Whyte, W. F. *Money and motivation.* New York: Harper & Row, 1955.

Expectancy Theory Predictions of Work Effectiveness

J. Richard Hackman
Lyman W. Porter[1]

While expectancy theory has enjoyed considerable currency among psychologists since its beginnings in the work of Tolman (1932) and Lewin (1938), until recently there have been relatively few studies testing the predictions of the theory in

From *Organizational Behavior and Human Performance*, 1968, **3**, 417–426. Copyright 1968 by Academic Press. Reprinted by permission.

[1]This research was carried out while the second author was a visiting Professor of Administrative Sciences at Yale University. The authors wish to thank Patrick Canavan for his assistance with the data analyses, and Douglas T. Hall for his comments on an earlier draft of the manuscript.

"real-world" performance situations. In recent years, the relevance and usefulness of the theory for understanding work behavior in organizations has been
demonstrated by Georgopoulos, Mahoney and Jones (1957), Vroom (1964), Galbraith and Cummings (1967) and Lawler and Porter (1967).

This study utilizes measurement techniques adapted from the attitude theory
of Fishbein (1963) to generate expectancy theory predictions of effort and performance in an on-going work situation. Since this methodology makes the *components* of the expectancy theory predictions operationally explicit, it has the
potential for considerably facilitating efforts to diagnose and change individuals'
motivation. Thus, the present research has the dual purpose of assessing the
usefulness of the Fishbein methodology for generating expectancy theory predictions, and of providing additional data on the relationship between these predictions and performance effectiveness in a field setting.

METHOD

The Measurement Strategy

Expectancy theory states that the strength of the tendency for an individual to
perform a particular act is a function of (a) the strength with which he expects
certain outcomes to be obtained from the act, times (b) the attractiveness to him
of the expected outcomes. Thus, the theory frequently is summarized by the
phrase "Force equals expectancy times valence" ($F = E \times V$). Since there usually are several different outcomes potentially associated with any given action,
most expectancy theorists sum the $E \times V$ component across the total number of
possible or relevant outcomes *(n)* to obtain an overall estimate of motivation or
"force" to act, yielding

$$F = \sum_{i=1}^{n} E_i \times V_i$$

In this study, expectancy theory is used to generate predictions of how hard
employees work on their jobs, and how effective their performance is. Thus, three
kinds of information must be obtained from the employees: (a) a list of outcomes
which they expect to obtain as a result of "working hard" on the job; (b) an
estimate of the level of certainty they have that the outcomes will in fact be
obtained as a result of working hard E_i); and (c) an estimate of the degree to
which they like or dislike the outcomes *(V_i)*.

Procedures developed for applications of Fishbein's (1963) attitude theory
offer an appropriate and relatively refined means of obtaining these data, since
the Fishbein theory parallels expectancy theory closely in form and content. In
brief, Fishbein specifies that an individual's attitude toward an objects equals

$$\sum_{i=1}^{n} B_i \times a_i$$

where B_i is the strength of a particular belief about the object (analogous to E_i in expectancy theory), a_i is the evaluation associated with that belief (analogous to V_i in expectancy theory), and n_i is the number of beliefs held by the individual about the object (analogous to the number of outcomes in expectancy theory). The means by which the Fishbein procedures were applied to obtain expectancy theory predictions are presented below.

The Research Setting

The study was conducted at three comparably-sized offices of a telephone company. Subjects were 82 female service representatives working at these offices who had been on the job for more than three months, and for whom it was possible to obtain complete predictor and criterion data. Service representatives are responsible for most aspects of customers' telephone service, including arranging new or changed service, handling complaints and special requests, maintaining records of customer services and charges, and servicing overdue accounts. The job involves both customer contact and clerical activities, and is generally described by the representatives as having considerable variety and responsibility. Although part of the "pace" of the work is determined by the rate of incoming calls from customers, the representatives reported that they had control over the pace and scheduling of a significant portion of their activities.

Predictor Scores

The expectancy theory formula was used to generate a single predictor score for each subject. The means by which the information required to compute these scores was obtained is presented below.

Obtaining a List of Expected Outcomes   In its most elegant form, expectancy theory requires that the outcomes which are utilized in the prediction equation be obtained from the particular individual whose behavior is to be predicted. A similar requirement exists for the Fishbein attitude theory; in order to best predict an individual's attitude, only those beliefs which are idiosyncratic to him should be employed. However, recent research by Hackman and Anderson (in press) and Kaplan and Fishbein (in press) has shown predictions of attitudes are not attenuated when beliefs are obtained on a group basis. That is, when only those beliefs which generally are held *in common* by subjects are used in prediction, the level of prediction is just as high as when idiosyncratic beliefs are used for each subject. Thus, to the extent that these findings about "beliefs about an object" also are relevant to "beliefs about outcomes" (as is reasonable to assume, given the strong parallels between the Fishbein attitude theory and expectancy theory), only those outcomes which are held in common by most of the service representatives need to be identified for use in the prediction equation. This procedure, of course, renders studies such as this one much more feasible to conduct, and more importantly allows direct comparison of the responses of different subjects, since all respondents deal with identically the same set of beliefs about outcomes.

A list of common outcomes or consequences of working hard on the job was obtained in the present study by interviewing 24 service representatives, 8 from each of the three research sites. A frequency distribution was computed and 14 outcomes which were mentioned by 3 or more interviewees were selected for use in computing predictions. Probably because of the generally high morale of the service representatives, there were very few *negative* consequences included in the set of outcomes. Therefore, 4 possible outcomes of moderately negative tone (e. g., "If a person works especially hard on this job, she will set too high a standard for other girls in the office") were added to the list to allow for as wide a range of response as possible. It was expected these negative items would turn out to have relatively low expectancy strengths for most representatives, and this was in fact the case. A complete list of outcomes used in the study, arranged in order of decreasing strength of expectancy, is presented in Table 1. (The questionnaire with which the expectancy measures were obtained is described below.)

Obtaining Indices of Expectancy and Valence A questionnaire was constructed to obtain measures of how strongly the representatives believed that each of the outcomes would in fact result from working hard on the job (E_i), and how positively (or negatively) the representatives evaluated each of the outcomes (V_i). In the first half of the questionnaire, designed to measure strength of expectancy, subjects responded to items of the following format:

If a person works especially hard on this job, *she is more likely to feel a sense of completion and accomplishment at the end of the day.* A seven-point scale was used, ranging from "not at all true" (meaning that the employee did not expect to obtain this outcome as a result of working hard) to "very true."

In the second half of the questionnaire the subjects used a seven-point scale to react evaluatively to the outcomes themselves, as a means of obtaining estimates of valence. This scale ranged from "very bad" to "very good" with "neither good nor bad" at the midpoint, and the items were the outcomes themselves, viz., "feeling a sense of completion and accomplishment." Thus, the responses of the subjects indicated the value which they placed on each of the outcomes.[2]

The questionnaire emphasized that the researchers were university-connected (and not company-connected), and that the subjects' responses would be seen

---

[2]Although there are zero values on both the E and V questionnaire scales, it is clear that these measurement procedures do not meet the criteria for ratio scales. Thus, it is not legitimate to claim that the $\Sigma E_i \times V_i$ predictor is a psychometrically valid measure of the "motivation" of individual subjects. Instead, the predictor is viewed as a numerical *score* which, given the measurement and arithmetic operations employed to obtain the score and the theory from which the operations were derived, should reflect gross differences in the motivation of subjects to work hard. Thus, the procedures used follow Comrey's (1951) and Hays (1963) note, such procedures are reasonable, as long as the scores are substantively meaningful on extramathematical grounds and so long as the scores do in fact relate to the criterion variables of interest.

Table 1 Beliefs about the Consequences of Working Hard Used in Predicting Work Behavior

If a person works especially hard on this job:
1. Time will seem to go faster.
2. She is likely to be of more help to her customers.
3. She is more likely to feel tired and fatigued at the end of the day.
4. She is more likely to feel a sense of completion and accomplishment at the end of the day.
5. She is more likely to receive thanks and gratitude from her customers.
6. She is not as likely to need the help of other girls to catch up on her work.
7. Her supervisor will expect it from her all the time.[a]
8. It is more likely that her office will win contestswith other offices.[b]
9. She is more likely to gain admiration and respect from her fellow workers.
10. She is likely to receive more compliments and praise from her supervisor.
11. She is more likely towin individual contests.[b]
12. Her supervisor is likely to check up on her work less frequently.
13. Her customers are likely to buy more service.
14. She is likely to receive a promotion more quickly.
15. She will simply get more work assigned to her.[a]
16. She is likely to receive a raise more quickly.
17. She will set too high a standard for other girls in the office.[a]
18. Her customers are more likely to get annoyed.[a]

Note.—Beliefs are listed in order of decreasing mean strength; i.e., the first belief listed was held most strongly by the subjects and the last one listed was held least strongly.
[a]"Moderately negative" beliefs supplied by the experimenters.
[b]The reference to contests has to do with company-initiated sales competitions.

only by the researchers. The questionnaires were administered to all service representatives at the three sites (not just those who had been interviewed). The subjects took the questionnaire in small groups, and the researchers re-emphasized the anonymity of the questionnaires as they were administered.

Criteria

Five criteria were utilized to test the adequacy of the expectancy theory predictions. These were:

1. Job involvement and effort. Ratings by the representatives' supervisors of the involvement of each representative in her job. Each representative was rated by two supervisors on four scales: (a) enthusiasm about the job itself, (b) effort and energy expended in doing her job, (c) personal involvement in the job itself, and (d) feelings of concern about the job. Ratings were made on a nine-point continuum for each scale, and a total score was obtained by summing across the four scales. Median intercorrelation among the four scales was .83. Interrater reliability for the judgments was .60; Spearman-Brown projected reliability for the summed judgments (across the four scales) was .86.

2. Employee Appraisal Form. Periodically each representative is assessed by her supervisor on seven scales as part of the company's regular appraisal process. These scales are: quality of work, quantity of work, cooperativeness, judgment, dependability, initiative, and ability to learn. Appraisals were obtained from company records for each representative in the sample.

3. Error rate. The company maintains complete records of errors made by the representatives in processing customer orders, and these data were obtained for all subjects.

4. Sales data. The company also maintains data on each representative's sales effectiveness, and these data were obtained for all subjects. Error rate and sales data were converted to standard scores within each of the three research sites before analysis, to compensate for minor differences in the way in which these data were compiled at the three locations.

5. Composite criterion. The job involvement, error rate and sales data were converted to standard scores and combined to yield one "overall" index of work effectiveness.

RESULTS

The expectancy theory predictor of how hard the subjects would work on the job

$$\left(\sum_{i=1}^{n} E_i \times V_i \right)$$

correlated .40 with the composite criterion of work effectiveness. In addition, the predictor was significantly related to supervisors' ratings of effort, to sales, to error rate (negatively), and to five of the seven scales of the Employee Appraisal Form. These results are summarized in Table 2.[3]

DISCUSSION

Magnitude of the Results

The relationships between the expectancy theory predictions and the performance criteria, while statistically significant, are not strikingly large. Yet there are reasons for optimism about them. First, as is noted in reviews by Brayfield and Crockett (1955), Vroom (1964) and others, attitude measures have been notoriously poor predictors of performance in work situations. The present relationships, in which (following Fishbein) the expectancy theory predictions can be viewed as *attitudes toward actions,* appear quite strong in this context. Further, the present results serve to emphasize the contention of Porter and Lawler (1968)

---

[3]Expectancy theory, as can be seen from the $\Sigma E_i \times V_i$ formula, implies that it is the *interaction* between expectancy and valence which will yield the best predictions of behavior. To check this, other combinations of the data were correlated with the criteria, and these relationships compared to those presented in Table 2. In particular, the two components of the predictor (ΣE_i and ΣV_i) and the sum of the components ($\Sigma E_i + \Sigma V_i$) each were correlated with the criteria. The results supported the multiplicative model in each case. The correlations between the ΣE_i term and the eleven criteria (reversing the sign of the correlation with error rate) ranged from $-.8$ to .23, with a median of .11; for the ΣV_i term the correlations ranged from .08 to .33, with a median of .16; and for the $\Sigma E_i + \Sigma V_i$ term the correlations ranged from $-.01$ to .27, with a median of .17. All three sets of correlations are lower than those obtained using the $\Sigma E_i \times V_i$ predictor, which ranged from .08 to .40, with a median of .27.

Table 2   Correlations between Expectancy Theory Predictions and Criteria

Criterion Measure	Correlation with $\Sigma E_i \times V_i$ Predictor
Supervisor ratings of involvement and effort	.27**
Employee Appraisal Form	
Quality of work	.06
Quantity of work	.37**
Cooperativeness	.13
Judgment	.25**
Dependability	.36**
Initiative	.28**
Ability to learn	.25**
Error rate	.23*
Sales	.31**
Composite criterion	.40**

*$p \leqslant .05$
**$p \leqslant .01$

that specific attitudes about expectancies (or "path-goal relationships") and out-comes are a more appropriate basis for making predictions about performance effectiveness than are general attitudes toward the task or the performance set-ting.

Secondly, the present results were obtained using *only* the subjects' percep-tions of the consequences of working hard as the basis of prediction. There obviously are other factors which have substantial impacts on performance as well, such as ability and personality predispositions. If measures of individual differences on dimensions such as these had been included, the magnitude of the results might have been substantially increased.

Prediction of Work Quality

The relationship between the predictor scores and supervisors' appraisals of work quality (primarily assessments of thoroughness, neatness, and accuracy) was near zero. This finding is not unexpected, since the predictor was derived on the basis of outcomes which were expected to result from "working especially hard" (not working especially *well*).

The differentiation between "hard work" and "high quality work" also was evident in the interviews which were conducted early in the study. When the representatives discussed "hard work" on the job, they frequently would inquire "What do you mean by 'hard work'?" When the question was returned by asking the interviewee what *she* meant by "hard work" the answer invariably was some-thing about "doing a lot" in a day—often because of an especially heavy load of incoming calls on a particular day, or because of a decision, say, to try to get all the paperwork cleared up before going home. Thus, the conception of hard work held by the service representatives seemed generally to have more to do with quantity than with quality, and they tended to perceive quantity and quality as independent aspects of their performance. (This perceived independence also was borne out in supervisors' appraisals, in which judgments of quantity and quality correlated only .07.)

Thus, it is not surprising to find that the questionnaire-derived predictions were much more closely associated with quantity of work than with work quality. Nevertheless, the predictions were not entirely irrelevant to work quality, since there was a significant negative relationship between the predictor and one objective measure of work quality, namely, error rate.

Implications of the Findings

The results and the methodology of the study have considerable relevance to the problem of *diagnosing* a performance situation in motivational terms, and for effectively *changing* aspects of the situation so as to obtain higher levels of effort from the performers. According to expectancy theory as it has been applied in this research, there are three factors which affect the level of effort an individual exerts in a performance situation: (a) the particular outcomes which the performer perceives as occurring as a result of working hard on the job; (b) the strength of expectancy, i. e., the level of certainty which the performer has that he actually will obtain particular outcomes by working hard; and (c) the valence of outcomes, i. e., the evaluations which the performer makes of the perceived outcomes.

Use of a methodology (such as that of the present study) which makes explicit these three components allows an investigator to identify those aspects of a performer's perceptions and evaluations which tend to enhance his motivation to work hard, and those which tend to detract from it. For example, outcomes which have high expectancies and high positive valences will, according to the results of this study, enhance a performer's motivation to work hard. Outcomes with high expectancies and high negative valences will detract from his motivation. Outcomes with relatively low expectancies or with neutral valences will have no substantial impact on the performer's motivation. By examining the expectancies and valences associated with a performer's perceived outcomes of hard work, an investigator can identify the motivational problems and opportunities which are inherent in the performance situation.

Once a diagnosis of the situation is made (as suggested above), changes can be instituted to improve the performer's motivation to work hard. Such changes can involve (a) instituting new outcomes which will be valued by the performer and which will be seen by him as resulting from hard work; (b) changing the expectancies of existing outcomes so that the link between hard work and positively valued outcomes is strengthened and that between hard work and negatively valued outcomes is weakened; or (c) changing the valences of existing outcomes. The first two alternatives probably are much more amenable to external change than is the last one; it should be much easier to change aspects of the situation so that the performer will perceive it differently than it would be to change the evaluations which a performer makes of various outcomes.

The discussion above has focussed only on the use of expectancy theory in understanding and changing the level of effort which performers put into their work. The same kinds of analyses and similar suggestions could be made as well for other performance and decision-making situations. To the extent that the findings are generalizable to these other situations, the present study suggests that expectancy theory can be a broadly useful tool in understanding behavior in "real world" settings.

REFERENCES

Brayfield, A. H., and Crockett, W. H. Employee attitudes and employee performance. *Psychological Bulletin,* 1955, **52,** 396–424.

Comrey, A. L. Mental testing the logic of measurement. *Educational and Psychological Measurement,* 1951, **11,** 323–334.

Fishbein, M. An investigation of the relationships between beliefs about an object and the attitude toward that object. *Human Relations,* 1963, **16,** 233–239.

Galbraith, J., and Cummings, L. L. An empirical investigation of the motivational determinants of task performance: Interactive effects between instrumentality-valence and motivation-ability. *Organizational Behavior and Human Performance,* 1967, **2,** 237–257.

Georgopoulos, B. S., Mahoney, G. M., and Jones, N. W., Jr. A path-goal approach to productivity. *Journal of Applied Psychology,* 1957, **41,** 345–353.

Hackman, J. R., and Anderson, L. R. The strength, relevance and source of beliefs about an object in Fishbein's attitude theory. *Journal of Social Psychology,* in press.

Hays, W. L. *Statistics for psychologists.* New York: Holt, 1963.

Kaplan, K. J., and Fishbein, M. The source of beliefs, their saliency, and prediction of attitude. *Journal of Social Psychology,* in press.

Lawler, E. E., III, and Porter, L. W. Antecedent attitudes of effective managerial performance. *Organizational Behavior and Human Performance,* 1967, **2,** 122–142.

Lewin, K. *The conceptual representation and measurement of psychological forces.* Durham, N.C.: Duke University Press, 1938.

Porter, L. W., and Lawler, E. E., III. *Managerial attitudes and performance.* Homewood, Illinois: Irwin-Dorsey, 1968.

Tolman, E. C. *Purposive behavior in animals and men.* New York: Century, 1932.

Vroom, V. *Work and motivation.* New York: Wiley, 1964.

Instrumentality Theories: Current Uses in Psychology

Terence R. Mitchell
Anthony Biglan[1]

This study reviews the literature on instrumentality theories in psychology. These theories are distinguished by the hypothesis that the behavior of an individual is

Abridged from *Psychological Bulletin,* 1971, **76,** 432–454. Copyright by the American Psychological Association. Reprinted by permission.

[1]The preparation of this review was supported by Contract NR 177–472, N00014–67–A– 0102–0012, Office of Naval Research, Department of the Navy (Fred E. Fiedler, Principal Investigator), and by Contract NR 177–473, N00014–67–A–0102–0013, Advanced Research Projects Agency, Office of Naval Research, Department of the Navy (Fred E. Fiedler, Principal Investigator). The authors are indebted to Gerald R. Oncken and Fred E. Fiedler for their invaluable suggestions.

in part determined by *(a)* his expectations that the behavior will lead to various outcomes and *(b)* his evaluation of these outcomes. . . .

The concept of instrumentality is not new to psychology. Both Lewin (1935) and Tolman (1932) emphasized the link between behavior and its perceived outcomes. However, reference to internal, organismic processes as determinants of behavior has not been readily accepted in the United States. This seems due to two closely linked factors. First, stimulus-response theories have dominated psychology in this country, and these theories emphasize factors, external to the organism, that affect behavior. Second, the prevailing behaviorist logic was not adequate for supporting statements containing constructs that refer to internal organismic processes, and there existed no alternate logic that was adequate.

Georgopoulos, Mahoney, and Jones (1957) first tested an instrumentality hypothesis in the industrial area. They suggested that worker productivity could be predicted from the worker's perception of the degree to which his productivity is a path to the attainment of his personal goals. If the worker sees high productivity as a path to his goals, then he will be a high producer; if he sees low productivity as a path to these goals, then he will be a low producer.

Georgopoulos et al. tested this hypothesis in a household appliances company. They obtained measures of the perceived instrumentality of high and low productivity for each of 10 goals. Their sample of 621 workers was split into high- and low-need groups on the basis of their ranking of three of these goal items: "making money in the long run"; "getting along well with the work group"; and "promotion to a higher base rate." Thus, the high-need group ranked these items as higher in importance to them than did the low-need group. The measure of productivity was based on subject reports of the percentage above or below the company-set standard they had reached. This measure was the form in which productivity was typically dealt with in the plant; hence, it was not alien to the workers. Finally, workers were split into high- and low-freedom groups on the basis of their ability to set their own work pace (if they could, they were in the high-freedom group), their age (20–59 years was high-freedom group), and their amount of experience (more than 6 months was high-freedom group).

The results of this study support the basic goal path or instrumentality hypothesis. First, high productivity was associated with the perception that high productivity leads to each of the three goals in question. Second, for workers who ranked a goal as being important to them personally, the relationship between productivity and perceived instrumentality was stronger. Third, the relationship between perceived instrumentality and productivity was significantly higher for those who were classified as "free." Finally, for workers who were both "free" and had a high need on an item, there was a stronger relationship between perceived instrumentality and productivity than for workers with any other combination of these two factors. To summarize, the above study supports the hypothesis that productivity is related to its perceived instrumentality for the attainment of goals and that degree of attraction to the goals and freedom of action mediate this relationship.

In a similar study, Porter and Lawler (1968) examined attitudes toward pay as they related to the performance of managers in industrial and governmental organizations. They compared the performance of the third of their sample that perceived pay as a probable outcome of performance with the third that saw little relation between performance and pay. Performance (as rated by the subjects and their superiors) was significantly higher for the former group. When samples were split according to the rated importance of pay to the subjects, the relationship between performance and the expectancy that pay results from performance was stronger for the high-importance group than for the low-importance group. This suggests that performance is highest for those who perceive it as leading to *valued* outcomes and is consistent with the Georgopoulos et al. (1957) study.

A more complete statement of instrumentality theory in industrial psychology was presented by Vroom. His statement of the theory has been the basis for most of the subsequent work in this area. Vroom (1964) presented two models, the first for the prediction of the valences of outcomes, and the second for the prediction of force toward behavior. An outcome is simply anything an individual might want to attain. The valence of an outcome for a person is defined conceptually as the strength of his positive or negative affective orientation toward it. Similar to Lewin's use of the term, valence refers to the anticipated satisfaction associated with an outcome, and is distinguished from the value of the outcome—the actual satisfaction resulting from attainment of the outcome.

The valence model states that the valence of an outcome to a person is a monotonically increasing function of the algebraic sum of the products of the valences of all other outcomes and his conceptions of the specific outcome's instrumentality for the attainment of these other outcomes. Symbolically,

$$V_j = f \sum_{k=1}^{n} (V_k I_{jk}),$$

where

V_j = the valence of outcome j;

I_{jk} = the cognized instrumentality of outcome j for the attainment of outcome k;

V_k = valence of outcome k;

n = the number of outcomes.

Cognized or perceived instrumentality is defined conceptually by Vroom (1964) as the degree to which the person sees the outcome in question as leading to the attainment of other outcomes. Instrumentality varies from -1 (meaning that the outcome in question is perceived as always leading to not attaining the second outcome) to $+1$ (meaning that the outcome is perceived as always leading to the attainment of the second outcome).

Although this model can be used to predict the valence of any outcome, it has been applied most frequently to the prediction of job satisfaction. In essence, the model says that the worker's satisfaction with his job results from the instrumentality of the job for attaining other outcomes and the valence of those outcomes. In the remainder of this section we refer to this model as the *job satisfaction model.*

Vroom's second model predicts the force toward behavior. The force on a person to perform an act is conceptualized by Vroom as a monotonically increasing function of the algebraic sum of the products of the valences of all outcomes, and the strength of his expectancies that the act will be followed by the attainment of these outcomes (Vroom, 1964). Symbolically,

$$F_i = \sum_{j=1}^{n} (E_{ij} V_j)$$

where

F_i = the force on the individual to perform act i;
E_{ij} the strength of the expectancy that act i will be followed by outcome j;
V_j = the valence of outcome j;
n = the number of outcomes.

The individual's expectancy is defined by Vroom as his belief concerning the probability that the behavior in question will be followed by the outcome of interest. An expectancy is a perceived probability, and therefore ranges from zero to plus one. It is distinguished from instrumentality in that it is an action-outcome association, while instrumentality is an outcome-outcome association. While expectancies are perceived probabilities, instrumentalities are perceived correlations.

Vroom suggested that this second model can be used to predict choice of occupation, remaining on the job, and effort. In practice, it has been tested with respect to job performance, and we, therefore, refer to it as the *job performance model.* Specifically, Vroom stated that the force on the individual to exert a given amount of effort is a function of the algebraic sum of the products of the valence of each level of performance and the person's expectation that each level of performance will be attained by that amount of effort. Note that the amount of effort, not performance, is predicted by Vroom; effort is considered to be a behavior, while performance is an outcome.

Galbraith and Cummings (1967) elaborated and tested Vroom's job performance model. They began by distinguishing between first- and second-level outcomes. A first-level outcome is one which has a valence that the investigator is interested in predicting—in their case, performance on the job. They defined second-level outcomes as events to which the first-level outcomes are expected to lead. It should be noted that Galbraith and Cummings' definition of second-level outcomes suggests that only those outcomes actually expected by the individual to result from the first-level outcome may be considered. In fact, outcomes not perceived by the individual as resulting from the first-level outcome may be included in the equation, since their instrumental value will be zero; and they will, therefore, not degrade the prediction of the valence of the first-level outcome.

Galbraith and Cummings described three sources of second-level outcomes that might be expected to result from performance. First, the organization as a whole may provide money, fringe benefits, and promotions for performance. Second, the supervisor may be supportive. Third, the work group may be accepting. Essentially, Galbraith and Cummings are providing an a priori list of the outcomes they feel are important to the prediction of the valence of high performance. The problem with this approach is that the investigators may fail to support the instrumentality hypothesis because they choose the second-level outcomes that are not important to the subjects, rather than because of any inadequacy of the hypothesis.

Galbraith and Cummings did not study the effects of expectancy in this investigation. Rather they attempted to predict performance for a sample of subjects considered likely to have expectancies of +1 about the relationship between their behavior and high performance. Workers were chosen whose attainment of performance did not depend on other workers and whose work pace was not dependent on a machine. Their sample consisted of 32 workers in an Indiana heavy equipment plant. Measures of instrumentality of performance for each of the second-level outcomes and the valence of each second-level outcome were obtained from subjects. The measure of performance was obtained from company records. This measure took the form of a percentage of the company standard for a 1-month period.

The instrumentality hypothesis was tested separately for each of the second-level outcomes. Significant prediction of performance was obtained only for the outcome, supportiveness of the supervisor. Neither the valence of this outcome nor the instrumentality of performance for the outcome was related to performance by itself, but the interaction of the two was related to performance. This result is as Vroom's job performance model predicts.

The instrumentality hypothesis was also tested for all outcomes taken together. Stepwise multiple regression was used. In this analysis, the interaction of valence and instrumentality was significantly related to performance for both the supportiveness and money outcomes. It should be noted that the analysis of these data did not include a test of the association between the *sum* of the products of instrumentality and valence ratings. This sum was central to Vroom's statement of the instrumentality hypothesis, but Galbraith and Cummings (1967) gave no explanation for the absence of this test.

Despite the author's conclusions, we do not feel these results provide impressive support for instrumentality theory. The failure to obtain strong support of the instrumentality hypothesis may be due to a number of factors besides the inadequacy of the hypothesis. First, subjects' expectancies that their behavior leads to high performance may not have been controlled at $+1$ as the authors hoped. According to Vroom's hypothesis, even when high performance is positively valent, the individual will not exert a given amount of effort if he does not *expect* that his effort will lead to high performance. Thus, if subjects' expectancies were not at $+1$, the theory would not predict that the sum of the products of the valence of second-level outcomes multiplied by the instrumentality of performance for those second-level outcomes would be related to performance.

Second, the a priori set of outcomes used in this study may have excluded outcomes related to performance. For example, a feeling of accomplishment may be an important outcome of achieving high performance for some individuals. Negative outcomes, such as getting fired and being bored, may also affect performance. For example, some individuals may perceive many positively valued outcomes as resulting from performance, but also perceive boredom as a result. If boredom is strongly negatively valenced, it may lead the individual to forego the possibility of attaining positive outcomes.

A third reason for the failure of Galbraith and Cummings' (1967) study to support the theory is that amount of effort and performance may not have been related in this sample. Recall that Vroom's (1964) model predicts effort, not performance. Thus, if Galbraith and Cummings had measured workers' intentions to exert effort or actual effort exerted, they might have found that the model adequately predicted these variables.

Lawler and Porter (1967) did attempt to predict *effort* from subjects' perceived instrumentalities. They studied 154 managers in five different organizations, and ratings of the importance of seven outcomes were collected: pay, promotion, prestige, security, autonomy, friendship, and opportunity to use skills and abilities. A composite measure of the subject's expectancies was based on the sum of his ratings of the degree to which (a) effort, (b) high productivity, and (c) good job performance led to the seven outcomes. Ratings of effort and performance were obtained from superiors, peers, and the subject. Multiple correlations between the Expectancy $\times$ Importance ratings for each of the seven outcomes, and the supervisor, peer, and self-ratings of effort, were .27 ($p < .10$), .30 ($p < .05$), and .44 ($p < .01$), respectively. Prediction of performance from the Expectancy $\times$ Outcome scores was less successful; the multiple correlations were .18 *(ns)*, .21 *(ns)*, and .38 ($p < .01$) for the supervisor, peer, and self-performance ratings. With seven predictors, these multiple correlations are hardly strong support for the instrumentality hypothesis. As in the Galbraith and Cummings (1967) study, Lawler and Porter's use of multiple correlations is not consistent with Vroom's (1964) model (nor with their own statement of the model). A simple sum of the Importance $\times$ Expectancy scores would have been the appropriate predictor. Moreover, the authors used an a priori set of outcomes. The problem with this approach was discussed above.

A study by Lawler (1968) provides support for the causal status of subjects' instrumentalities. Six rewards were rated by 55 managers as to their importance. Subjects' expectations of the degree to which effort and job performance led to each of the six rewards was also rated. Peer, supervisor, and self-ratings of performance were obtained at the same time. All of these measures were obtained at the beginning and end of a 1-year interval. Multiple correlations were generated to assess the ability of the six Expectancy × Importance scores to predict performance. For the supervisors' ratings, these correlations were .44 (Time 1), .52 (Time 2), .55 (Time 1 Expectancy × Importance with the Time 2 Performance), and .39 (Time 2 Expectancy × Importance with the Time 1 Performance). The first three coefficients were significant ($p < .05$). The corresponding correlations for peer ratings were .52, .30, .45, and .30 ($p < .05$ for the first and third coefficients), and for the self-performance ratings they were .43, .48, .65, and .52 ($p < .05$ for the last three). The causal status of the expectancy attitudes is supported by the fact that Time 1 Expectancy × Importance measures are more highly related to Time 2 performance measures than Time 2 Expectancy × Importance measures are related to Time 1 performance. Again, however, multiple correlation with six Expectancy × Importance predictors was used, and the rewards were not generated by the subjects themselves.

Another experiment by Hackman and Porter (1968) avoided some of the problems with the above studies. These authors used instrumentality theory to predict the effectiveness of 82 telephone company service representatives. Instead of developing their own outcomes, they had 24 service representatives generate relevant outcomes. The 14 most frequently mentioned outcomes were included, as well as 4 negative outcomes which they added. The 82 subjects were then asked to evaluate each outcome and the probability that working hard on the job would lead to each outcome. The sum of the products of expectations and valence was then correlated with 11 effectiveness measures. The correlations ranged from .25 to .40, and 9 of the 11 were significant ($p < .05$). These results suggest that instrumentalities are important, but not the only factor related to employee performance.

Graen (1969) tested Vroom's job performance and job satisfaction models and examined some factors affecting perceived instrumentality. His results define important boundary conditions for instrumentality theory. In addition, he proposed some useful modifications and extensions of the theory.

Graen began by clarifying the distinction between first- and second-level outcomes. A first-level outcome is called a work role. A work role is defined as a set of behaviors expected by the organization and considered appropriate for the occupant of a position in the organization. For example, "effective job performer," "team member," and "group leader" are work roles. Work roles are attained and maintained through the performance of the expected behaviors in such a way that minimal organizational expectations are met. Second-level outcomes are called role outcomes. They are the outcomes that accrue to the individual as a result of his attainment or maintenance of the work role. Graen focused on two work roles: *effective performer* and *job incumbent*. Eight role outcomes (second level) are included in his study: accomplishment, achievement feedback, salary, human relations, recognition, policies and practices, responsibility, and working conditions. As in the Galbraith and Commings (1967) study, the role outcomes were derived on an a priori basis.

According to [Graen], job satisfaction is a matter of satisfaction with the job-incumbent work role. It is predicted to be a monotonically increasing function of the sum of the products of the instrumentality of the job-incumbent work role for attaining role outcomes and the valence of those role outcomes. Job performance, on the other hand, is predicted to be a positive function of the valence of the effective performer work role and the perceived expectancy that increased effort will lead to attainment of this work role.

The study was an experimental simulation in which women were hired for part-time, temporary employment by a fictitious company. In the first task, subjects had to find certain correlations from a 155 × 155 matrix and transcribe them. The second task was the same as the first, except that the correlations were to be rounded to two places before transcription. There were three treatment groups. The first, the achievement group, was rewarded for prior effective performance. The second group, the incentive group, was offered money as an inducement for subsequent performance. The third group was a control group: the money they obtained was not contingent on performance. Subjects were run during two sessions, and the treatments were introduced in the second session. These treatments were intended to permit a test of the boundary conditions of the instrumentality theory and to examine the factors affecting perceived instrumentality. Upon completion of the task activity, measures of the following were obtained: the attraction of the work-role outcomes, the perceived instrumentality of the two work roles (the particular job and "effective performer") fo the attainment of each of the *eight* role outcomes, and the perceived expectancy that increased effort would lead to more effective performance.

A separate job satisfaction measure based on the Hoppock Job Satisfaction Blank (Hoppock, 1935) was used to measure job satisfaction. Performance measures used were the number of items completed (quantity) and proportion correct (quality). Both a raw score and a gain score (pre- to posttreatment) for both quantity and quality measures were used in the final analysis.

Perceived instrumentality varied according to the treatment condition. It will be recalled that the achievement treatment group was rewarded for prior effective performance and that the incentive treatment group received money as an inducement for subsequent good performance. For the achievement treatment group, the perceived instrumentality of the job-incumbent work role for achievement and recognition was significantly higher than it was for the incentive and control groups. For the incentive treatment group, the perceived instrumentality of the job-incumbent work role for money was significantly higher than it was for the other two groups. Graen (1969) also looked at the perceived instrumentality of the effective performer work role. The achievement treatment group rated the instrumentality of the effective performer work role. The achievement treatment group rated the instrumentality of this work role for achievement and recognition significantly higher than did the groups in the other two treatment conditions. However, the perceived instrumentality of the effective performer work role for money was *not* greater for the incentive treatment group.

The results of this study provide partial support for the job satisfaction model and suggest some limitations for it. The specific model tested in this study states that satisfaction with the work role of job incumbent is a monotonically increasing function of the sum of the products of the valences of role outcomes and the perceived instrumentality of the work role for these outcomes. The model was tested separately for intrinsic outcomes (accomplishment, achievement feedback, recognition, and responsibility), and extrinsic outcomes (human relations, policies and practices, salary, and working conditions), and for all outcomes taken together. It was found that the model predicted both job satisfaction (i. e., the Hoppock scale scores) and gains in satisfaction for the achievement-feedback treatment group when intrinsic outcomes and all outcomes were considered. These correlations were .36 (intrinsic outcomes) and .37 (all outcomes) for the raw scores, and .32 and .29 for the gain scores ($p < .05$ for all coefficients). Since the achievement-feedback group was the only treatment group for which a contingency between the work role and certain role outcomes was clearly stated, Graen concluded that the job satisfaction model is limited to situations where the contingencies between work roles and role outcomes are stated in a concrete manner.

The job performance model (effective performer) failed to predict either the quality or quantity raw performance scores. In other words, there was no correlation between the raw scores and the product of the expectation that effort would lead to the role of effective performer and the evaluation of that role. However, the model was partially successful in predicting residual gain scores. These scores were obtained by partialing out pretreatment performance scores so that the variance in posttreatment performance due to ability, and pretreatment motivation is minimized. The effective performer model significantly predicted these scores for the achievement-treatment group when intrinsic and extrinsic role outcomes were considered separately and when all outcomes were considered at the same time. These correlations were .29, .22, and .28 for one task, and .41, .31, and .39 for another ($p < .05$ for all six coefficients). The model did not predict residual gain scores for the other treatment groups.

Together with the job satisfaction results, the just-mentioned results define boundary conditions for the instrumentality theory models. Graen suggested that the theory will be successful only when the contingencies between work roles and role outcomes are clearly stated.

These data also suggest, though less clearly, that the models will only be successful for the specific role outcomes that are linked to the work role. This conclusion is based on the fact that the job satisfaction model successfully predicted job satisfaction only for the intrinsic outcomes, and these outcomes were the only outcomes specifically linked to the job. Moreover, in the case of the relationship between the job performance model and performance for the achievement group, the correlations were higher for the intrinsic outcomes than they were for the extrinsic outcomes.

EXTENDED MODELS

Both Graen (1969) and Porter and Lawler (1968) suggested extensions of the basic instrumentality model to predict performance and job satisfaction. The latter authors suggested that the effort-performance relationship is moderated by ability and role perception variables. The relevant role perceptions are concerned with the types of effort an individual believes are essential to effective job performance. They argued that an accuracy of role perceptions score should be multiplied by an Effort × Ability score to predict performance. They presented some evidence that role perceptions do indeed moderate the effort-performance relationship (Lawler & Porter, 1967; Porter & Lawler, 1968), but no data have been presented that measure all three variables and combine them in the suggested manner.

Graen proposed a number of modifications of the models in addition to the distinction between work roles (first-level outcomes) and role outcomes (second-level outcomes). First, Graen suggested that the focus of the model be on gains in performance or satisfaction rather than raw scores. Besides being consistent with his results, he argued, this focus makes the model a dynamic one and provides the model with developmental implications. It is not clear why the prediction of changes in performance or satisfaction is more important than the prediction of raw scores, but Graen's modified model, if successful, would make explicit the factors that are important for increasing production or satisfaction.

Graen (1969) suggested additional predictors of performance and satisfaction. In addition to the Expectancy × Valence term, gains in performance are predicted from (a) the perceived expectations of others and pressure to comply with the others and (b) the sum of the valence of intrinsic consequences of the performance gain multiplied by the expectancy that the gain will lead to these consequences. The latter term reflects the subject's internally felt pressure toward increased performance.

Gains in satisfaction that are associated with gains in performance are predicted from the same model, except that the term referring to others' expectations is the amount of pressure consonant with increased performance *relative* to all pressure and the intrinsic instrumentality term refers to the amount of internally felt pressure that is consonant with increased performance relative to all internal pressure.

It can be seen that both Porter and Lawler's and Graen's work are conceptually similar to that of Fishbein and Dulany in that they include other sources of influence on behavior besides instrumentalities. Empirical support for these extensions, however, still must be presented.

In summary, instrumentalities appear to be an important factor in predicting the satisfaction and behavior of personnel in organizational settings. However, if we compare the amount of variance accounted for in the organization studies with the amount accounted for in the attitude and verbal conditioning areas, it appears that the use of instrumentalities has been less successful in the former area. There are at least two reasons why this might be the case. First, the phenomena that the industrial psychology studies are attempting to predict are more complex than those predicted in the various game and verbal conditioning settings. Second, the situations in the industrial settings are less controllable than those in the attitude and verbal conditioning areas.

REFERENCES

Galbraith, J., & Cummings, L. L. An empirical investigation of the motivational determinants of task performance. Interactive effects between instrumentality-valence and motivation-ability. *Organizational Behavior and Human Performance,* 1967, **2,** 237–257.

Georgopoulos, B. S., Mahoney, G. M., & Jones, N. W., Jr. A path-goal approach to productivity. *Journal of Applied Psychology,* 1957, **41,** 345–353.

Graen, G. Instrumentality theory of work motivation: Some experimental results and suggested modifications. *Journal of Applied Psychology Monograph,* 1969, **53,** (2, part 2).

Hackman, J. R., & Porter, L. W. Expectancy theory predictions of work effectiveness. *Organizational Behavior and Human Performance,* 1968, **3,** 417–426.

Hoppock, R. *Job satisfaction.* New York: Harper and Brothers, 1935.

Lawler, E. E. A correlational-causal analysis of the relationship between expectancy attitudes and job performance. *Journal of Applied Psychology,* 1968, **52,** 462–468.

Lawler, E. E., & Porter, L. W. Antecedent attitides of effective managerial performance. *Organizational Behavior and Human Performance,* 1967, **2,** 122–142.

Lewin, K. *A dynamic theory of personality.* New York: McGraw-Hill, 1935.

Porter, L. W., & Lawler, E. E. *Managerial attitudes and performance.* Homewood, Ill.: Irwin-Dorsey, 1968.

Tolman, E. C. *Purposive behavior in animals and men.* New York: Appleton-Century, 1932.

Vroom, V. H. *Work and motivation.* New York: Wiley, 1964.

QUESTIONS FOR DISCUSSION

1 Compare and contrast equity theory and expectancy/valence theory.
2 Why is expectancy/valence theory a multipicative model?
3 Evaluate the research evidence in support of the expectancy/valence model of motivation.
4 What, if anything, is really different between expectancy/valence theory and the theories covered earlier? (Consult the analytical framework in Chapter 1.)
5 What factors might possibly affect the valence levels attached to various outcomes by individuals?
6 If managers wanted to increase the motivational levels of their subordinates, would it generally be easier for them to manipulate their subordinates' expectancies or their valences? Why?
7 How can various rewards, like money, affect motivational processes under expectancy/valence theory?
8 When studying the expectancy/valence model of motivation, what benefits can be derived from dividing expectancies into two "types" ($E \rightarrow$ and $P \rightarrow O$)?
9 Of what practical value is the expectancy/valence model for line managers? What can managers learn from the model that would improve their effectiveness on the job?

Part Three

Central Issues in Motivation at Work

Chapter 7

Motivation, Performance, and Satisfaction

OVERVIEW

The relationship between job attitudes and job behavior has long been a topic of ✓ interest to both practicing managers and organizational researchers. Such interest dates back at least to the human relations movement of the 1930s, when it was generally felt that a happy worker was a productive one. A causal relationship was largely assumed during this time whereby job satisfaction "caused" improved job performance. The managerial implication was thus quite simple: keep your employees satisfied.

As time went on, however, research evidence began to call into question the veracity of this simple pronouncement. Based on an extensive review of investigations in the area, Brayfield and Crockett (1955) concluded that little evidence existed of any simple or even appreciable relation between job satisfaction and resulting performance. Somewhat later, Vroom (1964) analyzed the results of twenty studies which measured both satisfaction and performance and found that the two variables had a median correlation of .14. Correlation coefficients ranged from +.86 to −.31 across these studies.

These revelations sparked considerable controversy concerning the causal relationship—if any—between these variables. Did job satisfaction in fact lead to job performance or was the reverse true? Or was there a third alternative? Was it possible, for example, that other important intervening variables served to moderate the relationship?

In the two selections that follow, we shall consider this "controversy." Schwab and Cummings compare the evidence relating to three competing hypotheses: (1) that satisfaction leads to performance; (2) that satisfaction leads to performance, as moderated by a number of additional variables; and (3) that performance leads to satisfaction. Following this, Greene reviews additional research relating to this topic and argues, based on these data, that rewards, far more than performance, are the major factors that determine satisfaction. This contention is similar to earlier positions taken by Porter and Lawler (1968). Implications of such findings for the practicing manager are also discussed.

REFERENCES AND SUGGESTED ADDITIONAL READINGS

Brayfield, A. H., & Crockett, W. H. Employee attitudes and employee performance. *Psychological Bulletin,* 1955, **52,** 396–424.

Herzberg, F., Mausner, B., Peterson, R. O., & Capwell, D. *Job attitudes: Review of research and opinion.* Pittsburgh: Psychological Service of Pittsburgh, 1957.

Lawler, E. E., III, & Porter, L. W. The effect of performance on job satisfaction. *Industrial Relations,* 1967, **7**(1), 20–28.

Porter, L. W., & Lawler, E. E., III. *Managerial attitudes and performance.* Homewood, Ill.: Irwin, 1968.

Porter, L. W., & Lawler, E. E., III. What job attitudes tell us about motivation. *Harvard Business Review,* 1968, **46**(1), 118–126.

Vroom, V. H. *Work and motivation.* New York: Wiley, 1964.

Theories of Performance
and Satisfaction: A Review
Donald P. Schwab
Larry L. Cummings

. . . the animals worked like slaves. But they were happy in their work; they grudged no effort or sacrifice, well aware that everything that they did was for the benefit of themselves and those of their kind who would come after them. . . .[1]

A sizable portion of behavioral science research in organizations has focused on possible connections between job attitudes, particular job satisfaction, and various job behaviors.[2] Industrial psychologists and labor economists, for example, have explored the relationship between job satisfaction and job tenure.[3] Other scholars from various disciplines have examined the association between job satisfaction and such behavioral variables as absences, accidents, grievances, illnesses,[4] and even life expectancy.[5] More recently, a growing number of studies suggesting a controversy have emerged concerning the relationship between technology and task design and satisfaction with the job.[6]

Unquestionably, however, it is the hypothesized connection between employee satisfaction and job performance which has generated the greatest re-

From *Industrial Relations*, 1970, **7**, 408-430. Copyright by the Regents of the University of California. Reprinted by permission.

[1] George Orwell, *Animal Farm* (New York: New American Library, Signet Classics, 1959), p. 63.

[2] The authors thank H. G. Heneman, Jr., H. G. Heneman, III, R. U. Miller, and W. E. Scott, Jr., for their critical comments on an earlier draft of this paper. Portions of this paper were presented at the American Psychological Association Convention, September 1970, Miami Beach.

[3] For a review of psychological research on this relationship, see Victor H. Vroom, *Work and Motivation* (New York: Wiley, 1964), pp. 175–178. For more recent research investigating the relationship from a psychological point of view, see Charles L. Hulin, "Effects of Changes in Job Satisfaction Levels on Employee Turnover," *Journal of Applied Psychology*, LII (April, 1968), 122–126; Charles L Hulin, "Job Satisfaction and Turnover in a Female Clerical Population," *Journal of Applied Psychology*, L (August, 1966), 280–285, and Patricia S. Mikes and Charles L. Hulin, "Use of Importance as a Weighting Component of Job Satisfaction," *Journal of Applied Psychology*, LII (October, 1968), 394–398. Labor economists have tended to be concerned with the relative impact of differing types of satisfaction on turnover. In particular, they have sought to determine the importance of satisfaction with money income in the decision to remain with or leave an organization. In this regard, see the studies by Lloyd G. Reynolds, *The Structure of Labor Markets* (New York: Harper, 1951), pp. 79–101, and Charles A. Myers and George P. Shultz, *The Dynamics of a Labor Market* (New York: Prentice-Hall, 1951), pp. 102–134. These and other economically oriented studies are reviewed in Herbert S. Parnes, *Research on Labor Mobility* (New York: Social Science Research Council, 1954), pp. 147–156. For a discussion which attempts to explain the labor market findings within the context of classical economic theory, see Simon Rottenberg, "On Choice in Labor Markets," *Industrial and Labor Relations*, IX (January, 1956), 183–199.

[4] Studies investigating these relationships are reviewed in Arthur H. Brayfield and Walter H. Crockett, "Employee Attitudes and Employee Performance," *Psychological Bulletin*, LII (September, 1955), 396–424; Frederick H. Herzberg, Bernard M. Mausner, Richard O. Peterson, and Dora F. Capwell, *Job Attitudes: Review of Research and Opinion* (Pittsburgh: Psychological Service of Pittsburgh, 1957), pp. 107–111, and Vroom, *op. cit.*, pp. 178–181.

[5] See, for example, Francis C. Madigan, "Role Satisfactions and Length of Life in a Closed Population," *American Journal of Sociology*, LXVII (May, 1962), 640–649.

[6] A recent study by Shepard concluded that job satisfaction and functional job specialization are

search and theoretical interest. In the last 40 years, investigators have examined these two variables in a wide variety of work situations: (1) among organization members ranging from the unskilled to managers and professionals, (2) in diverse administrative and technological environments, (3) using individuals or groups as the unit of analysis, and (4) employing various measures of both satisfaction and performance. The methodologies employed in these studies, and their findings have been reviewed by Brayfield and Crockett; Herzberg, Mausner, Peterson and Capwell; and Vroom.[7]

Whereas earlier reviews have focused on empirical research, this paper reviews and evaluates *theoretical* propositions concerning the relationship between satisfaction and performance. Three major points of view are considered: (1) the view that satisfaction leads to performance, a position generally associated with early human relations concepts, (2) the view that the satisfaction-performance relationship is moderated by a number of variables, a position which gained acceptance in the fifties and continues to be reflected in current research, and (3) the view that performance leads to satisfaction, a recently stated position. Conceptualizations of satisfaction-performance relations which represent each of these positions are reviewed, even though several do not represent theories in any rigorous sense.

SATISFACTION → PERFORMANCE

. . . management has at long last discovered that there is greater production, and hence greater profit when workers are satisfied with their jobs. Improve the morale of a company and you improve production.[8]

Historical Perspective

Whatever their value as research, the Hawthorne studies had a significant impact on the thinking of a generation of behavioral scientists and business managers.[9] The quotation from Parker and Kleemeier was almost certainly inspired by the Hawthorne studies, although the original investigators probably never stated the

inversely related. Jon M. Shepard, "Functional Specialization and Work Attitudes, *Industrial Relations,* VIII (February, 1969), 185–194. However, a recent thorough review of the literature challenges much of the research which purportedly shows a relationship between job satisfaction and task design. Charles L. Hulin and Milton R. Blood, "Job Enlargement, Individual Differences and Worker Responses," *Psychological Bulletin,* LXIX (January, 1968), 41–55.

[7]Brayfield and Crockett, *op. cit.;* Herzberg, *et al., op. cit.;* and Vroom, *op. cit.*

[8]Willard E. Parker and Robert W. Kleemeier, *Human Relations in Supervision: Leadership in Management* (New York: McGraw-Hill, 1951), p. 10.

[9] Fritz J. Roethlisberger and William J. Dickson, *Management and the Worker,* Science Editions (New York: Wiley, 1964). For two highly critical interpretations of the Hawthorne studies as research, see A. J. M. Sykes, "Economic Interest and the Hawthorne Researchers: A Comment," *Human Relations,* XVIII (August, 1965), 253–263, and Alex Carey, "The Hawthorne Studies: A Radical Criticism," *American Sociological Review,* XXXII (June, 1967), 403–416. For less critical but earlier re-examinations, see Michael Argyle, "The Relay Assembly Test Room in Retrospect," *Occupational Psychology,* XXVII (April, 1953), 98–103, and Henry A. Landsberger, *Hawthorne Revisited* (Ithaca, New York: Cornell University, 1958).

relationship so unequivocally. Roethlisberger, for example, in discussing the implications of the study for managers, noted that " . . . the factors which make for efficiency in a business organization are not necessarily the same as those factors that make for happiness, collaboration, teamwork, morale, or any other word which may be used to refer to cooperative situations."[10]

Yet, despite Roethlisberger's caveat, the early human relationists have been interpreted as saying that satisfaction leads to performance. Vroom, for example, argues that " . . . human relations might be described as an attempt to increase productivity by satisfying the needs of employees."[11] Strauss states that " . . . early human relationists viewed the morale-productivity relationship quite simply: higher morale would lead to improved productivity." [12] In the final analysis the interpretation is perhaps more significant than the original views expressed.

A Current Satisfaction →
Performance Interpretation

The work of Herzberg and his colleagues provides perhaps the best illustration of current theory and research formulated on the view that satisfaction leads to performance. These researchers separate job variables into two groups, hygiene factors and motivators.[13] Included in the hygiene group are such variables as supervision, physical working conditions, regular salary and benefits, company policies, etc. These are viewed as potential sources of dissatisfaction, but not as sources of positive work attitudes. Among the motivators, Herzberg lists factors closely associated with work itself and its accomplishment, i. e., challenging assignments, recognition, the opportunity for professional growth, etc. These factors presumably contribute to work satisfaction and are the key factors associated with performance. Thus, Herzberg feels that low performance-satisfaction correlations obtained in other research studies can thus be explained since " . . . the usual morale measures are confounded . . . they tap both kinds of attitudes . . ." (i. e., satisfiers and dissatisfiers).[14]

In fairness to the original authors of *The Motivation to Work,* it should be recognized that the conclusion relating performance to the satisfiers but not to the dissatisfiers has escalated somewhat with the passage of time. In the original study, care was taken to report the actual percentages obtained and to at least raise alternative explanations of the findings.[15] These qualifications are not present in subsequent restatement of the original findings by Herzberg[16] or by other

[10]Fritz J. Roethlisberger, *Management and Morale* (Cambridge: Harvard University Press, 1941), p. 156.

[11]Vroom, *op. cit.,* p. 181.

[12]George Strauss, "Human Relations—1968 Style," *Industrial Relations,* VII (May, 1968), 264.

[13] Frederick Herzberg, Bernard Mausner, and Barbara Snyderman, *The Motivation to Work* (2nd edition; New York: Wiley, 1959), pp. 59–83.

[14]*Ibid.,* p. 87.

[15]*Ibid.,* pp. 86–87.

[16]Frederick Herzberg, *Work and the Nature of Man* (Cleveland: World Publishing, 1966), p. 74 and Frederick Herzberg, "One More Time, How Do You Motivate Employees?" *Harvard Business Review,* XLVI (January-February, 1968), 53–62.

advocates of the two-factor theory.[17] In short, it appears that the satisfaction-performance findings of *The Motivation to Work* are being overinterpreted in the same manner as were Roethlisberger and Dickson's findings in *Management and the Worker*.

Although there have been a number of partial replications of the two-factor theory,[18] they have not investigated the hypothesized performance consequences of job satisfaction and dissatisfaction.[19] Thus, the empirical validity of the satisfaction-performance relationship specified in the two-factor theory rests entirely on the original study of 200 accountants and engineers.[20]

Moreover, the evidence employed to support the premise that satisfaction leads to performance has been non-experimental in design. As such, the studies obviously do not show causality. In fact, neither human relationists in general, nor Herzberg in particular, have provided an adequate theoretical explanation for the causal relationship which they postulated.

In sum, it is our view that the popular interpretation of human relations research has probably been detrimental to the understanding of worker motivation. An essentially unsupported interpretation was so quickly and widely accepted that the underlying theory was neither questioned nor refined. By assuming, without adequate analysis, that observed satisfaction-performance linkages were causally and unidirectionally related, subsequent researchers may well have misinterpreted the meaning of their data.[21] Ultimately, however, it was probably the human relationist's failure to develop a sufficiently sophisticated theory, com-

---

[17]See, for example, David A. Whitsett and Erik K. Winslow, "An Analysis of Studies Critical of the Motivator-Hygiene Theory," *Personnel Psychology*, XX (Winter, 1967), 391–415.

[18]Nine such replications are discussed in Herzberg, *Work and the Nature of Man*, pp. 96–129. See, however, a study by Schwab and Heneman which suggests that the analytical procedure employed in the original study and in the replications overstates the theory's predictability of individual responses to satisfying and dissatisfying experiences. Donald P. Schwab and Herbert G. Heneman, III, "Aggregate and Individual Predictability of the Two-Factor Theory of Job Satisfaction," *Personnel Psychology*, XXIII (Spring, 1970), 55–66.

[19]See, for example, Frederick Herzberg, "The Motivation to Work Among Finnish Supervisors," *Personnel Psychology*, XVIII (Winter, 1965), 393–402; M. Scott Myers, "Who Are Your Motivated Workers?" *Harvard Business Review*, XLII (January—February, 1964), 73–88; Shoukry D. Saleh, "A Study of Attitde Change in the Pre-Retirement Period," *Journal of Applied Psychology*, XLVII (October, 1964), 310–312; and Milton M. Schwartz, Edmund Jenusaitis, and Harry Stark, "Motivational Factors Among Supervisors in the Utility Industry," *Personnel Psychology*, XVI (Spring, 1963), 45–53.

[20]Moreover, a recent study examining the relationship between job attitudes and performance effects did not find support for Herzberg's hypothesis. Among a group of 80 managers, it was found that the dissatisfiers were as closely associated with variations in performance effects as were the satisfiers. Donald P. Schwab, William W. Devitt and Larry L. Cummings, "A Test of the Adequacy of the Two-Factor Theory as a Predictor of Self-Report Performance Effects," *Personnel Psychology*, XXIV (Summer, 1971).

[21] Several findings of the Herzberg, *et al.*, study suggest, for example, an alternative interpretation. They reported that 74 percent of satisfying and 25 percent of the dissatisfying sequences included feelings of achievement and/or recognition for successful or unsuccessful job performance. (Cf. Herzberg, *et al.*, *The Motivation to Work*, pp. 72, 143.) In these instances, at least, it would seem plausible to argue that performance preceded, rather than followed, satisfaction. If one were to accept their conclusions about stated performance effects, it would seem appropriate to suggest a possible circular relationship between satisfaction and performance.

bined with ambiguous, often contradictory research evidence, which led to other formulations of the relationship between these two variables.

SATISFACTION—?—
PERFORMANCE

. . . high morale is no longer considered as a prerequisite of high productivity. But more than this, the nature of the relationship between morale and productivity is open to serious questioning. Is it direct? Is it inverse? Is it circular? Or, is there any relationahip at all between the two; are they independent variables?[22]

The Development of Uncertainty

The statement by Scott (and others similar to it)[23] reflects perhaps more than anything else the pervasive influence of the previously mentioned review by Brayfield and Crockett, along with the conclusions reached in some of the early research conducted at the Institute for Social Research, University of Michigan.[24]

The Michigan findings are important for at least two reasons. First, they represent early empirical evidence offering little reason for optimism about the association between satisfaction and performance. In the insurance and railroad studies only one of the four attitude measures (pride in work group) was found to be positively associated with the productivity measures employed.[25] Second, unlike much previous research reported, the investigators carefully spelled out the limitations of their design for making causal inferences and specifically suggested alternative causal hypotheses which their data might support.[26]

A capstone to the development of uncertainty regarding the satisfaction-performance relationship was provided by Brayfield and Crockett in 1955.[27]

[22]William G. Scott, *Human Relations in Management: A Behavioral Science Approach* (New York: McGraw-Hill, 1962), p. 93.

[23] See also, for example, March and Simon who stated that "Attempts to relate these variables (morale, satisfaction and cohesiveness) directly to productivity have failed to reveal any consistent simple relation." James G. March and Herbert A. Simon, *Organizations* (New York: Wiley, 1958), pp. 47–48. In the same vein, Carey, in commenting on the Hawthorne studies, noted " . . . the widespread failure of later (post-Hawthorne) studies to reveal any reliable relations between the social satisfaction of industrial workers and their work performance." Carey, *op. cit.*, p. 403. Even Davis, an avowed human relationist, deferred to Brayfield and Crockett, conceding that one must " . . . recognize that high morale and high productivity are not absolutely related to each other." Keith Davis, *Human Relations in Business* (New York: McGraw-Hill, 1957), p. 182.

[24]Daniel Katz, Nathan Maccoby, and Nancy C. Morse, *Productivity Supervision and Morale in an Office Situation* (Ann Arbor: University of Michigan, Survey Research Center, 1950) and Daniel Katz, Nathan Maccoby, Gerald Gurin, and Lucretia G. Floor, *Productivity, Supervision, and Morale Among Railroad Workers* (Ann Arbor: University of Michigan, Survey Research Center, 1951).

[25]Katz, et al., *Productivity . . . in an Office Situation*, p. 48 and Katz, et al., *Productivity . . . Among Railroad Workers*, pp. 24–30. Factor items and analyses differed somewhat between the two studies and thus they are not strictly comparable. In summarizing this research, Kahn stated that "The persistence with which managers and managerial consultants place them (satisfaction and performance) in juxtaposition is much more revealing of their own value structure, I believe, than it is indicative of anything in the empirical research data on organizations." Robert L. Kahn, "Productivity and Job Satisfaction," *Personnel Psychology*, XIII (Autumn, 1960), 275.

[26]Katz, et al., *Productivity . . . in an Office Situation*, pp. 14–15.

[27] Brayfield and Crockett, *op. cit.*

Their review of over 50 studies represents, depending on one's point of view, either a council of despair or a challenge for theory development and extended research. As we will illustrate, the latter (at least the theoretical dimension) seems to have prevailed.

Brayfield and Crockett hypothesized that employees govern their job seeking, job performing, and job terminating behavior by the law of effect, subsequently elaborated and relabeled by Vroom, and Porter and Lawler, as expectancy theory.[28] Regarding job terminating behavior, Brayfield and Crockett argued that: "One principal generalization suffices to set up an expectation that morale should be related to absenteeism and turnover, namely, that organisms tend to avoid those situations which are punishing and to seek out situations that are rewarding."[29]

Brayfield and Crockett encountered greater difficulty explaining satisfaction and job performance linkages through the simple application of the hedonistic principle. They suggested that satisfaction and job performance might be concomitantly rather than causally related. In addition, one ". . . might expect high satisfaction and high productivity to occur together when productivity is perceived as a path to certain important goals and when these goals are achieved. Under other conditions, satisfaction and productivity might be unrelated or even negatively related."[30]

Additional Models

Three lesser known theoretical expositions of the satisfaction-performance relation further illustrate the influence of the mixed and uncertain research findings in this area.[31] Each suggests that both satisfaction and performance can be viewed as criteria of organizational effectiveness. Moreover, each suggests that relationships between satisfaction and performance need be neither direct nor particularly strong.

A Theory of Work Adjustment   In the first of these, Dawis and his colleagues posit that work adjustment is a function of employee *satisfaction* and *satisfactoriness* (performance).[32] Satisfaction presumably results from the correspondence between the individual's need set and the organization's reinforcer system and has its major impact on individual decisions to remain with or with-

---

[28]Vroom, *op. cit.,* and Lyman W. Porter and Edward E. Lawler, III, *Managerial Attitudes and Performance* (Homewood, Ill.: Irwin, 1968).

[29]Brayfield and Crockett, *op. cit.,* p. 415.

[30]*Ibid.,* p. 416. The tone of this quote anticipates a portion of the Porter-Lawler model to be discussed subsequently; namely that performance can lead to satisfaction when mediated by relevant goals (rewards in the terminology of the Porter-Lawler model).

[31]Rene V. Dawis, George E. England, and Lloyd H. Lofquist, *A Theory of Work Adjustment: A Revision* (Minneapolis: University of Minnesota, Industrial Relations Center, 1968), Bulletin 47; Harry C. Triandis, "A Critique and Experimental Design for the Study of the Relationship Between Productivity and Job Satisfaction," *Psychology Bulletin,* LVI (July, 1959), 309–312, and March and Simon, *op. cit.*

[32]Dawis, *et al., op. cit.,* p. 8.

draw from the organization. Satisfactoriness, alternatively, refers to the organization's evaluation (in terms of its goals) of the behavior of its members. It is assumed to be a function of the correspondence between the requirements imposed by the job and the abilities possessed by the employee and can result in one of several consequences, e. g., promotion, transfer, termination, or retention in present position. Incorporated in the Dawis *et al.* model is the possibility of a relation between satisfaction and satisfactoriness, although its form and strength are not developed. Moreover, their model allows one to explain variations in employee satisfaction without reference to performance (either as a cause or consequence).

Pressure for Production as an Intervening Variable In a related statement, Triandis has proposed a theory which shares with Dawis *et al.* the notion that satisfaction and performance need not covary under all conditions.[33] Triandis hypothesized that organizational pressure for high production influences both satisfaction and performance, but not in the same fashion. As pressure increases, job satisfaction is hypothesized to decrease irrespective of the concomitant variation in performance. Employee performance, alternatively, is hypothesized to be curvilinearly related to production pressure. At several locations with the typical range of employee satisfaction increasing pressure is hypothesized to result in increased performance, while at other locations the relation between pressure and performance is assumed to be negative. Triandis also hypothesized that satisfaction and performance may be directly linked in certain circumstances. Finally, satisfaction may also lead to moderate performance under the utopian condition of no pressure to perform. This would be the case where a minimum level of performance is caused by intrinsic job satisfaction plus certain activity drives or needs for stimulus inputs and variation.[34]

Satisfaction and the Motivation to Produce A model proposed by March and Simon perhaps best bridges the theoretical gap between the satisfaction → performance view of the human relationists and the performance → satisfaction view to be discussed in the following section.[35] The model suggests that both performance and satisfaction can serve as dependent variables.

Beginning with performance as the dependent variable, March and Simon hypothesized: "Motivation to produce stems from a present or anticipated state of discontent and a perception of a direct connection between individual production and a new state of satisfaction." [36] The hypothesis states that performance is a function of two variables: (1) the degree of dissatisfaction experienced, and (2) the perceived instrumentality of performance for the attainment of valued rewards.

[33]Triandis, *op. cit.*
[34]For an elaborated treatment of the implications of activity drives or activation levels as correlates of task performance, see William E. Scott, Jr., "Activation Theory and Task Design," *Organizational Behavior and Human Performance,* I (September, 1966), 3–30.
[35]March and Simon, *op. cit.*
[36]*Ibid.*, p. 51.

Thus, the model suggests that a state of dissatisfaction is a necessary, but not sufficient, condition for performance. It is necessary because dissatisfaction of some sort is assumed to be required to activate the organism toward search behavior. It lacks sufficiency, however, because a dissatisfied employee may not perceive performance as leading to satisfaction or may perceive nonperformance as leading to greater perceived satisfaction.

March and Simon also specify conditions where performance may lead to satisfaction although the linkage appears weaker (moderated by a greater number of variables) in their model than the satisfaction → performance linkage.[37] This is due to three factors. First, we have already noted that the hypothesized job satisfaction may result from the receipt of rewards which are not based on performance. Second, even if improved performance is the behavioral alternative chosen by the employee, satisfaction need not necessarily result since the actual rewards of performance may not correspond to the anticipated consequences. Third, in the process of searching for an evaluating the consequences of alternative behaviors, the worker's level of aspiration may be raised as much or more than the expected value of the rewards associated with the behavior. Thus, even if performance is chosen as the best alternative and its consequences are perfectly anticipated, the worker may find himself no more and perhaps less satisfied than before.

The Models Compared   The above three models can most easily be contrasted on the independent variables hypothesized to influence employee performance. The theory of work adjustment implies that the major determinant of performance is the structural fit between employee skills and abilities on the one hand and technical job requirements on the other. Thus, its implications for organizational practice are largely in the areas of employee selection, placement, and training. In contrast, March and Simon focus primarily on two motivational determinants of performance; namely, expected value of rewards and aspiration levels. Finally, Triandis emphasizes the importance of pressure for production, an organizational variable. As such, the Triandis model ignores the impact of either skill and ability or motivational differences between individuals.

It is also interesting to contrast Triandis, March and Simon, and the Herzberg two-factor theory with regard to the circumstances leading to a causative linkage between performance and satisfaction. In the Triandis and March and Simon models, it is dissatisfaction which can have performance implications (negative in the former; positive in the latter). The two-factor theory alternatively suggests that it is predominantly satisfaction which leads to high performance.

PERFORMANCE → SATISFACTION

. . . good performance may lead to rewards, which in turn lead to satisfaction;

---

[37]Because March and Simon hypothesize that in certain circumstances performance leads to satisfaction, their theory could have been included in the following major section. We include it here because they hypothesize that performance is not necessary for satisfaction, while dissatisfaction is necessary for performance. Porter and Lawler's theory, discussed later, also hypothesizes a circular causal connection between satisfaction and performance. It reverses the emphasis of March and Simon, however, since it concentrates on the performance→satisfaction linkage.

this formulation then would say that satisfaction, rather than causing perfor-mance, as was previously assumed, is caused by it.[38]

The performance → satisfaction theory represents an important departure from earlier views about the relationship between these two variables. Human relationists, not without some qualification, postulated that high levels of satis-faction would result in high levels of performance. Subsequent models focused on the complexity of the relationship, incorporating ambiguous findings of empirical studies. The performance → satisfaction theory, while it retains the idea of inter-vening variables, stresses the importance of variations in effort and performance as causes of variations in job satisfaction.

The Porter-Lawler Model[39]

Just as the Brayfield and Crockett review significantly influenced subsequent theoretical developments on the satisfaction → performance issue, a later review published by Vroom in 1964 has apparently had a similar impact on recent theorizing. While noting the generally low correspondence observed between measured satisfaction and performance, Vroom nevertheless found that in 20 of 23 cases the correlation was positive and that the median correlation reported was +.14.[40] Porter and Lawler have cited this review and the generally positive nature of this association as a basis for suggesting that premature, pessimistic closure would be unwise and have expounded their model through a series of recent publications.[41]

Although the Porter-Lawler model posits circularity in the relationship be-tween performance and satisfaction, Figure 1 shows that the most direct linkage has performance as the causal and satisfaction as the dependent variable. That relationship is mediated only by rewards (intrinsic and extrinsic) and the per-ceived equity of those rewards.

When performance leads to rewards which are seen by the individual as equitable, it is hypothesized that high satisfaction will result.[42] The model sug-

---

[38]Edward E. Lawler, III, and Lyman W. Porter, "The Effect of Performance on Job Satisfac-tion," *Industrial Relations,* VII (October, 1967), p.23.

[39]The performance → satisfaction theory is attributed to Porter and Lawler because they have developed it most fully. As we have already noted, March and Simon suggested conditions when performance could cause satisfaction. Vroom also suggests that performance as a cause of satisfaction is somewhat more tenable than the reverse (*op. cit.,* p. 187).

[40]*Ibid.,* p. 183.

[41]Edward E. Lawler, III, and Lyman W. Porter, "Antecedent Attitudes of Effective Managerial Performance," *Organizational Behavior and Human Performance,* II (May, 1967), 122–142; Edward E. Lawler, III, "Attitude Surveys and Job Performance," *Personnel Administration,* XXX (September–October, 1967), 3-ff; Lawler and Porter, "The Effect of Performance on Job Satisfaction"; Lyman W. Porter and Edward E. Lawler, III, "What Job Attitudes Tell About Motivation," *Harvard Business Review,* XLVI (January–February, 1968), 118–136, and Porter and Lawler, *Managerial Attitudes and Performance.*

[42]The concept of equity does not play the central role in the Porter-Lawler theory as it does, say, in the works of Adams. See, for example, J. Stacy Adams, "Toward an Understanding of Inequity," *Journal of Abnormal and Social Psychology,* LXVII (November, 1963), 422–436, and "Wage Inequities, Productivity and Work Quality," *Industrial Relations* III (October, 1963), 9–16. In addition, at least one of the authors appears to have some serious reservations about the predictive utility of equity theory. See Edward E. Lawler, III, "Equity Theory as a Predictor of Productivity and Work Quality," *Psychological Bulletin,* LXX (December, 1968), 596–610.

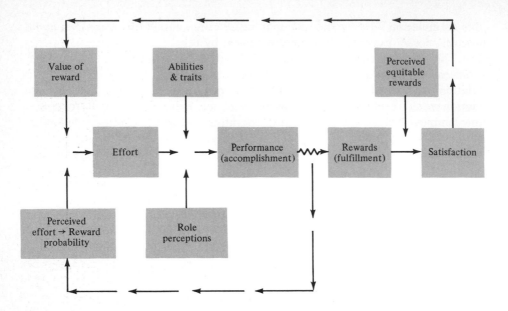

Figure 1 Performance → satisfaction. (*Adapted from Lyman W. Porter and Edward E. Lawler, III*, Managerial Attitudes and Performance, *Richard D. Irwin, Inc., Homewood, Ill., 1968, p. 17.*)

gests that the generally low performance-satisfaction relationships observed in previous empirical research may result from rewards, particularly extrinsic rewards, which are often not closely tied to performance.[43]

For satisfaction to exert an influence on performance in the Porter-Lawler model, it must affect the value of the rewards received, which in turn interacts with the perceived effort → reward linkage to determine the level of actual work effort. Finally, effort moderated by role perceptions and abilities and traits determines performance. Because of the number of intervening variables involved, it seems unlikely that satisfaction (or dissatisfaction) has as much impact on performance as performance has on satisfaction.

A Comparative Evaluation The March and Simon model probably provides the most salient comparison with the Porter-Lawler model because both explicitly postulate a circular performance-satisfaction relation. The theories can be contrasted regarding the conditions necessary to avoid entropy or the "running down" of the level of employee motivation. In the March and Simon model, the function is performed primarily by aspiration level. It is hypothesized that as the expected value of reward increases, level of aspiration increases, which in turn has a negative impact on satisfaction. Thus, the concept of aspiration level enables the model to be dynamic. That is, it is partially because of a rising aspiration level (resulting from the receipt of past rewards) that dissatisfaction is created, thereby leading to search behavior, one form of which can be performance.

Provision for the avoidance of entropy is more tenuous in the Porter-Lawler

[43]Lawler and Porter, "The Effect of Performance on Job Satisfaction," pp. 23–24.

model. To sustain effort and performance over time, it is necessary to assume that satisfaction experienced from the receipt of intrinsic rewards leads to enhanced value being attached to such rewards. One must assume, for example, that feelings of worthwhile accomplishment increase the attractiveness or valence of such achievement.[44] As the authors note, however, the relation between satisfaction and value of reward can be interpreted in contrasting ways.[45] There exists some physiological and psychological evidence to suggest that the greater the extrinsic reward satisfaction experienced, the less value attached to such rewards.[46] This would clearly lead to eventual entropy in the Porter-Lawler model. The point of contention between the two models on this issue centers on the causative factors in the continuity and preservation of behavior over time. Since both models are essentially based on need deprivation theories, some mechanism must be provided to prevent the system from attaining entropy.

Alternative Sources of Satisfaction   Porter and Lawler's model can be contrasted with both the March and Simon model and the theory of work adjustment on the question of sufficiency of performance for satisfaction. The Porter-Lawler model shown in Figure 1 implies that satisfaction results from rewards associated with performance. It does not, therefore, appear to take into account all sources of employee satisfaction. Consider, for example, an organization which bases its rewards on seniority or organizational longevity. For persons with relatively strong security needs and low task involvement, seniority may represent the most rational means to the attainment of valued rewards and satisfaction. That is, the performance → reward linkage is not a necessary condition for attainment of meaningful satisfactions. Nor is it necessarily a condition for organizational survival. There are industrial jobs where minimally acceptable levels of performance are sufficient conditions for sustained participation. If system rewards are based on participation rather than individual performance and if they are perceived to be administered equitably, then, logically, satisfaction may be evident. This possibility is accounted for in the theory of work adjustment through the correspondence between employee needs and the reinforcer system of the job. It is accounted for in March and Simon's theory by their explicit hypothesis that satisfaction may result from rewards associated with various forms of nonperformance.

Implications for Administrative Practice   The Porter-Lawler model is quite rich in terms of its administrative implications. For example, it shares with the theory of work adjustment implications for high performance through the modification of abilities and traits via selection and training processes. In addition, their theory more than the others suggests a role for performance appraisal and salary

[44]On this point, satisfaction or dissatisfaction having performance consequences, Porter and Lawler are clearly closer to Herzberg and the early human relationists than to March and Simon or Triandis.

[45]Porter and Lawler, *Managerial Attitudes and Performance*, pp. 39–40.

[46]Charles N. Cofer and Mortimer H. Appley, *Motivation: Theory and Research* (New York: Wiley, 1964), pp. 204–268.

administration in increasing employee performance levels. Both activities presumably have the potential of influencing the effort → reward and performance → reward probabilities. Furthermore, salary level, and particularly salary structure, would appear to be important determinants of perceived equity of rewards.

Alternatively, the Porter-Lawler model does not explicitly include supervisory and system pressure for high levels of effort and performance. These may be extremely important variables in some organizations. In this regard, Triandis' discussion is clearly more realistic. March and Simon's model also considers organizational pressure through its influence on the individual's evaluation of the perceived consequences of behavioral alternatives.

DISCUSSION

Two broad problems suggested by out review of the theoretical literature are discussed in the present section. First, although we have noted some obvious differences and points of contrast between various theoretical viewpoints, rigorous comparison and evaluation is made difficult by the fact that there are few commonly defined constructs across various theories. Second, it appears questionable whether present theorizing has adequately accounted for the variety of relevant variables that may moderate satisfaction-performance linkages in any specific work environment.

Conceptual Problems

In their review of empirical studies, Brayfield and Crockett observed: "Definitions are conspicuous by their absence in most current work in this area." [47] Much of the same conclusion can be stated after reviewing the theoretical literature, and the consequences are even more troublesome. In empirical research the measures employed ultimately define the variables. Thus, if operational procedures are adequately reported, one can identify the definitions and assess their appropriateness to the research question posed.[48] However, with regard to theory, it is impossible to ascertain the meaning of variables if the theoretician fails to define terms.

Satisfaction

The greatest ambiguity in theorizing about satisfaction-performance linkages has been in defining satisfaction. Three partially overlapping issues are raised by the literature reviewed here. First, it is often unclear whether satisfaction is being used in a "narrow," need deprivation sense, or in a "broad," attitudinal sense. Second, it is generally not clear which needs or which attitudinal referents are being considered. Third, there is a question whether feelings of job satisfaction are generated with or without reference to conditions on other jobs. These issues make comparisons among theoretical positions risky.

[47]Brayfield and Crockett, *op. cit.,* p. 397.
[48]Evans recently identified five definitions of satisfaction generated by alternative measuring procedures. Martin G. Evans, "Conceptual and Operational Problems in the Measurement of Various Aspects of Job Satisfaction," *Journal of Applied Psychology,* LIII (April, 1969), 93–101.

Beginning with the need deprivation versus attitude issue, satisfaction-dissatisfaction may be thought of in the context of "elementary" motivation theory.[49] Needs, demands, or drives generate tensions (feelings of dissatisfaction). The individual engages in behavior designed to obtain goals or incentives to reduce the tensions (satisfy the need).

Alternatively, satisfaction-dissatisfaction can be thought of as the evaluative component of an attitude. A person may respond affectively (feel satisfied or dissatisfied) about an object or referent in his work environment. Peak has argued that an attitude toward an object is a function of the object's perceived instrumentality for obtaining a valued end.[50] Thus, an object (e. g., economic rewards) could be positively valent (satisfying) in an attitudinal sense[51] while simultaneously deficient (dissatisfying) in a need sense. Illustrating these definitional differences, in the March and Simon model (dissatisfaction may lead to high performance), satisfaction appears to be defined in the need deprivation context.[52] Dissatisfaction (deprivation) in a sense, "pushes" the individual to behave. Satisfaction in the two-factor theory (satisfaction leads to performance), on the other hand, may refer to the affective feelings associated with certain job referents. A referent with positive valence may "pull" an individual to obtain it.[53]

Whether the theoretician chooses to work with needs or with attitudes he must still identify the need types or attitude referents about which the individual feels satisfied or dissatisfied. There is evidence suggesting that global job satisfaction is made up of at least partially independent subcomponents.[54] Recent research at Cornell on the Job Description Index and other satisfaction measures, for example, has identified five subcomponents of overall satisfaction (work, pay, promotion, supervision, and co-workers) showing adequate convergent and discriminant validity.[55] The Minnesota Satisfaction Questionnaire has 20 factors

[49] See, for example, David Drech and Richard S. Crutchfield, *Theory and Problems of Social Psychology* (New York: McGraw-Hill, 1948), pp. 40–43.

[50] Helen Peak, "Attitude and Motivation," in Marshall R. Jones, editor, *Nebraska Symposium on Motivation* (Lincoln, Nebraska: University of Nebraska Press, 1955), pp. 149–159. Note the similarity between attitude as defined by Peak and valence as defined by Vroom. In Vroom's model, motivation (force) is a function of valence (attitude) times the expectation that a particular behavior will lead to the desired outcome (*op. cit.*, pp. 15–19). Porter and Lawler use attitudes to refer to valence as well as other antecedents of job performance (*Managerial Attitudes and Performance* and "Antecedent Attitudes of Effective Managerial Performance"). For quite a different formulation of attitude, see Daryl J. Bem, "Self-Perception: The Dependent Variable of Human Performance," *Organizational Behavior and Human Performance*, II (May, 1967), 105–121. He argued attitudes result from behavior. For evidence on a similar theme, see Aaron Lowin and James R. Craig, "The Influence of Level of Performance on Managerial Style: An Experimental Object-Lesson in the Ambiguity of Correlational Data," *Organizational Behavior and Human Performance*, III (November, 1968), 440–458.

[51] And hence be a necessary, but not sufficient, condition for motivation given Vroom's model.

[52] Unfortunately, March and Simon do not define satisfaction in their discussion. In fact, they do not explicitly distinguish between satisfaction, morale, or cohesiveness (Organizations, pp. 47–48).

[53] While Herzberg *et at.* employ the term job attitude when referring to satisfaction, they do not define it (Herzberg, *et al., The Motivation to Work*, pp. 5–12). More importantly, they do not discuss the mechanism whereby performance is perceived as the path to the attainment of the satisfying referent. In this context, see Vroom's discussion of expectancy (*op. cit.*, pp. 17–18).

[54] For a review, see Vroom, *op. cit.*, pp. 101–105.

[55] Lorne M. Kendall, Patricia C. Smith, Charles L. Hulin, and Edwin A. Locke, "Cornell Studies of Job Satisfaction: IV The Relative Validity of the Job Description Index and Other Methods of

which have shown only moderately high intercorrelations.[56] Hinrichs factored a 60-item satisfaction questionnaire and obtained nine fairly independent factors.[57]

Despite (or, perhaps because of) this type of research, little is known about the number of satisfaction objects, their interrelationship or their relationship to more global feelings of satisfaction.[58] With such basic questions about job satisfaction unanswered, it is imperative that theoreticians be specific about the satisfaction objects they have in mind. Performance implications may well differ depending upon the type of satisfaction under study.

One illustration is sufficient to show the ambiguity which results if the theorist fails to adequately confront this issue. As noted previously, Triandis hypothesized that pressure leads to dissatisfaction. In light of the previous discussion one might well ask, what type of dissatisfaction?[59] Suppose the pressure is induced by the supervisor.[60] An increase in dissatisfaction with supervision might be expected. There seems little reason to believe, however, that satisfaction with referents such as pay, promotion opportunities, working conditions, or co-workers will decrease.[61] One might even hypothesize that increases in supervisory pressure, in some circumstances, would increase informal group cohesiveness,[62] which in turn may increase satisfaction with co-workers. The impact of supervisory pressure on overall satisfaction, to say nothing of performance, is very much in doubt.

Comparison of one of the theories reviewed with recent empirical work suggests another issue that may bear on hypothesized satisfaction-behavior relations. Specifically, the definition and model in the theory of work adjustment clearly imply that satisfaction is perceived as an intra-job phenomenon, i. e., judgments

Measurement of Job Satisfaction," unpublished paper, 1963. A recent thorough description of the development of the JDI can be found in Patricia C. Smith, Lorne M. Kendall, and Charles L Hulin, *The Measurement of Satisfaction in Work and Retirement* (Chicago, Ill.: Rand McNally, 1969).

[56]David J. Weiss, Rene V. Dawis, George W. England, and Lloyd H. Lofquist, *Manual for the Minnesota Satisfaction Questionnaire* (Minneapolis: University of Minnesota, Industrial Relations Center, 1967), Bulletin 45, pp. 93–100. McCormack has shown how erroneous it may be to assume that because two variables correlate fairly highly with each other (e.g., two satisfaction measures) both will correlate about the same with some third variable (e.g., performance). Robert L. McCormack, "A Criticism of Studies Comparing Item-Weighing Methods," *Journal of Applied Psychology*, XL (October, 1956), 343–344. See also Patricia C. Smith and Lorne M. Kendall, "Cornell Studies of Job Satisfaction: VI Implications for the Future," unpublished paper, 1963.

[57]John R. Hinrichs, "A Replicated Study of Job Satisfaction Dimensions," *Personnel Psychology*, XXI (Winter, 1968), 479–503.

[58]Weiss, *et al.,* found that the factor structure of measured satisfaction varied across occupational groups (*Manual for the Minnesota Satisfaction Questionnaire,* pp. 22–23). While the factor structure was relatively constant across five subsamples in Hinrichs' study, differences existed in terms of the degree to which various factors correlated with an overall measure of satisfaction (*op. cit.*).

[59]In fairness to Triandis, it should be noted that the same criticism could be made of most of the other models. Only Herzberg *et al.,* have specifically dealt with types of satisfaction.

[60]As noted above, Triandis did not specify the type of pressure induced either.

[61]All of these hypotheses are, of course, empirically researchable. We simply do not know whether increasing levels of supervisory pressure increase or decrease various types of dissatisfaction for all individuals and for all levels of pressure.

[62]If true, this would clearly complicate any pressure-satisfaction-performance linkage. Seashore, for example, concluded that identification with management goals moderated the relation between cohesiveness and performance. Stanley Seashore, *Group Cohesiveness in the Industrial Work Group* (Ann Arbor: University of Michigan, Survey Research Center, 1954).

of satisfaction or dissatisfaction are made without reference to the reinforcer system of other jobs in the same organization or jobs in other organizations.[63] Smith, on the other hand, suggests that job satisfaction may more appropriately be thought of in relative terms. She hypothesized that " . . . above a certain minimum, for example, a given annual income is a positive source of satisfaction, a source of dissatisfaction, or irrelevant to an individual, depending upon what other jobs might pay, upon what other people of comparable training, skills, and experience are obtaining (in the same labor market), upon what the same individual has earned in the past, and upon the financial obligations he has assumed and expenditures to which he has become accustomed."[64]

Without getting into the merits of the two approaches in an abstract sense, we simply wish to point out that expected relationships between satisfaction and other variables may differ depending upon the definition chosen. We would hypothesize, for example, that scores on an operational measure of Smith's definition would be more highly related to voluntary turnover than scores obtained from a measure conforming to the theory of work adjustment.[65] The former reflects labor market conditions, a variable which has been shown to influence voluntary turnover;[66] the latter does not.

The issues raised here do not exhaust those which might be considered when discussing conceptual problems associated with satisfaction. They do, however, serve to to show that comparisons between different theories are difficult, if not impossible, without explicit definitions on the part of the theorist. They also suggest that one might expect quite dissimilar relationships between satisfaction and other variables depending on one's definition of satisfaction.

Performance

In defining performance a fundamental issue pertains to the value of thinking in terms of some "ultimate" criterion as thougt it was a unidimensional construct.[67]

[63]Dawis, et al., op. cit., pp. 8, 13.

[64]Patricia C. Smith, "Cornell Studies of Job Satisfaction: I Strategy for the Development of a General Theory of Job Satisfaction," unpublished paper, 1963.

[65]It may be difficult to obtain an operational measure conforming to Dawis' et al., definition. Results from a study conducted by Hulin suggest that individuals may respond from a relative frame of reference even when asked about satisfaction with a specific job. He found, for example, that satisfaction with pay was inversely related to such community factors as median income, percentage of residents earning over $10,000, percentage of acceptable housing units, and per capita retail sales. Since type of organization, job level, and sex of respondents was held relatively constant across communities, Hulin concluded variance in satisfaction was due to job opportunity differences in the communities sampled. Charles L. Hulin, "Effects of Community Characteristics on Measure of Job Satisfaction," *Journal of Applied Psychology*, LIX (April, 1966), 185–192.

[66]See, for example, Hilde Behrend, "Absence and Labour Turnover in a Changing Economic Environment," *Occupational Psychology*, XXVII (April, 1953), 69–79; Gladys L. Palmer, *Labor Mobility in Six Cities* (New York: Social Science Research Council, 1954), and Reynolds, op. cit.

[67] For example, Bechtoldt defined the criterion as " . . . the performance of individuals on a success criterion." Harold P. Bechtoldt, "Problems of Establishing Criterion Measures," in Dewey B. Stuit, editor, *Personnel Research and Test Development in the Bureau of Naval Personnel* (Princeton: Princeton University, 1947), p. 357. At a somewhat more sophisticated level, Brogden and Taylor sought to qualify various performance dimensions on a single monetary continuum. H. E. Brogden and E. K. Taylor, "The Dollar Criterion: Applying the Cost Accounting Concept to Criterion Construction," *Personnel Psychology*, III (Summer, 1950), 133–154.

This global approach is partially the result of efforts to arrive at operational measures of performance through overall ratings or rankings of the workers' effectiveness.[68] Recent theory and research severely questions the adequacy of this point of view.[69] Research has shown, for example, that alternative criterion measures are neither particularly stable over time[70] nor highly intercorrelated.[71] This suggests, of course, that relations between other variables and performance will vary depending upon the performance measure employed.

Despite this evidence, theorists interested in satisfaction-performance relations have generally treated performance as a homogeneous variable.[72] This position is particularly troublesome when one thinks of measuring performance across different kinds of tasks, organizations, and occupations.[73] For example, on some jobs performance would appear to be heavily influenced by rule compliance and programmatic behavior, while on others problem solving and creative behavior are probably much more important. One might well expect differences in relationships between some satisfaction measure and these two types of performance.

Potential Moderator Variables

Definitions aside, a commendable trend in recent theorizing and research is the inclusion of variables hypothesized to moderate the relationship between satisfaction and performance. In an experimental study, Korman found that subjects' self-esteem (a variable not explicitly accounted for in previous theorizing) moderated the relationshp between task success (performance) and task liking (satisfaction).[74] Carlson recently reported that the measured correspondence between the

[68]Robert M. Guion, "Personnel Selection," *Annual Review of Psychology,* XVIII (1967), 191–216.

[69]For a brief but excellent discussion, see Marvin D. Dunnette, "A Note on The Criterion," *Journal of Applied Psychology,* XLVII (August, 1963), 251–254.

[70]Edwin E. Ghiselli and Mason Haire, "The Validation of Selection Tests in the Light of the Dynamic Character of Criteria," *Personnel Psychology,* XIII (Autumn, 1960), 225–231, and Edwin E. Ghiselli; "Dimensional Problems of Criteria," *Journal of Applied Psychology,* XL (February, 1956), 1–4.

[71]See, for example, Charles L. Hulin, "Relevance and Equivalence in Criterion Measures of Executive Success," *Journal of Industrial Psychology,* I (September, 1963), 67–78.

[72] Moreover, definitions differ among theories. Porter and Lawler identify but do not distinguish (in terms of relations with satisfaction) between three types of performance measures: objective, subjective-supervisor, and subjective-self (Porter and Lawler, *Managerial Attitudes and Performance,* pp. 26–28). Performance is measured by self-evaluations in the two-factor theory (Herzberg, *et al., The Motivation to Work,* pp. 51–52). In the theory of work adjustment performance (satisfactoriness) is measured by the organization (Dawis, *et al., The Theory of Work Adjustment,* p. 9). While Triandis does not explicitly define the term, he appears to be emphasizing quantity of performance (Triandis, "A Critique and Experimental Design . . . ," see especially footnote 1, p. 309). March and Simon employ the term *motivation to produce* which appears to be more closely related to Porter and Lawler's effort than to any of the performance measures used (March and Simon, *op. cit.,* pp. 52–53). With such variability in definitions, it is not surprising that hypothesized relationships between satisfaction and performance vary.

[73]In this regard, see Alexander W. Astin, "Criterion-Centered Research," *Education and Psychological Measurement,* XXIV (Winter, 1964), 807–822. He argued for the need to think of criteria in terms of relationships between the individual worker and his environment.

[74]Abraham K. Korman, "Task Success, Task Popularity, and Self-Esteem as Influences on Task Liking," *Journal of Applied Psychology,* LII (December, 1968), 484–490.

individual's ability and the ability requirements of the job moderated the relationship between satisfaction and performance.[75] This evidence offers some support for the theory of work adjustment. Katzell *et al.* concluded that the positive satisfaction-performance relationship observed in their study probably resulted from variation in "urbanization" among the workers studied.[76] Finally, Harding and Bottenberg found that satisfaction did not contribute significantly to explained variance in performance above that accounted for by biographical data.[77]

A much larger body of evidence suggests that satisfaction and performance, when treated separately as dependent variables, are complexly related to a number of other variables. To the extent that these variables differentially affect satisfaction and performance, they become potential moderators of satisfaction-performance relationships. For example, measures of need satisfaction on the job have been found to be functionally related to occupational,[78] organizational,[79] individual,[80] and community [81] variables. Moreover, evidence suggests that at least in the case of organizational characteristics these variables tend to be related to satisfaction in a nonadditive fashion.[82]

[75]Robert E. Carlson, "Degree of Job Fit as a Moderator of the Relationship Between Job Performance and Job Satisfaction," *Personnel Psychology,* XXII (Summer, 1969), 159–170.

[76]Raymond A. Katzell, Richard S. Barrett, and Treadway C. Parker, "Job Satisfaction, Job Performance, and Situational Characteristics," *Journal of Applied Psychology,* XLV (April, 1961), 65–72. Reanalysis of the data suggested that two factors, "urbanization," and "female employee syndrome" moderated the satisfaction-performance relation. Edward E. Cureton and Raymond A. Katzell, "A Further Analysis of the Relations Among Job Performance and Situational Variables," *Journal of Applied Psychology,* XLVI (June, 1962), 230.

[77]Francis. D. Harding and Robert A. Bottenberg, "Effect of Personal Characteristics on Relationships Between Attitudes and Job Performance," *Journal of Applied Psychology,* XLV (December, 1961), 428–430.

[78] For a review of studies, see Harold L. Wilensky, "Varieties of Work Experience," in Henry Borow, editor, *Man in a World of Work* (Boston: Houghton Mifflin, 1964), pp. 125–154. For a recent comprehensive study, see Gerald Gurin, Joseph Veroff, and Sheila Feld, *Americans View Their Mental Health* (New York: Basic Books, 1960). See also George W. England and Carroll I. Stein, "The Occupational Reference Group—A Neglected Concept in Employee Attitude Studies," *Personnel Psychology,* XIV (Autumn, 1961), 299–304.

[79]Porter and Lawler have conducted a series of studies investigating the relationship between satisfaction and organizational variables such as job level, line/staff, company size and structure, and pay. These and other studies are reviewed in L. L. Cummings and A. M. El Salmi, "Empirical Research on the Bases and Correlates of Managerial Motivation: A Review of the Literature," *Psychological Bulletin,* LXX (August, 1968), 127–144.

[80]For a review of studies, see Glenn P. Fournet, M. K. Disefano, Jr., and Margaret W. Pryer, "Job Satisfaction: Issues and Problems," *Personnel Psychology,* XIX (Summer, 1966), 165–183. See also studies by Charles L. Hulin and Patricia C. Smith, "Sex Differences in Job Satisfaction," *Journal of Applied Psychology,* XLVIII (April, 1964), 88–92; Charles L. Hulin and Patricia C. Smith, "A Linear Model of Job Satisfaction," *Journal of Applied Psychology,* XLIX (June, 1965), 209–216; and William H. Form and James A. Geschwender, "Social Reference Basis of Job Satisfaction: The Case of Manual Workers," *American Sociological Review,* XXVII (April, 1962), 228–237. In the latter study the subjects' job satisfaction was found to be associated with fathers' and brothers' job level.

[81]Hulin, "Effects of Community Characteristics on Job Satisfaction." For a study which bears on this issue indirectly, see Arthur N. Turner and Paul R. Lawrence, *Industrial Jobs and the Worker: An Investigation of Response to Task Attributes* (Boston: Harvard Graduate School of Business Administration, 1965). See also Hulin and Blood, "Job Enlargement, Individual Differences, and Worker Responses."

[82]In one study, for example, it was found that several organizational variables were interactively related to satisfaction (A. M. El Salmi and L. L. Cummings, "Managers' Perceptions of Needs and

Knowledge of the determinants of performance has come primarily from researchers interested in employee selection and employee motivation. Both groups have concentrated on the impact of individual variables on performance.[83] Selection researchers have been concerned primarily with the impact on performance of such variables as abilities and aptitudes,[84]personality characteristics,[85]and interests.[86] Students of industrial motivation have also begun to look seriously at the determinants of performance. Recently research having performance as the dependent variable has been conducted within the framework of equity,[87] expectancy, [88]and goal-setting[89]theories.

While the selection and motivational approaches to predicting performance have had some success, a relatively small amount of performance variance is typically explained in any one study.[90] Part of the problem is perhaps attributable

Need Satisfactions as a Function of Interactions Among Organizational Variables," *Personnel Psychology,* XXI (Winter, 1968), 465–477). In another study individual values were found to moderate the relationship between organizational climate variables and satisfaction (Frank Friedlander and Newton Margulies, "Multiple Impacts of Organizational Climate and Individual Value Systems Upon Job Satisfaction," *Personnel Psychology,* XXII (Summer, 1969), 171–183).

[83]Organizational variables have received less attention. Three exceptions are task complexity (see, again, Hulin and Blood, "Job Enlargement, Individual Differences, and Worker Responses"), supervision (for reviews see Stephen M. Sales, "Supervisory Style and Productivity: Review and Theory," *Personnel Psychology,* XIX (Autumn, 1966), 275–286; Abraham K. Korman, " 'Consideration,' 'Initiating Structure,' and Organizational Criteria—A Review," *Personnel Psychology,* XIX (Winter, 1966), 349–361), and wages (for a review see Robert L. Opsahl and Marvin D. Dunnette, "The Role of Financial Compensation in Industrial Motivation," *Psychological Bulletin,* LXVI (August, 1966), 94–118).

[84]Edwin E. Ghiselli, *The Validity of Occupational Aptitude Tests* (New York: Wiley, 1966).

[85]Robert M. Guion and Richard F. Gottier, "Validity of Personality Measures in Personnel Selection," *Personnel Psychology,* XVIII (Summer, 1965), 135–164.

[86]Allan N. Nash, "Vocational Interests of Effective Managers: A Review of the Literature," *Personnel Psychology,* XVIII (Spring, 1965), 21–37. For an excellent overview of the problems and accomplishments in predicting performance from a selection point of view, see Robert M. Guion, *Personnel Testing* (New York: McGraw-Hill, 1965).

[87]For an early formulation of equity theory, see Adams, "Toward an Understanding of Inequity." A large amount of research, sometimes nonsupportive, has been conducted on this theory. For a recent review, see Lawler, "Equity Theory as a Predictor of Productivity and Work Quality."

[88]See Basil S. Georgopoulos, Gerald M. Mahoney, and Nyle W. Jones, "A Path-Goal Approach to Productivity," *Journal of Applied Psychology,* XLI (December, 1957), 345–353; Jay Galbraith and L. L. Cummings, "An Empirical Investigation of the Motivational Determinants of Task Performance: Interactive Effects Between Instrumentality-Valence and Motivation-Ability," *Organizational Behavior and Human Performance,* II (August, 1967), 237–257; Edward E. Lawler, III, and Lyman W. Porter, "Antecedent Attitudes of Effective Managerial Performance," *Organizational Behavior and Human Performance,* II (May, 1967), 122–142; George Graen, "Instrumentality Theory of Work Motivation: Some Experimental Results and Suggested Modifications," *Journal of Applied Psychology Monograph,* LIII (April, 1969), 1–25; and J. Richard Hackman and Lyman W. Porter, "Expectancy Theory Predictions of Work Effectiveness," *Organizational Behavior and Human Performance,* III (November, 1968), 417–426.

[89] Locke and his colleagues have conducted a number of experimental studies on the impact of goal-setting on performance. These are reviewed in Edwin A. Locke, "Toward a Theory of Task Motivation and Incentives," *Organizational Behavior and Human Performance,* III (May, 1968), 157–189.

[90]In the selection context, see Edward A. Rundquist, "The Prediction Ceiling," *Personnel Psychology,* XXII (Summer, 1969), 109–116.

to measurement problems associated with both independent variables and performance. Part, however, is unquestionably due to the fact that insufficient attention has been paid to the variety of variables which may influence performance or to their probable interrelationships.[91]

While the discussion above does not exhaust the literature, one point is clear. Satisfaction and performance, studied alone or together, are associated with a large number of covariates. This suggests that even recent theoretical work has not accounted for a sufficient number of the variables which may influence the strength and perhaps even the direction of the relationship between satisfaction and performance. At the very least it suggests that if available theory were to be applied, these applications should be within the context of well-defined and specified individuals, organizations, occupations, and communities. However, the most pressing need would seem to be for additional research on the dimensionality of satisfaction and performance and on specific conditions under which they are related.

CONCLUSIONS

We close with a few recommendations for investigators interested in job satisfaction and performance. Although pleas for the use of standardized research instruments generally fall on deaf ears, we are unlikely to sample the necessary variety of work environments in a meaningfully comparable fashion unless there is greater utilization of common measures. We additionally urge researchers to obtain as much information about potential moderating variables as their data sources and methodological skills permit. Experimental studies obviously permit control and observation of potential moderators and should be employed more frequently than in the past. But additional survey research is also needed. Adequate controls can be obtained through subject selection and by the greater utilization of multivariate analytical techniques.

We are frankly pessimistic about the value of additional satisfaction-performance theorizing at this time. The theoretically inclined might do better to work on a theory of satisfaction *or* a theory of performance. Such concepts are clearly complex enough to justify their own theories. Prematurely focusing on relationships between the two has probably helped obscure the fact that we know so little about the structure and determinants of each.

[91]As a case in point, equity and goal-setting theory have developed more or less independently of each other. Only one study (P. Goodman and A. Friedman, "An Examination of the Effect of Wage Inequity in the Hourly Condition," *Organizational Behavior and Human Performance,* III (August, 1968), 340–352) has combined elements of the two theories. Interestingly, the goal-setting implications of their study are ignored by the authors.

The Satisfaction-Performance Controversy
Charles N. Greene

As Ben walked by smiling on the way to his office Ben's boss remarked to a friend: "Ben really enjoys his job and that's why he's the best damn worker I ever had. And that's reason enough for me to keep Ben happy." The friend replied: "No, you're wrong! Ben likes his job because he does it so well. If you want to make Ben happy, you ought to do whatever you can to help him further improve his performance."

Four decades after the initial published investigation on the satisfaction-performance relationship, these two opposing views are still the subject of controversy on the part of both practitioners and researchers. Several researchers have concluded, in fact, that "there is no present technique for determining the cause-and-effect of satisfaction and performance." Current speculations, reviewed by Schwab and Cummings, however, still imply at least in theory that satisfaction and performance are causally related although, in some cases, the assumed cause has become the effect, and, in others, the relationship between these two variables is considered to be a function of a third or even additional variables.[1]

THEORY AND EVIDENCE

"Satisfaction Causes Performance"

At least three fundamental theoretical propositions underlie the research and writing in this area. The first and most pervasive stems from the human relations movement with its emphasis on the well-being of the individual at work. In the years following the investigations at Western Electric, a number of studies were conducted to identify correlates of high and low job satisfaction. The interest in satisfaction, however, came about not so much as a result of concern for the individual as concern with the presumed linkage of satisfaction with performance.

According to this proposition (simply stated and still frequently accepted), the degree of job satisfaction felt by an employee determines his performance, that is, satisfaction causes performance. This proposition has theoretical roots, but it also reflects the popular belief that "a happy worker is a productive worker" and the notion that "all good things go together." It is far more pleasant to increase an employee's happiness than to deal directly with his performance whenever a performance problem exists. Therefore, acceptance of the satisfac-

From *Business Horizons*, 1972, **15**(5), 31–41. Copyright by Indiana University. Reprinted by permission.

[1]Initial investigation by A. A. Kornhauser and A. W. Sharp, "Employee Attitudes: Suggestions from a Study in a Factory," *Personnel Journal*, X (May, 1932), 393–401.

First quotation from Robert A. Sutermeister, "Employee Performance and Employee Need Satisfaction—Which Comes First?" *California Management Review*, XIII (Summer, 1971), p.43.

Second quotation from Donald P. Schwab and Larry L. Cummings, "Theories of Performance and Satisfaction: a Review," *Industrial Relations*, IX (October, 1970), pp. 408–30.

tion-causes-performance propostion as a solution makes good sense, particularly for the manager because it represents the path of least resistance. Furthermore, high job satisfaction and high performance are both good, and, therefore, they ought to be related to one another.

At the theoretical level, Vroom's valence-force model is a prime example of theory-based support of the satisfaction-causes-performance case.[2] In Vroom's model, job satisfaction reflects the valence (attractiveness) of the job. It follows from his theory that the force exerted on an employee to remain on the job is an increasing function of the valence of the job. Thus, satisfaction should be negatively related to absenteeism and turnover, and, at the empirical level, it is.

Whether or not this valence also leads to higher performance, however, is open to considerable doubt. Vroom's review of twenty-three field studies, which investigated the relationship between satisfaction and performance, revealed an insignificant median static correlation of 0.14, that is, satisfaction explained less than 2 percent of the variance in performance. Thus, the insignificant results and absence of tests of the causality question fail to provide support for this propostion.

"Performance Causes Satisfaction"

More recently, a second theoretical proposition has been advanced. According to this view, best represented by the work of Porter and Lawler, satisfaction is considered not as a cause but as an effect of performance, that is, performance causes satisfaction.[3] Differential performance determines rewards which, in turn, produce variance in satisfaction. In other words, rewards constitute a necessary intervening variable and, thus, satisfaction is considered to be a function of performance-related rewards.

At the empirical level, two recent studies, each utilizing time-lag correlations, lend considerable support to elements of this proposition. Bowen and Siegel, and Greene reported finding relatively strong correlations between performance and satisfaction expressed later (the performance-causes-satisfaction condition), which were significantly higher than the low correlations between satisfaction and performance which occurred during the subsequent period (the "satisfaction-causes-performance" condition).[4]

In the Greene study, significant correlations were obtained between performance and rewards granted subsequently and between rewards and subsequent satisfaction. Thus, Porter and Lawler's predictions that differential performance determines rewards and that rewards produce variance in satisfaction were upheld.

[2]Victor H. Vroom, *Work and Motivation* (New York: John Wiley & Sons, Inc., 1964).

[3]Lyman W. Porter and Edward E. Lawler, III, *Managerial Attitudes and Performance* (Homewood, Ill.: Richard D. Irwin, Inc., 1968).

[4]Donald Bowen and Jacob P. Siegel, "The Relationship Between Satisfaction and Performance: the Question of Causality," paper presented at the annual meeting of the American Psychological Association, Miami Beach, September, 1970.

Charles N. Greene, "A Causal Interpretation of Relationship Among Pay, Performance, and Satisfaction," paper presented at the annual meeting of the Midwest Psychological Association, Cleveland, Ohio, May, 1972.

"Rewards" as a Causal Factor

Closely related to Porter and Lawler's predictions is a still more recent theoretical position, which considers both satisfaction and performance to be functions of rewards. In this view, rewards cause satisfaction, and rewards that are based on current performance cause affect subsequent performance.

According to this proposition, formulated by Cherrington, Reitz, and Scott from the contributions of reinforcement theorists, there is no inherent relationship between satisfaction and performance.[5] The results of their experimental investigation strongly support their predictions. The rewarded subjects reported significantly greater satisfaction than did the unrewarded subjects. Furthermore, when rewards (monetary bonuses, in this case) were granted on the basis of performance, the subjects' performance was significantly higher than that of subjects whose rewards were unrelated to their performance. For example, they found that when a low performer was not rewarded, he expressed dissatisfaction but that his later performance improved. On the other hand, when a low performer was in fact rewarded for his low performance, he expressed high satisfaction but continued to perform at a low level.

The same pattern of findings was revealed in the case of the high performing subjects with one exception: the high performer who was not rewarded expressed dissatisfaction, as expected, and his performance on the next trial declined significantly. The correlation between satisfaction and subsequent performance, excluding the effects of rewards, was 0.000, that is, satisfaction does *not* cause improved performance.

A recent field study, which investigated the source and direction of causal influence in satisfaction-performance relationships, supports the Cherrington-Reitz-Scott findings.[6] Merit pay was identified as a cause of satisfaction and, contrary to some current beliefs, was found to be a significantly more frequent source of satisfaction than dissatisfaction. The results of this study further revealed equally significant relationships between (1) merit pay and subsequent performance and (2) current performance and subsequent merit pay. Given the Cherrington-Reitz-Scott findings that rewards based on current performance cause improved subsequent performance, these results do suggest the possibility of reciprocal causation.

In other words, merit pay based on current performance probably caused variations in subsequent performance, and the company in this field study evidently was relatively successful in implementing its policy of granting salary increases to an employee on the basis of his performance (as evidenced by the significant relationship found between current performance and subsequent merit pay). The company's use of a fixed (annual) merit increase schedule probably obscured some of the stronger reinforcing effects of merit pay on performance.

[5]David J. Cherrington, H. Joseph Reitz, and William E. Scott, Jr., "Effects of Contingent and Non-contingent Reward on the Relationship Between Satisfaction and Task Performance, *Journal of Applied Psychology*, LV (December, 1971) pp. 531–36.

[6]Charles N. Greene, "Source and Direction of Causal Influence in Satisfaction-Performance Relationships," paper presented at the annual meetings of the Eastern Academy of Management, Boston, May, 1972. Also reported in Greene, "Causal Connections Among Managers' Merit Pay, Satisfaction, and Performance." *Journal of Applied Psychology*, 1972 (in press).

Unlike the Cherrington-Reitz-Scott controlled experiment, the fixed merit increase schedule precluded (as it does in most organizations) giving an employee a monetary reward immediately after he successfully performed a major task. This constraint undoubtedly reduced the magnitude of the relationship between merit pay and subsequent performance.

IMPLICATIONS FOR MANAGEMENT

These findings have several apparent but nonetheless important implications. For the manager who desires to enhance the satisfaction of his subordinates (perhaps for the purpose of reducing turnover), the implication of the finding that "rewards cause satisfaction" is self-evident. If, on the other hand, the manager's interest in his subordinates' satisfaction arises from his desire to increase their performance, the consistent rejection of the satisfaction-causes-performance proposition has an equally clear implication: increasing subordinates' satisfaction will have no effect on their performance.

The finding that rewards based on current performance affect subsequent performance does, however, offer a strategy for increasing subordinates' performance. Unfortunately, it is not the path of least resistance for the manager. Granting differential rewards on the basis of differences in his subordinates' performance will cause his subordinates to express varying degrees of satisfaction or dissatisfaction. The manager, as a result, will soon find himself in the uncomfortable position of having to successfully defend his basis for evaluation or having to put up with dissatisfied subordinates until their performance improves or they leave the organization.

The benefits of this strategy, however, far outweigh its liabilities. In addition to its positive effects on performance, this strategy provides equity since the most satisfied employees are the rewarded high performers and, for the same reason, it also facilitates the organization's efforts to retain its most productive employees.

If these implications are to be considered as prescriptions for managerial behavior, one is tempted at this point to conclude that all a manager need to in order to increase his subordinates' performance is to accurately appraise their work and then reward them accordingly. However, given limited resources for rewards and knowledge of appraisal techniques, it is all too apparent that the manager's task here is not easy.

Moreover, the relationship between rewards and performance is often not as simple or direct as one would think, for at least two reasons. First, there are other causes of performance that may have a more direct bearing on a particular problem. Second is the question of the appropriateness of the reward itself, that is, what is rewarding for one person may not be for another. In short, a manager also needs to consider other potential causes of performance and range of rewards in coping with any given performance problem

Nonmotivational Factors

The element of performance that relates most directly to the discussion thus far is effort, that element which links rewards to performance. The employee who works hard usually does so because of the rewards or avoidance of punishment that he associates with good work. He believes that the magnitude of the reward he will receive is contingent on his performance and, further, that his performance is a function of how hard he works. Thus, effort reflects the motivational aspect of performance. There are, however, other nonmotivational considerations that can best be considered prior to examining ways by which a manager can deal with the motivational problem.

Direction   Suppose, for example, that an employee works hard at his job, yet his performance is inadequate. What can his manager do to alleviate the problem? The manager's first action should be to identify the cause. One likely possibility is what can be referred to as a "direction problem."

Several years ago, the Minnesota Vikings' defensive end, Jim Marshall, very alertly gathered up the opponent's fumble and then, with obvious effort and delight, proceeded to carry the ball some fifty yards into the wrong end zone. This is a direction problem in its purest sense. For the employee working under more usual circumstances, a direction problem generally stems from his lack of understanding of what is expected of him or what a job well done looks like. The action indicated to alleviate this problem is to clarify or define in detail for the employee the requirements of his job. The manager's own leadership style may also be a factor. In dealing with an employee with a direction problem, the manager needs to exercise closer supervision and to initiate structure or focus on the task, as opposed to emphasizing consideration or his relations with the employee.[7]

In cases where this style of behavior is repugnant or inconsistent with the manager's own leadership inclinations, an alternative approach is to engage in mutual goal setting or management-by-objectives techniques with the employee. Here, the necessary structure can be established, but at the subordinate's own initiative, thus creating a more participative atmosphere. This approach, however, is not free of potential problems. The employee is more likely to make additional undetected errors before his performance improves, and the approach is more time consuming than the more direct route.

Ability   What can the manager do if the actions he has taken to resolve the direction problem fail to result in significant improvements in performance? His subordinate still exerts a high level of effort and understands what is expected of him—yet he continues to perform poorly. At this point, the manager may begin, justifiably so, to doubt his subordinate's ability to perform the job. When this doubt does arise, there are three useful questions, suggested by Mager and Pipe, to which the manager should find answers before he treats the problem as an ability deficiency: Could the subordinate do it if he really had to? Could he do it

---

[7]For example, a recent study reported finding that relationships between the leader's initiating structure and both subordinate satisfaction and performance were moderated by such variables as role ambiguity, job scope, and task autonomy perceived by the subordinate. See Robert J. House, "A Path Goal Theory of Leader Effectiveness," *Administrative Science Quarterly,* **XVI** (September, 1971), pp. 321–39.

if his life depended on it? Are his present abilities adequate for the desired performance?[8]

If the answers to the first two questions are negative, then the answer to the last question also will be negative, and the obvious conclusion is that an ability deficiency does, in fact, exist. Most managers, upon reaching this conclusion, begin to develop some type of formal training experience for the subordinate. This is unfortunate and frequently wasteful. There is probably a simpler, less expensive solution. Formal training is usually required only when the individual has never done the particular job in question or when there is no way in which the ability requirement in question can be eliminated from his job.

If the individual formerly used the skill but now uses it only rarely, systematic practice will usually overcome the deficiency without formal training. Alternatively, the job can be changed or simplified so that the impaired ability is no longer crucial to successful performance. If, on the other hand, the individual once had the skill and still rather frequently is able to practice it, the manager should consider providing him greater feedback concerning the outcome of his efforts. The subordinate may not be aware of the deficiency and its effect on his performance, or he may no longer know how to perform the job. For example, elements of his job or the relationship between his job and other jobs may have changed, and he simply is not aware of the change.

Where formal training efforts are indicated, systematic analysis of the job is useful for identifying the specific behaviors and skills that are closely related with successful task performance and that, therefore, need to be learned. Alternatively, if the time and expense associated with job analysis are considered excessive, the critical incidents approach can be employed toward the same end.[9] Once training needs have been identified and the appropriate training technique employed, the manager can profit by asking himself one last question: "Why did the ability deficiency develop in the first place?"

Ultimately, the answer rests with the selection and placement process. Had a congruent man-job match been attained at the outset, the ability deficiency would have never presented itself as a performance problem.[10]

Performance Obstacles When inadequate performance is not the result of a lack of effort, direction, or ability, there is still another potential cause that needs attention. There may be obstacles beyond the subordinate's control that interfere with his performance. "I can't do it" is not always an alibi; it may be a real description of the problem. Performance obstacles can take many forms to the extent that their number, independent of a given situation, is almost unlimited.

---

[8]Robert F. Mager and Peter Pipe, *Analyzing Performance Problems* (Belmont, Calif.: Lear Siegler, Inc., 1970), p. 21.

[9] See, for example, J. D. Folley, Jr., "Determining Training Needs of Department Store Personnel," *Training Development Journal,* **XXIII** (January, 1969), pp. 24–27, for a discussion of how the critical incidents approach can be employed to identify job skills to be learned in a formal training situation.

[10]For a useful discussion of how ability levels can be upgraded by means of training and selection procedures, the reader can refer to Larry I. Cummings and Donald P. Schwab, *Performance in Organizations: Determinants and Appraisal* (Glenview, Ill.: Scott, Foresman & Co., 1972; in press).

However, the manager might look initially for some of the more common potential obstacles, such as a lack of time or conflicting demands on the subordinate's time, inadequate work facilities, restrictive policies or "right ways of doing it" that inhibit performance, lack of authority, insufficient information about other activities that affect the job, and lack of cooperation from others with whom he must work.

An additional obstacle, often not apparent to the manager from his face-to-face interaction with a subordinate, is the operation of group goals and norms that run counter to organizational objectives. Where the work group adheres to norms of restricting productivity, for example, the subordinate will similarly restrict his own performance to the extent that he identifies more closely with the group than with management.

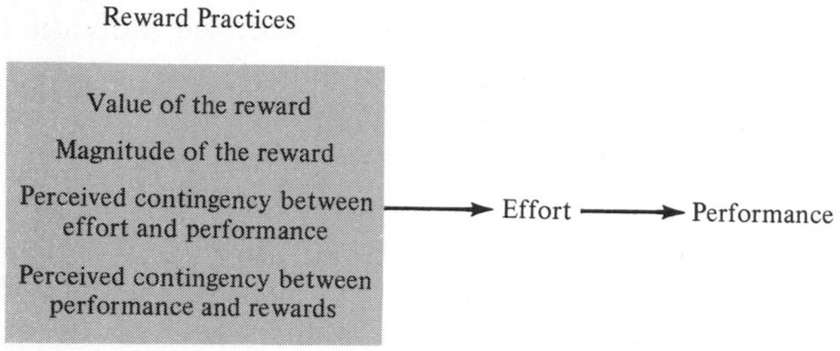

Figure 1   Rewards and effort.

Most performance obstacles can be overcome either by removing the obstacle or by changing the subordinate's job so that the obstacle no longer impinges on his performance. When the obstacle stems from group norms, however, a very different set of actions is required. Here, the actions that should be taken are the same as those that will be considered shortly in coping with lack of effort on the part of the individual. In other words, the potential causes of the group's lack of effort are identical to those that apply to the individual.

The Motivational Problem

Thus far, performance problems have been considered in which effort was not the source of the performance discrepancy. While reward practices constitute the most frequent and direct cause of effort, there are, however, other less direct causes. Direction, ability, and performance obstacles may indirectly affect effort through their direct effects on performance. For example, an individual may perform poorly because of an ability deficiency and, as a result, exert little effort on the job. Here, the ability deficiency produced low performance, and the lack of effort on the individual's part resulted from his expectations of failure. Thus, actions taken to alleviate the ability deficiency should result in improved performance and, subsequently, in higher effort.

Effort is that element of performance which links rewards to performance. The relationship between rewards and effort is, unfortunately, not a simple one. As indicated in the figure, effort is considered not only as a function of the (1) value and (2) magnitude of reward, but also as a function of the (3) individual's perceptions of the extent to which greater effort on his part will lead to higher performance, and (4) that his high performance, in turn, will lead to rewards. Therefore, a manager who is confronted with a subordinate who exerts little effort must consider these four attributes of reward practices in addition to the more indirect, potential causes of the lack of effort. The key issues in coping with a subordinate's lack of effort—the motivation problem—or in preventing such a problem from arising involve all four of the attributes of rewards just identified.[11]

Appropriateness of the Reward   Regardless of the extent to which the individual believes that hard work determines his performance and subsequent rewards, he will obviously put forth little effort unless he *values* those rewards—that is, the rewards must have value in terms of his own need state. An accountant, for example, may value recognition from his boss, an opportunity to increase the scope of his job, or a salary increase; however, it is unlikely that he will place the same value on a ten-year supply of budget forms.

In other words, there must be consistency between the reward and what the individual needs or wants and recognition that there are often significant differences among individuals in what they consider rewarding. Similarly, individuals differ in terms of the *magnitude* of that valued reward they consider to be positively reinforcing. A 7 or 8 percent salary increase may motivate one person but have little or no positive effect on another person at the same salary level. Furthermore, a sizable reward in one situation might be considered small by the same individual in a different set of circumstances.

These individual differences, particularly those concerning what rewards are valued, raise considerable question about the adequacy of current organization reward systems, virtually none of which make any formal recognition of individual differences. Lawler, for example, has suggested that organizations could profit greatly by introducing "cafeteria-style" wage plans.[12] These plans allow an employee to select any combination of cash and fringe benefits he desires. An employee would be assigned "X" amount in compensation, which he may then divide up among a number of fringe benefits and cash. This practice would ensure that employees receive only those fringe benefits they value; from the organization's point of view, it would reduce the waste in funds allocated by the organization to fringe benefits not valued by its members. As a personal strategy, however, the manager could profit even more by extending Lawler's plan to include the entire range of monmonetary rewards.

Rewards can be classified into two broad categories, extrinsic and intrinsic. Extrinsic rewards are those external to the job or in the context of the job, such as job security, improved working facilities, praise from one's boss, status symbols, and, of course, pay, including fringe benefits. Intrinsic rewards, on the other hand, are rewards that can be associated directly with the "doing of the job," such as a sense of accomplishment after successful performance, opportunities for advancement, increased responsibility, and work itself.

[11] The discussion in this section is based in part on Cummings and Schwab, *Performance in Organizations,* and Lyman W. Porter and Edward E. Lawler, III, "What Job Attitudes Tell About Motivation," *Harvard Business Review,* LXVI (January-February, 1968), pp. 118–26.

[12] Edward E. Lawler, III, *Pay and Organizational Effectiveness: a Psychological View* (New York: McGraw-Hill Book Company, 1971).

Thus, intrinsic rewards flow immediately and directly from the individual's performance of the job and, as such, may be considered as a form of self-reward. For example, one essentially must decide for himself whether his level of performance is worthy of a feeling of personal achievement. Extrinsic rewards, to the contrary, are administered by the organization; the organization first must identify good performance and then provide the appropriate reward.

Generally speaking, extrinsic rewards have their greatest value when the individual is most strongly motivated to satisfy what Maslow has referred to as lower level needs, basic physiological needs and needs for safety or security, and those higher level ego needs that can be linked directly to status. Pay, for example, may be valued by an individual because he believes it is a determinant of his social position within the community or because it constitutes a means for acquiring status symbols.

Intrinsic rewards are likely to be valued more by the individual after his lower level needs have been largely satisfied. In other words, there must be an adequate level of satisfaction with the extrinsic rewards before intrinsic rewards can be utilized effectively. In order to make the subordinate's job more intrinsically rewarding, the manager may want to consider several actions.

Perhaps most important, the manager needs to provide meaningful work assignments, that is, work with which the subordinate can identify and become personally involved. He should establish challenging yet attainable goals or, in some cases, it may be more advantageous for him to create conditions that greatly enhance the likelihood that his subordinate will succeed, thus increasing the potential for attaining feelings of achievement, advancement, and recognition. The manager may also consider such means as increased delegation and job enlargement for extending the scope and depth of the subordinate's job and thereby increasing the subordinate's opportunity to make the job into something more compatible with his own interests.

In short, the manager should as best he can match the rewards at his disposal, both extrinsic and intrinsic rewards, with what the subordinate indicates he needs or wants. Second, he should, by varying the magnitude and timing of the rewards granted, establish clearly in the subordinate's mind the desired effort-performance-reward contingencies.

Establishing the Contingencies   The contingency between effort and performance (that is, the extent to which the individual believes that by working harder, he will improve his performance) is largely a function of his confidence in his own abilities and his perceptions of the difficulty of the task and absence of obstacles standing in the way of successful task performance. When the effort-performance contingency is not clear for these reasons, the manager should consider several actions. He can reassign work or modify the task to be more consistent with the individual's perceptions of his own abilities; treat the problem as a "real" ability deficiency; remove the apparent performance obstacles; or simply reassure the individual.

The second contingency, the individual's belief that the rewards he receives reflect his accomplishments, is usually more difficult to establish. Here, two rather vexing predicaments are frequently encountered, both of which stem primarily from administration of extrinsic rewards. First, the instrument (usually a merit evaluation or performance appraisal device) may inaccurately measure the individual's contribution and thus his performance is rewarded in error. Reward schedules constitute the source of the second problem. Given fixed reward schedules (that is, the ubiquitous annual salary increase) adopted by the great majority of organizations, there is more frequently than not a considerable delay between task accomplishment and bestowal of the reward. As a result, the individual may not only fail to perceive the intended contingency but may incorrectly associate the reward with his behavior just prior to being rewarded. In other words, he may perceive a nonexistent contingency, and his subsequent behavior will reflect that contingency and, this time, go unrewarded.

Reward Schedules The manner in which a given reward, or reinforcer, is scheduled is as strong a determinant of the effectiveness of that reward as is the value of the reward itself, or, for that matter, any other attribute of the reward. In organizations, the only plausible forms of reward schedules are intermittent as opposed to the continuous reward schedule in which the reward or punishment is administered after every behavioral sequence to be conditioned. In the case of the intermittent schedules, the behavior to be conditioned is reinforced only occasionally. There are four schedules of interest to the manager, each with varying effects on performance as a number of investigations in the field of experimental psychology have revealed.

1 *Fixed-interval schedule* Rewards are bestowed after a fixed period, usually since the last reward was granted. This schedule is equivalent to the annual salary increase schedule in organizations, and its effects on performance are well-known. Typically, the individual "saves up," that is, he exerts a high level of effort just prior to the time of the reinforcement, usually his annual performance review. His performance more than likely will then taper off until the time just prior to his next annual review.

2 *Variable-interval schedule* Rewards are administered at designated time periods, but the intervals between the periods vary. For example, a reward may be given one day after the last rewarded behavior sequence, then three days later, then one week later, and so on, but only if the behavior to be conditioned actually occurs. This schedule results in fairly consistent rates of performance over long periods of time. Praise or other forms of social reinforcement from one's peers and superior, as an example, usually occur according to a variable-interval schedule, not by intention but simply because they are too involved with their own affairs to provide systematic reinforcement.

3 *Fixed-ratio schedule* Reinforcement is provided after a fixed number of responses or performances by the individual. Incentive wage plans so frequently utilized in organizations constitute the prime example of this type of schedule. It is characterized by higher rates of effort than the interval schedules unless the ratio is large. When significant delays do occur between rewards, performance, much like in the fixed schedule, declines immediately after the reward is bestowed and improves again as the time for the next reward approaches.

4 *Variable-ratio schedule* The reward is administered after a series of responses or performances, the number of which varies from the granting of one reward to the next.

For example, an individual on a 15:1 variable-interval schedule might be reinforced after ten responses, then fifteen responses, then twenty responses, then ten responses, and so on, an average of one reinforcement for every fifteen responses. This schedule tends to result in performance that is higher than that of a comparable fixed ratio schedule, and the variation in performance both before and after the occurrence of the reward or reinforcement is considerably less.

Virtually all managers must function within the constraints imposed by a fixed-interval schedule (annual salary schedule) or fixed ratio schedule (wage incentives). However, this fact should not preclude consideration of the variable schedules, even within the framework of fixed schedules. Given their more positive effects on performance, such consideration is indeed highly desirable. It is conceivable, at least in a sales organization, for example, that monetary rewards (bonuses in this case) could be administered according to a variable-ratio schedule. From a more practical point of view, the entire range of nonmonetary rewards could be more profitably scheduled on a variable-interval basis, assuming that such scheduling was done in a systematic fashion.

CONCLUSIONS

This article has reviewed recent research concerning the relationship between satisfaction and performance and discussed the implications of the results of this research for the practicing manager. As noted at the outset, current speculation on the part of most practitioners and researchers continue to imply that satisfaction and performance are causally related, although confusion exists concerning the exact nature of the relationship. While the performance-causes-satisfaction proposition is a more recent development, the contention that satisfaction causes performance, nonetheless, remains the more widely held of the two beliefs, particularly among practitioners.

The recent research findings, however, offer only moderate support of the former view and conclusively reject the latter. Instead, the evidence provides rather strong indications that the relationship is more complex: (1) rewards constitute a more direct cause of satisfaction than does performance and (2) rewards based on current performance (and not satisfaction) cause subsequent performance.

For the manager who is concerned about the well-being of his subordinates, the implication of the finding that rewards cause satisfaction is self-evident. In order to achieve this end, the manager must provide rewards that have value or utility in terms of the subordinate's own need state and provide them in sufficient magnitude to be perceived as positively reinforcing. The manager whose goal is to increase a subordinate's performance, on the other hand, is faced with a more difficult task for two reasons. First, the relationship between rewards and performance is not a simple one. Second, there are other causes of performance—direction, the subordinate's ability, and existence of performance obstacles standing in the way of successful task performance—which the manager must deal also with.

The relationship between rewards and performance is conplex because in reality there is at least one intervening variable and more than one contingency that needs to be established. An employee exerts high level effort usually because of the valued rewards he associates with high performance. Effort, the intervening variable, may be considered a function of the value and magnitude of the reward and the extent to which the individual believes that high effort on his part will lead to high performance and that his high performance, in turn, will lead to rewards.

Therefore, the manager in addition to providing appropriate rewards, must establish contingencies between effort and performance and between performance and rewards. The first contingency, the extent to which the individual believes that "how hard he works" determines his performance, is perhaps the more readily established. This contingency is a function, at least in part, of the individual's confidence in his own abilities, his perceptions of the difficulty of the task, and the presence of performance obstacles. When a problem does arise here, the manager can take those actions indicated earlier in this article to overcome an apparent ability deficiency or performance obstacle. The performance-reward contingency requires the manager, by means of accurate performance appraisals and appropriate reward practices, to clearly establish in the subordinate's mind the belief that his own performance determines the magnitude of the rewards he will receive.

The establishment of this particular contingency, unfortunately, is becoming increasingly difficult as organizations continue to rely more heavily on fixed salary schedules and nonperformance-related factors (for example, seniority) as determinants of salary progression. However, the manager can, as a supplement to organizationally determined rewards, place more emphasis on monmonetary rewards and both the cafeteria-style reward plans and variable-interval schedules for their administration.

It is apparent that the manager whose objective is to significantly improve his subordinates' performance has a difficult but by no means impossible task. The path of least resistance—that is, increasing subordinates' satisfaction—simply will not work.

However, the actions suggested concerning reward practices and, particularly, establishment of appropriate performance-reward contingencies will result in improved performance, assuming that such improvement is not restricted by ability or direction problems or by performance obstacles. The use of differential rewards may require courage on the part of the manager, but failure to use them will have far more negative consequences. A subordinate will repeat that behavior which was rewarded, regardless of whether it resulted in high or low performance. A rewarded low performer, for example, will continue to perform poorly. With knowledge of this inequity, the high performer, in turn, will eventually reduce his own level of performance or seek employment elsewhere.

QUESTIONS FOR DISCUSSION

1   Why is it so difficult to measure such factors as performance and job satisfaction objectively?

2   What role do job attitudes play in effective job performance?

3   Is job satisfaction an objective or a subjective concept? Explain.

4   Exactly how might rewards such as pay, promotion, and positive feedback affect the determination of job satisfaction? How might they affect performance?

5   Do you think it likely that we will soon have one universally accepted theory of work motivation? Why or why not?

6   Is it necessary for line managers to select one theory of motivation and remain with it in their day-to-day supervisory activities or could they use several theories simultaneously? Explain.

7   How does the position expressed by Greene differ from that of Schwab and Cummings?

Chapter 8

Attachment to Organizations

OVERVIEW

Most of the discussion up to this point has concentrated on what March and Simon (1958) term the "decision to produce." In other words, we have been concerned with factors which appear to influence an individual's willingness or desire to perform well on the job. There also exists a second and equally important type of motivated work behavior which has been called the "decision to participate." Here we focus on the processes by which individuals decide whether to form attachments, or linkages, with organizations or to sever such attachments.

The topic of attachment to organizations is indeed a broad one. When loosely defined, it includes such topics as why and how people select their occupations or careers, why they shift occupations, why they choose a particular organization, why the organization chooses them, and why individuals decide to remain with or withdraw from an organization. (Lawler [1973] has recently added a new dimension to this topic by suggesting the need for research into why people decide *not* to work at all!) In this chapter, we shall omit consideration of why or how people select careers or occupations (see Super & Bohn, 1970) and focus on the mutual decision by an organization and an individual to join together.

We are concerned, then, with what organizations want from their employees, and what employees want in exchange from their employers. It is important to recognize that an exchange relationship exists here. On the one hand, organizations want to be assured of receiving a certain quantity and quality of employee participation, or else they have little need of that employee. On the other hand, employees want to be sure that they can satisfy many of their own personal goals—such as adequate pay, promotion opportunities, coworker interactions— or else there is little purpose in their coming to work. Thus, linkages between individuals and organizations are a process in which both parties agree to some compromise situation in which both organizational and personal goal-attainment are facilitated.

One side of this individual-organization linkage—what organizations expect from their members—is discussed in the selection by Katz. This excellent theoretical piece proposes a conceptual framework for understanding the types of behavior required of individuals if an organization is to survive and function effectively in a dynamic and competitive world. Concern is given not only to these behavioral requirements, but also to the mechanisms (such as reward systems) used by organizations to secure such behavior and to the consequences of their use.

The other side of the linkage is the individual's decision to remain with or withdraw from organization activities. Withdrawal may take many forms, including turnover, absenteeism, alcoholism and drugs, or simply inactivity or minimal compliance. We are concerned here primarily with the more overt withdrawal forms of turnover and absenteeism.

Considerable research has been carried out on the causes of turnover and absenteeism. It has generally been concluded that a major factor is the degree of job satisfaction or dissatisfaction experienced by the employee (see Brayfield & Crockett, 1955; Herzberg, Mausner, Peterson & Capwell, 1957; Vroom, 1964). However, it is argued in the second selection (by Porter & Steers) that the simple knowledge that dissatisfaction leads to withdrawal really tells us very little about the processes behind such withdrawal. Toward this end, Porter and Steers review some sixty empirical investigations aimed at identifying specific causes of turnover and absenteeism. Based on these findings, general conclusions are drawn and a hypothetical model is proposed in an attempt to better understand the process by which individuals decide whether to participate in, or withdraw from, their employing organization. In addition, specific implications of such a model are identified in an attempt to help organizations to reduce such behavior, assuming they wish to.

REFERENCES AND SUGGESTED ADDITIONAL READINGS

Brayfield, A. H., & Crockett, W. H. Employee attitudes and employee performance. *Psychological Bulletin,* 1955, **52**, 396–424.

Hall, D. T., & Schneider, B. Correlates of organizational identification as a function of career pattern and organizational type. *Administrative Science Quarterly,* 1972, **17,** 340–350.

Herzberg, F., Mausner, B., Peterson, R. O., & Capwell, D. F. *Job attitudes: Review of research and opinion.* Pittsburgh: Psychological Service of Pittsburgh, 1957.

Hrebiniak, L. G., & Alutto, J. A. Personal and role-related factors in the development of organizational commitment. *Administrative Science Quarterly,* 1972, **17,** 555–573.

Lawler, E. E., III. *Motivation in work organizations.* Monterey, Calif.: Brooks/Cole, 1973.

March, J. G., & Simon, H. A. *Organizations.* New York: Wiley, 1958.

Porter, L. W., Steers, R. M., Mowday, R. T., & Boulian, P. V. Organizational commitment, job satisfaction, and turnover among psychiatric technicians. *Journal of Applied Psychology,* 1974, **59,** 603–609.

Schuh, A. The predictability of employee tenure: A review of the literature. *Personnel Psychology,* 1967, **20,** 133–152.

Sheldon, M. E. Investments and involvements as mechanisms producing commitment to the organization. *Administrative Science Quarterly,* 1971, **16,** 143–150.

Super, E. E., & Bohn, M. J. *Occupational psychology.* Belmont, Calif.: Wadsworth, 1970.

Vroom, V. H. *Work and motivation.* New York: Wiley, 1964.

The Motivational Basis of Organizational Behavior
Daniel Katz

The basic problem to which I shall address myself is how people are tied into social and organizational structures so that they become effective functioning units of social systems. What is the nature of their involvement in a system or their commitment to it?

The major input into social organizations consists of people. The economist or the culturologist may concentrate on inputs of resources, raw materials, technology. To the extent that human factors are recognized, they are assumed to be constants in the total equation and are neglected. At the practical level, however, as well as for a more precise theoretical accounting, we need to cope with such organizational realities as the attracting of people into organizations, holding them within the system, insuring reliable role performance, and in addition stimulating actions which are generally facilitative of organizational accomplishment. The material and psychic returns to organizational members thus constitute major determinants, not only of the level of effectiveness or organizational functioning, but of the very existence of the organization.

The complexities of motivational problems in organizations can be understood if we develop an analytic framework which will be comprehensive enough to identify the major sources of variance and detailed enough to contain sufficient specification for predictive purposes. The framework we propose calls for three steps in an analysis process, namely, the formulation of answers to these types of questions: (1) What are the types of behavior required for effective organizational functioning? Any organization will require not one, but several patterns of behavior from most of its members. And the motivational bases of these various behavioral requirements may differ. (2) What are the motivational patterns which are used and which can be used in organizational settings? How do they differ in their logic and psycho-logic? What are the differential consequences of the various types of motivational patterns for the behavioral requirements essential for organizational functioning? One motivational pattern may be very effective in bringing about one type of necessary behavior and completely ineffective in leading to another. (3) What are the conditions for eliciting a given motivational pattern in an organizational setting? We may be able to identify the type of motivation we think most appropriate for producing a given behavioral outcome but we still need to know how this motive can be aroused or produced in the organization (Katz, 1962).

BEHAVIORAL REQUIREMENTS

Our major dependent variables are the behavioral requirements of the organization. Three basic types of behavior are essential for a functioning organization:

Abridged from *Behavioral Science*, 1964, **9**, 131–146. Reprinted by permission.

(1) People must be induced to enter and remain within the system. (2) They must carry out their role assignments in a dependable fashion. (3) There must be innovative and spontaneous activity in achieving organizational objectives which go beyond the role specifications.

Attracting and Holding People in a System

First of all, sufficient personnel must be kept within the system to man its essential functions. People thus must be induced to enter the system at a sufficiently rapid rate to counteract the amount of defection. High turnover is costly. Moreover, there is some optimum period for their staying within the system. And while they are members of the system they must validate their membership by constant attendance. Turnover and absenteeism are both measures of organizational effectiveness and productivity, though they are partial measures. People may, of course, be within the system physically but may be psychological absentees. The child may be regular and punctual in his school attendance and yet daydream in his classes. It is not enough, then, to hold people within a system.

Dependable Role Performance

The great range of variable human behavior must be reduced to a limited number of predictable patterns. In other words, the assigned roles must be carried out and must meet some minimal level of quantity and quality of performance. A common measure of productivity is the amount of work turned out by the individual or by the group carrying out their assigned tasks. Quality of performance is not as easily measured and the problem is met by quality controls which set minimal standards for the pieces of work sampled. In general, the major role of the member is clearly set forth by organizational protocol and leadership. The man on the assembly line, the nurse in the hospital, the teacher in the elementary school all know what their major job is. To do a lot of it and to do it well are, then, the most conspicuous behavioral requirements of the organization. It may be, of course, that given role requirements are not functionally related to organizational accomplishment. This is a different type of problem and we are recognizing here only the fact that some major role requirements are necessary.

Innovative and Spontaneous Behavior

A neglected set of requirements consists of those actions not specified by role prescriptions which nevertheless facilitate the accomplishment of organizational goals. The great paradox of a social organization is that it must not only reduce human variability to insure reliable role performance but that it must also allow room for some variability and in fact encourage it.

There must always be a supportive member of actions of an innovative or relatively spontaneous sort. No organizational planning can foresee all contingencies within its operations, or can anticipate with perfect accuracy all environmental changes, or can control perfectly all human variability. The resources of people in innovation, in spontaneous co-operation, in protective and creative behavior are thus vital to organizational survival and effectiveness. An organization which depends solely upon its blueprints of prescribed behavior is a very fragile social system.

Co-operation

The patterned activity which makes up an organization is so intrinsically a co-operative set of interrelationships, that we are not aware of the co-operative nexus any more than we are of any habitual behavior like walking. Within every work group in a factory, within any division in a government bureau, or within any department of a university are countless acts of co-operation without which the system would break down. We take these everyday acts for granted, and few, if any, of them form the role prescriptions for any job. One man will call the attention of his companion on the next machine to some indication that his machine is getting jammed, or will pass along some tool that his companion needs, or will borrow some bit of material he is short of. Or men will come to the aid of a fellow who is behind on his quota. In a study of clerical workers in an insurance company one of the two factors differentiating high-producing from low-producing sections was the greater co-operative activity of the girls in the high-producing sections coming to one another's help in meeting production quotas (Katz, Maccoby, & Morse, 1950). In most factories specialization develops around informal types of help. One man will be expert in first aid, another will be expert in machine diagnosis, etc. We recognize the need for co-operative relationships by raising this specific question when a man is considered for a job. How well does he relate to his fellows, is he a good team man, will he fit in?

Protection

Another subcategory of behavior facilitative of organizational functioning is the action which protects the organization against disaster. There is nothing in the role prescriptions of the worker which specifies that he be on the alert to save life and property in the organization. Yet the worker who goes out of his way to remove the boulder accidentally lodged in the path of a freight car on the railway spur, or to secure a rampant piece of machinery, or even to disobey orders when they obviously are wrong and dangerous, is an invaluable man for the organization.

Constructive Ideas

Another subcategory of acts beyond the line of duty consists of creative suggestions for the improvement of methods of production or of maintenance. Some organizations encourage their members to feed constructive suggestions into the system, but coming up with good ideas for the organization and formulating them to management is not the typical role of the worker. An organization that can stimulate its members to contribute ideas for organizational improvement is a more effective organization in that people who are close to operating problems can often furnish informative suggestions about such operations. The system which does not have this stream of contributions from its members is not utilizing its potential resources effectively.

Self-training

Still another subcategory under the heading of behavior beyond the call of duty concerns the self-training of members for doing their own jobs better and self-education for assuming more responsible positions in the organization. There may be no requirement that men prepare themselves for better positions. But the organization which has men spending their own time to master knowledge and skills for more responsible jobs in the system has an additional resource for effective functioning.

Favorable Attitude

Finally, members of a group can contribute to its operations by helping to create a favorable climate for it in the community, or communities, which surround the organization. Employees may talk to friends, relatives, and acquaintances about the excellent or the poor qualities of the company for which they work. A favorable climate may help in problems of recruitment, and sometimes product disposal.

In short, for effective organizational functioning many members must be willing on occasion to do more than their job prescriptions specify. If the system were to follow the letter of the law according to job descriptions and protocol, it would soon grind to a halt. There have to be many actions of mutual co-operation and many anticipations of organizational objectives to make the system viable.

Now these three major types of behavior, and even the subcategories, though related, are not necessarily motivated by the same drives and needs. The motivational pattern that will attract and hold people to an organization is not necessarily the same as that which will lead to higher productivity. Nor are the motives which make for higher productivity invariably the same as those which sustain co-operative interrelationships in the interests of organizational accomplishment. Hence, when we speak about organizational practices and procedures which will further the attainment of its mission, we need to specify the type of behavioral requirement involved.

TYPES OF MOTIVATIONAL PATTERNS

It is profitable to consider the possible motivational patterns in organizations under six major headings. Before considering their specific modes of operation and their effects, let me briefly describe the six motivational patterns which seem most relevant. These patterns are: (1) conformity to legal norms or rule compliance; (2) instrumental system rewards; (3) instrumental individual rewards; (4) intrinsic satisfaction from role performance; (5) internalization of organizational goals and values; and (6) involvement in primary-group relationships.

Rule Compliance or Conformity to System Norms   Conformity constitutes a significant motivational basis for certain types of organizational behavior. Though people may conform for different reasons I am concerned here with one common type of reason, namely a generalized acceptance of the rules of the game. Once people enter a system they accept the fact that membership in the system means complying with its legitimate rules. In our culture we build up during the course of the socialization process a generalized expectation of conforming to the recognized rules of the game if we want to remain in the game. We develop a role readiness, i. e., a readiness to play almost any given role according to the established norms in those systems in which we become involved.

Instrumental System Rewards   These are the benefits which accrue to invidiuals by virtue of their membership in the system. They are the across-the-board rewards which apply to all people in a given classification in an organization. Examples would be the fringe benefits, the recreational facilities, and the working conditions which are available to all members of the system or subsystem. These rewards are instrumental in that they provide incentives for entering and remaining in the system and thus are instrumental for the need satisfaction of people.

Instrumental Reward Geared to Individual Effort or Performance   System rewards apply in blanket fashion to all members of a subsystem. Individual rewards of an instrumental character are attained by differential performance. For example, the piece rate in industry or the singling out of individuals for honors for their specific contributions would fall into this category of instrumental individual rewards.

Intrinsic Satisfactions Accruing from Specific Role Performance   Here the gratification comes not because the activity leads to or is instrumental to other satisfactions such as earning more money but because the activity is gratifying in itself. The individual may find his work so interesting or so much the type of thing he really wants to do that it would take a heavy financial inducement to shift to a job less congenial to his interests. It is difficult to get professors in many universities to take administrative posts such as departmental chairmanships or deanships because so many of them prefer teaching and research. This motivational pattern has to do with the opportunities which the organizational role provides for the expressions of the skills and talents of the individual.

Internalized Values of the Individual Which Embrace the Goals of the Organization   Here the individual again finds his organizational behavior rewarding in itself, not so much because his job gives him a chance to express his skill, but because he has taken over the goals of the organization as his own. The person who derives his gratifications from being a good teacher could be equally happy in teaching in many institutions but unhappy as an administrator in any one. The person who has identified himself with the goals of his own particular university and its specific problems, potentialities, and progress wants to stay on at his university and, moreover, is willing to accept other assignments than a teaching assignment.

Social Satisfactions Derived from Primary Group Relationships   This is an important source of gratification for organizational members. One of the things people miss most when they have to withdraw from organizations is the sharing of experiences with like-minded colleagues, the belonging to a group with which they have become identified. Whether or not these social satisfactions become channelled for organizational objectives leads us to a consideration of the two basic questions with which we started: (1) What are the consequences of these motivational patterns for the various organizational requirements of holding people in the system, maximizing their role performances, and stimulating innovative behavior? and (2) What are the conditions under which these patterns will lead to a given organizational outcome?

MOTIVATIONAL PATTERNS: CONSEQUENCES AND CONDITIONS

Compliance with Legitimized Rules

In discussing bureaucratic functioning Max Weber pointed out that the acceptance of legal rules was the basis for much of organizational behavior (Weber, 1947). Compliance is to some extent a function of sanctions but to a greater extent a function of generalized habits and attitudes toward symbols of authority. In other words, for the citizen of modern society the observance of legitimized rules has become a generalized value. A great deal of behavior can be predicted once we know what the rules of the game are. It is not necessary to take representative samplings of the behavior of many people to know how people will conduct themselves in structured situations. All we need is a single informant who can tell us the legitimate norms and appropriate symbols of authority for given types of behavioral settings. Individuals often assume that they can control their participation with respect to organizational requirements when they enter an organization. Before they are aware of it, however, they are acting like other organizational members and complying with the rules and the authorized decisions.

The major impact of compliance with the legitimate rules of the organization primarily concerns only one type of organizational requirement, namely reliable role performance. The way in which any given role occupant is to perform in carrying out his job can be determined by the rules of the organization. But individuals cannot be held in the system by rule enforcement save for exceptions like the armed services. Nor can innovative behavior and actions beyond the call of duty be prescribed.

Though compliance with legitimate rules is effective for insuring reliable role performance it operates to insure minimal observance of role requirements. In other words, the minimal standards for quantity and quality of work soon become the maximum standards. The logic of meeting legal norms is to avoid infractions of the rules and not to go beyond their requirements, for as Allport has pointed out (1934), it is difficult, if not impossible, to be more proper than proper. Why, however, cannot the legal norms be set to require high standards with respect to both quantity and quality of production? Why cannot higher production be legislated? It can, but there is an important force working against such raising of standards by changing rules. The rule which sets a performance standard in a large organization is also setting a uniform standard for large numbers of people. Hence it must be geared to what the great majority are prepared to do. If not, there will be so many defections that the rule itself will break down. Timing of jobs in industry illustrates this principle. Management does not want a loose standard, but if the standards are set so that many workers can meet them only with difficulty, management is in for trouble.

In the third area of behavior necessary for effective organizational functioning, namely innovative and spontaneous acts which go beyond the call of duty, rule compliance is useless by definition. There can be exceptions, in that rules can be devised to reward unusual behavior under specified conditions. The army, for example, will move the man who has pulled off a brilliant military exploit from a court martial to a court of honors. Though such exceptions may occur, organizations cannot stimulate innovative actions by decreeing them. In general the greater the emphasis upon compliance with rules the less the motivation will be for individuals to do more than is specified by their role prescriptions. The great weakness of a system run according to rules is the lack of the corrective factor of human enterprise and spontaneity when something goes wrong. Two years ago in a hospital in New York State several infants died because salt rather than sugar was put into the formula. The large container for sugar had been erroneously filled with salt. The tragic fact was that day after day for about a week the nurses fed the babies milk saturated with salt in spite of the fact that the infants reacted violently to the food, crying and vomiting after each feeding session. But the hospital continued poisoning the children until many of them died. Not a single nurse, attendant, supervisor, or person connected with the nursery tasted the milk to see what was wrong. The error was discovered only when a hospital employee broke a rule and used some of the substance in the sugar container in her own coffee.

Conditions Conducive to the Activation of Rule Acceptance

Though compliance with rules can bring about reliable role performance, the use of rules must take account of the following three conditions for maximum effectiveness: (1) the appropriateness of the symbols of authority and the relevance of rules to the social system involved; (2) the clarity of the legal norms and rule structure; and (3) the reinforcing character of sanctions.

Appropriateness and Relevance   The acceptance of communications and directives on the basis of legitimacy requires the use of symbols and procedures recognized as the proper and appropriate sources of authority in the system under consideration. The worker may grumble at the foreman's order but he recognizes the right of the foreman to give such an order. The particular directives which are accepted as legitimate will depend upon their matching the type of authority structure of the system. The civilian in the army with officer status, uniform, and unassimilated rank is not accepted by the enlisted man as the proper giver of orders. In a representative democracy a policy decision of an administrator may be rejected since it lacks the legal stamp of the accepted procedures of the system. An industrial company may have a contract with a union that changes in the speed of the assembly line have to be agreed to by both organizations. The workers accordingly will accept a speedup in the line if it is santioned by the union management agreement, but not if it is the work of a foreman attempting to impress his superiors.

The acceptance of legal rules is also restricted to the relevant sphere of activity. Union policy as formulated in its authority structure is binding upon its members only as it relates to relations with the company. The edicts of union officials on matters of desegregation or of support of political parties are not necessarily seen as legal compulsions by union members. In similar fashion, employees do not regard the jurisdiction of the company as applying to their private lives outside the plant. And areas of private behavior and personal taste are regarded in our democratic society as outside the realm of coercive laws. The most spectacular instance of the violation of a national law occurred in the case of the Volstead Act. While people were willing to accept laws about the social consequences resulting from drinking, such as reckless driving, many of them were not willing to accept the notion that their private lives were subject to federal regulation.

Another prerequisite to the use of rules as the appropriate norms of the system is their impersonal character. They are the rules of the system and are not the arbitary, capricious decisions of a superior aimed at particular individuals. The equivalents of bills of attainder in an organization undermine rule compliance. We speak of the officiousness of given individuals in positions of authority when they use their rank in an arbitary and personal fashion.

Clarity   A related condition for the acceptance of legal norms is the clarity of authority symbols, of proper procedures, and the content of the legitimized decisions. Lack of clarity can be due to the vagueness of the stimulus situation or to the conflict between opposed stimulus cues. In some organizations, symbols may lack such clarity of definition. One difficulty of using group decisions in limited areas in an otherwise authoritarian structure is that group members may not perceive the democratic procedure as legitimized by the structure. They will question the compelling effect of any decisions they reach. And often they may be right. Moreover, the procedure for the exercise of power may not be consistent with the type of authority structure. The classic case is that *of ordering* a people to be democratic.

Specific laws can be ambiguous in their substance. They can be so complex, so technical, or so obscure that people will not know what the law is. The multiplication of technical rulings and the patchwork of legislation with respect to tax structure means that while people may feel some internal compulsion to pay taxes, they also feel they should pay as little as they can without risking legal prosecution. A counter dynamic will arise to the tendency to comply with legal requirements, namely, the use of legal loopholes to defy the spirit of the law. Any complex maze of rules in an organization will be utilized by the guardhouse lawyers in the system to their own advantage.

Though our argument has been that legal compliance makes for role performance rather than for holding people in a system, the clarity of a situation with well-defined rules is often urged as a condition making for system attractiveness. People know what is expected of them and what they should expect in turn from others, and they much prefer this clarity to a state of uncertainty and ambiguity. There is merit in this contention, but it does not take into account all the relevant variables. The armed services were not able to hold personnel after World War II, and recruitment into systems characterized by rules and regulations is traditionally difficult in the United States. The mere multiplication of rules does not produce clarity. Even when certainty and clarity prevail they are not relished if it means that individuals are certain only of nonadvancement and restrictions on their behavior.

In brief, the essence of legal compliance rests upon the psychological belief that there are specific imperatives or laws which all good citizens obey. If there is doubt about what the imperative is, if there are many varying interpretations, then the law is not seen as having a character of its own but as the means for obtaining individual advantage. To this extent, the legitimacy basis of compliance is undermined.

Reinforcement To maintain the internalized acceptance of legitimate authority there has to be some reinforcement in the form of penalties for violation of the rules. If there is no policing of laws governing speeding, speed limits will lose their force over time for many people. Sometimes the penalties can come from the social disapproval of the group as well as from legal penalties. But the very concept of law as an imperative binding upon everyone in the system requires penalties for violation either from above or below. Where there is no enforcement by authorities and no sanctions for infractions from the group itself, the rule in question becomes a dead letter.

Instrumental System Rewards

It is important to distinguish between rewards which are administered in relation to individual effort and performance and the system rewards which accrue to people by virtue of their membership in the system. In the former category would belong piecerate incentives, promotion for outstanding performance, or any special recognition bestowed in acknowledgment of differential contributions to organizational functioning. In the category of system rewards would go fringe benefits, recreational facilities, cost of living raises, across-the-board upgrading, job security save for those guilty of moral turpitude, pleasant working conditions. System rewards differ, then, from individual rewards in that they are not allocated on the basis of differential effort and performance but on the basis of membership in the system. The major differentiation for system rewards is seniority in the system—a higher pension for thirty years of service than for twenty years of service. Management will often overlook the distinction between individual and system rewards and will operate as if rewards administered across the board were the same in their effects as individual rewards.

System rewards are more effective for holding members within the organization than for maximizing other organizational behaviors. Since the rewards are distributed on the basis of length of tenure in the system, people will want to stay with an attractive setup which becomes increasingly attractive over time. Again the limiting factor is the competition with the relative attraction of other systems. As the system increases its attrations, other things being equal, it should reduce its problems of turnover. In fact, it may sometimes have the problem of too low turnover with too many poorly motivated people staying on until retirement.

System rewards will do little, moreover, to motivate performance beyond the line of duty, with two possible exceptions. Since people may develop a liking for the attractions of the organization they may be in a more favorable mood to reciprocate in co-operative relations with their fellows toward organizational goals, provided that the initiation of task-oriented co-operation comes from some other source. Otherwise, they may just be co-operative with respect to taking advantage of the system's attractions, such as the new bowling alley. Another possible consequence of system rewards for activity supportive of organizational goals is the favorable climate of opinion for the system in the external environment to which the members contribute. It may be easier for a company to recruit personnel in a community in which their employees have talked about what a good place it is to work.

Though the effects of system rewards are to maintain the level of productivity not much above the minimum required to stay in the system, there still may be large differences between systems with respect to the quantity and quality of production as a function of system rewards. An organization with substantially better wage rates and fringe benefits than its competitors may be able to set a higher level of performance as a minimal requirement for its workers than the other firms and still hold its employees. In other words, system rewards can be related to the differential productivity of organizations as a whole, though they are not effective in maximizing the potential contributions of the majority of individuals within the organization. They may account for differences in motivation between systems rather than for differences in motivation between individuals in the same system. They operate through their effects upon the minimal standards for all people in the system. They act indirectly in that their effect is to make people want to stay in the organization; to do so people must be willing to accept the legitimately derived standards of role performance in that system. Hence, the direct mechanism for insuring performance is compliance with legitimacy, but the legal requirements of the organization will not hold members if their demands are too great with respect to the demands of other organizations. The mediating variable in accounting for organizational differences based upon system rewards is the relative attractiveness of the system for the individual compared to other available systems in relation to the effort requirements of the system. If the individual has the choice of a job with another company in the same community which requires a little more effort but offers much greater system rewards in the way of wages and other benefits, he will in all probability take it. If, however, the higher requirements of the competing system are accompanied by very modest increases in system rewards, he will probably stay where he is.

Conditions Conducive to Effective System Rewards

We have just described one of the essential conditions for making system rewards effective in calling attention to the need to make the system as attractive as competing systems which are realistic alternatives for the individual. In this context seniority becomes an important organizational principle in that the member can acquire more of the rewards of the system the longer he stays in it. The present trends to permit the transfer of fringe benefits of all types across systems undercuts the advantages to any one system of length of membership in it, though of course there are other advantages to permitting people to retain their investment in seniority when they move across systems.

Another condition which is important for the effective use of system rewards is their uniform application for all members of the system or for major groupings within the system. People will perceive as inequitable distinctions in amounts of rewards which go to members by virtue of their membership in the system where such differences favor some groups over other groups. Management is frequently surprised by resentment of differential system rewards when there has been no corresponding resentment of differential individual rewards. One public utility, for example, inaugurated an attractive retirement system for its employees before fringe benefits were the acceptable pattern. Its employees were objectively much better off because of the new benefits and yet the most hated feature about the whole company was the retirement system. Employee complaints centered on two issues: years of employment in the company before the age of thirty did not count toward retirement pensions, and company officials could retire on livable incomes because of their higher salaries. The employees felt intensely that if they were being rewarded for service to the company it was unfair to rule out years of service before age thirty. This provision gave no recognition for the man who started for the company at age twenty compared to the one who started at age thirty. Moreover, the workers felt a lifetime of service to the company should enable them to retire on a livable income just as it made this possible for company officials. The company house organ directed considerable space over a few years to showing how much the worker actually benefited from the plan, as in fact was the case. On the occasion of a company-wide survey, this campaign was found to have had little effect. The most common complaint still focused about the patent unfairness of the retirement system.

The critical point, then, is that system rewards have a logic of their own. Since they accrue to people by virtue of their membership or length of service in an organization, they will be perceived as inequitable if they are not uniformly administered. The perception of the organization member is that all members are equal in their access to organizational benefits. Office employees will not be upset by differences in individual reward for differences in responsibility. If, however, their organization gives them free meals in a cafeteria and sets aside a special dining room for their bosses, many of them will be upset. In our culture we accept individual differences in income but we do not accept differences in classes of citizenship. To be a member of an organization is to be a citizen in that community, and all citizens are equal in their membership rights. A university which does not extend the same tenure rights and the same fringe benefits accorded its teaching staff to its research workers may have a morale problem on its hands.

Instrumental Individual Rewards

The traditional philosophy of the free-enterprise system gives priority to an individual reward system based upon the quality and quantity of the individual effort and contribution. This type of motivation may operate effectively for the entreprenueur or even for the small organization with considerable independence of its supporting environment. It encounters great difficulties, however, in its application to large organizations which are in nature highly interdependent co-operative structures. We shall examine these difficulties in analyzing the conditions under which individual rewards of an instrumental character are effective.

Basically the monetary and recognition rewards to the individual for his organizational performance are directed at a high level of quality and quantity of work. In other words, they can be applied most readily to obtain optimal role performance rather than to innovative and nonspecific organizational needs. They may also help to hold the individual in the organization, if he feels that his differential efforts are properly recognized. Nonetheless there is less generalization, or rubbing off, of an instrumental individual reward to love for the organization than might be anticipated. If another organization offers higher individual rewards to a person, his own institution may have to match the offer to hold him.

Individual rewards are difficult to apply to contributions to organizational functioning which are not part of the role requirements. Spectacular instances of innovative behavior can be singled out for recognition and awards. In the armed services, heroism beyond the call of duty is the basis for medals and decorations, but the everyday co-operative activities which keep an organization from falling apart are more difficult to recognize and reward. Creative suggestions for organizational improvement are sometimes encouraged through substantial financial rewards for employees' suggestions. The experience with suggestion systems of this sort has not been uniformly positive though under special conditions they have proved of value.

Conditions Conducive to Effective Individual Instrumental Rewards

If rewards such as pay incentives are to work as they are intended they must meet three primary conditions. (1) They must be clearly perceived as large enough in amount to justify the additional effort required to obtain them. (2) They must be perceived as directly related to the required performance and follow directly on its accomplishment. (3) They must be perceived as equitable by the majority of system members many of whom will not receive them. These conditions suggest some of the reasons why individual rewards can work so well in some situations and yet be so difficult of application in large organizations. The facts are that most enterprises have not been able to use incentive pay, or piece rates, as reliable methods for raising the quality and quantity of production (McGregor, 1960).

In terms of the first criterion many companies have attempted incentive pay without making the differential between increased making the differential between increased effort and increased reward proportional from the point of view of the worker. If he can double his pay by working at a considerably increased tempo, that is one thing. But if such increased expenditure means a possible 10 percent increase, that is another. Moreover, there is the tradition among workers, and it is not without some factual basis, that management cannot be relied upon to maintain a high rate of pay for those making considerably more than the standard and that their increased efforts will only result in their "being sweated." There is, then, the temporal dimension of whether the piece rates which seem attractive today will be maintained tomorrow.

More significant, however, is the fact that a large-scale organization consists of many people engaging in similar and interdependent tasks. The work of any one man is highly dependent upon what his colleagues are doing. Hence individual piece rates are difficult to apply on any equitable basis. Group incentives are more logical, but as the size of the interdependent group grows, we move toward system rather than toward individual rewards. Moreover, in large-scale production enterprises the performance is controlled by the tempo of the machines and their co-ordination. The speed of the worker on the assembly line is not determined by his decision but by the speed of the assembly line. An individual piece rate just does not accord with the systemic nature of the co-ordinated collectivity. Motivational factors about the amount of effort to be expended on the job enter the picture not on the floor of the factory but during the negotiations of the union and management about the manning of a particular assembly line. Heads of corporations may believe in the philosophy of individual enterprise, but when they deal with reward systems in their own organizations they become realists and accept the pragmatic notion of collective rewards.

Since there is such a high degree of collective interdependence among rank-and-file workers the attempts to use individual rewards are often perceived as inequitable. Informal norms develop to protect the group against efforts which are seen as divisive or exploitive. Differential rates for subsystems within the organization will be accepted much more than invidious distinctions within the same subgrouping. Hence promotion or upgrading may be the most potent type of individual reward. The employee is rewarded by being moved to a different category of workers on a better pay schedule. Some of the same problems apply, of course, to this type of reward. Since differential performance is difficult to assess in assembly-type operations, promotion is often based upon such criteria as conformity to company requirements with respect to attendance and absenteeism, observance of rules, and seniority. None of these criteria are related to individual performance on the job. Moreover, promotion is greatly limited by the technical and professional education of the worker.

It is true, of course, that many organizations are not assembly-line operations, and even for those which are, the conditions described here do not apply to the upper echelons. Thus General Motors can follow a policy of high individual rewards to division managers based upon the profits achieved by a given division. A university can increase the amount of research productivity of its staff by making publication the essential criterion for promotion. In general, where assessment of individual performance is feasible and where the basis of the reward system is clear, instrumental individual rewards can play an important part in raising productivity.

Intrinsic Job Satisfaction

The motivational pathway to high productivity and to high-quality production can be reached through the development of intrinsic job satisfaction. The man who finds the type of work he delights in doing is the man who will not worry about the fact that the role requires a given amount of production of a certain quality. His gratifications accrue from accomplishment, from the expression of his own abilities, from the exercise of his own decisions. Craftmanship was the old term to refer to the skilled performer who was high in intrinsic job satisfaction. This type of performer is not the clock watcher, not the shoddy performer. On the other hand, such a person is not necessarily tied to a given organization. As a good carpenter or a good mechanic, it may matter little to him where he does work, provided that he is given ample opportunity to do the kind of job he is interested in doing. He may, moreover, contribute little to organizational goals beyond his specific role.

Conditions Conducive to Arousal of Intrinsic Job Satisfaction

If intrinsic job satisfaction or identification with the work is to be aroused and maximized, then the job itself must provide sufficient variety, sufficient complexity, sufficient challenge, and sufficient skill to engage the abilities of the worker. If there is one confirmed finding in all the studies of worker morale and satisfaction, it is the correlation between the variety and challenge of the job and the gratifications which accrue to workers (Morse, 1953). There are, of course, people who do not want more responsibility and people who become demoralized by being placed in jobs which are too difficult for them These are, however, the exceptions. By and large people seek more responsibility, more skill-demanding jobs than they hold, and as they are able to attain these more demanding jobs, they become happier and better adjusted. Obviously, the condition for securing higher motivation to produce, and to produce quality work, necessitates changes in organizational structure—specifically job enlargement rather than job fractionation. And yet the tendency in large-scale organizations is toward increasing specialization and routinization of jobs. Workers would be better motivated toward better quality work if we discarded the assembly line and moved toward the craftsmanlike operations of the old Rolls Royce type of production. Industry has demonstrated, however, that it is more efficient to produce via assembly-line methods with lowered motivation and job satisfaction than with highly motivated craftsmen with a large area of responsibility in turning out their part of the total product. The preferred path to the attainment of production goals in turning out cars or other mass physical products is, then, the path of organizational controls and not the path of internalized motivation. The quality of production may suffer somewhat, but it is still cheaper to buy several mass-produced cars, allowing for programming for obsolescence, than it is to buy a single quality product like the Rolls Royce.

In the production of physical objects intended for mass consumption, the assembly line may furnish the best model. This may also apply to service operations in which the process can be sufficiently simplified to provide service to masses of consumers. When, however, we move to organizations which have the modifications of human beings as their product, as in educational institutions, or when we deal with treating basic problems of human beings, as in hospital, clinics, and remedial institutions, we do not want to rely solely upon an organizational control to guarantee minimum effort of employees. We want employees with high motivation and high indentification with their jobs. Jobs cannot profitably be fractionated very far and standarized and co-ordinated to a rigorous time schedule in a research laboratory, in a medical clinic, in an educational institution, or in a hospital.

In addition to the recognition of the inapplicability of organizational devices of the factory and the army to all organizations, it is also true that not all factory operations can be left to institutional controls without regard to the motivations of employees. It frequently happens that job fractionation can be pushed to the point of diminishing returns even in industry. The success of the Tavistock workers in raising productivity in the British coal mines through job enlargement was due to the fact that the specialization of American long-wall methods of coal mining did not yield adequate returns when applied to the difficult and variable conditions under which British miners had to operate (Trist & Bamforth, 1951). The question of whether to move toward greater specialization and standardization in an industrial operation or whether to move in the opposite direction is generally an empirical one to be answered by research. One rule of thumb can be applied, however. If the job can be so simplified and standardized that it is readily convertible to automated machines, then the direction to take is that of further institutionalization until automation is possible. If, however, the over-all performance requires complex judgment, the differential weighing of factors which are not markedly identifiable, or creativity, then the human mind is a far superior instrument to the computer.

The paradox is that where automation is feasible, it can actually increase the motivational potential among the employees who are left on the job after the changeover. Mann and Hoffman (1960) conclude from their study of automation in an electric power plant that the remaining jobs for workers can be more interesting, that there can be freer association among colleagues, and that the limination of supervisory levels brings the top and bottom of the organization closer together.

Internalization of Organizational Goals and Values

The pattern of motivation associated with value expression and self-identification has great potentialities for the internalization of the goals of subsystems and of the total system, and thus for the activation of behavior not prescribed by specific roles. Where this pattern prevails individuals take over organizational objectives as part of their own personal goals. They identify not with the organization as a safe and secure haven but with its major purposes. The internalization or organizational objectives is generally confined to the upper echelons or to the officer personnel. In voluntary organizations it extends into some of the rank-and-file, and in fact most voluntary organizations need a core of dedicated people who are generally referred to as the dedicated damn fools.

Now the internalization of organizational goals is not as common as two types of more partial internalization. The first has to do with some general organizational purposes which are not unique to the organization. A scientist may have internalized some of the research values of his profession but not necessarily of the specific institution to which he is attached. As long as he stays in that institution, he may be a well-motivated worker. But he may find it just as easy to work for the things he believes in in another institution. There is not the same set of alternative organizations open to liberals who are political activists and who are part of the core of dedicated damn fools in the Democratic party. They have no other place to go, so they find some way of rationalizing the party's deviation from their liberal ideals.

A second type of partial internalization concerns the values and goals of a subsystem of the organization. It is often easier for the person to take over the values of his own unit. We may be attached to our own department in a university more than to the goals of the university as a whole.

Conditions Conducive to Internalization of System Goals

Internalization of organization objectives can come about through the utilization of the socialization process in childhood or through the adult socialization which takes place in the organization itself. In the first instance, the selective process, either by the person or the organization, matches the personality with the system. A youngster growing up in the tradition of one of the military services may have always thought of himself as an Air Force officer. Similarly, the crusader for civil liberties and the American Civil Liberties Union find one another.

The adult socialization process in the organization can build upon the personal values of its members and integrate them about an attractive model of its ideals. People can thus identify with the organizational mission. If the task of an organization has emotional significance, the organization enjoys an advantage in the creation of an attractive image. If the task is attended by hazard as in the tracking down of criminals by the FBI, or of high adventure, as in the early days of flying, or of high service to humanity, as in a cancer research unit, it is not difficult to develop a convincing model of the organization's mission.

The imaginative leader can also help in the development of an attractive picture of the organization by some new conceptualization of its mission. The police force entrusted with the routine and dirty business of law enforcement carried out by dumb cops and "flatfeet" can be energized by seeing themselves as a corps of professional officers devoted to the highest form of public service. Reality factors limit the innovative use of symbols for the glorification of organizations. Occupational groups, however, constantly strive to achieve a more attractive picture of themselves, as in the instances of press agents who have become public relations specialists or undertakers who have become morticians.

Internalization of subgroup norms can come about through identification with fellow group members who share the same common fate. People take over the values of their group because they identify with their own kind and see themselves as good group members, and as good group members they model their actions and aspirations in terms of group norms. This subgroup identification can work for organizational objectives only if there is agreement between the group norms and the organizational objectives. Often in industry the norms of the work group are much closer to union objectives than to company objectives.

This suggests three additional factors which contribute to internalization of group objectives: (1) participating in important decisions about group objectives; (2) contributing to group performance in a significant way; and (3) sharing in the rewards of group accomplishment. When these three conditions are met, the individual can regard the group as his, for he in fact has helped to make it.

Social Satisfactions from Primary-Group Relationships

Human beings are social animals and cannot exist in physical or psychological isolation. The stimulation, the approval, and the support they derived from interacting with one another comprise one of the most potent forms of motivation. Strictly speaking, such affiliative motivation is another form of instrumental-reward-seeking, but some of its qualitative aspects are sufficiently different from the instrumental system and individual rewards previously described to warrant separate discussion.

The desire to be part of a group in itself will do no more than hold people in the system. The studies of Elton Mayo and his colleagues during World War II showed that work groups which provided their members social satisfactions had less absenteeism than less cohesive work groups (Mayo & Lombard, 1944). Mann and Baumgartel (1953) corroborated these findings in a study of the Detroit Edison Company. With respect to role performance, moreover, Seashore (1954) has demonstrated that identification with one's work group can make for either above-average or below-average productivity depending upon the norms of the particular group. In the Seashore study the highly-cohesive groups, compared to the low-cohesive groups, moved to either extreme in being above or below the production standards for the company.

Other studies have demonstrated that though the group can provide important socioemotional satisfactions for the members it can also detract from task orientation (Bass, 1960). Members can have such a pleasnat time interacting with one another that they neglect their work. Again the critical mediating variable is the character of the values and norms of the group. The affiliative motive can lead to innovative and co-operative behavior, but often this assumes the form of protecting the group rather than maximizing organizational objectives. So the major question in dealing with the affiliative motive is how this motive can be harnessed to organizational goals.

REFERENCES

Allport, F. H. The J-curve hypothesis of conforming behavior. *J. Soc. Psychol.,* 1934, **5,** 141–183.

Bass, B. M. *Leasership, psychology, and organizational behavior.* New York: Harper, 1960.

Katz, D. Human interrelationships and organizational behavior. In S. Mailick and F. H. Van Ness (Eds.), *Concepts and issues in administrative behavior,* New York: Prentice-Hall, 1962, pp. 166–186.

Katz, D., Maccoby, N., & Morse, Nancy. *Productivity supervision and morale in an office situation.* Ann Arbor, Mich.: Institute for Social Research, Univ. of Michigan, 1950.

Mann, F. C., & Baumgartel, H. J. *Absences and employee attitudes in an electric power company.* Ann Arbor, Mich.: Institute for Social Research, Univ. of Michigan, 1953.

Mayo, E., & Lombard, G. *Teamwork and labor turnover in the aircraft industry of Southern California. Business Res. Studies No. 32.* Cambridge, Mass.: Harvard Univ., 1944.

McGregor, D. *The human side of enterprise.* New York: McGraw-Hill, 1960.

Morse, Nancy. *Satisfactions in the white collar job.* Ann Arbor, Mich.: Institute for Social Research, Univ. of Michigan, 1953.

Seashore, S. *Group cohesiveness in the industrial work group.* Ann Arbor, Mich.: Institute for Social Research, Univ. of Michigan, 1954.

Trist, E., & Bamforth, K. W. Some social and psychological consequences of the long wall method of coal-getting. *Hum. Relat.,* 1951, **4,**3–38.

Weber, M. *The theory of social and economic organization.* Glencoe, Ill.: Free Press, 1947.

Organizational, Work, and Personal Factors
in Employee Turnover and Absenteeism

Lyman W. Porter
Richard M. Steers[1]

To those concerned with studying the behavior of individuals in organizational settings, employee turnover and absenteeism represent both interesting and important phenomena. They are relatively clear-cut acts of behavior that have potentially critical consequences both for the person and for the organization. It is probably for this reason that turnover and absenteeism have been investigated in a relatively large number of studies to date and are likely to remain a key focus of personnel research by psychologists. . . .

In the past, there have been some four reviews of the literature dealing with turnover and absenteeism. Three of these (Brayfield & Crockett, 1955; Herzberg, Mausner, Peterson, & Capwell, 1957; Vroom, 1964) are now somewhat dated in relation to all of the research carried out during the past decade or so, and the fourth (Schuh, 1967) represents a highly specialized review of only a portion of the available literature. Before proceeding to our own analysis of the recent literature, it will be helpful to summarize briefly what was uncovered by these previous reviews.

Brayfield and Crockett (1955) and Herzberg et al. (1957) both found evidence of a strong relationship between employee dissatisfaction and withdrawal behavior (i. e., both turnover and absenteeism). Brayfield and Crockett went further, however, to point out major methodological weaknesses in a number of the studies, such as the failure to obtain independent measures and the use of weak or ambiguous measurement techniques. In fact, such flaws were so prevalent that they questioned whether methodological changes alone would substantially alter the magnitude or direction of many of the obtained relationships. In general, then, Brayfield and Crockett pointed as much to a need for increased rigor in research techniques as toward the acceptance or rejection of an attitude-withdrawal relationship.

Several years later, Vroom (1964) again reviewed the literature pertaining to job satisfaction and withdrawal. The results of his analysis generally reinforced the earlier conclusions. Vroom reported that the studies he reviewed showed a consistent negative relationship between job satisfaction and the propensity to leave. In addition, he found a somewhat less consistent negative relationship between job satisfaction and absenteeism. Vroom interpreted the findings concerning job satisfaction and withdrawal as being consistent with an expectancy/valence theory of motivation; namely, workers who are highly attracted to their

Abridged from *Psychological Bulletin*, 1973, **80,** 151–176. Copyright by the American Psychological Association. Reprinted by permission.

[1]This research was supported by a grant from the Office of Naval Research, Contract No. N00014–69– A–0200–9001, NR 151–315. The authors wish to express their appreciation to Richard T. Mowday, Eugene F. Stone, Joseph E. Champoux, and William J. Crampon for their valuable comments on an earlier draft.

jobs are presumed to be subject to motivational forces to remain in them, with such forces manifesting themselves in increased tenure and higher rates of attendance.

Schuh's (1967) review focused primarily on studies of the prediction of turnover by the means of personality and vocational inventories and biographical information. From his review, he concluded that there was not a consistent relationship between turnover and scores on intelligence, aptitude, and personality tests. On the other hand, some evidence was found that vocational interest inventories and scaled biographical information blanks could be used to fairly accurately predict turnover. Moreover, a very small number of older studies pertaining to job satisfaction were cited in the review, and these too seemed predictive of turnover.

Taken as a whole, these reviews and their conclusions point to the importance of job satisfaction as a central factor in withdrawal. In the review that follows, we attempt to build on the previous ones by citing the rather extensive recent literature (over 60 studies) that for the most part has not been previously covered. First, recent studies concerning the role of *overall* job satisfaction in withdrawal are reviewed. Next, and more specifically, the literature is categorized according to (a) organization-wide factors, (b) immediate work environment factors, (c) job content factors, and (d) personal factors. These seem to us to be meaningful groupings in terms of the variety of possible "internal factors" (i. e., variables related to an individual's interaction with the work situation) that could be involved in withdrawal behavior. Omitted from the present analysis is the obviously crucial set of "external" factors pertaining to such things as economic conditions, the availability of specific job opportunities, and various unavoidable causes of withdrawal (e. g., pregnancy, illness, etc.).

Throughout this review we are particularly concerned with the potential role that "met expectations" may have on withdrawal behavior. The concept of met expectations may be viewed as the discrepancy between what a person encounters on his job in the way of positive and negative experiences and what he expected to encounter. Thus, since different employees can have quite different expectations with respect to payoffs or rewards in a given organizational or work situation, it would not be anticipated that a given variable (i. e., high pay, unfriendly work colleagues, etc.) would have a uniform impact on withdrawal decisions. We would predict, however, that when an individual's expectations —whatever they are—are not substantially met, his propensity to withdraw would increase. We will return to the possible role of met expectations following our review of the various segments of the recent literature on withdrawal.

JOB SATISFACTION AND WITHDRAWAL

Subsequent to the publication of the earlier reviews, a number of new investigations have appeared concerning the relationship of overall job satisfaction to turnover and absenteeism. These findings are briefly summarized here in order to determine how they relate to the earlier findings as previously reviewed.

In two related predictive studies of particular merit, Hulin investigated the impact of job satisfaction on turnover among female clerical workers. Using the Job Descriptive Index as a measure of job attitudes, Hulin's (1966) first study matched each subject who subsequently left the company over a 12-month period with two "stayers" along several demographic dimensions. Significant differences were found between the stayer and leaver groups on mean satisfaction scores. Hulin concluded that at least in this sample, subsequent leavers *as a group* could be accurately distinguished from stayers based on a knowledge of the workers' degree of job satisfaction up to 12 months prior to the act of termination.

These findings raised the question as to the possibility of reducing this turn-over by increasing a worker's degree of satisfaction on the job. Toward this end, the company instituted new policies in the areas of salary administration and promotional opportunities. Approximately 1–1 ½ years after these changes, Hulin (1968) again administered the Job Descriptive Index to a sample similar to the previous one. Subsequent leavers were matched with two stayers each, and again it was found that termination decisions were significantly related to the degree of worker satisfaction. Equally important was the finding that satisfaction scores with four of the five Job Descriptive Index scales rose significantly between the first and second studies. Simultaneously, the department's turnover rate between these two periods dropped from 30 % during the first study period to 12 % during the second.

Other important studies have yielded essentially the same results among life insurance agents (Weitz & Nuckols, 1955), male and female office workers (Mikes & Hulin, 1968), retain store employees (Taylor & Weiss, 1969a, 1969b), and female operatives (Wild, 1970).

Taking a somewhat different approach to the topic, Katzell (1968) and Dunnette, Arvey, and Banas[2] investigated the role of employee expectations at the time of hire as they related to later job experiences and turnover. In both studies, no significant differences were found to exist at the time of entry between the expectation levels of those who remained and those who later decided to leave. However, as time went on, significant differences did emerge; those who remained generally felt their original expectations were essentially met on the job, while those who left felt their expectations had not been met.

Also relevant to the role of met expectations in the participation decision are the field experiments of Weitz (1956), Youngberg (1963), and Macedonia (1969). These studies (described in greater detail below) found that where individuals were provided with a realistic picture of the job environment—including its difficulties—prior to employment, such subjects apparently adjusted their job expectations to more realistic levels. These new levels were then apparently more easily met by the work environment, resulting in reduced turnover.

Many studies, therefore, point to the importance of job satisfaction as a predictor of turnover. However, it appears that expressed intentions concerning future participation may be an even better predictor. In a large scale investigation

[2]M. D. Dunnette, R. Arvey, & P. Banas. Why do they leave? Unpublished manuscript, 1969.

of managerial personel, Kraut[3] consistently found significant correlations between expressed intent to stay and subsequent employee participation. Such findings were far stronger than relationships between expressed satisfaction and continued participation. And, in a study of turnover among Air Force pilots, Atchison and Lefferts (1972) found that the frequency with which individuals thought about leaving their job was significantly related to rate termination. Based on these preliminary findings, an argument can be made that an expressed intention to leave may represent the next logical step after experienced dissatisfaction in the withdrawal process.

While considerable investigation has been carried out since the previous reviews concerning the relation of job satisfaction to turnover, only two studies have been found considering such satisfaction as it relates to absenteeism. Talacchi (1960), using the Science Research Associates' Employee Inventory, found a significant inverse relation between job satisfaction and absenteeism among office workers. He did not, however, find such a relation concerning turnover. And Waters and Roach (1971), using the Job Descriptive Index with clerical workers, found significant inverse relations between job satisfaction and both turnover and absenteeism.

In summary, the recent evidence concerning the impact of job satisfaction on withdrawal (especially on turnover) is generally consistent with the findings as reviewed by Brayfield and Crockett (1955), Herzberg et al. (1957), and Vroom (1964). (These new findings are summarized in Table 1.) It appears, however, that the major asset of these more recent findings is not simply their confirming nature but rather their increased methodological rigor over those studies reviewed previously. Most of the earlier studies contained several design weaknesses (see, e. g., the discussion by Brayfield & Crockett) which the more recent studies have overcome to a significant degree. For example, 12 of the 15 new studies reviewed here were predictive in nature. In addition, several of the research instruments used in the more recent studies (e. g., the Job Descriptive Index) appear to be more rigorously designed in terms of validity, reliability, and norms. Thus, these newer studies go a long way in the direction of providing increased confidence in the importance of job satisfaction as a force in the decision to participate.

SPECIFIC FACTORS RELATED TO WITHDRAWAL

While consideration of the role of overall job satisfaction in the decision to participate is important, it tells us little about the roots of such satisfaction. Knowing that an employee is dissatisfied and about to leave does not help us understand *why* he is dissatified, nor does it help us determine what must be changed in an effort to retain him. For the answer to these critical questions, it is necessary to look more closely at the various factors of the work situation as they potentially relate to the propensity to withdraw. We begin our discussion with

[3]A. I. Kraut. The prediction of turnover by employee attitudes. Unpublished manuscript, 1970.

Table 1   Studies of Relation of Job Satisfaction to Turnover and Absenteeism

Investigator(s)	Population	n^a	Type of with- drawal studied	Relation to withdrawal
Weitz & Nuckols (1955)	Insurance agents	990	Turnover	Negative
Weitz (1956)	Insurance agents	474	Turnover	Negative
Talacchi (1960)	Departmental workers	NA	Turnover	Zero
			Absenteeism	Negative
Youngberg (1963)	Insurance salesmen	NA	Turnover	Negative
Hulin (1966)	Female clerical workers	129	Turnover	Negative
Hulin (1968)	Female clerical workers	298	Turnover	Negative
Katzell (1968)	Student nurses	1852	Turnover	Negative
Mikes & Hulin (1968)	Office workers	660	Turnover	Negative
Dunnette et al. (see Footnote 2)	Lower level managers	1020	Turnover	Negative
Macedonia (1969)	Military academy cadets	1160	Turnover	Negative
Taylor & Weiss (1969a, 1969b)	Retail store employees	475	Turnover	Negative
Kraut (see Footnote 3)[b]	Computer salesmen	Varied	Turnover	Negative
Wild (1970)	Female manual workers	236	Turnover	Negative
Waters & Roach (1971)	Female clerical workers	160	Turnover	Negative
			Absenteeism	Negative
Atchison & Lefferts (1972)[b]	Air Force pilots	52	Turnover	Negative

Note. NA = not available.
[a] Sample sizes reported here and on the following tables reflect the actual number of subjects used in the data analysis from which the reported results were derived.
[b] Both Kraut, and Atchison and Lefferts found that an expressed intention to leave represented an even more accurate predictor of turnover than job satisfaction.

those factors that are generally organization-wide in their impact on employees and move toward those factors that are more unique to each individual.

Organization-Wide Factors

Organization-wide factors for purposes of this discussion can be defined as those variables affecting the individual that are primarily determined by persons or events external to the immediate work group. Under this rubric would fall such factors as pay and promotion policies and organization size. . . .

Pay and promotional considerations often appear to represent significant factors in the termination decision. [See Table 2.] While several of the recent studies reviewed above simply confirmed such a conclusion, other studies investigated the reasons behind such a relationship. These studies fairly consistently pointed out the importance of perceived equity and met expectations as important forces in such a decision. The size of the pay raise or the rate of promotion, while important in and of themselves, are, in addition, weighed by an employee in the light of his expectations, given his level of self-perceived contribution. The resulting determination of his degree of satisfaction or dissatisfaction then apparently inputs into his decision to remain or to search for preferable job alternatives.

The results of one study indicated that turnover rates appear to be fairly constant among organizations of varying sizes, while absenteeism is significantly

Table 2   Studies of Relations between Organization-wide Factors and Turn-over and Absenteeism

Factor	Population	n	Type of withdrawal studied	Relation to withdrawal
Satisfaction with pay and promotion				
Patchen (1960)	Oil refinery workers	487	Absenteeism	Negative
Friedlander & Walton (1964)	Scientists and engineers	82	Turnover	Negative
Knowles (1964)	Factory workers	56	Turnover	Negative
Saleh et al. (1965)	Nurses	263	Turnover	Negative
Bassett (1967)[a]	Engineers	200	Turnover	Negative
Ronan (1967)	Administrative & professional personnel	91	Turnover	Negative
Hulin (1968)	Female clerical workers	298	Turnover	Netative
Dunnette et al. (see Footnote 2)	Lower level managers	1020	Turnover (pay)	Zero
			Turnover (promotion)	Negative
Kraut (see Footnote 3)	Computer salesmen	Varied	Turnover	Negative
Telly et al. (1971)	Factory workers	900	Turnover	Zero[b]
Conference Board (1972)	Salesmen; management trainees	Varied	Turnover	Negative
Participation in compensation plan design				
Lawler & Hackman (1969)	Custodians	83	Absenteeism	Negative
Scheflen et al. (1971)	Custodians	NA	Absenteeism	Nogativo
Organization size				
Ingham (1970)	Factory workers	8 units	Turnover	Zero
			Absenteeism	Positive

Note. NA = not available.
[a] Bassett posited such a relationship but did not specifically test for it.
[b] This relation was explained by the nature of the union contract, which standardized pay and promotion procedures based essentially on seniority.

higher in larger firms than in smaller ones. Some theoretical considerations were offered to explain this variance but were not effectively substantiated by empirical data.

Immediate Work Environment Factors

A second set of factors instrumental in the decision to withdraw centers around the immediate work situation in which the employee finds himself. In previous reviews, Brayfield and Crockett (1955) found that negative employee attitudes toward their job context (especially at the lower levels) were significantly related to absenteeism and, to a lesser extent, to turnover. And Herzberg et al. (1957) found that such factors as the nature of the social work group were of particular importance in the decision to participate.

Since these reviews were published, significant research has been carried out which tends to supplement existing knowledge concerning the importance of immediate work environment factors in withdrawal. Factors to be considered here include *(a)* supervisory style, *(b)* work unit size, and *(c)* the nature of peer group interaction. . . .

The findings, summarized in Table 3, provide a relatively clear picture of the relation of at least three immediate work environment factors to an employee's decision to participate or withdraw. Several studies have pointed to the importance of supervisory style as a major factor in turnover. Apparently, when one's expectations concerning what the nature of supervision should be like remain substantially unmet, his propensity to leave increases. No studies, however, have been found relating supervisory style to absenteeism. This neglect of absenteeism studies is rather surprising considereing the widely accepted notion of the centrality of the supervisor as a factor in such withdrawal.

The size of the working unit has been shown to be related to both turnover and absenteeism among blue-collar workers; however, insufficient evidence is available to draw conclusions concerning such influence on managerial or clerical personnel.

Finally, most of the research in the area of co-worker satisfaction demonstrates the potential importance of such satisfaction in retention. Such findings, however, are not universal. A possible explanation for the divergent findings is that some people have a lower need for affiliation than others and may place less importance on satisfactory co-worker relations. Alternatively, it is possible that some organizational settings provide for a greater degree of peer group interaction, thereby increasing the probability that one's level of expectations would be met in this area. In either event, co-worker dissatisfaction cannot be overlooked as a possible cause of attrition.

Job Content Factors

It has long been thought that the duties and activities required for the successful performance of an individual's particular job can have a significant impact on his decision to remain with and participate in the employing organization. Such job requirements are presumed to represent for the individual either a vehicle for personal fulfillment and satisfaction or a continual source of frustration, internal conflict, and dissatisfaction. In recent years, several new investigations have appeared which provide added clarity to the role of such job-related factors in the withdrawal process. Four such factors will be discussed here: *(a)* the overall reaction to job content, *(b)* task repetitiveness, *(c)* job autonomy and responsibility, and *(d)* role clarity. . . .

In general, turnover has been found to be positively related to dissatisfaction with the content of the job among both blue- and white-collar workers. Insufficient evidence is available, however, to draw any such conclusions concerning absenteeism, but initial investigations point to a similar relationship. More specifically, the available data tend to indicate that both absenteeism and turnover are positively associated with task repetitiveness, although such a conclusion may represent an oversimplification of the nature of the relationship (see, e. g., Hulin & Blood, 1968). Finally, a strong positive relation has been found consistently between both forms of withdrawal and a perceived lack of sufficient job autonomy or responsibility.

Table 3   Studies of Relations between Immediate Work Environment Factors and Turnover and Absenteeism

Factor	Population	n	Type of with-drawal studied	Relation to withdrawal
Satisfaction with supervisory relations				
Fleishman & Harris (1962)	Production workers	NA[a]	Turnover	Negative (curvilinear)
Saleh et al. (1965)	Nurses	263	Turnover	Negative
Ley (1966)	Production workers	100	Turnover	Negative
Hulin (1968)	Female clerical workers	298	Turnover	Negative
Skinner (1969)	Production workers	85	Turnover	Negative (curvilinear)
Taylor & Weiss (1969a, 1969b)	Retail store employees	475	Turnover	Zero
Telly et al. (1971)	Production workers	900	Turnover	Negative
Receipt of recognition and feedback				
Ross & Zander (1957)	Female skilled workers	507	Turnover	Negative
General Electric Company (1964a)	Engineers	36	Turnover	Negative
Supervisory experience				
Bassett (1967)	Technicians and engineers	200	Turnover	Negative
Work unit size				
Kerr et al. (1951)	Production workers	894	Turnover	Positive
			Absenteeism	Positive
Acton Society Trust (1953)	Factory workers	91	Absenteeism	Positive
Hewitt & Parfitt (1953)	Factory workers	179	Absenteeism	Positive
Metzner & Mann (1953)	Blue-collar workers	251	Absenteeism	Positive
	White-collar workers	375	Absenteeism	Zero
Mandell (1956)	Clerical workers	320	Turnover	Positive
Argyle et al. (1958)	Production departments	86	Turnover	Zero
			Absenteeism	Positive (curvilinear)
Revans (1958)	Factory workers	Varied	Absenteeism	Positive
Baumgartel & Sobol (1959)	Blue- and white-collar workers	3900	Absenteeism	Positive
Indik & Seashore (1961)	Factory workers	NA	Turnover	Positive
			Absenteeism	Positive
Satisfactory peer group interactions				
Evan (1963)[b]	Management trainees	300	Turnover	Negative
Hulin (1968)	Female clerical workers	298	Turnover	Negative
Taylor & Weiss (1969a, 1969b)	Retail store employees	475	Turnover	Zero
Farris (1971)	Scientists and engineers	395	Turnover	Negative
Telly et al. (1971)	Production workers	900	Turnover	Negative
Waters & Roach (1971)	Clerical workers	160	Turnover	Zero
			Absenteeism	Negative

Note. NA = not available.

[a] A total of 56 foremen plus approximately 3 subordinates of each foreman took part in the study: specific *N* not reported.

[b] Inference based on study results

Table 4 Studies of Relations between Job Content Factors and Turnover and Absenteeism

Factor	Population	n	Type of withdrawal studied	Relation to withdrawal
Satisfaction with job content				
Saleh et al. (1965)	Nurses	263	Turnover	Negative
Hulin (1968)	Clerical workers	298	Turnover	Zero
Katzell (1968)	Student nurses	1852	Turnover	Negative
Dunnette et al. (see Footnote 4)	Lower-level managers	1020	Turnover	Negative
Taylor & Weiss (1969a, 1969b)	Retail store employees	475	Turnover	Negative
Kraut (see Footnote 5)	Computer salesmen	Varied	Turnover	Negative
Wild (1970)	Female manual workers	236	Turnover	Negative
Telly et al. (1971)	Production workers	900	Turnover	Negative
Waters & Roach (1971)	Clerical workers	160	Turnover	Negative
			Absenteeism	Negative
Task repetitiveness				
Guest (1955)	Automobile assembly line workers	18	Turnover	Positive
Kilbridge (1961)	Production workers	568	Turnover	Zero
		331	Absenteeism	Positive
Lefkowitz & Katz (1969)	Factory workers	80	Turnover	Positive
Taylor & Weiss (1969a, 1969b)	Retail store employees	475	Turnover	Positive
Wild (1970)	Female manual workers	236	Turnover	Positive
Job autonomy and responsibility				
Guest (1955)	Automobile assembly line workers	18	Turnover	Negative
Ross & Zander (1957)	Female skilled workers	507	Turnover	Negative
Turner & Lawrence (1965)	Blue-collar workers	403	Absenteeism	Negative
Taylor & Weiss (1969a, 1969b)	Retail store employees	475	Turnover	Negative
Hackman & Lawler (1971)	Telephone operators and clerks	208	Absenteeism	Negative·
Waters & Roach (1971)	Clerical workers	160	Turnover	Negative
Role clarity				
Weitz (1956)	Insurance salesmen	474	Turnover	Negative
Youngberg (1963)	Insurance salesmen	NA	Turnover	Negative
Macedonia (1969)	Military academy cadets	1260	Turnover	Negative
Lyons (1971)	Nurses	156	Turnover	Negative

Note. NA = not available.

The degree of role clarity on the part of the individual can apparently affect turnover in two ways. First, an accurate picture of the actual tasks required by the organization can function to select out, prior to employment, those who do not feel the rewards offered justify doing such tasks. And, secondly, accurate role perceptions can serve to adjust the expectations of those already employed to more realistic levels as to what is expected of them in terms of performance. The resulting increased congruence between expectations and actual experience apparently can serve to increase satisfaction and continued participation. No conclusions can be drawn concerning the effect of role clarity on absenteeism due to a lack of investigations on the subject.

The results of those studies relating to job content are summarized in Table 4 on page 284.

Personal Factors

Factors unique to the individual also appear to have a significant impact on the problems of turnover and absenteeism. Such factors include *(a)* age, *(b)* tenure with the organization, *(c)* similarity of job with vocational interest, *(d)* personality characteristics, and *(e)* family considerations. While often overlooked by investigators, the inclusion of such items are central to developing a comprehensive model explaining the dynamics of work participation. . . .

The findings concerning personal factors in withdrawal are summarized in Table 5. Age is strongly and negatively related to turnover, while being somewhat postively (though weakly) related to absenteeism. Similarly, increased tenure appears to be strongly related to propensity to remain. One possible explanation here may be that increases in tenure result in increases in personal investment on the part of the employee in the organization (i. e., after a while, he may not be able to "afford" to quit). No solid conclusions can be drawn concerning the impact of tenure on absenteeism, however, due to conflicting results.

From limited studies, turnover appears to be inversely related to the similarity between job requirements and vocational interests. No studies were found that related such interests to absenteeism, however. Predicting turnover or absenteeism from interest inventories (assuming they are properly validated) represents an important possibility for organizations because such data can be collected *prior* to employment. Such an advantage does not exist for most predictors of withdrawal.

The majority of studies investigating the relationship between personality traits and withdrawal center around turnover so no conclusions can be drawn about their relation to absenteeism. Apparently, the possession of more extreme personality traits may lead to an increased tendency to leave the organization. While further investigation is definitely in order here, a tendency exists for employees manifesting very high degrees of anxiety, emotional instability, aggression, independence, self-confidence, and ambition to leave the organization at a higher rate than employees possessing such traits in a more moderate degree. The implications of such a phenomenon, if borne out by further research, need also to be investigated for their effects on organizational efficiency and effectiveness. That is, if such a pattern really exists, research is needed as to the desirability for the organization of accepting a higher turnover rate in exchange for possible resulting increases in performance from such mobile employees. No research has been found that demonstrates that low-turnover employees (those possessing more moderate personality traits) are in fact better performers. Thus, reduced

Table 5 Studies of Relations between Personal Factors and Turnover and Absenteeism

Factor	Population	n	Type of withdrawal studied	Relation to withdrawal
Age				
Minor (1958)	Female clerical workers	440	Turnover	Negative
Naylor & Vincent (1959)	Female clerical workers	220	Absenteeism	Zero
Fleishman & Berniger (1960)	Female clerical workers	205	Turnover	Negative
de la Mare & Sergean (1961)	Industrial workers	140	Absenteeism	Positive
Shott et al. (1963)	Male office workers	561	Turnover	Zero
	Female office workers		Turnover	Negative
Cooper & Payne (1965)	Construction workers	392	Absenteeism	Positive
Ley (1966)	Factory workers	100	Turnover	Negative
Bassett (1967)	Technicians and engineers	200	Turnover	Negative
Downs (1967)	Public service organization trainees	1736	Turnover	Positive
	Public service organization employees (after training)		Turnover	Negative
Stone & Athelstan (1969)	Clerical workers	453	Turnover	Negative
Farris (1971)	Scientists and engineers	395	Turnover	Negative
Robinson (1972)	Female clerical workers	200	Turnover	Negative
Tenure				
Hill & Trist (1955)	Factory workers	289	Absenteeism	Zero
Baumgartel & Sobol (1959)	Male blue-collar workers	3900	Absenteeism	Negative
	Female blue-collar, male and female white-collar workers		Absenteeism	Positive
Fleishman & Berniger (1960)	Female clerical workers	205	Turnover	Negative
Shott et al. (1963)	Male and female office workers	561	Turnover	Negative
Knowles (1964)	Factory workers	56	Turnover	Negative
Robinson (1972)	Female clerical workers	200	Turnover	Negative
Congruence of job with vocational interests				
Ferguson (1958)	Insurance salesmen	520	Turnover	Negative
Boyd (1961)	Engineers	326	Turnover	Negative
Mayeske (1964)	Foresters	125	Turnover	Negative
"Extreme" personality characteristics[a]				
Cleland & Peck (1959)	Ward attendants	54	Turnover	Positive
Hakkinen & Toivainen (1960)	Miners	135	Turnover	Positive
MacKinney & Wolins (1960)	Male production foremen	175	Turnover	Positive
Meyer & Cuomo (1962)	Engineers	1360	Turnover	Positive
Sinha (1963)	Industrial workers	110	Absenteeism	Positive
Farris (1971)	Technical personnel	395	Turnover	Positive
Family size				
Naylor & Vincent (1959)	Female clerical workers	220	Absenteeism	Positive
Knowles (1964)	Male factory workers	56	Turnover	Negative
Stone & Athelstan (1969)	Female physical therapists	453	Turnover	Positive
Family responsibilities				
Guest (1955)	Male auto assembly line workers	18	Turnover	Positive
Minor (1958)	Female clerical workers	440	Turnover	Positive
Fleishman & Berniger (1960)	Female clerical workers	205	Turnover	Positive
Saleh et al. (1965)	Nurses	263	Turnover	Positive
Robinson (1972)	Female clerical workers	200	Turnover	Positive

[a] See text for more detailed description.

turnover may be an undesirable goal if it is bought at the price of reduced work-force effectiveness.

Finally, family size and family responsibilities were generally found to be positively related to turnover and absenteeism among women, while their impact on men appears to be mixed.

SUMMARY AND DISCUSSION

The foregoing review clearly shows that a multiplicity of organizational, work, and personal factors can be associated with the decision to withdraw. It is possible, however, to summarize briefly those factors for which sufficient evidence exists to draw meaningful conclusions concerning their relation to withdrawal.

In general, very strong evidence has been found in support of the contention that *overall* job satisfaction represents an important force in the individual's participation decision. In addition, based on preliminary evidence, such satisfaction also appears to have a significant impact on absenteeism. These trends have been demonstrated among a diversity of work group populations and in organizations of various types and sizes. Moreover, the methodologies upon which these findings are based are generally of a fairly rigorous nature.

However, as noted earlier, it is not sufficient for our understanding of the withdrawal process to simply point to such a relationship. It is important to consider what constitutes job satisfaction. Under the conceptualization presented here, job satisfaction is viewed as the sum total of an individual's met expectations on the job. The more an individual's expectations are met on the job, the greater his satisfaction. Viewing withdrawal within this framework points to the necessity of focusing on the various factors that make up the employee's expectation set.

We have proposed four general categories, or "levels" in the organization, in which factors can be found that affect withdrawal. Sufficient evidence exists to conclude that important influences on turnover can be found in each of these categories. That is, some of the more central variables related to turnover are organization-wide in their derivation (e. g., pay and promotion policies), while others are to be found in the immediate work group (e. g., unit size, supervision, and co-worker relations). Still others are to be found in the content of the job (e. g., nature of job requirements) and, finally, some are centered around the person himself (e. g., age and tenure). Thus, based on these findings, the major roots of turnover appear to be fairly widespread throughout the various facets of organizational structure, as they interact with particular types of individuals.

On a more tentative level, initial findings indicate that role clarity and the receipt of recognition and feedback are also inversely related to turnover. However, not all of the possible factors reviewed here have been found to be clearly or consistently related to termination. For example, conflicting data exist concerning the influence of task repetitiveness and of family size on such withdrawal.

Much less can be concluded about the impact of these factors on absenteeism due to a general lack of available information. Sufficient evidence does exist, however, to conclude with some degree of confidence that increased unit size is strongly and directly related to absenteeism. In addition, tentative evidence suggests that opportunities for participation in decision making and increased job autonomy are inversely related to such behavior.

One further point warrants emphasis here concerning the turnover studies reviewed above. To a large extent, there is an underlying assumption, often inferred but sometimes stated, that the reduction of all turnover is a desirable goal. Such an assumption may be questioned on several grounds. First, from the individual's point of view, leaving an unrewarding job may result in the procurement of a more satisfying one. Second, from the organization's standpoint, some of those who leave may be quite ineffective performers, and their departure would open positions for (hopefully) better performers. The important point here is that a clear distinction should be made in future research efforts between effective and ineffective leavers. The loss of an effective employee may cost far more than the loss of an ineffective one, and the costs of efforts to retain the latter may well exceed the benefits. Third, given the present state of technological flux, turnover may in some ways be considered a necessary evil. It may be necessary to simply accept certain levels of turnover as the price for rapid change and increased efficiency.

Met Expectations and Turnover

The preceding review of turnover and absenteeism studies highlights the fact that there is an abundance of findings concerning the former and a relative paucity of findings concerning the latter. Because of this difference and because of the potential danger of undue generalizations from a joint treatment of the topics, the role of met expectations on turnover *only* are discussed here. A later section will consider the problem of absenteeism.

The major turnover findings of this review, when taken together, point to the centrality of the concept of met expectations in the withdrawal decision. Under such a conceptualization, each individual is seen as bringing to the employment situation his own unique set of expectations for his job. It is likely, based on the results presented here, that most employees place a fairly high valence on the attainment of their expectations in certain areas, such as pay, promotion, supervisory relations, and peer group interactions. In addition, however, each individual appears to place varying importance on a host of other potential "rewards" available from his job. For some, the most important factor may be challenging work, while for others it may be the status attached to one's job; for some, it may be both. Whatever the composition of the individual's expectation set, it is important that *those* factors be substantially met if the employee is to feel it is worthwhile to remain with the organization. Doubling the salary of a man who is genuinely disinterested in money may have little effect in ensuring his continued participation. While this set of expectations may be modified over time in response to past rewards, available alternatives, and other factors, it is toward the present or anticipated satisfaction of this fairly unique set of expectations that we must direct our attention if we are to understand the termination decision.

In general, then, the decision to participate or withdraw may be looked upon as a process of balancing received or potential rewards with desired expectations. Such an explanation, however, raises questions as to what the organization can do if it wants to reduce such turnover. Based on the literature, several seemingly contradictory approaches result. In an effort to clarify these apparent contradictions, we will discuss in detail the findings of six of the more important studies as they apply to the problem at hand.

Ross and Zander (1957), Katzell (1968), and Dunnette et al. (see Footnote 2) found that the mean levels of *initial* expectations of those who remained and those who later decided to leave were essentially the same. Thus, while individuals may vary considerably in terms of their own expectation set, no significant differences were found between stayers and leavers as a group at the time of entry into the organization. However, those who later left reported significantly lower levels of met expectations as time went on. Since the original expectations were similar, the significant differences between the two groups in the degree to which such expectations were actually met could have resulted from the existence of differential reward levels. Those who left may have failed, in general, to meet their expectation on the job and sought satisfaction elsewhere. Following this approach, turnover could presumably be reduced somewhat through an increase in the reward levels so they would be more congruent with the more stationary expection levels.

Weitz (1956), Youngberg (1963), and Macedonia (1969), on the other hand, altered the experimental groups' initial expectations, resulting in distinct differences between the stayers' and leavers' mean levels of expectation at the time of entry into the organization. Those who later decided to remain presumably had more realistic levels upon entry. A unitary reward system can be inferred from these findings, suggesting that one key to the reduction of turnover would be to clarify expectations among entering personnel so as to bring them into closer alignment with the available rewards.

While the first set of findings here appears to be in conflict with the second set, closer analysis demonstrates that it is quite possible to achieve a viable synthesis. It appears from these investigations that both expectation levels and reward levels are variable within certain limits. Such possible fluctuations are depicted in the hypothetical example shown in Figure 1. Following this example, we can first apply the results of Ross and Zander, Katzell, and Dunnette et al. where both stayers and leavers entered the organization with similar mean expectation levels, represented in Figure 1 by the column labeled E_1. As a result of differential reward levels, represented in Figure 1 by R_1, R_2, and R_3, some employees would tend to perceive that rewards met or exceeded expectations (in the case of R_1), resulting in increased satisfaction an an increased propensity to participate. Other employees, however, would perceive rewards to be below their expectations (in the case of R_2 and R_3), resulting in decreased satisfaction and an increased propensity to leave.

Next, we can apply the model to the findings of Weitz (1956), Youngberg (1963), and Macedonia (1969). Here, the mean expectation level of those who later left remained unchanged (represented by E_1), while the mean level of those who stayed was generally adjusted downward (to E_2), by increasing the employ-ees' knowledge about the nature of the job. Thus, even with the impact of differ-ential reward levels, it can be seen that, on the whole, a greater number of those who stayed would be more likely to experience met expectations than those who later left. The stayers, with more realistic expectations levels, would have a great-er number of potential reward levels (R_1 and R_2) lying above their expectation levels than would the leavers (R_1 *only*), thereby increasing the chances of meeting of exceeding their expectations or the job.

The use of such a model points to at least three actions that the organization might attempt in its effort to reduce turnover. First, attempts can be made to enrich the total amount of potentially available rewards. This action should serve to increase the probability that reward expectations will be met. Such a proce-dure may have limited applicability, of course, due to structural and financial constraints on the organization. Various feasible approaches do exist, however, for improving rewards in such areas as supervisory and co-worker interactions, recognition and feedback on performance, and fairness (if not increases) in com-pensation policies. Second, organizations may consider the installation of cafete-ria-style compensation plans (Lawler, 1971) to allow the employee a greater selection of rewards toward which to work. Such increased selection should serve in part to increase the likelihood that more of his expectations can be met on the job. Third, and perhaps most important, the organization can attempt to increase the present or potential employee's accuracy and realism of expectations through increased communications concerning the nature of the job and the probable potential payoffs for effective performance. Where the employee fully under-stand what is expected of him and what the organization offers in return, the likelihood of him forming unrealistic expectations should decrease, resulting in increased possibilities that his expectations are actually met.

The clarification for the employee of both expectations and potential re-wards, then, should have the effect of generally increasing the degree to which such expectations are met. Where these expectations have been essentially satis-fied and where the employee has no reason to believe they will not continue to be satisfied in the future, we would expect an increased tendency to leave.

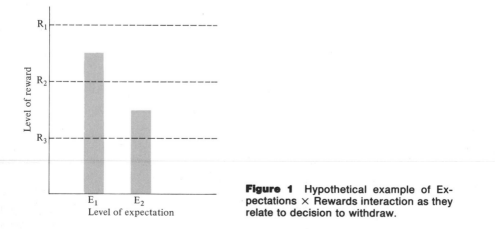

Figure 1 Hypothetical example of Ex-pectations × Rewards interaction as they relate to decision to withdraw.

Met Expectations and Absenteeism

The organization's tendency not to accept even minimal turnover appears often to be matched by a somewhat unconcerned attitude toward absenteeism. Perhaps this is due, in part, to an inability in many cases to distinguish accurately between avoidable and unavoidable absenteeism for purposes of measurement. It may be, however, that the costs to the organization due to poor attendance may be far greater than the costs of turnover. The studies reviewed here indicate that those employees in which the organization has the least investment (young, low-tenured employees) have the greatest incidences of turnover, while those employees who are older and more mature (and in whom the organization typically has greater investment) apparently have increased incidences of absenteeism. If this is the case, a redirection of effort may be in order away from the study of turnover and toward a better understanding of the more temporary forms of withdrawal. Too often in the past, absenteeism has been considered simply an analogue of turnover, and it has been assumed, with sufficient evidence, that the two shared identical roots.

Several important dimensions exist along which absenteeism as a form of withdrawal can be distinguished from turnover: (a) The negative consequences for the individual that are associated with absenteeism are usually much less than those associated with turnover. For example, with the prevalence of company sick leave policies, an employee can miss work (up to a point) without salary loss. (b) Absenteeism is more likely to be a spontaneous and relatively easy decision, while the act of termination can be assumed to be more carefully considered over time in most cases. (c) Absenteeism may sometimes represent a substitute type of behavior for turnover, particularly where alternative employment is unavailable. In this sense, absenteeism may allow for temporary avoidance of an unrewarding situation without the loss of the benefits of employment; turnover, on the other hand, represents a complete severance of the individual from such benefits.

In view of some of these differences, it is important to compare the two types of withdrawal as they simultaneously relate to specific factors in the work environment. March and Simon (1958) hypothesize that no differences exist between absenteeism and turnover insofar as the factors inducing such forms of behavior are concerned. However, the evidence as reviewed above does not entirely support such a position (e. g., Kilbridge, 1961; Waters & Roach, 1971). In fact, of the 22 tested relationships on the studies reviewed here where data were available on both turnover and absenteeism among the same samples, only 6 found significant relations in the same direction between the factors under study and *both* types of withdrawal. The remainder found certain factors significantly related to one form of withdrawal but not the other. Such findings suggest that some important differences may exist between the causes of turnover and those of absenteeism.

Whether a model similar to that proposed for turnover (Figure 1) also applies in a somewhat modified version to absenteeism remains to be demonstrated. Even so, one can speculate that such a model is applicable but that different thresholds exist for the two forms of withdrawal. That is, it is possible that the failure by and large to meet one's expectations on the job would lead to increased tendencies both to terminate and to go absent. However, a far greater disparity between such expectations and rewards may be necessary for an individual to decide to quit than to simply decide not to come to work on a particular day.

Future Directions for Research

Based on this review, several fairly obvious voids exist in our knowledge of turnover and absenteeism which require further study. To begin with, much more emphasis should be placed in the future on the psychology of the withdrawal *process*. While correlational studies abound (particularly with respect to turnover) which relate various factors to withdrawal, our understanding of the manner in which the actual decision is made is far from complete.

Second, a major focus should be placed on differential expectation levels at the time of entry into the organization and the extent to which these expectations are met or altered over the course of employment. This strongly suggests the need for as much attention to expectations as to reactions to the work situation.

Third, some attention should be directed toward the study of differentially valued employees in relation to withdrawal. Organizational investments (e. g., compensation, additional training, experience) in employees can vary considerably across hierarchical levels and functions. Similarly, some employees are rated higher by the organization in terms of performance and potential. Little is known about the relation of these factors to withdrawal. It is possible that the more valued employees quit or exhibit high rates of absenteeism for quite different reasons than those who are less valued.

Fourth, more investigation is necessary which simultaneously studies both turnover and absenteeism among the same samples as they are affected by various factors in the organizational situation. Such designs would increase our knowledge not only of the potentially different roots of each type of withdrawal but also of possible interactive effects between the two.

Finally, future research should include more emphasis on determining the effects of specific organizational interventions on turnover and absenteeism. The increased use of longitudinal designs and well-controlled field experiments would significantly increase the confidence we could place in the presumed impact of significant variables on withdrawal.

REFERENCES

Acton Society Trust. *Size and morale.* London: Author, 1953.

Argyle, M., Gardner, G., & Cioffi, I. Supervisory methods related to productivity, absenteeism and labor turnover. *Human Relations,* 1958, **11**, 23–40.

Atchison, T. J., & Lefferts, E. A. The prediction of turnover using Herzberg's job satisfaction technique. *Personnel Psychology,* 1972, **25**, 53–64.

Bassett, G. A. *A study of factors associated with turnover of exempt personnel.* Crotonville, N.Y.: Behavioral Research Service, General Electric Company, 1967.

Baumgartel, H., & Sobol, R. Background and organizational factors in absenteeism. *Personnel Psychology,* 1959, **12**, 431–443.

Boyd, J. B. Interests of engineers related to turnover, selection, and management. *Journal of Applied Psychology,* 1961, **45**, 143–149.

Brayfield, A. H., & Crockett, W. H. Employee attitudes and employee performance. *Psychological Bulletin,* 1955, **52**, 396–424.

Cleland, C. C., & Peck, R. F. Psychological determinants of tenure in institutional personnel. *American Journal of Mental Deficiency,* 1959, **64,** 876–888.

Conference Board. *Salesmen's turnover in early employment.* New York: Author, 1972.

Cooper, R., & Payne, R. Age and absence: A longitudinal study in three firms. *Occupational Psychology,* 1965, **35,** 31–43.

De La Mare, G., & Sergean, R. Two methods of studying changes in absence with age. *Occupational Psychology,* 1961, **35,** 245–252.

Downs, S. Labour turnover in two public service organizations. *Occupational Psychology,* 1967, **41,** 137–142.

Evan, W. M. Peer-group interaction and organizational socialization: A study of employee turnover. *American Sociological Review,* 1963, **28,** 436–440.

Ferris, G. F. A predictive study of turnover. *Personnel Psychology,* 1971, **24,** 311–328.

Ferguson, L. W. Life insurance interest, ability and termination of employment. *Personnel Psychology,* 1958, **11,** 189–193.

Fleishman, E. A. A leader behavior description for industry. In R. M. Stogdill & A. E. Coons (Eds.), *Leader behavior: Its description and measurement.* (Ohio Studies in Personnel; Research Monograph No. 88) Columbus: Ohio State University, Bureau of Business Research, 1957. (a)

Fleishman, E. A. The Leadership Opinion Questionnaire. In R. M. Stogdill & A. E. Coons (Eds.), *Leader behavior: Its description and measurement.* (Ohio Studies in Personnel; Research Monograph No. 88) Columbus: Ohio State University, Bureau of Business Research, 1957. (b)

Fleishman, E. A. *Revised Manual for Leadership Opinion Questionnaire.* Chicago: Science Research Associates, 1968.

Fleishman, E. A., & Berniger, J. One way to reduce office turnover. *Personnel,* 1960, **37,** 63–69.

Fleishman, E. A., & Harris, E. F. Patterns of leadership behavior related to employee grievances and turnover. *Personnel Psychology,* 1962, **15,** 43–56.

Friedlander, F., & Walton, E. Positive and negative motivations toward work. *Administrative Science Quarterly,* 1964, **9,** 194–207.

General Electric Company, Behavioral Research Service. *Attitudes associated with turnover of highly regarded employees.* Crotonville, N. Y.: Author, 1964. (a)

General Electric Company, Behavioral Research Service. *A comparison of work planning program with the annual performance appraisal interview approach.* Crotonville, N. Y.: Author, 1964. (b)

Guest, R. H. A neglected factor in labour turnover. *Occupational Psychology,* 1955, **29,** 217–231.

Hackman, J. R., & Lawler, E. E., III. Employee reactions to job characteristics. *Journal of Applied Psychology,* 1971, **55,** 259–286.

Hakkinen, S., & Toivainen, Y. Psychological factors causing labour turnover among underground workers. *Occupational Psychology,* 1960, **34,** 15–30.

Herzberg, F., Mausner, B., Peterson, R. O., & Capwell, D. F. *Job attitudes: Review of research and opinion.* Pittsburgh: Psychological Service of Pittsburgh, 1957.

Hewitt, D., & Parfitt, J. A note on working morale and size of group. *Occupational Psychology,* 1953, **27,** 38–42.

Hill, J. M., & Trist, E. L. Changes in accidents and other absences with length of service. *Human Relations,* 1955, **8,** 121–152.

Hulin, C. L. Job satisfaction and turnover in a female clerical population. *Journal of Applied Psychology,* 1966, **50,** 280–285.

Hulin, C. L. Effects of changes in job-satisfaction levels on employee turnover. *Journal of Applied Psychology,* 1968, **52,** 122–126.

Hulin, C. L., & Blood, M. R. Job enlargement, individual differences, and worker responses. *Psychological Bulletin,* 1968, **69,** 41–55.

Indik, B., & Seashore, S. *Effects of organization size on member attitudes and behavior.* Ann Arbor: University of Michigan, Survey Research Center of the Institute for Social Research, 1961.

Ingham, G. *Size of industrial organization and worker behaviour.* New York: Wiley, 1964.

Kahn, R., Wolfe, D., Quinn, R., Snoek, J., & Rosenthal, R. *Organizational stress: Studies in role conflict and ambiguity.* New York: Wiley, 1964.

Katz, D., Maccoby, E., Gurin, G., & Floor, L. *Productivity, supervision and morale among railroad workers.* Ann Arbor: University of Michigan, Survey Research Center, 1951.

Katz, D., Maccoby, N., & Morse, N. *Productivity, supervision and morale in an office situation.* Ann Arbor: University of Michigan, Institute for Social Research, 1950.

Katzell, M. E. Expectation and dropouts in schools of nursing. *Journal of Applied Psychology,* 1968, **52,** 154–157.

Kerr, W., Koppelmeier, G., & Sullivan, J. Absenteeism, turnover and morale in a metals fabrication factory. *Occupational Psychology,* 1951, **25,** 50–55.

Kilbridge, M. Turnover, absence, and transfer rates as indicators of employee dissatisfaction with repetitive work. *Industrial and Labor Relations Review,* 1961, **15,** 21–32.

Knowles, M. C. Personal and job factors affecting labour turnover. *Personnel Practice Bulletin,* 1964, **20,** 25–37.

Lawler, E. E., III. *Pay and organizational effectiveness: A psychological view.* New York: McGraw-Hill, 1971.

Lawler, E. E., III, & Hackman, J. R. Impact of employee participation in the development of pay incentive plans: A field experiment. *Journal of Applied Psychology,* 1969, **53,** 467–471.

Lefkowitz, J., & Katz, M. Validity of exit interviews. *Personnel Psychology,* 1969, **22,** 445–455.

Ley, R. Labour turnover as a function of worker differences, work environment, and authoritarianism of foremen. *Journal of Applied Psychology,* 1966, **50,** 497–500.

Lyons, T. Role clarity, need for clarity, satisfaction, tension and withdrawal. *Organizational Behavior and Human Performance,* 1971, **6,** 99–110.

Macedonia, R. M. Expectation-press and survival. Unpublished doctoral dissertation, Graduate School of Public Administration, New York University, June 1969.

MacKinney, A. C., & Wolins, L. Validity information exchange. *Personnel Psychology,* 1960, **13,** 443–447.

Mandell, M. *Recruiting and selecting office employees.* New York: American Management Association, 1956.

March, J. G., & Simon, H. A. *Organizations.* New York: Wiley, 1958.

Mayeske, G. W. The validity of Kuder Preference Record scores in predicting forester turnover and advancement. *Personnel Psychology,* 1964, **17,** 207–210.

Metzner, H., & Mann, F. Employee attitudes and absences. *Personnel Psychology,* 1953, **6,** 467–485.

Meyer, H., & Cuomo, S. *Who leaves? A study of background characteristics of engineers associated with turnover.* Crotonville, N.Y.: General Electric Company, Behavioral Science Research, 1962.

Mikes, P. S., & Hulin, C. Use of importance as a weighting component of job satisfaction. *Journal of Applied Psychology,* 1968, **52,** 394–398.

Minor, F. J. The prediction of turnover of clerical employees. *Personnel Psychology,* 1958, **11,** 393–402.

Naylor, J. E., & Vincent, N. L. Predicting female absenteeism. *Personnel Psychology,* 1959, **12,** 81–84.

Patchen, M. Absence and employee feelings about fair treatment. *Personnel Psychology,* 1960, **13,** 349–360.

Porter, L. W., & Lawler, E. E., III. Properties of organization structure in relation to job attitudes and job behavior. *Psychological Bulletin,* 1965, **64,** 23–51.

Porter, L. W., & Lawler, E. E., III. *Managerial attitudes and performance.* Homewood, Ill.: Irwin, 1968.

Revans, R. Human relations, management and size. In E. M. Hugh-Jones (Ed.), *Human relations and modern management.* Amsterdam: North-Holland Publishing, 1958.

Robinson, D. D. Prediction of clerical turnover in banks by means of a weighted application blank. *Journal of Applied Psychology,* 1972, **56,** 282.

Ronan, W. W. A study of some concepts concerning labour turnover. *Occupational Psychology,* 1967, **41,** 193–202.

Ross, I. C., & Zander, A. Need satisfaction and employee turnover. *Personnel Psychology,* 1957, **10,** 327–338.

Saleh, S. D., Lee, R. J., & Prien, E. P. Why nurses leave their jobs—An analysis of female turnover. *Personnel Administration,* 1965, **28,** 25–28.

Scheflen, K. C., Lawler, E. E., III, & Hackman, J. R. Long-term impact of employee participation in the development of pay incentive plans: A field experiment revisited. *Journal of Applied Psychology,* 1971, **55,** 182–186.

Schuh, A. The predictability of employee tenure: A review of the literature. *Personnel Psychology,* 1967, **20,** 133–152.

Shott, G. L., Albright, L. E., & Glennon, J. R. Predicting turnover in an automated office situation. *Personnel Psychology,* 1963, **16,** 213–219.

Sinha, A. K. P. Manifest anxiety affecting industrial absenteeism. *Psychological Reports,* 1963, **13,** 258.

Skinner, E. Relationships between leadership behavior patterns and organizational situational variables. *Personnel Psychology,* 1969, **22,** 189–194.

Stogdill, R., & Coons, A. (Eds.) *Leader behavior: Its description and measurement.* Columbus: Ohio State University, Bureau of Business Research, 1957.

Stone, T. H., & Athelstan, G. T. The SVIB for women and demographic variables in the prediction of occupational tenure. *Journal of Applied Psychology,* 1969, **53,** 408–412.

Talacchi, S. Organization size, individual attitudes and behavior: An empirical study. *Administrative Science Quarterly,* 1960, **5,** 398–420.

Science Quarterly, 1960, **5,** 398–420.

Taylor, K., & Weiss, D. Prediction of individual job termination from measured job satisfaction and biographical data. (Research Report No. 30) Minneapolis: University of Minnesota, Work Adjustment Project, October 1969. (a)

Taylor, K., & Weiss, D. Prediction of individual job turnover from measured job satisfaction. (Research Report No. 22) Minneapolis: University of Minnesota, Work Adjustment Project, May 1969. (b)

Telly, C. S., French, W. L., & Scott, W. G. The relationship of inequity to turnover among hourly workers. *Administrative Science Quarterly,* 1971, **16,** 164–172.

Turner, A. N., & Lawrence, P. R. *Industrial jobs and the worker: An investigation of response to task attributes.* Boston: Harvard University Press, Division of Research, 1965.

Vroom, V. *Work and motivation.* New York: Wiley, 1964.

Walker, C. R., & Guest, R. H. *The man on the assembly line.* Cambridge: Harvard University Press, 1952.

Waters, L. K., & Roach, D. Relationship between job attitudes and two forms of withdrawal from the work situation. *Journal of Applied Psychology,* 1971, **55,** 92–94.

Weitz, J. Job expectancy and survival. *Journal of Applied Psychology,* 1956, **40,** 294–300.

Weitz, J., & Nuckols, R. C. Job satisfaction and job survival. *Journal of Applied Psychology,* 1955, **39,** 294–300.

Wild, R. Job needs, job satisfaction, and job behavior of women manual workers. *Journal of Applied Psychology,* 1970, **54,** 157–162.

Youngberg, C. F. An experimental study of "job satisfaction" and turnover in relation to job expectancies and self expectations. Unpublished doctoral dissertation, New York University, 1963.

QUESTIONS FOR DISCUSSION

1 Provide several examples that demonstrate why each of Katz's three "behavioral requirements" is necessary for the effective functioning of organizations.

2 How might the causes of turnover and absenteeism differ between managerial and blue-collar workers? How widespread do you feel such differences may be?

3 Why might the causes of turnover differ from the causes of absenteeism among the same group of employees?

4 Given the large number of empirical studies of turnover and absenteeism, why do you feel that withdrawal continues to be so widespread?

5 What would you consider the most important things a manager could do to reduce turnover and absenteeism?

6 List several of the more important disadvantages associated with high withdrawal rates from organizations. What are some advantages of high withdrawal rates?

7 Aside from monetary considerations, what specific factors in the organizational milieu do you consider most important in keeping employees "attached" to their organization?

8 Can employees be physically attached to an organization, in that they continue to come to work for it, but not be psychologically attached? If so, does their lack of psychological attachment really make any difference?

Chapter 9

Organizational Environment and Work Behavior

OVERVIEW

It was pointed out in Chapter 8 that sources of attachment to organizations (or, conversely, sources of withdrawal from organizations) can be found in many elements of the organizational situation. These sources include organizationwide factors, immediate work environment factors, job-related factors, and personal factors. In the chapters that follow, we intend to examine each of these areas as they affect job attitudes and behavior other than withdrawal behavior. In this chapter we analyze the role of organizationwide factors—or organizational environment—as they affect such attitudes and behavior.

Central to a discussion of organizational environment is the concept of "organizational climate." Climate is a broad term designed to include the relatively constant variables in a work environment that are considered important to the efficient use of human resources. Examples of climate factors would be the type of supervision, the nature and direction of communication flows, the perceived reward-punishment structure, and so forth. These variables are assumed to be measurable and manipulatable at least to some extent and are considered the defining characteristics which distinguish one organization's working environment from another. Litwin and Stringer describe the concept as:

> . . . a set or cluster of expectancies and incentives [that represent] . . . a property of environments that is perceived directly or indirectly by the individuals in the environment. It is a molar construct which (1) permits analysis of the determinants of motivated behavior in actual, complex social situations, (2) simplifies the problem of measurement of situational determinants by allowing the individuals in the situation to think in terms of bigger, more integrated chunks of their experience, and (3) makes possible the characterization of the total situational influence of various environments, so that they may be mapped and categorized, and so that cross-environmental comparisons can be made.[1]

In other words, organizational climate can be thought of in one sense as the "personality" of the organization. Moreover, climate is believed by many to serve as a basis for individuals to interpret situations, to act as a source of pressure and/or constraint for directing individual activity, and to determine in large measure the reward-punishment system within the organization (Forehand & Gilmer, 1964; Pritchard & Karasick, 1973).

It is generally held that climatic factors affect behavior—not by themselves, but rather to the extent that they interact with other individual or personal factors. The importance of this interrelationship was first discussed by Lewin (1938, 1951). Lewin proposed a model of human behavior, based upon his research, which took into account both individual or personal differences *(P)* and the climate or environment surrounding the individual *(E)*. In brief, Lewin posited that human behavior *(B)* was a function of the interaction of both P and E. This hypothesis has been traditionally abbreviated $B = f(P,E)$. More recently, several management researchers, most notably Likert (1961, 1967), Katz and Kahn (1966), and Vroom (1964), have attempted to develop more complex models based upon this basic equation.

Organizational climate is created as the result of several forces (Litwin & Stringer, 1968). First, past experiences (including climate) play a major role in the determination of present climate. Second, climate is viewed as being affected by the constraints imposed by the formal organizational system and by the nature of the tasks required of the employees. Compare, for example, the climate of a highly structured, bureaucratic military organization with that of a free-form, unstructured R&D laboratory, or "think tank." Third, it is thought that the particular needs, expectations, and values of organizational members represent a significant input into climate determination. However, the most important determinant of climate is probably the leadership style of management. Litwin and Stringer (1968, p. 188) argue that "the emphasis a leader puts on adherence to rules, the kinds of goals and standards he sets, and perhaps most important, the

---

[1] G. H. Litwin & R. A. Stringer, Jr., *Motivation and organizational climate,* Boston: Harvard University, Graduate School of Business Administration, Division of Research, 1968, p. 29–30.

nature of his informal relationships and communications with his people, have very great impact on the climate." Supervisors who foster open, two-way communications with their subordinates, for instance, may indeed create an environment where their employees feel comfortable in expressing their true feelings on matters of importance to the organization. The opposite type of supervisory behavior, on the other hand, may lead to the creation of a work group of rule-oriented "yes men" who tell their superiors what they want to hear and seldom suggest innovations that deviate significantly from company norms or policies.

In the selection that follows, the general nature of environmental variation is discussed as it relates to human behavior at work. This selection reviews some definitional problems with the climate construct, several taxonomies of organizational climate factors, and a good portion of the recent research.

Also discussed are several of the problems associated with the concept. For example, it is difficult to secure a universally accepted measure of the various climate dimensions of a particular organization because of differential perceptions by the various employees. Thus, organizational climate is to some extent in the eye of the beholder. One employee may see his or her supervisor as arbitrary and autocratic while a second employee may see the same supervisor as relatively considerate. To study such a phenomenon, however, we must look at the prevailing or modal perceptions of the various climate dimensions. In other words, for the concept of organizational climate to have any meaning for managers or behavioral researchers, we must analyze *trends* in climate perceptions across individuals. If no trends exist, we must seriously question the meaningfulness or utility of the concept.

A second problem that is often raised with the climate construct is the cause and effect relationship involved. Do "considerate" supervisors help to improve performance or does improved performance allow the supervisor to be more considerate? Or both? Third, there is a problem of "level." Is climate truly an organizationwide phenomenon or is it in actuality a departmentwide or even sectionwide phenomenon? If your immediate superior is considerate and open, but his or her boss is autocratic, what type of climate do you have? Is it possible that organizations have several climates, depending upon which department you work in or where you stand in the organizational hierarchy? Based on problems such as these, Guion (1973) recently questioned whether the construct of organizational climate had any meaningful purpose at all! It should be evident from these questions and from the selection that follows that a great deal more information is needed on the topic before an accurate assessment can be made of its value.

REFERENCES AND SUGGESTED ADDITIONAL READINGS

Argyris, C. Some problems of conceptualizing climate: A case study of a bank. *Administrative Science Quarterly,* 1958, **2,** 501–520.

Forehand, G. A., & Gilmer, B. V. H. Environmental variation in studies of organizational behavior. *Psychological Bulletin,* 1964, **62,** 361–482.

Friedlander, F., & Margulies, N. Multiple impacts of organizational climate and individual value systems upon job satisfaction. *Personnel Psychology,* 1969, **22,** 171–183.

Gellerman, S. W. *Motivation and productivity.* New York: American Management Association, 1963.

Guion, R. M. A note on organizational climate. *Organizational Behavior and Human Performance,* 1973, **9,** 120–125.

Hall, J. W. A comparison of Halpin and Croft's organizational climates with Likert and Likert's organizational systems. *Administrative Science Quarterly,* 1972, **17,** 586–590.

Halpin, A. W., & Crofts, D. B. *The organizational climate of schools.* Chicago: University of Chicago, Midwest Administration Center, 1963.

Hellriegel, D., & Slocum, J. W., Jr. Organizational climate: Measures, research, and contingencies. *Academy of Management Journal,* 1974, **17,** 255–280.

Kaczra, E. E., & Kirk, R. V. Managerial climate, work groups, and organizational performance. *Administrative Science Quarterly,* 1967, **12,** 253–272.

Katz, D., & Kahn, R. L. *The social psychology of organizations.* New York: Wiley, 1966.

Lewin, K. *The conceptual representation and the measurement of psychological forces.* Durham, N.C.: Duke University Press, 1938.

Lewin, K. *Field theory in social science.* New York: Harper, 1951.

Likert, R. *New patterns in management.* New York: McGraw-Hill, 1961.

Likert, R. *The human organization.* New York: McGraw-Hill, 1967.

Litwin, G. H., & Stringer, R. A. *Motivation and organizational climate.* Boston: Harvard University, Graduate School of Business Administration, Division of Research, 1968.

Payne, R. L., & Mansfield, R. Relationships of perceptions of organizational climate to organizational structure, context, and hierarchical position. *Administrative Science Quarterly,* 1973, **18,** 515–526.

Pervin, L. A. Performance and satisfaction as a function of individual-environmental fit. *Psychological Bulletin,* 1968, **69,** 56–68.

Porter, L. W., & Lawler, E. E., III. Properties of organizational structure in relation to job attitudes and job behavior. *Psychological Bulletin,* 1965, **64,** 23–51.

Prien, E. P., & Ronan, W. W. An analysis of organizational characteristics. *Organizational Behavior and Human Performance,* 1971, **6,** 215–234.

Pritchard, R. D., & Karasick, B. W. The effects of organizational climate on managerial job performance and job satisfaction. *Organizational Behavior and Human Performance,* 1973, **9,** 126–146.

Schneider, B. Organizational climate: Individual preferences and organizational realities. *Journal of Applied Psychology,* 1972, **56,** 211–217.

Schneider, B., & Bartlett, C. J. Individual differences and organizational climate as the multi-trait, multi-rater matrix. *Personnel Psychology,* 1970, **23,** 493–512.

Sorcher, M., & Danzig, S. Chartering and changing the organizational climate. *Personnel,* 1969, **46,** 16–28.

Steers, R. M., & Porter, L. W. The role of task goal attributes in employee performance. *Psychological Bulletin,* 1974, **81,** 434–452.

Tagirui, R., & Litwin, G. H. (eds.), *Organizational climate.* Boston: Harvard University, Division of Research, 1968.

Vroom, V. H. *Work and motivation.* New York: Wiley, 1964.

Environmental Variation and Managerial Effectiveness

John P. Campbell
Marvin D. Dunnette
Edward E. Lawler, III
Karl E. Weick, Jr.

It is very easy to speak of situational or environmental "determinants" of managerial performance as if the linkage of environmental differences to behavior was easily understood and the causal nature of the relationships was known or could be assumed. Obviously, at the present time it is more proper to speak of correlates than determinants, even though a few experimental studies do exist. What is perhaps not so obvious is a corresponding ambiguity in the form of the correlational relationship between a situational variable and a measure of performance.

Can an environmental variable be used as a predictor of behavior or should a direct relationship with performance be ruled out? Would it make better sense to conceive of environmental characteristics as a moderator of the relationship between characteristics of individuals and their performance on the job? Another way of phrasing the question is to ask whether situational variables combine additively or interactively with the previously discussed correlates (e. g., individual differences) of performance. For example, does an autonomous environment enhance or detract from everyone's performance in similar fashion, and are differences in autonomy thereby correlated with performance, or is there an interactive relationship, with particular individual differences correlated with performance only for certain levels of autonomy? The distinction is crucial in terms of how research on situational variables should be pursued and the kinds of data that should be collected. Further, successful a priori specification of the nature and magnitudes of the relationships would add considerably to the theoretical understanding of environmental characteristics. To date, the nature of the linkage between situational variables and job behavior has not been very well conceptualized.

How the Environment Influences the Individual Forehand and Gilmer (1964) discuss the problem of specifying how organizational environment differences are translated to differences in behavior. They mention three mechanisms:

1 *Definition of stimuli.* Environmental characteristics such as the structure of an organization, the implicit theories held by its management, or the economic condition of the industry have considerable influence on the relevant stimuli which impinge on an individual in his work role. For example, a shrinking market may elicit managerial skills associated with holding cost down, preventing waste and increasing market share rather than those concerned with increasing production and developing new products.

2 *Constraints upon freedom.* Certain attributes of the situation may actually prevent certain behaviors from occurring. The structure of the organization may place a number of restraints on management communication or the degree of autonomy. Such structurally imposed constraints may be either deleterious or facilitative, relative to performance effectiveness.

3 *Reward and punishment.* Besides influencing what sorts of stimuli will be perceived and what types of responses are permitted, the environment can also specify the reinforcement contingencies for various managerial behaviors. It seems intuitively obvious that the situation should help determine the behavior-reward contingencies in an organization. For example, a manager in a very autonomous organization would make much broader decisions without consulting his superior than a comparable manager in a very nonautonomous organization. The situation is one in which a great deal of independent action is rewarded. Supposedly, a lack of independent action would be punished in some fashion.

The situation a manager is in should also affect his behavior by arousing various motives. If we consider the theory of need achievement, people have a certain "amount" of different needs (e. g., *n* Ach, *n* Aff, *n* Pow) which are relatively permanent characteristics. However, for these motives or needs to have a significant effect on behavior, they must be aroused. In this formulation scores on need for achievement will not predict performance unless the situation arouses this need by inducing cognitions of competition with a standard of excellence. The essential point is whether different situations elicit or arouse different needs. It would seem quite likely that this is the case. For example, the need for power might be elicited more in one organization than in another.

These effects on behavior must also be considered in relation to individual differences. People have different needs and see various outcomes as more or less desirable, and these differences must be considered. As Litwin and Stringer (1966) point out, different individuals may expect different rewards and punishments for various kinds of behavior. Climate, for example, should not act in the same way for all individuals as an arouser of needs or motives. . . .

DIMENSIONAL ANALYSES OF SITUATIONAL VARIABLES

Perhaps the most frustrating feature of an attempt to deal with situational variables in a model of management performance is the enormous complexity of the environment itself (Sells, 1963). It makes the definition and measurement of situational characteristics very difficult, and a fruitful taxonomy of environments is the key to unraveling this portion of our model. Although it is here that a certain amount of empirical work has been done, the surface has barely been scratched.

Researchers concerned with a taxonomy of situational characteristics have borrowed heavily from the methodology of differential psychology and have made considerable use of the factor analytic approach. In so doing they have tended to use the term "organizational climate" in place of "environment" or "situation."

Climate Factors

One way to get a firmer grasp on the concept of organizational climate is to consider some potential properties of climate. Forehand and Gilmer (1964) feel that climate consists of a set of characteristics that describe an organization, distinguish it from other organizations, are relatively enduring over time, and influence the behavior of the people in it. Georgopoulos (1965) speaks of a normative structure of attitudes and behavioral standards which provide a basis for interpreting the situation and act as a source of pressure for directing activity. Litwin and Stringer (1966) add the notion that these properties must be perceivable by the people in the organization and that an important aspect of climate is the "patterns of expectations and incentive values that impinge on and are created by a group of people that live and work together." H. H. Meyer (1967) expands on one aspect of the Litwin and Stringer definition by suggesting that climate arises as the result of the style of management, the organization's policies, and its general operating procedures. Gellerman (1959) feels the goals and tactics of the men whose attitudes "count" are a significant determiner of climate.

From this collection of properties, components, and determiners that various authors feel contribute to climate, we might define climate as a set of attributes specific to a particular organization that may be induced from the way that organization deals with its members and its environment. For the individual member within the organization, climate takes the form of a set of attitudes and expectancies which describe the organization in terms of both static characteristics (such as degree of autonomy) and behavior-outcome and outcome-outcome contingencies.

When organizational climate is defined in this way, it can be seen that many kinds of organizational factors are potentially relevant contributors to it. The crucial elements are the individual's perceptions of the relevant stimuli, constraints, and reinforcement contingencies that govern his job behavior. For this reason, the basic data used by a number of investigators to organize a taxonomy of "climate" factors are individual perceptions of organizational properties.

For example, Litwin and Stringer (1966) report a questionnaire developed to measure organizational members' perception in six different areas:

1 *Structure.* Perception of the extent of organizational constraints, rules, regulations and "red tape"
2 *Individual responsibility.* Feelings of autonomy, of "being one's own boss"
3 *Rewards.* Feelings related to being confident of adequate and appropriate rewards—pay, praise, special dispensations—for doing the job well

4 *Risk and risk taking.* Perceptions of the degree of challenge and risk in the work situation

5 *Warmth and support.* Feelings of general good fellowship and helpfulness prevailing the work settings

6 *Tolerance and conflict.* Degree of confidence that the climate can tolerate differing opinions

These dimensions proved to distinguish among various organizational subunits and have been incorporated into some experimental studies to be reviewed in a later section.

A broader and somewhat more systematic study of climate dimensions is described by B. Schneider and Bartlett (1968). The research sites were a group of sales agencies making up two different insurance companies. An item pool of 299 items describing various characteristics of the agencies was administered to 143 management personnel, and the responses were factor analyzed. Among other things, the respondents were asked to indicate what managers did in the agencies, what agents did, how people were treated, and what kinds of people were in the agencies. Thus, the 143 managers were not describing their own climate (i. e., the organization above them), but what they perceived the climate of the organization below them to be. Schneider and Bartlett admit the possible biasing effect of having managers describe their own agencies.

Six factors emerged. Their labels and descriptions are given below:

1 *Managerial support.* Similar to the factor of consideration found in the Ohio State studies. It refers to managers taking an active interest in the progress of their agents, backing them up with the home office, and maintaining a spirit of friendly cooperation.

2 *Managerial structure.* Refers to the manager requiring agents to adhere to budgets, be knowledgeable regarding sales material, and produce new customers. It tends to be a "sales-or-else" factor.

3 *Concern for new employees.* Most of the items are typified by a concern for the selection orientation, and training of a new agent.

4 *Intra-agency conflict.* Refers to the presence of ingroups or outgroups within an agency and the undercutting of managerial authority by the agents.

5 *Agent independence.* These items describe agents who tend to run their own business and do not pay much attention to management.

6 *General satisfaction.* Refers to the degree to which the agency sponsors periodic social get-togethers and the agents express satisfaction with various management and agency activities.

The final form of the questionnaire contains 80 items for the six factors. At a conceptual level Schneider and Bartlett view the agency climate factors both as possible predictors of later performance and as potential moderators of the relationship between selection information and performance measures. In the predictor instance an individual would be asked to respond with his preferences for climate characteristics and/or his expectancies, and they could then be correlated with later performance.

The climate factors derived in the above two efforts are meant to generalize across the perceptions of all individuals in the organization. In contrast, the two studies described below were specifically aimed at specifying climate dimensions as perceived by managers.

Taguiri (1966) asked a small sample of managers participating in a Harvard management course to name the things that mattered most to them in their organizations. From their replies, he developed a standardized questionnaire which he administered to a larger sample of managers and then factor analyzed their responses. Five factors resulted:

1. Practices related to providing a sense of direction or purpose to their jobs—setting of objectives planning, and feedback
2. Opportunities for exercising individual initiative
3. Working with a superior who is highly competitive and competent
4. Working with cooperative and pleasant people
5. Being with a profit-minded and sales-oriented company

One phase of a large study on role conflict reported by Kahn, Wolfe, Quinn, Snoek, and Rosenthal (1964) also bears on the dimensional analysis of climate. During the course of the study, 53 "focal" supervisory and management positions were selected to represent the full spectrum of the managerial hierarchy. Next, an average of seven "role senders" (usually superiors and subordinated) were chosen for each focal position on the basis of the closeness of their interaction. The role senders were then asked to respond to 36 questionnaire items indicating the degree to which they advocated compliance or noncompliance with normative or expected *role* behaviors on the part of the focal individuals. The responses were factor analyzed, and five factors seemed to emerge: (1) rules orientation, or the degree to which company-oriented rules are followed; (2) the nurturance of subordinates, or communicating and consulting with subordinates, taking an interest in them, and taking responsibility for their training morale; (3) closeness of supervision, or supervising the work pace and work methods of subordinates; (4) universalism, or the degree to which the individual should identify with the organization as a whole rather than with his particular work group; and (5) promotion-achievement orientation, or the degree to which an individual should try to take advantage of every opportunity for promotion, try to make himself look good in the eyes of his superiors, and come up with original ideas for handling work.

It is extremely difficult to draw generalizations from and integration of the results of these four studies. The individual perceptions which make up the data were obtained from vastly different orientations, or "sets." Taguiri asked managers to rate the importance, or valence, of various organizational characteristics in terms of their motivating properties. Kahn *et al.* asked individuals (not necessarily managers) to indicate what a particular manager should do relative to a specific set of role behaviors. The implication is that respondents felt such role characteristics were necessary for the effective operation of the organization. In contrast, the Schneider and Bartlett items asked managers to describe their work groups.

A Synthesis   Even though these are very different sets relative to what was required of the respondents, a good deal of communality seemed to result, at least in the outward appearance of the factors. All the studies yielded either five or six factors, and at least four seem to be common across all the investigations. Our composite view of these recurring factors is as follows:

1   *Individual autonomy.* This is perhaps the clearest composite and includes the *individual responsibility, agent independence,* and *rules orientation* factors found by Litwin and Stringer, Schneider and Bartlett, and Kahn et al., respectively, and Taguiri's factor dealing with opportunities for exercising individual initiative. The keystone of this dimension is the freedom of the individual to be his own boss and reserve considerable decision-making power for himself. He does not have to be constantly accountable to higher management.

2   *The degree of structure imposed upon the position.* Litwin and Stringer's *structure;* Schneider and Bartlett's *managerial structure;* Taguiri's first factor dealing with direction, objectives, etc.; and Kahn et al.'s *closeness of supervision* seem similar enough to be lumped under this label. The principal element is the degree to which the objectives of, and methods for, the job are established and communicated to the individual by superiors.

3   *Reward orientation.* Another meaningful grouping includes Litwin and Stringer's *reward* factor. Schneider and Bartlett's *general satisfaction* factor, which seems to convey reward overtones; Kahn et al.'s *promotion-achievement orientation,* and Taguiri's being with a profit-minded and sales-oriented company. These factors do not hang together quite as well as the previous two groups and seem to vary a great deal in breadth. However, the reward element appears to be present in all.

4   *Consideration, warmth, and support.* This dimension lacks the clarity of the previous three. Managerial support from the Schneider and Bartlett study and nurturance of subordinates from Kahn et al. seem quite similar. Litwin and Stringer's *warmth* and *support* also seems to belong here since apparently this is a characteristic attributable to supervisory practices. Taguiri's mention of working with a superior who is highly competitive and competent does not fit quite so easily, but nevertheless seems to refer to the support and stimulation received from one's superior. However, the human relations referent is not as clear as in the factors derived from the other studies.

It is tempting to label a fifth group and include Litwin and Stringer's "tolerance of conflict." Schneider and Bartlett's "presence of conflict," Taguiri's "working with cooperative and pleasant people," and Kahn et al.'s "universalism." All these factors seem to represent interpersonal relationships between peers, but from somewhat different perspectives. The Schneider and Bartlett and the Taguiri factors appear to fall on opposite ends of the same continuum, a kind of "cooperativeness" dimension, while the Litwin and Stringer factor reflects more of a willingness to be honest and open about interpersonal conflict, and the Kahn et al. factor represents the effect of group identification on how interpersonal relationships are handled.

A question that might be asked at this point concerns whether the comparability that does seem to exist should be a cause for rejoicing. Probably not. The factors or clusters that result from a dimensional analysis are a function of the types of individual measures that were initially included in the study. Even though the sets required of the respondents were different, perhaps the content of the stimuli (items) was very similar across the four studies. Also, the relatively small number of factors which were found implies that a great deal of environmental variation remains to be uncovered. The tendency for researchers to cull items from the previous literature, especially that relating to studies of job satisfaction or job attitudes, may contribute to both of the above shortcomings.

SOME EMPIRICAL RESULTS

As we emphasized at the beginning of this chapter, the research literature concerning the influence of the situation on managerial effectiveness is meager. Furthermore, the studies that do exist vary widely in terms of the variables and conceptual relationships that are studied. There is very little communality on which to build integrative conclusions.

Experimental Studies

Organizational Climate Both Frederiksen (1966) and Litwin and Stringer (1966) have carried out laboratory studies using "climate" dimension as independent variables. The Frederiksen study is the most extensive and the most directly relevant for the present chapter. A total of 260 middle managers employed by the state of California worked through an In-basket Test designed to simulate the job of chief of the field service division of the Department of Commerce. Four treatment combinations designed to create differences in climate were arranged in a 2 by 2 design. One treatment dichotomy had to do with the general prevalence of "rules and regulations." Half the subjects were informed via instructions and In-basket materials that the Department of Commerce encouraged new ideas, innovation, and creative problem solving. They were told that rules existed but that they could be broken if they got in the way. The other half were told that a very substantial set of rules and regulations had been built up over the years and had proved very valuable and that they were not to be violated except under extreme circumstances. The second treatment factor was concerned with the closeness of supervision, and the subjects were told either that the organization preferred a subordinate's work to be closely monitored or that subordinates should be allowed to work out details for themselves.

The In-basket can be scored on a large number of indexes (e. g., explains action to peers, postpones decision, involves subordinates, and takes final action). In previous research, some sixty of these initial scores were reduced to a smaller number of first-order factors, and the dependent variable in this particular study was a second-order factor labeled "productivity," or the sheer amount of work accomplished. The subjects also provided a large amount of test and biographical data which served as 21 different predictor variables. The actual dependent variable under consideration was the predictability of In-basket performance by the 21 predictors.

In general it was found that predictability was higher under the innovative climate. The details of the analysis are too numerous to give here, but Friederiksen (1966, p. 13) summarizes them with the following statement:

> It appears that the amount of administrative work in the simulated job is more predictable in a climate that encourages innovation than in one that encourages standard procedures, and that in an innovative climate (but not in a rules climate) greater productivity can be expected of people with skills and attitudes that are associated with independence of thought and action and the ability to be productive in free, unobstructed situations.

Frederiksen also found that performance was more predictable for subjects who worked in a consistent climate (innovation + loose supervision or rules + close supervision) than for those who had to operate in an inconsistent environment (innovation + close supervision or rules + loose supervision).

In further analyses of the same study (Frederiksen, 1968) it was demonstrated that inconsistent climates also have a negative effect on productivity. Specifically, those subjects who were placed in a climate that encouraged innovation and was at the same time characterized by detailed supervision worked at a substantially reduced level of output. Digging still deeper in the data, Frederiksen (1968) was able to show that subjects employed different work methods under different climate conditions. For example, in the In-basket under the climate conditions permitting more freedom, administrators dealt more directly with peers, while in the restrictive climates, they tended to work through more formal channels.

In sum, the Frederiksen study yields a glimpse of the wide range of influences that climate differences can exhibit. It also demonstrates the potential power of this kind of research strategy. The conclusion is inescapable that a sophisticated research technology of organizational simulation would yield many new insights into management behavior. The research enterprise should take strong steps in that direction.

Litwin and Stringer (1966) used 45 students from the Harvard Business School and divided them into three "firms," which then had to compete in the construction and marketing of "radar equipment" manufactured from Erector Set materials. The buyer was a simulated government agency, and competition for contract awards was intense. The simulated operation, or game, required considerable organization and cooperation on the part of the 15 players. Three different climates were created. (1) *an authoritarian-structured* business, with strong emphasis on careful definition of duties, the exercise of formal authority, etc.; (2) *a democratic-friendly* business, where cooperative behavior, group loyalty, teamwork, freedom from punishment, and a loose informal structure were emphasized; and (3) *an achieving* business, where innovation was encouraged, competitive feedback was given, pride in the organization was fostered, a certain amount of risk taking was deemed desirable, and high personal goals were encouraged.

The principal means for creating the climate differences was the president of the company who was a member of the research staff and who adopted the appropriate leadership "style." The expected differences were found on a questionnaire designed to measure the six climate factors discussed earlier in this chapter. Playing of the game was continued over an eight-day period.

Significant differences in performance and satisfaction were found. The achieving business produced the most in terms of dollar volume, number of new products, and cost-saving innovations. However, the authoritarian-structured business produced finished goods with the highest quality, primarily by never deviating from the government specifications laid out in the game. After playing for seven days, the subjects in the democratic-friendly business rated themselves as being more satisfied with their jobs than subjects in the other two firms.

Several features of these two experiments have relevance for some of the more general issues with which we are trying to deal in this chapter. The dependent variable under consideration in the Litwin and Stringer study is much broader, but the source of climate differences is given a much narrower focus. That is, Litwin and Stringer consider the effects on the entire simulated organization of climate differences produced by the president of the company, while Frederiksen generates differences from much more diffuse and generalized sources, but notes their effects on only a particular organizational role. Future researchers must devote considerable attention to specifying the breadth of effect they wish to investigate if a meaningful integration of research results is to be possible. In "climate" terms, what is preceived as bad weather for one part of the organization may be good for another.

A second point illustrates a paradox that tends to arise when the experimental studies are related to the previous taxonomic efforts. Developing *dimensions* of environmental variation implies that differences among organizations along these dimensions are important. However, the treatment variables in the Litwin and Stringer study really represent modal types and not variations in a particular variable. The effects of differences in types can in no way be causally related back to the original taxonomic study. In the Frederiksen study the treatment differences do seem to reflect differences in two situational variables (rules orientation and closeness of supervision), but no indication is given as to why these treatments happened to be the ones selected or whether the two dichotomies do indeed represent two levels of the same dimension. Obviously, if experimental work is to have any scientific utility, there must be some means for relating independent variables to one another.

Third, the two studies adopted a very different view regarding the functional relationship of climate to performance. Litwin and Stringer emphasized the determinant or direct causal effects of climate differences while Frederiksen viewed his experimental treatments as moderators of the relationship between other measures of individual differences and performance. Neither study tried to compare the relative amount of variance accounted for by main effects versus interactive effects. . . .

Correlational and Field Studies

We would now like to consider empirical studies that were conducted in naturally occurring organizational contexts. Obviously, the direction of causality is difficult to infer in such studies, but the variables tend to be "richer" in content, and fruitful hypothesis can be suggested for later experimentation.

Job Challenge   Berlew and Hall (1966) performed analyses on data gathered in the AT&T Management Progress Study. Several performance measures were obtained for 62 individuals originally hired as managers by two companies of the Bell System in 1956 and 1957. These included the 1962 salary adjusted for starting salary, a global appraisal at the end of either the fourth or the fifth year, a composite of these two, the average of the yearly effectiveness ratings over the four- or five-year period (depending on which of the two companies the individual entered), and indexes of "contribution" and "overcontribution." These latter two criteria are related to a measure of how much the company expected of the individual on his first managerial assignment. Company expectations were rated by both superiors and subjects on 18 categories (communication skills, technical competence, etc.), and the ratings were summed. The contribution score was obtained by rating the individual's actual performance on the same 18 categories, and overcontribution was simply the comparison of expectations and actual performance. The crucial findings from the study were the significant correlations between company expectations for the first year (i. e., initial job challenge) and measures of later performance. These relationships could not be accounted for by initial differences in ability since none of the variables in the Management Progress Study designed to measure various aptitudes and skills correlated with the expectation measure. Differences in expectations seemed to be a function of the job itself.

In an earlier study using the same data, Berlew and Hall (1964) demonstrated that an individual will tend to change his performance (either up or down) to bring himself in line with company expectations. The company will also change its expectations to achieve an equilibrium with an individual's performance. The significance of both these effects was demonstrated via a partial correlation technique. To the extent that they are valid, the results suggest a dynamic aspect of situational effects that must be reckoned with. The situation may change as a function of the type of people that enter it.

Although the subjects were not managers, two other studies bear on the effects of job challenge. Peres (1966) did a follow-up study of 475 engineers hired by General Electric during the mid-1950s and attempted to determine what individual and organizational factors contributed to "salary success." At the time of hire, each subject had completed a lengthy battery of tests and biographical questionnaires from which a prediction could be made concerning future performance "potential." At the time of the Peres study, the subjects were asked to describe certain characteristics pertaining to their first full-time job assignment. The results suggested an interaction between the nature of the first job and success potential. High potential individuals achieved higher salary success if their first job was seen as difficult, challenging, and not easily handled by falling back on their college training, while the low potential subjects attained high salary success if they could successfully cope with their first assignment by direct use of their college training.

Pelz and Andrews (1967) studied 1,300 research and development engineers and scientists in five industrial laboratories, five government laboratories, and seven departments in a large university. In addition to objective measures such as reports, published papers, and patents, scientific contribution was judged by a panel of colleagues. The most successful individuals seemed to be those who occupied a position of "creative tension" between otherwise conflicting aims, such as specialized activity in a particular area versus opportunity to participate in a number of activities, or colleagues who shared similar interests but differed in technical style and strategy. Also, the most creative individuals were not those who spent all their time on research but those who had to deal with other organizational problems and tasks as well.

Obviously, the correlational nature of the above studies leaves considerable room for competing explanations. However, they provide useful hypotheses to follow up with more controlled investigation. . . .

Organizational Climate   In an interesting study which deserves to serve as a prototype for many others, J. D. W. Andrews (1967) examined the effect of the congruence of organizational and individual values on managerial performance and advancement. Two Mexican firms that provided a clear-cut contrast in value orientations were used as criterion organizations. One firm was judged to be highly achievement-oriented, progressive, expansion-minded, and economically successful, while the second firm was assessed as being much more conservative, less achievement-oriented, more oriented toward power relations, and less successful. All top level managers in the two firms were measured on n Ach and n Pow via the Thematic Appreception Test (TAT) and success was indexed by the number of promotions and salary increase received by an individual during the previous four years. There were no significant differences on the TAT scores between managers from the two firms, but in an analysis of variance framework, there was a significant interaction between motivational needs and type of firm. That is, advancement was greater for those individuals who had motivational needs congruent with the values of the organization. As is always the case in a field study, competing explanations are possible; however, the investigation of these kinds of interactions deserves to be pursued with vigor.

Similar research from college and university settings is reviewed by Pervin (1968). He cites date from Funkenstein (1962), Stern (1962), and his own research (Pervin, 1967) showing that a lack of congruence between measured personality characteristics, or self perceptions, and environmental characteristics predicts dropouts in a number of institutions. Since voluntary turnover is such an important outcome in the managerial population, this kind of research deserves considerable emulation in the organizational setting.

SUMMARY

In this chapter we have attempted to identify some of the conceptual difficulties inherent in investigating situational effects, review research dealing with taxonomic efforts, and review the empirical evidence on situational effects. On a conceptual level there is a polyglot of variables that can be subsumed under the rubric the "situation." We grouped these under the following four headings: (1) structural properties, (2) environmental characteristics, (3) organizational climate, and (4) formal role characteristics. The relationship of a situational variable to managerial performance may be conceptualized as an experimental main effect, a predictor (in the correlational sense), a moderator, or some combination of these. Research studies have tended to focus on only one of the three at any one time. There are also serious problems regarding the "level of explanation" associated with the relationship between a situational variable and managerial performance. If the independent variable is a structural property such as organization size, the connecting chain is certainly much longer than in the case of a climate variable which is assessed by means of the individual's *perceptions* of what the organization is like.

Most of the taxonomic research has centered around dimensions of organizational climate. Even though there have been relatively few studies and they varied widely in their approach, four factors appear common to them. These we have labeled (1) autonomy, (2) structure, (3) general reward level, and (4) warmth and support. Further research should build on these efforts and attempt to determine the nature of the factor structure in different settings and how it interacts with individual differences. Unfortunately, no such beginning taxonomic work exists with regard to other types of situational variables.

At the empirical level things have not progressed very far, but perhaps a few inferences can be made. The simulation studies by Frederiksen (1966, 1968) and Litwin and Stringer (1966) strongly suggest a number of beneficial effects for organizations which maintain a consistent climate. They further suggest that if individual differences are not taken into account, there is little reason to expect *mean* differences in performance under different climate conditions. One thing these studies do not do is suggest how the influence of climate differs for different tasks. Studies of climate should take a cue from a laboratory experiment by

Roby, Nicol, and Farrell (1963) which showed that a decentralized structure was best if the task required cooperative effort but that a centralized structure was best if individuals (students in this case) worked independently toward a common goal.

Perhaps one of the most important findings to emerge from the empirical research is the importance of the initial job assigned to an individual. His expectations and aspirations regarding his career in an organization seem to be very much a function of the skill requirements and difficulty level of his first few jobs. It should be the aim of every organization to "stretch" its personnel by offering them appropriate challenges. If it does not, a self-defeating circle could be created, for the analyses by Berlew and Hall (1964) suggest that over time an individual's expectations for himself tend to approximate those the organization has for him.

In sum, the "situation" has been shown to encompass an exceedingly complex set of variables, especially when their dynamic and interactive properies are considered. Again, not much research has been forthcoming, but there is considerable promise for the future.

REFERENCES

Andrews, J. D. W. The achievement motive and advancement in two types of organizations. *Journal of Personality and Social Psychology,* 1967, **6,** 163–169.

Berlew, E. E., & Hall, D. T. Some determinants of early managerial success. Working paper No. 81–64, Alfred P. Sloan School of Management. Cambridge, Mass.: Massachusetts Institute of Technology, 1964.

Berlew, E. E., & Hall, D. T. The socialization of managers: Effects of expectations on performance. *Administrative Science Quarterly,* 1966, **11,** 207–224.

Forehand, G. A., & Gilmer, B. v. H. Environmental variation in studies of organizational behavior. *Psychological Bulletin,* 1964, **62,** 361–382.

Frederiksen, N. Some effects of organizational climates on administrative performance. Research Memorandum RM–66–21, Educational Testing Service, 1966.

Frederiksen, N. Administrative performance in relation to organizational climate. Paper presented at a symposium on measuring managerial effectiveness, American Psychological Association, San Francisco, September 1968.

Funkenstein, D. H. Failure to graduate from medical school. *Journal of Medical Education,* 1962, **37,** 585–603.

Gellerman, S. W. The company personality. *Management Review,* 1959, **48,** 69–76.

Georgopoulos, B. S. Normative structure variables and organizational behavior. *Human Relations,* 1965, **18,** 115–170.

Kahn, R. L., Wolfe, D. M., Quinn, R. P., Snoek, J. D., & Rosenthal, R. A. *Organizational stress: Studies in role conflict and ambiguity.* New York: Wiley, 1964.

Litwin, G. H., & Stringer, R. The influence of organizational climate on human motivation. Paper presented at a conference on organizational climate, Foundation for Research on Human Behavior, Ann Arbor, Mich., March 1966.

Meyer, H. H. Differences in organizational climate in outstanding and average sales offices: A summary report. General Electric, Behavioral Research Service and Public Relations Personnel Service, 1967.

Pelz, D. C., & Andrews, F. M. *Scientists in organizations.* New York: Wiley, 1966.

Peres, S. H. Factors which influence careers at General Electric. General Electric, Behavioral Research Service, 1966.

Pervin, L. A. A twenty-college study of student + college interaction using TAPE (transactional analysis of personality and environment): Rationale reliability, and validity. *Journal of Educational Psychology,* 1967, **58,** 290–302.

Pervin, L. A. Performance and satisfaction as a function of individual-environmental fit. *Psychological Bulletin,* 1968, **69,** 56–68.

Roby, T. B., Nicol, E. H., & Farrell, F. M. Group problem solving under two types of executive structure. *Journal of Abnormal and Social Psychology,* 1963, **67,** 550–556.

Sells, S. B. (Ed.) *Stimulus determinants of behavior.* New York: Ronald Press, 1963.

Stern, G. G. Environments for learning. In N. Stanford (Ed.) *The American college.* New York: Wiley, 1962.

Taguiri, R. Comments on organizational climate. Paper presented at a conference on organizational climate, Foundation for Research on Human Behavior, Ann Arbor, Mich., March 1966.

QUESTIONS FOR DISCUSSION

1 Do you feel the concept of organizational climate is a useful one for managers? Explain.
2 What is the general process by which a particular climate is created?
3 Is it fair to say that there is a universally desirable climate for all work organizations? Why or why not?
4 How might organizational climate affect expectancies and/or valences under expectancy/valence theory?
5 Why have some people argued that supervisory style is the most important climate factor? Do you agree or disagree?
6 How might you alter organizational climate to change patterns of employee attachment to an organization?
7 Specifically, how might climate affect work behavior?
8 How could climate affect job attitudes and satisfaction?
9 How might different climates (a) be more effective in terms of job performance; and (b) be more satisfying for employees?
10 How does the concept of organizational climate relate to equity theory?
11 Does Herzberg's theory encompass organizational climate variables?
12 Is the concept of organizational climate really different from the sum of employees' various job attitudes?

ROUTING/CALL MEMO		INITIAL & DATE		ACTION
				CIRCULATE
1. **TO** *(Name, Office Symbol or Location)*				COORDI- NATION
MAJ D.				FILE
2.				INFO
				NOTE & RETURN
3.				PER CON- VERSATION
				SEE ME
4.				SIGNATURE
				MEMO OF CALL

NAME OF CALLER/VISITOR	TEL NO.	TIME
Evers		1000

☒ PLEASE CALL ☐ WILL CALL AGAIN ☐ LEFT MSG

REMARKS OR MESSAGE *(Use Reverse If Needed)*

226 - 0780

FROM *(Name, Office Symbol or Location)*	DATE
	12 OJ 77
	TEL NO.
LINDA	

AF FORM FEB 75 1271   ☆ U.S.GPO: 1976—221-222

Chapter 10

Group Influences on Behavior

OVERVIEW

Since the early work of Allport (1924), Mayo (1933), and Roethlisberger and Dickson (1939), a considerable body of research data has accumulated on the topic of group processes at work. In fact, under the initial leadership of Kurt Lewin, there has arisen a group dynamics school which tends to view group processes as the basic unit of analysis in the study of organizations (see, for example, Cartwright & Zander, 1968). We intend in this chapter to look at such processes as they influence motivation and work behavior.

Defining precisely what constitutes a "group" is no easy task. The boundaries of group membership tend to be rather permeable, with new members joining and old ones leaving at a fairly consistent rate. Moreover, members of one group are generally also members of several additional groups, thereby dividing their time and loyalties. Because of problems such as these, we tend to discuss and define groups more in terms of processes than in terms of specific members and their personal characteristics. Thus, a typical definition of a group would include the notion of a collectivity of people who share a set of norms (or common viewpoints), who generally have differentiated roles among members, and who jointly pursue common goals. While it is not possible to specify the "required" size of such a collectivity, the number usually averages between four and seven.

Groups form for a variety of reasons. Some groups result simply from proximity. The day-to-day interactions with one's immediate coworkers tend to facilitate group formation. Other groups form for economic reasons. For example, where bonuses are paid to workers based on *group* productivity, an incentive exists to band together for mutual gain. Still other groups form as the result of various social-psychological forces. Such groups can satisfy employees' social needs for interaction, reinforce feelings of self-worth, and provide emotional support in times of stress. Whatever the reason for their formation, they can be a potent factor in the determination of both individual job effort and individual job satisfaction.

Primarily as a result of the Hawthorne studies (Roethlisberger & Dickson, 1939) and the later research which they stimulated, we have developed a fairly clear picture of some of the more common characteristics of a group. To begin with, as mentioned above, there are generally rather detailed norms, or shared beliefs, that are held by the group members and that guide their behavior. In addition, various members often have specific duties, or role prescriptions, for which they are responsible. Groups usually have acknowledged control procedures, such as ostracism, to minimize deviant behavior from their norms. They also develop their own systems or patterns of communications, which often include special or technical words (jargon). They tend to have an informal leader whose responsibility it is to enforce the norms and assure goal attainment. Finally, groups provide a useful source of support for their members. Employees who find little satisfaction in a dull, repetitive job may refrain from quitting because they really enjoy their coworkers, who provide comfort, support, and satisfaction in an otherwise meaningless job. Moreover, groups also provide support in a different sense where the group intends to regulate its rate of output. If one member restricts his output, a very real possibility exists that he will be punished or even terminated by the organization. However, if all group members restrict output in unison, there is much less chance of "retribution" by the company.

From a motivational standpoint, perhaps the most important group process is the tendency toward conformity (Asch, 1958; Sherif, 1936). One of the basic prerequisites for continued group membership is adherence to group standards, norms, and so forth. Once a work group has determined an acceptable rate of output, for example, it tends to punish or reject members whose output is above ("rate-busters") or below ("goldbrickers") this rate. If a company offers individual incentives for increased output, but the group decide the new rate of output is too high (perhaps out of fear of working themselves out of a job), the group will exert force on its members not to increase output, despite the potential short-run monetary gain. On the other hand, however, if group support can be won for the new rate of output, conformity could then lead to increased output. The application of this latter example can be seen in such programs as the Lincoln Electric and the Scanlon plans, where workers have a significant voice in the determination of production rates and in the introduction of new production techniques.

Under such plans, participation in program formulation *and* in the rewards from the new techniques appears to lead to group acceptance of the innovations, resulting in increased output.

In summary, research indicates that groups often serve useful functions for their members and must be taken into account as potential moderator variables in any program designed by the organization to increase employee effort and performance. These effects of group dynamics on behavior are discussed in the two selections that follow. First, Kolasa reviews much of the research on social influence processes, with particular emphasis on the role of group norms. The effects of group cohesiveness, competition, participation, and problem solving are also examined as each relates to the behavior of group members.

Following this discussion, Cartwright sets forth a series of propositions, based on early research, which attempts to demonstrate how group processes can be used to facilitate change in behavior patterns of individuals. The role of the group as both the target and the medium of change is discussed.

REFERENCES AND SUGGESTED ADDITIONAL READINGS

Allport, F. H. *Social psychology.* New York: Houghton Mifflin, 1924.

Asch, S. E. The effects of group pressure upon the modification and distortion of judgments. In E. E. Maccoby, T. E. Newcomb, & E. L. Hartley (eds.), *Readings in social psychology.* New York: Holt, 1958.

Cartwright, D., & Zander, A. (eds.). *Group dynamics.* (3rd ed.) Evanston, Ill.: Row, Peterson, 1968.

Hare, A. P. *Handbook of small group research.* New York: Free Press, 1962

Hinton, B. L., & Reitz, H. J. (eds.). *Groups and organizations.* Belmont, Calif.: Wadsworth, 1971.

Hollander, E. P. *Leaders, groups, and influence.* New York: Oxford University Press, 1964.

Homans, G. C. *The human group.* New York: Harcourt, Brace & World, 1950.

Katz, E., & Kahn, R. L. *The social psychology of organizations.* New York: Wiley, 1966.

Kemp, C. G. *Perspectives on group processes.* Boston: Houghton Mifflin, 1970.

Mayo, E. *The human problems of an industrial civilization.* New York: Macmillan, 1933.

Olmstead, M. S. *The small group.* New York: Random House, 1959.

Patchen, M. Supervisory methods and group performance norms. *Administrative Science Quarterly,* 1962, **7,** 275–294.

Roethlisberger, F. J., & Dickson, W. J. *Management and the worker.* Boston: Harvard University Press, 1939.

Schachter, S. *The psychology of affiliation.* Palo Alto, Calif.: Stanford University Press, 1959.

Tannenbaum, A. S. *Social psychology of the work organization.* Belmont, Calif.: Wadsworth, 1966.

Thibaut, J., & Kelley, H. *The social psychology of groups.* New York: Wiley, 1959.

Whyte, W. F. *Organizational behavior: Theory and application.* Homewood, Ill.: Irwin-Dorsey, 1969.

Social Influence of Groups
Blair J. Kolasa

SOCIAL INFLUENCE

The influence of the group on its members can take place in many ways. Often there are well-known and accepted norms to follow, but where the standards are not very clear the actions of the individual members are affected still more by their view of the patterns of behavior exhibited by others in the group. Even definite criteria are followed, however, because of the real or implied pressures of the social group. What is of greater importance, however, is that the mere presence of other people affects the performance of a person.

In an early and well-known experiment, Sherif (1936) asked subjects in a darkened room to estimate the extent and direction of movement of a tiny pinpoint of light. (The light really did not move although people ordinarily perceived movement—a phenomenon known as the *autokinetic effect).* Individual estimates were very close together when made in a group and did not diverge significantly when the subjects were later asked to make estimates while alone. When Sherif started with subjects making estimates when no other members were present, the estimates were quite divergent. When later gathered into a group, the estimates of individuals began to converge and, while they were very close, these were not as close as the nearly identical estimates given by members of the group that started out together as a group. The earlier individual experiences clearly played a role even though the group influences were more significant.

A closer look at the influence processes in a group setting reveals the role of already familiar social concepts such as norms in the specific context of interaction in groups.

Group Norms

Norms [are] very important in human affairs; this is no less true when we look more closely into the functioning of groups. The rules of behavior that are important for the functioning of the group become even more important when the group or the task becomes larger. Some guidelines are necessary to help the group reach a goal, although, as Thibaut and Kelley (1959) point out, the norm structure can become so complex that it interferes with the effective functioning of the group. In this situation it is likely that more attention is paid to the following of the rules to the letter than to the fulfillment of the functions those rules were intended to serve originally. Norms may be described in various ways, depending on the focus of attention. There may be a concentration on the processes at work in the social situation or on the effects of the functioning of norms. Looking at the norms as sanctions emphasizes their role as a process; common behavior of group members is an immediate effect, and the support of group activity may be regarded as an only slightly more distant effect.

Real or imagined pressures to conform to the norms of the group often have been described by casual observers of the social scene. There is some general opinion that the very notion of conformity is antagonistic to individual fulfillment and, eventually, the attainment of societal well-being. Indeed it might, but such superficial pronouncements overlook the positive and sometimes necessary aspects of conformity to group norms. Cartwright and Zander (1960, p. 159) point out that pressures for conformity can help the group accomplish its goals by providing information on "reality" to its members so that the group can maintain itself. These social pressures can provide stability and information for both individual members and the total group in the common pursuit of functional goals.

The influence of the group toward conformity can be demonstrated in many ways. An early experiment by Asch (1952) indicated that even simple tasks could be altered by group pressures. Asch had members of a small group make judgments in the presence of each other. The subjects were to match a criterion line with one of three lines presented along with it; this was a task so simple that a large number of subjects given the choices earlier made virtually no mistakes. The experimental group itself was composed of individuals who were unaware of the fact that some of the other members were instructed by the experimenter to give incorrect answers occasionally. The naive subjects, when faced with unanimous choices by the other members, often gave the same incorrect choices. This did not occur with some subjects, and even those who did conform did not always do so; the number of incorrect choices, however, was quite high. Asch varied the experiment by changing the number in the group and in the majority. A majority of three was found to be as influential as any larger ones (up to 16 were tried). If one other person was present who supported the naive subject, this was enough to reduce the influence of the majority or even eliminate it entirely.

The Asch experiment called for very simple judgments—ones where there should have been little doubt as to outcome. If the group influence was strong with respect to easy judgments of lengths of lines, it should not be too surprising to find strong group influences in more common social situations where the "correct" choices are less easy to find than are the group guidelines.

Other experimenters have confirmed the basic results of Asch's study (Rosenberg, 1961). Milgram (1964) also found that naive subjects administered more pain to other subjects under the social pressure of a group (accomplices of the experimenter) than they would on their own initiative.

Some individuals find it easier to conform than do others; the differences between the independent and the submissive undoubtedly are based in personality factors. Steiner and Johnson (1963) confirm the generally accepted guess that authoritarians are more conforming than are nonauthoritarians. The authors found an easy acceptance of the decisions of a respected group of peers. When strong needs for social approval are considered in addition to the authoritarian pattern, subjects for social approval are considered in addition to the authoritarian pattern, subjects who are highly motivated with respect to this factor are more likely to agree with expressed opinions of their peers (Stickland and Crowne, 1962).

Other variables play a role too, however. Older subjects are less likely to conform (DiVesta and Cox, 1960). The same authors found also that females and those with less intellectual ability showed more conformity. Milgram (1964) supported the latter point in finding that college graduates conformed less than those in lower educational brackets.

There is substantial evidence to support a statement that when an individual takes a stand publicly, he is more likely to be influenced by group norms than when he arrives at a conclusion in private. Raven (1959) found greater pressure to conform to the group norm when the individual either had to communicate his opinion or where possibility of rejection for nonconformity existed. Kelley and Volkart (1952) found similar results when they presented a critical speech to a group of boy scouts. Half the group was told that the results of a latter questionnaire about the speech would be made public while the other half was assured that their responses would not be disclosed. Those boy scouts who were told their questionnaires would be made public tended to agree more with the speaker.

Cohesiveness

The perceptions of the bonds between individuals are important aspects of group functioning. There is even some doubt as to whether there will be any unifying adherence to group norms without cohesiveness, the condition defined as "that group property which is inferred from the number and strength of mutual positive attitudes among the members of a group" (Lott, 1961, p. 279).

It might be expected that the influence a group will exert upon its members will be related to the cohesiveness of the group, that is, the greater the cohesiveness the greater the influence. Festinger et al. (1950) found this to be the case. The same authors described the basis for the influence as being in the attractiveness of the group for its members. Individuals may want to belong to the group for several reasons—the group may be the mediator for certain goals that are important for members, being a member of the group may have certain attractions in itself, or people may want to belong to the group simply because they like the other members.

Since norms involve criteria for behavior, they tend to reduce any anxiety about what is "right" or proper. The more homogeneous the group, the more consistent the criteria are likely to be; this, in turn, makes the group more cohesive, and so on, in a reinforcing cycle. The more the values of the group are shared, the more cohesive the group is likely to be. The more the values of the group are shared, the more cohesive the group is likely to be. The "tightly knit group" means a greater sharing of values and more identification with group perspectives.

Cohesiveness of the group will be greater if changes in the membership of the group occur less or not at all (Lasswell and Kaplan, 1950). A few new members may not be resisted or may even be welcomed by the existing membership; when there is a chance of the intrusion of a large number of new participants, there is less likely to be acceptance of the new members. The newcomers, on the other hand, may come into the new situation with trepidation or feelings of inferiority (Shils, 1950). Cohesiveness may be enhanced in many different ways or through the use of many different techniques. It has been characteristic of many "in" groups that their existence has been furthered by the use of secret symbols, passwords, or any mystical arrangements that unify them and set them apart from others.

Cohesiveness of a group influences communications within it and, at the same time, communications have some effect on cohesiveness. Festinger and Thibaut (1951) found that where there was a wide range of opinion in decision-making groups, there was a tendency for communications to be directed to those members who were at the extremes of the range of opinions. There are more communications to the deviate from group norms, since these are attempts to bring him "back into the fold." The attempts are made partly because the deviate may represent a threat to the existence and stability of the group. Because of this threat, there is, in addition, hostility often expressed toward the nonconformist, the rejection being particularly strong in high-cohesiveness groups (Schachter, 1951).

Lott (1961) suggests that a more cohesive group has a higher level of communication between the members. There is also some suggestion that cohesiveness will increase if communication among members of a group increases, particularly if there are visible rewards in this procedure for the various members. This may be similar to the point that Homans (1950) has indicated, that interaction between members of a group and attractiveness were directly related. This would mean that interaction and communication would bring increased liking of other members and vice versa.

As might be expected, a cohesive group is more likely to arise in a situation calling for cooperative activity and is likely to be more effective in performance than is one where competition occurs internally. Klein (1956) has indicated that compatibility of members and similarity in characteristics of individuals lead to more effective collaboration and performance. He indicates that the badly organized group is no better than one that is composed of members in competition with one another where individuals hinder others in attainment of a goal. There is also more likelihood of communication of hostile feelings, criticism, withholding of information, and less communication in a poorly organized group. What communication does occur may be largely irrelevant or unrelated to the task.

Group discussions of problems to be faced and procedures to be followed is probably more effective in carrying out group performance than is any individual educational effort.

Competition

A competitive atmosphere involving groups may play an important role in their functioning in many practical situations. It may be commonly believed, especially in industrial concerns, that competition between individuals and groups within the company is of the value in stimulating higher performance. Whether this is so or not is important to determine.

Some contribution to an understanding of the effects of competition and cooperation on individual and group performance is gained through a reading of results of a basic experiment by Mintz (1951). Mintz arranged metal cones in a bottle with an opening just large enough for the cones to be withdrawn one at a time. Water was introduced into the jar from below in the experiment while the subjects were instructed to withdraw the cones without getting them wet. There were two experimental conditions; in one a reward was promised to the person who retrieved his cone without getting it wet; a fine was paid if the cone was dampened by the rising water. The second experimental variation indicated that a similar group of students succeeded in cooperating and getting their cones out within a short period of time. There were no "traffic jams" under the cooperative pattern of behavior while the reward-and-fine conditions produced blockage and nonadaptive behavior over half the time. The experimenter obtained this result with no more than the threat of a mild fear of failure or the payment of a 10 cent fine.

Another of the earlier experimental studies of competition versus cooperation was done by Deutsch (1949). His subjects performed tasks ranging from simple puzzles to more complex problems of human relations. On most tasks the cooperative groups produced at a higher level than did the competitive groups, perhaps because of greater coordination in the cooperative teams. An added feature was a friendlier spirit among the cooperators. A later attempt by Jones and Vroom (1964) to isolate key factors in a similar situation led to the conclusion that the more effective performance of cooperative groups was the result of an effective division of labor. Performance was likely to be adversely affected when members had strong preferences for a particular task. This was true in cooperative as well as competitive groups.

These results and those of other researchers give some indication of the influence of group norms and the resulting cohesiveness on the performance of the members' conformity to norms. Hammond and Goldman (1961, p. 60) phrase it in terms of "noncompetition (being) more favorable to the group process."

Participation

In one way or another, various group studies have buttressed the view that a significant factor contributing to the effectiveness of the group is that of participation by the members in its functioning. Several research studies, particularly in industry, have indicated the importance of this factor.

The "Hawthorne studies" represent one of the most significant conceptual influences in the area of organizational behavior, particularly in an industrial setting. While the experiments focused on the influence of the group on productivity of workers, the deeper implications for a general theory of human behavior and the applications of it in an administrative framework have had great impact on organizational theorists and practitioners. These studies, begun in the 1920's in the Hawthorne plant of the Western Electric Company, have been discussed by many, including Roethlisberger and Dickson (1947) and Homans (1950).

The original interest of the experimenters in this series of studies was in the effects of environmental factors on work performance. They varied the level of illumination, for instance, and related this to measures of output, using small groups of workers selected from the general work force as subjects placed in specially prepared test facilities. During the course of the experiments, the investigators recognized that variables other than those with which they were concerned were playing a very important role in the final output. It was the recognition of the social factors contribution to performance for which these studies became justly famous. The girls who were selected for the test room experience participated in the planning of the experiment, and their views were taken into account throughout. The girls felt "it was fun" and, even though the number of observers was greater and their attention higher in the test situation than in the ordinary work environment, the girls felt no sense of anxiety because of tight control. The group developed leadership and common purpose; the work situation became a very cohesive one, where, when individuals may not have felt up to par, the other members of the group "carried" them. In short, there emerged an effectively functioning social group in a warm relationship with its supervisors. What about the original dependent variable—work output? There need not be any concern on this score by those who concentrated only on production. Output progressed to consistently higher levels without stress on the individuals and, of course, while this could not continue indefinitely, the workers were highly motivated to show increasing improvement.

This was in distinct contrast to the situation the workers said existed in their original work stations. It was also distinctly different from the situation existing in another work group that was observed without any of the preliminary discussion or participation by the workers in the new investigation. Even though there was a wage incentive system in this group, which should have provided some increase in output and wages, production figures remained remarkably constant over a period of time. Work procedures and the resulting output were influenced by the shared attitudes and values of the group; the work group set norms which maintained a ceiling on output. Those workers who exceeded the ceiling were given evidence of social disapproval, verbally or physically. Output was not exceedingly low, however, since the group norms included a floor for production, below which employees could not fall without being called a "chiseler" or something similar.

This work unit proved to be less cohesive than the original experimental one. While there was a common set of values and sentiments, the main group was characterized by a set of cliques, each with limited interests. Relationships with supervisors were less friendly and more formal than in the cohesive participating group. Workers felt more closely supervised when, in reality, there was less overall supervision in the regular work situation than in the test group. Both groups seemed to be organized; the difference arose from the fact that the test group was organized in cooperation with management for a common purpose while the second informal work group was organized in opposition to management. In both cases, however, an analysis of the informal group clearly indicated the strong influence of social factors on individual and group performance.

Another well-known study of the importance of participation in the functioning of groups was done at the Harwood Manufacturing Corporation by Coch and French (1948). While the study focused on the change process and the specific techniques possible in the overcoming of resistance to change, the techniques used and the results illustrate several aspects of group dynamics. The experiment was conducted at a time when the factory was involved in a style change that necessitated a revision of work roles and procedures. The investigators arranged to have matched groups of employees exposed to three degrees of participation in determining the new work assignments. One group had virtually no participation in the process; they were assigned tasks from the very beginning. The second group participated indirectly through a group of representatives selected from the original group. The final variation involved complete participation in the determining of programs and assignments in the changeover. After the changeover, the no-participation group showed little or no improvement in their performance. Resistance was notable among the members of the production crew, and many examples of hostility and aggression between workers and supervisors were common. The group that participated through representatives worked well with the supervisor or staff man and showed a substantial increase in performance, particularly in the second week after the change. The total participation group adapted to the change very rapidly and progressed to levels that were significantly higher than their earlier performance. The emotional tone of the group was very good; there was excellent cooperation between individuals in the group and the supervisor, and no aggression was evident.

At the end of the month, the no-participation group had made no progress and were assigned to new jobs somewhere else in the factory. When they were reassembled after a few months and permitted to participate in still another change, this group operated at the same high levels that earlier participation groups achieved, a level that, again, was significantly higher than the positions reached where they were not permitted to participate. The experimenters felt that such participation leads to higher morale or better labor-management relations in addition to higher production. The entire management of the company felt that the practical results were very valuable, over and above any of the theoretical additions this study has made to concepts of group processes and intergroup relations generally.

It may be, however, that, while there is a strong motivational basis for individual participation, the strength of this factor may not be uniform for all individuals. Vroom (1959) related personality with group participation and performance. He found the highest satisfaction in the job and the best performance in those individuals who had a high need for independence. Individuals who are highly dependent and were authoritarian-oriented were affected less by the opportunity to participate and showed no relationship between felt participation and job performance. This study indicates that, while participation is related to performance and is important in group functioning, we should also look to variations in individuals in terms of the need for participation.

Broader situational and demographic variables are not, of course, without their influence on the interaction within the small group. A series of studies on an important small group in the legal area, the jury, has indicated several avenues of influence from outside the immediate group situation. Strodtbeck, James, and Hawkins (1958) determined the influence of socioeconomic status and occupation on the interaction in the mock jury. It was found that those individuals who participated more were most often chosen as foreman. Men participated in jury deliberations much more frequently than did women, and there was much more activity from those individuals in higher socioeconomic brackets.

Group Problem Solving

One of the aspects of group functioning that has attracted considerable interest down through the years is that of group problem solving. The basic question has been whether the product of the intellectual functioning of a group is superior to that of a group of individuals functioning separately.

In one of the earliest studies on the question of group versus individual problem solving, Allport (1920) found a difference in favor of the group because a greater variety of ideas arose in that social setting. Lorge and Solomon (1960) replicated an earlier study by Shaw (1932) and found (as Shaw did) that, generally, groups were superior to individuals. Level of aspiration was a significant factor; no individual without aspiration was able to solve the problem, while groups were not affected as strongly. Argyle (1957) agreed in terms of superiority of the group. He isolated two factors in the process, namely, the improvement of judgment through prior judgment and the superiority achieved through a combination of individual judgments. Group problem solving increased the number of alternatives available and stimulated activity toward a typical solution to identify blind alleys that individuals might find themselves in if they pursue the task alone.

It is safe to say that most of the studies in this area report a superiority of group over individual approaches although at least one (Moore and Anderson, 1954) does not. It may be that the source of disagreement lies mainly in the conditions surrounding the task and in the individuals who are subjects. The preponderance of expert opinion, however, is in favor of superiority of the group in problem-solving performance.

There has been further interest in a specific variant of group problem solving known popularly as "brainstorming" where the focus is on unrestricted and uninhibited associative responses by members of an assembled group. The group is under instructions to be unconcerned about the logic or validity of an idea and to respond with as many as possible.

Results of experiments in this area have been somewhat controversial. Osborn (1957), among others, has noted evidence for a greater variety and creativity in group solutions under the brainstorming instructions to provide ideas without concern for their value or logic. Taylor et al. (1958) indicate that this has not been true in their experience. The latter findings may represent, however, an inability of the individuals in the group to rid themselves of limiting attitudes; other situational and relational factors also may be playing an inhibiting role.

REFERENCES

Allport, F. (1920). The influence of the group upon association and thought. *Journal of Experimental Psychology, 3,* 159–182.

Argyle, M. (1957). Social pressure in public and private situations. *Journal of Abnormal and Social Psychology,* **54,** 172–175.

Asch, S. (1952). *Social psychology.* Englewood Cliffs, N. J.: Prentice-Hall.

Cartwright, D., and Zander, A. eds (1960). *Group dynamics: research and theory* (2nd ed.). New York: Harper & Row.

Coch, L., and French, J. (1948). Overcoming resistance to change. *Human Relations.* **1,** 512–534.

Deutsch, M. (1949). An experimental study of the effects of cooperation and competition upon group processes. *Human Relations, 2,* 199–231.

DiVesta, F., and Cox, L. (1960). Some dispositional correlates of conformity behavior. *The Journal of Social Psychology,* **52,** 259–268.

Festinger, L., Schachter, S., and Back, K. (1950). *Social pressures in informal groups: A study of a housing project.* New York: Harper.

Festinger, L., and Thibaut, J. (1951). Interpersonal communication in small groups. *Journal of Abnormal and Social Psychology,* **46,** 92–99.

Hammond, L., and Goldman, M. (1961). Competition and non-competition and its relationship to individual and group productivity. *Sociometry,* **24,** 46–60.

Homans, G. (1950). *The human group.* New York: Harcourt, Brace and World.

Jones, S., and Vroom, V. (1964). Division of labor and performance under cooperative and competitive conditions. *Journal of Abnormal and Social Psychology,* **68,** 313–320.

Kelley, H., and Volkhart, E. (1952). The resistance to change of group-anchored attitudes. *American Sociological Review,* **17,** 453–465.

Klein, J. (1956). *The study of groups.* London: Routledge.

Lasswell, H., and Kaplan, A. (1950). *Power and society: a framework for political inquiry.* New Haven, Conn.: Yale University Press.

Lorge, I., and Solomon, H. (1960). Group and individual performance in problem solving related to previous exposure to problem, level of aspiration, and group size. *Behavioral Science,* **5,** 28–38.

Lott, B. (1961). Group cohesiveness: A learning phenomenon. *The Journal of Social Psychology,* **55,** 275–286.

Milgram, S. (1964). Group pressure and action against a person. *Journal of Abnormal and Social Psychology,* **69,** 137–143.

Mintz, A. (1951). Nonadaptive group behavior. *The Journal of Abnormal and Social Psychology,* **46,** 150–159.

Moore, O., and Anderson, S. (1954). Search behavior in individual and group problem solving. *American Sociological Review,* **19,** 702–714.

Osborn, A. (1957). *Applied imagination.* New York: Scribner's.

Raven, B. (1959). Social influence on opinions and the communication of related content. *Journal of Abnormal and Social Psychology, 58,* 119–128.

Roethlisberger, F., and Dickson, W. (1939). *Management and the worker.* Cambridge, Mass.: Harvard University Press.

Rosenberg, L. (1961). Group size, prior experience, and conformity. *Journal of Abnormal and Social Psychology, 63,* 436–437.

Schachter, S. (1951). Deviation, rejection, and communication. *Journal of Abnormal and Social Psychology, 46,* 190–207.

Shaw, M. (1932). A comparison of individuals and small groups in the rational solution of complex problems. *American Journal of Psychology, 44,* 491–504.

Sherif, M. (1936). *The psychology of social norms.* New York: Harper.

Shils, E. (1950). Primary groups in the American army. In Merton, R. and Lazarsfeld, P. (eds). *Continuities in social research: Studies in the scope and method of "the American soldier,"* New York: Free Press.

Steiner, I., and Johnson, H. (1963). Authoritarianism and conformity. *Sociometry, 26,* 21–34.

Strickland, B., and Crowne, D. (1962). Conformity under conditions of simulated group pressure as a function of the need for social approval. *The Journal of Social Psychology, 58,* 171–181.

Strodtbeck, F., James, R., and Hawkins, C. (1958). Social status in jury deliberations. In Maccoby, E., Newcomb, T., and Hartley, E. (eds). *Readings in social psychology,* (3rd ed.) New York: Holt.

Taylor, D., Berry, P., and Block, C. (1958). Does group participation when using brainstorming facilitate or inhibit creative thinking? *Administrative Science Quarterly, 3,* 23–47.

Thibaut, J., and Kelley, H. (1959). *The social psychology of groups,* New York: Wiley.

Vroom, V. (1959). Some personality determinants of the effects of participation. *Journal of Abnormal and Social Psychology, 59,* 322–327.

Achieving Change in People: Some Applications of Group Dynamics Theory

Dorwin Cartwright

I

We hear all around us today the assertion that the problems of the twentieth century are problems of human relations. The survival of civilization, it is said, will depend upon man's ability to create social inventions capable of harnessing, for society's constructive use, the vast physical energies now at man's disposal. Or, to put the matter more simply, we must learn how to change the way in which people behave toward one another. In broad outline, the specifications for a good

From *Human Relations,* 1951, **4,** 381–392. Reprinted by permission.

society are clear, but a serious technical problem remains: How can we change people so that they neither restrict the freedom nor limit the potentialities for growth of others; so that they accept and respect people of different religion, nationality, color, or political opinion; so that nations can exist in a world without war, and so that the fruits of our technological advances can bring economic well-being and freedom from disease to all the people of the world? Although few people would disagree with these objectives when stated abstractly, when we become more specific, differences of opinion quickly arise. How is change to be produced? Who is to do it? Who is to be changed? These questions permit no ready answers.

Before we consider in detail these questions of social technology, let us clear away some semantic obstacles. The word "change" produces emotional reactions. It is not a neutral word. To many people it is threatening. It conjures up visions of a revolutionary, a dissatisfied idealist, a trouble-maker, a malcontent. Nicer words referring to the process of changing people are education, training, orientation, guidance, indoctrination, therapy. We are more ready to have others "educate" us than to have them "change" us. We, ourselves, feel less guilty in "training" others than in "changing" them. Why this emotional response? What makes the two kinds of words have such different meanings? I believe that a large part of the difference lies in the fact that the safer words (like education or therapy) carry the implicit assurance that the only changes produced will be good ones, acceptable within a currently held value system. The cold, unmodified word "change," on the contrary, promises no respect for values; it might even tamper with values themselves. Perhaps for this very reason it will foster straight thinking if we use the word "change" and thus force ourselves to struggle directly and self-consciously with the problems of value that are involved. Words like education, training, or therapy, by the very fact that they are not so disturbing, may close our eyes to the fact that they too inevitably involve values.

Another advantage of using the word "change" rather than other related words is that it does not restrict our thinking to a limited set of aspects of people that are legitimate targets of change. Anyone familiar with the history of education knows that there has been endless controversy over what it is about people that "education" properly attempts to modify. Some educators have viewed education simply as imparting knowledge, others mainly as providing skills for doing things, still others as producing healthy "attitudes," and some have aspired to instill a way of life. Or if we choose to use a word like "therapy," we can hardly claim that we refer to a more clearly defined realm of change. Furthermore, one can become inextricably entangled in distinctions and vested interests by attempting to distinguish sharply between, let us say, the domain of education and that of therapy. If we are to try to take a broader view and to develop some basic principles that promise to apply to all types of modifications in people, we had better use a word like "change" to keep our thinking general enough.

The proposal that social technology may be employed to solve the problems of society suggests that social science may be applied in ways not different from those used in the physical sciences. Does social science, in fact, have any practically useful knowledge which may be brought to bear significantly on society's most urgent problems? What scientifically based principles are there for guiding programs of social change? In this paper we shall restrict our considerations to certain parts of a relatively new branch of social science known as "group dynamics." We shall examine some of the applications for social action which stem from research in this field of scientific investigation.

What is "group dynamics"? Perhaps it will be most useful to start by looking at the derivation of the word "dynamics." It comes from a Greek word meaning force. In careful usage of the phrase, "group dynamics" refers to the forces operating in groups. The investigation of group dynamics, then, consists of a study of these forces: what gives rise to them, what conditions modify them, what consequences they have, etc. The practical application of group dynamics (or the technology of group dynamics) consists of the utilization of knowledge about these forces for the achievement of some purpose. In keeping with this definition, then, it is clear that group dynamics, as a realm of investigation, is not particularly novel, nor is it the exclusive property of any person or institution. It goes back at least to the outstanding work of men like Simmel, Freud, and Cooley.

Although interest in groups has a long and respectable history, the past 15 years have witnessed a new flowering of activity in this field. Today, research centers in several countries are carrying out substantial programs of research designed to reveal the nature of groups and of their functioning. The phrase "group dynamics" has come into common usage during this time and intense efforts have been devoted to the development of the field, both as a branch of social science and as a form of social technology.

In this development the name of Kurt Lewin has been outstanding. As a consequence of his work in the field of individual psychology and from his analysis of the nature of the pressing problems of the contemporary world, Lewin became convinced of society's urgent need for a *scientific approach* to the understanding of the dynamics of groups. In 1945 he established the Research Center for Group Dynamics to meet this need. Since that date the Center has been devoting its efforts to improving our scientific understanding of groups through laboratory experimentation, field studies, and the use of techniques of action research. It has also attempted in various ways to help get the findings of social science more widely used by social management. Much of what I have to say in this paper is drawn from the experiences of this Center in its brief existence of a little more than five years (2).

II

For various reasons we have found that much of our work has been devoted to an attempt to gain a better understanding of the ways in which people change their behavior or resist efforts by others to have them do so. Whether we set for ourselves the practical goal of improving behavior or whether we take on the intellectual task of understanding why people do what they do, we have to investigate processes of communication, influence, social pressure—in short, problems of change.

In this work we have encountered great frustration. The problems have been most difficult to solve. Looking back over our experience, I have become convinced that no small part of the trouble has resulted from an irresistible tendency to conceive of our problems in terms of the individual. We live in an individualistic culture. We value the individual highly, and rightly so. But I am inclined to believe that our political and social concern for the individual has narrowed our thinking as social scientists so much that we have not been able to state our research problems properly. Perhaps we have taken the individual as the unit of observation and study when some larger unit would have been more appropriate. Let us look at a few examples.

Consider first some matters having to do with the mental health of an individual. We can all agree, I believe, that an important mark of a healthy personality is that the individual's self-esteem has not been undermined. But on what does self-esteem depend? From research on this problem we have discovered that, among other things, repeated experiences of failure or traumatic failures on matters of central importance serve to undermine one's self-esteem. We also know that whether a person experiences success of failure as a result of some undertaking depends upon the level of aspiration which he has set for himself. Now, if we try to discover how the level of aspiration gets set, we are immediately involved in the person's relationships to groups. The groups to which he belongs set standards for his behavior which he must accept if he is to remain in the group. If his capacities do not allow him to reach these standards, he experiences failure, he withdraws or is rejected by the group and his self-esteem suffers a shock.

Suppose, then, that we accept a task of therapy, of rebuilding his self-esteem. It would appear plausible from our analysis of the problem that we should attempt to work with variables of the same sort that produced the difficulty, that is to work with him either in the groups to which he now belongs or to introduce him into new groups which are selected for the purpose and to work upon his relationships to groups as such. From the point of view of preventive mental health, we might even attempt to train the groups in our communities—classes in schools, work groups in business, families, unions, religious and cultural groups— to make use of practices better designed to protect the self-esteem of their members.

Consider a second example. A teacher finds that in her class she has a number of troublemakers, full of aggression. She wants to know why these children are so aggressive and what can be done about it. A foreman in a factory has the same kind of problem with some of his workers. He wants the same kind of help. The solution most tempting to both the teacher and the foreman often is to transfer the worst troublemakers to someone else, or if facilities are available, to refer them for counselling. But is the problem really of such a nature that it can be solved by removing the troublemaker from the situation or by working on his individual motivations and emotional life? What leads does research give us? The evidence indicates, of course, that there are many causes of aggressiveness in people, but one aspect of the problem has become increasingly clear in recent years. If we observe carefully the amount of aggressive behavior and the number of troublemakers to be found in a large collection of groups, we find that these characteristics can vary tremendously from group to group even when the different groups are composed essentially of the same kinds of people. In the now classic experiments of Lewin, Lippitt, and White (7) on the effects of different styles of leadership, it was found that the same group of children displayed markedly different levels of aggressive behavior when under different styles of leadership. Moreover, when individual children were transferred from one group to another, their levels of aggressiveness shifted to conform to the atmosphere of the new group. Efforts to account for one child's aggressiveness under one style of leadership merely in terms of his personality traits could hardly succeed under these conditions. This is not to say that a person's behavior is entirely to be accounted for by the atmosphere and structure of the immediate group, but it is remarkable to what an extent a strong, cohesive group can control aspects of a member's behavior traditionally thought to be expressive of enduring personality traits. Recognition of this fact rephrases the problem of how to change such behavior. It directs us to a study of the sources of the influence of the group on its members.

Let us take an example from a different field. What can we learn from efforts to change people by mass media and mass persuasion? In those rare instances when educators, propagandists, advertisers, and others who want to influence large numbers of people, have bothered to make an objective evaluation of the enduring changes produced by their efforts, they have been able to demonstrate only the most negligible effects (1). The inefficiency of attempts to influence the public by mass media would be scandalous if there were agreement that it was important or even desirable to have such influences strongly exerted. In fact, it is no exaggeration to say that all of the research and experience of generations has not improved the efficiency of lectures or other means of mass influence to any noticeable degree. Something must be wrong with our theories of learning, motivation, and social psychology.

Within very recent years some research data have been accumulating which may give us a clue to the solution of our problem. In one series of experiments directed by Lewin, it was found that a method of group decision, in which the group as a whole made a decision to have its members change their behavior, was from two to ten times as effective in producing actual change as was a lecture presenting exhortation to change (6). We have yet to learn precisely what produces these differences of effectiveness, but it is clear that by introducing group forces into the situation a whole new level of influence has been achieved.

The experience has been essentially the same when people have attempted to increase the productivity of individuals in work settings. Traditional conceptions of how to increase the output of workers have stressed the individual: select the right man for the job; simplify the job for him; train him in the skills required; motivate him by economic incentives; make it clear to whom he reports; keep the lines of authority and responsibility simple and straight. But even when all these conditions are fully met we are finding that productivity is far below full potential. There is even good reason to conclude that this individualistic conception of the determinants of productivity actually fosters negative consequences. The individual, now isolated and subjected to the demands of the organization through the commands of his boss, finds that he must create with his fellow employees informal groups, not shown on any table of organization, in order to protect himself from arbitrary control of his life, from the boredom produced by the endless repetition of mechanically sanitary and routine operations, and from the impoverishment of his emotional and social life brought about by the frustration of his basic needs for social interaction, participation, and acceptance in a stable group. Recent experiments have demonstrated clearly that the productivity of work groups can be greatly increased by methods of work organization and supervision which give more responsibility to work groups, which allow for fuller participation in important decisions, and which make stable groups the firm basis for support of the individual's social needs (3). I am convinced that future research will also demonstrate that people working under such conditions become more mature and creative individuals in their homes, in community life, and as citizens.

As a final example, let us examine the experience of efforts to train people in workshops, institutes, and special training courses. Such efforts are common in various areas of social welfare, intergroup relations, political affairs, industry, and adult education generally. It is an unfortunate fact that objective evaluation of the effects of such training efforts has only rarely been undertaken, but there is evidence for those who will look that the actual change in behavior produced is most disappointing. A workshop not infrequently develops keen interest among the participants, high morale and enthusiasm, and a firm resolve on the part of many to apply all the wonderful insights back home. But what happens back home? The trainee discovers that his colleagues don't share his enthusiasm. He learns that the task of changing others' expectations and ways of doing things is discouragingly difficult. He senses, perhaps not very clearly, that it would make all the difference in the world if only there were a few other people sharing his enthusiasm and insights with whom he could plan activities, evaluate consequences of efforts, and from whom he could gain emotional and motivational support. The approach to training which conceives of its task as being merely that of changing the individual probably produces frustration, demoralization, and disillusionment in as large a measure as it accomplishes more positive results.

A few years ago the Research Center for Group Dynamics undertook to shed light on this problem by investigating the operation of a workshop for training leaders in intercultural relations (9). In a project, directed by Lippitt, we set out to compare systematically the different effects of the workshop upon trainees who came as isolated individuals in contrast to those who came as teams.

Since one of the problems in the field of intercultural relations is that of getting people of good will to be more active in community efforts to improve intergroup relations, one goal of the training workshop was to increase the activity of the trainees in such community affairs. We found that before the workshop there was no difference in the activity level of the people who were to be trained as isolates and of those who were to be trained as teams. Six months after the workshop, however, those who had been trained as isolates were only slightly more active than before the workshop whereas those who had been members of strong training teams were now much more active. We do not have clear evidence on the point, but we would be quite certain that the maintenance of heightened activity over a long period of time would also be much better for members of teams. For the isolates the effect of the workshop had the characteristic of a "shot in the arm" while for the team member it produced a more enduring change because the team provided a more enduring change because the team provided continuous support and reinforcement for its members.

III

What conclusions may we draw from these examples? What principles of achieving change in people can we see emerging? To begin with the most general proposition, we may state that the behavior, attitudes, beliefs, and values of the individual are all firmly grounded in the groups to which he belongs. How aggressive or cooperative a person is, how much self-respect and self-confidence he has, how energetic and productive his work is, what he aspires to, what he believes to be true and good, whom he loves or hates, and what beliefs and prejudices he holds—all these characteristics are highly determined by the individual's group memberships. In a real sense, they are properties of groups and of the relationships between people. Whether they change or resist change will, therefore, be greatly influenced by the nature of these groups. Attempts to change them must be concerned with the dynamics of groups.

In examining more specifically how groups enter into the process of change, we find it useful to view groups in at least three different ways. In the first view, the group is seen as a source of influence over its members. Efforts to change behavior can be supported or blocked by pressures on members stemming from the group. To make constructive use of these pressures the group must be used *as a medium of change*. In the second view, the group itself becomes the *target of change*. To change the behavior of individuals it may be necessary to change the standards of the group, its style of leadership, its emotional atmosphere, or its stratification into cliques and hierarchies. Even though the goal may be to change the behavior of *individuals,* the target of change becomes the group. In the third view, it is recognized that many changes of behavior can be brought about only by the organized efforts of groups as *agents of change*. A committee to combat intolerance, a labor union, an employers association, a citizens group to increase the pay of teachers—any action group will be more or less effective depending upon the way it is organized, the satisfaction it provides to its members, the degree to which its goals are clear, and a host of other properties of the group.

An adequate social technology of change, then, requires at the very least a scientific understanding of groups viewed in each of these ways. We shall consider here only the first two aspects of the problem: the group as a medium of change and as a target of change.

The Group as a Medium of Change

Principle No. 1. If the group is to be used effectively as a medium of change, those people who are to be changed and those who are to exert influence for change must have a strong sense of belonging to the same group.

Kurt Lewin described this principle well: "The normal gap between teacher and student, doctor and patient, social worker and public, can . . . be a real obstacle to acceptance of the advocated conduct." In other words, in spite of whatever status differences there might be between them, the teacher and the student have to feel as members of one group in matters involving their sense of values. The chances for reeducation seem to be increased whenever a strong we-feeling is created (5). Recent experiments by Preston and Heintz have demonstrated greater changes of opinions among members of discussion groups operating with participatory leadership than among those with supervisory leadership (12). The implications of this principle for classroom teaching are far-reaching. The same may be said of supervision in the factory, army, or hospital.

Principle No. 2. The more attractive the group is to its members the greater is the influence that the group can exert on its members.

This principle has been extensively documented by Festinger and his co-workers (4). They have been able to show in a variety of settings that in more cohesive groups there is a greater readiness of members to attempt to influence others, a greater readiness to be influenced by others, and stronger pressures toward conformity when conformity is a relevant matter for the group. Important for the practitioner wanting to make use of this principle is, of course, the question of how to increase the attractiveness of groups. This is a question with many answers. Suffice it to say that a group is more attractive the more it satisfies the needs of its members. We have been able to demonstrate experimentally an increase in group cohesiveness by increasing the liking of members for each other as persons, by increasing the perceived importance of the group goal, and by increasing the prestige of the group among other groups. Experienced group workers could add many other ways to this list.

Principle No. 3. In attempts to change attitudes, values, or behavior, the more relevant they are to the basis of attraction to the group, the greater will be the influence that the group can exert upon them.

I believe this principle gives a clue to some otherwise puzzling phenomena. How does it happen that a group, like a labor union, seems to be able to exert such strong discipline over its members in some matters (let us say in dealing with management), while it seems unable to exert nearly the same influence in other matters (let us say in political action)? If we examine why it is that members are attracted to the group, I believe we will find that a particular reason for belonging seems more related to some of the group's activities than to others. If a man joins a union mainly to keep his job and to improve his working conditions, he may be largely uninfluenced by the union's attempt to modify his attitudes toward national and international affairs. Groups differ tremendously in the range of matters that are relevant to them and hence over which they have influence. Much of the inefficiency of adult education could be reduced if more attention were paid to the need that influence attempts be appropriate to the groups in which they are made.

> *Principle No. 4.* The greater the prestige of a group member in the eyes of the other members, the greater the influence he can exert.

Polansky, Lippitt, and Redl (11) have demonstrated this principle with great care and methodological ingenuity in a series of studies in children's summer camps. From a practical point of view it must be emphasized that the things giving prestige to a member may not be those characteristics most prized by the official management of the group. The most prestige-carrying member of a Sunday school class may not possess the characteristics most similar to the minister of the church. The teacher's pet may be a poor source of influence within a class. This principle is the basis for the common observation that the official leader and the actual leader of a group are often not the same individual.

> *Principle No. 5.* Efforts to change individuals or subparts of a group which, if successful, would have the result of making them deviate from the norms of the group will encounter strong resistance.

During the past few years a great deal of evidence has been accumulated showing the tremendous pressures which groups can exert upon members to conform to the group's norms. The price of deviation in most groups is rejection or even expulsion. If the member really wants to belong and be accepted, he cannot withstand this type of pressure. It is for this reason that efforts to change people by taking them from the group and giving them special training so often have disappointing results. This principle also accounts for the finding that people thus trained sometimes display increased tension, aggressiveness toward the group, or a tendency to form cults or cliques with others who have shared their training.

These five principles concerning the group as a medium of change would appear to have readiest application to groups created for the purpose of producing changes in people. They provide certain specifications for building effective training or therapy groups. They also point, however, to a difficulty in producing change in people in that they show how resistant an individual is to changing in any way contrary to group pressures and expectations. In order to achieve many kinds of changes in people, therefore, it is necessary to deal with the group as a target of change.

The Group as a Target of Change

> *Principle No. 6.* Strong pressure for changes in the group can be established by creating a shared perception by members of the need for change, thus making the source of pressure for change lie within the group.

Marrow and French (9) report a dramatic case study which illustrates this principle quite well. A manufacturing concern had a policy against hiring women over 30 because it was believed that they were slower, more difficult to train, and more likely to be absent. The staff psychologist was able to present to management evidence that this belief was clearly unwarranted at least within their own company. The psychologist's facts, however, were rejected and ignored as a basis for action because they violated accepted beliefs. It was claimed that they violated accepted beliefs. It was claimed that they went against the direct experience of the foremen. Then the psychologist hit upon a plan for achieving change which differed drastically from the usual one of argument, persuasion, and pressure. He proposed that management conduct its own analysis of the situation. With his help management collected all the facts which they believed were relevant to the problem. When the results were in they were now their own facts rather than those of some "outside" expert. Policy was immediately changed without further resistance. The important point here is that facts are not enough. The facts must be the accepted property of the group if they are to become an effective basis for change. There seems to be all the difference in the world in changes actually carried out between those cases in which a consulting firm is hired to do a study and present a report and those in which technical experts are asked to collaborate with the group in doing its own study.

> *Principle No. 7.* Information relating to the need for change, plans for change, and consequences of change must be shared by all relevant people in the group.

Another way of stating this principle is to say that change of a group ordinarily requires the opening of communication channels. Newcomb (10) has shown how one of the first consequences of mistrust and hostility is the avoidance of communicating openly and freely about the things producing the tension. If you look closely at a pathological group (that is, one that has trouble making decisions or effecting coordinated efforts of its members), you will certainly find strong restraints in that group against communicating vital information among its members. Until these restraints are removed there can be little hope for any real and lasting changes in the group's functioning. In passing it should be pointed out that the removal of barriers to communication will ordinarily be accompanied by a sudden increase in the communication of hostility. The group may appear to be falling apart, and it will certainly be a painful experience to many of the members. This pain and the fear that things are getting out of hand often stop the process of change once begun.

> *Principle No. 8.* Changes in one part of a group produce strain in other related parts which can be reduced only by eliminating the change or by bringing about readjustments in the related parts.

It is a common practice to undertake improvements in group functioning by providing training programs for certain classes of people in the organization. A training program for foremen, for nurses, for teachers, or for group workers is established. If the content of the training is relevant for organizational change, it must of necessity deal with the relationships these people have with other subgroups. If nurses in a hospital change their behavior significantly, it will affect their relations both with the patients and with the doctors. It is unrealistic to assume that both these groups will remain indifferent to any significant changes in this respect. In hierarchical structures this process is most clear. Lippitt has proposed on the basis of research and experience that in such organizations attempts at change should always involve three levels, one being the major target of change and the other two being the one above and the one below.

IV

These eight principles represent a few of the basic propositions emerging from research in group dynamics. Since research is constantly going on and since it is the very nature of research to revise and reformulate our conceptions, we may be sure that these principles will have to be modified and improved as time goes by. In the meantime they may serve as guides in our endeavors to develop a scientifically based technology of social management.

In social technology, just as in physical technology, invention plays a crucial role. In both fields progress consists of the creation of new mechanisms for the accomplishment of certain goals. In both fields inventions arise in response to practical needs and are to be evaluated by how effectively they satisfy these needs. The relation of invention to scientific development is indirect but important. Inventions cannot proceed too far ahead of basic scientific development, nor should they be allowed to fall too far behind. They will be more effective the more they make good use of known principles of science, and they often make new developments in science possible. On the other hand, they are in no sense logical derivations from scientific principles.

I have taken this brief excursion into the theory of invention in order to make a final point. To many people "group dynamics" is known only for the social inventions which have developed in recent years in work with groups. Group dynamics is often thought of as certain techniques to be used with groups. Role playing, buzz groups, process observers, postmeeting reaction sheets, and feedback of group observations are devices popularly associated with the phrase "group dynamics." I trust I have been able to show that group dynamics is more than a collection of gadgets. It certainly aspires to be a science as well as a technology.

This is not to underplay the importance of these inventions nor of the function of inventing. As inventions they are all mechanisms designed to help accomplish important goals. How effective they are will depend upon how skilfully they are used and how appropriate they are to the purposes to which they are put. Careful evaluative research must be the ultimate judge of their usefulness in comparison with alternative inventions. I believe that the principles enumerated in this paper indicate some of the specifications that social inventions in this field must meet.

REFERENCES

1 Cartwright, D. Some principles of mass persuasion: Selected findings of research on the sale of United States war bonds. *Human Relations,* 1949, **2**(3), 253–67.
2 Cartwright, D. *The research center for group dynamics: A report of five years' activities and a view of future needs.* Ann Arbor: Institute for Social Research, 1950.
3 Coch, L. and French, J. P., Jr. Overcoming resistance to change. *Human Relations,* 1948, **1**(4), 512–32.
4 Festinger, L., et al. *Theory and experiment in social communication: Collected papers.* Ann Arbor: Institute for Social Research, 1950.
5 Lewin, K. *Resolving social conflicts,* p. 67. New York: Harper & Bros., 1948.
6 Lewin, K. *Field theory in social science,* pp. 229–236. New York: Harper & Bros., 1951
7 Lewin, K., Lippitt, R., and White, R. K. Patterns of aggressive behavior in experimentally created "social climates." *Journal of Social Psychology,* 1939, **10,** 271–99.
8 Lippitt, R. *Training in Community Relations.* New York: Harper & Bros., 1949.
9 Marrow, A. J., and French, J. R. P., Jr. Changing a stereotype in industry. *Journal of Social Issues,* 1945, **1**(3), 33–37.
10 Newcomb, T. M. Autistic hostility and social reality. *Human Relations,* 1947, **1**(1), 69–86.
11 Polansky, N., Lippitt, R., and Redl, F. An investigation of behavioral contagion in groups. *Human Relations,* 1950, **3**(4), 319–48.
12 Preston, M. G., and Heintz, R. K. Effects of participatory vs. supervisory leadership on group judgment. *Journal of Abnormal and Social Psychology,* 1949, **44,** 345–55.

QUESTIONS FOR DISCUSSION

1　What relationships exist between group aspiration level and individual performance on the job?
2　What motivationally relevant functions do groups serve in organizations?
3　What role do group processes play in equity theory?
4　How can group processes influence motivation to perform, as analyzed using expectancy/valence theory?

5   What does achievement motivation theory say about the influence of the group on employee motivation?
6   What influence might the nature of the task have on the effectiveness of participative decision making?
7   If you were a manager trying to increase performance among your subordinates, would you use group or individual incentives? Why?
8   What is the role of group norms in the motivational process?
9   Under what circumstances would you expect competition among group members for rewards to result in higher performance than cooperation? When might cooperation lead to higher performance than competition? Explain why such differences can occur.

Chapter 11

Leadership and Motivation

OVERVIEW

The topic of leadership has been consistently popular throughout the literature on organization behavior. Countless articles and books have appeared which attempted to prescribe the "correct" leadership style or approach to managing people at work. As one reviews this literature, however, at least two important conclusions emerge. First, it becomes evident that the amount of theoretical and/ or prescriptive material on leadership far outweighs the amount of empirical research on the topic. One is easily led to the conclusion that almost every practicing manager has strong feelings about the "best" way to lead subordinates and that such feelings are based more on past experiences and attitudes than on objective data.

Second, it becomes evident that there is little agreement as to what "leadership" as a concept really means. Some people use the term to describe a *position* in the organizational hierarchy. Under this definition, the president of a company is a "leader" by virtue of holding high office. Other people use the term to describe particular *personal characteristics*. How often have we heard the phrase, "a natural born leader"? Finally, a more recent definition has emerged in which leadership is described as a *category of behavior*. In this last description, leadership is seen as a dynamic process in which one person behaves in a certain manner, thereby causing others to follow. Phrasing this third definition in more formal terms, Katz and Kahn (1966, p. 302) state that leadership is "the influential increment over and above mechanical compliance with the routine directives of the organization." If we view leadership in a dynamic state, particularly as it relates to motivation, then it appears that this third approach is far more valuable for our purposes here.

Using such a definition, effective leadership is something beyond power or authority in that it implies some form of voluntary compliance on the part of the followers. That is, effective leadership can be understood in terms of an individual's ability to stimulate and direct subordinates to perform specific tasks deemed important by the leader. As such, the concept of leadership really reduces to a question of motivation. In other words, using the Katz and Kahn or similar definitions, leaders are only effective to the extent that they can motivate their subordinates or followers to perform.

This crucial relationship between motivation and leadership can also be seen when one considers the various "functions" which leaders are believed to serve within organizations at one time or another. Krech, Crutchfield, and Ballachey (1962) have provided a rather extensive list of these functions. They include: (1) executive, or coordinator of group activities; (2) planner, or strategist; (3) policy maker; (4) expert, or source of information; (5) group representative to nongroup members; (6) controller of internal group relations; (7) purveyor of rewards and punishment; (8) arbitrator and mediator; (9) exemplar; (10) symbol of the group; (11) substitute for individual responsibility; (12) ideologist; (13) parent figure; and (14) scapegoat, when things go wrong.

On a more abstract level, Katz and Kahn (1966) have argued that leadership serves four general functions in ongoing organizations: (1) it fills the voids left by the incompleteness and imperfections of organization design; (2) it maintains the stability of an organization in a turbulent environment, allowing the organization to respond and adjust to changing external conditions; (3) it maintains internal coordination and adjudication through periods of internal change and growth; and (4) it attempts to maintain human membership in the organization. Although these lists are not empirically derived, they should suggest that not only is the leadership function quite broad-based but also that it is centrally related to the ability of the leader to motivate subordinates.

Having considered both various definitions of leadership and some functions which leaders purportedly serve, we can now examine several general "theories" of leadership that have been prominent at one time or another. Viewed historically, the earliest theory is generally termed the "great man" theory. This approach dates from the time of the ancient Greeks but it maintained its popularity into the early twentieth century. Briefly, it assumed that true leaders possessed two quite dissimilar characteristics: (1) they were capable of "instrumental" behavior, such as planning, organizing, controlling subordinate activities; and (2) they showed concern for their subordinates and fostered sound group interrelationships (Bales, Borgatta, & Couch, 1954). Persons who showed both of these traits simultaneously were considered "great men" and it was generally believed that they would be effective leaders in *any* given situation. Moreover, it was assumed that such leaders were born with these qualities; learned behavior was not considered relevant.

With the emergence of the behavioral school of psychology in the early 1900s, researchers began to reexamine the "great man" theory. There were at least two reasons for this reexamination. First, it was argued that if there were in fact "great men," or true leaders, it should be possible scientifically to investigate the qualities, or traits, that were common across such individuals. By so investigating, it was felt that valuable insight would be gained into the nature of leadership. This concern for the identification of "traits" closely paralleled the emergence of the instinct theory of motivation, both in time and in nature. Second, it was largely believed that if these traits could be identified accurately, it might be possible for individuals to acquire these leadership qualities through experience and learning. In other words, this newer "trait" theory of leadership rejected the more passive "great man" approach by arguing that leadership could to some degree be *learned.*

Between approximately 1930 and 1950, numerous studies were undertaken in search of universal traits (physical, mental, and personality) that might be related to leadership. In general, some support was found for the conclusion that good leaders tended: (1) to have appealing physical characteristics (for example, they were physically dominating, and so on); (2) to have certain personality traits (such as high needs for achievement and dominance, social maturity, and the like); and (3) to be well above average in intelligence (Gibb, 1954; Mann, 1959; Stogdill, 1948). However, such findings were generally weak and often inconsistent. Partially because of this latter fact, researchers began to challenge the existence of universal traits. Based on the early work of Kurt Lewin (Lewin, Lippitt, & White, 1939) and the later studies at the University of Michigan (Katz, Maccoby, Gurin, & Floor, 1951; Katz, Maccoby, & Morse, 1950) and Ohio State University (Fleishman, Harris, & Burtt, 1955; Shartle, 1952; Stogdill & Coons, 1957), important evidence began to emerge that one set of traits or one style of leadership might not be equally appropriate in all situations. In general, these studies, which formed the basis of the "behavioral" theory of leadership, suggested that there were two fairly distinct *styles* of leadership: task oriented (also called "production centered," "instrumental," and "initiating structure") and employee oriented (or "people centered," "expressive," and "consideration"). A third style of leadership, laissez faire, was used by Lewin and his associates but was later dropped from both theory and research after it was discovered to have no practical relationship to performance or satisfaction (Lewin et al., 1939).

Some disagreement has existed in the literature concerning the nature of the relationship between task orientation and employee orientation. Some researchers believe the two are relatively independent factors, while others believe they are opposite ends of a single continuum. Evidence generally tends to support the former approach. That is, most research tends to indicate that leadership style may be high on both dimensions (task orientation *and* employee orientation), low on both dimensions, or high on one and low on the other. If we consider the relation of these styles of leadership to motivation, it appears that both styles have relevance. The task-oriented supervisor can increase motivation by clarifying the connection between successful task accomplishment and the receipt of desired rewards. The employee-oriented supervisor can increase motivation by providing as many rewarding situations as possible and by creating a supportive environment.

Most recently, a series of newer theories have emerged which use the environment, or situation, as the basic unit of analysis in a theory of leadership instead of the style itself. These theories, known generally as situational or contingency models, typically argue that effective leadership is really a function of the interaction of several variables. For example, under Fiedler's (1967) model, effective leadership is seen as largely a function of: (1) the favorableness of superior-subordinate relations; (2) the power distribution between superior and subordinates; and (3) the degree of task structuring on the job. Tannenbaum and Schmidt (1958) present a similar, though less complex, model. While a more thorough discussion of these contingency models is reserved for later in this chapter, it is important to note here that these newer models see the most effective leadership style—task oriented or employee oriented—as a direct function of additional factors in the work situation.

In the selections that follow, we shall examine several approaches to the topic of leadership, particularly as it relates to motivation. Our aim is to provide a broad understanding of how these two variables interact and how both, in concert, affect employee performance. The first selection (Hollander and Julian) presents a review of contemporary approaches to the analysis of leadership processes in general. This review sets the stage for the more specific discussion by Locke of the role of the supervisor as motivator. Finally, two contemporary theories of leadership are presented by Fiedler and by House and Mitchell. (See also Tannenbaum & Schmidt, 1958; Yukl, 1971.) Each article cites supportive evidence consistent with the positions taken. The final theory presented here (by House and Mitchell) specifically views leadership within a motivational framework. It is felt that both of these last two theoretical statements provide an excellent opportunity for a detailed analysis and discussion of the interactive dynamics between leadership style, motivation, and employee performance and satisfaction on the job.

REFERENCES AND SUGGESTED ADDITIONAL READINGS

Bales, R.F., Borgatta, E. F., & Couch, A. S. Some findings relevant to the great-man theory of leadership. *American Sociological Review,* 1954, **19,** 755–759.

Bowers, D. G., & Seashore, S. E. Predicting organizational effectiveness with a four-factor theory of leadership. *Administrative Science Quarterly,* 1966, **11,** 238–263.

Day, R. C., & Hamblin, R. L. Some effects of close and punitive styles of supervision.

American Journal of Sociology, 1964, **69,** 499–510.

Evans, M. G. The effects of supervisory behavior on the path-goal relationship. *Organizational Behavior and Human Performance,* 1970, **5,** 277–298.

Fiedler, F. E. *A theory of leadership effectiveness.* New York: McGraw-Hill, 1967.

Fiedler, F. E. Validation and extension of the contingency model of leadership effectiveness: A review of empirical findings. *Psychological Bulletin,* 1971, 76, 128–148.

Fiedler, F. E., & Chemers, M. M. *Leadership and effective management.* Glenview, Ill.: Scott, Foresman, 1974.

Fleishman, E. A., Harris, E., & Burtt, H. E. *Leadership and supervision in industry.* Columbus, Ohio: Ohio State University, Bureau of Educational Research, 1955.

Gibb, C. Leadership. In G. Lindzey (ed.), *Handbook of social psychology.* Reading, Mass.: Addison-Wesley, 1954.

Hill, W. A. Leadership style: Rigid or flexible. *Organizational Behavior and Human Performance,* 1973, **9,** 35–47.

Hunt, J. G., & Larson, L. L. (eds.), *Contingency approaches to leadership.* Carbondale, Ill.: Southern Illinois University Press, 1974.

Katz, D. The motivational basis of organizational behavior. *Behavioral Science,* 1964, **9,** 131–146.

Katz, D., & Kahn, R. L. *The social psychology of organizations.* New York: Wiley, 1966.

Katz, D., Maccoby, N. M., & Morse, N. *Productivity supervision and morale in an office situation.* Ann Arbor, Mich.: University of Michigan, Survey Research Center, 1950.

Katz, D., Maccoby, N., Gurin, G., & Floor, L. *Productivity, supervision, and morale among railroad workers.* Ann Arbor, Mich.: University of Michigan, Institute for Social Research, 1951.

Korman, A. K. "Consideration," "initiating structure," and organizational criteria—A review. *Personnel Psychology,* 1966, **19,** 349–361.

Krech, D., Crutchfield, R. S., & Ballachey, E. L. *Individuals in society.* New York: McGraw-Hill, 1962.

Lewin, K., Lippitt, R., & White, R. K. An experimental study of leadership and group life. In E. Maccoby, T. M. Newcomb, & E. L. Hartley (eds.), *Readings in social psychology.* New York: Holt, Rinehart & Winston, 1958. (First published in 1939.)

Mann, R. D. A review of the relationships between personality and performance in small groups. *Psychological Bulletin,* 1959, **56,** 241–270.

Sales, S. M. Supervisory style and productivity: Review and theory. *Personnel Psychology,* 1966, **19,** 275–286.

Shartle, C. L. *Executive performance and leadership.* Columbus, Ohio: The Ohio State University Research Foundation, 1952.

Stogdill, R. M. Personal factors associated with leadership: A survey of the literature. *Journal of Psychology,* 1948, **25,** 35–71.

Stogdill, R. M., & Coons, A. E. *Leader behavior: Its description and measurement.* Columbus, Ohio: Ohio State University, Bureau of Business Research, 1957.

Tannenbaum, R., & Schmidt, W. H. How to choose a leadership pattern. *Harvard Business Review,* 1958, **36,** 95–101.

Vroom, V. H. *Work and motivation.* New York: Wiley, 1964.

Yukl, G. Toward a behavioral theory of leadership. *Organizational Behavior and Human Performance,* 1971, **6,** 414–440.

Contemporary Trends in the Analysis of Leadership Processes

Edwin P. Hollander
James W. Julian[1]

The history of leadership research is a fitful one. Certainly as much, and perhaps more than other social phenomena, conceptions and inquiry about leadership have shifted about. The psychological study of leadership in this century began with a primary focus on the personality characteristics which made a person a leader. But the yield from this approach was fairly meager and often confused, as Stogdill (1948) and Mann (1959) among others documented in their surveys of this literature. In the 1930s, Kurt Lewin and his co-workers (Lewin, Lippitt, & White, 1939) turned attention to the "social climates" created by several styles of leadership, that is, authoritarian, democratic, or laissez-faire. Together with developments in the sociometric study of leader-follower relations (e.g., Jennings, 1943), this work marked a significant break with the past.

Two residues left by Lewin's approach fed importantly into later efforts, even with the limited nature of the original study. One was the concern with "leader style," which still persists, especially in the work on administrative or managerial leadership (see e.g., McGregor, 1960, 1966; Preston & Heintz, 1949). The other was the movement toward a view of the differential contexts of leadership, ultimately evolving into the situational approach which took firm hold of the field by the 1950s (cf. Gouldner, 1950).

For the most part, the situational movement was spurred by the growing recognition that there were specialized demands made upon leadership, depending upon the nature of the group task and other aspects of the situation. Clearly, a deficiency in the older approach was its acceptance of "leader" as a relatively homogeneous role, independent of the variations in leader-follower relationships across situations. The disordered state in which the trait approach left the study of leadership was amply revealed by Stogdill in his 1948 survey, which marked a point of departure for the developing situational emphasis. The publication in 1949 of Hemphill's *Situational Factors in Leadership* contributed a further push in this direction.

The main focus of the situational approach was the study of leaders in different settings, defined especially in terms of different group tasks and group structure. Mainly, though not entirely, through laboratory experimentation, such matters as the continuity in leadership across situations with variable tasks was studied (e.g., Carter, Haythorn, Meirowitz, & Lanzetta, 1951; Carter & Nixon,

From *Psychological Bulletin*, 1969, **71**, 387–397. Copyright by the American Psychological Association. Reprinted by permission.

[1]The preparation of this paper was facilitated by the support of a program of research under ONR Contract 4679 from the group Psychology Branch, Office of Naval Research.

1949; Gibb, 1947). The findings of this research substantially supported the contention that who became a leader depended in some degree upon the nature of the task. With this movement, however, there came a corresponding deemphasis on the personality characteristics of leaders or other group members. Though a number of studies systematically placed people in groups on the basis of their scores on certain personality dimensions (e.g., Berkowitz, 1956; Haythorn, Couch, Haefner, Langham, & Carter, 1956; Scodel & Mussen, 1953; Shaw, 1955), more typically laboratory experimentation tended to disregard personality variables. In McGrath and Altman's (1966) review of small-group research, for example, they reported that of some 250 studies reviewed, only 16 employed such measures as variables of study. Thus, in little more than a decade, the pendulum swung very much away from the leader as the star attraction.

Within the present era, characterized by a greater sensitivity to the social processes of interaction and exchange, it becomes clearer that the two research emphases represented by the trait and situational approaches afforded a far too glib view of reality. Indeed, in a true sense, neither approach ever represented its own philosophical underpinning very well, and each resulted in a caricature. The purpose here is to attempt a rectification of the distortion that these traditions represented, and to point up the increasing signs of movement toward a fuller analysis of leadership as a social influence process, and not as a fixed state of being.

AN OVERVIEW

By way of beginning, it seems useful to make a number of observations to serve as an overview. First, several general points which grow out of current research and thought on leadership are established. Thereafter, some of the directions in which these developments appear to be heading are indicated, as well as those areas which require further attention.

One overriding impression conveyed by surveying the literature of the 1960s, in contrast to the preceding two decades, is the redirection of interest in leadership toward processes such as power and authority relationships (e.g., Blau, 1964; Emerson, 1962; Janda, 1960; Raven, 1965). The tendency now is to attach far greater significance to the interrelationship between the leader, the followers, and the situation (see, e.g., Fielder, 1964, 1965, 1967; Hollander, 1964; Hollander & Julian, 1968; Steiner, 1964). In consequence, the problem of studying leadership and understanding these relationships is recognized as a more formidable one than was earlier supposed (cf. Cartwright & Zander, 1968). Several of the particulars which signalize this changing emphasis may be summarized under four points, as follows:

1. An early element of confusion in the study of *leadership* was the failure to distinguish it as a process from the *leader* as a person who occupies a central role in that process. Leadership constitutes an influence relationship between two, or usually more, persons who depend upon one another for the attainment of cer-

tain mutual goals within a group situation. This situation not only involves the task but also comprises the group's size, structure, resources, and history, among other variables.

(2). This relationship between leader and led is built *over time,* and involves an exchange or *transaction* between leaders and followers in which the leader both gives something and gets something. The leader provides a *resource* in terms of adequate role behavior directed toward the group's goal attainment, and in return receives greater influence associated with status, recognition, and esteem. These contribute to his "legitimacy" in making influence assertions, and in having them accepted.

3. There are differential tasks or functions attached to being a leader. While the image of the leader frequently follows Hemphill's (1961) view of one who "initiates structure," the leader is expected to function too as a mediator within the group, as a group spokesman outside it, and very often also as the decision maker who sets goals and priorities. Personality characteristics which may fit a person to be a leader are determined by the perceptions held by followers, in the sense of the particular role expectancies and satisfactions, rather than by the traits measured via personality scale scores.

4. Despite the persisting view that leadership traits do not generalize across situations, leader effectiveness can and should be studied as it bears on the group's achievement of desired outputs (see Katz & Kahn, 1966). An approach to the study of leader effectiveness as a feature of the group's success, in system terms, offers a clear alternative to the older concern with what the leader did do or did not do.

A richer, more interactive conception of leadership processes would entertain these considerations as points of departure for further study. Some evidence for a trend toward this development is considered in what follows.

WHITHER THE "SITUATIONAL APPROACH"?

What was the essential thrust of the situational approach, after all? Mainly, it was to recognize that the qualities of the leader were variously elicited, valued, and reacted to as a function of differential group settings and their demands. Hemphill (1949a) capped the point in saying "there are no absolute leaders, since successful leadership must always take into account the specific requirements imposed by the nature of the group which is to be led, requirements as diverse in nature and degree as are the organizations in which persons band together [p. 225]."

Though leadership events were seen as outcomes of a relationship that implicates the leader, the led, and their shared situation, studies conducted within the situational approach, usually left the *process* of leadership unattended. Much of the time, leaders were viewed in positional terms, with an emphasis on the outcome of their influence assertions. Comparatively little attention was directed to followers, especially in terms of the phenomenon of emergent leadership (cf.

Hollander, 1961). With a few exceptions, such as the work of McGregor (see 1966) and others (e.g., Slater & Bennis, 1964), the leader's maintenance of his position was emphasized at the expense of understanding the attainment of it through a process of influence.

But even more importantly, the situational view made it appear that the leader and the situation were quite separate. Though they may be separable for analytic purposes, they also impinge on one another in the perceptions of followers. Thus, the leader, from the follower's vantage point, is an element in the situation, and one who shapes it as well. As an active agent of influence he communicates to other group members by his words and his actions, implying demands which are reacted to in turn. In exercising influence, therefore, the leader may set the stage and create expectations regarding what he should do and what he will do. Rather than standing apart from the leader, the situation perceived to exist may be his creation.

It is now possible to see that the trait and situational approaches merely emphasize parts of a process which are by no means separable. One kind of melding of the trait and situational approaches, for example, is found in the work of Fiedler. His essential point, sustained by an extensive program of research (see 1958, 1964, 1965, 1967), is that the leader's effectiveness in the group depends upon the structural properties of the group and the situation, including interpersonal perceptions of both leader and led. He finds, for example, that the willingness of group members to be influenced by the leader is conditioned by leader characteristics, but that the quality and direction of this influence is contingent on the group relations and task structure (1967). This work will be discussed further in due course.

Another kind of evidence about the importance to group performance of the leader's construction of the situation is seen in recent research on conflict. Using a role-playing test situation involving four-person groups, Maier and Hoffman (1965) found that conflict is turned to productive or nonproductive ends, depending on the attitude of the discussion leader. Where the leader perceived conflict in terms of "problem subordinates," the quality of the decision reached in these discussion groups was distinctly inferior to that reached under circumstances in which the discussion leader perceived disagreements as the source for ideas and innovation. In those circumstances, innovative solutions increased markedly.

A leader, therefore, sets the basis for relationships within the group, and thereby can affect outcomes. As Hemphill (1961) suggested, the leader initiates structure. But more than just structure in a concrete sense, he affects the process which occurs within that structure. Along with other neglected aspects of process in the study of leadership is the goal-setting activity of the leader. Its importance appears considerable, though few studies give it attention. In one of these, involving discussion groups, Burke (1966) found that the leader's failure to provide goal orientations within the group led to antagonism, tension, and absenteeism. This effect was most acute when there was clear agreement within the group regarding who was to act as the leader. Though such expectations about the leader undoubtedly are pervasive in groups studied in research on leadership, they are noted only infrequently.

LEGITIMACY AND SOCIAL EXCHANGE IN LEADERSHIP

Among the more substantial features of the leader's role is his perceived legitimacy—how he attains it and sustains it. One way to understand the process by which the leader's role is legitimated is to view it as an exchange of rewards operating to signalize the acceptance of his position and influence.

In social exchange terms, the person in the role of leader who fulfills expectations and achieves group goals provides rewards for others which are reciprocated in the form of status, esteem, and heightened influence. Because leadership embodies a two-way influence relationship, recipients of influence assertions may respond by asserting influence in return, that is, by making demands on the leader. The very sustenance of the relationship depends upon some yielding to influence on both sides. As Homans (1961) put it, "Influence over others is purchased at the price of allowing one's self to be influenced by others [p. 286]." To be influential, authority depends upon esteem, he said. By granting esteem itself, or symbolic manifestations of it, one may in turn activate leadership, in terms of a person taking on the leader role.

The elicitation of leader behavior is now a demonstrable phenomenon in various experimental settings. In one definitive study conducted by Pepinsky, Hemphill, and Shevitz (1958), subjects who were low on leader activity were led to behave far more actively in that role by the group's evident support for their assertions. Alternatively, other subjects known to be high on leader activity earlier were affected in precisely the opposite way by the group's evident disagreement with their statements. In simplest terms, an exchange occurs between the group and the target person. The group provides reinforcement which in turn elicits favored behaviors. In other terms, the reinforcement of a person's influence assertions substantiates his position of authority.

Other, more recent, work suggested that even the use of lights as reinforcers exerts a significant effect on the target person's proportion of talking time as well as his perceived leadership status (Bavelas, Hastorf, Gross, & Kite, 1965; Zdep & Oakes, 1967). Thus, the lights not only produced a heightening of leader acts, but also created the impression of greater influence with the implication of legitimacy as well.

In a similar vein, Rudraswamy (1964) conducted a study in which some subjects within a group were led to believe they had higher status. Not only did they attempt significantly more leadership acts than others in their group, but they even outdistanced those subjects who were given more relevant information about the task itself.

It is also clear that agreement about who should lead has the effect in groups of increasing the probability of leader acts (e.g., Banta & Nelson, 1964). Relatedly, in a study of five-man groups involving changed as against unchanged leadership. Pryer, Flint, and Bass (1962) found that group effectiveness was enhanced by early agreement on who should lead.

When a basis is provided for legitimately making influence assertions, it is usually found that individuals will tend to act as leaders. This, of course, does not deny the existence of individual differences in the propensity for acting, once these conditions prevail. In a recent study by Gordon and Medland (1965), they found that positive peer ratings on leadership in army squads was consistently related to a measure of "aspiration to lead." Similarly, research findings on discussion groups (e.g., Riecken, 1958) indicated that the more vocal members obtain greater reinforcement, and hence experience the extension of legitimacy.

The "idiosyncrasy credit" concept (Hollander, 1958) suggests that a person's potential to be influential arises out of the positive dispositions others hold toward him. In simplest terms, competence in helping the group achieve its goals, and early conformity to its normative expectations for members, provide the potential for acting as a leader and being perceived as such. Then, assertions of influence which were not tolerated before are more likely to be acceptable. This concept applies in an especially important way to leadership succession, since it affords the basis for understanding how a new leader becomes legitimized in the perceptions of his peers. Further work on succession phenomena appears, in general, to be another area of fruitful study. There are many intriguing issues here, such as the question of the relative importance in legitimacy of factors such as "knowledge" and "office," in Max Weber's terms, which deserve further consideration (see, e.g., Evan & Zelditch, 1961).

THE PERCEPTION OF LEADERSHIP FUNCTIONS WITHIN GROUP STRUCTURE

A major deficiency in the older trait approach was its conception of "traits" within the framework of classic personality typologies. Personality measures were applied to leaders, often in profusion, without reference either to the varying nature of leadership roles or the functions they were to fulfill. As Mann's (1959) review revealed, such measures indeed do yield inconsistent relationships among leaders, variously defined. To take a common instance, dominance and extroversion are sometimes related positively to status as the leader, but mainly are neither related positively nor negatively to this status. On the other hand, Stogdill (1948) reported that such characteristics as "originality," "initiative," and "adaptability" have a low but positive relationship with leader status.

Granting that some essentially personality-type variables are more often found among those designated as leaders than among those designated as nonleaders, there can be no dismissing the widespread failure to treat the characteristics of the leader as they are perceived—and, what is more, as they are perceived *as relevant*—by other group members within a given setting. As Hunt (1965) and Secord and Backman (1961) pointed out, traits are viewed relative to the interpersonal context in which they occur. In short, followers hold expectations regarding what the leader ought to be doing here and now, and not absolutely.

One probable source for the disparate findings concerning qualities of the leader is the existence of differential expectations concerning the functions the leader is to perform. In simplest terms, there are various leadership roles. Without nearly exhausting the roster, it helps to realize that the leader in various time-space settings may be a task director, mediator, or spokesman, as well as a decision maker who, as Bavelas (1960) put it, "reduces uncertainty."

Whether in the laboratory or the field, studies of the perceptions of the leader's functions often have depended upon a sociometric approach (cf. Hollander, 1954). Thus, Clifford and Cohen (1964) used a sociometric device to study leadership roles in a summer camp, with 79 boys and girls, ranging in age from 8 to 13 years. Over a period of 4 weeks, they had nine elections by secret ballot asking the youngsters to indicate how the others would fit into various roles, including such things as planner, banquet chairman, swimming captain, and so forth. Their results indicated that the perceived attributes of campers were tied variously to their election for different leader roles. In line with the earlier point about the interpersonal context of leader traits, these researchers say, "the problem should be rephrased in terms of personality variables required in a leader role in a specific situation, which is in turn a function of the follower's perceptions [p. 64]."

Apart from personality traits, one prevailing expectation which does yield consistent findings across situations is that the leader's competence in a major group activity should be high. Dubno (1965), for example, reported that groups are more satisfied when leaders are demonstrably competent in a central function and do most of the work associated with that function. This is seen, too, in an experiment with five-man discussion groups, from which Marak (1964) found that the rewards associated with the leader's ability on a task led to greater perceived as well as actual influence. In general, the greater influence of a leader perceived to be more competent was verified experimentally by Dittes and Kelley (1956) and by Hollander (1960), among others.

Another leader attribute which evidently determines the responsiveness of followers is his perceived motivation regarding the group and its task. This was seen in Rosen, Levinger, and Lippitt's (1961) finding that helpfulness was rated as the most important characteristic leading to high influence potential among adolescent boys. In a more recent study of the role dimensions of leader-follower relations, Julian and Hollander (1966) found that, aside from the significance of task competence, the leader's "interest in group members" and "interest in group activity" were significantly related to group members' willingness to have a leader continue in that position. This accords with the finding of a field study by Nelson (1964) among 72 men who spent 12 months together in the Antarctic. While those men most liked as leaders had characteristics highly similar to those who were most liked as followers, Nelson reported that perceived motivation was the major factor which distinguished the two. Hollander (1958) considered this as one critical factor determining the leader's ability to retain status, even though nonconforming. In Nelson's study, the highly liked leaders were seen significantly more to be motivated highly toward the group in line with his hypothesis that "a critical expectation held of the leader, if he is to maintain esteem, is that he display strong motivations to belonging to the group [p. 165]."

A study by Kirkhart (1963) investigated group leadership among Negro college students as a function of their identification with their minority group. In terms of follower expectations, he found that those selected most frequently by their peers for leadership roles, in both the "internal system" and the "external system" activities of the group, scored higher on a questionnaire expressing Negro identification. This quality of being an examplar of salient group characteristics was noted long ago by Brown (1936) as a feature of leadership. Its relationship to processes of identification with the leader is discussed shortly.

SOURCE AND NATURE OF
LEADER AUTHORITY

The structural properties of groups affect the processes which occur within them. In leadership, the source of the leader's authority constitutes a significant element of structure. Yet, experimentation on leadership has given little attention to this variable, apart from some promising earlier work by Carter et al. (1951) with appointed and emergent leaders, and the previously mentioned work by Lewin and his associates on the style of the leader and its consequences to the group's social climate (Lewin et al., 1939; Preston & Heintz, 1949). More recently, Cohen and Bennis (1961) demonstrated that where groups could elect their leaders, the continuity of leadership was better maintained than where their leaders were appointed. In research on the productivity of groups, Goldman and Fraas (1965) found that differences occurred among four conditions of leader selection, including election and appointment.

With four-man discussion groups, Julian, Hollander, and Regula (1969) employed a multifactor design to study three variables: the source of a leader's authority, in either election or appointment; his competence, in terms of perceived capability on the task; and his subsequent task success. Their main dependent measure was the members' acceptance of the leader as a spokesman for the group. The findings of this experiment indicated that the latter two variables were significantly related to this acceptance, but that these relationships were differentially affected by whether the leader was appointed or elected. The shape of the three-way interaction suggested that election, rather than making the leader more secure, made him more vulnerable to censure if he were either initially perceived to be incompetent or subsequently failed to secure a successful outcome as spokesman for the group. While this finding alone does not sustain a generalization that the appointed leader necessarily is more firmly entrenched, it does support the conclusion that the leader's source of authority is perceived and reacted to as a relevant element in the leadership process.

Other work on a differentiation of the leader's role, through the social structure, was conducted by Anderson and Fiedler (1964). In their experiment with four-man discussion groups, half the groups had leaders who were told to serve as a "chairman" in a participatory way, and the other groups had leaders who were told to serve as an "officer in charge" in a supervisory way. They found that the nature of the leadership process was affected markedly by this distinction, thus paralleling the main findings of Preston and Heintz (1949). In general, the more participatory leaders were significantly more influential and made more of a contribution to the group's performance. But, more to the point, the relationship between leader attributes, such as intelligence and group performance, was significant for certain tasks under the participatory condition, though not for any of the tasks under the supervisory condition. The conclusion that Anderson and Fiedler reached, therefore, is that the characteristics of a leader, including intelligence and other personality attributes, become more salient and more highly relevant to group achievement under conditions of participation by the leader, as against circumstances where a highly formal role structure prevails.

EFFECTIVENESS OF THE LEADER

By now it is clear that an entire interpersonal system is implicated in answering the question of the leader's effectiveness. The leader is not effective merely by being influential, without regard to the processes at work and the ends achieved. Stressing this point, Selznick (1957) said that, "far more than the capacity to mobilize personal support . . . (or) the maintenance of equilibrium through the routine solution of everyday problems," the leader's function is "to define the ends of group existence, to design an enterprise distinctively adapted to these ends, and to see that the design becomes a living reality [p. 37]."

As Katz and Kahn (1966) observed, any group operates with a set of resources to produce certain outputs. Within this system, an interchange of inputs for outputs occurs, and this is facilitated by leadership functions which, among other things, direct the enterprise. The leader's contribution and its consequences vary with system demands, in terms of what Selznick referred to as "distinctive competence." Taken by itself, therefore, the typical conception of leadership as one person directing others can be misleading, as already indicated. Though the leader provides a valued resource, the group's resources provide the basis for functions fulfilled in the successful attainment of group goals, or, in other terms, group outputs.

Given the fact that a group must work within the set of available resources, its effectiveness is gauged in several ways. Stogdill (1959), for one, distinguished these in terms of the group's performance, integration, and member satisfaction as group outputs of a leadership process involving the use of the group's resources. Thus, the leader and his characteristics constitute a set of resources contributing to the effective utilization of other resources. A person who occupies the central role of leader has the task of contributing to this enterprise, within the circumstances broadly confronting the group.

One prominent exemplification of the system's demands and constraints on the leader's effectiveness is seen in Fiedler's "contingency model" (1964, 1965, 1967). He predicted varying levels of effectiveness for different *combinations* of leader and situational characteristics. Thus, depending upon the leader's orientation toward his co-workers, in the context of three situational variables—the quality of leader-member liking, the degree of task structure, and the position power of the leader—he finds distinct variations in this effectiveness.

In a recent test of his model, Fiedler (1966) conducted an experiment to compare the performance of 96 three-man groups that were culturally and linguistically homogeneous or heterogeneous. Some operated under powerful and other under weak leadership positions on three types of tasks varying in structure and requirements for verbal interaction. Despite the communication difficulties and different backgrounds, heterogeneous groups performed about as well on the nonverbal task as did the homogeneous group. Groups with petty officers as leaders (powerful) did about as well as the groups with recruits as leaders (weak). The main finding of the experiment was support for the hypothesis from the contingency model that the specific leadership orientation required for effectiveness is contingent on the favorableness of the group-task situation. Partial support for this hypothesis came also from a study by Shaw and Blum (1966) in which they manipulated some of the same variables with five-person groups, and with three tasks selected to vary along a dimension reflecting different levels of favorability for the leader. Their results indicated that the directive leader was more effective than the nondirective leader only when the group-task situation was highly favorable for the leader but not otherwise.

IDENTIFICATION WITH THE LEADER

For any leader, the factors of favorability and effectiveness depend upon the perceptions of followers. Their identification with him implicates significant psychological ties which may affect materially his ability to be influential. Yet the study of identification is passé in leadership research. Though there is a recurring theme in the literature of social science, harking back to Weber (see 1947), about the so-called "charismatic leader," this quality has a history of imprecise usage; furthermore, its tie with identification processes is by no means clear. Putting the study of the sources and consequences of identification with the leader on a stronger footing seems overdue and entirely feasible.

Several lines of work in social psychology appear to converge on identification processes. The distinction made by Kelman (1961) regarding identification, internalization, and compliance, for example, has obvious relevance to the relationship between the leader and his followers. This typology might be applied to the further investigation of leadership processes. The work of Sears (1960) and of Bandura and Walters (1963), concerning the identification of children with adult models, also has implications for such study.

One point which is clear, though the dynamics require far more attention, is that the followers' identification with their leader can provide them with social reality, in the sense of a shared outlook An illustration of this is seen in work on the social psychology of political leadership by Hollander (see 1963). In two phases, separated by an interval of 8 years, he studied Republicans in 1954 who had voted for President Eisenhower in 1952 and who would or would not vote for him again in 1954; and then in 1962, he studied Democrats who had voted for President Kennedy in 1960 and who would or would not vote for him again in 1962. He found that continuing loyalty to the President of one's party, among these respondents, was significantly associated with their views on issues and conditions and with their votes for the party in a midterm congressional-senatorial election. The defectors showed a significant shift in the precise opposite direction, both in their attitudes and in their voting behavior. In both periods, the ideology of loyalists was highly consistent with the leader's position. In the economic realm, for example, even where actual well-being varied considerably among loyalists, this identification with the President yielded highly similar attitudes regarding the favorability of the economic picture facing the nation.

With appropriate concern for rectifying the balance, there may be virtue in reopening for study Freud's (1922) contention that the leader of a group represents a common "ego ideal" in whom members share an identification and an ideology. Laboratory experimentation on groups offers little basis for studying such identification in light of the ephemeral, ad hoc basis for the creation of such groups. In fact, a disproportionate amount of our current knowledge about leadership in social psychology comes from experiments which are methodologically sophisticated but bear only a pale resemblance to the leadership enterprise that engages people in persisting relationships.

There also is the problem of accommodating the notion of identification within prevailing conceptions of leader-follower transactions and social exchange. But that is not an insurmountable difficulty with an expansion of the reward concept to include, for instance, the value of social reality. In any case, as investigators move increasingly from the laboratory to studies in more naturalistic settings, one of the significant qualities that may make a difference in leadership functioning is precisely this prospect for identification.

SOME CONCLUSIONS AND IMPLICATIONS

The present selective review and discussion touches upon a range of potential issues for the further study of leadership. The discussion is by no means exhaustive in providing details beyond noting suggestive developments. It is evident, however, that a new set of conceptions about leadership is beginning to emerge after a period of relative quiescence.

In providing a bridge to future research here, these newer, general ideas are underscored in a suggestive way. The methodologies they demand represent a challenge to imaginative skill, especially toward greater refinements in the conduct of field experiments and field studies which provide a look at the broader system of leadership relationships. Then, too, there is a need to consider the two-way nature of the influence process, with greater attention paid to the expectations of followers within the system. As reiterated here, the key to an understanding of leadership rests in seeing it as an influence process, involving an implicit exchange relationship over time.

No less important as a general point is the need for a greater recognition of the system represented by the group and its enterprise. This recognition provides a vehicle by which to surmount the misleading dichotomy of the leader and the situation which so long has prevailed. By adopting a systems approach, the leader, the led, and the situation defined broadly, are seen as interdependent inputs variously engaged toward the production of desired outputs.

Some release is needed from the highly static, positional view of leadership if we are to analyze its processes. A focus on leadership maintenance has weighted the balance against a more thorough probe of emerging leadership and succession phenomena. Investigators should be more aware of their choice and the differential implications, as between emerging and ongoing leadership. In this regard, the significance of the legitimacy of leadership, its sources, and effects requires greater attention in future investigations.

In studying the effectiveness of the leader, more emphasis should be placed on the outcomes for the total system, including the fulfillment of expectations held by followers. The long-standing overconcern with outcome, often stated only in terms of the leader's ability to influence, should yield to a richer conception of relationships geared to mutual goals. Not irrelevantly, the perception of the leader held by followers, including their identification with him, needs closer scrutiny. In this way, one may approach a recognition of stylistic elements allowing given persons to be effective leaders.

Finally, it seems plain that research on task-oriented groups must attend more to the organizational frameworks within which these groups are imbedded. Whether these frameworks are industrial, educational, governmental, or whatever, they are implicated in such crucial matters as goal-setting, legitimacy of authority, and leader succession. Though not always explicit, it is the organizational context which recruits and engages members in particular kinds of tasks, role relationships, and the rewards of participation. This context deserves more explicitness in attempts at understanding leadership processes.

REFERENCES

Anderson, L. R. and Fiedler, F. E. The effect of participatory and supervisory leadership on group creativity. *Journal of Applied Psychology,* 1964, **48,** 227–36.

Bandura, A. and Walters, R. H. *Social learning and personality development.* New York: Holt, Rinehart & Winston, 1963.

Banta, T. J., and Nelson, C. Experimental analysis of resource location in problem-solving groups. *Sociometry,* 1964, **27,** 488–501.

Bavelas, A. Leadership: Man and function. *Administrative Science Quarterly,* 1960, **4,** 491–98.

Bavelas, A., Hastorf, A. H., Gross, A. E., & Kite, W. R. Experiments on the alteration of group structure, *Journal of Experimental Social Psychology,* 1965, **1,** 55–70.

Berkowitz, L. Personality and group position. *Sociometry,* 1956, **19,** 210–22.

Blau, P. *Exchange and power in social life.* New York: Wiley, 1964.

Brown, J. F. *Psychology and the social order.* New York: McGraw-Hill, 1936.

Burke, P. J. Authority relations and descriptive behavior in small discussion groups. *Sociometry,* 1966, **29,** 237–50.

Carter, L. F., Haythorn, W., Meirowitz, B., and Lanzetta, J. The relation of categorizations and ratings in the observation of group behavior. *Human Relations,* 1951, **4,** 239–53.

Carter, L. F., and Nixon, M. An investigation of the relationship between four criteria of leadership ability for three different tasks. *Journal of Psychology,* 1949, **27,** 245–61.

Cartwright, D. C., and Zander, A. (eds.) *Group dynamics: Research and theory.* (3rd ed.) New York: Harper & Row, 1968.

Clifford, E., and Cohen, T. S. The relationship between leadership and personality attributes perceived by followers. *Journal of Social Psychology,* 1964, **64,** 57–64.

Cohen, A. M., and Bennis, W. G. Continuity of leadership in communication networks. *Human Relations,* 1961, **14,** 351–67.

Dittes, J. E., and Kelley, H. H. Effects of different conditions of acceptance upon conformity to group norms. *Journal of Abnormal and Social Psychology,* 1956, **53,** 100–7.

Dubno, P. Leadership, group effectiveness, and speed of decision. *Journal of Social Psychology,* 1965, **65,** 351–60.

Emerson, R. M. Power-dependence relations. *American Sociological Review,* 1962, **27,** 31–41.

Evan, W. M., and Zelditch, M. A laboratory experiment on bureaucratic authority. *American Sociological Review,* **26,** 883–93.

Fiedler, F. E. *Leader attitudes and group effectiveness.* Urbana: University of Illinois Press, 1958.

Fiedler, F. E. A contingency model of leadership effectiveness. In L. Berkowitz (ed.), *Advances in experimental social psychology.* Vol. 1. New York: Academic Press, 1964.

Fiedler, F. E. The contingency model: A theory of leadership effectiveness. In H. Proshansky & B. Seidenberg (eds.), *Basic studies in social psychology.* New York: Holt, Rinehart & Winston, 1965.

Fiedler, F. E. The effect of leadership and cultural heterogeneity on group performance: A test of a contingency model. *Journal of Experimental Social Psychology,* 1966, **2,** 237–64.

Fiedler, F. E. *A theory of leadership effectiveness.* New York: McGraw-Hill, 1967.

Freud, S. *Group psychology and the analysis of the ego.* London and Vienna: International Psychonalytic Press, 1922.

Gibb, C. A. The principles and traits of leadership. *Journal of Abnormal and Social Psychology,* 1947, **42,** 267–84.

Goldman, M., and Frass, L. A. The effects of leader selection on group performance. *Sociometry,* 1965, **28,** 82–88.

Gordon, L. V., and Medland, F. F. Leadership aspiration and leadership ability. *Psychological Reports,* 1965, **17,** 388–90.

Gouldner, A. W. (ed.) *Studies in leadership.* New York: Harper, 1950.

Haythorn, W., Couch, A., Haifner, D., Langham, P., and Carter, L. F. The effects of varying combinations of authoritarian and equalitarian leaders and followers. *Journal of abnormal and Social Psychology,* 1956, **53,** 210–19.

Hemphill, J. K. The leader and his group. *Educational Research Bulletin,* 1949, **28,** 225–29, 245–46 (a)

Hemphill, J. K. *Situational factors in leadership.* Columbus: Ohio State University, Bureau of Educational Research, 1949. (b)

Hemphill, J. K. Why people attempt to lead. In L. Petrullo and B. M. Bass (eds.), *Leadership and interpersonal behavior,* New York: Holt, Rinehart & Winston, 1961.

Hollander, E. P. Authoritarianism and leadership choice in a military setting. *Journal of Abnormal and Social Psychology,* 1954, **49,** 365–70.

Hollander, E. P. Conformity, status, and idiosyncrasy credit. *Psychological Review,* 1958, **65,** 117–27.

Hollander, E. P. Competence and conformity in the acceptance of influence. *Journal of Abnormal and Social Psychology,* 1960, **61,** 365–69.

Hollander, E. P. Emergent leadership and social influence. In L. Petrullo & B. M. Bass (eds.), *Leadership and interpersonal behavior.* New York: Holt, Rinehart & Winston, 1961.

Hollander, E. P. The "pull" of international issues in the 1962 election. In S. B. Withey (Chm.), Voter attitudes and the war-peace issue. Symposium presented at the American Psychological Association Philadelphia, August, 1963.

Hollander, E. P. *Leaders, groups, and influence.* New York: Oxford University Press, 1964.

Hollander, E. P., and Julian, J. W. Leadership. In E. F. Borgatta and W. W. Lambert (eds.), *Handbook of personality theory and research.* Chicago: Rand McNally, 1968.

Homans, G. C. *Social Behavior: Its elementary forms.* New York: Harcourt, Brace & World, 1961.

Hunt, J. McV. Traditional personality theory in the light of recent evidence. *American Scientist,* 1965, **53,** 80–96.

Janda, K. F. Towards the explication of the concept of leadership in terms of the concept of power. *Human Relations,* 1960, **13,** 345–63.

Jennings, H. H. *Leadership and isolation.* New York: Longmans, 1943.

Julian, J. W., and Hollander, E. P. A study of some role dimensions of leader-follower relations. Technical Report No. 3, April 1966, State University of New York at Buffalo, Department of Psychology, Contract 4679, Office of Naval Research.

Julian, J. W., Hollander, E. P., and Regula, C. R. Endorsement of the group spokesman as a function of his source of authority, competence, and success. *Journal of Personality and Social Psychology,* 1969, **11,** 42–49.

Katz, D., and Kahn, R. *The social psychology of organizations,* New York: Wiley, 1966.

Kelman, H. C. Processes of opinion change. *Public Opinion Quarterly,* 1961, **25,** 57–78.

Kirkhart, R. O. Minority group identification and group leadership. *Journal of Social Psychology,* 1963, **59,** 111–17.

Lewin, K., Lippitt, R., and White, R. K. Patterns of aggressive behavior in experimentally created "social climates," *Journal of Social Psychology,* 1939, **10,** 271–99.

Maier, N. R., and Hoffman, L. R. Acceptance and quality of solutions as related to leader's attitudes toward disagreement in group problem solving. *Journal of Applied Behavioral Science,* 1965, **1,** 373–86.

Mann, R. D. A review of the relationships between personality and performance in small groups. *Psychological Bulletin,* 1959, **56,** 241–70.

Marak, G. E. The evolution of leadership structure. *Sociometry,* 1964, **27,** 174–82.

McGrath, J. E., and Altman. I. *Small group research: A critique and synthesis of the field.* New York: Holt, Rinehart & Winston, 1966.

McGregor, E. *The human side of enterprise.* New York: McGraw-Hill, 1960.

McGregor, D. *Leadership and motivation.* (Essays edited by W. G. Bennis & E. H. Schein) Cambridge, Mass.: M.I.T. Press, 1966.

Nelson, P. D. Similarities and differences among leaders and followers. *Journal of Social Psychology,* 1964, **63,** 161–67.

Pepinsky, P. N., Hemphill, J. K., and Shevitz, R. N. Attempts to lead, group productivity, and morale under conditions of acceptance and rejection. *Journal of Abnormal and Social Psychology.* 1958, **57,** 47–54.

Preston, M. G., and Heintz, R. K. Effects of participatory versus supervisory leadership on group judgment. *Journal of Abnormal and Social Psychology,* 1949, **44,** 345–55.

Pryer, M. W., Flint, A. W., and Bass, B. M. Group effectiveness and consistency of leadership. *Sociometry,* 1962, **25,** 391–97.

Raven, B. Social influence and power. In I. D. Steiner & M. Fishbein (eds.), *Current studies in social psychology.* New York: Holt, Rinehart & Winston, 1965.

Riecken, H. W. The effect of talkativeness on ability to influence group solutions to problems. *Sociometry,* 1958, **21,** 309–21.

Rosen, S., Levinger, G., and Lippitt, R. Perceived sources of social power. *Journal of Abnormal and Social Psychology,* 1961, **62,** 439–41.

Rudraswamy, V. An investigation of the relationship between perceptions of status and leadership attempts. *Journal of the Indian Academy of Applied Psychology,* 1964, **1,** 12–19.

Scodel, A., and Mussen, P. Social perception of authoritarians and nonauthoritarians. *Journal of Abnormal and Social Psychology,* 1953, **48,** 181–84.

Sears, R. R. The 1958 summer research project on identification. *Journal of Nursery Education,* 1960, **16,** (2).

Secord, P. F., and Backman, C. W. Personality theory and the problem of stability and change in individual behavior: An interpersonal approach. *Psychological Review,* 1961, **68,** 21–33.

Selznick, P. *Leadership in administration.* Evanston: Row, Peterson, 1957.

Shaw, M. E. A comparison to two types of leadership in various communication nets. *Journal of Abnormal and Social Psychology,* 1955, **50,** 127–34.

Shaw, M. E., and Blum, J. M. Effects of leadership style upon group performance as a function of task structure. *Journal of Personality and Social Psychology,* 1966, **3,** 238–42.

Slater, P. E., and Bennis, W. G. Democracy is inevitable. *Harvard Business Review,* 1964, **42,** (2), 51–59.

Steiner, I. Group dynamics. *Annual review of psychology,* 1964, **15,** 421–46.

Stogdill, R. M. Personal factors associated with leadership: A survey of the literature. *Journal of Psychology,* 1948, **25,** 35–71.

Stogdill, R. M. *Individual behavior and group achievement,* New York: Oxford University Press, 1959.

Weber, M. *The theory of social and economic organization.* (Trans. and ed. by T. Parsons & A. M. Henderson.) New York: Oxford University Press, 1947.

Zdep, S. M., and Oakes, W. I. Reinforcement of leadership behavior in group discussion. *Journal of Experimental Psychology,* 1967, **3,** 310–20.

The Supervisor as "Motivator": His Influence on Employee Performance and Satisfaction

Edwin A. Locke[1]

It is widely recognized that supervisors can influence the "motivation" of their subordinates. However, the precise nature and mechanism of this influence (and its limitations) have not been clearly identified in the literature.

There are two interrelated aspects of motivation that must be considered in this context: satisfaction with the job (and supervisor) and work performance. Let us first consider how a supervisor can influence employee satisfaction.

The Supervisor and Satisfaction

An individual's degree of satisfaction with his job reflects the degree to which he believes (explicitly or implicitly) that it fulfills or allows the fulfillment of his job values. (Locke, 1969). It follows that a supervisor can influence employee satisfaction by facilitating or blocking subordinate value attainment. There are two broad categories of job values over which a supervisor may have some control.[2]

(1) Task Values Individuals have different degrees of intrinsic interest in different task activities. If a supervisor has any options with respect to task assignment, he can facilitate satisfaction by assigning workers tasks which they enjoy doing. Within limits he may even allow or promote restructuring of the job to increase its interest to the worker.

Furthermore, most employees have implicit or explicit performance goals in their work, (quantity, quality, time limits, deadlines, quotas, budgets, etc.) Work goal achievement has been found repeatedly to be a major source satisfaction on the job. (Friedlander, 1964; Herzberg, 1966; Hoppock, 1935; Wernimont, 1966). A supervisor can either help or hinder his subordinates in the pursuit of their work goals and will affect their satisfaction accordingly.

A study by Hahn of several hundred Air Force officers found that when actions of superiors were judged to be responsible for causing a "good day on the job" these actions entailed work goal facilitation 33% of the time. When the actions of superiors were seen as causing a "bad day on the job," it was percieved to be caused by work goal blockage or hinderance 56% of the time.[3]

From B. M. Bass, R. Cooper, & J. A. Haas (Eds.), *Managing for accomplishment*, p. 57– 67. Copyright 1970 by Lexington Books, D. C. Heath and Company. Reprinted by permission.

[1]Preparation of this paper was facilitated by Grant No. 10542 from the American Institutes for Research.

[2]These categories are discussed in more detail in Locke, (1970).

[3]These percentages were computed from unpublished data supplied by Clifford P. Hahn of the American Institutes for Research.

There is a crucial respect in which a supervisor has more *potential* for causing employee dissatisfaction than for causing satisfaction, as implied by the above data. A supervisor can help an employee attain his work goals but he cannot attain them for him. The subordinate himself must be at least *one* of the agents responsible for the accomplishment of his own work. However, the converse is not necessarily true. A supervisor can hinder or prevent goal attainment regardless of the actions of his subordinates—such as by refusing to give him the permission, or time, or facilities, money, helpers, authority etc. needed to achieve them.

Similarly a supervisor can allow a subordinate to work on tasks which the subordinate finds intrinsically interesting but he cannot create interests himself. However, a supervisor can prevent an employee from working on tasks which interest him without the latter's consent or participation.

The above should not be taken as supporting Herzberg's (1966) theory of motivation as it now stands. Herzberg claims that supervision can cause only dissatisfaction with the job whereas task factors such as achievement can only cause satisfaction. Herzberg's supporting data, however, are virtually meaningless since his classification system confuses *events* (what happened) with *agents* (who made it happen). When incidents reported as causing satisfaction and dissatisfaction on the job are classified separately as to agent and event, it is found that the *same class of events* (namely, task-related events, such as achievement and failure) are seen as the main cause of *both* satisfaction and dissatisfaction, but that *different agents* are judged to be predominantly responsible for these events. The self is typically given credit for good day events (successes) while others (supervisors) are usually blamed for bad day events (failures). It must be added that the latter relationship is only statistical. Some individuals do blame themselves for failures and give others (partial) credit for their successes.[4] Furthermore defensiveness could lead them to underestimate their actual degree of responsibility for failures.

(2) Non-Task Values A supervisor also administers rewards and punishments for performance, both directly and indirectly. He has direct control, for example, over the giving of praise and recognition for a job well done and of criticism for a poor job. By recommending or criticizing an employee to his own superiors, a supervisor can indirectly affect a subordinate's chances for raises and promotions.

Employees value supervisors who have influence in the organization (Mann and Hoffman, 1960; Pelz, 1952). Influence is what enables a supervisor to gain values for his subordinates from the organization, e.g., raises, promotions, time off, good equipment, better working conditions, etc.

---

[4]Much of this data has been gathered and analyzed by Joseph Schneider of the University of Maryland in partial fulfillment of his Master's degree. The unpublished data of Hahn, some of which were referred to above, yielded similar results.

Rosen (1969) found that two of the characteristics which best differentiated between the most and least-liked foremen in a furniture factory were the ability to "get things for his men" and to "organize the work." Since these workers were on a piece-rate incentive, there is little doubt that money was one thing a good foreman could help his men to get, especially if he knew how to organize the work.

There is an interconnection between task and non-task values in that the former can be a means to attaining the latter. By helping his subordinates attain high production, solve problems, and do competent work, a supervisor can help them make high earnings and gain promotions.

If an employee sees his supervisor as instrumental in gaining him important job values, he will not only like the job he will like the supervisor as well. Employees also like supervisors who are "pleasant," "considerate" and "friendly" (Mann and Hoffman, 1960; Rosen, 1969; Vroom, 1964). At first glance these traits might seem to be completely unrelated to the idea of functional utility; but a closer look suggests otherwise. A supervisor may be described as unpleasant and inconsiderate because in the past he has blocked value attainment by subordinates or because he projects the kind of personality that *would* do so if given the chance. An unfriendly supervisor is typically one who does not acknowledge or reward work or who unjustly condemns or punishes marginal work or who looks as though he might do these things.

Individuals also like people who are like themselves, with whom they have important traits in common. This too can be interpreted (partly) in functional terms. A supervisor who values the same things as his subordinates, for example, is more likely to be of benefit to them than one whose values are opposite to theirs.

The functional (utility) implications of being pleasant or having values similar in one's subordinates do not exhaust the reasons a supervisor could be liked. Individuals may value each other not only as a means to an end but as ends in themselves. The value in such a case is associated with the person rather than in what he can do for you. One can respond to a supervisor *qua* individual as well as *qua* supervisor.

A discussion of the reasons individuals value those who respond to them as persons is beyond the scope of this paper.[5] Suffice it to say that this principle is probably less crucial to an understanding of supervisor-subordinate relationships than is the principle of functional utility.

The Supervisor and Performance

A subordinate who likes his supervisor will desire to approach (interact with) him, to seek or take his advice, and/or (within limits) to do favors for him. There is nothing inherent in the fact of liking a supervisor, however, that necessarily leads to high production.

---

[5]The basic psychological principle involved here was first discussed to the author's knowledge, in N. Branden's "Self-esteem and Romantic Love," *The Objectivist*, 1967, VI, No. 12, 1–8.

A subordinate who dislikes his supervisor will want to avoid him, or persuade him to change his ways, or file a grievance against him or refuse to do favors for him or possibly to quit the job altogether. There is nothing inherent in fact of disliking, however, that necessitates low production, although such a reaction is possible (if the employee sees it as an appropriate means of "getting even" with the supervisor and thinks he can get away with it).

In short there is no causal connection—divorced from the individual's other values, his beliefs and expectations and his understanding of the total job— between satisfaction with the job or supervisor and productivity (for a detailed theoretical discussion of this issue, see Locke, 1969b).

I have argued previously (Locke, 1970) that the most direct motivational determinant of an individual's performance on the job is his specific performance goal or intention (Locke, Carteledge and Knerr, 1970). Let us now discuss the relationship between goals and performance.

Goal Content and Performance

Goals and values have two major attributes: content and intensity (Rand, 1966). The attribute of content pertains to the *what,* to the nature of the activity or end sought. The attribute of intensity pertains to the *how much,* to the importance of the goal or value in the individual's value hierarchy.

The effects of goal content are most fundamentally directive in nature. This is true with respect to both mental and physical action. If a (normal) individual's purpose is to think about how he will spend his next pay check, he will think of that topic rather than about something else. A man whose goal is to walk across the street will walk there rather than to another location.

This is not to claim that all goals led to the activity or end specified by the goal. To attain a desired goal successfully an individual must possess sufficient ability and mental health and be given sufficient opportunity. Goal attainment may be prevented by lack of knowledge, capacity or determination on his part, or by external interference. Furthermore, goal conflicts may render efficacious action and efficacious thinking impossible.

Even when action is abortive or unsuccessful, it is typically set in motion and guided by some goal or intention. For example, a person who accidentally hits a shot out of bounds in tennis still intended to hit the ball, even if it did not go where he wanted it to go. Further, the degree of discrepancy between the place he intended to hit the ball and the place he did hit it might be only a matter of inches.

If an individual's goal is long range, or difficult, or complex, he may have to establish a series of *subgoals* and develop a coordinated *plan of action* in order to reach it. The *means* by which a goal can be attained may not be known initially and may have to be discovered. For this reason goals may indirectly stimulate creativity and the seeking of new knowledge. This was illustrated in a study done at General Electric by Stedry and Kay (1964; see also a study by Chaney, 1969). A group of foremen were assigned quantitative production goals with respect to both quantity and quality. Some of these who were assigned difficult goals, rather than simply exhorting their subordinates to work harder, made an effort to discover the causes of and to eliminate unproductive time. The latter procedure generally led to greater performance improvement than the former. A laboratory study by Eagle and Leiter (1964) found that individuals who had an intention to memorize certain materials did so more effectively if they developed a specific learning plan than if they simple "tried" to learn the material.

The pursuit of any goal requires action, whether it be mental or physical, and action requires effort. A second function of goal content, with is necessarily entailed in the directive function, is the *regulation of energy expenditure.* Different goals require different amounts of effort. More energy is required to run the marathon than to walk across the room; more mental concentration is needed to write a book than to write one's name. Typically, a person mobilizes an amount of energy that is appropriate to the perceived difficulty of the goal sought. For instance, Bryan and Locke (1967) found that when people are given different amounts of time to complete the same task, those given the shorter time limits worked faster than those given longer time limits. These authors noted that:

> Because the phenomenon [of adjusting effort level to the perceived difficulty of the task] is so much a part of our everyday life, it is often taken for granted and we do not always think about it consciously. But it can become particularly salient when errors of . . . [judgment] occur. For example, if a weight lifter's weights are secretly replaced by wooden blocks painted to resemble the real weights, he will be likely to jerk [them] right through the ceiling [on his first try] . . . (Bryan and Locke, 1967, p. 259)

Goal importance may also influence direction and level of effort by affecting the individual's degree of commitment to his goal. The greater a man's commitment, the longer he should persist at a task in the face of failure, fatigue and stress.

Most studies of the effect of goals have focused on the relationship of goal content to performance on simple laboratory tasks. (See Locke, 1968a for a review.) In these tasks performance could be influenced relatively directly by effort or choice; the acquisition of new knowledge and long range planning were not required. Two categories of studies have stressed the directing function of goals, while two other categories have stressed the energizing as well as the directing effects of goal content. Studies representative of each category are described below:

(1) Intentions and Response Selection　　In these studies, typified by the work of Dulany (1962, 1968) and Holmes (1967), subjects had to select (on each trial) one of a number of possible verbal responses and were "rewarded" or "punished" according to their choices. It was found that the individual's intentions with respect to responses were correlated as high as .94 with his actual responses, regardless of the "reinforcements" given for performance.

(2) Intentions and Task Choice　　In another group of studies subjects could choose, on each trial, the difficulty of the task they would work on and were offered various monetary incentives for succeeding at their chosen task. Correlations in the .70's and .80's were typically found between intentions with respect to future choices and actual choice distributions regardless of incentive condition. (Locke, Bryan and Kendall, 1968)

(3) Qualitatively Different Goals and Performance   Two types of studies fall into this category. In one, all subjects worked on the same task but tried to minimize or maximize their scores on different performance dimensions on different trials. The interest was in whether subjects could modify their scores on the various dimensions as intended. Locke and Bryan (1969a) found that subjects could lower their scores on two dimensions of automobile driving performance as intended 100% of the time. They also found that subjects committed fewer errors on an addition task when trying to minimize errors than when trying to maximize the number of problems correct.

In the second subcategory of studies only one performance dimension was involved (number of correct answers). Individuals trying to do "as well as possible" on a task were compared to those trying to reach difficult, quantitative goals. Subjects trying for the latter type of goal typically outperformed subjects trying for the former. (Locke, 1968a; Mace, 1935) One effect of trying for specific hard goals is to prevent performance from dropping below one's previous best level more often than is the case with the abstract goal of "do your best." (Locke and Bryan, 1966)

(4) Goal Level and Performance Level (Output)   Most studies of the effects of goals have focused on the relationship between the individual's level of aspiration (quantitative goal level) and his performance level on a task. A consistent finding has been that high, difficult goals lead to a higher level of performance than moderate or easy goals. The evidence thus far suggests that, provided the individual has the requisite ability, there is a positive, linear relationship between goal level and performance level. (Locke, 1968a) No claim is made that this linear relationship would hold across all possible levels of goal difficulty; some goals are obviously impossible to reach.

Let us now summarize the findings with respect to goals and performance. The results indicate than on simple repetitive tasks goals usually lead to the behavior specified by the goal, or else to outcomes correlated with the intended goal. Goals guide performance by determining the direction or content of mental and/or physical action; as a result they energize action by leading the individual to mobilize the effort necessary to attain the goal.

It should be stressed that the above findings presuppose that the individual has really *accepted* (is actually committed to) the goal(s) in question. This issue will be discussed further below.

Considerable research evidence indicates that the effects of external incentives on action depend on the goal and intentions individuals set in response to them. For it has been found in a number of laboratory studies that: (a) when incentives do affect behavior, they also affect goals and intentions; (b) when differential goal-setting is controlled or partialled out, there is no relationship of incentive condition to choice behavior or to level of performance; and (c) partialling out or controlling incentive differences does not vitiate the relationship between goals and performance.

These findings are most well documented with respect to three external incentives: *money* (Locke, Bryan and Kendall, 1968); *feedback* regarding overall task performance ("knowledge of results," Locke, 1967, 1968b; Locke and Bryan, 1968, 1969b; Locke, Cartledge and Koeppel, 1968); and so-called *verbal reinforcement*" (Dulany, 1962, 1968; Holmes, 1967). There is some documentation with respect to three other incentives: *instructions* (Eagle, 1967; Locke, et al., 1968); *time limits* (Bryan and Locke, 1967); and *participation* (Locke, 1968a; Meyer, Kay and French, 1965). Experimental evidence is still lacking for incentives such as competition, and praise and reproof. (See Locke, 1968a, for a theoretical analysis of these incentives.)

Goal Commitment and Performance

Very few studies have explored either the determinants or the affects of goal commitment. Theoretically, strength of goal commitment should be a function of the importance of the goal in the individual's value hierarchy. The importance of goal attainment should be a function of the importance of success and efficacy as ends in themselves and of the importance of the other values to which goal attainment leads (money, promotion) and/or of the disvalues which it avoids (lack of money, being fired, losing a promotion, etc.).

One procedure that may promote goal commitment is *participation* in the goal-setting process. A possible explanation for this is that making an overt agreement to strive for or attain a certain goal engages a value not previously engaged. It implies an overt test of one's *integrity:* (loyalty to one's stated values in action). Participation may also allow subordinates to choose tasks or methods of work which interest and challenge them to a greater extent than would be the case if supervisors made assignments on their own.

How the Supervisor Influences Goal-Setting

The implication of the above is that in order for a supervisor to influence the job performance of his subordinates, he must implicitly or explicitly influence the goals they set and/or their commitment to them. There are at least four ways he can try to do this, differing in degree of directness:

(1) Instructions   The simplest and most direct method is to tell the subordinate what is expected of him on the job, not only with respect to the content of the work but also with respect to the speed or proficiency level desired.

The effect of instructions on performance will depend upon their content and upon whether or not the employee *accepts* them. When goals assigned by a supervisor (or experimenter) are judged to be unreasonable or impossible, they may be rejected by the individual and easier ones (overtly or covertly) substituted in their place. (See Stedry, 1960; Stedry and Kay, 1964.) Or barring this, the individual may leave the situation (e.g., job) altogether.

Whether or not an employee accepts an assigned goal will depend upon other factors as well: whether he believes the demands to be morally legitimate; whether he sees them as just in the context of his ability and the nature of the job; whether the goal is congruent with his personal preferences; his desire to help or hurt the supervisor; the anticipated outcomes of compliance and noncompliance; the amount of "pressure" exerted, etc.

A study at General Electric by Miller (1965) found that direct instructions to production workers to improve the quality of their work sometimes resulted in an initial improvement in performance; but this improvement was not maintained unless it was made clear that punishments (loss of income) would be administered for noncompliance with this request. In other words, the instructions had to be backed up by (the threat of) sanctions for them to be effective.

(2) Participation   Rather than assigning goals to employees a supervisor may let his subordinates participate in the goal-setting process. It was mentioned earlier that such a procedure can enhance goal commitment by engaging the employee's integrity and his personal interests.

It must be stressed, however, that simply using the *method* of participation does not guarantee either increased job satisfaction or higher productivity as is often implied by advocates of the "human relations" approach to motivation. Its outcome will depend on such factors as: (a) the particular values of the employees (whether they want to participate); (b) the nature of the job (size of work group; need for rapid decisions); and (c) the content of the participation sessions. (The first factor is discussed in Vroom, 1964.)

With respect to the last point, a close examination of several experimental studies of participation by Locke (1968a) revealed that employees in the "participation" conditions were typically urged to aim for higher production goals than they had previously whereas employees in the "control" conditions received no such request. In other studies, supervisors of participation groups were given special training designed to correct their weaknesses and deficiencies. (Chaney, 1969) In a recent field study Meyer, Kay and French (1965) found that the goals employees set (or failed to set) during conferences with their supervisors had far more influence on subsequent performance than participation as such.

(3) Rewards and Punishments   Money is the most widely used incentive in industry. Not only is it an incentive to take a job or to switch jobs, it may be an incentive to perform competently on the job. The effectiveness of money in motivating effective performance will depend on such things as: (a) how the incentive system is structured; (b) what the employee believes it is given (or withheld) for; and (c) the degree to which he values money (in comparison to other rewards).

Many years ago F. W. Taylor (1911) argued that ordinary piece-rate incentives were not optimal for increasing production because workers often failed to set their output goals as high as they were capable of achieving. A key element of Taylor's Scientific Management system was to assign workers specific (and high) production quotas and to make monetary bonuses (and remaining on the job) contingent upon their attaining these quotas. Locke et al. (1968) found this method to produce higher output than offering piece-rate incentives alone in some recent laboratory studies.

Other studies have shown that the effectiveness of monetary incentives depends upon the degree to which workers believe that high effort and high performance will "pay-off" in higher earnings and on the degree to which they value money (Georgopoulos, Mahoney and Jones, 1957; Porter and Lawler, 1968). Dalton (in Whyte, 1955) found that incentive pay was not very effective for workers who valued the approval of their coworkers (which was contingent upon moderate to low production) more than maximizing earnings.

Praise and criticism are also commonly used incentives, but their effects on subsequent performance are from from simple. (See the review article by Kennedy and Willcutt, 1964.) A crucial determinant of the effect of praise is the subordinate's interpretation of what it *means*. If he interprets it to mean that his performance is adequate and he sees no other values to be gained by increasing production, it may be an incentive to maintain his present level of production. If the employee understands it to mean that if he keeps up the good work, he may be promoted, and he values promotion, it may encourage him to work even harder. If praise is seen as being insincere or manipulative in its intent, it may have no effect at all (or a negative effect) on performance.

The effects of criticism on subsequent performance also depend upon how the employee interprets it. For example, an individual may deliberately refrain from performance improvement after being criticized because it would be an implicit admission that the criticism was justified—which admission would threaten his self-esteem. Meyer, Kay and French (1965) found criticism by supervisors to inhibit subsequent performance improvement by subordinates because it produced defensiveness rather than constructive goal-setting.

Even if a man believed criticism to be justified (in the sense that performance was not up to the minimum requirements of the job), he would become apathetic if he believed that further improvement was totally impossible. Many individuals have implicit deterministic premises (to the effect that certain abilities are impossible to acquire or that certain things are not open to their understanding or that certain personality traits or emotional reactions are beyond their control). Such premises can severely undercut a man's motivation to persist in the face of difficulty and failure.

Under certain conditions, criticism will spur a man on to greater efforts. The necessary conditions for such an effect are not yet known but they would no doubt include: (a) the individual's belief that his performance was, in fact, inadequate; (b) his conviction that he can do better; and (c) his desire to improve.

(4) Setting an Example   Some results reported by Cooper[6] suggest a rela-

[6]R. Cooper, "Task-oriented Leadership and Subordinate Response," in B. M. Bass, R. Cooper, & J. A. Haas (Eds.) *Managing for accomplishment.* Lexington, Mass.: Heath-Lexington, 1970.

tively indirect way that supervisors may influence subordinate goals. He found positive correlations between the degree to which supervisors were rated by their superiors as "task oriented" and high work quality and low absence on the part of subordinates. Although several interpretations of these correlations are possible, the one suggested by Cooper is that employees implicitly adopted (some of) the work attitudes and standards of their supervisors.

It is not difficult to imagine how this might happen. A supervisor who comes late, who is frequently absent, who takes numerous coffee breaks, who is careless in his work and unconcerned with its outcome could not help but convey to a subordinate that the work is not very important, that he does not value it, and that low standards of performance are acceptable. (The employee may adopt such standards without any explicit purpose to do so, in the same way that a student may absorb or adopt the values of his teachers.)

Similarly, a supervisor who loves his job, who sets himself high standards and works to achieve them, who creates an atmosphere of dedication to hard work and high standards may help instill similar attitudes in his subordinates.

Satisfaction with Supervision and Productivity

The foregoing discussion indicated that high production (ability and knowledge being equal) was the result of setting high or hard work goals. It follows that the supervisor with high producing subordinates (ability being equal) will be the one whose subordinates set and attain high goals.

A supervisor may try to achieve high production by direct instructions backed up by threats of punishment. If employees see no short-run alternative to accepting hard goals, high production may result. But such high production would be accompanied by low satisfaction with the job and with supervision to the degree that: (a) employees fail to achieve fully their hard goals or goal attainment fails to gain them just extrinsic rewards; (b) supervisors interfere with their task performance, and/or (c) the supervisors' pressures are perceived as excessive and/or illegitimate. In the long run, of course, such actions as the above may lead to increased absences, grievances and turnover, depending on the workers' other values and the job market. (Locke, (1970)

Alternatively, a supervisor could offer positive incentives (monetary bonuses, recognition, increased responsibility) to employees who reached (or approached) high work goals, If high goals were set as a result, high production could occur. To the extent that the supervisor was perceived as helping his subordinates to achieve these goals and as giving just rewards for success, he would be liked. In this case, production and satisfaction with supervision would both be high.

An individual could also set high work goals on his own and not interact with his supervisor at all. If the person preferred to be left alone, high production would be accompanied by indifference toward the supervisor.

Many other patterns are possible. A supervisor might reward his subordinates for low production. If they actually set low goals as a result and personally valued low productivity, high satisfaction with supervision would accompany low production. Or, if a supervisor prevented his employees from achieving their work goals through interference and harassment, and then penalized them for their failure, low satisfaction and low production would result.

To repeat, there is no direct causal relationship between satisfaction with supervision (on the job) and productivity. The two effects are the results of different causes. Production level, to the degree that it is affected by motivation, depends (in the short run) upon the production goal the individual is actually trying for, *regardless of how or why he chose that goal* (The reasons why an employee has a particular goal, of course, have long range implications, since these factors determine how susceptible the goal is to change and under what conditions). Satisfaction with supervision depends (in the short run) upon the degree to which the supervisor is perceived as achieving or helping the employee to achieve his work and other goals *regardless of the particular content (level) of these goals.*[7]

Satisfaction is an outcome of action and an incentive to further action; thus it fulfills a crucial motivational function. But a man's emotional reactions do not determine the content of his values, or his goals, or his knowledge, or his thinking. (Locke, 1970)

Conclusion

A supervisor can contribute in important ways to an individual's job satisfaction and his motivation to produce. But there is a fundamental respect in which he cannot "motivate" an employee. To perform adequately on a job, an individual must choose to pursue values; he must gain the knowledge needed to perform the work; he must set goals; he must expend effort. A supervisor can help fulfill an employee's desires but he cannot provide him with desires; he can offer him new knowledge or the chance to gain new knowledge but he cannot force him to learn; he can assign goals to a worker but he cannot compel him to accept those goals. In short, a supervisor's influence is *limited;* what he can accomplish depends not simply on his own actions but on the values, knowledge, and goals of his subordinates.

To put the matter more generally, man is not a passive responder to external stimulation but an active agent. He is not an effect of the actions of others but a cause in his own right.

REFERENCES

Bryan, J. F., & Locke, E. A. Parkinson's law as a goal-setting phenomenon. *Organizational Behavior and Human Performance,* 1967, **2**, 258–275.

Chaney, F. B. Employee participation in manufacturing job design. *Human Factors,* 1969,

---

[7]One important qualification must be made to this statement. If an individual's goals and values are irrational (anti-life) or if he has value conflicts, he will not derive the same quality or duration or intensity of pleasure from attaining them as compared with rational values. This issue is discussed in Locke (1969) based on Rand (1964).

11, 101–106.

Dulany, D. E., Jr. The place of hypotheses and intentions: An analysis of verbal control in verbal conditioning. In C. W. Eriksen (Ed.), *Behavior and awareness,* Durham, N.C.: Duke University Press, 1962, 102–129.

Dulany, D. E., Jr. Awareness, rules and propositional control: A confrontation with S-R behavior theory. In D. Horton and T. Dixon (Eds.), *Verbal behavior and general behavior theory,* Englewood Cliffs, N.J.: Prentice-Hall, 1968, 340–348.

Eagle, M. N. The effect of learning strategies upon free recall. *American Journal of Psychology,* 1967, **80,** 421–425.

Eagle, M., & Leiter, E. Recall and recognition in intentional and incidental learning. *Journal of Experimental Psychology,* 1964, **68,** 58–63.

Friedlander F. Job characteristics as satisfiers and dissatisfiers. *Journal of Applied Psychology,* 1964, **48,** 388–392.

Georgopoulos, B. S., Mahoney, G. M., & Jones, N. W. A path-goal approach to productivity. *Journal of Applied Psychology,* 1957, **41,** 345–353.

Herzberg, F. *Work and the nature of man.* Cleveland: World Publishing Company, 1966.

Holmes, D. S. Verbal conditioning or problem solving and cooperation? *Journal of Experimental Research in Personality,* 1967, **2,** 289–294.

Hoppock, R. *Job satisfaction.* New York: Harper, 1935.

Kennedy, W. A., & Willcatt, H. C. Praise and blame as incentives. *Psychological Bulletin,* 1964, **62,** 323–332.

Locke, E. A. The motivational effects of knowledge of results: Knowledge or goal-setting? *Journal of Applied Psychology,* 1967, **51,** 324–329

Locke, E. A. Toward a theory of task motivation and incentives. *Organizational Behavior and Human Performance,* 1968, **3,** 157–189. (a)

Locke, E. A. The effects of knowledge of results, feedback in relation to standards and goals on reaction time performance. *American Journal of Psychology,* 1968, **81,** 566–574. (b)

Locke, E. A. What is job satisfaction? *Organizational Behavior & Human Performance,* 1969. (a)

Locke, E. A. Job satisfaction and job performance: A theoretical analysis. Unpublished manuscript, American Institutes for Research, 1969. (b)

Locke, E. A. Studies of the relationship between satisfaction, goal-setting, and performance. *Organizational Behavior and Human Performance,* 1970, **5,** 135–158.

Locke, E. A., & Bryan, J. F. Cognitive aspects of psychomotor performance: The effects of performance goals on level of performance. *Journal of Applied Psychology,* 1966, **50,** 286–291.

Locke, E. A., & Bryan, J. F. Goal-setting as a determinant of the effect of knowledge of score on performance. *American Journal of Psychology,* 1968, **81,** 398–406.

Locke, E. A., & Bryan, J. F. Knowledge of score and goal difficulty as determinants of work rate. *Journal of Applied Psychology,* 1969, **53,** 59–65.

Locke, E. A., Bryan, J. F., & Kendall, L.M. Goals and intentions as mediators of the effects of monetary incentives on behavior. *Journal of Applied Psychology,* 1968, **52,** 104–121.

Locke, E. A., Cartledge, N., & Koeppel, J. The motivational effects of knowledge of results: A goal-setting phenomenon? *Psychological Bulletin,* 1968, **70,**474–485.

Locke, E. A., Cartledge, N., & Knerr, C. Studies of the relationship between satisfaction, goal-setting and performance. *Organizational Behavior and Human Performance,*

1970, **5**, 135–158.

Mace, C. A. Incentives: Some experimental studies. Industrial Health Research Board (Great Britain), 1935, Report No. 72.

Mann, F. C., & Hoffman, L. R. *Automation and the worker.* New York: Holt, 1960.

Meyer, H. H., Kay, E., & French, J. R. P., Jr. Split roles in performance appraisal. *Harvard Business Review,* 1965, **43**, 123–129.

Miller, L. The use of knowledge of results in improving the performance of hourly operators. General Electric Co., Behavioral Research Service, 1965.

Pelz, D. C. Influence: A key to effective leadership in the first-line supervisor. *Personnel,* 1952, **3**, 209–217.

Porter, L. W., & Lawler, E. E. *Managerial attitudes and performance.* Homewood, Ill.: R. D. Irwin, 1968.

Rand, A. The Objectivist ethics. In A. Rand (Ed.), *The virtue of selfishness.* New York: Signet, 1964, 13–35.

Rand, A. Concepts of consciousness. *The Objectivist,* 1966, **5**(9), 1–8.

Rosen, N. A. *Leadership change and work-group dynamics.* Ithaca, N.Y.: Cornell University Press, 1969.

Stedry, A. C. *Budget control and cost behavior.* Englewood Cliffs, N.J.: Prentice-Hall, 1960.

Stedry, A. C., & Kay, E. The effects of goal difficulty on performance. General Electric Co., Behavioral Research Service, 1964.

Taylor, F. W. *The principles of scientific management.* New York: Harper, 1911.

Vroom, V. H. *Work and motivation.* New York: Wiley, 1964.

Wernimont, P. F. Intrinsic and extrinsic factors in job satisfaction. *Journal of Applied Psychology,* 1966, **50**, 41–50.

Whyte, W. F. *Money and motivation.* New York: Wiley, 1955.

Engineer the Job to Fit the Manager
Fred E. Fiedler

What kind of leadership style does business need? Should company executives be decisive, directive, willing to give orders, and eager to assume responsibility? Should they be human relations-oriented, nondirective, willing to share leadership with the men in their group? Or should we perhaps start paying attention to the more important problem of defining under what conditions each of these leadership styles works best and what to do about it?

The success or failure of an organization depends on the quality of its management. How to get the best possible management is a question of vital importance; but it is perhaps even more important to ask how we can make better use of the management talent which *we already have.*

To get good business executives we have relied primarily on recruitment, selection, and training. It is time for businessmen to ask whether this is the only way or the best way for getting the best possible management. Fitting the man to the leadership job by selection and training has not been spectacularly successful. It is surely easier to change almost anything in the job situation than a man's personality and his leadership style. Why not try, then, to fit the leadership to the man?

Executive jobs are surprisingly pliable, and the executive manpower pool is becoming increasingly small. The luxury of picking a "natural leader" from among a number of equally promising or equally qualified specialists is rapidly fading into the past. Business must learn how to utilize the available executive talent as effectively as it now utilizes physical plant and machine tools. Your financial expert, your top research scientist, or your production genius may be practically irreplaceable. Their jobs call for positions of leadership and responsibility. Replacements for these men can be neither recruited nor trained overnight, and they may not be willing to play second fiddle in their departments. If their leadership style does not fit the job, *we must learn how to engineer the job to fit their leadership style.*

In this article I shall describe some studies that illuminate this task of job engineering and adaptation. It will be seen that there are situations where the authoritarian, highly directive leader works best, and other situations where the egalitarian, more permissive, human relations-oriented leader works best; but almost always there are possibilities for changing the situation around somewhat to match the needs of the particular managers who happen to be available. The executive who appreciates these differences and possibilities has knowledge that can be valuable to him in running his organization.

To understand the problems that a new approach would involve, let us look first at some of the basic issues in organizational and group leadership.

STYLES OF LEADERSHIP

Leadership is a personal relationship in which one person directs, coordinates, and supervises others in the performance of a common task. This is especially so in "interacting groups," where men must work together cooperatively in achieving organizational goals.

In oversimplified terms, it can be said that the leader manages the group in either of two ways: He can:

1   Tell people what to do and how to do it.
2   Or share his leadership responsibilities with his group members and involve them in the planning and execution of the task.

There are, of course, all shades of leadership styles in between these two polar positions, but the basic issue is this: the work of motivating and coordinating group members has to be done either by brandishing the proverbial stick or by dangling the equally proverbial carrot. The former is the more orthodox job-centered, autocratic style. The latter is the more nondirective, group-centered procedure.

Research evidence exists to support both approaches to leadership. Which, then, should be judged more appropriate? On the face of it, the first style of leadership is best under some conditions, while the second works better under others. Accepting this proposition immediately opens two avenues of approach. Management can:

1 Determine the specific situation in which the directive or the nondirective leadership style works best, and then select or train men so that their leadership style fits the particular job.

2 Or determine the type of leadership style which is most natural for the man in the executive position, and then change the job to fit the man.

The first alternative has been discussed many times before; the second has not. We have never seriously considered whether it would be easier to fit the executive's job to the man.

NEEDED STYLE?

How might this be done? Some answers have been suggested by a research program on leadership effectiveness that I have directed under Office of Naval Research auspices since 1951.[1] This program has dealt with a wide variety of different groups, including basketball teams, surveying parties, various military combat crews, and men in open-hearth steel shops, as well as members of management and boards of directors. When possible, performance was measured in terms of objective criteria—for instance, percentage of games won by high school basketball teams; tap-to-tap time of open-hearth shops (roughly equivalent to the tonnage of steel output per unit of time); and company net income over a three-year period. Our measure of leadership style was based on a simple scale indicating the degree to which a man described, favorably or unfavorably, his least-preferred co-worker (LPC). This co-worker did not need to be someone he actually worked with at the time, but could be someone the respondent had known in the past. Whenever possible, the score was obtained before the leader was assigned to his group.

The study indicates that a person who describes his least-preferred co-worker in a relatively favorable manner tends to be permissive, human relations-oriented, and considerate of the feelings of his men. But a person who describes his least-preferred co-worker in an unfavorable manner—who has what we have come to call a low LPC rating—tends to be managing, task-controlling, and less

[1]Conducted under Office of Naval Research contracts 170–106, N6-ori-07135 and NR 177–472, Nonr-1834 (36).

concerned with the human relations aspects of the job. It also appears that the directive, managing and controlling leaders tend to perform best in basketball and surveying teams, in open-hearth shops, and (provided the leader is accepted by his group) in military combat crews and company managements. On the other hand, the nondirective, permissive, and human relations-oriented leaders tend to perform best in decision- and policy-making teams in groups that have a creative task—provided that the group likes the leader or the leader feels that the group is pleasant and free of tension.

Critical Dimensions

But in order to tell which style fits which situation, we need to categorize groups. Our research has shown that "it all depends" on the situation. After reviewing the results of all our work and the findings of other investigators, we have been able to isolate three major dimensions that seem to determine, to a large part, the kind of leadership style called for by different situations.

It is obviously a mistake to think that groups and teams are all alike and that each requires the same kind of leadership. We need some way of categorizing the group-task situation, or the job environment within which the leaser has to operate. If leadership is indeed a process of influencing other people to work together effectively in a common task, then it surely matters how easy or difficult it is for the leader to exert his influence in a particular situation.

Leader-Member Relations   The factor that would seem most important in determining a man's leadership influence is the degree to which his group members trust and like him, and are willing to follow his guidance. The trusted and well-liked leader obviously does not require special rank or power in order to get things done. We can measure the leader-member relationship by the so-called sociometric nomination techniques that ask group members to name in their group the most influential person, or the man they would most like to have as a leader. It can also be measured by a group-atmosphere scale indicating the degree to which the leader feels accepted and comfortable in the group.

The Task Structure   The second important factor is the "task structure." By this term I mean the degree to which the task *(a)* is spelled out step by step for the group and, if so, the extent to which it can be done "by the numbers" or according to a detailed set of standard operating instructions, or *(b)* must be left nebulous and undefined. Vague and ambiguous or unstructured tasks make it difficult to exert leadership influence, because neither the leader nor his members know exactly what has to be done or how it is to be accomplished.

Why single out this aspect of the task rather than the innumerable other possible ways of describing it? Task groups are almost invariably components of a larger organization that assigns the task and has, therefore, a big stake in seeing it performed properly. However, the organization can control the quality of a group's performance only if the task is clearly spelled out and programmed or structured. When the task can be programmed or performed "by the numbers," the organization is able to back up the authority of the leader to the fullest; the man who fails to perform each step can be disciplined or fired. But in the case of ill-defined, vague, or unstructured tasks, the organization and the leader have very little control and direct power. By close supervision one can ensure, let us say, that a man will correctly operate a machine, but one cannot ensure that he will be creative.

It is therefore easier to be a leader in a structured task situation in which the work is spelled out than in an unstructured one which presents the leader and his group with a nebulous, poorly defined problem.

Position Power   Thirdly, there is the power of the leadership position, as distinct from any personal power the leader might have. Can he hire or fire and promote or demote? Is his appointment for life, or will it terminate at the pleasure of his group? It is obviously easier to be a leader when the position power is strong than when it is weak.

Model for Analysis

When we now classify groups on the basis of these three dimensions, we get a classification system that can be represented as a cube; see Exhibit 1. As each group is high or low in each of the three dimensions, it will fall into one of the eight cells.

From examination of the cube, it seems clear that exerting leadership influence will be easier in a group in which the members like a powerful leader with a clearly defined job and where the job to be done is clearly laid out (Cell 1); it

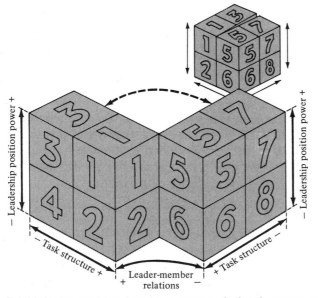

Exhibit I   A model for classifying group-task situations.

will be difficult in a group where a leader is disliked, has little power, and has a highly ambiguous job (Cell 8).

In other words, it is easier to be the well-esteemed foreman of a construction crew working from a blueprint than it is to be the disliked chairman of a volunteer committee preparing a new policy.

I consider the leader-member relations the most important dimension, and the position-power dimension the least important, of the three. It is, for instance, quite possible for a man of low rank to lead a group of higher-ranking men in a structured task—as is done when enlisted men or junior officers conduct some standardized parts of the training programs for medical officers who enter the Army. But it is not so easy for a disrespected manager to lead a creative, policy-formulating session well, even if he is the senior executive present.

Varying Requirements

By first sorting the eight cells according to leader-member relations, then task structure, and finally leader position power, we can now arrange them in order according to the favorableness of the environment for the leader. This sorting leads to an eight-step scale, as in Exhibit II. This exhibit portrays the results of a series of studies of groups performing well but (a) in different situations and

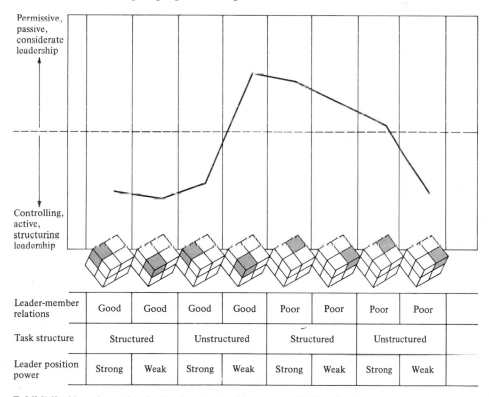

Leader-member relations	Good	Good	Good	Good	Poor	Poor	Poor	Poor	
Task structure	Structured		Unstructured		Structured		Unstructured		
Leader position power	Strong	Weak	Strong	Weak	Strong	Weak	Strong	Weak	

Exhibit II How the style of effective leadership varies with the situation.

conditions, and *(b)* with leaders using different leadership styles. In explanation:

> The *horizontal* axis shows the range of situations that the groups worked in, as described by the classification scheme used in Exhibit 1.
>
> The *vertical* axis indicates the leadership style which was best in a certain situation, as shown by the correlation coefficient between the leader's LPC and his group's performance.

A positive correlation (falling above the midline) shows that the permissive, nondirective, and human relations-oriented leaders performed best; a negative correlation (below the midline) shows that the task-controlling, managing leader performed best. For instance, leaders of effective groups in situation categories 1 and 2 had LPC-group performance correlations of -0.40 to -0.80, with the average between -0.50 and -0.60; whereas leaders of effective groups in situation categories 4 and 5 had LPC-group performance correlations of 0.20 to 0.80, with the average between 0.40 and 0.50.

Exhibit II shows that both the directive, managing, task-oriented leaders and the nondirective, human relations-oriented leaders are successful under some conditions. Which leadership style is the best depends on the favorableness of the particular situation for the leader. In very favorable or in very unfavorable situations for getting a task accomplished by group effort, the autocratic, task-controlling, managing leadership works best. In situations intermediate in difficulty, the nondirective, permissive leader is more successful.

This corresponds well with our everyday experience. For instance:

> Where the situation is very favorable, the group expects and wants the leader to give directions. We neither expect nor want the trusted air-line pilot to turn to his crew and ask, "What do you think we ought to check before takeoff?"
>
> If the disliked chairman of a volunteer committee asks his group what to do, he may be told that everybody ought to go home.
>
> The well-liked chairman of a planning group or research team must be nondirective and permissive in order to get full participation from his members. The directive, managing leader will tend to be more critical and to cut discussion short; hence he will not get the full benefit of the potential contributions by his group members.

The varying requirements of leadership styles are readily apparent in organizations experiencing dramatic changes in operating procedures. For example:

> The manager or supervisor of a routinely operating organization is expected to provide direction and supervision that the subordinates should follow. However, in a crisis the routine is no longer adequate, and the task becomes ambiguous and unstructured. The typical manager tends to respond in such instances by calling his principal assistants together for a conference. In other words, the effective leader changes his behavior from a directive to a permissive, nondirective style until the operation again reverts to routine conditions.
>
> In the case of a research planning group, the human relations-oriented and

permissive leader provides a climate in which everybody is free to speak up, to suggest, and to criticize. Osborn's brainstorming method[2] in fact institutionalizes these procedures. However, after the research plan has been completed, the situation becomes highly structured. The director now prescribes the task in detail, and he specifies the means of accomplishing it. Woe betide the assistant who decides to be creative by changing the research instructions!

Practical Tests

Remember that the ideas I have been describing emanate from studies of real-life situations; accordingly, as might be expected, they can be validated by organizational experience. Take, for instance, the dimension of leader-member relations described earlier. We have made three studies of situations in which the leader's position power was strong and the task relatively structured with clear-cut goals and standard operating procedures. In such groups as these the situation will be very favorable for the leader if he is accepted; it will be progressively unfavorable in proportion to how much a leader is disliked. What leadership styles succeed in these varying conditions? The studies confirm what out theory would lead us to expect:

> The first set of data come from a study of B-29 bomber crews in which the criterion was the accuracy of radar bombing. Six degrees of leader-member relations were identified, ranging from those in which the aircraft commander was the first choice of crew members and highly endorsed his radar observer and navigator (the key men in radar bombing), to those in which he was chosen by his crew but did not endorse his key men, and finally to crews in which the commander was rejected by his crew and rejected his key crew members. What leadership styles were effective? The results are plotted in Exhibit III.
>
> A study of anti-aircraft crews compares the 10 most chosen crew commanders, the 10 most rejected ones, and 10 of intermediate popularity. The criterion is the identification and "acquisition" of unidentified aircraft by the crew. The results shown in Exhibit III are similar to those for bomber crew commanders.
>
> Exhibit III also summarizes data for 32 small-farm supply companies. These were member companies of the same distribution system, each with its own board of directors and its own management. The performance of these highly comparable companies was measured in terms of percentage of company net income over a three-year period. The first quarter of the line (going from left to right) depicts endorsement of the general manager by his board of directors and his staff of assistant managers; the second quarter, endorsement by his board but not his staff; the third quarter, endorsement by his staff but not his board; the fourth quarter, endorsement by neither.

As can be seen from the results of all three studies, the highly accepted and strongly rejected leaders perform best if they are controlling and managing, while the leaders in the intermediate acceptance range, who are neither rejected nor accepted, perform best if they are permissive and nondirective.

[2]See Alex F. Osborn, *Applied imagination* (New York: Charles Scribner's Sons, 1953).

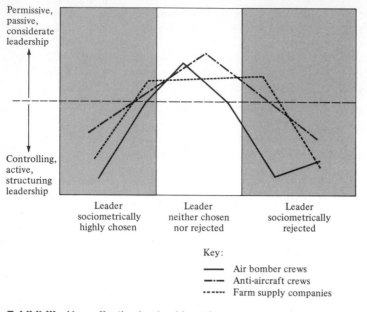

Exhibit III   How effective leadership styles vary depending on group acceptance.

Now let us look at some research on organizations in another country:

Recently in Belgium a study was made of groups of mixed language and cultural composition. Such teams, which are becoming increasingly frequent as international business and governmental activities multiply, obviously present a difficult situation for the leader. He must not only deal with men who do not fully comprehend one another's language and meanings, but also cope with the typical antipathies, suspicions, and antagonisms dividing individuals of different cultures and nationalities.

At a Belgian naval training center we tested 96 three-man groups, half of which were homogeneous in composition (all Flemish or all Waloon) and half heterogeneous (the leader differing from his men). Half of each of these had powerful leader positions (petty officers), and half had recruit leaders. Each group performed three tasks: one unstructured task (writing a recruiting letter); and two parallel structured tasks (finding the shortest route for ships through 10 ports, and doing the same for 12 ports). After each task, leaders and group members described their reactions—including group-atmosphere ratings and the indication of leader-member relations.

The various task situations were then arranged in order, according to their favorableness for the leader. The most favorable situation was a homogeneous group, led by a well-liked and accepted petty officer, which worked on the structured task of routing a ship. The situation would be especially favorable toward the end of the experiment, after the leader had had time to get to know his members. The least favorable situation was that of an unpopular recruit leader of a heterogeneous group where the relatively unstructured task of writing a letter came up as soon as the group was formed.

There were six groups that fell into each of these situations or cells. A correlation was then computed for each set of six groups to determine which type of leadership

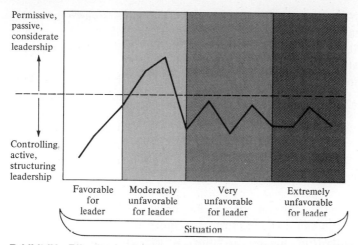

Exhibit IV Effective leadership styles vary depending on group acceptance.

style led to best team performance. The results, indicated in Exhibit IV, support the conclusions earlier described.

Of particular interest is the fact that the difficult heterogeneous groups generally required controlling, task-oriented leadership for good performance. This fits the descriptions of successful leader behavior obtained from executives who have worked in international business organizations.

CONCLUSION

Provided our findings continue to be supported in the future, what do these results and the theory mean for executive selection and training? What implications do they have for the management of large organizations?

Selection and Training

Business and industry are now trying to attract an increasingly large share of exceptionally intelligent and technically well-trained men. Many of these are specialists whose talents are in critically short supply. Can industry really afford to select only those men who have a certain style of leadership in addition to their technical qualifications? The answer is likely to be negative, at least in the near future.

This being the case, can we then train the man selected in one leadership style or the other? This approach is always offered as a solution, and it does have merit. But we must recognize that training people is at best difficult, costly, and time-consuming. It is certainly easier to place people in a situation compatible with their natural leadership style than to force them to adapt to the demands of the job.

As another alternative, should executives learn to recognize or diagnose group-task situations so that they can place their subordinates, managers, and department heads in the jobs best suited to their leadership styles? Even this procedure has serious disadvantages. The organization may not always happen to have the place that fits the bright young man. The experienced executive may not want to be moved, or it may not be possible to transfer him.

Should the organization try to "engineer" the job to fit the man? This alternative is potentially the most feasible for management. As has been shown already, the type of leadership called for depends on the favorableness of the situation. The favorableness, in turn, is a product of several factors. These include leader-member relations, the homogeneity of the group, and the position power and degree to which the task is structured, as well as other, more obvious factors such as the leader's knowledge of his group, his familiarity with the task, and so forth.

It is clear that management can change the characteristic favorableness of the leadership situation; it can do so in most cases more easily than it can transfer the subordinate leader from one job to another or train him in a different style of interacting with his members.

Possibilities of Change

Although this type of organizational engineering has not been done systematically up to now, we can choose from several good possibilities for getting the job done:

> **1** *We can change the leader's position power.* We can either give him subordinates of equal or nearly equal rank or we can give him men who are two or three ranks below him. We can either give him sole authority for the job or require that he consult with this group, or even obtain unanimous consent for all decisions. We can either punctiliously observe the channels of the organization to increase the leader's prestige or communicate directly with the men of his group as well as with him in person.
>
> **2** *We can change the task structure.* The tasks given to one leader may have to be clarified in detail, and he may have to be given precise operating instructions; another leader may have to be given more general problems that are only vaguely elucidated.
>
> **3** *We can change the leader-member relations.* The Belgian study, referred to earlier, demonstrates that changing the group composition changes the leader's relations with his men. We can increase or decrease the group's heterogeneity by introducing men with similar attitudes, beliefs and backgrounds, or by bringing in men different in training, culture, and language.

The foregoing are, of course, only examples of what could be done. The important point is that we now have a model and a set of principles that permit predictions of leadership effectiveness in interacting groups and allow us to take a look at the factors affecting team performance. This approach goes beyond the traditional notions of selection and training. It focuses on the more fruitful possibility of organizational engineering as a means of using leadership potentials in the management ranks.

Path-Goal Theory of Leadership
Robert J. House
Terence R. Mitchell

An integrated body of conjecture by students of leadership, referred to as the "Path-Goal Theory of Leadership," is currently emerging. According to this theory, leaders are effective because of their impact on subordinates' motivation, ability to perform effectively and satisfactions. The theory is called Path-Goal because its major concern is how the leader influences the subordinates' perceptions of their work goals, personal goals and paths to goal attainment. The theory suggests that a leader's behavior is motivating or satisfying to the degree that the behavior increases subordinate goal attainment and clarifies the paths to these goals.

HISTORICAL FOUNDATIONS

The path-goal approach has its roots in a more general motivational theory called expectancy theory, (Mitchell, 1974a). Briefly, expectancy theory states that an individual's attitudes (e. g., satisfaction with supervision or job satisfaction) or behavior (e. g., leader behavior or job effort) can be predicted from: (1) the degree to which the job, or behavior, is seen as leading to various outcomes called (expectancy) and (2) the evaluation of these outcomes called (valences). Thus, people are satisfied with their job if they think it leads to things that are highly valued, and they work hard if they believe that effort leads to things that are highly valued. This type of theoretical rationale can be used to predict a variety of phenomena related to leadership, such as why leaders behave the way they do (Nebeker and Mitchell, 1974) or it can help us to understand how leader behavior influences subordinate motivation.

This latter approach is the primary concern of this article. The implication for leadership is that subordinates are motivated by leader behavior to the extent that this behavior influences expectancies, e. g., goal paths and valences, e. g., goal attractiveness.

Several writers have advanced specific hypotheses concerning how the leader affects the paths and the goals of subordinates (Evans, 1970; Hammer and Dachler, 1973; Dansereau et al, 1973; House, 1971; Mitchell, 1973; Graen et al, 1972; House and Dessler, 1974). These writers focused on two issues: (1) how the leader affects subordinates' expectations that effort will lead to effective performance and valued rewards, and (2) how this expectation affects motivation to work hard and perform well.

While the state of theorizing about leadership in terms of subordinates' paths and goals is in its infancy, we believe it is promising for two reasons. First,

From *Journal of Contemporary Business*, Autumn 1974, 81–97. Reprinted with permission.

it suggests effects of leader behavior that have not yet been investigated but which appear to be fruitful areas of inquiry. And, second, it suggests with some precision the situational factors on which the effects of leader behavior are contingent.

The initial theoretical work by Evans (1970, 1974) asserts that leaders will be effective by making rewards available to subordinates and by making these rewards contingent on the subordinates accomplishment of specific goals. Evans argued that one of the strategic functions of the leader is to clarify for subordinates' the kind of behavior that leads to goal accomplishment and valued rewards. This function might be referred to as path clarification. Evans also argued that the leader increases the rewards available to subordinates by being supportive toward subordinates, i. e., by being concerned about their status, welfare and comfort. Leader supportiveness is in itself a reward that the leader has at his or her disposal, and the judicious use of this reward increases the motivation of subordinates.

Evans studied the relationship between the behavior of leaders and the subordinates' expectations that effort leads to rewards and also studied the resulting impact on ratings of the subordinates' performance. He found that when subordinates viewed leaders as being supportive (considerate of their needs) and when these superiors provided directions and guidance to the subordinates, there was a positive relationship between leadership behavior and subordinates' performance ratings.

However, leader behavior was only related to subordinates' performance when the leader's behavior also was related to the subordinates' expectations that their effort would result in desired rewards. Thus, Evans' findings suggest that the major impact of a leader on the performance of subordinates is clarifying the path to desired rewards and making such rewards contingent on effective performance.

Stimulated by this line of reasoning House, (1971) and House and Dessler (1974) advanced a more complex theory of the effects of leader behavior on the motivation of subordinates. The theory intends to explain the effects of four specific kinds of leader behavior on the following three subordinate attitudes or expectations: (1) the satisfaction of subordinates, (2) the subordinates'acceptance of the leader and (3) the expectations of subordinates that effort will result in effective performance and that effective performance is the path to rewards. The four kinds of leader behavior included in the theory are: (1) directive leadership, (2) supportive leadership, (3) participative leadership, and (4) achievement-oriented leadership. Directive leadership is characterized by a leader who lets subordinates know what is expected of them, gives specific guidance as to what should be done and how it should be done, makes his or her part in the group understood, schedules work to be done, maintains definite standards of performance and asks that group members follow standard rules and regulations. Supportive leadership is characterized by a friendly and approachable leader who shows concern for the status, well-being and needs of subordinates. Such a leader does little things to make the work more pleasant, treats members as equals and is friendly and approachable. Participative leadership is characterized by a leader who consults with his subordinates, solicits their suggestions and takes these suggestions seriously into consideration before making a decision. An achievement-oriented leader sets challenging goals, expects subordinates to perform at their highest level, continuously seeks improvement in performance *and* shows a high degree of confidence that the subordinates will assume responsibility, put forth effort and accomplish challenging goals. This kind of leader constantly emphasizes excellence in performance and simultaneously displays confidence that subordinates will meet high standards of excellence.

A number of studies suggest that these different leadership styles can be shown by the same leader in various situations (House and Dessler, 1974; Stogdill, 1965; House, Velancy and Van der Krabben, unpublished). For example, a leader may show directiveness toward subordinates in some instances and be participative or supportive in other instances (Hill, 1974). Thus, the traditional method of characterizing a leader as either highly participative and supportive *or* highly directive is invalid; rather, it can be concluded that leaders vary in the particular fashion employed for supervising their subordinates. Also, the theory, in its present stage, is a tentative explanation of the effects of leader behavior—it is incomplete because it does not explain other kinds of leader behavior and does not explain the effects of the leader on factors other than subordinate acceptance, satisfaction and expectations. However, the theory is stated so that additional variables may be included in it as new knowledge is made available.

PATH-GOAL THEORY

General Propositions

The first proposition of path-goal theory is that leader behavior is acceptable and satisfying to subordinates to the extent that the subordinates see such behavior as either an immediate source of satisfaction or as instrumental to future satisfaction.

The second proposition of this theory is that the leader's behavior will be motivational i. e., increase effort, to the extent that (1) such behavior makes satisfaction of subordinates' needs contingent on effective performance and (2) such behavior complements the environment of subordinates by providing the coaching, guidance, support and rewards necessary for effective performance.

These two propositions suggest that the leader's strategic functions are to enhance subordinates' motivation to perform, satisfaction with the job and acceptance of the leader. From previous research on expectancy theory of motivation (House, Shapiro, and Wahba, 1974) it can be inferred that the strategic functions of the leader consist of: (1) recognizing and/or arousing subordinates' needs for outcomes over which the leader has some control, (2) increasing personal payoffs to subordinates for work-goal attainment, (3) making the path to those payoffs easier to travel by coaching and direction, (4) helping subordinates clarify expectancies, (5) reducing frustrating barriers and (6) increasing the opportunities for personal satisfaction contingent on effective performance.

Stated less formally, the motivational functions of the leader consist of increasing the number and kinds of personal payoffs to subordinates for work-goal attainment, and making paths to these payoffs easier to travel by clarifying the paths, reducing road blocks and pitfalls and increasing the opportunities for personal satisfaction en route.

Contingency Factors

Two classes of situational variables are asserted to be contingency factors. A contingency factor is a variable which moderates the relationship between two other variables such as leader behavior and subordinate satisfaction. For example, we might suggest that the degree of structure in the task moderates the relationship between the leaders' directive behavior and subordinates' job satisfaction. Figure 1 shows how such a relationship might look. Thus, subordinates are satisfied with directive behavior in an unstructured task and are satisfied with nondirective behavior in a structured task. Therefore, we say that the relationship between leader directiveness and subordinate satisfaction is contingent upon the structure of the task.

The two contingency variables are (a) personal characteristics of the subordinates and (b) the environmental pressures and demands with which the subordinates must cope in order to accomplish the work goals and to satisfy their needs. While other situational factors also may operate to determine the effects of leader behavior, they are not presently known.

With respect to the first class of contingency factors, the characteristics of subordinates, path-goal theory asserts that leader behavior will be acceptable to subordinates to the extent that the subordinates see such behavior as either an immediate source of satisfaction or as instrumental to future satisfaction. Subordinates' characteristics are hypothesized to partially determine this perception.

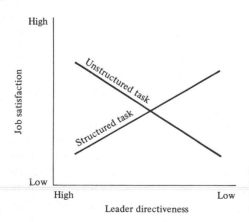

Figure 1 Hypothetical relationship between directive leadership and subordinate satisfaction with task structure as a contingency factor.

For example, Runyon (1973) and Mitchell (1974b) show that the subordinate's score on a measure called Locus of Control moderates the relationship between participative leadership style and subordinate satisfaction. The Locus-of-Control measure reflects the degree to which an individual sees the environment as systematically responding to his or her behavior. People who believe that what happens to them occurs because of their behavior are called internals; people who believe that what happens to them occurs because of luck or chance are called externals. Mitchell's (1974) findings suggest that internals are more satisfied with a participative leadership style and externals are more satisfied with a directive style.

A second characteristic of subordinates on which the effects of leader behavior are contingent is subordinates' perception of their own ability with respect to their assigned tasks. The higher the degree of perceived ability relative to task demands, the less the subordinate will view leader directiveness and coaching behavior as acceptable. Where the subordinate's perceived ability is high, such behavior is likely to have little positive effect on the motivation of the subordinate and to be perceived as excessively close control. Thus, the acceptability of the leader's behavior is determined in part by the characteristics of the subordinates.

The second aspect of the situation, the environment of the subordinate, consists of those factors that are not within the control of the subordinate but which are important to need satisfaction or to ability to perform effectively. The theory asserts that effects of the leader's behavior on the psychological states of subordinates are contingent on other parts of the subordinates' environment that are relevant to subordinate motivation. Three broad classifications of contingency factors in the environment are:

- The subordinates' tasks
- The formal authority system of the organization
- The primary work group

Assessment of the environmental conditions makes it possible to predict the kind and amount of influence that specific leader behaviors will have on the motivation of subordinates. Any of the three environmental factors could act upon the subordinate in any of three ways: first, to serve as stimuli that motivate and direct the subordinate to perform necessary task operations; second, to constrain variability in behavior. Constraints may help the subordinate by clarifying expectancies that effort leads to rewards or by preventing the subordinate from experiencing conflict and confusion. Constraints also may be counterproductive to the extent that they restrict initiative or prevent increases in effort from being associated positively with rewards. Third, environmental factors may serve as rewards for achieving desired performance, e. g., it is possible for the subordinate to receive the necessary cues to do the job and the needed rewards for satisfaction from sources other than the leader, e. g., coworkers in the primary work group. Thus, the effect of the leader on subordinates' motivation will be a function of how deficient the environment is with respect to motivational stimuli, constraints or rewards.

With respect to the environment, path-goal theory asserts that when goals and paths to desired goals are apparent because of the routine nature of the task, clear group norms or objective controls of the formal authority systems, attempts by the leader to clarify paths and goals will be both redundant and seen by subordinates as imposiing unnecessary, close control. Although such control may increase performance by preventing soldiering or malingering, it also will result in decreased satisfaction (see Figure 1). Also with respect to the work environment, the theory asserts that the more dissatisfying the task the more the subordinates will resent leader behavior directed at increasing productivity or enforcing compliance to organizational rules and procedures.

Finally, with respect to environmental variables the theory states that leader behavior will be motivational to the extent that it helps subordinates cope with environmental uncertainties, threats from others or sources of frustration. Such leader behavior is predicted to increase subordinates' satisfaction with the job context and to be motivational to the extent that it increases the subordinates' expectations that their effort will lead to valued rewards.

These propositions and specification of situational contingencies provide a heuristic framework on which to base future research. Hopefully, this will lead to a more fully developed, explicitly formal theory of leadership.

Figure II presents a summary of the theory. It is hoped that these propositions, while admittedly tentative, will provide managers with some insights concerning the effects of their own leader behavior and that of others.

EMPIRICAL SUPPORT

The theory has been tested in a limited number of studies which have generated considerable empirical support for our ideas and also suggest areas in which the theory requires revision. A brief review of these studies follows.

Figure 2   Summary of Path-Goal Relationships

Leader behavior and	Contingency factors	Cause	Subordinate attitudes and behavior
1 Directive	1 Subordinate characteristics		1 Job satisfaction Job → rewards
	Authoritarianism	Personal	
2 Supportive	Locus of control	Influence > perceptions	
	Ability		2 Acceptance of leader Leader → rewards
3 Achievement oriented	2 Environmental factors		
	The task	Influence > Motivational	
	Formal authority system	Stimuli	3 Motivational behavior Effort → performance
		Constraints	
4 Participative	Primary work group	Rewards	Performance → rewards

Leader Directiveness

Leader directiveness has a positive correlation with satisfaction and expectancies of subordinates who are engaged in ambiguous tasks and has a negative correlation with satisfaction and expectancies of subordinates engaged in clear tasks. These findings were predicted by the theory and have been replicated in seven organizations (House, 1971; House and Dessler, 1974; Sims and Szilagyi, 1974; Dermer, 1974; Smetana, 1974). They suggest that when task demands are ambiguous or when the organization procedures, rules and policies are not clear, a leader behaving in a directive manner complements the tasks and the organization by providing the necessary guidance and psychological structure for subordinates. However, when task demands are clear to subordinates, leader directiveness is seen more as a hindrance.

However, other studies have failed to confirm these findings (Weed, Mitchell, and Smyser, 1974; Dermer and Siegel, 1973; Schuler, 1973; Downey et al., 1974; Stinson and Johnson, 1974). A study by Dessler (1973) suggests a resolution to these conflicting findings—he found that for subordinates at the lower organizational levels of a manufacturing firm who were doing routine, repetitive, unambiguous tasks, directive leadership was preferred by closed-minded, dogmatic, authoritarian subordinates and nondirective leadership was preferred by nonauthoritarian, open-minded subordinates. However, for subordinates at higher organizational levels doing nonroutine, ambiguous tasks, directive leadership was preferred for both authoritarian and nonauthoritarian subordinates. Thus, Dessler found that two contingency factors appear to operate simultaneously: subordinate task ambiguity and degree of subordinate authoritarianism. When measured in combination, the findings are as predicted by the theory; however, when the subordinate's personality is not taken into account, task ambiguity does not always operate as a contingency variable as predicted by the theory. House, Burill and Dessler (unpublished) recently found a similar interaction between subordinate authoritarianism and task ambiguity in a second manufacturing firm, thus adding confidence in Dessler's original findings.

Supportive Leadership

The theory hypothesizes that supportive leadership will have its most positive effect on subordinate satisfaction for subordinates who work on stressful, frustrating or dissatisfying tasks. This hypothesis has been tested in 10 samples of employees, (House, 1971; House and Dessler, 1974; Sims and Szalagyi, 1974; Stinson and Johnson, 1974; Schuler, 1973; Downey et al, 1974; Weed et al, 1974) and in only one of these studies was the hypothesis disconfirmed (Sims and Szalagyi, 1974). Despite some inconsistency in research on supportive leadership the evidence is sufficiently positive to suggest that managers should be alert to the critical need for supportive leadership under conditions where tasks are dissatisfying, frustrating or stressful to subordinates.

Achievement-oriented Leadership

The theory hypothesizes that achievement-oriented leadership will cause subordinates to strive for higher standards of performance and to have more confidence in the ability to meet challenging goals. A recent study by House, Valency and Van der Krabben provides a partial test of this hypothesis among white collar employees in service organizations. For subordinates performing ambiguous, nonrepetitive tasks, they found a positive relationship between the amount of achievement orientation of the leader and subordinates' expectancy that their effort would result in effective performance. Stated less technically, for subordinates performing ambiguous, nonrepetitive tasks, the higher the achievement orientation of the leader, the more the subordinates were confident that their efforts would pay off in effective performance. For subordinates performing moderately unambiguous, repetitive tasks, there was no significant relationship between achievement-oriented leadership and subordinate expectancies that their effort would lead to effective performance. This finding held in four separate organizations.

Two plausible interpretations may be used to explain these data. First, people who select ambiguous, nonrepetitive tasks may be different in personality from those who select a repetitive job and may, therefore, be more responsive to an achievement-oriented leader. A second explanation is that achievement orientation only affects expectancies in ambiguous situations because there is more flexibility and autonomy in such tasks. Therefore, subordinates in such tasks are more likely to be able to change in response to such leadership style. Neither of the above interpretations have been tested to date; however, additional research is currently under way to investigate these relationships.

Participative Leadership

In theorizing about the effects of participative leadership it is necessary to ask about the specific characteristics of both the subordinates and their situation that would cause participative leadership to be viewed as satisfying and insturmental to effective performance.

Mitchell (1973) recently described at least four ways in which a participative leadership style would impact on subordinate attitudes and behavior as predicted by expectancy theory. First, a participative climate should increase the clarity of organizational contingencies. Through participation in decision making, subordinates should learn what leads to what. From a path-goal viewpoint participation would lead to greater clarity of the paths to various goals. A second impact of participation would be that subordinates, hopefully, should select goals they highly value. If one participates in decisions about various goals, it makes sense that this individual would select goals he or she wants. Thus, participation would increase the correspondence between organization and subordinate goals. Third, we can see how participation would increase the control the individual has over what happens on the job. If our motivation is higher (based on the preceding two points), then having greater autonomy and ability to carry out our intentions should lead to increased effort and performance. Finally, under a participative system, pressure towards high performance should come from sources other than the leader or the organization. More specifically, when people participate in the decision process they become more ego-involved; the decisions made are in some part their own. Also, their peers know what is expected and the social pressure has a greater impact. Thus, motivation to perform well stems from internal and social factors as well as formal external ones.

A number of investigations prior to the above formulation supported the idea that participation appears to be helpful (Tosi, 1970; Sadler, 1970; Wexley et al, 1973), and Mitchell (1973) presents a number of recent studies that support the above four points. However, it is also true that we would expect the relationship between a participative style and subordinate behavior to be moderated by both the personality characteristics of the subordinate and the situational demands. Studies by Tannenbaum and Alport (1966) and Vroom (1959) have shown that subordinates who prefer autonomy and self-control respond more positively to participative leadership in terms of both satisfaction and performance than subordinates who do not have such preferences. Also, the studies mentioned earlier by Runyon (1973) and Mitchell (1974b) showed that subordinates who were external in orientation were less satisfied with a participative style of leadership than were internal subordinates.

House (1974) has also reviewed these studies in an attempt to explain the ways in which the situation or environment moderates the relationship between participation and subordinate attitudes and behavior. His analysis suggests that where participative leadership is positively related to satisfaction, regardless of the predispositions of subordinates, the tasks of the subjects appear to be ambiguous and ego-involving. In the studies in which the subjects' personalities or predispositions moderate the effect of participative leadership, the tasks of the subjects are inferred to be highly routine, and/or nonego-involving tasks.

House reasoned from this analysis that the task may have an overriding effect on the relationship between leader participation and subordinate responses, and that individual predispositions or personality characteristics of subordinates may have an effect only under some tasks. It was assumed that when task demands are ambiguous, subordinates will have a need to reduce the ambiguity. Further, it was assumed that when task demands are ambiguous, participative problem solving between the leader and the subordinate will result in more effective decisions than when the task demands are unambiguous. Finally, it was assumed that when the subordinates are ego involved in their tasks they are more likely to want to have a say in the decisions that affect them. Given these assumptions, the following hypotheses were formulated to account for the conflicting findings reviewed above:

●When subjects are highly ego-involved in a decision or a task and the decision or task demands are ambiguous, participative leadership will have a positive effect on the satisfaction and motivation of the subordinate, *regardless* of the subordinate's predisposition toward self-control, authoritarianism or need for independence.

●When subordinates are not ego-involved in their tasks and the task demands are clear, subordinates who are not authoritarian and who have high needs for independence and self-control will respond favorably to leader participation and their opposite personality types will respond less favorably.

These hypotheses were derived on the basis of path-goal theorizing, i. e., the rationale guiding the analysis of prior studies was that both task characteristics and characteristics of subordinates interact to determine the effect of a specific kind of leader behavior on the satisfaction, expectancies and performance of subordinates. To date, one major investigation (Schuler, 1974) has supported some of these predictions in which personality variables, amount of participative leadership, task ambiguity and job satisfaction were assessed for 324 employees of an industrial manufacturing organization. As expected, in nonrepetitive, ego-involving tasks, employees (regardless of their personality) were more satisfied under a participative style than a nonparticipative style. However, in repetitive tasks which were less ego-involving the amount of authoritarianism of subordinates moderated the relationship between leadership style and satisfaction. Specifically, low authoritarian subordinates were *more satisfied* under a participative style. These findings are exactly as the theory would predict, thus it has promise in reconciling a set of confusing and contradictory findings with respect to participative leadership.

SUMMARY AND CONCLUSIONS

We have attempted to describe what we believe is a useful theoretical framework for understanding the effect of leadership behavior on subordinate satisfaction and motivation. Most theorists today have moved away from the simplistic notions that all effective leaders have a certain set of personality traits or that the situation completely determines performance. Some researchers have presented rather complex attempts at matching certain types of leaders with certain types of situations, e. g., the articles written by Vroom and Fiedler in this issue. But, we believe that a path-goal approach goes one step further. It not only suggests what type of style may be most effective in a given situation—it also attempts to explain *why* it is most effective.

We are optimistic about the future outlook of leadership research. With the guidance of path-goal theorizing, future research is expected to unravel many confusing puzzles about the reasons for and the effects of leader behavior that have, heretofore, not been solved. However, we add a word of caution: the theory, and the research on it, are relatively new to the literature of organizational behavior. Consequently, path-goal theory is offered more as a tool for directing research and stimulating insight than as a proven guide for managerial action.

REFERENCES

Atkinson, J. W. and Raynor, J. O. Motivation and achievement, V. H. Winston and Sons, Washington, D.C., 1974.

Dansereau, F., Jr., Cashman, J. and Graen, G. Instrumentality theory and equity theory as complementary approaches in predicting the relationship of leadership and turnover among managers. *Organizational Behavior and Human Performance,* **10,** 184–200, 1973.

Dermer, J. D. and Siegel, J. P. A test of path goal theory: disconfirming evidence and a critique. Unpublished mimeograph, Faculty of Management Studies, University of Toronto, 1973.

Dermer, J. D. Supervisory behavior and budget motivation. Unpublished manuscript, Working Paper W. P. Sloan School of Management, Massachusetts Institute of Technology, Cambridge, Massachusetts, 1974.

Dessler, G. An investigation of the path goal theory of leadership. Unpublished doctoral dissertation, Bernard M. Baruch College, City University of New York, 1973.

Downey, H. K., Sheridan, J. E. and Slocum, J. W., Jr. Analysis of relationships among leader behavior, subordinate job performance and satisfaction: a path goal approach. Unpublished mimeograph, 1974.

Evans, M. G. The effects of supervisory behavior on the path goal relationship. *Organization Behavior and Human Performance,* 1970, **55,** 277–298.

Evans, M. G. Extensions of a path goal theory of motivation. *Journal of Applied Psychology,* 1974, **59,** 172–178.

Graen, G., Dansereau, F., Jr. and Minami, T. Disfunctional leadership styles. *Organization Behavior and Human Performance,* 7, 216–236, 1972(a).

Graen, G., Dansereau, F., Jr. and Minami, T. An empirical test of the man-in-the-middle hypothesis among executives in a hierarchical organization employing a unit analysis, *Organization Behavior and Human Performance,* 8, 161–285, 1972(b).

Hammer, T. H. and Dachler, H. P. The process of supervision in the context of motivation theory, Research Report No. 3, Dept. of Psychology, University of Maryland, 1973.

Haythorn, W., Couch, A, Haefner, D., Langham, P. and Carter, L. The effects of varying combinations of authoritarian and equalitarian leaders and followers, *Journal of Abnormal Social Psychology,* 1956, **53,** 210–219.

Hill, W. A., and Ruhe, J. A. Attitudes and behavior of black and white supervisors in problem solving groups, *Organization Behavior and Human Performance,* (in press).

House, R. J. A path goal theory of leader effectiveness, *Administrative Science Quarterly,* **16,** 3, September, 1971, 321–338.

House, R. J. and Dessler, G. The path goal theory of leadership: some post hoc and a priori tests. To appear in Hunt, J. G. (Ed.) *Contingency Approaches to Leadership.* Carbondale, Illinois: Southern Illinois University Press, 1974.

House, R. J., Shapiro, H. J. and Wahba, M. A. Expectancy theory as a predictor of work behavior and attitude, a re-evaluation of empirical evidence. *Decision Sciences,* (in press).

House, R. J., Valency, A. and Van der Krabben, R. Some tests and extensions of the path goal theory of leadership, in preparation.

Mitchell, T. R. Expectancy model of job satisfaction, occupational preference and effort: A theoretical, methodological and empirical appraisal. *Psychological Bulletin,* (in press), 1974a.

Mitchell, T. R., Smyser, C. R., and Weed, S. E. Locus of control: supervision and work satisfaction, unpublished. Technical Report No. 74–56, University of Washington. (1974b)

Mitchell, T. R. Motivation and participation: an integration, *Academy of Management Journal.* 1973, **16,** (4,) 160–679.

Nebeker, D. M. and Mitchell, T. R. Leader behavior: An expectancy theory approach. *Organizational Behavior and Human Performance,* 1974.

Runyon, K. E. Some interactions between personality variables and management styles, *Journal of Applied Psychology,* 1973, **57,** (3), 288–294.

Sadler, J., Leadership style, confidence in management and job satisfaction, *Journal of Applied Behavioral Sciences,* 1970, **6,** 3–19.

Schuler, R. S. A path goal theory of leadership: an empirical investigation. Doctoral dissertation, Michigan State University, East Lansing, Michigan, 1973.

Schuler, R. S. Leader participation, task structure and subordinate authoritarianism, unpublished mimeograph, Cleveland State University, 1974.

Stinson, J. E. and Johnson, T. W. The path goal theory of leadership: a partial test and suggested refinement, *Proceedings,* 7th Annual Conference of the Mid-West, Division of the Academy of Management, Kent, Ohio, April, 1974, 18–36.

Stogdill, R. M. *Managers, employees, organization.* Bureau of Business Research, Division of Research, College of Commerce and Administration. The Ohio State University, 1965.

Szalagyi, A. D. and Sims, H. P. An exploration of the path goal theory of leadership in a health care environment. *Academy of Management Journal,* (in press).

Tannebaum, A. S. and Allport, F. H. Personality structure and group structure: an interpretive study of their relationship through an event-structure hypothesis. *Journal of Abnormal and Social Psychology,* 1956, **53,** 272–280.

Tosi, H. A re-examination of personality as a determinant of the effects of participation. *Personnel Psychology,* 1970, **23,** 91–99.

Vroom, V. H. Some personality determinants of the effects of participation, *Journal of Abnormal Social Psychology,* 1959, **59,** 322–327.

Weed, S. E., Mitchell, T. R. and Smyser, C. R. A test of House's path goal theory of leadership in an organizational setting. Paper presented at Western Psychological Association, 1974.

Wexley, K. N., Singh, J. P. and Yukl, J. A. Subordiante personality as a moderator of the effects of participation in three types of appraisal interviews, *Journal of Applied Psychology,* 1973, **83,** (1,) 54–59.

QUESTIONS FOR DISCUSSION

1 What major conclusions can you draw from the Hollander and Julian review article concerning the basic role of leadership in organizations?

2 How are the concepts of leadership and supervision related? How are these two concepts different?

3 What role does leadership play in motivating employees in general?

4 Where might differing styles of leadership be equally effective under different circumstances? Give examples.

5 Critically evaluate Locke's comments on the role of the supervisor as motivator. Are his comments universally applicable or only relevant under particular circumstances?

6 What similarities exist in the leadership theories of Fiedler and of House and Mitchell? What differences exist?

7 Critically evaluate the theories of Fiedler and of House and Mitchell. Which theory do you feel better explains leadership processes as they affect employee work behavior?

8 How might supervisory style affect employee motivation and performance under: *(a)* the two-factor theory; *(b)* equity theory; and *(c)* expectancy/valence theory?

9 What is the relationship between leadership and *group* performance?

10 Assume you are a middle manager in an organization. What type of leader or supervisor do you honestly believe you would be?

Chapter 12

Job Design Factors
In Motivation

OVERVIEW

Early managerial approaches to job design (see Chapter 1) focused primarily on attempts to simplify an employee's required tasks insofar as possible in order to increase production efficiency. It was felt that, since workers were largely economically motivated, the best way to maximize output was to reduce tasks to their simplest forms and then reward workers with money on the basis of units of output—a piece-rate incentive plan. In theory, such a system would simultaneously satisfy the primary goals of both the employees and the company. Evidence of such a philosophy can be seen in the writings of Taylor and other scientific management advocates.

This approach to simplified job design has reached its zenith from a technological standpoint in assembly-line production techniques such as those used by automobile manufacturers. (Piece-rate incentive systems have been largely omitted here, however.) On auto assembly lines, in many cases, the average length of "work cycle" (that is, the time allowed for an entire "piece" of work) ranges between 30 seconds and 1 ½ minutes. This means that workers would repeat the same task on an average of at least 500 times per day: Such a technique, efficient as it may be, is not without its problems, however. As workers have become better educated and more organized, they have begun demanding more from their jobs. Not only is this demand shown in recurrent requests for shorter hours and increased wages, it is also shown in several undesirable behavior patterns, such as higher turnover, absenteeism, dissatisfaction, sabotage, and so on.

While organizational psychologists and practicing managers have long sought ways of reducing such undesirable behavior, only recently have they begun to rigorously study it in connection with the task performed. As pointed out by Porter (1969, p. 415), ". . . at best, prior to the last few years, task factors have been underemphasized, if considered at all, in attempts to reveal the motivational and cognitive explanations for job behaviors." This omission has been largely alleviated by a series of recent investigations into ways to attack the problem of job redesign as it affects motivation, performance, and satisfaction. Somewhat surprisingly, many of the new "solutions" bear striking resemblance to the old craft type of technology of pre-assembly-line days.

A major thrust of many of the contemporary efforts at job redesign research represents a blend of two central factors. On the one hand, researchers are concerned with studying the motivational processes associated with redesigning jobs. On the other hand, they are equally concerned with the practical applications of such knowledge as it affects attempts to improve the work environment. In this sense, investigations in this area have generally represented applied research in the truest sense.

One of the first researchers in the area of job redesign as it affected motivational force and performance was Herzberg (Herzberg, Mausner, & Snyderman, 1959). He pointed to the necessity of considering such factors as challenge and meaningfulness of work as major variables affecting motivation. He and his associates differentiated between what they described as the older and less effective job redesign efforts, known as job *enlargement*, and the newer concept of job *enrichment* (Paul, Robertson, & Herzberg, 1969). The term "job enlargement," as used by Herzberg, means a *horizontal* expansion of an employee's job, giving him or her more of the same kinds of activities but not altering the necessary skills. "Job enrichment," on the other hand, means a *vertical* expansion of an employee's job, requiring an increase in the skills repertoire which ostensibly leads to increased opportunities. (It is important to note here, however, that, in contrast to Herzberg, many behavioral scientists use the term "job enlargement" to refer to both horizontal *and* vertical expansion.) As Paul et al. (1969, p. 61) described it, job enrichment " . . . seeks to improve both efficiency and human satisfaction by means of building into people's jobs, quite specifically, a greater scope for personal achievement and recognition, more challenging and responsible work, and more opportunity for individual advancement and growth."

Considerable evidence has come to light recently in support of positive behavioral and attitudinal consequences of such job enrichment efforts (Ford, 1969; Kuriloff, 1966; Lawler, 1973; Maher, 1971; Myers, 1970; Special Task Force, H.E.W., 1973; Vroom, 1964). In general, such efforts have tended to result in: (1) significantly reduced turnover and absenteeism; (2) improved job satisfaction; (3) improved quality of products; and (4) some, though not universal, improvements in productivity and output rates. On the negative side, the costs often associated with such programs are generally identified as: (1) increased training time and expense; and (2), occasionally, additional retooling costs where dramatic shifts toward group assembly teams have been instituted.

In the three articles that follow, we shall attempt to sample much of the recent work done in job design and job enrichment as they affect motivation at work. In the first selection, several contemporary experiments in job redesign in European organizations are reviewed. This selection describes how such programs originated and evolved, and also identifies many of the purported benefits and potential problems associated with such efforts.

In the second article, Lawler discusses the important role of variations in task designs as they affect worker expectations. It is argued here that the impact of job redesign efforts on performance will be largely determined by the manner in which such efforts affect a worker's beliefs concerning the performance-reward relationship (see Chapter 6).

Finally, Hulin reviews a portion of the psychological literature on the impact of job redesign efforts on both performance and satisfaction. This paper, which updates an earlier important work by Hulin and Blood (1968), attempts to place the various findings within a general conceptual framework capable of resolving some of the discrepancies that appear to exist in the data. Hulin stresses the necessity of avoiding unwarranted generalizations about the nature of human beings as they act and react in their work environment.

REFERENCES AND SUGGESTED ADDITIONAL READINGS

Alderfer, C. P. Job enlargement and the organizational context. *Personnel Psychology,* 1969, **22,** 418–426.

Bishop, R. C., & Hill, J. W. Job enlargement vs. job change and their effects on contiguous but non-manipulated work groups. *Journal of Applied Psychology,* 1971, **55,** 175–181.

Fitzgerald, T. H. Why motivation theory doesn't work. *Harvard Business Review,* 1971, **49**(4), 37–44.

Ford, R. N. *Motivation through the work itself.* New York: American Management Association, 1969.

Foulkes, F. *Creation of more meaningful work.* New York: American Management Association, 1969.

Hackman, J. R. Nature of the task as a determiner of job behavior. *Personnel Psychology,* 1969, **22,** 435–444.

Hackman, J. R., & Lawler, E. E., III. Employee reactions to job characteristics. *Journal of Applied Psychology,* 1971, **55,** 259–286.

Herzberg, F. *Work and the nature of man.* Cleveland: World, 1966.

Herzberg, F., Mausner, B., & Snyderman, B. *The motivation to work.* New York: Wiley, 1959.

Hulin, C. L., & Blood, M. R. Job enlargement, individual differences, and worker responses. *Psychological Bulletin,* 1968, **69,** 41–55.

Janson, R. Job enrichment: Challenge of the 70's. *Training and Development Journal,* June 1970, 7–9.

Kuriloff, A. H. *Reality in management.* New York: McGraw-Hill, 1966.

Lawler, E. E., III. Motivation in work organizations. Monterey, Calif.: Brooks/Cole, 1973.

Maher, J. R. (ed.). *New perspectives in job enrichment.* New York: Van Nostrand Reinhold, 1971.

Myers, M. S. *Every employee a manager.* New York: McGraw-Hill, 1970.

Paul, W. J., Robertson, K. B., & Herzberg, F. Job enrichment pays off. *Harvard Business Review,* 1969, **47**(2), 61–78.

Porter, L. W. Effects of task factors on job attitudes and behavior. *Personnel Psychology,* 1969, **22,** 415–418.

Reif, W. E., & Luthans, F. Does job enrichment really pay off? *California Management Review,* 1972, **14,** 30–37.

Rush, H. M. F. *Job design for motivation.* New York: The Conference Board, Report No. 515, 1971.

Special Task Force to the Secretary of Health, Education, and Welfare. *Work in America.* Cambridge, Mass.: M.I.T. 1973.

Turner, A. N., & Lawrence, P. R. *Industrial jobs and the worker.* Boston: Harvard University, Graduate School of Business Administration, 1965.

Vroom, V. H. *Work and motivation.* New York: Wiley, 1964.

Job Redesign on the Assembly Line:
Farewell to Blue-Collar Blues?
Editor, Organizational Dynamics

The authors of the much-quoted, much-praised, and much-criticized HEW report *Work in America* wound up their study with a rhetorical bang: "Albert Camus wrote that 'without work life goes rotten. But when work is soulless, life stifles and dies.' Our analysis of work in America leads to much the same conclusion: Because work is central to the lives of so many Americans, either the absence of work or employment in meaningless work is creating an increasingly intolerable situation."

Most who argue that the rhetoric in the report is exaggerated and the thesis overstated would exempt the assembly line, particularly the auto assembly line, from their dissent. The auto assembly line epitomizes the conditions that contribute to employee dissatisfaction: fractionation of work into meaningless activities, with each activity repeated several hundred times each workday, and with the employees having little or no control over work pace or any other aspect of working conditions.

Two generations of social scientists have documented the discontent of auto workers with their jobs. Yet the basic production process hasn't changed since Ford's first Highland Park assembly plant in 1913. We read a lot about the accelerating pace of technology: Here's a technology that's stood still for 60 years despite the discontent.

The social explanations are easy. The automakers—when they thought about the problem at all—dismissed it. The economic advantages of the assembly line seemingly outweighed any possible social costs—including the high wages, part of which might properly be considered discontentment pay. In short, the cash register rang more clearly than the gripes.

Recently, the situation has changed. The advent of an adversary youth culture in the United States, the rising educational levels, with a concomitant increase in employee expectations of the job, the expansion of job opportunities for all but the least skilled and the most disaffected, have raised the level of discontent. One of the big three automakers, for example, now has an annual turnover rate of close to 40 percent. G.M.'s famous Lordstown Vega plant, the latest triumph of production engineering—with the average time per job activity pared to 36 seconds and workers facing a new Vega component 800 times in each eight-hour shift—has been plagued with strikes, official and wildcat, slowdowns, and sabotage. At times, the line has shut down during the second half of the day to remedy the defects that emerged from the line during the first half.

From *Organizational Dynamics*, 1973, **2**(2), 51–67. Copyright 1973 by AMACOM, a division of American Management Association. Reprinted by permission.

IS JOB REDESIGN THE ANSWER?

Much has been written about the two automobile plants in Sweden, Volvo and Saab-Scania, that have practiced job redesign of the assembly line on a large scale. The results, variously reported, have appeared in the world press. Also receiving wide press coverage have been the efforts of Philips N.V. in The Netherlands to redesign jobs on the lines assembling black-and-white and color TV sets. So much for instant history!

We visited the three companies during a recent trip to Europe and shall attempt to evaluate and compare them. But first a caveat: We eschew chic terms, such as job enrichment, autonomy, job rotation, and employee participation, in favor of the drabber job redesign for several reasons. First, the other terms have taken on emotional connotations; they've become the rallying ground for true believers who view them as a partial answer or panacea to the problem of employee alienation in an industrial society. The term job redesign, by contrast, has no glamor and no followers. Second, most efforts at job redesign, certainly the three we're going to write about, include elements of job enrichment, autonomy, job rotation, and employee participation in varying degrees at different times, but none of the competing terms affords a sufficiently large umbrella to cover what's happened and what's planned in the three organizations. Last, true believers passionately define their faiths differently; using any of the other terms as central would involve us in tiresome and trivial questions of definition. Hence, our choice of job redesign. It's comprehensive, and noncontroversial.

"Job redesign—the answer to what?" might have been a more descriptive subhead than one implying that our sole concern would be the question of employee discontent and its converse, employee satisfaction. Ours is a wider net. We're going to ask and answer (the answers, of course, being partial and tentative) these questions:

1   What conditions on the assembly line are economically favorable to which forms of job redesign?

2   Do many employees resent and resist job redesign? Do they prefer monotonous, repetitious work?

3   Are the "best" results from job redesign obtained when it's at its most thorough (job rotation plus job enrichment plus autonomy plus employee participation)?

4   Is there any single element in job redesign that seems to account for the biggest increase in employee satisfaction?

5   What are the benefits of job redesign—both those we can measure and monetize and those that can only be described?

6   On balance, does management gain as much from job redesign as the employee whose job is redesigned?

7   Last, what's the impact of the overall culture and political system on job redesign? What's the evidence, pro or con, that the success of job redesign at Volve, Saab-Scania, or Philips—or the lack of it—would be replicated on similar assembly lines in the United States?

A tall order, but remember that we promised only tentative and partial answers to the seven questions.

JOB REDESIGN AT PHILIPS

First Generation, 1960–1965

We start with Philips because, of our three companies, Philips is the pioneer; its experience with job redesign goes back to 1960. We use the term first generation, second generation, and so on to mark the stages of the Philips program because this is Philips' terminology—obviously appropriated from computer lingo.

In the first experiment, concern was more with the deficiencies of long assembly lines than it was with improving job satisfaction. Breaking up the existing line of 104 workers into five shorter assembly lines, installing buffer stocks of components between groups, and placing inspectors at the end of each group instead of the whole assembly line reduced waiting times by 55 percent, improved feedback, and improved the balance of the system—various short chains being stronger than one long chain because the line can never travel faster than the worker with the longest average time per operation.

Almost incidentally, morale also improved: Only 29 percent of the workers on the assembly line responded positively to the survey question "I like doing my job," versus a 51 percent positive response from the test line. Furthermore, when the test line was restructured with half the number of workers, so that each one performed twice the original cycle and workplaces alternated with empty seats, production flowed more smoothly and quality improved. Dr. H. G. Van Beek, a psychologist on the original study team, drew a dual lesson from the experiment: "From the point of view of production, the long line is very vulnerable; from the point of view of morale—in the sense of job satisfaction—downright bad."

Subsequent experiments in several plants involved rotating workers between different jobs on the assembly line, enriching jobs by having employees set their own pace within overall production standards, and enlarging them by making employees responsible for inspecting their own work. Most of the gains from the experiments Philips entered under the heading of "social profit." In other words, morale and job satisfaction improved but bread-and-butter items such as productivity and scrap showed little improvement.

Second Generation, 1965–1968

The key feature of the second phase, a program that involved a few thousand employees scattered over 30 different locations, was the abolition of foremen. With supervisors' enlarged span of control, the men on the assembly line acquired autonomy and more control over their jobs. Even an authoritarian supervisor would find that he was spread too thin to exercise the same amount of control as the previous foreman had.

Once again, the bulk of the profits were social. The bill for waste and repairs dropped slightly, and, of course, Philips pocketed the money that had been paid to the foremen. Otherwise, the gains to Philips were nonmonetary.

Third Phase, 1968

This phase, one that is ongoing, has focused on giving various groups of seven or eight employees total responsibility for assembling either black-and-white TV sets or color selectors for color TV sets, a task equivalent in complexity to assembling a black-and-white set from scratch.

We want to emphasize the word *total:* The group responsible for assembling the black-and-white sets, for example, not only performs the entire assembling task but also deals directly with staff groups such as procurement, quality, and stores, with no supervisor or foreman to act as intermediary or expediter. If something is needed from another department or something goes wrong that requires the services of another department, it's the group's responsibility to deal with the department.

"This third phase has had its problems," concedes Den Hertog, staff psychologist. "Typically, it's taken about six months for the groups to shake down—adjust to the increased pressures and responsibilities." Establishing effective relationships with unfamiliar higher-status employees in staff departments has proved the biggest single problem. On the other hand, anyone in an experimental group can opt out at any time—an option that has yet to be taken up. Of course, it may be the satisfaction of being a member of a select group, even physically separated from other work groups by a wall of green shrubbery, that accounts for no employee's having made a switch. Hertog, however, believes that the increase in intrinsic job satisfactions has more than compensated for any pains of adjustments and accounts for the lack of turnover.

What about results? What's the measurable impact of the program? There have been additional costs, such as increased training costs; more important, small, autonomous groups require new and smaller machines to perform traditional assembly line tasks. On the other hand, there have been measurable benefits. Overall, production costs in manhours have dropped 10 percent, while waiting times have decreased and quality levels have increased by smaller but still significant amounts.

To restructure work and redesign jobs in ways that increase employee job satisfaction at no net cost to the company over the long run is all that Philips, as a matter of policy, requires of such programs. Short-term deficits caused by purchases of new equipment are something it's prepared to live with.

Where is Philips going from here? Obviously, the potential for effective job redesign is large. With 90,000 workers in 60 plants, Philips has barely scratched the surface. Part of the answer would seem to lie in the future strength of the movement for employee participation and power equalization that is particularly strong in Norway and Sweden and is gaining adherents in The Netherlands.

At Philips the primary response has been the establishment of worker consultation in some 20 different departments. Worker consultation is just what it sounds like: Employees meet with first- and second-level supervision to discuss problems of joint interest. Worker consultation exists at different levels in different departments, stresses Hertog, who attributes the difference to the level of maturity of the group itself: "In some groups we're still at the flower pot phase, talking about what should be done to improve meals in the cafeteria, while at other extremes we have departments where we have left the selection of a new supervisor for the group up to the workers."

It's significant that those groups who have considered the question of job redesign consistently have criticized Philips for not doing more of it. The expansion of job redesign, in part, would seem to depend on the expansion of work consultation and the pressures exerted by the workers themselves to get job redesign extended.

JOB REDESIGN AT SAAB-SCANIA

To claim that Saab-Scania has abolished the auto assembly line would misrepresent the facts. Saab-Scania, or to speak more precisely, the Scania Division, has instituted small-group assembly of auto engines—not the whole car—in its new engine plant. Even so, this effort is limited to 50 employees in a plant with a workforce of approximately 300, most of whom monitor automatic transfer machines that perform various machining tasks. (See Figure 1.) There's only one manual loading operation in the entire machining process.

More important, the humanization of the auto assembly line is the most dramatic single instance in a series starting in 1969 that Palle Berggen, the head of the industrial engineering department, characterized as "one phase in the development of enhanced industrial democracy."

We won't quarrel with his description, although we think he succumbed to the rhetoric of public relations. Scania, in its actions from 1969 on, has responded to some problems for which the best word is horrendous. Employee turnover was running around 45 percent annually, and in the auto assembly plant, 70 percent. Under such conditions, the maintenance of an even flow of production, something crucial in an integrated work system like Scania's, presented insuperable problems. Also, it was increasingly difficult to fill jobs on the shop floor at all. A survey taken in 1969 indicates what Scania was up against: Only four out of 100 students graduating from high school in Sweden indicated their willingness to take a rank-and-file factory job. In consequence, Scania became heavily dependent on foreign workers—58 percent of the current workforce are non-Swedes. This in turn created problems, both expected and otherwise—among the former problems of training and communications, among the latter, an epidemic of wildcat strikes, previously unknown in Sweden, that largely resulted from the manipulation by extreme left elements of foreign workers ignorant of the tradition among Swedish employees of almost total reliance upon the strong trade union organization to protect their interests.

Any response to these conditions *had* to have as its number one objective the maintenance of productivity. To assert anything else is window dressing—unconvincing as well as unnecessary. No one can fault an industrial organization for undertaking a program whose primary goal is the maintenance of productivity.

This is not to deny that one byproduct of the program has been "enhanced industrial democracy." What happened is that the pursuit of productivity led to an examination of the conditions that created job satisfactions; these, in turn, suggested the series of actions "that enhance industrial democracy"—a term subject to almost as many definitions as there are interpreters.

Production Groups and Development Groups

Employee representation is nothing new at Scania. Like every company in Sweden with more than 50 employees, it's had an employee-elected Works Council since 1949. However, these bodies have no decision-making function; their role is limited to receiving and responding to information from top management, and their effectiveness depends on the willingness of top management to seriously consider suggestions from the Works Council. David Jenkins, in his recent book *Job Power,* tells of asking a company president if he had ever been influenced by worker suggestions. His reply: "Well, yes. We were going to build a new plant and we showed the workers the plans at one of the meetings. They objected very much to the fact that the plant would have no windows. So we changed the plans and had some windows put in. It doesn't cost much more and, actually, the building looks better. And the workers feel better."

The production and development groups initiated in the truck chassis assembly plant in 1969, by contrast, have real decision-making power. Production groups of five to 12 workers with related job duties decide among themselves how they will do their jobs, within the quality and production standards defined by higher management; they can rotate job assignments—do a smaller or larger part of the overall task. At the same time, the jobs of all members of the production group were enlarged by making them jointly responsible for simple service and maintenance activities, housekeeping, and quality control in their work area, duties formerly performed by staff personnel.

Development groups, a parallel innovation, consist of foremen, industrial engineers, and two representatives of one or more production groups whose function is to consider ideas for improving work methods and working conditions. Representatives of the production groups are rotated in a way that guarantees that every member of a production group will serve each year on a development group.

Employee reception of the production group has been mixed but largely positive. The results appear to be favorable, although Scania has done little or nothing to measure them quantitatively. However, impressions have been sufficiently favorable so that within four years production and development groups have expanded to include 2,200 out of the 3,600 employees in the main plant at Södertälje, and within the year they will be extended throughout the company.

Work Design in the Engine Plant

The four machine lines for the components in the engine factory—the cylinder block, the cylinder head, the connecting rod, and the crankshaft—mainly consist of transfer machines manned or monitored by individual operations. Group assembly is restricted to the seven final assembly stations, each of which contains a team of fitters that assemble an entire engine.

Team members divide the work among themselves; they may decide to do one-third of the assembly on each engine—a ten-minute chore—or follow the engine around the bay and assemble the entire engine—a 30-minute undertaking. In fact, only a minority prefer to do the total assembly job. (Using traditional assembly line methods, each operation would have taken 1.8 minutes.) The team also decides its own work pace, and the number and duration of work breaks within the overall requirement of assembling 470 engines in each ten-day period, a specification that allows them a good deal of flexibility in their pacing. Incidentally, over half the employees in the engine plant are women, while the assembly teams are over 80 percent female. We personally saw four assembly teams with only a single man in the lot.

Benefits and Costs

Kaj Holmelius, who is responsible for planning and coordination of the production engineering staff, ticked off the principal credits and debits, along with a few gray areas in which it would be premature to estimate results. On the plus side, he cited the following:

1 Group assembly has increased the flexibility of the plant, making it easier to adjust to heavy absenteeism.

2 The group assembly concept is responsible for a lower balancing loss due to a longer station time.

3 Less money is invested in assembly tools. Even allowing for the fact that you have to buy six or seven times as many tools, the simpler tools make for a smaller overall cost.

4 Quality has definitely improved, although by how much it's hard to estimate.

5 Productivity is higher than it would have been with the conventional assembly line—although once more, there is no proof. Lower production speed per engine, because it's not economical to use some very expensive automatic tools, is outweighed by higher quality and reduced turnover.

6 Employee attitudes have improved, although there have been no elaborate surveys taken. To Holmelius the best indication of job satisfaction is that it's impossible to fill all the requests to transfer from other parts of the plant to the assembly teams.

On the negative side, in addition to the reduced production speed, group assembly takes up considerably more space than the conventional assembly line.

In the neutral corner is the impact on absenteeism and turnover. Absenteeism is actually higher in the engine plant—18 percent versus 15 percent for overall plant operations at Södertälje. However, Holmelius attributes the difference to the fact that the engine plant employs a heavier percentage of women. As for turnover, with the plant in operation for a little more than a year, it's too early to tell. Because of an economic slowdown, turnover generally is down from the 45 percent crisis level of 1969 to 20 percent, and it's Holmelius' belief that turnover in the assembly teams will prove significantly lower than average.

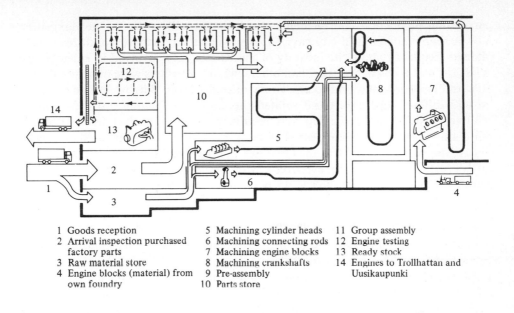

1 Goods reception
2 Arrival inspection purchased
   factory parts
3 Raw material store
4 Engine blocks (material) from
   own foundry

5 Machining cylinder heads
6 Machining connecting rods
7 Machining engine blocks
8 Machining crankshafts
9 Pre-assembly
10 Parts store

11 Group assembly
12 Engine testing
13 Ready stock
14 Engines to Trollhattan and
   Uusikaupunki

Figure 1 Diagram of engine plant, Saab-Scania.

What's the Future of Group Assembly?

It's easier to point out the directions in which Scania does *not* plan to extend group assembly. An experiment with having employees assemble an entire truck diesel engine—a six-hour undertaking involving 1,500 parts—was abandoned at the employees' request; they couldn't keep track of all the parts. Similarly, group assembly wouldn't work with the body of the trucks—truck bodies are too complex, and group assembly would require twice the space currently needed. The moot question at the moment is car assembly. So far, group assembly has been applied only to assembling doors. We suspect that in any decision, economic calculations will predominate, including, of course, the inherently fuzzy calculation about the economic value of job satisfaction.

JOB REDESIGN AT VOLVO

Job redesign at Volvo began, almost accidentally, in the upholstery shop of the car assembly plant during the mid-1960s, but a companywide effort had to wait until 1969, when Volvo faced the same problems that plagued Scania—wildcat strikes, absenteeism, and turnover that were getting out of hand and an increasing dependence on foreign workers. Turnover was over 40 percent annually; absenteeism was running 20 to 25 percent, and close to 45 percent of the employees of the car assembly plant were non-Swedes. One other event in 1971 made a difference: Volvo acquired a young, hard-driving new managing director, Pehr Gyllenhammar, who developed a keen interest in the new methods of work organization.

Ingvar Barrby, head of the upholstery department, started job redesign by persuading production management to experiment with job rotation along the lines he had read about in Norway. The overwhelmingly female workforce complained frequently about the inequity of the various jobs involved in assembling car seats; some jobs were easier than others, while still others were more comfortable and less strenuous, and so on. To equalize the tasks, Barrby divided the job into 13 different operations and rotated the employees among tasks that were relatively arduous and those that were relatively comfortable. Jealousy and bickering among employees disappeared: First, jobs were no longer inequitable; second, employees perceived that they had exaggerated the differences between jobs anyway—the grass-is-greener syndrome. More important, turnover that had been running 35 percent quickly fell to 15 percent, a gain that has been maintained over the years.

Job Alternation and "Multiple Balances"

Volvo uses these phrases instead of the more commonly used job rotation and job enrichment, but the concepts are the same. In job alternation or job rotation, the employee changes jobs once or several times daily, depending on the nature of the work in his group. Take Line IV A, for example, whose function is to do the external and internal sealing and insulation of car bodies. Because internal sealing is such uncomfortable work—employees work in cramped positions inside the car body—the work is alternated every other hour. The remaining jobs are rotated daily.

"Multiple balances" is our old friend, job enrichment, under another name. One example involves the overhead line where the group follows the same body for seven or eight stations along the line for a total period of 20 minutes—seven or eight times the length of the average job cycle.

Not all employees have had their jobs rotated or enriched—only 1,500 out of 7,000 in the car assembly at Torslanda are affected by the program. Because participation is strictly voluntary, the figures at first glance seem to indicate a massive show of disinterest on the part of Volvo employees. Not so. True, some employees prefer their jobs the way they are. The bigger problem is that Volvo has, to date, lacked the technical resources to closely scrutinize many jobs to determine whether and how they can be enlarged or enriched, or it has scrutinized them and determined that it isn't economically feasible to enlarge or enrich them. A company spokesman gave the job of coating under the car body to prevent rust as an example of a thoroughly unpleasant job that so far has defied redesign.

Production Teams at Volvo Lundbyverken

In the truck assembly plant at Lundbyverken, Volvo has carried job redesign several steps further, with production teams who, in form and function, roughly duplicate the production groups previously described at Scania. The production team, a group of five to 12 men with a common work assignment, elects its own chargehand, schedules its own output within the standards set by higher management, distributes work among its members, and is responsible for its own quality control. In these teams, group piecework replaces individual piecework and everyone earns the same amount, with the exception of the chargehand. Currently, there are 23 production teams involving 100 out of the plant's 1,200 employees. Plans call for the gradual extension of the production team approach to cover most, if not all, of the factory workforce.

The Box Score at Volvo

Have the various forms of job redesign, job rotation, job enrichment, and production teams paid off for Volvo? If so, what forms have the payoff taken? Anything we can measure or monetize? Or are we reduced to subjective impressions and interesting although iffy conjectures about the relationship between factors such as increased job satisfaction and reduced turnover?

The two plants deserve separate consideration: Absenteeism and turnover traditionally have been lower at the truck assembly plant than at the car assembly plant. The jobs are inherently more complex and interesting—even before job enrichment, some individual jobs took up to half an hour. The workers, in turn, are more highly skilled and tend to regard themselves as apart from and above the rank-and-file auto worker. They see themselves more as junior engineers. Within this context, it's still true that the introduction of production teams has led to further improvement: less labor turnover, less absenteeism, an improvement in quality, and fewer final adjustments.

At the auto assembly plant the picture isn't clear. Turnover is down from 40 to 25 percent. However, an economic slowdown undoubtedly accounts for some of the decline, while other actions unrelated to job redesign may account for part of the remainder. When Volvo surveyed its employees to probe for the causes of turnover and absenteeism, most of the causes revealed were external—problems with housing, child care, long distances traveling to the plant, and so on. Volvo responded with a series of actions to alleviate these causes, such as extending the bus fleet, together with the community, to transport employees, loaning money to employees to purchase apartments at very favorable rates of interest, putting pressure on the community to expand day care centers, and so on. Such measures presumably contributed to the decline of turnover. Nevertheless, Gyllenhammar is convinced that "we can see a correlation between increased motivation, increased satisfaction on the job, and a decrease in the turnover of labor." Absenteeism is a sadly different picture: It's double what it was five years ago, a condition that Gyllenhammar attributes to legislation enabling workers to stay off the job at practically no cost to themselves.

As for output in that part of the auto assembly plant covered by job enrichment or job enlargement, there was no measurable improvement. Quality, on balance, has improved, and the feeling is that improved quality and decreased turnover had more than covered the costs of installing the program.

The Future of Job Redesign at Volvo

Despite the relatively ambiguous success of Volvo's job redesign efforts, whatever Volvo has done in the past is a pale prologue to its future plans. In about nine months, Volvo's new auto assembly plant at Kalmar will go on stream. And, for once, that overworked term "revolutionary" would seem justified.

Physically, the plant is remarkable. Gyllenhammar describes it as "shaped like a star and on each point of the star you have a work group finishing a big share of the whole automobile—for example, the electrical system or the safety system or the interior." Assembly work takes place along the outer walls, while component parts are stored in the center of the building. Architecturally, the building has been designed to preserve the atmosphere of a small workshop in a large factory, with each work team having its own entrance, dressing room, rest room, and so on. Each team is even physically shielded from a view of the other teams. (See Figure 2.)

Each work team, of 15 to 25 men, will distribute the work among themselves and determine their own work rhythm, subject to the requirement of meeting production standards. If the team decides to drive hard in the morning and loaf in the afternoon, the decision is theirs to make. As with production teams in the truck assembly plant, the team will choose its own boss, and deselect him if he turns out poorly.

The new plant will cost about 10 percent more—some 10 million Swedish kroner—than a comparable conventional auto assembly plant. Time alone will tell whether the extra investment will be justified by the decreased turnover, improved quality, and even reduced absenteeism that its designers confidently expect at the new facility. In announcing the plan for the new factory, Gyllenhammar's economic objectives were modest enough, his social objectives more ambitious. "A way must be found to create a workplace that meets the needs of the modern working man for a sense of purpose and satisfaction in his daily work. A way must be found of attaining this goal without an adverse effect on productivity." With luck, he may achieve both.

WHAT DOES IT ADD UP TO?

On the basis of what we learned at Philips, Saab-Scania, and Volvo, what answers—tentative and partial—do we have to the seven questions that we raised earlier in the article? Or are the results of the programs so ambiguous and inconclusive that, as long as we restrict ourselves to the context of these three companies, we must beg off attempting to answer some of the questions at all? That none of the companies answered all of the questions, and that many of the answers rely on subjective impressions haphazardly assembled, rather than on quantitative data systematically collected, of necessity, limit our answers, but they don't prevent us from presenting them—with the appropriate caveats.

1. *What conditions on the assembly line are economically favorable to which forms of job redesign?*

The basic question here is under what conditions can a man-paced assembly line replace a machine-paced assembly line? Unless this is economically feasible, no form of job redesign is likely to be adopted. Even allowing for rhetoric, none of our three companies—and no other organization of which we are aware—has indicated a willingness to suffer economic losses in order to increase the satisfactions employees might feel if they switched over from machine-paced to man-paced assembly lines. Take the case of manufacturing a pair of man's pants in a garment factory. Give the job to one man and he will take half a day; divide the work among many people on a line with each one using advanced technical equipment, and it takes one man-hour to produce a pair of trousers. The future of job redesign is not bright in a pants factory.

The man-paced assembly line, however, has a couple of widely recognized advantages over the machine-paced line: First, it's much less sensitive to disruption; the whole line doesn't have to stop because of one breakdown—human or technical; second, extensive and costly rebalancing need not be undertaken every time production is increased or decreased. You simply add more people or groups. Of course, there are advantages to machine-paced production, the outstanding one being speed of production, which depends, in turn, on an even flow of production.

There's the rub—and there's the number one cause for job redesign, certainly at Volvo and Saab-Scania. Absenteeism and turnover had risen to the point where they canceled out the economic advantages of machine-paced production. At the same time, evidence had accumulated that job redesign organized around a man-paced assembly line might strike at the root causes of inordinate turnover and absenteeism.

If you look at the design of the new engine plant at Scania, it incorporates

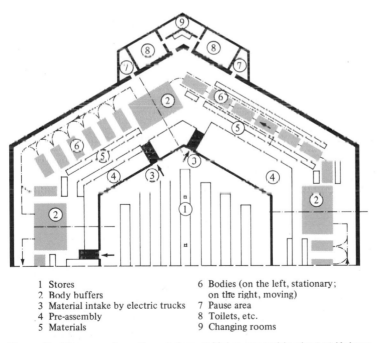

1 Stores	6 Bodies (on the left, stationary;
2 Body buffers	on the right, moving)
3 Material intake by electric trucks	7 Pause area
4 Pre-assembly	8 Toilets, etc.
5 Materials	9 Changing rooms

Figure 2 Diagram of small workshop at Volvo assembly plant at Kalmar.

Drucker's insight that "the worker is put to use to use a poorly designed one-purpose machine tool, but repetition and uniformity are two qualities in which human beings are weakest. In everything but the ability to judge and coordinate, machines can perform better than man." In the new engine plant, everything that can be automated economically has been—probably 90 percent of the total task—with the final assembly paced by teams on the assumption that the relatively slight increases in production time will be more than compensated for by better balancing and decreased disruption—improvements inherent in the technical change—and improvements in quality, turnover, and absenteeism, the anticipated byproducts of job satisfaction.

The results, as you have seen, are sketchy. However, we can affirm that none of the three organizations, by their own testimony, has lost economically by the changeover from a machine-paced to a man-paced assembly line. How much they have gained is decidedly a more iffy question.

2. *Do many employees resent and resist job redesign? Do they prefer monotonous, repetitious work?*

A flip answer might be "God only knows—and he isn't talking." Any answer, at best, is based largely on conjecture. Joseph E. Godfrey asserts that "workers may complain about monotony, but years spent in the factories lead me to believe that they like to do their jobs automatically. If you interject new things you spoil the rhythm of the job and work gets fouled up." As head of the General Motors Assembly Line Division he is qualified, but biased. But even Fred Herzberg, whose bias is obviously in the other direction, concedes that "individual reaction to job enrichment is as difficult to forecast in terms of attitudes as it is in terms of performance. Not all persons welcome having their job enriched." The Survey Research Center at The University of Michigan in a 1969 study concluded that factors such as having a "nutrient supervisor, receiving adequate help, having few labor standard problems all seem to relate at least as closely to job satisfaction as having a challenging job with 'enriching demands.' " One thing does seem clear: Assuming the job level is held constant, education is inversely related to satisfaction. And when Pehr Gyllenhammar foresaw a near future in which 90 percent of the Swedish population would at least have graduated from high school, he was realistically anticipating a situation in which Volvo would become almost entirely dependent on foreign employees unless it found ways of enriching the auto assembly jobs.

3. *Are the "best" results from job redesign obtained when it's at its most thorough (job rotation plus job enrichment plus autonomy plus employee participation)?*

Work in America flatly endorses the thesis that "it is imperative that employers be made aware of the fact that thorough efforts to redesign work, not simply 'job enrichment' or 'job rotation,' have resulted in increases of productivity from 5 to 40 percent. In no instance of which we have evidence has a major effort to increase employee participation resulted in a long-term decline in productivity." Obviously, in this context "best" results means increased productivity.

Before we can answer the question and respond to the claims asserted in

Work in America a few definitions are necessary. Most descriptions of the elements that enter into a satisfying job concentrate on three: (1) variety, (2) responsibility, and (3) autonomy. Variety defines itself. Responsibility is more complex; it involves both working on a sufficiently large part of the total job to feel that it is a meaningful experience, and also having a sufficient amount of control over what you are doing to feel personally responsible.

Companies responding to this need for more responsibility may add set-up and inspection the employee's duties or ask him to assemble one-third of an engine instead of a single component—both examples of horizontal job enrichment; and the employee may be permitted to control the pace at which he works—an example of vertical job enrichment. Everything that is subsumed under vertical job enrichment is included in autonomy but it also means something else and something more—giving to the employee himself some control over how his job should be enlarged or enriched—a clear demarcation point between almost all American approaches to job enrichment and some European.

We're describing a circular process; the worker in Sweden and The Netherlands places a higher value on autonomy than the worker in the United States. Therefore, job redesign that incorporates increased autonomy for the employee will be more appreciated and lead to more job satisfaction than comparable efforts would in the United States. Here, Huey Long's concept of a satisfying job, with allowances for the regional overtones, and the hyperbole, still makes sense: "There shall be a real job, not a little old sowbelly black-eyed pea job, but a real spending money beefsteak, and gray Chevrolet Ford in the garage, new suit, Thomas Jefferson, Jesus Christ, red, white, and blue job for every man." The employee did then and still does define, although to a progressively decreasing degree, a satisfying job in terms of how much it pays. For a measure of the difference, take the definition of a dissatisfying job by Malin Lofgren, a 12-year-old Swedish schoolboy: "A bad job is one where others make all the decisions, and you have to do what others say."

Now that the tedious, although necessary, business of definition is out of the way, how do we answer the question with reference to our three companies? Inconclusively. If we define "best" results in terms of gains in productivity, the only certifiable gain occurred with the Philips production groups that scored high on both horizontal and vertical job enrichment, and in which employees were consulted in advance about the ways in which their job should be enriched. In the body of the article, we didn't go into their institutional arrangements, but suffice it to say that both Saab-Scania and Volvo have comparable consultative institutions. Thus, the autonomy factor assumes less significance. The only significant differences would appear to be: (1) The increased status caused by making the production groups at Philips wholly responsible for liaison with other departments, (2) the Hawthorne, or, as the Philips personnel call it, the "Princess" effect—the groups having been visited and complimented by such dignitaries as Queen Juliana and Marshal Tito. On the other hand, the groups at Volvo that chose their own supervisors—certainly a measure of autonomy—have not increased their productivity. Quality, turnover, attendance had improved. But with productivity, there was no measurable impact.

4. *Is there any single element in job redesign that seems to account for the biggest increase in employee satisfaction?*

In a word—no. But that requires an explanation. Our failure to respond principally reflects lack of evidence; none of the organizations concerned asked themselves the question. None tried on any systematic basis to relate what they were doing in redesigning jobs to what they were accomplishing in increased job satisfaction. Word-of-mouth testimony and more cheerful figures—as in the case of Volvo and Saab-Scania with turnover—seemed sufficient to confirm the efficacy of past efforts and sanction future ones, on similar although expanded lines.

5. *What are the benefits of job redesign—both those we can measure and monetize and those that can only be described?*

We begin with a proposition shared by a generation of social scientists who have studied the problem and attempted to answer the question: Employee attitudes and job satisfaction are correlated much more clearly with factors such as absenteeism, turnover, and quality than they are with productivity.

The three companies reinforce this finding. Only one experiment at Philips establishes a positive correlation between job satisfaction and productivity, while several—Philips with productivity groups in Phase III, Saab-Scania in the engine plant and the truck assembly plant, and Volvo in its truck plant—all report improvements in quality, the problem in each case being the absence of quantifiable data. Turnover is another area in which the responses are positive, but suggestive rather than conclusive—"probably lower" in the Scania engine plant; lower in the truck assembly plant; down in both the truck assembly and auto assembly plant at Volvo—but there are no firm figures at the Volvo truck assembly line, while the decrease in turnover at the auto assembly plant is partly attributed to causes unrelated to job redesign. Philips proffers no comparisons of absenteeism or turnover before and after job redesign. All we know is that so far no one in the production groups has decided to quit. In short, the evidence—what there is of it—is positive, but fragmented and based more on impressions than on data.

6. *On balance, does management gain as much from job redesign as the employee whose job is redesigned?*

A two-headed question that logically requires both extensive employee attitude surveys before and after job redesign, along with firm measurements that demonstrate the impact of job redesign on factors such as quality, output, absenteeism, and turnover. As we have seen, we have very little of either. The only attitude surveys were first, the one conducted at the Volvo auto assembly plant to determine the causes of excessive absenteeism and turnover—most of which had nothing to do with job satisfaction and where the subsequent substantial drop in turnover at best could only partially be ascribed to job redesign—and the survey at Philips, where the switchover from machine-paced to man-paced assembly line improved employees' satisfaction with their jobs.

On balance, as previously stated, management has achieved at least an economic draw from its efforts at job redesign, along with a measure of insurance against a fretful future in which employee expectations will become increasingly difficult to fulfill and the job redesign carried out or contemplated will, it is hoped, help to meet those expectations.

As for the satisfactions the employees have gained from the collective efforts at enlarging and enriching their jobs, we can only guess. We have a few pieces of anecdotal evidence, such as the flood of applications to work in the final assembly at Scania's engine plant, or the absence of turnover among the production groups at Philips. In short, we know too little to generalize.

7. *Last, what's the impact of the overall culture and political system on job redesign? What's the evidence, pro or con, that the success of job redesign at Volvo, Saab-Scania, or Philips—or lack of it—would be replicated in similar assembly lines in the United States?*

Technologically, there are no convincing reasons why assembly lines in new automobile factories or television plants in the United States couldn't be redesigned along lines similar to what has been done at Philips, Saab-Scania, and Volvo. It might prove prohibitively expensive in existing plants—after all, job redesign at Volvo's auto assembly plant was largely restricted, on economic grounds, to job rotation. However, new plants in the United States should present no more inherent problems of job redesign than new plants in Sweden. Yet auto executives in the United States have gone on record as feeling that the situation is hopeless. A 1970 report of the Ford Foundation found that none of the corporation executives interviewed "really believe that assembly line tasks can be significantly restructured," and "no one really believes that much can be done to make the assembly jobs more attractive."

Not that all the features of job redesign at Philips, Saab-Scania, and Volvo are equally exportable. The three companies exist in a different political and social ethos, one in which both management and the workers have gone much further in accepting the idea of employee participation in decision making than all but a handful of managers and a small minority of workers in the United States. A survey of Swedish managers in 1970, for example, showed that 75 percent favored more employee decision making in all departments. Even the idea of replacing the decision of the supervisor with collective employee decisions elicited a favorable response from 11 percent of the managers. Given this different ethos, it is not surprising that all three companies have experimented with what would be in the United States the radical step of either dispensing with first-level supervision or leaving it up to the employees to choose their own supervisor. It is a form of autonomy that few managements in the United States would consider for an instant, and one in which few employees would take much interest.

But why not consider it, as long as management continues to set overall standards of production and quality and to hold the group responsible for meeting them? The experiment of having employees choose their own bosses with the experimental groups in the truck assembly plant at Volvo works so well that it has been incorporated as one of the basic design features in the new auto assembly plant. Employees demonstrated that, given the opportunity, they would choose as leaders men who could organize the work and maintain order and discipline.

Let's indulge in speculation. The single quality that most clearly distinguishes between the efforts at job enrichment here and in the three companies we visited is the emphasis abroad on letting the employees have a part—and sometimes a decisive part—in deciding how their jobs should be enriched. By contrast, most exponents of job enrichment in the United States take the "papa-knows-best" approach. Fred Herzberg, the best-known work psychologist, asserts that when people took part in deciding how to change their own jobs, "the results were disappointing." We suspect that Herzberg's real objection is not to the results themselves, but to the difficulty of selling most managements on the idea that employee participation should be an integral part of any process of job enrichment. The experiences at Volvo, Saab-Scania, and Philips suggest that the objection to the employee's participating in how his own job should be enriched or redesigned has its roots in symbolism, rather than substance, in the irrational preoccupation with management prerogatives, rather than in any real or potential threat to productivity or profits.

What about the future? Technologically, there seem to be no compelling reasons why Ford, G.M., and Chrysler cannot take a leaf from Volvo and Saab-Scania. Whether they will is another question. The combination of inertia, custom, and commitment is a formidable one. So far the automakers have chosen to move in the opposite direction: shorter work cycles, smaller jobs, more rapidly moving lines. We should recall that it took a crisis—nothing less than the probability that most people would refuse to work at all or only for uneconomic periods on the jobs the organization had to offer them—to "break the cake of custom" at Volvo and Saab-Scania. Even today, it is clear that there are limits to which auto assembly jobs can be enriched, a limitation obvious in Gyllenhammar's bitter observation that " 'absenteeism with pay' is based on the very utopian hypothesis that people love to work, and no matter what happens they will strive to go to their job every morning." Still, the situation he is in is preferable to the situation he faced. And some of the difference is due to job redesign.

We suspect that it will take a crisis of similar magnitude, together with the belief that they have no choice, to unfreeze the attitudes of automakers in the United States and get them moving in the direction of man-paced assembly lines and the forms of job redesign they facilitate. That such a development, over the long run, is in the cards we strongly believe, but how long it will take for the cards to show up, we leave to the astrologers.

SELECTED BIBLIOGRAPHY

On the general subject of job redesign we strongly recommend three books: The H.E.W. *Work in America,* MIT Press (Cambridge, 1971) is scarcely unbiased but it pulls together much material in the whole area of employee discontent—what causes it and what can be done about it. David Jenkins' *Job Power: Blue and White Collar Democracy*, Doubleday (New York, 1973), is remarkable for the number of case studies of job redesign both here and in Europe—all based on personal visits to the organizations described. Jenkins, like the various authors of *Work in America*, is convinced of the need for wholesale job redesign as the prime means of alleviating growing employee discontent. Last, *Design of Jobs*, Penguin Books Ltd. (Harmondsworth, England, 1972) is a first-rate collection of papers on different aspects of job design. All are worth reading, but of spectial interest are J. Richard Hackman and Edward E. Lawler III, "Conditions Under Which Jobs Will Facilitate Internal Motivation" (pp. 141–154) and James C. Taylor, "Some Effects of Technology in Organizational Change" (pp. 391–414).

On Philips, there is a suggestive article on the first phase of job redesign that shows clearly that Philips' interest in getting away from the machine-paced assembly line arose mainly from technical and economic dissatisfactions with the line—H. G. Van Beek, "The Influence of Assembly Line Organization on Output, Quality and Morale," *Occupational Psychology*, Volume 38, pp. 161–172. On Scania, there's a section on the company—but not identified by name—in Hans Lindestad and Jan-Peter Norstedt, *Autonomous Groups and Payment by Result*, Swedish Employers Confederation (Stockholm, 1973). The Employers Confederation also has published a detailed account of job redesign at Saab-Scania that is being translated into English but that, unfortunately, was not available at the time the article was written.

Job Design and Employee Motivation
Edward E. Lawler, III

The psychological literature on employee motivation contains many claims that changes in job design can be expected to produce better employee job performance. Very few of these claims, however, are supported by an explanation of why changes in job design should be expected to affect performance except to indicate that they can affect employee motivation. Thus, I would like to begin by considering the WHY question with respect to job design and employee performance. That is, I want to focus on the reasons for expecting changes in job design to affect employee motivation and performance. Once this question is answered, predictions will be made about the effects on performance of specific changes in job design (e. g., job enlargement and job rotation).

From *Personnel Psychology*, 1969, **22,** 426–435. Reprinted by permission.

A THEORY OF MOTIVATION

Basic to any explanation of why people behave in a certain manner is a theory of motivation. As Jones (1959) has pointed out, motivation theory attempts to explain "how behavior gets started, is energized, is sustained, is directed, is stopped and what kind of subjective reaction is present in the organism." The theory of motivation that will be used to understand the effects of job design is "expectancy theory." Georgopoulos, Mahoney, and Jones (1957), Vroom (1964) and others have recently stated expectancy theories of job performance. The particular expectancy theory to be used in this paper is based upon this earlier work and has been more completely described elsewhere (e. g., Lawler & Porter, 1967; Porter & Lawler, 1968). According to this theory, an employee's motivation to perform effectively is determined by two variables. The first of these is contained in the concept of an effort-reward probability. This is the individual's subjective probability that directing a given amount of effort toward performing effectively will result in his obtaining a given reward or positively valued outcome. This effort-reward probability is determined by two subsidary subjective probabilities; the probability that effort will result in performance and the probability that performance will result in the reward. Vroom refers to the first of these subjective probabilities as an expectancy and to the second as an instrumentality.

The second variable that is relevant here is the concept of reward value or valence. This refers to the individual's perception of the value of the reward or outcome that might be obtained by performing effectively. Although most expectancy theories do not specify why certain outcomes have reward value, for the purpose of this paper I would like to argue that the reward value of outcomes stems from their perceived ability to satisfy one or more needs. Specifically relevant here is the list of needs suggested by Maslow that includes security needs, social needs, esteem needs, and self-actualization needs.

The evidence indicates that, for a given reward, reward value and the effort-reward probability combine multiplicatively in order to determine an individual's motivation. This means that if either is low or nonexistent then no motivation will be present. As an illustration of this point, consider the case of a manager who very much values getting promoted but who sees no relationship between working hard and getting promoted. For him, promotion is not serving as a motivator, just as it is not for a manager who sees a close connection between being promoted and working hard but who doesn't want to be promoted. In order for motivation to be present, the manager must both value promotion and see the relationship between his efforts and promotion. Thus, for an individual reward or outcome the argument is that a multiplicative combination of its value and the appropriate effort-reward probability is necessary. However, an individual's motivation is influenced by more than one outcome. Thus, in order to determine an individual's motivation it is necessary to combine data concerned with a number of different outcomes. This can be done for an individual worker by considering all the outcomes he values and then summing the products obtained from multiplying the value of these outcomes to him by their respective effort-reward probabilities.

According to this theory, if changes in job design are going to affect an individual's motivation they must either change the value of the outcomes that are seen to depend upon effort, or positively affect the individual's beliefs about the probability that certain outcomes are dependent upon effort. The argument in this paper is that job design changes can have a positive effect on motivation, because they can change an individual's beliefs about the probability that certain rewards will result from putting forth high levels of effort. They can do this because they have the power to influence the probability that certain rewards will be seen to result from good performance, not because they can influence the perceived probability that effort will result in good performance. Stated in Vroom's language, the argument is that job design changes are more likely to affect the instrumentality of good performance than to affect the expectancy that effort will lead to performance.

Before elaborating on this point, it is important to distinguish between two kinds of rewards. The first type are those that are extrinsic to the individual. These rewards are part of the job situation and are given by others. Hence, they are externally-mediated and are rewards that can best be thought of as satisfying lower order needs. The second type of rewards are intrinsic to the individual and stem directly from the performance itself. These rewards are internally-mediated since the individual rewards himself. These rewards can be thought of as satisfying higher order needs such as self-esteem and self-actualization. They involve such outcomes as feelings of accomplishment, feelings of achievement, and feelings of using and developing one's skills and abilities. The fact that these rewards are internally-mediated sets them apart from the extrinsic rewards in an important way. It means that the connection between their reception and performance is more direct than is the connection between the reception of externally-mediated rewards and performance. Hence, potentially they can be excellent motivators because higher effort-reward probabilities can be established for them than can be established for extrinsic rewards. They also have the advantage that for many people rewards of this nature have a high positive value.

Job content is the critical determinant of whether employees believe that good performance on the job leads to feelings of accomplishment, growth, and self-esteem; that is, whether individuals will find jobs to be intrinsically motivating. Job content is important here because it serves a motive arousal function where higher order needs are concerned and because it influences what rewards will be seen to stem from good performance. Certain tasks are more likely to arouse motives like achievement and self-actualization, and to generate, among individuals who have these motives aroused, the belief that successful performance will result in outcomes that involve feelings of achievement and growth. It is precisely because changes in job content can affect the relationship between performance and the reception of intrinsically-rewarding outcomes that it can have a strong influence on motivation and performance.

There appear to be three characteristics which jobs must possess if they are to arouse higher order needs and to create conditions such that people who perform them will come to expect that good performance will lead to intrinsic rewards. The first is that the individual must receive meaningful feedback about his performance. This may well mean the individual must himself evaluate his own performance and define the kind of feedback that he is to receive. It may also mean that the person may have to work on a whole product or a meaningful part of it. The second is that the job must be perceived by the individual as requiring him to use abilities that he values in order for him to perform the job effectively. Only if an individual feels that his significant abilities are being tested by a job can feelings of accomplishment and growth be expected to result from good performance. Several laboratory studies have in fact shown that, when people are given tasks they see as testing their valued abilities, greater motivation does appear (e. g., Alper, 1946; French, 1955). Finally, the individual must feel he has a high degree of self-control over setting his own goals and over defining the paths to these goals. As Argyris (1964) points out, only if this condition exists will people experience psychological "success" as a result of good performance.

Thus, it appears that the answer to the *why* question can be found in the ability of job design factors to influence employees' perceptions of the probability that good performance will be intrinsically rewarding. Certain job designs apparently encourage the perception that it will, while others do not. Because of this, job design factors can determine how motivating a job will be.

JOB DESIGN CHANGES

Everyone seems to agree that the typical assembly line job is not likely to fit any of the characteristics of the intrinsically-motivating job. That is, it is not likely to provide meaningful knowledge of result, test valued abilities, or allow self-control. Realizing this, much attention has been focused recently on attempts to enlarge assembly line jobs, and there is good reason to believe that enlarging assembly line jobs can lead to a situation where jobs are more intrinsically motivating. However, many proponents of job enlargement have failed to distinguish between two different kinds of job enlargement. Jobs can be enlarged on both the horizontal dimension and the vertical dimension. The horizontal dimension refers to the number and variety of the operations that an individual performs on the job. The vertical dimension refers to the degree to which the job holder controls the planning and execution of his job and participates in the setting of organization policies. The utility man on the assembly line has a job that is horizontally but not vertically enlarged, while the worker who Argyris (1964) suggests can participate in decision making about his job while he continues to work on the assembly line, has a vertically but not a horizontally-enlarged job.

The question that arises is, what kind of job enlargement is necessary if the job is going to provide intrinsic motivation? The answer, that is suggested by the three factors that are necessary for a task to be motivating, is that jobs must be enlarged both vertically and horizontally. It is hard to see, in terms of the theory, why the utility man will see more connection between performing well and intrinsic rewards than will the assembly line worker. The utility man typically has no more self-control, only slighly more knowledge of results, and only a slighly greater chance to test his valued abilities. Hence, for him, good performance should be only slightly more rewarding than it will be for the individual who works in one location on the line. In fact, it would seem that jobs can be over-enlarged on the horizontal dimension so that they will be less motivating than they were originally. Excessive horizontal enlargement may well lead to a situation where meaningful feedback is impossible, and where the job involves using many additional abilities that the worker does not value. The worker who is allowed to participate in some decisions about his work on the assembly line can hardly be expected to perceive that intrinsic rewards will stem from performing well on the line. His work on the line still is not under his control, he is not likely to get very meaningful feedback about it, and his valued abilities still are not being tested by it. Thus, for him it is hard to see why he should feel that intrinsic rewards will result from good performance.

On the other hand, we should expect that a job which is both horizontally and vertically enlarged will be a job that motivates people to perform well. For example, the workers Kuriloff (1966) has described, who make a whole electronic instrument, check and ship it, should be motivated by their jobs. This kind of job does provide meaningful feedback, it does allow for self-control, and there is a good chance that it will be seen as testing valued abilities. It does not, however, guarantee that the person will see it as testing his valued abilities since we don't know what the person's valued abilities are. In summary, then, the argument is that if job enlargement is to be successful in increasing motivation, it must be enlargement that affects both the horizontal and the vertical dimensions of the job. In addition, individual differences must be taken into consideration in two respects. First and most obviously, it must only be tried with people who possess higher order needs that can be aroused by the job design and who, therefore, will value intrinsic rewards. Second, individials must be placed on jobs that test their valued abilities.

Let me now address myself to the question of how the increased motivation, that can be generated by an enlarged job, will manifest itself in terms of behavior. Obviously, the primary change that can be expected is that the individual will devote more effort to performing well. But will this increased effort result in a higher quality work, higher productivity, or both? I think this question can be answered by looking at the reasons we gave for the job content being able to affect motivation. The argument was that it does this by affecting whether intrinsic rewards will be seen as coming from successful performance. It would seem that high quality work is indispensable if most individuals are to feel they have performed well and are to experience feelings of accomplishment, achievement, and self-actualization. The situation is much less clear with respect to productivity. It does not seem at all certain that an individual must produce great quantities of a product in order to feel that he has performed well. In fact, many individuals probably obtain more satisfaction from producing one very high quality product than they do from producing a number of lower quality products.

There is a second factor which may cause job enlargement to be more likely to lead to higher work quality than to higher productivity. This has to do with the advantages of division of labor and mechanization. Many job enlargement changes create a situation in which, because of the losses in terms of machine assistance and optimal human movements, people actually have to put forth more energy in order to produce at the prejob enlargement rate. Thus, people may be working harder but producing less. It seems less likely that the same dilemma would arise in terms of work quality and job enlargement. That is, if extra effort is devoted to quality after job enlargement takes place, the effort is likely to be translated into improved quality. This would come about because the machine assistance and other features of the assembly line jobs are more of an aid in bringing about high productivity than they are in bringing about high quality.

THE RESEARCH EVIDENCE

There have been a number of studies that have attempted to measure the effects of job enlargement programs. These were examined to determine if the evidence supports the contention stated previously that both horizontal and vertical job enlargement are necessary if intrinsic motivation is to be increased. Also sought was an indication of whether the effects of any increased motivation was more likely to result in higher quality work than in high productivity.

In the literature search, reports of ten studies where jobs had been enlarged on both the horizontal and the vertical dimensions were found. Table 1 presents a brief summary of the results of these studies. As can be seen, every study shows that job enlargement did have some positive effect since every study reports that job enlargement resulted in higher quality work. However, only four out of ten studies report that job enlargement led to higher productivity. This provides support for the view that the motivational effects produced by job enlargement are more likely to result in higher quality work than in higher productivity.

There are relatively few studies of jobs enlarged only on either the horizontal or the vertical dimension so that it is difficult to test the prediction that both kinds of enlargement are necessary if motivation is to be increased. There are a few studies which have been concerned with the effects of horizontal job enlargement (e. g., Walker & Guest, 1952), while others have stressed its advantages. However, most of these studies have been concerned with its effects on job satisfaction rather than its effects on motivation. None of these studies appears to show that horizontal enlargement tends to increase either productivity or work quality. Walker and Guest, for example, talk about the higher satisfaction of the

Table 1

Research Study	Higher Quality	Higher Productivity
Biggane and Stewart (1963)	Yes	No
Conant and Kilbridge (1965) Kilbridge (1960)	Yes	No
Davis and Valfer (1965)	Yes	No
Davis and Werling (1960)	Yes	Yes
Elliott (1953)	Yes	Yes
Guest (1957)	Yes	No
Kuriloff (1966)	Yes	Yes
Marks (1954)	Yes	No
Rice (1953)	Yes	Yes
Walker (1950)	Yes	No

utility men but they do not report that they work harder. Thus, with respect to horizontal job enlargement, the evidence does not lead to rejecting the view that it must be combined with vertical in order to increase production.

The evidence with respect to whether vertical job enlargement alone can increase motivation is less clear. As Argyris (1964) has pointed out, the Scanlon plan has stressed this kind of job enlargement with some success. However, it is hard to tell if this success stems from people actually becoming more motivated to perform their own job better. It is quite possible that improvements under the plan are due to better overall decision making rather than to increased motivation. Vroom (1964) has analyzed the evidence with respect to the degree to which participation in decision making *per se* leads to increased motivation. This evidence suggests that vertical job enlargement can lead to increased motivation when it leads to the employees' committing themselves to higher production goals.

The evidence with respect to whether vertical job enlargement alone can increase motivation is less clear. As Argyris (1964) has pointed out, the Scanlon plan has stressed this kind of job enlargement with some success. However, it is hard to tell if this success stems from people actually becoming more motivated to perform their own job better. It is quite possible that improvements under the plan are due to better overall decision making rather than to increased motivation. Vroom (1964) has analyzed the evidence with respect to the degree to which participation in decision making *per se* leads to increased motivation. This evidence suggests that vertical job enlargement can lead to increased motivation when it leads to the employees' committing themselves to higher production goals.

Perhaps the crucial distinction here is whether the participation involves matters of company policy or whether it involves matters directly related to the employees' work process. Participation of the former type would seem much less likely to lead to increased motivation than would participation of the latter type.

Thus, it seems to be crucial to distinguish between two quite different types of vertical job enlargement, only one of which leads to increased motivation. Considered together, the evidence suggests that, of the two types of job enlargement, vertical is more important than horizontal. Perhaps this is because it can lead to a situation in which subjects feel their abilities are being tested and where they can exercise self-control even though horizontal enlargement does not take place. Still, the evidence, with respect to situations where both types of enlargement have been jointly installed, shows that much more consistent improvements in motivation can be produced by both than can be produced by vertical alone.

SUMMARY

It has been argued that, when a job is structured in a way that makes intrinsic rewards appear to result from good performance, then the job itself can be a very effective motivator. In addition, the point was made that, if job content is to be a source of motivation, the job must allow for meaningful feedback, test the individual's valued abilities, and allow a great amount of self-control by the job holder. In order for this to happen, jobs must be enlarged on both the vertical and horizontal dimensions. Further, it was predicted that job enlargement is more likely to lead to increased product quality than to increased productivity. A review of the literature on job enlargement generally tended to confirm these predictions.

REFERENCES

Alper, Thelma G. "Task-orientation vs. Ego-orientation in Learning and Retention." *American Journal of Psychology,* XXXVIII (1946), 224–238.

Argyris, C. *Integrating the Individual and the Organization.* New York: John Wiley & Sons, 1964.

Biggane, J. F., and Stewart, P. A. *Job Enlargement: A Case study.* Research Series No. 25 Bureau of Labor and Management, State University of Iowa, 1963.

Conant, E. H., and Kilbridge, M. D. "An Interdisciplinary Analysis of Job Enlargement: Technology, Costs, and Behavioral Implications." *Industrial and Labor Relations Review,* XVIII (1965), 377–395.

Davis, L. E., and Valfer, E. S. "Intervening Responses to Changes in Supervisor Job Designs." *Occupational Psychology,* XXXIX (1965), 171–189.

Davis, L. E., and Werling, R. "Job Design Factors." *Occupational Psychology,* XXXIV (1960), 100–132.

Elliot, J. D. "Increasing Office Productivity through Job Enlargement." *The Human Side of the Office Manager's Job.* A.M.A. Office Management Series, No. 134, New York, 1953, 5–15.

French, Elizabeth G. "Some Characteristics of Achievement Motivation." *Journal of Experimental Psychology,* L (1955), 232–236.

Georgopoulos, B. S., Mahoney, G. M., and Jones, M. N. "A Path-goal Approach to Productivity." *Journal of Applied Psychology,* XLI (1957), 345–353.

Guest, R. H. "Job Enlargement: A Revolution in Job Design." *Personnel Administration,* XX (1957), 9–16.

Jones, M. R., (Editor), *Nebraska Symposium on Motivation.* Lincoln, Nebr.: Nebraska University Press, 1959.

Kilbridge, M. D. "Reduced Costs through Job Enlargement: A Case." *Journal of Business,* XXXIII (1960), 357–362.

Kuriloff, A. H. *Reality in Management.* New York: McGraw-Hill, 1966.

Lawler, E. E., and Porter, L. W. "Antecedent Attitudes of Effective Managerial Performance." *Organizational Behavior and Human Performance,* II (1967), 122–142.

Marks, A. R. N. "An Investigation of Modifications of Job Design in an Industrial Situation and Their Effects on Some Measures of Economic Productivity." Unpublished Ph.D. dissertation. University of California, Berkeley, 1954.

Porter, L. W., and Lawler, E. E. *Managerial Attitudes and Performance.* Homewood, Ill.: Irwin-Dorsey, 1968.

Rice, A. K. "Productivity and Social Organization in an Indian Weaving Shed." *Human Relations,* VI (1953), 297–329.

Vroom, V. H. *Work and Motivation.* New York: John Wiley & Sons, 1964.

Walker, C. R. "The Problem of the Repetitive Job." *Harvard Business Review,* XXVIII (1950), 54–59.

Walker, C. R., and Guest, R. H. *The Man on the Assembly Line.* Cambridge, Mass.: Harvard University Press, 1952.

Individual Differences and Job Enrichment—The Case Against General Treatments

Charles L. Hulin†

According to the job enrichment advocates, as jobs become increasingly specialized and less autonomous, the monotony (perception of the unchanging characteristics of the job from minute-to-minute) increases. Short time cycle, simplified jobs are assumed to lead to monotony. Monotony is supposedly associated with

Abridged from J. R. Maher (ed.), *New perspectives in job enrichment,* pp. 162–168 and 182–191. Copyright 1971 by Van Nostrand Reinhold Company. Reprinted by permission.

Author's note: I would like to express my appreciation to Jeanne Brett Herman who read and commented on an earlier draft of this paper. Her criticisms and comments substantially improved this final product.

†Portions of this selection have appeared in an article by C. L. Hulin and M. R. Blood entitled "Job Enlargement, Individual Differences, and Worker Responses." *Psychological Bulletin,* **69,** 41–55 (1968).

feelings of boredom and job dissatisfaction. Boredom and job dissatisfaction lead to undesirable (from management's point of view) behavior. This reasoning could be diagrammed as follows:

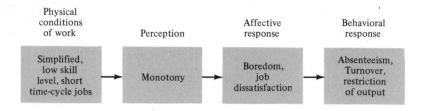

An alternative, more positive, way of stating the job enlargement hypothesis is presented in Figure 1.

Figure 1 graphically indicates the hypothesized positive, monotonic relationship between job variety (job size) and the experienced job satisfaction of the incumbents. (Note that even though the relationship in Figure 1 is linear, any monotonic positive function could be substituted.) There is also the implicit assumption that as job variety and job satisfaction increase, the motivation of the workers shows a concomitant increase.

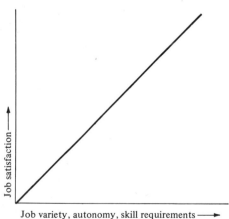

Figure 1 Hypothesized general relationship between job variety and job satisfaction.

The assumptions implicit in this line of reasoning deserve to be discussed. First, consider the assumption that repetitiveness leads to monotony and, conversely, that uniqueness and change lead to lack of monotony. Smith has demonstrated there are substantial individual differences in susceptibility to monotony among workers on the same job.[1] According to Smith, some workers do not report feelings of monotony even in the face of a job with an extremely short work cycle. Further, Baldamus has pointed out that repetitive work can be positively motivating and tends to "pull the worker along."[2] This notion of traction has been experimentally verified by Smith and Lem using a sample of industrial workers.[3] Thus, it would seem that the assumption that repetitiveness leads to monotony could be questioned on two grounds—effects of individual differences and positive motivational characteristics of repetition.

The second assumption is monotony leads to boredom and job dissatisfaction. Even if we grant the tenuous supposition that the physical reality of short time cycles or repetition leads to monotony, can we presume that the workers will respond with negative affect to this perception? It would seem this can be questioned on much the same grounds as the first. At the very least, we should allow the possibility that some workers prefer the safety of not being required to make decisions regarding their jobs. Vroom has demonstrated that not all workers are satisfied when they are allowed to take part in the decision making process about their jobs, and there are significant individual differences (F-scale scores) between workers who respond positively to the opportunity to make decisions about their jobs and those who do not.[4] These data indicate the possibility that some workers prefer routine, repetition, and specified work methods.

Finally, we have the assumption that boredom and job dissatisfaction are associated with undesirable behavior on the part of the job incumbent. This assumption is probably the least crucial to the argument since, trite as it may seem, a high level of job satisfaction among industrial workers may be an appropriate goal in itself. Thus, if job enrichment had no other result than decreased boredom and increased job satisfaction, it could be an appropriate manipulation. Also, there is evidence that in certain circumstances an individual's job satisfaction is significantly related to his subsequent decision to quit his job.[5,6,7] The relationship between satisfaction and productivity and other on-the-job behaviors is somewhat more elusive. The fact that this relationship has been so difficult to document with data indicates the weakness of the final assumption of the traditional model.

AN ALTERNATIVE VIEWPOINT

Let us propose that for some workers, all of the above assumptions are incorrect and that for all workers, the assumptions are true only in varying degrees. In other words, there may exist in the American work force identifiable subgroups whose motivation to work does *not* coincide with the idea that hard work is a virtue and that work is intrinsically rewarding; nor do they feel that it is a sin to work for money, social contact, or status. Let us further entertain the idea that

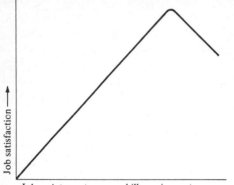

Figure 2 Hypothetical relationship between job variety and job satisfaction for a group of workers with a strong desire for a demanding job.

the psychological maturity and mental health of these subgroups of workers is neither better nor worse than that of any other identifiable subgroup.

I am suggesting that the ethnomorphising* of the white middle class social scientists, excutives, and managers may be as responsible for the job enrichment thesis as any set of data. That is, these influential individuals, starting with Adam Smith,† with their years of education and their frame of reference developed by exposure to the academic environment and administrative jobs respond nega-

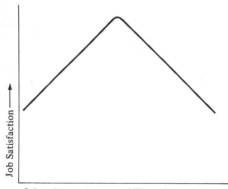

Figure 3 Hypothetical relationship between job variety and job satisfaction for a group of workers with a moderate desire for a demanding job.

*Ethnomorphising: The tendency to attribute to all members of a population the values, desires and aspirations possessed by one's own peer group or sub-culture.
†See Adam Smith's *An inquiry into the nature and causes of the wealth of nations.*

tively to a routine job and make the assumption that all mature, healthy workers will do the same.

This set of counter assumptions would lead to the rejection of the view that the relationship shown in Figure 1 is a general relationship which is true for all members of the American workforce. Rather this particular positive, monotonic relationship should be regarded as only *one* of a number of possible relationships between job variety and job satisfaction. We should be willing to consider also the hypotheses summarized in Figures 2 through 4. These figures portray a family of curves relating job variety to satisfaction, with the optimal amount of variety (in terms of producing the greatest amount of satisfaction) occurring at different points for different groups of workers.

The thrust of this alternative point of view may be summarized as follows: There exist identifiable subgroups of workers within the American workforce whose motivations to work are predictably and lawfully different from the general work motivation assumed by the job enrichment proponents. The problem confronting the researcher, then, is one of determining and assessing those variables which differentiate between these various subgroups, rather than assuming we understand work and what motivates men. The next step must be to determine the characteristics of the job and work situation which serve as positive sources of motivation for these different, independently defined work groups. Finally, if we discover that substantial differences exist between workers and that certain groups of workers are positively motivated by money or even a repetitive job, then *such differences must simply be regarded as part of the description of the world as it exists.* Whether or not this is the way the psychologist would like the world to be is a completely separate issue. In short, if the investigation of the differences between workers reveals that substantial numbers of these workers are motivated by so-called "lower-order needs" (such as money) then no value judgments need be made nor pejorative paragraphs written. (As an acquaintance

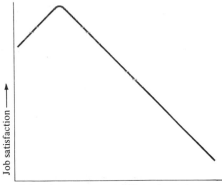

Job variety, autonomy, skill requirements ⟶

Figure 4 Hypothetical relationship between job variety and job satisfaction for a group of workers with a weak desire for a demanding job.

once said, "Money won't buy happiness but it sure takes the sting out of being miserable." Or as a famous blues singer put it, "I've been rich and I've been poor. Rich is better." Or alternatively, "It's better to be rich and healthy than poor and sick.")

The hypothesis that work (as a concept) has substantially different meanings to different groups of people is neither new nor startling. An examination of the anthropological literature suggests that the differences in the meaning of work from one culture to another are striking. For example, among the Tikopians of Oceania, work as a general concept is "good" and idleness is an evil similar to a religious offense. The people of Tikopia start work early, take few breaks and often compete with each other to see who can accomplish the most. (The similarity between these conceptions of work and idleness and the writings of John Calvin is obvious.) On the other hand, work is but a necessary evil for the Siriono of the Amazon Basin. They work when absolutely necessary, and only to obtain food. When food is available, they rest and there are no group or cultural sanctions for idleness.[8]

It would be all too easy for us to fall into the trap of making value judgments about the cultural differences described above and conclude that the Siriono are somehow less good than the people of Tikopia. These would be value judgments and *nothing more.* Such judgments are neither demanded by the data nor warranted by logic. A third example, somewhat closer to home, is found in the study by Morse and Weiss.[9] In this study people were asked if they would continue to work if they suddenly inherited enough money so they no longer needed to. The majority, 80%, said they would. However, the percentage of people who said they would *not* continue to work *increased* steadily from the white collar workers, to the skilled workers, and finally to the unskilled workers, with only 50% of the unskilled workers expressing a desire to continue working.

The study by Morse and Weiss provides evidence that work has different meanings within the different subcultures (defined by job levels) of the United States. Work is likely to be seen as a means to an economic end by the unskilled worker, while it has intrinsic meaning for the white collar worker. Again, no pious value judgments need be made.

SOME INDIRECT EVIDENCE

Let us now turn to an examination of some of the studies relating to job level and job enrichment. It is unfortunate that most of these studies provide indirect evidence, at best, and a certain amount of interpretation must be done before the results can be seen as relevant to the issue. Many of these studies have been poorly controlled, and most of the authors have attempted to generalize from severely limited data. . . .

[This] literature . . . presents a confused picture. Some investigators have reported results which show positive results of job enrichment programs and/or strong positive relationships between job level and job satisfaction. Other investigators have reported less positive or even negative results. There are three possible conclusions which can be drawn from such a collection of studies, each of which has certain merit. We could conclude that job enrichment is but another oversold, over-promoted gimmick in the long dreary history of research on job motivation and that the positive results are attributable to the Hawthorne effect and the Messianic fervor of the disciples of the model. Alternatively, we could conclude that job enrichment is the answer to our problems and the negative results are due to sloppy implementation of the program by inept investigators. Neither conclusion seems appropriate. A more reasonable conclusion would be that either positive or negative results may be expected from a program of job enrichment and the type of result depends to a great extent on the motivations of the workforce involved (among other things). The studies reviewed demonstrate this if nothing else. Precisely what characteristics of the workforce result in a positive or a negative response to job enrichment is still open to conjecture. Only a little research has been done on this question. This is unfortunate since this research should have been done first rather than last. The result is that job enrichment has by now been oversold to industry and in the literature. Any critical study or studies which might now be done and which indicate the presence of moderating influences (including groups which may respond negatively to job enrichment) are likely to be rejected.

INDIVIDUAL DIFFERENCES AND JOB ENRICHMENT

Our analysis of the problem of job enrichment and/or job simplification is limited by our lack of a definition of what we mean by "task" or "job." Few of the investigators working in this area have defined "job" either implicitly or explicitly. Two notable examples are the studies by Turner and Lawrence[10] and Hackman and Lawler.[11] Both of these teams of investigators described a job as a point in a 10-dimensional space. Their descriptions may be useful as a first approximation to a definition. Their studies will be considered from this point of view. Turner and Lawrence used "object variety" (number of different kinds of objects, tools, and controls worked on), "motor variety" (change in work pace, change in physical location, change in required physical operations), "autonomy" (latitude in choice of method, sequence, pace, importing outside services), "required interaction" (number of persons with whom the job requires interaction, quantity of interaction), "interaction opportunities: on-the-job" (number of people available for interaction, quantity), "interaction opportunities: off-the-job" (amount of time subject is free to choose to interact by going off the job without reprimand), knowledge and skill (learning time), "responsibility" (ambiguity of remedial action for routine problems, time span of discretion, probability of serious error), "task identity" (clarity of cycle, visibility of transformation to operator, magnitude of transformation), "cycle time" (duration of major job cycle), and "working conditions." They then collapsed these dimensions into one composite measure which they labeled "Requisite Task Attribute scale." Thus, while they started out conceptualizing a job as a point in a ten-dimensional space, they ended up combining the ten dimensions so that a job becomes a point in a complex continuum. This combining of the ten measures unfortunately masks any differences which may exist among the different dimensions of the job.

Hackman and Lawler used the research of Turner and Lawrence as their starting point and used six dimensions of jobs related to those used by Turner and Lawrence (labeled as variety, autonomy, task identity, feedback, dealing with others, and friendship opportunities). They found that the six dimensions were indeed related in different ways to the workers' responses. This study has been summarized above. The problem with this research is that of the choice of the dimensions used to describe the jobs. It is unclear if the 10 dimensions used by Turner and Lawrence or the six used by Hackman and Lawler are the dimensions which should be used to characterize jobs.

How one goes about establishing the appropriate dimensions is itself a controversial topic. We could assume a radical empiricism posture and attempt to develop dimensions which would maximize the standard score differences between any pair of jobs. This approach would yield a set of dimensions which would discriminate efficiently between jobs and locate them in an n-dimensional space with a minimum of confusion between the points. It is not clear, however, that these dimensions would be useful for studying psychological responses to the jobs. An example of the use of this method of developing defining dimensions is the approach used by Cattell* to describe the personality of an individual. Cattell, using the radical empiricism approach, has developed measures which will indeed discriminate between individuals. Unfortunately, the evidence relating his 16 personality measures to behavioral responses is scarce indeed. Therefore, their usefulness for understanding human behavior is limited.

Another approach is the method used by the Dictionary of Occupational Titles (DOT) to define or describe jobs. The DOT discriminates between jobs in terms of the abilities required to perform the job. The DOT may be a useful device to consult when selection and placement studies are undertaken. It is not clear, however, that the DOT definitions or dimensions are even remotely related to psychological responses to the job of the types we are considering.

It is possible that enough research has been done concerning the way people respond to the job so that we are further down the road than Cattell was when he began his research on personality. The problem remains, however, that this is only an assumption, and the dimensions we use to characterize jobs, while they may be related to psychological responses (as demonstrated by Hackman and Lawler), may be associated with only a very small portion of the variance of the psychological responses to the job. The net result of our lack of attention to this problem is that at the present time we can only assume we know which dimensions are important and we can only assume that we are measuring reliably at

---

*See Cattell, R. B. *Description and Measurement of Personality.* New York: World Book Co., 1946.

least some of these important dimensions. The basic research has not been done and we find ourselves locked into a program of job change when we are not even sure what variables should be changed if we are to enrich jobs.

It is also evident that our knowledge concerning those dimensions of individuals which are important in determining their response to a job is inadequate. Turner and Lawrence used a variable which they labeled "anomie" as their explanatory variable.[10] They defined anomie as feelings of normlessness and powerlessness. Hulin and Blood rejected the notion of anomie by arguing that simply because workers do not share the dominant values and norms does not mean they are normless.[12] Instead, Hulin and Blood substituted "alienation from middle-class work values" as the individual difference which determined the way workers responded to a job.

Hackman and Lawler used a variable labeled "higher-order need strength" as their individual difference variable. They operationalized "higher-order need strength" by means of a questionnaire requesting expressions of belief or disbelief in a number of statements related to Maslow's self actualization needs.

The only thing common to these three approaches is that they have organized a large amount of data and the results make sense. This, however, is a very weak base on which to build a theory of work, jobs, and motivation.

We find ourselves in the unfortunate position of having to assume that we know what the important individual differences are in determining workers' responses to their jobs. We have little knowledge that the dimensions we use are associated with more than a trivial amount of the variance. Until parametric research is undertaken, we are in little better shape regarding individual differences among workers than we are comparing differences among jobs. Nevertheless, the following tentative model relating job enrichment, job satisfaction, and individual differences is presented.

Earlier, Hulin and Blood presented a model which they felt would summarize the available data regarding individuals' responses to job enrichment or their responses to high level jobs.[12] Their model will be reviewed here for historical interest. Basically this model postulated that the response of a worker to a job enrichment program could vary from positive to negative depending on the extent to which the worker had internalized the work values of the middle class. To the extent that the worker had internalized the beliefs that hard work is a virtue and idleness is a sin; if you work hard you will get ahead; you are what you do, to do nothing is to be nothing; material rewards are but a small part of the rewards one gets from working; etc., then one could expect that the worker would respond favorably to a job enrichment program. However, if a worker had not internalized such a value system, then there is no reason to expect that he would respond favorably to an opportunity to take on a more responsible, more demanding job. In fact, if a worker received his major rewards from the money he received from his job and used the monetary reward to obtain off-the-job satisfactions, then he might even resent being asked to expend more of his psychological energy on his job.

Hulin and Blood felt that a reasonable predictor of a worker's response to his job could be found in certain characteristics of the community in which he was reared or in which he was living. Their argument was that blue-collar workers who are living in small towns or rural areas would not be members of a work group which would be large enough to develop and sustain its own work norms and values. Such workers would more likely be in closer contact with the dominant middle class. On the other hand, blue-collar workers living and working in large metropolitan industrialized areas would likely be members of a working class population which was large enough to develop a set of norms particular to that culture.

There is no compelling reason to believe that the norms developed by an urban working class subculture would be the same as those of the middle class. However, it should not be necessary to use an argument based on numbers of blue collar workers and social heterogeneity. One could argue that the dominant norms and values that all children learn in school and at home are those brought by the Anglo-Saxon Protestants from Europe in the 17th and 18th centuries. These norms and values have become the standard in American middle class society. Children are taught these values in school by their middle class teachers and attempt to reach goals defined in terms of these values and by means of behavior consistent with these values. However, children raised in slums, where the cost of living is high and where there is a great deal of migration, are likely to be frustrated in their attempts to reach such goals. Also, the lower class American city dweller is more likely to be non-Anglo-Saxon Protestant (Turner and Lawrence)[10] and less sympathetic to American middle class values. Therefore, the acquisition by the lower class city dweller of goals consistent with the Anglo-Saxon Protestant value system is likely to be met with criticism from his peer group.[13] Such frustration or negative reinforcement should extinguish behavior and beliefs consistent with American middle class ideals.*

The model developed by Hulin and Blood as well as the earlier model spelled out by Turner and Lawrence seem, in retrospect, to take an unnecessarily indirect approach to the problem. They invoke a set of social demographic variables (urbanization, extent of slums, industrialization) to explain differences in the extent to which workers have internalized middle class work values. These differences in work values are then used to explain differences in workers' responses to their jobs. It is easy to understand why this long chain of reasoning took place. The only data available *at the time* were the descriptions of the workers' responses to the programs and (usually) where the study was done. In addition, few investigators had directly studied the effects of plant location. In general, Hulin and Blood's explanation seemed to account for the data. However, a more direct

---

*It is interesting to note the similarity between this "sociological" model developed by Hulin and Blood and some data obtained from a sample of Yugoslavian workers (Jezernik).[14] Jezernik's explanation of his data was based in terms of the change from a revolutionary society to a consumer society. The differences in the terminology from that of Hulin and Blood only serves to dramatize the similarity of the ideas.

approach might summarize the data more efficiently and, in addition, prove to be more easily testable.

Such a direct approach is typified by the study of Hackman and Lawler. In their study they directly assessed a variable related to individual differences in motivation. This variable, labeled by Hackman and Lawler as "higher-order need strength," was found to moderate significantly the responses workers made to high level jobs. Workers who were categorized as being motivated by "higher-level needs" typically reported greater satisfaction if they were on jobs described (by observers) as having a great deal of variety and autonomy. The responses of these workers were similar to the responses of workers described by Hulin and Blood as non-alienated. The workers low on the "higher-order need" scale responded as the workers Hulin and Blood described as being alienated.

The findings of studies which relate individual differences to workers' responses to jobs can be understood within the following framework.

1 Work role outcomes* are valued to the extent that such outcomes meet the needs, aspirations or desires of the worker.

2 All workers do not have the same needs, aspirations and desires.

3 To the extent that jobs can be engineered so as to provide for the needs, aspirations and desires of individuals, these jobs will be satisfying for these individuals.

4 Workers will adopt a particular work role if the adoption of such a work role will lead to desired outcomes.

These four propositions are not new with this chapter. They have been presented in different contexts, using different emphases many times before.[15] Such propositions do, however, point out the complexity of the industrial world. They should also serve to reiterate that any given worker may be motivated by more than one job characteristic *and* that workers can differ greatly from each other in terms of what job characteristics are motivating to them. In addition, any differences between workers who are motivated by different outcomes are a matter for data, not assumption. If the data indicate that workers who are motivated by a desire for money (as opposed to workers who are motivated by a desire for "self-actualization") are psychologically immature, produce less, are absent more frequently, or are more likely quit their job, then such is the case. Until these data are available, however, we should start with the viewpoint that different workers may well be motivated by strikingly different job characteristics and we should design jobs accordingly. Such an approach will not lead to job enrichment programs in all plants, but it is an indication that as complicated a problem as motivation cannot be written off with the solution of job enrichment alone.

*Work role outcome is defined as being the result(s) of a particular work role. Work role is defined as a set of behaviors which are used to categorize different groups of employees. Being an incumbent of a tool and die makers job is an example of a work role. Being a highly productive salesman (as opposed to an unproductive salesman) is another example.

REFERENCES

1 Smith, Patricia C. Individual differences in suseptibility to industrial monotony. *J. Applied Psychology,* **39,** 322–29 (1955).
2 Baldamus, W. *Efficiency and effort.* London: Tavistock, 1961.
3 Smith, Patricia C., and Lem, C. Positive aspects of motivation in repetitive work: effects of lot size upon spacing of voluntary rest periods. *J. Applied Psychology,* **39,** 330–33 (1955).
4 Vroom, V. H. *Some personality determinants of the effects of participation.* Englewood Cliffs: Prentice-Hall, 1960.
5 Hulin, C. L. Job satisfaction and turnover in a female clerical population. *J. Applied Psychology,* **50,** 280–85 (1966).
6 Hulin, C. L. The effects of changes in job satisfaction levels on turnover. *J. Applied Psychology,* **52,** 122–26 (1968).
7 Weitz, J., and Nuckols, R. C. The validity of direct and indirect questions in measuring job satisfaction. *Personnel Psychology,* **6,** 487–94 (1953).
8 Holmberg, A. *Nomads of the long bow.* Washington: Smithsonian Institution, 1950.
9 Morse, N. C., and Weiss, R. S. The function and meaning of work and the job. *American Sociological Review,* **20,** 191–98 (1955).
10 Turner, A. N., and Lawrence, P. R. *Industrial jobs and the worker: an investigation of response to task attributes.* Boston: Harvard University Press, 1965.
11 Hackman, J. R., and Lawler, E. E. *Jobs and motivation.* Mimeographed copy. School of Administrative Sciences, Yale University, 1970.
12 Hulin, C. L., and Blood, M. R. Job enlargement, individual differences, and worker responses. *Psychological Bulletin,* **69,** 41–55 (1968).
13 Whyte, W. F. *Money and motivation.* New York: Harper, 1955.
14 Jezernick, M. D. Changes in the hierarchy of motivational factors and social values in Slovenian industry. *J. Social Issues,* **24,** No. 2, 103–11 (1968).
15 Graen, G. B. Instrumentality theory of work motivation: some experimental results and suggested modifications. *J. Applied Psychology Monograph,* **53,** No. 2 Part 2, 1–25 (1969).

QUESTIONS FOR DISCUSSION

1 How might variations in job design affect employee motivation? Explain using *(a)* Maslow's need hierarchy theory, and *(b)* expectancy/valence theory.
2 Why might individual differences among employees play an important role in the determination of the impact of job characteristics on motivation?
3 What are several potential drawbacks to job enrichment and job redesign efforts?
4 How might job enrichment efforts differ between managerial and blue-collar jobs?
5 How would you go about enriching an assembly-line worker's job without actually doing away with the assembly line?
6 How important a factor do you feel an individual's task requirements really are in determining his or her motivation to perform? In determining his or her level of job satisfaction? Why?
7 What role do various cultural factors play in employee reactions to job redesign?

Chapter 13

Goal-Setting and Performance

OVERVIEW

In this chapter, we discuss the role of goals and goal-setting in organizations as they affect employee motivation and performance. Before analyzing this role, however, we should first consider what is meant by the concept of goals itself. Traditionally, there have been two definitional approaches. First, goals can be conceptualized as future states of desired affairs (Etzioni, 1964; Vroom, 1960). In this sense, they are statements of where the individual or organization wants to be at some future time. Second, goals can be seen as constraints placed on present and future behavior as a result of past and present decisions and commitments (Cyert & March, 1963; Simon, 1964).

Although the literature on goals has generally treated these approaches as two distinct entities (Porter, Lawler, & Hackman, 1975; Steers, 1971), it appears that they are more complementary than mutually exclusive. That is, it is possible to envision the concept of goals as a dynamic process by which individuals and organizations determine their future aspirations within certain known limitations. Once these aspirations (or objectives) have been set, however, they tend to rule out the possibility of pursuing other potential goals because of the limit of resources. Hence, goal-setting really becomes a process of allocating one's resources—such as manpower, money, time. Such a dynamic approach to goals—viewing goal-setting as a continual decision and reevaluation process—subsumes both of the definitional approaches discussed above.

Once goals have been formulated, they tend to serve several *functions* for the goal-setter. First—and perhaps most important—goals guide and direct behavior; they focus attention and effort in specific directions. In this sense, they provide a rationale for organizing resources. Second, goals often serve as a standard against which judgments can be made as to the relative effectiveness and efficiency with which individuals or organizations achieve (or fail to achieve) their purposes. Third, goals may also serve as a source of legitimacy, justifying various activities and the use of resources necessary to pursue them. Fourth, on an organizational level, goals often significantly affect the structure of the organization itself. The activities, practices, and technological processes necessary for goal attainment can impose restrictions on the activities of the membership, as well as on the acquisition and distribution of resources. Such basic social phenomena as communication patterns, authority and power relations, division of labor, and status orderings can thus be directly affected. Fifth, the study of goals can provide significant insight that is not found elsewhere into the underlying motives and character—and thus behavior—of both individuals and organizations. In this sense, goals are statements of what the goal-setter thinks is important and worthy of pursuit.

When specifically viewing the role of goals in employee motivation and performance, it is important to ask which *type* of goals we are considering. There appear to be at least three important types that have a bearing on the individual's effort and performance. First, there are organizationwide (or, at least, departmentwide) goals. These goals represent statements concerning future directions for large segments of the organization's population. Making a suitable profit or increasing a company's market share might be examples of organizational goals. (See the Steers and Porter selection, immediately following, for a discussion of official versus operational organizational goals.) Such goals may affect employee effort by giving individuals a general idea of the types of performance desired. Moreover, they may serve as a source of identification for employees, enhancing to some extent their feelings of self-worth through such identification. (How often have we heard people, when asked what they do, respond by saying they work for such-and-such corporation?)

A second major type of goal is the task-goal. Task-goals are specific objectives assigned to an individual, or small group of individuals. Broad organizational goals may lack significant influence for employees unless they are translated into task-goals so that each employee knows the extent of his or her own responsibilities.

A third distinct type of goal is the personal goal, or level of aspiration. Personal goals differ from task-goals in that they are internally generated; they are the goals set by the individual himself. For example, salespersons who have been assigned a task-goal of increasing their sales by 10 percent may think that, realistically, they can increase their sales by only 5 percent. This 5 percent goal, then, becomes their personal goal (or aspiration level)—the goal for which they are really *trying*.

When these three types of goals are taken into consideration, goal-setting behavior at the level of the individual employee can be viewed as a bargaining process between the individual and the organization (usually represented by the employee's immediate supervisor). On the one hand, management attempts to set employee task-goals that are consistent with the larger organizational purpose and of sufficient scope and magnitude to justify hiring the employee. On the other hand, the employees themselves must ultimately determine what level of aspiration on assigned tasks they think is fair or desirable and worth pursuing. This bargaining process—whether overt or implicit—is an important force in the determination of individual performance in complex organizations. In theory, the closer an employee's aspiration levels are to his or her assigned task-goals, the greater is the likelihood that the task-goal will be realized.

These two sides of the bargaining process are discussed in the selections that follow. The first selection, by Steers and Porter, analyzes the role of task-goal in employee performance. These findings are then analyzed within an expectancy/ valence motivational framework in an effort to develop a clearer understanding of the role of goals in motivational process. (See also Steers, 1975.) The basic nature of formalized goal-setting programs, like "management by objectives" (MBO), is then discussed from a managerial standpoint by Tosi, Rizzo, and Carroll.

Finally, the role of personal aspiration levels in performance is reviewed by Locke, Cartledge, and Knerr. Locke and his associates propose a model which posits that behavior is largely the result of intentional actions taken by individuals. In short, it is argued that people set personal goals on various activities and that these goals guide their behavior. Locke reviews several laboratory experiments which are largely consistent with his basic theoretical formulations. Moreover, he compares his model to other motivational theories, pointing out several unique features of his own model.

In summary, we have two quite distinct views of goal-setting behavior set forth in this chapter. The first view analyzes goal-setting from the standpoint of variations in task-goals as they impact upon employee behavior. Several conclusions are drawn with regard to what organizations can do to coordinate the activities of their employees for organizational goal attainment. The second view attempts to develop a theory of task motivation and performance based on employee aspiration levels. It would seem that both approaches are necessary if we are to understand more fully the dynamics of goal-setting. That is, performance in organizations can be seen as a function of what the organization expects from its employees in the way of task performance *and* of what the employees are willing to offer in the form of personal levels of aspiration on the job.

REFERENCES AND SUGGESTED ADDITIONAL READINGS

Bryan, J. F., & Locke, E. A. Goal-setting as a means of increasing motivation. *Journal of Applied Psychology,* 1967, **51,** 274–277.

Carroll, S. J., Jr., & Tosi, H. L., Jr. Goal characteristics and personality factors in a management-by-objective program. *Administrative Science Quarterly,* 1970, **15,** 295–305.

Carroll, S. J., Jr., & Tosi, H. L., Jr. *Management by objectives: Applications and research.* Macmillan, 1973.

Cyert, R. M., & March, J. G. *A behavioral theory of the firm.* Englewood Cliffs, N.J.: Prentice-Hall 1963.

Etzioni, A. *Modern organizations.* Englewood Cliffs, N.J.: Prentice-Hall, 1964.

French, J. R., Kay, E., & Meyer, H. H. Participation and the appraisal system. *Human Relations,* 1966, **19,** 3–19.

Humble, J. W. *Management by objectives in action.* London: McGraw-Hill, 1970.

Ivancevich, J. M. A longitudinal assessment of management by objectives. *Administrative Science Quarterly,* 1972, **17,** 126–138.

Locke, E. A. The motivational effects of knowledge of results: Knowledge or goal-setting? *Journal of Applied Psychology,* 1967, **51,** 324–329.

Locke, E. A. Toward a theory of task performance and incentives. *Organizational Behavior and Human Performance,* 1968, **3,** 157–189.

Locke, E. A., & Bryan, J. F. The directing function of goals in task performance. *Organizational Behavior and Human Performance,* 1969, **4,** 35–42.

Meyer, H. H., Kay, E., & French, J. R. Split roles in performance appraisal. *Harvard Business Review,* 1965, **43,** 123–129.

Porter, L. W., Lawler, E. E., III, & Hackman, J. R. *Behavior in organizations.* New York: McGraw-Hill, 1975.

Raia, A. P. Goal setting and self control. *Journal of Management Studies,* 1965, **2,** 34–53.

Raia, A. P. A second look at goals and controls. *California Management Review,* 1966, **8(4),** 49–58.

Simon, H. A. On the concept of organizational goal. *Administrative Science Quarterly,* 1964, **9,** 1–22.

Stedry, A. C., & Kay, E. The effects of goal difficulty on performance: A field experiment. *Behavioral Science,* 1966, **11,** 459–470.

Steers, R. M. The concept of organizational goals: A research review. Unpublished manuscript, 1971.

Steers, R. M. Task goal attributes, n achievement, and supervisory performance. *Organizational Behavior and Human Performance,* 1975, in press.

Tosi, H. L., Jr., & Carroll, S. J., Jr. Managerial reaction to management by objectives. *Academy of Management Journal,* 1968, **11,** 415–426.

Vroom, V. H. The effects of attitudes on perception of organizational goals. *Human Relations,* 1960, **13,** 229–240.

The Role of Task-Goal Attributes in Employee Performance

Richard M. Steers
Lyman W. Porter[1]

Organizational researchers and practicing managers have long been concerned with discovering methods for improving the effectiveness and efficiency of on-going organizations. The determination of organizational effectiveness has traditionally been seen as the extent to which an organization is successful in accomplishing its operative goals, while organizational efficiency is typically defined as the cost-benefit ratio incurred in pursuit of those goals (Barnard, 1938). Considerable theory exists on an abstract level concerning the nature of organizational goal formulation and goal attainment, particularly as it relates to the external environment (Cyert & March, 1963; Etzioni, 1964; Lawrence & Lorsch, 1967; March & Simon, 1958; Perrow, 1961, 1970; Simon, 1964; Thompson & McEwen, 1958). However, little attempt has been made empirically to understand how such broad-based objectives become translated into specific activities which can be carried out by the individual members of an organization; that is, our knowledge of the relationship between the pursuit of *organizational* goals and the required tasks of *individuals* appears lacking in several respects. What is needed is a clearer understanding of the factors which eventually go to determine how well an organization achieves its stated intentions.

It is the purpose of this paper to review systematically the relevant research dealing with the role played by *task*-goals in employee performance. The findings of these investigations will be placed in the larger organizational context as they ultimately relate to the attainment of organization-wide goals. We first briefly consider the association between organizational goals and task-goals. Next, we review the research relating various aspects of task-goals to individual performance on the job. Finally, the role of task-roles will be discussed within the theoretical context of an employee's motivational force to perform and how such performance relates to the larger issue of organizational effectiveness.

To begin with, it is important to consider, at least in theory, how the goals of an organization become translated into manageable tasks for employees to perform. A typical formalized goal-setting program designed to maximize organizational goal attainment, while simultaneously minimizing unnecessary expenditure of human resources, can be seen as proceeding on two levels. The first step in this (ideal) process would involve what March and Simon (1958) term a "means-ends

Abridged from *Psychological Bulletin*, 1974, **81**, 434–452. Copyright 1974 by the American Psychological Association. Reprinted by permission.

[1]This paper was supported in part by a grant from the Graduate Division, University of California, Irvine, and by funds supplied under Office of Naval Research Contract No. N00014–69–020 0–9001, NR 151–315.

analysis." Briefly defined, such an analysis represents an attempt on an organization-wide basis to refine operative goals (i. e., the real objectives or intentions of the organization) into operational (i. e., specific, manageable, and measurable) goals. This means-ends analysis, which would finally culminate in fairly specific and tangible organizational goals, is generally *horizontal* in nature; that is, goal refinements typically would remain organization-wide, or at least department-wide, in scope and responsibility.

Next, a vehicle must be found to translate these organization-wide operational goals into smaller segments which are of sufficient size to be suitably managed by individuals or sub-groups in the organization. In other words, the second step in the process involves extending the means-ends chain *vertically* down through the various levels of the organization in such a way as to marshall organizational resources efficiently for goal-directed activities. When this sequential process becomes formalized into a goal-setting system where each member, or small group, has specific goals and time parameters for task accomplishment, it often goes under the rubric of "Management-By-Objectives," or MBO. The basic motivational *assumption* of such goal-setting programs is that effort—and consequently performance—is increased by providing individuals with clear targets toward which to direct their energies. Thus, search behavior is theoretically reduced, allowing for greater effort to be concentrated in a single direction. Such a system has as its major purpose, then, the maximization of organizational goal attainment through the efficient use of an organization's resources. In other words, the contribution of each member to organizational effectiveness is theoretically maximized.

It becomes clear from the foregoing discussion that the common denominator of such a goal-setting system is the individual "task-goals" assigned to the various members of the organization. *Task-goals* may be defined as relatively specific targets or objectives which an employee (or a small group of employees) is responsible for accomplishing within a specified time period. Typically, task-goals are tied to some form of systematic performance appraisal and review. Assuming that such goals have been set with reference to the larger organizational purpose, the degree to which these task-goals are met (or not met) in large measure should determine the ultimate success or failure of an organization in meeting its overall objectives.

While formalized goal-setting programs had their beginnings among managerial and supervisory personnel, the techniques have more recently been applied to blue-collar workers. Myers (1970) argues that meaningful goals can provide a sense of purpose for almost any type of activity. He describes goals which potentially have maximum motivational value as those task-goals which are influenced by the employee and which are visible, desirable, challenging, and attainable. Such goals are hypothesized to lead to the satisfaction of an individual's needs for growth, achievement, responsibility, recognition, affiliation, and security (1970:42). Thus, *in theory,* goal-setting techniques, such as those employed in MBO-type programs, should have a significant and beneficial impact not only upon performance but also upon employee attitudes and need satisfaction. Unfortunately, much of this theory remains largely untested.

The books written on formalized goal-setting systems are legion in number (e. g., Batten, 1966; Beck & Hillmar, 1972; Drucker, 1954; Hughes, 1965; Koontz, 1971; E. Miller, 1968; Morrisey, 1970; Odiorne, 1965; Schleh, 1961; Valentine, 1966; Wikstrom, 1968). By and large, these works represent "how-to-do-it" manuals based primarily on anecdotal evidence and are often void of empirical support for the theories expounded. (A notable exception to this trend is a recent book by Carroll and Tosi [1973].) This situation leaves both the researcher and the organizational decision-maker in a position of either accepting the utility of goal-setting programs on face value or rejecting them out of hand due to an absence of supportive evidence. Neither of these positions appears desirable. In an attempt to resolve this dilemma, an effort will be made here to bring together in an integrated fashion the available research that does exist to provide a better understanding of the performance implications of various aspects of such systems.

RESEARCH ON TASK-GOALS AND PERFORMANCE

When the research on task-goals is considered *in toto,* strong and consistent evidence emerges that the act of setting clear goals on an individual's job (as opposed to only broadly defining his areas of responsibility) does generally result in increased performance. Such findings have been demonstrated both in the laboratory (Bryan & Locke, 1967a; Fryer, 1964; Mace, 1935) and in the field (French, Kay & Meyer, 1966; Humble, 1970a, 1970b; Lawrence & Smith, 1955; Meyer, Kay & French, 1965; Raia, 1965, 1966). However, knowing that goal-setting techniques are relatively successful does not explain *why* they work or *what* can be done to improve their effectiveness. A more complete picture of the nature of goal-setting may be obtained by studying the role played by various attributes of a goal-setting system as they relate to performance.

Toward this end, studies relating various "task-goal attributes" to performance will be reviewed. A *task-goal attribute* is defined here as a characteristic or dimension of an employee's task-goals. While research has been carried out on numerous—and often overlapping—attributes, a recent study using factor analytic techniques (Steers, 1973) demonstrated the existence of five relatively autonomous attributes: (1) goal specificity; (2) participation in goal-setting; (3) feedback on goal progress; (4) peer competition for goal attainment; and (5) goal difficulty. In addition, we shall include "goal acceptance" here as a sixth attribute. While the goal acceptance dimension was not derived from the factor analytic study, recent research has pointed to its potential importance for employee performance under goal-setting conditions. The relevant research relating to each of these attributes will be analyzed separately. . . .[2]

DISCUSSION AND CONCLUSIONS

It has been argued throughout this review that the simple knowledge that goal-setting "works" is insufficient for our understanding of the goal-setting process;

[2]Due to space limitations, the review section of this paper has been omitted. The interested reader is referred to the original source for a more detailed analysis of the specific investigations.

we must know how and why it works. Toward this end, some 80 empirical studies relating to six factor-analytically derived attributes of task-goals were examined. Based on this review, several specific conclusions can be drawn.

To begin with, increases in goal specificity were found to be consistently and positively related to performance across both field and laboratory investigations. We would expect such a finding in view of the centrality of goal specification in formalized goal-setting programs; in fact, goal specificity may in many ways be considered a defining characteristic of such programs. In addition, the available research indicates that acceptance of task-goals is also strongly and positively related to performance. However, this conclusion rests on only a few empirical studies, and final judgment must await further investigation.

Less consistent findings have been demonstrated for the three attributes of goal difficulty, participation in goal-setting, and feedback on goal effort. While the majority of findings concerning each of these attributes tends to indicate positive relationships with performance, a number of important exceptions exist. For example, while the laboratory studies of goal difficulty consistently point to a positive relationship with performance, the field studies generally indicate either more complex or null relationships. Moreover, many investigations of these three attributes found important intervening variables which influenced performance relationships. Thus, while the tendencies for all three task-goal attributes are in the direction of positive associations with performance, no definitive relationships were found. Finally, no consistent relationship emerged between the degree of peer competition and employee performance, again suggesting the existence of important intervening variables which influence the relationship.

From these data, a possible case could be made that the "key" to successful goal-setting programs in work situations, such as MBO, lies primarily in discovering those specific task-goal attributes most closely associated with performance and then "loading" an employee's task-goals with these attributes. This approach has often been taken in some of the more prescriptive literature on goal-setting. However, such actions by themselves appear less than desirable for at least two reasons. First, the singular attention to the role of task-goal attributes in performance ignores several additional factors which have been shown to have an important bearing on performance. Second, and perhaps more important from a psychological standpoint, such action really tells us very little about the dynamics behind the effects of goal-setting. That is, knowing that goal specificity, for example, is consistently related to task performance does not explain the process by which it affects such performance.

A more comprehensive analysis of the role of task-goal attributes in employee performance can be derived by analyzing from a theoretical standpoint the psychological processes involved in such activities. The question posed here, then, is how various attributes in a goal-setting program affect an individual's motivational force to perform. We shall consider this question by viewing the effects of goal-setting programs within an Expectancy/Valence motivational framework. While many theories of motivation exist, the Expectancy/Valence model has been selected as a framework for analysis for several reasons. First, it represents a reasonably well-developed and comprehensive approach to explaining human behavior at work. It attempts to account for important variables not only within the individual but also within the work environment in which he finds himself. Second, some research has begun to emerge which generally provides some support for the effectiveness of this model in explaining the decision to perform at a given level (Campbell et al., 1970; Galbraith & Cummings, 1967; Georgopoulos, Mahoney, & Jones, 1957; Graen, 1969; Heneman & Schwab, 1972; Mitchell & Biglan, 1971; Porter & Lawler, 1968; Vroom, 1964).

In simplified form, Expectancy/Valence theory posits that the motivational force of an individual to perform is a multiplicative function of his subjective probability that effort will lead to the receipt of certain rewards and the valence he places on those rewards. For example, if an individual really believes that increasing his effort will lead to the receipt of a pay raise, and if he values having this additional income, we would expect his effort on the job to be high. (It should be noted that, while more complex elaborations of this theory exist, this simplified form will suffice for our purposes here.)

When the major findings of this review are placed within such a framework, it becomes possible to understand more fully—at least on a theoretical level— why certain task-goal attributes can play such important roles at times in the determination of employee performance under a goal-setting system. Under this conceptualization, it would appear that the various task-goal attributes affect performance because—and to the extent that—they affect the components comprising the motivational force equation. In other words, varying the amounts of certain of these attributes on the job may serve to alter an employee's expectancies, valences, or both, thereby affecting his motivation to perform. Three brief examples should serve to clarify this point.

First, consider the example of goal specificity. Giving an employee a set of goals that are highly specific in nature should allow him to know more precisely what is expected of him on the job. Such reduced search behavior should, in turn, make it easier for the individual to see the relationship between effort and resulting performance (and presumably rewards), thus clarifying his level of expectations on that job.

A second example can be seen by examining the potential motivational effects of allowing employee participation in goal-setting. It is possible that such participation may at times affect the valence an individual places on goal attainment. If an employee is allowed to play a central role in the determination of his task-goals, he may become more ego-involved in the outcome of those goals (Vroom, 1960) and place a higher value on goal attainment. Thus, assuming constant expectancies, increasing an employee's valence for potential rewards should lead to increased effort. We would expect, however, that these participation effects would be affected at least to some extent by the personality traits exhibited by the employee. For example, an employee with a high need for achievement might be more prone to become ego-involved in performance outcomes (and increase his valences accordingly) when allowed greater participation than someone who has a low need for achievement.

Finally, take the more complex example of peer competition for goal attainment. Where a situation approaches a zero-sum game (i. e., where there can be only one "winner"), we might expect a competitive atmosphere to lead to somewhat increased valences concerning outcomes, while at the same time lowering certain expectancy levels. A salesman, for instance, generally realizes that there are attractive benefits (e. g., bonuses, etc.) for ranking first among his peers in sales and that, simultaneously, there are undesirable penalties for ranking last (e. g., the possibility of termination). Under such circumstances, we would expect such competitive effects to lead to an increase in the valence attached to the available (and scarce) rewards. However, realization that one's peers are probably also putting forth maximum effort to gain such desirable rewards (and avoid such severe penalties) may tend to reduce one's expectancies that increased effort will, in fact, lead to increased performance and rewards. We may thus have a situation where increased peer competition would lead to increased valences, but the impact of such a change may be largely negated by a concomitant reduction in expectancies.

On the other hand, when the situation tends toward a non-zero-sum game (i. e., where there can be more than one "winner"), there is little reason to believe that perceived competitive effects would have a substantial influence on either expectancies or valences. The removal of both the extreme positive *and* the extreme negative consequences in the above example would tend to reduce in large measure the valence attached to goal attainment in and of itself. Subjective perceptions of the ease of goal attainment (expectancies) may be somewhat higher, however, because the individual may not perceive his peers as trying quite so hard, thereby making *relative* performance somewhat easier. Thus, while certain expectancies here may be somewhat higher, the corresponding reward valences would probably tend to be lower, again cancelling out any substantive gains in employee effort.

We have attempted here to provide three hypothetical examples of how goal-setting effects can be better understood by placing them within a specific motivational framework. Other examples could be provided. It is important to realize, however, that these examples are conjectural in nature and are meant simply to be illustrative of how a framework like the Expectancy/Valence model could be utilized to learn more about the processes behind goal-setting dynamics. It is argued here that one explanation for such a process is that variations in the attributes of an employee's task goals tend to affect effort and performance to the extent that they alter his level of path-goal expectancies or the valences he attaches to expected outcomes on the job. More specific descriptions of such a process awaits further investigation.

Viewing formalized goal-setting programs, like MBO, within such a motivational model leads to several fairly specific implications for the practicing manager. To begin with, it appears as though greater consideration should be given in the design and application of such programs to the nature of the particular attributes which characterize an employee's task-goals. For example, it was generally found in the above review that goal specificity was positively associated with task performance. Following this finding, greater attention could be paid in the formulation of task-goals to insuring that such goals are clearly specified and well understood by the employee. Similarly, increased effort on the part of management could be directed toward securing employee acceptance of these goals in the form of personal levels of aspiration. In short, greater care should be given to insuring that the final goal-setting program design is consistent with existing knowledge concerning the performance implications of the various task-goal attributes. Such a practice has apparently not been the case in many existing MBO-type programs (Carroll & Tosi, 1973; Raia, 1965, 1966).

In addition, increased attention could be paid to drawing a suitable linkage between existing programs and relevant motivational theories of work behavior. For example, consideration should be directed toward a better understanding of the consequences to be obtained from a clarification for employees of the relationship between task performance and potential rewards. Moreover, increased attention could be focused on improving our knowledge as to which rewards employees truly value. If employees consistently attach a low valence to the traditional rewards offered for goal attainment, the motivational value of such rewards would tend to be less than desirable.

Third, some concern appears in order as to the potential negative attitudinal consequences which may be associated with certain aspects of goal-setting programs that could hamper program effectiveness. Some research has indicated that when goals are perceived as being far too difficult or far too rigid, the credibility of the program itself may be seriously jeopardized, leading to poor performance. Care must be taken, in other words, to insure that the general parameters of the program are fairly widely accepted by program participants.

Finally, it would appear highly desirable if management would increase their willingness to subject their MBO-type programs to continual empirical examination in an effort to monitor both attitudinal and performance consequences of such programs. Some research has demonstrated that goal-setting programs tend to lose their potency over time but little effort has been directed toward discovering why such a phenomenon occurs. A continuing monitoring system could hopefully assist in the identification of such trends and possibly point to potential remedies.

Assuming that such factors are taken into account, we would expect this increased understanding of the nature of goal-setting and of the role played by the various task-goal attributes to lead to at least some improvement in program effectiveness. However, one cannot assume that variations in the nature of task-goals would account solely for performance variances related to goal-setting. Sufficient evidence exists to demonstrate that several other factors must be taken into account if we are to more fully understand how level of effort is determined. For example, many studies point to the importance of certain additional situational and environmental factors (e. g., openness of communication, leadership style, etc.) in determining effort (French et al., 1966; Ivancevich, 1972; Litwin & Stringer, 1968). Moreover, characteristics unique to the individual employee must be considered. Not only have some individual difference factors (e. g., need for achievement, level of aspiration) been shown to be somewhat effective predictors of performance by themselves (Cummin, 1967; E. French, 1955, 1958a, 1958b; Locke, 1968), but such factors have also been shown to represent important modifiers of the effects of certain task-goal attributes on performance (Carroll & Tosi, 1970, 1973; French et al., 1966; Steers, 1973; Vroom, 1960). These considerations must not be overlooked when attempting to understand more fully formalized goal-setting systems.

Thus, performance under goal-setting conditions appears to be a function of at least three important variables: the nature of task-goals, additional situational-environmental factors, and individual differences. Certainly, only when all three factors are duly considered can a greater understanding result concerning the extent of the role played by task-goals in employee performance. Such a conclusion must caution against the casual use of the *ceteris paribus* assumption when analyzing the performance implications of various task-goal attributes. We must begin to view the role of task-goal attributes within more complex frameworks which can adequately account for several additional variables which have been shown to represent important factors in employee performance. Moreover, there is a clear need to carry out these analyses within well-developed conceptualizations of the motivational process. One attempt at such a synthesis of empirical evidence with current work motivation theory has been made here, but more work is needed to test the applicability of such models to the goal-setting environment.

Finally, in addition to viewing individual performance on task-goals within a motivational framework, the role of task-goals must also be considered within the larger organizational context. More information is needed, for example, about the relation between task-goals and organizational goals. While much theorizing exists concerning such a relationship, in point of fact the bodies of research data on these two "types" of goals are virtually unrelated. Sound empirical investigation—as opposed to exhortative prescriptions—is needed on how (or whether) operational organizational goals become translated into employee task-goals and how such a process affects employee performance. Conversely, and equally important, we need to know how (or whether) task-goals impact upon organizational goals. Findings from such research should help us understand better how both types of goals affect the larger issue of organizational effectiveness.

REFERENCES[3]

Barnard, C. *The functions of the executive.* Cambridge, Mass.: Harvard University Press, 1938.

Batten, J. D. *Beyond management by objectives.* New York: American Management Association, 1966.

---

[3]References abridged.

Beck, A. C., Jr., & Hillmar, E. D. *A practical approach to organization development through MBO—Selected readings.* Reading, Mass.: Addison-Wesley, 1972.

Bryan, J. F., & Locke, E. A. Goal setting as a means of increasing motivation. *Journal of Applied Psychology*, 1967, **51**, 274–277. (a)

Campbell, J. P., Dunnette, M. D., Lawler, E. E., III, & Weick, K. E. *Managerial behavior, performance and effectiveness.* New York: McGraw-Hill, 1970.

Carroll, S. J., Jr., & Tosi, H. L., Goal characteristics and personality factors in a management-by-objectives program. *Administrative Science Quarterly*, 1970, **15**, 295–305.

Carroll, S. J., & Tosi, H. L., Jr. *Management by objectives: Applications and research.* New York: Macmillan, 1973.

Cummin, P. C. TAT correlates of executive performance. *Journal of Applied Psychology*, 1967, **51**, 78–81.

Cyert, R. M., & March, J. G. *A behavioral theory of the firm.* Englewood Cliffs, N.J.: Prentice-Hall, 1963.

Drucker, P. *The practice of management.* New York: Harper, 1954.

Etzioni, A. *Modern organizations.* Englewood Cliffs, N.J.: Prentice-Hall, 1964.

French, E. G. Some characteristics of achievement motivation. *Journal of Experimental Psychology*, 1955, **50**, 232–236.

French, E. G. Effects of the interaction of motivation and feedback on task performance. In J. W. Atkinson (Ed.), *Motives in fantasy, action, and society.* Princeton, N.J.: Van Nostrand, 1958. (a)

French, E. G. The interaction of achievement motivation and ability in problem solving success. *Journal of Abnormal Social Psychology*, 1958, **57**, 306–309. (b)

French, J. R., Kay, E., & Meyer, H. H. Participation and the appraisal system. *Human Relations*, 1966, **19**, 3–19.

Fryer, F. W. *An evaluation of level of aspiration as a training procedure.* Englewood Cliffs, N.J.: Prentice-Hall, 1964.

Galbraith, J., & Cummings, L. L. An empirical investigation of the motivational determinants of task performance: Interactive effects between instrumentality-valence and motivation-ability. *Organizational Behavior and Human Performance*, 1967, **2**, 237–257.

Georgopoulos, B., Mahoney, G., & Jones, N. A path-goal approach to productivity. *Journal of Applied Psychology*, 1957, **41**, 345–353.

Graen, G. Instrumentality theory of work motivation: Some experimental results and suggested modifications. *Journal of Applied Psychology Monograph*, 1969, **53** (2, Pt. 2).

Heneman, H. G., III, & Schwab, D. P. An evaluation of research on expectancy theory predictions of employee performance. *Psychological Bulletin*, 1972, **78**, 1–9.

Hughes, C. L. *Goal setting: Key to individual and organizational effectiveness.* New York: American Management Association, 1965.

Humble, J. W. *Improving business results.* London: McGraw-Hill, 1970. (a)

Humble, J. W. *Management by objectives in action.* London: McGraw-Hill, 1970. (b)

Ivancevich, J. M. A longitudinal assessment of management by objectives. *Administrative Science Quarterly*, 1972, **16**, 126–138.

Koontz, H. *Appraising managers as managers.* New York: McGraw-Hill, 1971.

Lawrence, L. C., & Smith, P. C. Group decision and employee participation. *Journal of Applied Psychology*, 1955, **39**, 334–337.

Lawrence, P. R., & Lorsch, J. *Organization and environment.* Boston: Division of Research, Graduate School of Business Administration, Harvard University, 1967.

Litwin, G. H., & Stringer, R. A., Jr. *Motivation and organizational climate.* Boston: Division of Research, Graduate School of Business Administration, Harvard University, 1968.

Locke, E. A. Toward a theory of task performance and incentives. *Organizational Behavior and Human Performance,* 1968, **3,** 157–189.

Mace, C. A. Incentives: Some experimental studies. London: Industrial Health Research Board, 1935, Report No. 72.

March, J. G., & Simon, H. A. *Organizations.* New York: Wiley, 1958.

Meyer, H., Kay, E., & French, J. R. Split roles in performance appraisal. *Harvard Business Review,* 1965, **43,** 123–129.

Miller, E. C. *Objectives and standards of performance in financial management.* New York: American Management Association, 1968.

Mitchell, T. R., & Biglan, A. Instrumentality theories: Current uses in psychology. *Psychological Bulletin,* 1971, **76,** 432–454.

Morrisey, G. L. *Management by objectives and results.* Reading, Mass.: Addison-Wesley, 1970.

Myers, M. S. *Every employee a manager.* New York: McGraw-Hill, 1970.

Odiorne, G. *Management by objectives.* New York: Pitman, 1965.

Perrow, C. The analysis of goals in complex organizations. *American Sociological Review,* 1961, **26,** 859–866.

Perrow, C. *Organizational analysis: A sociological view.* Belmont, Cal.: Wadsworth, 1970.

Porter, L. W., & Lawler, E. E., III. *Managerial attitudes and performance.* Homewood, Ill.: Irwin, 1968.

Raia, A. P. Goal setting and self control. *Journal of Management Studies,* 1965, **2,** 34–53.

Raia, A. P. A second look at goals and controls. *California Management Review,* 1966, **8** (4), 49–58.

Schleh, E. C. *Management for results.* New York: McGraw-Hill, 1961.

Steers, R. M. *Task goals, individual need strengths, and supervisory performance.* Unpublished doctoral dissertation, Graduate School of Administration, University of California, Irvine, June 1973.

Thompson, J. D., & McEwen, W. J. Organizational goals and environment. *American Sociological Review,* 1958, **23,** 23–30.

Valentine, R. F. *Performance objectives for managers.* New York: American Management Association, 1966.

Vroom, V. H. *Some personality determinants of the effects of participation.* Englewood Cliffs, N.J.: Prentice-Hall, 1960.

Vroom, V. *Work and motivation.* New York: Wiley, 1964.

Wikstrom, W. S. *Managing by and with objectives.* New York: National Industrial Conference Board, 1968.

Setting Goals
in Management
by Objectives

Henry L. Tosi
John R. Rizzo
Stephen J. Carroll

"Management By Objectives" (MBO) is a process in which members of complex organizations, working in conjunction with one another, identify common goals and coordinate their efforts toward achieving them. It emphasizes the future and change, since an objective or goal is an end state, or a condition to be achieved or have in effect at some future time. The emphasis is on where the organization is going—the what and the how of its intended accomplishments. Objectives can be thought of as statements of purpose and direction, formalized into a system of management. They may be long-range or short-range. They may be general, to provide direction to an entire organization, or they may be highly specific to provide detailed direction for a given individual.

One purpose of MBO is to facilitate the derivation of specific from general objectives, seeing to it that objectives at all levels in the organization are meaningfully located structurally and linked to each other. Sets of objectives for an organizational unit are the bases which determine its activities. *A set of objectives for an individual determines his job,* and can be thought of as a different way to provide a job description. Once objectives are determined and assumed by organizational units and by individuals, it is possible to work out the means or performance required for accomplishing the objectives. Methods of achieving objectives, resources required, timing, interactions with others, control, and evaluation must have continuing attention.

Objectives may or may not require change. The goal or end-state may be one of insuring that no change occurs   for example, and important recurring organizational operation. However, the emphasis still remains on change and the future, and "no change" conditions can be thought of as making finer change discriminations in the management process. However, MBO is deemed most appropriate in situations where activities tend not to be recurring or repetitious, where change toward new or improved conditions is sought. Typically, these would be innovative endeavors, problem-solving situations, improvements, and personal development.

Objectives may originate at any point in the organization structure. Quite naturally, they should be derived from the general purposes of the organization, and consistent with its philosophy, policies, and plans. It is beyond the scope of this paper to discuss the details of policy formulation and planning. Rather, it is recognized that these activities take place and that the setting of the objectives can, and often does, occur in concern and consonance with them. For example, plans can specify the phasing and timing of organizational operations, out of which are derived objectives for those involved in implementing them. Objectives are not considered as substitutes for plans, but rather as a basis for developing them. Stating objectives accomplishes the following.

1   Document expectations in superior-subordinate relationship regarding what is to be done and the level of attainment for the period covered by the goal.
2   Provide members with a firmer base for developing and integrating plans and personal and departmental activity.
3   Serve as the basis for feedback and evaluation of subordinate's performance.
4   Provide for coordination and timing of individual and unit activities.
5   Draw attention to the need for control of key organizational functions.
6   Provide a basis for work-related rewards as opposed to personality-based systems.
7   Emphasize change, improvement, and growth of the organization and the individual.

OBJECTIVES AS MEANS-END DISTINCTIONS

The formulation of objectives throughout an organization represents a kind of means-end analysis, which is an attempt to factor general requirements into specific activities. Means-end analysis starts "with the general goal to be achieved, (2) discovering a set of means, very generally specified, for accomplishing this goal, (3) taking each of these means, in turn, as a new sub-goal and discovering a more detailed set of means for achieving it, etc."[1]

MBO is predicted on this concept. It is assumed that a means-end analysis can occur with a degree of precision and accuracy. The end represents a condition or situation that is desired, a purpose to be achieved. Here, the concept of *end* is equated with *goal* or *objective*. Objectives may represent required inputs to other sectors of the organization. They may be specific achievement levels, such as product costs, sales volume and so on. They may also be completed projects. For instance, the market research department may seek to complete a sales forecast by a particular date so the production facilities may be properly coordinated with market demands. Objectives, or end states, are attained through the performance of some activity. These activities are the *means* to achieve the *end*. It is important to distinguish between ends and means in the use of the "objectives approach" since there are implications for measurement and assessment which will be discussed later in the paper.

It is obvious that a malfunction or break in such a process may lead to major problems in implementing management by objectives. It is for this reason that commitment, effort, support, and use by top management is critical at all levels to obtain consensus of objectives, cooperation in achievement, and the use of objectives as criteria for evaluation. But there are some problems in doing this. This paper is directed toward these: stating objectives, areas they should cover, the question of measurement, as well as some suggestions for dealing with them.

THE OBJECTIVE

The objectives for any position should reflect the means-end distinction discussed earlier. The first critical phase of objectives-setting is the statement which describes the end state sought. It should be:

1   Clear, concise and unambiguous.
2   Accurate in terms of the true and end-state or condition sought.
3   Consistent with policies, procedures, and plans as they apply to the unit.
4   Within the competence of the man, or represent a reasonable learning and developmental experience for him.
5   Interesting, motivating, and/or challenging whenever possible.

Some examples of goal statements might be written as: increase sales by 10 percent; reduce manufacturing costs by 5 percent; reduce customer complaints; increase sales by 5 percent by December 1; increase quality within a 5 percent increase in production control costs; develop understanding and implementation of computer techniques among subordinates.

Notice that these goal statements have at least two key components. First, each clearly suggests an *area of activity* in which accomplishment occurs. Second, some clearly specify a level of achievement, the quantity or deadlines to be met. We will refer to the desired level of achievement *as performance level.* The need for this distinction is obvious. It indicates the evaluation criterion by specifying the *level* or the condition which should exist. This has clear implications for both measurement and appraisal. Before discussing these implications, however, a more detailed examination of the scope and types of objectives in the MBO process is required.

Scope and Type of Objectives

It would be difficult to conceive of developing objectives for a manager which would cover each and every area of responsibility. The structure of most jobs is simply too complex. Yet once objectives are set for a position, they should comprise the major description of the job, and their achievement in light of what is known about total job requirements should be assessed. A sense of interference or conflict between objectives and other job requirements should be prevented.

Two major types of objectives may be delineated: *performance* objectives and *personal development* objectives.[2] *Performance objectives* refer mainly to those goals and activities that relate to the individual's position assignment. *Personal development* goals have to do with increasing the individual's skills, competence, or potential. Delineating types of objectives in this manner, more importantly, allows for an assessment of how MBO is being used and what emphases are deriving from it. For instance:

1   Once all objectives are set for a person, a basis exists to ensure that there is a "balance" of different types, that he is problem solving, developing, and maintaining critical functions.
2   Some estimates can be made regarding the importance of objectives and consequences of failure to achieve them. For example, a man who fails on a difficult creative objective should not be evaluated the same as one who fails to maintain a critical recurring operation.

Performance Objectives

A performance objective is derived directly from the job assignment, from the major areas of responsibility and activity of the individual that he must sustain or manage. Among them would be the maintenance of recurring or routine activities, the solving of problems, or the creation of innovative ideas, products, services, and the like. Some of these may take on the form of special activities or projects not normally part of the normal job requirements, they are goals which may take on special importance for a number of reasons—emergencies, changes in priorities, or simply management decisions.

A special activity for one position may be routine for another. A special project goal for a lower-level manager might be routine goal for his boss. Developing a computer-based information system for personnel records may be a highly creative objective for the personnel department, yet would probably be considered a routine goal for a systems analysis group.

Discretionary Areas and Other Problems

By its very nature, organization imposes restrictions on individuals. The structure of an organization defines legitimate areas of influence and decision making for an individual. Specialization and definition of function tend to limit decisions and activities to those defined for the incumbent.

If the objectives process is intended to, and does, facilitate subordinate participation and involvement, we must recognize the implicit nature of power. A lower-level manager cannot *legitimately* influence goal levels and action plans in areas in which he has no discretion, unless he has the *approval of his superior.* Therefore, it is necessary to spell out areas in which the subordinate has some latitude so that he knows what his decision limits are. Otherwise he may be misled into believing that he can participate in departmental and organizational decisions which have been defined, either procedurally or by managerial fiat, as being outside his discretion area. When you expect to participate and then cannot, negative consequences may occur. It is for this reason that it is important to determine and *communicate to the subordinate* what these discretion areas are.

One way to define discretion areas is to determine whether an individual should influence means or ends. If the activity operates primarily across the boundaries of the organization and is affected by conditions beyond its control, then the individual charged with performing it may be in a better positions to determine both the goals (or ends) and the most appropriate manner to achieve them. For instance, the marketing executives in constant touch with the external environment are in a better position to determine possible sales penetration and programs than others in the organization. However, not having discretion over goal levels should not preclude involvement in goal setting. Here the MBO process should focus on developing the best *means* (later called action plans) for goal attainment.

High levels of skill and technology required in a particular function may make the specialist better able than a nontechnical person to assess what can be done in a technical field. Thus, he should be involved in determining goal levels, as well as in carrying out activities. This is not to suggest that organizational constraints and requirements be entirely removed. Budget limitations, sales quotas, and production requirements are boundaries or restrictions which may not be removed but may have to be made more flexible.

If performance levels are set, for any reason, at higher organization levels, then there is little option but to focus on the determination of the "best" activities to achieve these levels. Internal definition of goal levels will most probably be for activities which function primarily within the boundaries of the organization. The assumption, of course, is that the one defining the objective, or level, is either competent to do so or must because of its critical importance.

An important limitation on discretion is organizational level. The lower the organizational level, the more and more narrow the zone of a manager's discretion. That is, the manager at the lower levels is responsible for fewer, more specific, and more measurable activities and can commit smaller quantities of resources than those at higher levels.[3]

Another factor which causes variation in the discretion range for a particular job is the changing competency levels of the incumbent. A person learning a job may need more guidance from the superior. However, as his skills increase, the superior may spend less time since the subordinate can capably handle more activities and make more decisions. The objectives approach, incidentally, may help the superior make assessments of the subordinate's competence to expand the decision area. As a subordinate becomes more successful in achieving goals, additional and more challenging goals within the parameters of the job could be added. When the incumbent can perform these adequately, then consideration should be given to possible promotion and transfer.

What about those decision areas beyond the discretion limits? We are not suggesting that the subordinate should have no part in these decisions. His role may be contributing information and assistance, such as providing inputs to the decision-making process of the superior, which the superior may choose to accept or reject. But this type of activity must be differentiated from *goal setting participation*, in which the individual *has something to say about the final shape and form* of the goals and activities. However, discretion boundaries are not rigid. While a particular decision may fall within the discretion range under normal circumstances, emergencies might develop which would result in the decision being made by the boss. These conditions cannot be foreseen, and consequently not planned for.

PERSONAL DEVELOPMENT OBJECTIVES

First, it is important to stress that these must be based on problems or deficiencies, current or anticipated, in areas such as improvements in technical skills or interpersonal problems. They may also be directed at developing one for movement within the organization. The critical nature of these objectives lies in their potential as means to combat obsolescence under a rapid expansion of knowledge, to prepare people for increased responsibility, and to overcome problems in organizational interactions.

Setting development goals is probably more difficult than setting performance goals, since they are personal in nature and, as such, must be handled with care and tact. This difficulty may be avoided by simply not setting them. It could be argued that they should be avoided since they are an intrusion into the individual's privacy by the boss or the organization. However, when perceived personal limitations hinder effective performance, the problem must be treated.

Thus, if at any time the superior believes an individual's limitations stand clearly in the way of the unit's goal achievement, it should be made known to the individual. He may not be aware that he is creating problems and would gladly change—if he knew. Many technically competent people have been relieved from positions because of human problems they ostensibly create. Many might have been retained had they only known that problems existed or were developing.

Personal development objectives should be a basic part of the MBO program, *when there is a need for them.* But, if they are included only to meet formal program requirements and are not problem-based, little value will obtain. Then personal improvement goals will probably be general and ambiguous, tenable only if the organization wishes to invest in "education for education's sake." For other than a philosophical or value-based justification, personal development should attack deficiencies related to performance, containing specific action proposals for solving the problems. This may be done in the following manner.

A. *Pinpoint a problem area.*—Parties involved in goal setting should continually be alert to negative incidents resulting from personal incapacities. The boss is in a particularly important position for recognizing problems. When situations occur which he believes are due to either personal or technical limitations, he should be aware of who was involved, and make some determination of the cause of these problems. Other individuals in the unit may bring problems to the fore. Those with whom an individual interacts may be in a reasonably good position to judge his technical competence or to determine when problems are due to his behavior. If colleagues are continually complaining about another person, additional investigation into the problem is warranted. Perhaps the most important source of these negative incidents is the subordinate himself. He may be very aware of problems in which he is involved and by discussing them may determine those in which he has been the primary cause.

These negative incidents should be relatively significant in effect and frequency and not simply a single event that has caused some notice to be taken. This does not mean, however, that an important incident which occurs one time should be overlooked if it suggests serious deficiencies.

There are at least three areas in which personal development objectives should be set.

1 **Improve interpersonal relations.** Inability to maintain reasonably effective working relationships may be due to a person's lack of awareness or his inability to cooperate. This may arise from personality deficiencies or simple lack of awareness of his impact upon others. He may be unable to recognize that he is precipitating problems.

2 **Improve current skills.** A manager may be, for instance, unable to prepare a budget or to engage in research because he has not had adequate training in these areas or because his training is not up to date. His general performance may be acceptable, but his skills should be improved.

3 **Prepare for advancement.** Another possibility covers either technical or human skills required for different or higher level positions. These are truly developmental goals which focus on preparation for advancement. There are many ways in which they may be achieved. In some cases the individual may be given advanced work assignments; in others, they may be achieved by exposure in training situations to new concepts. In any event, they represent a *potential* problem area.

B. *Assess the causes of the problem.*—Once it has been established that a problem exists, the cause needs to be determined. Causes should be sought jointly, a result of investigation and discussion by both the superior and subordinate after both have thought of possible causes.

Possible causes of problems may be grouped into three general categories:

1 **Procedures and structure.** The structure of the organization itself may induce disturbances. Interpersonal conflict may develop because of the interdependence of work activities. For instance, if formal requirements cause a delay in information transmission, those who need it may develop negative attitudes and feelings.

2 **Others with whom an individual must work.** Problems with subordinates or managerial peers of the goal setter may be caused by personality incompatibility or lack of certain technical skills. While this may represent an important cause of problems, it is too easy to blame negative incidents on others.

3 **The person himself.** The *individual* may have habits and characteristics which are not congruent with those of subordinates or colleagues. Or, he may lack the technical skills requisite to carry out certain responsibilities.

Attempting to define problems and causes facilitates converting development objectives into achievable goals. Like other objectives, they can be general (attend a sensitivity training course or role-playing seminar), or more specific (attend XYZ course in financial planning, use PERT techniques on Project X).

Self-improvement goals may be designed to improve current performance, or may be specifically intended to develop skills required at higher levels, or in different jobs (where it may be impossible to describe the end state of affairs to be achieved because success can be determined only in the future, or in other positions).

For development objectives it is necessary simply to rely upon the determination that the action plan has been carried out and that the individual has learned something. Suppose, for instance, that a development goal for an engineer destined to be a supervisor read as follows: "To meet with members of the financial, marketing, and production groups in order to learn how product release schedules affect their areas." Currently, he may have to know little about this since he may now have little impact on product release schedules. The question is, "How do you know that the activity produced the desired learning?" You don't. At some point in time, the superior, who presumably has some knowledge in the goal area, should discuss the results of the meeting with the subordinate, emphasizing particularly the important points that should have been learned. If this is done the subordinate will have the learning experience of the meeting and the reinforcement from discussion.

There is obviously no way to determine if these activities will improve the current, or future, performance of the manager. Managerial judgment is important here. We must simply assume that the superior is able to work with the subordinate to define activities of value in future work assignments.

Finally, it should be clear that performance and development objectives may well be derived from and related to management training and development efforts. These efforts must account for current organizational problems and future needs, and treat development as an integrated organization-wide effort. MBO should therefore be integrally tied to them.

PERFORMANCE REQUIRED: THE ACTION PLAN

Some of the problems inherent in MBO can be overcome by stating and discussing the specifics of the performance required to accomplish an objective. Earlier, the differentiation of means and ends was stressed. The goal statements reflected the ends: here, the performance or "action plan" refers to the means to accomplish an objective. It describes the manner in which it is to be attained. These means reflect alternatives which lead to the desired end and performance level.

The action plan may be brief statements, but it should summarize what is to be done. The action plan for a complex activity should be broken down into major subprograms and should represent the "best" alternative, of possibly many, which would achieve the goal level. The action plan provides an initial basis for a total action program for the individual or department. These action plans might be stated in the following manner:

1 *For the sales increase,* develop more penetration in a particular market area by increasing the number of calls to dealers there.
2 *For the reduced manufacturing costs,* analyze the overtime activities and costs and schedule more work during regular hours.

Subordinates may base their own action plans on those developed by their manager, using his plan to guide their own roles in the unit's effort. Thus, clear differentiation of means from ends can facilitate lower-level use of the objectives process.

Including both means and ends permits comparing performance with some criteria and determining if events occurred which are presumed to lead to a desired outcome. It is important to recognize the distinction between measuring an objective and determining if an event has occurred. If we are unable to quantify or specify the goal level adequately, then we simply *assume that the desired goal level will be achieved* if a particular event or set of activities takes place. For example, while it is very difficult to measure if a manager is developing the talents of subordinates by means of any hard criteria, we can determine if he has provided them with development opportunities. If they have participated in seminars, attended meetings, or gone off to school, it may be *assumed* that the development activity is being properly conducted.

Some further benefits and opportunities provided by adequate attention to an action plan are as follows:

1 Aids in search for better, more efficient methods of accomplishing the objective.
2 Provides an opportunity to test the feasibility of accomplishing the objective as stated.
3 Develops a sounder basis to estimate time or cost required and deadline for accomplishment.
4 Examines the nature and degree of reliance on other people in the organization toward coordination and support needed.
5 Uncovers anticipated snags or barriers to accomplishment.
6 Determines resources (manpower, equipment, supplies, facilities) required to accomplish the objective.
7 Facilitates control if the performance is well specified and agreed upon; reporting need only occur when problems arise in implementing. This is a form of planning ahead; when plans are sufficiently complete, only deviations from it need be communicated.
8 Identifies areas in which the superior can provide support and assistance.
9 Facilitates the delegation process.

Successful achievement or failure of an objective may depend upon the contribution and performance of other individuals or departments. Therefore, since they may be extremely critical to successful performance, they must be considered.

Some contingencies apply to all objectives and need not be documented on each. For example, delays in the availability of resources, change in support or priorities from higher management, equipment failures, delayed information or approval, and the like, which are unplanned, should relieve some responsibility for objective accomplishment.

Other contingencies, specific to the objective, should be discussed. Among these might be inadequate authority of the subordinate, lack of policy covering aspects of the objective, possible failure to gain other's cooperation, known delays in the system, and so on. Once these are uncovered, several actions are possible:

1 Reexamination of the objective (e. g., alternation of a deadline) when and if the contingency occurs.
2 Commitment of the superior to aid by overcoming or preventing the contingency.
3 Revision of the performance required to accomplish the objective.
4 Establishment of a new objective. If a contingency is serious enough, an objective aimed at overcoming the problem may be justified.

MEASUREMENT AND APPRAISAL

Management by objectives carried with it most of the familiar difficulties and complications of measurement and appraisal processes. Its emphasis on performance, as opposed to personality traits or criteria presumed related to performance, makes it potentially more effective. But this potential cannot be realized unless measurement and appraisal are reasonably valid, reliable, objective, and equitable.

Means, Ends, and Evaluation

Performance evaluations should rarely be based only on whether or not the objective was accomplished, or on the sheer number accomplished. They should include:

1 Quantitative aspects. (Was cost reduced 5 percent as planned?)
2 Qualitative aspects. (Have good relations been established with Department X? Has an evaluation technique been established?)
3 Deadline considerations. (Was the deadline beaten? Was it met?)
4 Proper allocation of time to given objectives.
5 Type and difficulty of objectives.
6 Creativity in overcoming obstacles.
7 Additional objectives suggested or undertaken.
8 Efficient use of resources.

9   Use of good management practices in accomplishing objectives (cost reduction, delegation, good planning, etc.)

10   Coordinative and cooperative behavior; avoidance of conflict-inducing or unethical practices, etc.

Evaluation and measurement, therefore, require considering both means and ends, being concerned with both the objective (number, type, difficulty, etc.) and the means to its achievement (cost, cooperativeness, time consumed, etc.). Unless this is done, an important opportunity to communicate expectations, feedback performance results, and setting effective goals may be lost. It must be fully understood that evaluation has obvious links to action plans, as well as to desired end states.

Further Consideration in Measurement

Some goals lend themselves more easily than others to measurement—scrap rates, production costs, sales volume, and other "hard" measures. These measures pertain most to lower organizational levels and to areas such as production, marketing, or other major functional activities of the organization and least to most staff and specialist units. The measurement problem often reduces to finding the appropriate, agreed-upon criterion for each objective, realizing that some will apply to many situations while others are unique to a single objective.

We have already detailed the distinction between performance and personal development objectives. Another distinction relevant to the measurement problem is the difference between routine and special project objectives. Classifying objectives according to these types permits some important refinements in evaluation and control. By examining the nature of the mix of objectives for a set of positions it is possible to determine any or all of the following:

1   The extent to which each individual has some personal development objectives.

2   That sufficient problem-solving or innovative activities were forthcoming in units where they might be required.

3   The priorities for performance or personal development objectives

Routine objectives are basic to the job, a core part of the job description. How should they be measured? The most appropriate method for evaluating if an individual has achieved them is first to insure that he is aware of these activities and required levels. The manager must tell the subordinate—early in the relationship—what the activities of the job are and what the desired level of performance is. Evaluation should not occur after a period of service unless there has been previous discussion of criteria.

At the same time that the criteria are being specified, acceptable tolerance limits should be developed. Measurement of the routine should be a major part of the objectives process, yet it should be of most concern *when performance falls outside acceptable levels*. Essentially, we are proposing that minimum performance levels be set for routine activities. Therefore, evaluation of routine goals is *by exception,* or when these standards are not met. Naturally, the ability to manage by exception demands good plans or clear standards from which exceptions can be specified in advance. Odiorne cites the following example:

> The paymaster, for example, may report that his routine duties cluster around getting the weekly payroll out every Friday. It is agreed that the measure of exception will be zero—in other words, the boss should expect no exceptions to the diligent performance of this routine duty. Thus, the failure any week to produce the payroll on Friday will be considered an exception that calls for explanation by the subordinate. If the cause were reasonably under his control or could have been averted by extra care or effort, the absence of the payroll will be considered a failure on the part of the subordinate.[4]

What About Superior Performance?

When a subordinate frequently exceeds the performance levels, the manager should let him know that his outstanding performance has been noticed. Positive feedback should occur, especially to let the individual know when he is performing his major job responsibilities exceptionally well.

Generally, routine job responsibilities or goals are expressed as job standards, or other "hard" performance measures. Although appraisal and evaluation essentially compare performance to the standard, this may be relatively shortsighted and suboptimal. Recall that the manager should also evaluate the activities or the manner in which performance was carried out. Often costs may be reduced by foregoing other expenditures, which may have negative long-run effects. There can be substantial distortions of behavior when only quantitative criteria are used in measurement.

Problem-solving, special project, or *creative objectives* are more difficult to quantify than the essentially routine. If the ends are truly creative, determining an adequate performance level may necessarily rely on intuitive judgment. Since innovation and invention are needed in their very formulation, we cannot generally measure results in these areas adequately, or directly. It is usually possible, however, to judge if an activity has been performed appropriately even though the ends, or the performance levels, are neither quantifiable nor measurable. Furthermore, constraints may be set on the activities. We can assess that they have occurred, but also within some tolerance limit such as of target dates, budget constraints, or a quality assessment by the manager. It becomes possible under these conditions to establish review points, thus giving attention to the outcomes of activities when they occur. Deliberations on these outcomes can serve to reevaluate both objectives and means. Thus changes are possible, and both flexibility and control are assured where they appear to be most needed— where predictions, plans, and standards could not be specified or articulated in advance.

Deadlines and budget constraints can be strictly specified in some cases and not in others. A great deal depends on:

1 The importance of the objective.

2   The ability to determine the time or costs required in performance.

3   Whether or not written plans or objectives of other people require coordinated completion dates.

4   The amount of time and money the subordinate will spend on the particular objective under discussion.

5   The predictability of problems or barriers to accomplishment.

Discussing these constraints allows greater understanding between superiors and subordinates and establishes their use in evaluation. Expectations become known; realities can be tested. Deadlines and costs should be viewed as "negotiable," and should be reasonably and rationally arrived at whenever possible. Deadlines especially should not be set simply to insure that action is initiated.

We wish to re-emphasize the importance of this criterion problem. A fundamental requirement for MBO is the development and use of sound criteria for evaluation, appraisal, and feedback. This is critical to achieve meaningful changes in behavior. "Hard" criteria must be used with extreme care. They are best viewed as ends or levels; they indicate nothing about attaining either. "Soft" criteria involve not a particular level of achievement, but determination that an event or condition has or has not occurred. These soft criteria are a vital and fundamental part of MBO. Without them, the approach cannot be well implemented.

To some managers, the development and communication of goals comes naturally. There are those who are able intuitively to determine and specify appropriate measures, criteria, goals, and the most satisfactory methods for achieving them. They innately sense what must be observed and measured and communicate this effectively to subordinates. This, of course, is the behavior which management by objectives seeks to develop and reinforce.

SUMMARY

Research and experience strongly support the relationship between the degree of a subordinate's acceptance of the objectives approach and his perception of its support and reinforcement from top management.[5] Organization support is critical for two reasons.

1   Top management may be an important reference group for lower level managers. Ambitious employees are likely to emulate managerial behavior. They identify with the top management and act similarly. If top management uses a particular method of managing, lower level managers are likely to use it also.

2   Consistent factoring and communication of goals to lower organizational levels is necessary. The general objective of the organization must be continually broken down into smaller and smaller units. The boss must learn what is expected, must communicate this to his subordinates, and must work with them to achieve these objectives. If this process breaks down at any point, then the whole approach is difficult to use.

Objectives must be written down for the entire organization, but the degree of detail and precision cannot easily be specified. This may be a matter for organizational policy and procedure, or it may be determined by mutual superi-or-subordinate agreement. However this is resolved, the varied aspects of objec-tives-setting should be attended to, discussed, and resolved as fully as possible to benefit from the MBO process.

Most important is that the approach must be intrinsically built into the job of managing. It must be related to other organizational processes and procedures, such as budgeting. It should be fundamentally incorporated into planning and development activities. It should be one of the major inputs to the performance appraisal and evaluation process. If not, it is likely that unless a manager intui-tively uses this approach, it is easier to do other things. There are costs involved in MBO. There must be some value or payoff which managers can recognize; otherwise they will view it as a waste of time.

REFERENCES AND NOTES

1 J. March and H. Simon, *Organizations.* New York: Wiley, 1958, p. 191.
2 These categories are similar to those proposed by Odiorne. See his *Management by Objectives.* New York: Pitman, 1964, especially Chapters 7, 8 & 9.
3 H. Tosi and S. Carroll, "Some Structural Factors Related to Goal Influence in the Management by Objectives Process," *Business Topics* (Spring 1969), 45–50.
4 Odiorne, p. 104.
5 H. Tosi and S. Carroll, "Managerial Reactions to Management by Objectives," *Academy of Management Journal* (December 1968), 415–426.

Studies of the Relationship between Satisfaction, Goal-Setting, and Performance

Edwin A. Locke
Norman Cartledge
Claramae S. Knerr

In several previous papers (Locke, 1968a, 1969; Locke, Bryan, & Kendall, 1968), a partial model of task motivation has been proposed which may be summarized as follows: *(a)* the most immediate, direct motivational determinant of task per-formance is the individual's goal or intention; *(b)* external incentives affect action through their effects on the individual's goals and intentions; *(c)* affective reac-tions are the result of evaluations, which consist of estimating the relationship between the existents one perceives and one's values or value standards. The model is schematized in the following:

Revised and abridged from *Organizational Behavior and Human Performance*, 1970, **5,** 135–139 and 151–158. Copyright by Academic Press. Reprinted by permission of the authors and publisher.

existents:	cognition	affective reactions (?)	goal-setting	action
incentives,	(evaluation)	emotions	intentions	
persons,	values			
actions,				
outcomes,				
etc.				
(1)	(2)	(3)	(4)	(5)

This model is organized in terms of the functions[1] of consciousness: cognition, evaluation, and the regulation of action.

(a) Cognition. In order to survive man has to act. In order to act he has to know the world, i. e., know something about the nature and properties of things which exist. Man gains knowledge through perception and the exercise of reason. The present model is not concerned with the problem of the validity of man's cognitions. It is assumed that he acts on the basis of his interpretation of the tasks and situations which confront him.

(b) Evaluation. Man's existence is conditional; it depends upon taking actions which will fulfill his needs. To survive man has to judge the significance of the existents he perceives for his own life and well-being. Furthermore, at any given time man holds far more information "in his head" than he could possibly act upon. His capacity to act is limited; thus, he needs a means of choosing among alternative courses of action (Locke, Cartledge, & Koeppel, 1968). To make choices he must make value judgments. Certain value judgments are biologically programmed; the physical sensations of pleasure and pain inform man as to whether a particular on-going course of action or object is physically harmful or beneficial. Physical sensations, however, will not guide a man's actions through the course of a lifetime. To do this man must acquire an (explicit or implicit) code of values: a set of standards by which to judge what is good or bad, right or wrong, for or against his interests (Rand, 1964).

A "value is that which one acts to gain and/or keep" (Rand, 1964, p. 25). In making evaluations man estimates (subconsciously) the relationship between what he perceives and his value standards. He asks, in effect, "Is this (object, situation, incentive, person) for me or against me (according to my values)?"

The form in which one experiences one's value judgments are emotions. (Rand, 1964). Man's most basic emotions are those of joy and suffering. (For a related view of the nature of emotions, see Arnold, 1960.)

(c) Regulation of action. Most human action is purposive; it is regulated by goals and intentions. The most fundamental effects of goals on (mental and/or physical) action are directive in nature. They guide man's thoughts and overt acts to one end rather than another. Since the pursuit of some goals require greater mental concentration and/or physical effort than others, goals, in the process of directing action, also regulate energy expenditure. For example, if a man decides

[1]This research was supported by Grants No. MH 12103–01 and 12103–02 from the National Institutes of Mental Health to the American Institutes for Research.

to mow his lawn rather than watch television, this action necessarily entails the expenditure of more effort than would have been required to watch TV.

This is not to claim that every goal leads to the activity or end specified by the goal. A particular goal may not lead to efficacious action because it conflicts with the individual's other goals. Or the situation at a given time may be perceived as inappropriate for action. An individual may not have sufficient knowledge, ability, or determination to carry out his plan of action. Further, external factors may interfere with his performance. Even abortive action, however, is (typically) initiated and guided by goals, and such action may still be highly correlated with the action intended.

Previous research has focused on several aspects of the above model:

(i) The directing function of goals and intentions has been emphasized in studies of choice behavior. In these studies individuals had to choose among alternative responses (Dulany, 1968) or among alternative tasks (Locke, Bryan, & Kendall, 1968), or had to decide which of the number of performance dimensions to maximize or minimize (Locke & Bryan, 1969). In all cases, substantial correlations were found between intended choices or goals and actual behavior.

(ii) A second category of studies stressed the energizing function of goals. All individuals worked on the same task and only their performance with respect to a single dimension was considered (e. g., output quantity). It was found that with simple, repetitive tasks, there was a positive linear correlation between goal level and performance level, i. e., the higher the goal, the higher the performance (see Locke, 1968a, for a summary of these studies). Even when individuals tried for goals which were so high that they rarely, if ever, were reached, they performed better than individuals with easy goals. (There is a point, of course, at which an increment in one's goal level would not lead to further improvement, i. e., there are limits to human performance.)

(iii) Other studies have shown that external incentives motivate action through their effects on the individual's goals and intentions. This is evidenced by the facts that: *(a)* when incentives do effect changes in performance, they bring about corresponding changes in the individual's goals and intentions; *(b)* when goal and intention differences are controlled or partialed out, the correlation between incentive condition and performance is vitiated. Thus far, the above relationships are most well documental with respect to three incentives: money (Locke *et al.,* 1968); feedback regarding one's overall score on a task (Locke, 1967a, 1968b; Locke & Bryan, 1968b, 1969b); and "verbal reinforcement" (Dulany, 1962, 1968).

(iv) Another series of studies have explored the effect of the judged relationship between the individual's values and what he perceives on his affective reactions (Locke, 1969). For example, work satisfaction was shown to be a function of the relationship between (or discrepancy between) what one perceives one's work as being like and what one wants from it (or wants it to be like). Satisfaction with performance was shown to be the result of perceiving one's performance as fulfilling or facilitating the fulfillment of one's performance goals. Job and per-

formance dissatisfaction were shown to be the result of perceiving one's job as frustrating one's job values or perceiving one's performance as being discrepant from one's performance goals, respectively.

Referring to the numbers in the above schematic, research to date has focused on relationships between: *(a)* Steps 4 and 5: goals and action; *(b)* Steps 1, 4, and 5: incentives, goals, and action; and *(c)* Steps 2 and 3: value judgments and emotional reactions. A missing link in this research is that between Steps 3 and 4; namely, how, specifically, are goals generated?

Arnold (1960) has argued that emotions contain inherent action tendencies, these action tendencies being experienced as desires. The basic desires are those of approach and avoidance. An unpleasant emotion entails the desire to avoid the object or situation that caused it, while a pleasant emotion entails the desire to approach or retain the object or situation that caused it.

If one is dissatisfied with one's performance on a task (and is constrained from leaving the situation altogether), one should desire and thus set a goal to change one's level of performance. Conversely, satisfaction with one's past performance should produce the desire and thus the goal to maintain this previous performance level.

In most real life situations, the process of setting a specific goal is enormously complex. It is the result of one's integration of numerous separate value judgments and cognitions. For the purposes of the present research, therefore, it was necessary to severely limit the range of phenomena investigated and the number of alternatives permitted.

Previous studies of the determinants of goal-setting (known generally as "level of aspiration" studies) have dealt primarily with situations where: *(a)* probability of success or difficulty was a major determinant of goal selection; and *(b)* the individual was free to set virtually any goal he wanted on the task, i. e., there were no external constraints on goal-setting. (For a summary and discussion of typical studies in this area, see Atkinson, 1964.). . .

THE REVISED MODEL

(1) Satisfaction. Our findings confirm previous work (Locke, 1969) showing that satisfaction with performance is a function of the degree to which one's performance achieves one's desired goal or is discrepant from one's value standard. The present results also extend the earlier findings which dealt only with goals as ends in themselves to include goals which are a means to an end. Subgoal attainment is valued to the extent that it is seen as instrumental in achieving one's overall (end) goal.

In Studies 3, 4, and 5 the use of goal-performance discrepancy to predict satisfaction added significantly (*F* tests) to the variance in satisfaction accounted for by instrumentality alone. Evidently the subjects valued hitting their subgoals as ends in themselves and not just as a means to an end. The wider or more general value that probably accounts for both relationships is that of "efficacy."

In order to achieve values (and therefore to survive) man has to be able to predict and control (to some extent) the outcomes of his actions. In attaining the goals he sets for himself, he develops and reinforces the conviction that he is competent to pursue and attain values in general.

(2) Goal-setting. When an individual's goal level remains constant, dissatisfaction with previous performance will correlate highly with the difference between previous performance level and subsequent goal level.

When a person has an overall end goal on a task, he will set subgoals according to their judged instrumentality in achieving this end goal. Judged instrumentality will correlate highly with anticipated satisfaction.

(3) Performance. To the degree that performance is affected by motivational factors, it is a result of the goals and intentions individuals set on the task. Goals guide action (and thought) and indirectly regulate energy expenditure.

The revised model is illustrated schematically in the following:

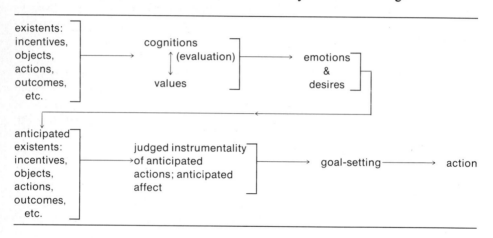

This model is by means complete, but only outlines the major processes that lead to goal setting and task performance.

(1) The model is not intended to be "hedonistic." It should be stressed that we do not assert that people pursue pleasure as such, but that they pursue goals. Goals are chosen with an awareness of their affective consequences, but these immediate consequences are not (typically) the sole criterion used in selecting them.

It is true that a "pure hedonist" would focus only on the immediate pleasures and displeasures to be gained from his actions. But few (if any) individuals follow this pattern. Most men choose subgoals as a means to an end goal. Their focus in choosing a subgoal is not on the immediate pleasure to be gained from it but on its instrumentality in achieving their long-range goals.

Men differ enormously in the time span across which they project their actions and in the criteria they use to choose their goals. An important individual difference variable in this context would be the degree to which an individual stresses immediate affective consequences as opposed to long-range instrumentality in selecting goals. The latter type should be willing to endure many more hardships and persist far longer in the face of frustration and dissatisfaction than the hedonist type.

(2) It should not be assumed that individuals precede their every action with an exhaustive "rational analysis" of all possible alternatives and their outcomes. Men differ greatly in the degree to which they think before they act in the number of alternatives they consider before acting, in the degree to which they are aware of their own values, and in the number of value conflicts they experience.

Furthermore, over time a given individual may encounter the same situation over and over. When this happens, he becomes habituated to the outcomes and alternatives. The more familiar he becomes with a situation the less reflection and foresight are necessary in order to make a choice. Considerations which were initially conscious and deliberate become subconscious and automatic.

We would argue that even in these cases, however, the same basic processes are occurring as specified above, the main difference being in the speed with which they take place, and the degree to which the individual is aware of them.

(3) The model does not delineate the factors which influence the establishment and acceptance of (end) goals and general values (e. g., "achievement") in the first place. In the studies reported here end goals were assigned and acceptance was facilitated by the "demand characteristics" of the experimental situation. In industrial situations, however, instructions are not always accepted. ("Participation" is one method that has been used to help insure goal acceptance by work-group members.) A series of studies by Miller (1965) at General Electric found that workers did not continue to try for assigned goals unless the instructions were backed up with rewards and punishments for goal attainment and failure, respectively.

The problem of where goals come from is often dismissed with the assertion that they are absorbed unthinkingly from "significant others." We believe that this is a somewhat over-simplified and misleading view of the matter. Individuals are often highly selective in the values they accept from society and with respect to whom they consider significant. Furthermore, some individuals generate their own goals and values.

(4) As stated earlier, the process by which an individual, in real life, decides to pursue a given goal and/or to change goals is enormously complex. For example, new knowledge (cognitions) from external sources and new insights based on self-generated thinking may intrude at any stage of this model and hence change the outcome. Subconscious value conflicts and premises may make actions difficult to predict from direct questioning of the individual. Our model, therefore, is only a very rough sketch of the major processes which appear to be involved in choosing a goal. The above experiments were able to show certain interconnections among the stages only because all or most extraneous factors were controlled.

RELATION TO OTHER THEORIES

There are a number of other theories of task performance which are similar in one or more respects to our model. It will only be possible to discuss some of them briefly here.

Dulany (1968) has proposed a theory to explain verbal response selection in laboratory studies of "verbal conditioning." The immediate determinant of response selection in this model is the "behavioral intention" which is similar to our "goal." Behavioral intentions are viewed as determined by the subject's hypotheses about what the experimenter wants him to do, what responses will gain him (sensory) reinforcement, and his desire to comply with the experimenter and to get the (sensory) reinforcement.

Dulany explicitly includes cognitive anticipations (i. e., hypotheses) in his model, but does not use the term "anticipated satisfaction." However, this idea is implicit in his concept of "desire." The desires to please the experimenter and to get (sensory) "reinforcement" (in this case, puffs of air to the face) are not the only types of rewards men will seek. But it might be possible to extend Dulany's model to cover other (real life) situations.

Atkinson and Feather (1966) have offered a theory based on individual differences in the desire to "achieve" or perform well on tasks (which they call "need for achievement"). They view achievement-motivated action as a joint function of the strength of the motivation to achieve, the anticipated satisfaction to be gained from success, and the estimated probability that a given course of action will produce success.

The subjective value of success is defined as the product of the importance of the motive to achieve and the anticipated satisfaction to be attained from achievement. The justification for this definition is questionable; it was argued in an earlier paper (Locke, 1969), that valid ratings of satisfaction already reflect value importance, so that multiplying one by the other is redundant.

Atkinson and Feather assume that the value of success is an inverse function of the probability (frequency) of success; however, their assumption has not always been empirically supported (e. g., see Locke, 1967b). Further, their model does not include goal-setting as a part of the process leading to action. This has led to different predictions as to the effects of difficult goals or tasks on performance. Atkinson and Feather argue that moderately difficult tasks lead to the highest level of performance, while Locke (1968a) has found that hard goals or tasks produce a higher level of performance than moderately difficult tasks or goals.

Vroom (1964) and Porter and Lawler (1968) see action as the result of cognitive and affective anticipations (i. e., the instrumentality of a given course of action in achieving valued goals), and view satisfaction as a function of the attainment of rewards (reward appears similar in meaning to what we call values). Porter and Lawler, however, see satisfaction as the result of value-percept discrepancy only, rather than value-percept discrepancy and value importance (see Locke, 1969, for a discussion of this issue).

Porter and Lawler view anticipated satisfaction and perceived probability of success as leading directly to the expenditure of effort; explicit goal-setting is not incorporated into the model. We would argue that the individual, on the basis of his anticipations, first chooses a goal and then mobilizes or expends the amount and type of effort that is appropriate to the goal or task he has chosen.

Like Atkinson and Feather, Vroom, and Porter and Lawler appear to view performance as a multiplicative function of anticipated satisfaction and the probability of success in attaining the desired outcome. We would agree that probability of success is taken into account in any decision to try for a goal. But, the empirical problem is how to combine measures of satisfaction and probability which are measured in very different units. Further, as noted above, we now believe that instrumentality is a more appropriate predictor of goal-setting than satisfaction.

Miller, Galanter, and Pribram (1960) view action as guided by plans, a concept which resembles what we call subgoals. Plans represent the sequence and order of actions to be taken so as to attain some end. The equivalent term to our end goal, or value, is Miller et al.'s concept of image (the image, however, also includes all stored knowledge and memories). These authors write that: "A motive is comprised of two independent parts: value and intention. A value refers to an Image, whereas an intention refers to a Plan" (1960, p. 62). According to Miller et al. each action outcome is compared to the image and the degree of "match" or similarity noted. Then new action is taken, guided by the plan, and the process is repeated until a match is obtained. The procedure of testing outcomes against the image and modifying future actions accordingly is called a "TOTE" (test-operator-test-exit) unit.

The similarity of the above model to ours is obvious. Our major reservation with Miller et al.'s position concerns their overly literal use of a computer analogy. We view conscious experience as being fundamentally different from the operation of a machine, whereas they (evidently) do not.

Finally, our interest in goals and intentions as determinants of performance is related to the approach to motivation advocated by Ryan (1958)[2] some years ago (see also Mace, 1935). Historically, interest in the effects of goals and tasks on behavior arose from the work of the Wurzburg School (Kulpe, Watt, Ach) around the turn of the century. Due primarily to the influence of behaviorism, this work has received limited attention from American psychologists to date.

REFERENCES

Arnold, Madga B. *Emotion and personality.* Vol. I. *psychological aspects.* New York: Columbia, Press, 1960.

Atkinson, J. W. *An introduction to motivation.* New York: Van Nostrand, 1964.

Atkinson, J. W., & Feather, N. T. *A theory of achievement motivation.* New York: Wiley, 1966.

Cartledge, N. Some determinants of goal-setting. Unpublished Master's Thesis, U. of Georgia, 1968.

Dulany, D. E., Jr. The place of hypotheses and intentions: An analysis of verbal control in verbal conditioning. In. C. W. Eriksen (Ed.), *Behavior and awareness.* Durham, N.C.: Duke University Press, 1962, Pp. 102–129.

Dulany, D. E., Jr. Awareness, rules and propositional control: A confrontation with S-R behavior theory. In D. Horton and T. Dixon (Eds.), *Verbal behavior and general*

[2]A book by Ryan giving his expanded views on this subject is now in press.

behavior theory. Englewood Cliffs, N.J.: Prentice Hall, 1968. Pp. 340–388.

Dunnette, M. *Personnel selection and placement.* Belmont, Cal.: Wadsworth, 1966.

Eagle, M. N. The effect of learning strategies upon free recall. *American Journal of Psychology,* 1967, **80,** 421–425.

Locke, E. A. The motivational effects of knowledge of results: Knowledge or goal-setting? *Journal of Applied Psychology,* 1967, **51,** 324–329. (a)

Locke, E. A. The relationship of success and expectation to affect on goal-seeking tasks. *Journal of Personality and Social Psychology,* 1967, **7,** 125–134. (b)

Locke, E. A. Toward a theory of task motivation and incentives. *Organizational Behavior and Human Performance,* 1968, **3,** 157–189. (a)

Locke, E. A. The effects of knowledge of results, feedback in relation to standards and goals on reaction time performance. *American Journal of Psychology,* 1968, **81,** 566–574. (b)

Locke, E. A. What is job satisfaction? *Organizational Behavior and Human Performance,* 1969, **4,** 309–336.

Locke, E. A., & Bryan, J. F. Grade goals as determinants of academic achievement. *Journal of General Psychology,* 1968, **79,** 217–228. (a)

Locke, E. A., & Bryan, J. F. Goal-setting as a determinant of the effect of knowledge of score on performance. *American Journal of Psychology,* 1968, **81,** 398–407. (b)

Locke, E. A., & Bryan, J. F. The directing function of goals in task performance. *Organizational Behavior and Human Performance,* 1969, **4,** 35–42. (a)

Locke, E. A., & Bryan, J. F. Knowledge of score and goal difficulty as determinants of work rate. *Journal of Applied Psychology,* 1969, **53,** 59–63. (b)

Locke, E. A., Cartledge, N., & Koeppel, J. The motivational effects of knowledge of results: A goal-setting phenomenon? *Psychological Bulletin,* 1968, **70,** 474–485.

Locke, E. A., Bryan, J. F., & Kendall, L. M. Goals and intentions as mediators of the effects of monetary incentives on behavior. *Journal of Applied Psychology,* 1968, **52,** 104–121.

Mace, C. A. Incentives: Some experimental studies. Report No. **72,** 1935, Industrial Health Research Board (Great Britain).

Miller, L. The use of knowledge of results in improving the performance of hourly operators. General Electric Co., Behavioral Research Service, 1965.

Miller, G., Galanter, E., & Pribram, K. *Plans and the structure of behavior.* New York: Holt, 1960.

Porter, L., & Lawler, E., *Managerial attitides and performance,* Homewood, Illinois: Dorsey, 1968.

Rand, Ayn. The Objectivist ethics. In Ayn Rand (Ed.), *The virtue of selfishness.* New York: Signet, 1964. Pp. 13–35.

Ryan, T. A., Drives, tasks, and the initiation of behavior. *American Journal of Psychology,* 1958, **71,** 74–93.

Vroom, V. *Work and motivation.* New York: Wiley, 1964.

QUESTIONS FOR DISCUSSION

1 How does Locke's theory of task motivation differ from the theories and models discussed earlier?

2 How does Locke's theory relate to the propositions expressed by Tosi and his associates?

3 Discuss the role of goal-setting in the determination of employee attitudes.
4 What role does goal-setting play in equity theory?
5 In general, why does MBO often result in increased performance?
6 Under what circumstances might MBO-type programs be more successful? Less successful? Why?
7 What effects might an MBO program have on organizational climate?
8 How could you use expectancy/valence theory in designing MBO-type programs?
9 What are some negative *consequences* that could arise from the implementation of an MBO program?
10 What are some of the major problems that might arise in trying to implement an MBO program?

Chapter 14

Operant Conditioning and Work Behavior

OVERVIEW

While Skinner's (1953) research on the effects of positive reinforcement on be-havior have been widely publicized in the psychological literature, it is only re-cently that attention has been paid to the application of such principles to work settings in organizations. Only in the last several years have management re-searchers attempted to experiment with these techniques in such diverse areas as job design, compensation, organizational climate, and so forth.

The results claimed by those organizations that have attempted such experi-ments with operant conditioning and positive reinforcement are impressive—at least on the surface. An air freight firm, for example, estimates that its new performance-improvement system, which is largely based on Skinnerian princi-ples, has saved the company over $2 million during a three-year period (*Psycholo-gy Today,* 1972). And in a large Midwest public utility, operant conditioning techniques were used to attack the problem of absenteeism, with the result that the rate dropped from 7 1/2 percent to 4 1/2 percent (*Business Week,* 1972).

Other positive results, using more rigorous measurement procedures, have been reported by Adam (1972) and by Jablonsky and DeVries (1972).

The basic concept of operant conditioning is simple. Briefly, it assumes that human behavior can be engineered, shaped, or altered by manipulating the reward structures of various forms of behavior. This process is called "positive reinforcement." Performance standards are clearly set, and improvement results—at least in theory—from the application of frequent *positive* feedback and from recognition for satisfactory behavior. Negative feedback is not used. It is assumed that the employee's desire for the rewards of positive feedback and recognition will in large measure motivate him or her to perform satisfactorily in anticipation of such rewards.

While operant conditioning applications in work organizations may appear appealing on the surface, they have not been universally accepted. Whyte, for example, in the second selection following, points out that most of the research in support of Skinner's theory is laboratory based, primarily using animals under highly controlled conditions. He argues that such principles may not apply when one attempts to use them in the more complex world of organizations. While not completely rejecting Skinner, Whyte raises four problems with applying his principles to "real-life" behavior.

First, much of Skinner's research has ignored complex social processes that can moderate any incentive system. (See, for example, the discussion of group influences on performance in Chapter 10.) If group performance norms are set in contravention to the positive reinforcement incentive system for improving performance, such incentives may have little impact. Second, there is the problem of conflicting stimuli. For example, the use of positive reinforcement to gain increased productivity may stimulate employees' desires to improve output, yet simultaneously arouse their fears that this improved output will only lead to the permanent establishment of still higher performance standards.

Third, there is the traditional problem of obtaining employee trust that management is truly acting with the employees' interests in mind and not simply trying to exploit them. Fourth, there is what Whyte terms the "one-body problem." An employee is motivated by experiences and anticipations that come from a variety of sources (family, friends, coworkers, and so on). If operant conditioning principles are to be effectively implemented, Whyte argues, all these forms of input would need to be controlled simultaneously so that a unified system of positive reinforcement could be attained. This would certainly be no easy task.

While little research has actually been carried out in ongoing organizations, the positive reinforcement principles of operant conditioning do appear to be a promising approach that warrants further investigation. Final decisions as to applicability to organization settings must, however, await this investigation. In the first selection that follows, Hamner discusses the potential role of operant conditioning in just such settings. The concept of reinforcement is reviewed in detail, followed by some suggestions for the practicing manager who is attempting to implement these techniques. Finally, several controversial issues surrounding operant conditioning are discussed. The second selection, by Whyte, is a short critique of the use of operant conditioning in organizations. Whyte raises several questions that must be considered by the manager who is thinking of using these techniques.

REFERENCES AND SUGGESTED ADDITIONAL READINGS

Adam, E. E., Jr. An analysis of changes in performance quality with operant conditioning procedures. *Journal of Applied Psychology,* 1972, **56,** 480–486.

Adam, E. E., Jr., & Scott, W. E., Jr. The application of behavioral conditioning procedures to the problems of quality control. *Academy of Management Journal,* 1971, **14,** 175–193.

Aldis, O. Of pigeons and men. *Harvard Business Review,* 1961, **39**(4), 59–63.

Bandura, A. *Principles of behavior modification.* New York: Holt, Rinehart & Winston, 1969.

Business Week. Where Skinner's theories work. December 2, 1972, No. 2257, 64–65.

Jablonsky, S. F., & DeVries, D. L. Operant conditioning principles extrapolated to the theory of management. *Organizational Behavior and Human Performance,* 1972, **7,** 340–358.

Luthans, F., & White, D. D., Jr. Behavior modification: Application to manpower management. *Personnel Administration,* 1971, **34,** 41–47.

Nord, W. R. Beyond the teaching machine: The neglected area of operant conditioning in the theory and practice of management. *Organizational Behavior and Human Performance,* 1969, **4,** 352–377.

Organizational Dynamics. At Emery Air Freight: Positive reinforcement boosts performance. Winter, 1973.

Psychology Today. New tool: Reinforcement for good work. April, 1972, 68–69.

Reynolds, G. S. *A primer of operant conditioning.* Glenview, Ill.: Scott, Foresman, 1968.

Skinner, B. F. *Science and human behavior.* New York: Free Press, 1953.

Spielberger, C. D., & De Nike, L. D. Descriptive behaviorism versus cognitive theory in verbal operant conditioning. *Psychological Review,* 1966, **73,** 306–325.

Reinforcement Theory and Contingency Management in Organizational Settings
W. Clay Hamner

Traditionally management has been defined as the process of getting things done through other people. The succinctness of this definition is misleading in that, while it may be easy to say *what* a manager does, it is difficult to describe the determinants of behavior, i. e. to tell *how* the behavior of the manager influences the behavior of the employee toward accomplishment of a task. Human behavior in organizational settings has always been a phenomenon of interest and concern. However, it has only been in recent years that a concerted effort has been made by social scientists to describe the principles of reinforcement and their implications for describing the determinants of behavior as they relate to the theory and practice of management (e. g. see Nord, 1969; Wiard, 1972; Whyte, 1972; Jablonsky and DeVries, 1972; Hersey and Blanchard, 1972; and Behling, Schrisheim, and Tolliver, in press).[1]

Organizational leaders must resort to environmental changes as a means of influencing behavior. Reinforcement principles are the most useful method for this purpose because they indicate to the leader how he might proceed in designing or modifying the work environment in order to effect specific changes in behavior (Scott and Cummings, 1973). A reinforcement approach to management does not consist of a bag of tricks to be applied indiscriminately for the purpose of coercing unwilling people (Michael & Meyerson, 1962). Unfortunately, many people who think of Skinnerian applications (Skinner, 1969) in the field of management and personnel think of manipulation and adverse control over employees. Increased knowledge available today of the positive aspects of conditioning as applied to worker performance should help to dispel these notions.

The purpose of this paper is to describe the determinants of behavior as seen from a reinforcement theory point of view, and to describe how the management of the contingencies of reinforcement in organizational settings is a key to successful management. Hopefully, this paper will enable the manager to understand how his behavior affects the behavior of his subordinates and to see that in most cases the failure or success of the worker at the performance of a task is a direct function of the manager's own behavior. Since a large portion of the manager's time is spent in the process of modifying behavior patterns and shaping them so that they will be more goal oriented, it is appropriate that this paper begin by describing the processes and principles that govern behavior.

LEARNING AS A PREREQUISITE FOR BEHAVIOR
Learning is such a common phenomenon that we tend to fail to recognize its occurrence. Nevertheless, one of the major premises of reinforcement theory is

From H. L. Tosi and W. C. Hamner (eds.), *Organizational behavior and management: A contingency approach*. Chicago: St. Clair Press, 1974. Reprinted by permission.

that all behavior is learned—a worker's skill, a supervisor's attitude and a secretary's manners. The importance of learning in organizational settings is asserted by Costello and Zalkind when they conclude:

> Every aspect of human behavior is responsive to learning experiences. Knowledge, language, and skills, of course; but also attitudes, value systems, and personality characteristics. All the individual's activities in the organization—his loyalties, awareness of organizational goals, job performance, even his safety record have been learned in the largest sense of that term (1963, p. 205).

There seems to be general agreement among social scientists that learning can be defined as *a relatively permanent change in behavior potentiality that results from reinforced practice or experience.* Note that this definition states that there is change in behavior potentiality and not necessarily in behavior itself. The reason for this distinction rests on the fact that we can observe other people responding to their environments, see the consequences which accrue to them, and be vicariously conditioned. For example, a boy can watch his older sister burn her hand on a hot stove and "learn" that pain is the result of touching a hot stove. This definition therefore allows us to account for "no-trial" learning. Bandura (1969) describes this as imitative learning and says that while behavior can be *acquired* by observing, reading, or other vicarious methods, "*performance* of observationally learned responses will depend to a great extent upon the nature of the reinforcing consequences to the model or to the observer" (p.128).

Luthans (1973, p. 362) says that we need to consider the following points when we define the learning process:

1 Learning involves a change, though not necessarily an improvement, in behavior. Learning generally has the connotation of improved performance, but under this definition bad habits, prejudices, stereotypes, and work restrictions are learned.

2 The change in behavior must be relatively permanent in order to be considered learning. This qualification rules out behavioral changes resulting from fatigue or temporary adaptations as learning.

3 Some form of practice or experience is necessary for learning to occur.

4 Finally, practice or experience must be reinforced in order for learning to occur. If reinforcement does not accompany the practice or experience, the behavior will eventually disappear.

From this discussion, we can conclude that learning is the acquisition of knowledge, and performance is the translation of knowledge into practice. The primary effect of reinforcement is to strengthen and intensify certain aspects of ensuing behavior. Behavior that has become highly differentiated (shaped) can be understood and accounted for only in terms of the history of reinforcement of that behavior (Morse, 1966). Reinforcement generates a reproducible behavior process in time. A response occurs and is followed by a reinforcer, and further responses occur with a characteristic temporal patterning. When a response is reinforced it subsequently occurs more frequently than before it was reinforced. Reinforcement may be assumed to have a characteristic and reproducible effect on a particular behavior, and usually it will enhance and intensify that behavior (Skinner, 1938; 1953).

TWO BASIC LEARNING PROCESSES

Before discussing in any detail exactly how the general laws or principles of reinforcement can be used to predict and influence behavior, we must differentiate between two types of behavior. One kind is known as *voluntary* or *operant* behavior, and the other is known as *reflex* or *respondent* behavior. Respondent behavior takes in all responses of human beings that are *elicited* by special stimulus changes in the environment. An example would be when a person turns a light on in a dark room (stimulus change), his eyes contract (respondent behavior).

Operant behavior includes an even greater amount of human activity. It takes in all the responses of a person that may at some time be said to have an effect upon or do something to the person's outside world (Keller, 1969). Operant behavior *operates* on this world either directly or indirectly. For example, when a person presses the up button at the elevator entrance to "call" the elevator, he is operating on his environment.

The process of learning or acquiring reflex behavior is different from the processes of learning or acquiring voluntary behavior. The two basic and distinct learning processes are known as *classical conditioning* and *operant conditioning*. It is from studying these two learning processes that much of our knowledge of individual behavior has emerged.

Classical Conditioning[2]

Pavlov (1902) noticed, while studying the automatic reflexes associated with digestion, that his laboratory dog salivated (unconditioned response) not only when food (unconditioned stimulus) was placed in the dog's mouth, but also when other stimuli were presented before food was placed in the dog's mouth. In other words, by presenting a neutral stimulus (ringing of a bell) every time food was presented to the dog, Pavlov was able to get the dog to salivate to the bell alone.

A stimulus which is not a part of a reflex relationship (the bell in Pavlov's experiment) becomes a *conditioned stimulus* for the response by repeated, temporal pairing with an *unconditioned* stimulus (food) which already elicits the response. This new relationship is known as a conditioned reflex, and the pairing procedure is known as classical conditioning.

While it is important to understand that reflex behavior is conditioned by a different process than is voluntary behavior, classical conditioning principles are of little use to the practicing manager. Most of the behavior that is of interest to society does not fit in the paradigm of reflex behavior (Michael and Meyerson, 1962). Nevertheless, the ability to generalize from one stimulus setting to another is very important in human learning and problem solving, and for this reason, knowledge of the classical conditioning process is important.

Operant Conditioning[3]

The basic distinction between classical and operant conditioning procedures is in terms of the *consequences* of the conditioned response. In classical conditioning, the sequence of events is independent of the subject's behavior. In operant conditioning, consequences (rewards and punishments) are made to occur as a consequence of the subject's response or failure to respond. The distinction between these two methods is shown in Figure 1.

In Figure 1, we see that classical conditioning involves a three stage process. In the diagram, let *S* refer to *stimulus* and *R* to *response.* We see that in stage 1, the unconditioned stimulus (food) elicits an unconditioned response (salivation). In stage 2, a neutral stimulus (bell) elicits no known response. However, in stage 3, after the ringing of the bell is repeatedly paired with the presence of food, the bell alone becomes a conditioned stimulus and elicits a conditioned response (salivation). The subject has no control over the unconditioned or conditioned response, but is "at the mercy" of his environment and his past conditioning history.

Note however, that for voluntary behavior, the consequence is dependent on the behavior of the individual in a given stimulus setting. Such behavior can be said to "operate" (Skinner, 1969) on the environment, in contrast to behavior which is "respondent" to prior eliciting stimuli (Michael and Meyerson, 1962). Reinforcement is not given every time the stimulus is presented, but is *only* given when the correct response is made. For example, if an employee taking a work break, puts a penny (R) in the soft drink machine (S), nothing happens (consequence). However, if he puts a quarter (R) in the machine (S), he gets the soft

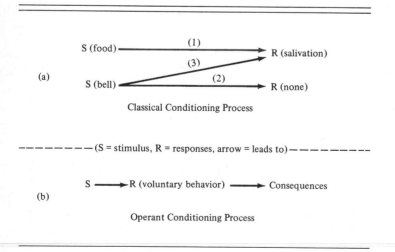

Figure 1   Classical vs. operant conditioning.

drink (consequence). In other words, the employee's behavior is *instrumental* in determining the consequences which accrue to him.

The interrelationships between the three components of (1) *stimulus* or environment, (2) *response* or performance, and (3) consequences or *reinforcements* are known as the *contingencies* of reinforcement. Skinner (1969) says "The class of responses upon which a reinforcer is *contingent* is called an operant, to suggest the action on the environment followed by reinforcements (p. 7)." Operant conditioning presupposes that human beings explore their environment and act upon it. This behavior, randomly emitted at first, can be constructed as an operant by making a reinforcement contingent on a response. Any stimulus present when an operant is reinforced acquires control in the sense that the rate of response for that individual will be higher when it is present. "Such a stimulus does not act as a *goal;* it does not elicit the response (as was the case in classical conditioning of reflex behavior)[4] in the sense of forcing it to occur. It is simply an essential aspect of the occasion upon which response is made and reinforced (Skinner, 1969, p. 7)."

Therefore, an adequate formulation of the interaction between an individual and his environment must always specify three things: (1) the occasion upon which a response occurs, (2) the response itself and (3) the reinforcing consequences. Skinner holds that the consequences determine the likelihood that a given operant will be performed in the future. Thus to change behavior, the consequences of the behavior must be changed, i. e. the contingencies must be rearranged (the ways in which the consequences are related to the behavior) (Behling, *et al.*, in press). For Skinner, this behavior generated by a given set of contingencies can be accounted for without appealing to hypothetical inner states (e. g. awareness or expectancies). "If a conspicuous stimulus does not have an effect, it is not because the organism has not attended to it or because some central gatekeeper has screened it out, but because the stimulus plays no important role in the prevailing contingencies (Skinner 1969, p. 8)."

Arrangement of the Contingencies of Reinforcement

In order to *understand* and *interpret* behavior, we must look at the interrelationship among the components of the contingencies of behavior. If one expects to influence behavior, he must also be able to manipulate the consequences of the behavior (Skinner, 1969). Haire (1964) reports the importance of being able to manipulate the consequences when he says,

> Indeed, whether he is conscious of it or not, the superior is bound to be constantly shaping the behavior of his subordinates by the way in which he utilizes the rewards that are at his disposal, and he will inevitably modify the behavior patterns of his work group thereby. For this reason, it is important to see as clearly as possible what is going on, so that the changes can be planned and chosen in advance, rather than simply accepted after the fact.

After appropriate reinforcers that have sufficient incentive value to maintain

stable responsiveness have been chosen, the contingencies between specific performances and reinforcing stimuli must be arranged (Bandura, 1969). Employers
intuitively use rewards in their attempt to modify and influence behavior, but
their efforts often produce limited results because the methods are used improp-
erly, inconsistently, or inefficiently. In many instances considerable rewards are
bestowed upon the workers, but they are not made conditional or contingent on
the behavior the manager wishes to promote. Also, "long delays often intervene
between the occurrence of the desired behavior and its intended consequences;
special privileges, activities, and rewards are generally furnished according to
fixed time schedules rather than performance requirements; and in many cases,
positive reinforcers are inadvertently made contingent upon the wrong type of
behavior (Bandura, 1969, pp. 229–230)."

One of the primary reasons that managers fail to "motivate" workers to
perform in the desired manner is due to a lack of understanding of the power of
the contingencies of reinforcement over the employee and of the manager's role
in arranging these contingencies. The laws or principles for arranging the contingencies are not hard to understand, and if students of behavior grasp them firmly, they are powerful managerial tools which can be used to increase supervisory
effectiveness.

As we have said, operant conditioning is the process by which behavior is
modified by manipulation of the contingencies of the behavior. To understand
how this works, we will first look at various *types* (arrangements) of contingencies, and then at various *schedules* of the contingencies available. Rachlin (1970)
described the four basic ways available to the manager of arranging the contingencies—*positive reinforcement, avoidance learning, extinction,* and *punishment.*
The difference among these types of contingencies depends on the consequence
which results from the behavioral act. Positive reinforcement and avoidance
learning are methods of strengthening *desired* behavior, and extinction and punishment are methods of weakening *undesired* behavior.

Positive Reinforcement "A positive reinforcer is a stimulus which, when
added to a situation, strengthens the probability of an operant response (Skinner,
1953, p. 73)." The reason it strengthens the response is explained by Thorndike's
(1911) Law of Effect. This law states simply that behavior which appears to lead
to a positive consequence tends to be repeated, while behavior which appears to
lead to a negative consequence tends not to be repeated. A positive consequence
is called a reward.

Reinforcers, either positive or negative, are classified as either: (1) unconditioned or primary reinforcers, or (2) conditioned or secondary reinforcers. Primary reinforcers such as food, water, and sex are of biological importance in that
they are innately rewarding and have effects which are independent of past experiences. Secondary reinforcers such as job advancement, praise, recognition, and
money derive their effects from a consistent pairing with other reinforcers (i. e.,
they are conditioned). Secondary reinforcement, therefore, depends on the indi-

vidual and his past reinforcement history. What is rewarding to one person may not be rewarding to another. Managers should look for a reward system system which has maximal reinforcing consequences to the group he is supervising.

Regardless of whether the positive reinforcer is primary or secondary in nature, once it has been determined that the consequence has reward value to the worker, it can be used to increase the worker's performance. So the *first step* in the successful application of reinforcement procedures is to select reinforcers that are sufficiently powerful and durable to "maintain responsiveness while complex patterns of behavior are being established and strengthened" (Bandura, 1969, p. 225).

The *second step* is to design the contingencies in such a way that the reinforcing events are made contingent upon the desired behavior. This is the rule of reinforcement which is most often violated. Rewards must result from performance, and the greater the degree of performance by an employee, the greater should be his reward. Money as a reinforcer will be discussed later, but it should be noted that money is not the only reward available. In fact, for unionized employees, the supervisor has virtually no way to tie money to performance. Nevertheless, other forms of rewards, such as recognition, promotion and job assignments, can be made contingent on good performance. Unless a manager is willing to discriminate between employees based on their level of performance, the effectiveness of his power over the employee is nil.

The arrangement of positive reinforcement contingencies can be pictured as follows:

Stimulus → Desired response → Positive consequences

$(S \rightarrow R \rightarrow R^+)$

The stimulus is the work environment which leads to a response (some level of performance). If this response leads to positive consequences, then the probability of that response being emitted again increases (Law of Effect). Now, if the behavior is undesired, then the supervisor is conditioning or teaching the employee that undesired behavior will lead to a desired reward. It is important therefore that the reward administered be equal to the performance input of the employee. Homans (1950) labels this as the rule of distributive justice and stated that this reciprocal norm applies in both formal (work) and informal (friendship) relationships. In other words, the employee *exchanges* his services for the rewards of the organization. In order to maintain desired performance, it is important that the manager design the reward system so that the level of reward administered is proportionately contingent on the level of performance emitted.

The *third step* is to design the contingencies in such a way that a reliable procedure for eliciting or inducing the desired response patterns is established; otherwise, if they never occur there will be few opportunities to influence the desired behavior through contingent management. If the behavior that a manager wishes to strengthen is already present, and occurs with some frequency, then contingent applications of incentives can, from the outset, increase and maintain the desired performance patterns at a high level. However, as Bandura (1969) states, "When the initial level of the desired behavior is extremely low, if the criterion for reinforcement is initially set too high, most, if not all, of the person's responses go unrewarded, so that his efforts are gradually extinguished and his motivation diminished (p. 232)."

The nature of the learning process is such that acquiring the new response patterns can be easily established. The principle of operant conditioning says that an operant followed by a positive reinforcement is more likely to occur under similar conditions in the future. Through the process of *generalization,* the more nearly alike the new situation or stimulus is to the original one, the more the old behavior is likely to be emitted in the new environment. For example, if you contract with an electrician to rewire your house, he is able to bring with him enough old behavioral patterns which he generalized to this unfamiliar, but similar, stimulus setting (the house) in order to accomplish the task. He has learned through his past reinforcement history that, when in a new environment, one way to speed up the correct behavior needed to obtain reward is to generalize from similar settings with which he has had experience. Perhaps one reason an employer wants a person with work experience is because the probability of that person emitting the correct behavior is greater and thus the job of managing that person simplified.

Just as generalization is the ability to react to similarities in the environment, *discrimination* is the ability to react to differences in a new environmental setting. Usually when an employee moves from one environment (a job, a city, an office) to another he finds that only certain dimensions of the stimulus conditions change. While all of the responses of the employee in this new setting will not be correct, by skilled use of the procedures of reinforcement currently being discussed, we can bring about the more precise type of stimulus control called discrimination. When we purchase a new car, we do not have to relearn how to drive a car (generalizable stimulus). Instead we need only learn the differences in the new car and the old car so that we can respond to these differences in order to get reinforced. This procedure is called *discrimination training.* "If in the presence of a stimulus a response is reinforced, and in the absence of this stimulus it is extinguished, the stimulus will control the probability of the response in high degree. Such a stimulus is called a *discriminative stimulus* (Michael and Meyerson, 1962)."

The development of effective discriminative repertoires is important for dealing with many different people on an interpersonal basis. Effective training techniques will allow the supervisor to develop the necessary discriminative repertoires in his new employees (e. g. see Bass and Vaughan, 1966, *Training in Industry: The Management of Learning*).

Using the principles of generalization and discrimination in a well-designed training program allows the manager to accomplish the third goal of eliciting or inducing the desired response patterns. Training is a method of *shaping* desired behavior so that it can be conditioned to come under the control of the reinforcement stimuli. Shaping behavior is necessary when the response to be learned is not currently in the individual's repertoire and when it is a fairly complex behavior. In shaping, we teach a desired response by reinforcing the series of successive steps which lead to the final response. This method is essentially the one your parents used when they first taught you to drive. You were first taught how to adjust the seat and mirror, fasten the seat belt, turn on the lights and windshield wipers, and then how to start the engine. Each time you successfully completed each stage you were positively reinforced by some comment. You then were allowed to practice driving on back roads and in empty lots. By focusing on one of these aspects at a time and reinforcing proper responses, your parents were able to shape your driving behavior until you reached the final stage of being able to drive. After your behavior was shaped, driving other cars or driving in new territories was accomplished successfully by the process of generalization and discrimination. This same process is used with a management trainee who is rotated from department to department for a period of time until he has "learned the ropes." After his managerial behavior has been minimally shaped, he is transferred to a managerial position where, using the principles of generalization and discrimination, he is able to adjust to the contingencies of the work environment.

Avoidance Learning   The second type of contingency arrangement available to the manager is called escape, or avoidance learning. Just as with positive reinforcement, this is a method of strengthening desired behavior. A contingency arrangement in which an individual's performance can terminate an already noxious stimulus is called *escape* learning. When behavior can prevent the onset of a noxious stimulus the procedure is called *avoidance learning*. In both cases, the result is the development and maintenance of the desired operant behavior (Michael and Meyerson, 1962).

An example of this kind of control can be easily found in a work environment. Punctuality of employees is often maintained by avoidance learning. The noxious stimulus is the criticism by the shop steward or office manager for being late. In order to avoid criticism other employees make a special effort to come to work on time. A supervisor begins criticizing a worker for "goofing off." Other workers may intensify their efforts to escape the criticism of the supervisor.

The arrangement of an escape reinforcement contingency can be diagrammed as follows:

Noxious stimulus → Desired response → Removal of noxious stimulus
$(S^- \rightarrow R \not\Vdash S^-)$

The distinction between the process of strengthening behavior by means of positive reinforcement techniques and avoidance learning techniques should be noted carefully. In one case, the individual works hard to gain the consequences from the environment which results from good work, and in the second case, the individual works hard to avoid the noxious aspects of the environment itself. In both cases the same behavior is strengthened.

While Skinner (1953) recognizes that avoidance learning techniques can be used to condition desired behavior, he does not advocate their use. Instead a Skinnerian approach to operant conditioning is primarily based on the principles of positive reinforcement.

Extinction While positive reinforcement and avoidance learning techniques can be used by managers to strengthen desired behavior, extinction and punishment techniques are methods available to managers for reducing undesired behavior. When positive reinforcement for a learned or previously conditioned response is withheld, individuals will continue to exhibit that behavior for an extended period of time. Under repeated nonreinforcement, the behavior decreases and eventually disappears. This decline in response rate as a result of nonrewarded repetition of a task is defined as *extinction.*

The diagram of the arrangement of the contingency of extinction can be shown as follows:

(1) Stimulus → Response → Positive consequences
  $(S \rightarrow R \rightarrow R^+)$

(2) Stimulus → Response → Withholding of positive consequences
  $(S \rightarrow R \nrightarrow R^+)$

(3) Stimulus → Withholding of response
  $(S \nrightarrow R)$

The behavior which was previously reinforced because (a) it was desired or (b) by poor reinforcement practices is no longer desired. To extinguish this behavior in a naturally recurring situation, response patterns substained by positive reinforcement (Stage 1) are frequently eliminated (Stage 3) by discontinuing the rewards (Stage 2) that ordinarily produce the behavior. This method when combined with a positive reinforcement method is the procedure of behavior modification recommended by Skinner (1953). It leads to the least negative side effects and when the two methods are used together, it allows the employee to get the rewards he desires and allows the organization to eliminate the undesired behavior.

Punishment A second method of reducing the frequency of undesired behavior is through the use of punishment. Punishment is the most controversial method of behavior modification, and most of the ethical questions about operant methods of control center around this technique. "One of the principal objections to aversive control stems from the widespread belief that internal, and often unconscious, forces are the major determinant of behavior. From this perspective, punishment may temporarily suppress certain expressions, but the underlying impulses retain their strength and press continuously for discharge through alternative actions (Bandura, 1969, p. 292)." While Skinner (1953) discounts the internal state hypothesis, he recommends that extinction rather than punishment be used to decrease the probability of the occurrence of a particular behavior.

Punishment is defined as presenting an aversive or noxious consequence contingent upon a response, or removing a positive consequence contingent upon a response. Based on the Law of Effect, as rewards strengthen behavior, punishment weakens it. This process can be shown as follows:

(1) Stimulus → Undesired Behavior → Noxious consequence or withhold-

    $(S \rightarrow R \rightarrow R^-)$ ing of positive consequence

    $(\quad \text{or} \not\rightarrow R^+)$

(2) Stimulus $\not\rightarrow$ Undesired behavior

    $(S \not\rightarrow R)$

Notice carefully the difference in the withholding of rewards in the punishment process and the withholding of rewards in the extinction process. In the extinction process, we withhold rewards for behavior that has previously been administered the rewards because the behavior was desired. In punishment, we withhold a reward because the behavior is undesired, has never been associated with the reward before, and is in fact a noxious consequence. For example, if your young son began imitating an older neighborhood boy's use of profanity and you thought it was "cute," you might reinforce the behavior by laughing or by calling public attention to it. Soon, the son learns one way to get the recognition he craves is to use profanity—even though he may have no concept of its meaning. As the child reaches an accountable age, you decide that his use of profanity is no longer as cute as it once was. To stop the behavior you can do one of three things: (1) You can withhold the previous recognition you gave the child by ignoring him (extinction), (2) You can give the child a spanking (punishment by noxious consequence), or (3) You can withhold his allowance or refuse to let him watch television (punishment by withholding of positive consequences not previously connected with the act).

It should be noted that method 2 and perhaps method 3 would be considered cruel because of the parent's own inconsistencies. Punishment should rarely be used to extinguish behavior that has previously been reinforced if the person administering the punishment is the same person who previously reinforced the behavior. However, had the parent failed to extinguish the use of profanity prior to sending the child out in society (e. g. school, church), it is possible that the society may punish the child for behavior that the parent is reinforcing or at least tolerating. It is often argued therefore that the failure to use punishment early in the life of a child for socially unacceptable behavior (e. g. stealing, driving at excessive speeds, poor table manners) is more cruel than the punishment itself, simply because the society will withhold rewards or administer adversive consequences for the behavior which the parents should have extinguished.

The use of aversive control is frequently questioned on the assumption that it produces undesirable by-products. In many cases this concern is warranted. Bandura (1969) states that it depends on the circumstances and on the past reinforcement history of the reinforcement agent and the reinforcement target as to whether punishment or extinction should be used. He says:

> Many of the unfavorable effects, however, that are sometimes associated with punishment are not necessarily inherent in the methods themselves but result from the faulty manner in which they are applied. A great deal of human behavior is, in fact, modified and closely regulated by natural aversive contingencies without any ill effects. On the basis of negative consequences people learn to avoid or to protect themselves against hazardous falls, flaming or scalding objects, deafening sounds, and other hurtful stimuli. . . . In instances where certain activities can have injurious effects, aversive contingencies *must* be socially arranged to ensure survival. Punishment is rarely indicated for ineffectiveness or deleterious side effects when used, for example, to teach young children not to insert metal objects into electrical outlets, not to cross busy thoroughfares . . . Certain types of negative sanctions, if applied considerately, can likewise aid in eliminating self-defeating and socially detrimental behavior without creating any special problems (p. 294).

Rules for Using Operant Conditioning Techniques

Several rules concerning the arrangement of the contingencies of reinforcement should be discussed. While these rules have common sense appeal, the research findings indicate that these rules are often violated by managers when they design control systems.

Rule 1. Don't reward all people the same. In other words, differentiate the rewards based on performance as compared to some defined objective or standard. We know that people compare their own performance to that of their peers to determine how well they are doing ("Social Comparison Theory," Festinger, 1954) and they compare their rewards to the rewards of their peers ("Equity Theory," Adams, 1965) in order to determine how to evaluate their rewards. While some managers seem to think that the fairest system of compensation is one where everyone in the same job classification gets the same pay, employees want differentiation so that they know their importance to the organization. Based on social comparison and equity theory assumptions, it can be argued that managers who reward all people the same are encouraging, at best, only average performance. Behavior of high performance workers is being extinguished (ignored) while the behavior of average performance and poor performance workers is being strengthened by positive reinforcement.

Rule 2. Failure to respond has reinforcing consequences. Managers who find the job of differentiating between workers so unpleasant that they fail to respond must recognize that failure to respond modifies behavior. "Indeed, whether he is conscious of it or not, the superior is bound to be constantly shaping the behavior of his subordinates by the way in which he utilizes the rewards that are at his disposal, and he will inevitably modify he behavior of his work group (Haire, 1964)." Managers must be careful that they examine the performance consequence of their non-action as well as their action.

Rule 3. Be sure to tell a person what he can do to get reinforced. By making clear the contingencies of reinforcement to the worker, a manager may be actually increasing the individual freedom of the worker. The employee who has a standard against which to measure his job will have a built-in feedback system which allows him to make judgements about his own work. The awarding of the reinforcement in an organization where the worker's goal is specified will be associated with the performance of the worker and not based on the biases of the supervisor. The assumption is that the supervisor rates the employee accurately (see Scott and Hamner, 1973a) and that he then reinforces the employee based on his ratings (see Scott and Hamner, 1973b). If the supervisor fails to rate accurately or administer rewards based on performance, then the stated goals for the worker will lose stimulus control, and the worker will be forced to search for the "true" contingencies, i. e. what behavior should he perform in order to get rewarded (e. g. ingratiation? loyalty? positive attitude?).

Rule 4. Be sure to tell a person what he is doing wrong. As a general rule, very few people find the act of failing rewarding. One assumption of behavior therefore is that a worker wants to be rewarded in a positive manner. A supervisor should never use extinction or punishment as a sole method for modifying behavior, but if used judiciously in conjunction with other techniques designed to promote more effective response options (Rule 3) such combined procedures can hasten the change process. If the supervisor fails to specify why a reward is being withheld, the employee may associate it with past desired behavior instead of the undesired behavior that the supervisor is trying to extinguish. The supervisor then extinguishes good performance while having no effect on the undesired behavior.

Rules 3 and 4, when used in combination, should allow the manager to control behavior in the best interest of reaching organizational goals. At the same time they should give the employee the clarity he needs to see that his own behavior and not the behavior of the supervisor controls his outcomes.

Rule 5. Don't punish in front of others. The reason for this rule is quite simple. The punishment (e. g. reprimand) should be enough to extinguish the undesired behavior. By administering the punishment in front of the work group, the worker is doubly punished in the sense that he is also put out of face (Goffman, 1959). This additional punishment may lead to negative side-effects in three ways. First, the worker whose self-image is damaged may feel that he must retaliate in order to protect himself. Therefore, the supervisor has actually increased undesired responses. Secondly, the work group may misunderstand the reason for the punishment and through "avoidance learning" may modify their own behavior in ways not intended by the supervisor. Third, the work group is also being punished in the sense that observing a member of their team being reprimanded has noxious or aversive properties for most people. This may result in a decrease in the performance of the total work group.

Rule 6. Make the consequences equal to the behavior. In other words be fair. Don't cheat the worker out of his just rewards. If he is a good worker, tell him. Many supervisors find it very difficult to praise an employee. Others find it very difficult to counsel an employee about what he is doing wrong. When a manager fails to use these reinforcement tools, he is actually reducing his effectiveness. When a worker is overrewarded he may feel guilty (Adams, 1965) and based on the principles of reinforcement, the worker's current level of performance is being conditioned. If his performance level is less than others who get the same reward, he has no reason to increase his output. When a worker is underrewarded, he becomes angry with the system (Adams, 1965). His behavior is being extinguished and the company may be forcing the good employee (underrewarded) to seek employment elsewhere while encouraging the poor employee (overrewarded) to stay.

An Argument for Positive Reinforcement

Most workers enter the work place willingly if not eagerly. They have a sense of right and wrong and have been thoroughly conditioned by their parents and by society. By the time they reach adulthood, it can be assumed that they are mature. For these reasons, it is argued here as well as by others (Skinner, 1953; Wiard, 1972), that the only tool needed for worker motivation is the presence or absence of positive reinforcement. In other words, managers do not, as a general rule, need to use avoidance learning or punishment techniques in order to control behavior.

Whyte (1972) says "positive reinforcers generally are more effective than negative reinforcers in the production and maintenance of behavior" (p. 67). Wiard (1972) points out, "There may be cases where the use of punishment has resulted in improved performance, but they are few and far between. The pitfalls of punishment can be encountered with any indirect approach" (p. 16). However, a positive reinforcement program is geared toward the desired results. It emphasizes what needs to be done, rather than what should not be done. A positive reinforcement program is result oriented, rather than process oriented. A well designed program encourages individual growth and freedom, whereas negative approach (avoidance learning and punishment) encourages immaturity in the indivudual and therefore eventually in the organization itself.

The reason organizations are ineffective according to Skinner (1969) is because they insist on using avoidance learning or punishment techniques, and because they fail to use a positive reinforcement program in an effective manner. He says:

> The contingencies of positive reinforcement arranged by governmental and religious agencies are primitive, and the agencies continue to lean heavily on the puritanical solution. Economic reinforcement might seem to represent an environmental solution, but it is badly programmed and the results are unsatisfactory for both the employer (since not much is done) and the employee (since work is still work). Education and the management of retardates and psychotics are still largely aversive. In short, as we have seen, the most powerful forces bearing on human behavior are not being effectively used. . . . Men are happy in an environment in which active, productive, and creative behavior is reinforced in effective ways (pp. 63–64).

Schedules of Positive Reinforcement

The previous discussion was primarily concerned with methods of arranging the contingencies of reinforcement in order to modify behavior. Two major points were discussed. First, some type of reinforcement is necessary in order to produce a change in behavior. Second, a combined program of positive reinforcement and extinction are more effective for use in organizations than are programs using punishment and/or avoidance learning techniques. The previous discussion thus tells what causes behavior and why it is important information for the manager, but it does not discuss the several important issues dealing with the scheduling or administering of positive reinforcement.

According to Costello and Zalkind (1963), "The speed with which learning takes place and also how lasting its effects will be is determined by the timing of reinforcement" (p. 193). In other words, the effectiveness varies as a function of the schedule of its administration. A reinforcement schedule is a more-or-less formal specification of the occurrence of a reinforcer in relation to the behavioral sequence to be conditioned, and effectiveness of the reinforcer depends as much upon its scheduling as upon any of its other features (magnitude, quality and degree of association with the behavioral act) (Adam and Scott, 1971).

There are many conceivable arrangements of a positive reinforcement schedule which managers can use to reward his workers (Ferster and Skinner, 1957). Aldis (1961) identifies two basic types of schedules which have the most promise concerning possible worker motivation. These schedules are *continuous* and *partial reinforcement* schedules.

Continuous Reinforcement Schedule   Under this schedule, every time the correct operant is emitted by the worker, it is followed by a reinforcer. With this schedule, behavior increases very rapidly but when the reinforcer is removed (extinction) performance decreases rapidly. For this reason it is not recommended for use by the manager over a long period of time. It is also difficult or impossible for a manager to reward the employee continuously for emitting desired behavior. Therefore a manager should generally consider using one or more of the partial reinforcement schedules when he administers both financial and nonfinancial rewards.

Partial Reinforcement Schedules   Partial reinforcement, where reinforcement does not occur after every correct operant, leads to slower learning but stronger retention of a response than total or continuous reinforcement. "In other words, *learning is more permanent when we reward correct behavior only part of the time*" (Bass and Vaughan, 1966, p. 20). This factor is extremely relevant to the observed strong resistance to changes in attitudes, values, norms, and the like.

Ferster and Skinner (1957) have described four basic types of partial reinforcement schedules for operant learning situations. They are:

1. Fixed Interval Schedule   Under this schedule a reinforcer is administered only when the desired response occurs after the passage of a specified period of time since the previous reinforcement. Thus a worker paid on a weekly basis would receive a full pay check every Friday, assuming that the worker was performing minimally acceptable behavior. This method offers the least motivation for hard work among employees (Aldis, 1961). The kind of behavior often observed with fixed interval schedules is a pause after reinforcement and then an increase in rate of responding until a high rate of performance occurs just as the interval is about to end. Suppose the plant manager visits the shipping department each day at approximately 10:00 A.M. This fixed schedule of supervisory recognition will probably cause performance to be at its highest just prior to the plant manager's visit and then performance will probably steadily decline thereafter and not reach its peak again until the next morning's visit.

2. Variable Interval Schedule   Under this schedule, reinforcement is administered at some variable interval of time around some average. This schedule is not recommended for use with a pay plan (Aldis, 1961), but it is an ideal method to use for administering praise, promotions, and supervisory visits. Since the reinforcers are dispensed unpredictably, variable schedules generate higher rates of response and more stable and consistent performance (Bandura, 1969). Suppose our plant manager visits the shipping department on an *average* of once a day but at randomly selected time intervals, i. e., twice on Monday, once on Tuesday, not on Wednesday, not on Thursday, and twice on Friday, all at different times during the day. Performance will be higher and have less fluctuation than under the fixed interval schedule.

3. Fixed Ratio Schedule   Here a reward is delivered only when a fixed number of desired responses take place. This is essentially the piece-work schedule for pay. The response level here is significantly higher than that obtained under any of the interval (or time-based) schedules.

4. Variable Ratio Schedule   Under this schedule, a reward is delivered only after a number of desired responses with the number of desired responses changing from the occurrence of one reinforcer to the next, around an average. Thus a person working on a 15 to 1 variable ratio schedule might receive reinforcement after ten responses, then twenty responses, then fifteen responses, etc., to an average of one reinforcer per fifteen responses. Gambling is an example of a variable ratio reward schedule. Research evidence reveals that of all the variations in scheduling procedures available, this is the most powerful in sustaining behavior (Jablonsky and DeVries, 1972). In industry, this plan would be impossible to use as the only plan for scheduling reinforcement. However, Aldis (1961) suggests how this method could be used to supplement other monetary reward schedules:

> Take the annual Christmas bonus as an example. In many instances, this "surprise" gift has become nothing more than a ritualized annual salary supplement which everybody expects. Therefore, its incentive-building value is largely lost. Now suppose that the total bonus were distributed at irregular intervals throughout the year and in small sums dependent upon the amount of work done. Wouldn't the workers find their urge to work increased? (p. 63).

An important point to remember is that to be effective a schedule should always include the specification of a contingency between the behavior desired and the occurrence of a reinforcer. In many cases it may be necessary to use each of the various schedules for administering rewards—for example, base pay on a fixed interval schedule, promotions and raises on a variable interval schedule, recognition of above average performance with a piece-rate plan (fixed ratio) and supplementary bonuses on a variable ratio schedule. The effect of each of the types of reinforcement schedules and the various methods of arranging reinforcement contingencies on worker performance is summarized in Table 1.

The necessity for arranging appropriate reinforcement contingencies is dramatically illustrated by several studies in which rewards were shifted from a response-contingent (ratio) to a time-contingent basis (interval). During the period in which rewards were made conditional upon occurrence of the desired behavior, the appropriate response patterns were exhibited at a consistently high level. When the same rewards were given based on time and independent of the worker's behavior, there was a marked drop in the desired behavior. The reinstatement of the performance-contingent reward schedule promptly restored the high level of responsiveness (Lovaas, Berberich, Perloff, and Schaeffer, 1966;

Table 1   Operant Conditioning Summary

Arrangement of reinforcement contingencies	Schedule of reinforcement contingencies	Effect on behavior when applied to the Individual	Effect on behavior when removed from the individual
	Continuous reinforcement	Fastest method to establish a new behavior	Fastest method to extinguish a new behavior
	Partial reinforcement	Slowest method to establish a new behavior	Slowest method to extinguish a new behavior
	Variable partial reinforcement	More consistent response frequencies	Slower extinction rate
	Fixed partial reinforcement	Less consistent response frequencies	Faster extinction rate
Positive reinforcement Avoidance reinforcement		Increased frequency over preconditioning level	Return to preconditioning level
Punishment extinction		Decreased frequency over preconditioning level	Return to preconditioning level

(Adapted from Behling et al., reprinted with permission of the author from "Present Theories and New Directions in Theories of Work Effort," *Journal Supplement and Abstract Service* of the American Psychological Corporation.)

Baer, Peterson, and Sherman, 1967). Similar declines in performance were obtained when workers were provided rewards in advance without performance requirements (Ayllen and Azrin, 1965; Bandura and Perloff, 1967).

Aldis (1961) encourages businessmen to recognize the importance of a positive reinforcement program. He also says that experimentation with various schedules of positive reinforcement is the key to reducing job boredom and increasing worker satisfaction. He concludes:

> Most of us fully realize that a large proportion of all workers hold jobs that are boring and repetitive and that these employees are motivated to work not by positive rewards but by various oblique forms of threat. . . . The challenge is to motivate men by positive rewards rather than by negative punishments or threats of punishments. . . . Businessmen should recognize how much their conventional wage and salary systems essentially rely on negative reinforcement.
>
> Thus the promise of newer methods of wage payments which rely on more immediate rewards, on piece-rate pay, and greater randomization does not lie only in the increase in productivity that might follow. The greater promise is that such experiments may lead to happier workers as well (p. 63).

MANAGEMENT AND THE DISSEMINATION OF KNOWLEDGE

Previously we defined *learning* as the acquisition of knowledge (by the process of operant conditioning), and performance as the translation of knowledge into behavior (depending on the consequences). It can be argued therefore that what managers do is disseminate knowledge to those they manage in order to gain the desired level of performance. The question that remains to be answered is "What is knowledge, i.e., what information should one disseminate to control behavior?

There are two types of knowledge according to Skinner (1969). *Private knowledge* (Polanyi, 1960; Bridgeman, 1959) is knowledge established through experience with the contingencies of reinforcement. Skinner says "The world which establishes contingencies of reinforcement of the sort studied in an operant analysis is presumably 'what knowledge is about.' A person comes to know that world and how to behave in it in the sense that he acquires behavior which satisfies the contingencies it maintains" (1969, p. 156). The behavior which results from private knowledge is called *contingency-shaped* behavior. This is the knowledge which one must possess in order to perform correctly in order to get rewarded. This knowledge does not assume any awareness on the part of the person but is based entirely on the person's past reinforcement history. A person can "know how" to play golf, for example, as indicated by a series of low scores—yet it is an entirely different thing to be able to tell others how to play golf. A machine operator may be an excellent employee, but make a poor foreman. One reason may be that, while he possesses private knowledge about his job, he is unable to verbalize the contingencies to other people.

Public knowledge, then, is the ability to derive rules from the contingencies, in the form of injunctions or descriptions which specify occasions, responses, and consequences (Skinner, 1969, p. 160). The behavior which results from public knowledge is called *rule-governed* behavior.

The reason the possession of public knowledge is important to the manager is simple. The employee looks to the manager for information about what behavior is required, how to perform the desired behavior, and what the consequences of the desired behavior will be. Before a manager can give correct answers to these questions, he must understand the true contingencies himself, since his business is not in doing, but in telling others how to do. The point is to be able to analyze the contingencies of reinforcement found in the organization and "to formulate rules or laws which make it unnecessary to be exposed to them in order to behave appropriately" (Skinner, 1969, p. 166).

After living in a large city for a long time, a person is able to go from Point A to Point B with little trouble. The knowledge of how to get around in the city was shaped by the past history with the environment. This behavior is an example of contingency-shaped behavior. If a stranger arrives in the same city and desires to go from Point A to Point B he too will have little trouble. He will look at a map of the city, and follow the path specified by the map. This behavior is an example of rule-governed behavior. Whether or not a person will continue to follow the map (rule) in the future is dependent on the consequences of following the map in the past. If the rule specified the correct contingencies, he probably will continue to use the map, but if a person found the map to be in error, then he will probably look to other sources of information (e. g., asking someone with private knowledge). The same thing happens in industry. If a manager is correct in the specification of the rules, i. e., the new worker follows the rules and receives a reward, then the worker will probably follow the other rules specified by the manager. If the manager specifies incorrect rules, then the worker may look to his peers or to other sources for informantion (e. g., the union steward) and specification of rules which describe behavior that will be rewarded.

There are two kinds of rules the manager can specify to the employee. A command or *mand* is a rule that specifies behavior and consequences of the bahavior, where the consequences are arranged by the person giving the command. The specified or implied consequences for failure to act are usually aversive in nature and the judgment of the correctness of the behavior is made by the person giving the command. A foreman who tells the worker to be on time for work is giving the worker a command. The implied consequence is that if the employee fails to report on time, the foreman will take action.

Advice and warnings are called *tacts* and involve rules which specify the reinforcements contingent on prior stimulation from rules, or laws. They specify the same contingencies which would directly shape behavior (private knowledge). The specification of the tact speeds up the conditioning process. If a secretary tells her boss he should take an umbrella when he goes to lunch she is describing a tact. She has no control over the consequences (getting wet) of the behavior (not carrying the umbrella). Instead it is determined by the environment itself (weather). Skinner (1969) says:

Go west, young man is an example of advice (tacting) when the behavior it specifies will be reinforced by certain consequences which do not result from action taken by the advisor. We tend to follow advice because previous behavior in response to similar verbal stimuli has been reinforced. Go west, young man is a command when some consequences of the specified action are arranged by the commander—say, the aversive consequences arranged by an official charged with relocating the inhabitants of a region. When maxims, rules, and laws are advice, the governed behavior is reinforced by consequences which might have shaped the same behavior directly in the absence of the maxims, rules, and laws. When they are commands, they are effective only because special reinforcements have been made contingent upon them. (p. 148).

While a manager must possess public knowledge as well as private knowledge in order to accomplish his task of "getting things done through other people" in keeping with a plea for positive reinforcement and unbiased reward systems, tacting is the method of rule specification recommended. Skinner (1969) recommends that by specifying the contingencies in such a way that the consequences are positive in nature and failure to respond is met with the withholding of a reward rather than by aversive stimuli, "the 'mand' may be replaced by a 'tact' describing conditions under which specific behavior on the part of the listener will be reinforced (p. 158)." Instead of saying "Give me that report" say "I need the report." "The craftsman begins by ordering his apprentice to behave in a given way; but he may later achieve the same effect simply by describing the relation between what the apprentice does and the consequences" (Skinner, 1969, p. 158). Thus, the technique which managers use to direct the employee can make a lot of difference in the acceptance of the rule by the employee. A mand operates from an avoidance learning base while a tact operates from a positive reinforcement base. A tact is more impersonal and gives the employee freedom in that it does not "enjoin anyone to behave in a given way, it simply describes the contingencies under which certain kinds of behavior will have certain kinds of consequences" (Skinner, 1969, p. 158).

CONTROVERSIES SURROUNDING AN OPERANT APPROACH TO MANAGEMENT

The reinforcement approach to the study and control of human behavior has met with resistance and criticism, primarily through a lack of understanding of its recommended uses and limitations. Goodman (1964) said, "Learning theory has two simple points to make and does so with talmudic ingenuity, variability, intricacy, and insistence. They are reinforcement and extinction. What has to be left out. . . . is thought."

While the criticism would be too numerous to mention here, an attempt will be made to examine three of the major controversies surrounding an operant approach to the management of people in organizational settings.

1. *The application of operant conditioning techniques ignores the individuality of man.* Ashby (1967) said "now the chief weakness of programmed instruction is

that it rewards rote learning, and worse than that—it rewards only those responses which are in agreement with the programme." Proponents of an operant approach to contingency management recognize that a poorly designed program can lead to rigidity in behavior. This is one of the major reasons that they recommend a program of reinforcement which best fits the group or individuals being supervised. It is untrue, however, that behaviorists ignore the individuality of man. Each man is unique based on his past reinforcement history. When personnel psychologists build sophisticated selection models to predict future performance, they are actually trying to identify those applicants who will perform well under the contingencies of that particular organization. That does not mean that a person rejected cannot be motivated, but only that the current reward system of that organization is better suited for another applicant.[5]

In other words, the problem a manager faces is not to design contingencies that will be liked by all men, "but a way of life which will be liked by those who live it" (Skinner, 1969, p. 41). As Hersey and Blanchard (1972) point out, "Positive reinforcement is anything that is rewarding to the individual being reinforced. Reinforcement, therefore, depends on the individual (p. 22)." What is reinforcing to one may not be reinforcing to someone else based on the person's past history of satiation, deprivation and conditioning operations. A manager can do two things to insure that the contingencies of reinforcement are designed to support the individuality of the worker. First, as noted earlier he can strive to hire the worker who desires the rewards offered by the firms; i. e., can the person be happy or satisfied with this firm? Secondly, if it seems that the contingencies are ineffective, the manager can change the contingencies by using a democratic process—letting the employees design their own reward structure, within the limits set by the organization. "Democracy is an effort to solve the problem by letting the people design the contingencies under which they are to live or—to put it another way—by insisting that the designer himself live under the contingencies he designs" (Skinner, 1969, p. 43).

In summary, therefore, it can be concluded that in a voluntary society, where man has freedom to move from one organization to another, operant methods of control should not ignore the individuality of man. Instead man should seek work where his individuality can best be appreciated and industries should select employees who can best be motivated by the contingencies available to them. It should be noted, however, that through the unethical application of conditioning principles, some employers may exploit workers. The overall evidence would seem to indicate that this is not due to the weakness in behavioral theory, but due to the weakness of man himself.

   2. The application of operant conditioning techniques restricts freedom of choice.

> Discussion of the moral implications of behavioral control almost always emphasize the Machiavellian role of change agents and the self-protective maneuvers of controllers. . . . The tendency to exaggerate the powers of behavioral control by psychologi-

cal methods alone, irrespective of willing cooperation by the client, and the failure to recognize the reciprocal nature of interpersonal control obscure both the ethical issues and the nature of the social influence processes (Bandura, 1969, p. 85).

Kelman (1965) noted that the primary criterion that one might apply in judging the ethical implications of social influence approaches is the degree to which they promote freedom of choice. If individualism is to be guaranteed, it must be tempered by a sense of social obligation by the individual and by the organization.

Bandura (1969) noted that a person is considered free insofar as he can partly influence future events by managing his own behavior. A person in a voluntary society can within limits exert some control over the variables that govern his own choices. Skinner (1969) noted that "Men are happy in an environment in which active, productive, and creative behavior is reinforced in effective ways" (p. 64). One method of effectively reinforcing behavior is by allowing the employee some determination in the design of the reinforcement contingencies. Another method is to design self-control reinforcement systems in which individuals regulate their own activities (Ferster, Nurenberger and Levitt, 1962; Harris, 1969).

While it cannot be denied that reinforcers which are "all too abundant and powerful" (Skinner, 1966) can restrict freedom of choice, it is not true that a behavioral or Skinnerian approach is against freedom of choice; the opposite is true. As Bandura noted, "Contrary to common belief, behavioral approaches not only support a humanistic morality, but because of their relative effectiveness in establishing self-determination these methods hold much greater promise than traditional procedures for enhancement of behavioral freedom and fulfillment of human capabilities" (p. 88).

3. *Operant theory, through its advocacy of an external reward system, ignores the fact that individuals can be motivated by the job itself.* Deci (1971, 1972) among others (Likert, 1967; Vroom and Deci, 1970) criticizes behaviorists for advocating a system of employee motivation that only utilizes externally mediated rewards, i. e., rewards such as money and praise administered by someone other than the employee himself. In so doing, according to Deci, management is attempting to control the employee's behavior so he will do what he is told. The limitations of this method of worker motivation, for Deci, is that it only satisfies man's "lower-order" needs (Maslow, 1943) and does not take into account man's "higher-order" needs for self-esteem and self-actualization. Deci states, "It follows that there are many important motivators of human behavior which are not under the direct control of managers and, therefore, cannot be contingently administered in a system of piece-rate payments" (1972, p. 218).

Deci recommends that we should move away from a method of external control, and toward a system where individuals can be motivated by the job itself. He says that this approach will allow managers to focus on higher-order needs where the rewards are mediated by the person himself (intrinsically motivated). To motivate employees intrinsically, tasks should be designed which are interesting, creative and resourceful, and workers should have some say in decisions which concern them "so they will feel like causal agents in the activities which they engage in" (Deci, 1972, p. 219). Deci concludes his argument against a contingency approach to management by saying:

> . . . It is possible to pay workers and still have them intrinsically motivated. Hence the writer favors the prescription that we concentrate on structuring situations and jobs to arouse intrinsic motivation, rather than trying to structure piece-rate and other contingency payment schemes. Workers would be intrinsically motivated and would seek to satisfy their higher-order needs through effective performance. The noncontingent payments (or salaries) would help to satisfy the workers and keep them on the job, especially if the pay were equitable (Adams, 1965; Pritchard, 1969), (1972, p. 227).

Deci levels criticism at a positive reinforcement contingency approach on the basis of four issues: (1) advocating that external rewards be administered by someone else, (2) ignoring the importance of the task environment, (3) ignoring the importance of internal rewards, and (4) advocating a contingent payment plan. Deci makes two errors, from a reinforcement theory point of view, when he advocates noncontingent equitable pay plans. First, equity theory (Adams, 1965) assumes that rewards are based on performance. If they weren't, then the pay would be equal, not equitable. Second, and more crucial, is Deci's assumption that a pay plan can be noncontingent. Bandura notes that "all behavior is inevitably controlled, and the operation of psychological laws cannot be suspended by romantic conceptions of human behavior, any more than indignant rejection of the law of gravity as antihumanistic can stop people from falling" (1969, p. 85). Homme and Tosti (1965) made the point that, "either one manages the contingencies or they get managed by accident. Either way there will be contingencies, and they will have their effect" (p. 16): In other words, if managers instituted a pay plan that was "noncontingent," they would in fact be rewarding poor performance and extinguishing good performance (see Rules 1, 2, and 6).

The assertion that a contingency approach advocates that the rewards always be administered by someone else is false. Skinner specifically (1969, p. 158) recommends that manding behavior be replaced by tacting methods for achieving the same effect. Skinner suggested that one safeguard against exploitation is to make sure that the designed of the contingencies never controls. In addition to recommending that the contingencies be so designed that they are controlled by the environment (tacting), operant theorists have advocated self-control processes in which individuals regulate their own behavior by arranging appropriate contingencies for themselves (Ferster, Nurenberger and Levitt, 1962). Bandura (1969) concluded that:

> The selection of well-defined objectives, both intermediate and ultimate, is an essential aspect of any self-directed program of change. The goals that individuals choose for themselves must be specified in sufficiently detailed behavioral terms to provide adequate guidance for the actions that must be taken daily to attain desired outcomes . . . .Individuals can, therefore, utilize objective records of behavioral changes as an additional source of reinforcement for their self-controlling behavior (p. 255).

Studies which have explored the effect of self-reinforcement on performance have shown that systems which allowed workers to keep a record of their own output to use as a continuous feedback system and for reinforcement purposes helped the workers to increase their performance (Kolb, Winter and Berlew, 1968; Fox, 1966). Michigan Bell Telephone Company and the Emery Air Freight Corporation are two of several firms which are currently using self-reinforcement programs in order to increase worker motivation and performance. Both programs have been immensely successful (see *Business Week,* December 18, 1971; and December 2, 1972).

It should be noted that even though the individual is determining his own reward in the self-feedback program, the reinforcers are both externally (money, recognition, praise) and internally (self-feedback) mediated. According to Skinner (1957) and Bem (1967) the self-report feedback is a "tract" or description of an internal feeling state. In both cases, the rewards must be contingent on performance for effective control of the behavior to take place.

Deci's recommendation that jobs should be designed so that they are interesting, creative, and resourceful is wholehartedly supported by proponents of a positive reinforcement program. Skinner (1969) warns managers that too much dependency on force and a poorly designed monetary reward system may actually reduce performance, while designing the task so that it is automatically reinforcing can have positive effects on performance. Skinner says:

> The behavior of an employee is important to the employer, who gains when the employee works industriously and carefully. How is he to be induced to do so? The standard answer was once physical force: men worked to avoid punishment or death. The by-products were troublesome, however, and economics is perhaps the first field in which an explicit change was made to positive reinforcement. Most men now work, as we say, 'for money'.
>
> Money is not a natural reinforcer; it must be conditioned as such. Delayed reinforcement, as in a weekly wage, raises a special problem. No one works on Monday morning because he is reinforced by a paycheck on Friday afternoon. The employee who is paid by the week works during the week to avoid losing the standard of living which depends on a weekly system. Rate of work is determined by the supervisor (with or without the pacing stimuli of a production line), and special aversive contingencies maintain quality. The pattern is therefore still aversive. It has often been pointed out that the attitude of the production-line worker toward his work differs conspicuously from that of the craftsman, who is envied by workers and industrial managers alike. One explanation is that the craftsman is reinforced by more than monetary consequences, but another important difference is that when a craftsman spends a week completing a given set object, each of the parts produced during the week is likely to be automatically reinforcing because of its place in the completed object (p. 18).

Skinner (1969) also agrees with Deci that the piece-rate may actually reduce performance in that it is so powerful it is most often misused, and "it is generally opposed by those concerned with the welfare of the worker (and by workers themselves when, for example, they set daily quotas)" (p. 19).

It appears therefore, that critics of operant conditioning methods misunderstand the recommendations of behaviorists in the area of worker motivation. Operant theory does advocate interesting job design and self-reinforcement feedback systems, where possible. It does not advocate force or try to control the employee's behavior by making the employee "do what he is told." It is not against humanistic morality; rather it advocates that workers be rewarded on their performance and not on their needs alone.

While other controversies about operant conditioning could be reviewed, the examination of these three issues should give the reader a flavor of the criticisms which surround the use of a contingency approach to behavioral control.

ETHICAL IMPLICATIONS FOR WORKER CONTROL

The deliberate use of positive and negative reinforcers often gives rise to ethical concern about harmful effects which may result from such practices. Poorly designed reward structures can interfere with the development of spontaneity and creativity. Reinforcement systems which are deceptive and manipulative are an insult to the integrity of man. The employee should be a willing party to the influence attempt, with both parties benefiting from the relationship.

The question of whether man should try to control human behavior is covered in a classic paper by Rogers and Skinner (1956). The central issue discussed was one of personal values. Rogers contends that "values" emerge from the individual's "freedom of choice," a realm unavailable to science. Skinner, in rebuttal, points out that the scientific view of man does not allow for such exceptions, and that choice and the resulting values are, like all behavior, a function of man's biology and his environment. Since biology and environment lie within the realm of science, "choice" and "value" must be accessible to scientific inquiry. Skinner and Rogers are both concerned with abuse of the power held by scientists, but Skinner is optimistic that good judgment will continue to prevail. Krasner (1964) agrees with Skinner that we should apply scientific means to control behavior, but warns that behavioral control can be horribly misused unless we are constantly alert to what is taking place in society.

Probably few managers deliberately misuse their power to control behavior. Managers should realize that the mismanagement of the contingencies of reinforcement is actually self-defeating. Workers will no longer allow themselves to be pushed around, but instead will insist that the work environment be designed in such a way that they have a chance at a better life. The effective use of a positive reinforcing program is one of the most critical challenges facing modern management.

The first step in the ethical use of behavioral control in organizations is the understanding by managers of the determinants of behavior. Since reinforcement is the single most important concept in the learning process, managers must learn how to design effective reinforcement programs that will encourage creative, productive, satisfied employees. This paper has attempted to outline the knowledge available for this endeavor.

NOTES

1 The author is indebted to Professor William E. Scott, Jr., Graduate School of Business, Indiana University for sharing with him his Skinnerian philosophy.
2 Classical conditioning is also known as respondent conditioning and Pavlovian conditioning.
3 Operant conditioning is also known as instrumental conditioning and Skinnerian conditioning.
4 Parentheses added.
5 This is true because the criterion variable is some measure of performance, and performance is directly tied to the reinforcement consequences for the current employees used to derive the selection model.

REFERENCES

Adam, E. E., and Scott, W. E., The application of behavioral conditioning procedures to the problems of quality control, *Academy of Management Journal,* 1971, **14,** 175–193.

Adams, J. S., Inequity in social exchange, in L. Berkowitz (ed.), *Advances in Experimental Psychology,* Academic Press, 1965, 157–189.

Aldis, O., Of pigeons and men, *Harvard Business Review,* 1961, **39,** 59–63.

Ayllon, T., and Azrin, N. H., The measurement and reinforcement of behavior of psychotics, *Journal of the Experimental Analysis of Behavior,* 1965, **8,** 357–383.

Ashby, Sir Eric, Can education be machine made?, *New Scientist,* February 2, 1967.

Baer, D. M., Peterson, R. F., and Sherman, J. A., The development of imitation by reinforcing behavioral similarity to a model. *Journal of the Experimental Analysis of Behavior, 1967,* **10,** 405–416.

Bandura, A., and Perloff, B., The efficacy of self-monitoring reinforcement systems, *Journal of Personality and Social Psychology,* 1967, **7,** 111–116.

Bandura, A., *Principles of Behavior Modification,* Holt, Rinehart and Winston, Inc., New York, 1969.

Bass, B. M., and Vaughan, J. A., *Training in Industry: The Management of Learning,* Wadsworth Publishing Company, Belmont, Calif., 1966.

Behling, O., Schriesheim, C., and Tolliver, J., Present theories and new directions in theories of work effort, *Journal Supplement Abstract Service* of the American Psychological Corporation, in press.

Bem, D. J., Self-perception: An alternative interpretation of cognitive dissonance phenomena, *Psychological Review,* 1967, **74,** 184–200.

Bridgeman, D. W. *The Way Things Are,* Harvard Press, Cambridge, Mass., 1959.

Costello, T. W., and Zalkind, S. S., *Psychology in Administration,* Prentice-Hall, Inc., Englewood Cliffs, N.J., 1963.

Deci, E. L., The effects of contingent and noncontingent rewards and controls on intrinsic motivation, *Organizational Behavior and Human Performance,* 1972, **8,** 217–229.

Deci, E. L., The effects of externally mediated rewards on intrinsic motivation, *Journal of Personality and Social Psychology,* 1971, **18,** 105–115.

Festinger, L., A theory of social comparison processes, *Human Relations,* 1954, **7,** 117–140.

Ferster, C. B., and Skinner, B F., *Schedules of Reinforcement,* Appleton-Century-Crofts, New York, 1957.

Ferster, C. B., Nurenberger, J. I., and Levitt, E. B., The control of eating, *Journal of Mathematics,* 1962, **1,** 87–109.

Fox, L., The use of efficient study habits, In R. Ulrich, T. Stachnik, and J. Mabry (Eds.), *Control of Human Behavior,* Scott, Foresman, Glenview, Ill., 1966, 85–93.

Goffman, E., *The Presentation of Self in Everyday Life,* Doubleday, New York, 1959.

Goodman, Paul, *Compulsory Mis-education,* Horizon Press, New York, 1964.

Haire, Mason, *Psychology in Management,* 2nd ed., McGraw-Hill, New York, 1964.

Harris, M. B., A self-directed program for weight control: a pilot study, *Journal of Abnormal Psychology,* 1969, **74,** 263–270.

Henry, Jules, Review of human behavior: An inventory of scientific findings by Bernard Berelson and Gary A. Steiner, *Scientific American,* July, 1964.

Hersey, P., and Blanchard, K. H., The management of change: Part 2, *Training and Development Journal,* February, 1972, 20–24.

Hilgard, E. R., *Theories of Learning,* 2nd ed., Appleton-Century-Crofts, New York, 1956.

Homme, L. E., and Tosti, D. T., Contingency management and motivation, *Journal of the National Society for Programmed Instruction,* 1965, **4,** 14–16.

Jablonsky, S., and DeVries, D., Operant conditioning principles extrapolated to the theory of management, *Organizational Behavior and Human Performance,* 1972, **7,** 340–358.

Keller, F. S., *Learning: Reinforcement Theory,* Random House, New York, 1969.

Kelman, H. C., Manipulation of human behavior: An ethical dilemma for the social scientist, *Journal of Social Issues,* 1965, **21,** 31–46.

Kolb, D. A., Winter, S. K., and Berlew, D. E., Self-directed change: Two studies, *Journal of Applied Behavioral Science,* 1968, **4,** 453–471.

Krasner, L., Behavior control and social responsibility, *American Psychologist,* 1964, **17,** 199–204.

Likert, R., *New Patterns of Management,* Likert, R., *New Patterns of Management,* McGraw-Hill, New York, 1961.

Lovaas, O. I., Berberich, J. P., Perloff, B. F., and Schaeffer, B., Acquisition of imitative speech for schizophrenic children, *Science,* 1966, **151,** 705–707.

Luthans, F., *Organizational Behavior,* McGraw-Hill, New York, 1973.

Maslow, A. H., A theory of human motivation, *Psychological Review,* 1943, **50,** 370–396.

McGregor, D., *The Human Side of Enterprise,* New York, McGraw-Hill, 1960.

Michael, J., and Meyerson, L., A behavioral approach to counseling and guidance, *Harvard Educational Review,* 1962, **32,** 382–402.

Morse, W. H., Intermittent reinforcement, in W. K. Honig, (ed.), *Operant Behavior,* Appleton-Century-Crofts, New York, 1966.

New tool: Reinforcement for good work, *Business Week,* December 18, 1971, 68–69.

Nord, W. R., Beyond the teaching machine: The neglected area of operant conditioning in the theory and practice of management, *Organizational Behavior and Human Performance,* 1969, 375–401.

Pavlov, I. P., *The Work of the Digestive Glands,* (Translated by W. H. Thompson), Clarles Griffin, London, 1902.

Polanyi, M., *Personal Knowledge,* Univ. of Chicago Press, 1960.

Rachlin, H., *Modern Behaviorism,* W. H. Freeman and Co., New York, 1970.

Rogers, Carl R., and Skinner, B. F., Some issues concerning the control of human behavior: A symposium, *Science,* 1956, **124,** 1057–1066.

Scott, W. E., and Cummings, L. L., *Readings in Organizational Behavior and Human Performance,* Revised Edition, Irwin, Homewood, Ill., 1973.

Scott, W. E., and Hamner, W. Clay, The effects of order and variance in performance on supervisory ratings of workers, Paper presented at the *45th Annual Meeting,* Midwestern Psychological Association, Chicago, 1973.

Scott, W. E., and Hamner, W. Clay, The effect of order and variance in performance on the rewards given workers by supervisory personnel, mimeo, Indiana University, 1973.

Scott, W. E., Activation theory and task design, *Organizational Behavior and Human Performance,* 1966, **1,** 3–30.

Skinner, B. F., *The Behavior of Organisms,* New York: Appleton-Century, 1938.

Skinner, B. F., *Walden Two,* New York: The Macmillan Company, 1948.

Skinner, B. F., Are theories of learning necessary? *Psychological Review,* 1950, **57,** 193–216.

Skinner, B. F., *Science and Human Behavior.* New York: The Macmillan Company, 1953.

Skinner, B. F., Freedom and the control of men, *American Scholar,* 1956, **25,** 47–65.

Skinner, B. F., Some issues concerning the control of human behavior, *Science,* 1956, **124,** 1056–1066.

Skinner, B. F., *Verbal Behavior.* New York: Appleton-Century-Crofts, 1957.

Skinner, B. F., Behaviorism at fifty. *Science,* 1963a, **134,** 566–602.

Skinner, B. F., Operant behavior. *American Psychologist,* 1963b, **18,** 503–515.

Skinner, B. F., *Contingencies of Reinforcement,* Appleton-Century-Crofts, New York, 1969.

Skinner, B. F., *Beyond Freedom and Dignity,* New York: Alfred A. Knopf, 1971.

Thorndike, E. L., *Animal Intelligence,* Macmillan, New York, 1911.

Vroom, V. H., and Deci, E. L., An overview of work motivation, in V. H. Vroom and E. L. Deci (eds.), *Management and Motivation,* Penguin Press, Baltimore, 1970, 9–19.

Wiard, H., Why manage behavior? A case for positive reinforcement, *Human Resource Management,* Summer, 1972, 15–20.

Where Skinner's theories work, *Business Week,* December, 1972, 64–65.

Whyte, W. F., Skinnerian theory in organizations, *Psychology Today,* April, 1972, 67–68, 96, 98, 100.

Skinnerian Theory in Organizations
William F. Whyte

As a long-time consultant and researcher in industry, I often come in contact with the executive who has just discovered the importance of "the human element."

"What we must do is change people's attitudes," he usually says.

As politely as I can, I tell him to forget attitudes. The problem is to change the conditions to which people are responding. If he does that, people will behave differently and he will find that attitudes—if they still interest him—will adjust themselves to the new situation.

Problems My line of argument sounds purely Skinnerian, of course. And I do, in fact, agree with B. F. Skinner's basic formulation. Behavioral scientists should abandon their preoccupation with the inner life of man and concentrate on the relations between man and environment, Skinner argues. Behavior is shaped and maintained by its consequences; these conquences (or reinforcers, as Skinner calls them) can be either positive or negative, but positive reinforcers generally are more effective than negative reinforcers in the production and maintenance of behavior.

Despite this basic agreement, however, my experiences in industry have let me to conclude that when we move out of the laboratory into the complexities of real life, Skinner's operant-conditioning theory tells us very little about the prediction and control of behavior. As I see it, Skinner fails to deal with four crucial elements in real-life behavior: 1) the cost-benefit ratio and the social-comparison process; 2) the problem of conflicting stimuli; 3) the problem of time lag and trust; and 4) the one-body problem.

Control In the industrial field, incentive systems provide a useful focus for analyzing these four elements because such systems are explicit attempts by management to control behavior through reinforcement: more production, more pay. I am aware, of course, that Skinner himself is no advocate of piece-rate pay, but I believe that the system nevertheless can be used to illustrate the problems we fact in attempting to apply Skinner's basic theory to real-life situations. My studies of incentive systems in U.S. industry point to some of the necessary qualifications that we must build into the Skinner schema.

1 THE COST-BENEFIT RATIO AND THE SOCIAL-COMPARISON PROCESS

Laboratory experimenters, from Pavlov with his dogs to Skinner with his pigeons, could disregard the costs of the action to the actor, for they were trifling compared to the benefits the experimental animal received as a consequence of his action. That is generally not the case in human affairs. The important rewards a person seeks usually involve substantial effort.

In analyzing individual piece-rate incentive systems, we can ignore the question of whether the person will produce more if he gets more money for putting out additional effort and applying superior skill. Other things being equal, most persons would rather have more money than less and will make some effort to get more. The important question is: How much effort in relation to how much more money?

More This question focuses on the rate-setting problem. Management commonly assumes that workers on piece rates will produce 25 to 30 percent more than they would produce if they were paid a flat, hourly rate. In the abstract, the rate-setting problem is simple: if we determine the number of pieces the average worker produces on time or hourly rates and call this number 100 percent, then the worker on piece rates will produce more and get about 130 percent of his hourly rate. For example, if a time-study man determines that a worker with a base pay of $2.00 an hour should produce 10 units an hour, the equation yields a price of 20 cents per unit produced. At an incentive pace, therefore, the worker should average 13 pieces an hour, raising his pay to $2.60.

But this assumption depends on the accuracy of the time-study man's estimates, which he makes by observing and measuring the work of fast, average, and slow workers under normal working conditions, and by throwing in adjustments for such factors as personal time and fatigue. Workers are well aware that if they can get the time-study man to decide that eight units an hour is a fair nonincentive pace, making the price per piece 25 cents instead of 20 cents, they can make more money with the same effort or the same amount of money with less effort.

Motion   The rate-setting process leads to elaborate charades played by workers for the benefit of the time-study man. Experienced workers learn how to slow down while appearing to work with maximum effort. They add extra motions that appear to be necessary but that can be eliminated after the rate has been set. If the time-study man demands that a worker operate his machine at a faster speed, the worker can find ways to damage the machine to prove that the speed demanded was excessive.

Of course, these maneuvers do not entirely fool the time-study man. He knows that workers try to mislead him, but he does not know how much. To the measurements he makes, he plugs in an estimate of how much he is being fooled. Thus he combines scientific observation and measurement with a guessing game.

If the worker fools the time-study man more than the time-study man allows for, the result is a loose rate on which the worker can make high earnings without excessive effort. If the time-study man overcompensates for the amount he thinks he is being fooled, the result is a tight rate on which the worker finds it difficult or impossible to make the incentive pay he seeks. If the rate is loose, workers are happy; but management is unhappy because it is paying too high a price for the units produced. If the rate is tight, workers are unhappy because they cannot make their expected earnings without excessive effort.

Levels   In more general terms, we are dealing with what George Homans calls the relationship between investments and rewards. Out of their experience, persons develop ideas about an equitable level of rewards in terms of their personal investments (level of education or training, years of service, skill, effort). If the person is not receiving rewards that he considers comparable to the investments he has made, he becomes dissatisfied and searches for ways to achieve a better balance.

The person also judges the equity of his investment-reward (or cost-benefit) ratio in terms of what another person with similar investments is getting in the way of rewards. If the other person seems to be getting more than the person is getting for similar investments, the person complains or reduces the level of his investments (producing less, giving less attention to quality, and so on).

In other words, providing positive reinforcers for production in the industrial situation is a highly complex problem that involves observation-and-measurement procedures embedded in a network of relationships among the person, the time-study man, the supervisor, and other workers.

2 CONFLICTING STIMULI

The problem of conflicting stimuli has not escaped the attention of stimulus-response or operant-conditioning psychologists. In fact, Ivan Pavlov entered into this field when he conditioned dogs to respond, in anticipation of food, to a light in the shape of a full moon, and to cringe, in anticipation of an electric shock, in response to a light in the shape of a new moon. By varying the shapes of the lights so that the stimuli came to resemble each other ever more closely, Pavlov produced experimental neuroses in his animals. With these experiments the question was whether a given stimulus stood for a potential reward or a potential penalty—a situation that occurs frequently outside the laboratory. However, situations in which a given behavior of a person may yield both rewards and penalties probably are even more frequent.

Conflict   One such case, passed on to me by Robert Kahn, involved the incentive system and the suggestion system in a factory. By itself, the suggestion system would appear to have no aversive consequences, but the conflicting stimuli become apparent when the suggestion system is combined with the incentive system.

Those who do research on incentive systems find that workers, out of their experience and skill on the job, often devise improved work methods or tools that enable them to increase their output or to produce the same amount with less effort. Since the rate set on the particular job is based on methods described by the time-study man, and since any official change in job methods or tools or machines entitles management to make a new study and set a new rate, workers naturally keep these improvements to themselves. They also keep an eye out for the time-study man and revert to the official job methods or hide their inventions when he comes by.

Prowl   In the plant studied by Kahn and his associates, the time-study man, well aware of worker customs, often went on the prowl, hoping to discover a hidden invention and thereby gain the right to restudy the job. If the workers lost out in this hide-and-seek game, the improvements they themselves had invented would become part of the official job methods, a new piece rate would be set, and their earnings on the job would be reduced or they would have to work harder to maintain the same level of earnings. In this way, the workers could lose all the benefits of their own ingenuity.

Gain   Through the suggestion system, workers could gain rewards for their inventions. If a person wrote up a new job method and put it into the suggestion box before the time-study man had observed it, management would study the economic gains involved in the improvement and present a reward to the person—possibly a substantial fraction of the gains that would accrue to management. But management also would invoke the time-study and rate-setting procedures, just as it would have done if the time-study man had invented the improvement, and the result would be a piece-rate cut. The person might well gain a financial reward substantially greater than what he would lose through the reduction of the rate on the job, but for his fellow workers the consequences would be entirely aversive.

Workers who face the conflicting stimuli of the incentive system and the suggestion system find that any action offers prospects of both rewarding and aversive consequences. If they conceal the invention successfully from management, they all are rewarded; but if management discovers it they all lose. If the person puts in his suggestion, he gains but the others lose.

This case illustrates the complexities that human beings find in many real-life situations. They do indeed respond, as Skinner argues, in terms of the consequences of past behavior. But many situations provide such conflicting stimulus conditions that we cannot predict any response simply by analyzing the relationship between the person and the anticipated reinforcement.

3 TIME LAG AND TRUST

Few of a person's acts bring immediate reward to him. The time span between behavior and reinforcement may be only a few minutes—but it also may be many months. Psychologists and sociologists, interpreting the problems caused by time lag in terms of deferred gratification, have noted that individuals differ in their responsiveness to delayed rewards and that middle-class persons generally are more responsive to them than are lower-class persons.

Time lag also involves the problem of the predictability of the environment—and for a person, other human beings are a major part of that environment. If another person tells the person to do something to gain a reward a year later, the person bases his decision to act only in part on his estimate of the probability that the actions proposed will produce the reward promised. He also asks himself: Can I trust the other person? His answer depends in part upon his past experiences with the other person (and with personnel in like positions).

Cuts The piece-rate field again provides a useful illustration. It is standard practice for management to promise that it will not cut piece rates on a given job no matter how much workers earn on the job. Nevertheless, workers widely fear rate cuts, and they restrict their output to conceal loose rates. Why? Does management violate its pledges? No doubt such abuses sometimes happen, but much more common are the problems of interpreting rights and procedures. Union contracts generally allow management to make a new time study and set a new rate when it has introduced a "major" or "substantial" change in methods, tools, or equipment used on a job. Between workers and management, we find frequent disagreements as to what constitutes a "major" change.

Furthermore, a series of minor changes over a period of months or years

could well add up to a major change; but at what point does management intervene to change the rate? How can we expect workers to respond if, as in the case
I described earlier, the workers themselves introduced the changes?

Workers tell us that exceptionally high earnings on a given incentive job are
sure to attract attention. Time-study men who note deviations from expected
results are likely to restudy a job to determine whether changes have occurred
that would justify new time studies and new rates. If they cannot show that the
nature of the job has changed substantially, they have still another option: to
"re-engineer" the job on management's initiative to such an extent that there can
no longer be any question that a major change has been introduced.

Such responses by time-study men are to be expected under the conditions
prevailing in most piece-rate operations. The existence of a job that produces
out-of-line earnings demonstrates to management that the time-study man has
made mistakes in his fundamental task of rate-setting. In other words, the behavior of workers in reponding to positive reinforcement produces aversive consequences for the time-study man.

Further, the requirements of the wage-and-salary system push management
to seek ways to get around its pledge against rate-cutting. In the experimental
laboratory, the psychologist can isolate the experimental animal from all other
tasks, reinforcements, and experimental animals. In the factory situation such
isolation is impossible. Both workers and management see each rate as part of a
total system of payments. A major change in one element of the system can have
disturbing effects on other parts of the system.

Up   For example, let's look at two hypothetical jobs, A and B. A pays $2.00
an hour, B pays $2.25 an hour, and the line of promotion runs from A to B. The
two jobs are now put on piece rates. A turns up with a loose rate that yields
earnings of $3.00 an hour, whereas B has a tight rate on which earnings average
$2.65 an hour.

In these conditions workers quite natually do not want to take "promotions"
from A to B. If management requires them to do so, as it can in some contracts,
the workers are likely to respond with actions that prove aversive to management.
In other words, as management acts to keep rates in line, the workers have good
reason to believe that while responding strongly to a given rate will bring short-
term positive reinforcement, in the long run it will have aversive consequences:
the rate will be cut so that they will get less money for their work or will have to
do more work for the same money. How strongly workers feel and how decisively
they act to create aversive consequences for management when they have grievances will depend also upon the nature of their past relations with management—
which is another way of expressing the degree of trust that workers will have
about management's future behavior.

4   THE ONE-BODY PROBLEM

In studying the laboratory experiments of Pavlov or Skinner, we are interested
only in the environmental conditions that induce the dog or the pigeon to behave
in a certain way. We are not concerned with the motivation of Ivan Pavlov or

B. F. Skinner, who are manipulating these environmental conditions. When we deal with human beings outside the laboratory, however, we will be able to predict and control very little if we limit our concern to the contingencies affecting the behavior of the individual. Since many if not most of the contingencies to which a person responds are provided by another person (or by several others), we must learn to deal simultaneously and systematically with the contingencies affecting the behavior of both the person and the other person.

Part   In a sense this point involves a restatement of issues I have already raised. In discussing the cost-benefit ratio, the problem of conflicting stimuli, and the time-lag and trust problem, I have not been able to limit our attention to the person. The worker is part of a social system in which he interacts with the time-study man, the foreman, other workers, union officers, and management. We cannot explain his behavior except in terms of the behavior of others with whom he interacts. More importantly, for practical purposes, if we want to change his behavior we cannot limit ourselves to a strategy designed simply to change the contingencies to which he is exposed. We must include in our strategy plans for changing the contingencies affecting the behavior of the principal other persons with whom he is interacting.

Vacuum   It may appear that all I am saying is that social psychology is better than individual psychology, but there is much more to be said than that. We do indeed have to deal with interpersonal relations, but those relations do not occur in a social or technological vacuum. Relations among persons tend to be structured through organizations, and within these organizational contexts behavior is linked to reinforcements in structured ways.

In industry we find many situations in which the behavior that produces rewards for a person also produces aversive consequences for another person and frequently such conflicts are built into the functional differences between departments or work groups. Salesmen who often get rewards solely on the basis of their sales volumes naturally try to sell as much as possible, and they give little attention to the credit ratings of potential customers. On the other hand, management evaluates the performance of the credit department in terms of its experience in collecting bills, so credit people naturally tend to disallow orders from customers who appear to be poor credit risks. By vetoing an order, the credit man deprives the salesman of a reward and produces further aversive consequences on the customer relations the salesman is trying to develop. Yet, if the credit man approves the order and the bill goes unpaid, the credit man suffers aversive consequences.

Tension   Friction-causing problems also crop up frequently in work-flow relations, in which work passes regularly from one group to another. In studies of busy restaurants, for instance, we observed a common friction point: the service counter where waitresses give food orders to countermen and pick up food when it is ready. Tension always mounts as the rush hour advances, with waitresses competing to place orders and yelling at countermen to hurry up, while countermen yell back at waitresses.

In such situations we can understand readily that concentrating on the behavior of the individual salesman, credit man, waitress, or counterman will yield little useful knowledge. But, while recognizing the need to examine interpersonal relations simply as the interplay of personalities. They occur in a highly patterned structure. Unless we can change the pattern, we can do little to change the behavior.

Network   At its simplest level, the problem of the prediction and control of behavior involves creating conditions in which the behavior that positively reinforces one person also positively reinforces the other person (in the same group or organization)—or at least does not produce aversive consequences for the other person. To do this, we can examine the current interpersonal behavior of the person and the other person, noting how the behavior of one rewards or penalizes the other. Then, on the basis of this analysis, we can seek to devise a more rewarding task structure and network of interpersonal relations.

In some cases, the introduction of changes in the immediate interpersonal situation can produce decisive changes in the balance of positive and negative reinforcers. Often we can accomplish such changes in interpersonal relations by changing the technology or work flow. For example, we found that some restaurants had eliminated the aversive conflict between waitresses and countermen by erecting a service counter high enough to provide a physical barrier and introducing a spindle on which waitresses place their written orders. Countermen pulled orders off in sequence and set out filled trays with order slips in the same sequence.

Plan   We should also recognize that we cannot resolve many problems of human conflict and frustration by tinkering at the immediate interpersonal level. Here again the individual piece-rate incentive system provides a convenient example. While students of incentive problems have devised ways to alleviate some of the more severe conflicts, we have had to realize that the system itself operates so as to produce tensions and frustrations and that only a far-reaching system change can get at the basic problem.

Various innovators have tried to meet the problems of reinforcement for work performance through a broad-based collective-reward system, which eliminates the problems of individual work measurement, rate-setting and their attendant conflicts. Such is the approach of the Scanlon Plan, which provides for a plant-wide sharing in the fruits of increased productivity, supported by worker and supervisor participation in a series of departmental and plant-wide committees that generate, evaluate and recommend changes leading to increased productivity. A similar rationale underlies profit-sharing plans, though the link between profits and work performance is much less direct than in the Scanlon Plan, and profit-sharing plans do not always involve worker participation in the development of ideas for improving performance.

We also need to examine even more fundamental structural changes whereby the workers in an enterprise, through their representatives, control policies and procedures on wages, bonuses, production, and so on. Such changes have arisen in isolated instances in the United States, particularly in the plywood industry on the West Coast. The system exists on a national scale in Yugoslavia, and its apparent success in both human and physical terms has led increasing numbers of social scientists and politicians from other countries to examine the theory and practice of the Yugoslav approach.

Rhetoric   In examining these broader structural changes, we should not let the current rhetoric regarding Marxism versus capitalism mislead us. The Yugoslavs say they are Communists—in fact, they claim to be the only ones who are acting out the authentic Marx—but their industrial system is distinctly different from that of the Soviet Union—or of the United States. Given what we know about the expectable characteristics of large-scale organizations, we are likely to find, in the government-run enterprises of the Soviet Union as in the privately owned enterprises of the United States, many of the same situations in which a person and another person characteristically find themselves on collision-course reinforcement schedules. If we are to devise new organizational systems that maximize both performance and positive reinforcement for organizational members, we need to come down from the sphere of political ideology and undertake detailed analyses of the sociotechnical system: the system of interpersonal relations that is linked with a structure of technology, work flow, and task organization.

Let us not abandon Skinner, but let us not assume either that his schema carries us beyond the beginning point in the prediction and control of human behavior. Until we shift our attention from the one-body problem and develop formulations in terms of two or more bodies interacting together within an organizational framework and with specified tasks, we will not be able to devise strategies that will effectively control the contingencies of reinforcement for both a person and another person.

QUESTIONS FOR DISCUSSION

1   Why do operant conditioning principles stress the necessity of avoiding negative feedback?
2   From a managerial standpoint, what is really new and innovative about operant conditioning?
3   How might you employ operant conditioning principles in designing an MBO program.
4   What potential drawbacks exist when you attempt to use operant conditioning at work?

5 Would operant conditioning tend to work better among blue- or white-collar employees? Why?

6 Would the general principles of operant conditioning be as applicable to solving the problems of turnover and absenteeism as they would to solving those of performance? Why or why not? Cite examples to illustrate your answer.

7 What effects might operant conditioning have on organizational climate? Explain.

8 How could a manager tie operant conditioning principles to achievement motivation theory? To the dual-factor theory?

9 How would you respond to Whyte's criticisms of the use of operant techniques in organization settings?

Chapter 15

Money and Motivation

OVERVIEW

For reasons not fully understood, the role of financial compensation in employee motivation and performance remains one of the most frequently discussed but most underresearched areas in organizational psychology. All too often, writers have tended to set forth data-free pronouncements on the role of money at work, and investigators have employed less-than-rigorous research methodologies to test relatively simplistic models of such relationships. Similarly, in work settings, practicing managers have tended to use reward systems that are based primarily on past practices or current fads (Dunnette & Bass, 1963), thus apparently trying both to save themselves time and yet find effective methods of compensation that are simple to administer. In many cases little concern is given to discovering the underlying relationships between organizational compensation practices and resulting motivation and performance. Such a trend has led to the creation of a series of myths concerning the exact role that is played by money.

A primary reason for the emergence of these myths—or misconceptions—about money and motivation can be found by tracing the history of the research efforts on the topic. The earliest systematic effort to study compensation practices in relation to productivity dates from the scientific management movement around the turn of the century. During this period, Frederick Taylor and his associates emphasized the use of piece-rate incentive systems for blue-collar workers, feeling that these systems provided the most efficient way to simultaneously maximize both productivity and worker income. Taylor saw such systems, when used in conjunction with his work redesign techniques, as being the fairest for both the organization and its employees. These scientific management notions had their roots in the "economic man" assumption that people work only (or primarily) for money. Thus, according to this line of reasoning, efforts to increase productivity meant using money as the basic incentive.

Most research during this period focused on comparative studies of various types of piece-rate incentive systems as each was related to improved work performance. Little or no concern was shown for possible variations across individuals, such as differences in personality, need strengths, and the like. In fact, it was primarily this failure to acknowledge the role of psychological variables in motivation and performance that led to the demise of the scientific management movement (Lawler, 1971; Schein, 1972) and allowed for the emergence of the human relations philosophy.

The human relations theorists, writing primarily in the 1930s and 1940s, substituted the concept of "social man" for "economic man." They contended that people in work settings were generally motivated by group forces, such as group pressures, social relations, and organizational structure. Pay was seen as less important. Unfortunately, little sound research was carried out to support such a proposition, and the data that did emerge were often misinterpreted. For example, when one reexamines the data from the classic Hawthorne studies (specifically the relay-assembly test-room experiments), it becomes apparent that almost half of the performance improvement that occurred was attributable to manipulations of the wage incentive system (Roethlisberger & Dickson, 1939). Such facts were often lost in the philosophical statements of the human relationists.

Beginning in the early 1960s, money again emerged as an important topic of concern—this time to the behavioral scientists. During this period, it was realized how little hard data really existed on the role of money in motivation. These contemporary theorists and researchers argued that any comprehensive theory of work motivation must take into account the role of financial compensation practices. In contrast to the early scientific management proponents, however, contemporary theorists tend to view money as only one of *several* important influences. They hold that such additional factors as perceived equity of pay, group influences, and individual need strength differences may also play important roles in determining performance levels on the job. Considerable disagreement still exists, however, over the relative importance of all these factors.

The selections that follow point up the diversity of current opinions concerning the relation of money to motivation. First, Opsahl and Dunnette discuss several important roles that are played by financial compensation in industrial settings. Second, McClelland discusses both various factors that are thought to be associated with employee performance and how money can affect these factors. Different incentive plans are then discussed within the context of work motivation. Throughout, McClelland emphasizes the role of variations in need strengths as a major influence on compensation practices as they affect individual performance at work.

Finally, Lawler reviews the experience of several organizations that attempted to tie pay to performance. He then discusses methods of relating pay to performance and evaluates the effectiveness of such methods. Next, he examines several factors that can often influence the success of different compensation plans, focusing specifically on how such factors relate to the larger issue of motivation and performance. Finally, he described several instances in which organizations may choose *not* to use money to motivate performance, and ends with a brief note on the behavioral and attitudinal implications of pay secrecy.

REFERENCES AND SUGGESTED ADDITIONAL READINGS

Andrews, I. R. *Managerial compensation.* Ann Arbor, Mich.: Foundation for Research on Human Behavior, 1965.

Andrews, I. R., & Henry, M. M. Management attitudes toward pay. *Industrial Relations,* 1963, **3,** 29–39.

Dunnette, M. D. The motives of industrial managers. *Organizational Behavior and Human Performance,* 1967, **2,** 176–182.

Dunnette, M. D., & Bass B. M. Behavioral scientists and personnel management. *Industrial Relations,* 1963, **2,** 115–130.

Haire, M., Ghiselli, E. E., & Porter, L. W. Psychological research on pay: An overview. *Industrial Relations,* 1963, **3,** 3–8.

Lawler, E. E., III. The mythology of management compensation. *California Management Review,* 1966, **9,** 11–22.

Lawler, E. E., III. Secrecy about management compensation. *Organizational Behavior and Human Performance,* 1967, **2,** 182–189.

Lawler, E. E., III. *Pay and organizational effectiveness: A psychological view.* New York: McGraw-Hill, 1971.

Lawler, E. E., III, & Porter, L. W. Perceptions regarding management compensation. *Industrial Relations,* 1963, **3,** 41–49.

Lawler, E. E., III, & Porter, L. W. Predicting managers' pay and their satisfaction with their pay. *Personnel Psychology,* 1966, **19,** 363–373.

Opsahl, R. L. Managerial compensation: Needed research. *Organizational Behavior and Human Performance,* 1967, **2,** 208–216.

Porter, L. W., & Lawler, E. E., III. *Managerial attitudes and performance.* Homewood, Ill.: Irwin, 1968.

Roethlisberger, F. J., & Dickson, W. J. *Management and the worker.* Cambridge, Mass.: Harvard, 1939.

Schein, E. H. *Organizational psychology.* Englewood Cliffs, N.J.: Prentice-Hall, 1972.

Tosi, H. J., House, R. J., & Dunnette, M. D. (eds.). *Managerial motivation and compensation: A selection of readings.* East Lansing, Mich.: Michigan State University, 1972.

Vroom, V. H. *Work and motivation.* New York: Wiley, 1964.

Weick, K. E. Dissonance and task enhancement: A problem for compensation theory. *Organizational Behavior and Human Performance,* 1967, **2,** 189–208.

Wernimont, P. F., & Fitzpatrick, S. The meaning of money. *Journal of Applied Psychology,* 1972, **56,** 218–226.

The Role of Financial Compensation
in Industrial Motivation[1]

Robert L. Opsahl
Marvin D. Dunnette

Widespread interest in money as a motivational tool for spurring production was first stimulated in this country by Frederick Taylor. Some years before the turn of the century, Taylor observed an energetic steelworker, who, after putting in a 12-hour day of lifting pigs of iron, would run 12 miles up a mountainside to work on his cabin. If this excess energy could be used to produce more on the job, thought Taylor, higher profits from lower fixed costs could be used to pay the worker significantly more for his increased efforts. Such was the beginning of *scientific management,* which is based essentially on the assumption that workers will put forth extra effort on the job to maximize their economic gains. This became a guiding principle in pay practices until the late 1920s when the *human relations movement* in industrial psychology was ushered in with the Western Electric studies directed by Elton Mayo. As a result of these studies, recognition of man's ego and social needs became widespread, and job factors other than pay came to be emphasized as the major reasons why men work. To a large extent, these later ideas are still with us. Yet, few would disagree that money has been and continues to be the primary means of rewarding and modifying human behavior in industry.

Strangely, in spite of the large amounts of money spent and the obvious relevance of behavioral theory for industrial compensation practices, there is probably less solid research in this area than in any other field related to worker performance. We know amazingly little about how money either interacts with other factors or how it acts individually to affect job behavior. Although the relevant literature is voluminous, much more has been written about the subject than is actually known. Speculation, accompanied by compensation fads and fashions, abounds; research studies designed to answer fundamental questions about the role of money in human motivation are all too rare.

THEORIES OF THE ROLE OF MONEY

Does money serve to stimulate job effort? If so, why does it do so? How does it take on value in our industrial society? There are at least five theories or interpre-

Abridged from *Psychological Bulletin,* 1966, **66,** 94–96. Copyright 1966 by the American Psychological Association. Reprinted by permission.

[1]This investigation was supported in part by a Public Health Service Fellowship (5-F1-MH-21, 814-03 PS) from the National Institute of Mental Health, United States Public Health Service, and in part by a behavioral science research grant to Marvin D. Dunnette from the General Electric Foundation.

tations of the role of money in affecting the job of employees.

Money as a Generalized Conditioned Reinforcer

One widely held hypothesis is that money acts as a generalized conditioned rein-forcer because of its repeated pairings with primary reinforcers (Holland & Skin-ner, 1961; Kelleher & Gollub, 1962; Skinner, 1953). Skinner (1953) has stated that such a generalized reinforcer should be extremely effective because some deprivation will usually exist for which the conditioned reinforcer is appropriate. Unfortunately, solid evidence of the behavioral effectiveness of such reinforcers is lacking, and what evidence there is has been based almost entirely on animal studies.

In a series of experiments conducted by Wike and Barrientos (1958) a goal box (containing wet mash) paired with both food and water deprivation proved to be a more effective reinforcer for rats than different goal boxes paired with food or water deprivation alone. The implications of these results are that money ought to be more potent when its attainment is paired with many, rather than only single, needs. Unfortunately, the magnitude of the difference in preferences in the above study, though statistically significant, was extremely small. In 15 test trials in a T-maze, rats turned to the goal box previously paired with both depri-vations an average of only 0.62 trials more often than to the goal box paired only with food deprivation.

Moreover, this and most other studies on generalized conditioned reinfor-cers can be criticized because of the nonindependence of food and water as primary reinforcers (Grice & Davis, 1957; Verplanck & Hayes, 1953). A water-deprived rat eats less than his normal intake of food. What is needed are studies with human subjects in which a stimulus has been paired with many independent reinforcers. In one such study (Ferster & DeMeyer, 1962), coins paired with games and candy were used successfully with autistic children to develop and maintain complex operant behaviors. Although the effectiveness of the coins was well-demonstrated by the increased frequencies of responding contingent on their presentation, their effectiveness under different conditions of deprivation was not studied, nor was their relative effectiveness compared with that of coins operating as simple conditional reinforcers.

Some theorists (e. g., Brown, 1961; Dollard & Miller, 1950) have referred to the token-reward studies of Wolfe (1936) and Cowles (1937) as examples of how money acquires value. In these studies, initially neutral poker chips apparently acquired reinforcement value because they could be exchanged for various foods. The analogy between the poker chips and the industrial use of money as wages is incomplete, however, because the reinforcement value of the poker chips came about because of their association with removing deprivation in a single primary area, whereas the theory of money's generalized reinforcing role would hypothe-size that it is valued quite aside from and independent of any particular state of deprivation. It should be apparent that evidence in support of money as a generalized conditioned reinforcer is, at best, limited and inconclusive.

Money as a Conditioned Incentive

According to this hypothesis, repeated pairings of money with primary incentives[1] establish a new learned drive for money (Dollard & Miller, 1950). For example, in Wolfe's (1936) study, the sight of a poker chip out of reach served as an incentive to motivate the chimpanzee to pull it in. The fact that chimpanzees refused to work if given a free supply of poker chips suggests that the act of obtaining the chips served a drive-reducing function (Dollard & Miller, 1950). Presumably, money could become a generalized conditioned incentive in the same manner that it is presumed by some to become a generalized conditioned reinforcer—that is, by many pairings with many different types of incentives. Perhaps the main difference between the conditioned reinforcer and conditioned incentive interpretations is the introduction of drive reduction in the incentive hypothesis. In contrast, no such drive need be hypothesized under empirical reinforcement principles.

Money as an Anxiety Reducer

Brown (1953, 1961) also utilized the concept of drive in an effort to explain how money affects behavior. He suggested that one learns to become anxious in the presence of a variety of cues signifying the absence of money. Presumably, anxiety related to the absence of money is aquired in childhood through a process of higher-order conditioning. The first stage consists of pairings of pain with cues of warning or alarm provided by adults. For example, before a child actually touches a hot stove, a nearby adult may provide facial gestures of alarm and warnings such as "Look out, you'll get hurt!" These cues eventually elicit anxiety without the unconditioned stimulus. In the second stage, anxiety-arousing warnings are conditioned to a wide variety of cues, indicating lack of money. After such learning, the child becomes anxious upon hearing phrases such as "That costs too much money," or "We can't afford to buy you that." The actual presence of money produces cues for the cessation of anxiety. This concept of anxiety as a learned motivating agent for money-seeking responses in no way contradicts the possible action of money according to the two previous hypotheses; money as an anxiety-reducer could operate jointly with them as an additional explanatory device.

Harlow (1953), however, has taken issue with Brown's thesis, stating: "It is hard to believe that parental expression at the time a child suffers injury is identical with or highly similar to a parent's expression when he says 'we have no money' [p. 22]." Harlow pointed out further that an infant's ability to recognize emotional expression when suffering pain has not been reliably demonstrated. Unfortunately, Brown presented no experimental evidence bearing on his theory.

[1]Incentive: "an object or external condition, perceived as capable of satisfying an aroused motive, that tends to elicit action to obtain the object or condition [English & English, 1958]."

Money as a "Hygiene Factor"

Herzberg, Mausner, and Snyderman (1959) postulated that money is a so-called "hygiene factor" serving as a potential dissatisfier if it is not present in appropriate amounts, but not as a potential satisfier or positive motivator. According to them, improvements in salary may only remove impediments to job satisfaction but do not actually generate job satisfaction. The main value of money, according to them, is that it leads to both the avoidance of economic deprivation and the avoidance of feelings of being treated unfairly. Thus, its hygienic role is one of avoiding pain and dissatisfaction ("disease") but not one of promoting heightened motivation ("health"). These notions were originally derived from content analyses of anecdotal accounts of unusually satisfying and unusually dissatisfying job events elicited from 200 engineers and accountants. Fifteen percent of their descriptions of satisfying events involved the mention of salary and 17 percent of their descriptions of dissatisfying events involved salary. Moreover, Herzberg *et al.* suggested that salary may be viewed as a "dissatisfier" because its impact on favorable job feelings was largely short-term while its impact on unfavorable feelings was long-term—extending over periods of several months. Herzberg *et al.'s* use of this finding to argue that money acts only as a potential dissatisfier is mystifying. It becomes even more so when their data are examined more carefully. In all of the descriptions of unusually good job feelings, salary was mentioned as a major reason for the feelings 19 percent of the time. Of the unusually good job feelings that lasted several months, salary was reported as a causal factor 22 percent of the time; of the short-term feelings, it was a factor 5 percent of the time. In contrast, salary was named as a major cause of unusually bad feelings only 13 percent of the time. Of the unusually bad job feelings lasting several months, it was mentioned only 18 percent of the time (in contrast with the 22 percent of the long-term good feelings, mentioned above).

These data seem inconsistent with the interpretations and lend no substantial support to hypotheses of a so-called differential role for money in leading to job satisfaction or job dissatisfaction.

Money as an Instrument for Gaining Desired Outcomes

Vroom's (1964) cognitive model of motivation has implications for understanding how money functions in affecting behavior. According to Vroom's interpretation, money acquires valence as a result of its perceived instrumentality for obtaining other desired outcomes. The concept of valence refers simply to affective orientations toward particular outcomes and has no direct implications for behavioral consequences. However, the "force" impelling a person toward action was postulated to be the product of the valence of an outcome and the person's expectancy that a certain action will lead to attainment of the outcome. Thus, for example, if money is perceived by a given person as instrumental to obtaining security, and if security is desired, money itself acquires positive valence. The probability, then, of his making money-seeking responses depends on the degree of his desire for security *multiplied* by his expectancy that certain designated job behaviors lead to attaining money. Although Vroom summarized studies giving general support to his theory, the specific role of money in his theory was not dealt with in any detail.

Gellerman's (1963) statement of how money functions in industry also stressed its instrumental role. According to him money in itself has no intrinsic meaning and acquires significant motivating power only when it comes to symbolize intangible goals. Money acts as a symbol in different ways for different persons, and for the same person at different times. Gellerman presented the interesting notion that money can be interpreted as a projective device—a man's reaction to money "summarizes his biography to date: his early economic environment, his competence training, the various nonfinancial motives he has acquired, and his current financial status [p. 166]." Gellerman's evidence was largely anecdotal, but nonetheless rather convincing.

Summary of Theoretical Speculations

Much remains to be learned before we will understand very well what meaning money has for different persons, how it affects their job behaviors, which motives it serves, and how its effectiveness may come about. It is probably doubtful that there will ever be a "theory of money" in the sense that money will be given a unique or special status as a psychological variable. It is true that money functions in many ways, depending upon the setting, the antecedent conditions, and the particular person involved. According to Brown, money must be present to avoid anxiety. For Herzberg *et al.,* it serves to avoid feelings of being unfairly treated or economically deprived. Reinforcement theories, on the other hand, seem to treat money either as a generalized entity, functioning independently of specific deprivations, or as a general incentive that has been coupled with variously valued goals during a person's total learning history. Obviously, the answers are not yet available, and it is probably best to view money symbolically, as Vroom and Gellerman do, and to begin to learn and measure the personal, situational, and job parameters that may define more fully what it is the symbol of and what its attainment is instrumental to. Only by mapping the domain in this way will we come to know the relevant factors associated with money as a "motivator" of behavior in industry.

REFERENCES

Brown, J. S. Problems presented by the concept of acquired drives. In, *Current theory and research in motivation: A symposium.* Lincoln: University of Nebraska Press, 1953, pp. 1–21.

Brown, J. S. *The motivation of behavior.* New York: McGraw-Hill, 1961.

Cowles, J. T. Food-tokens as incentives for learning by chimpanzees. *Comparative Psychology Monographs,* 1937, **14,** 1–96.

Dollard, J. and Miller, N. E. *Personality and psychotheraphy.* New York: McGraw-Hill, 1950.

Ferster, C. B., and DeMeyer, M. K. A method for the experimental analysis of the behavior of autistic children. *American Journal of Orthopsychiatry,* 1962, **32,** 89–98.

Gellerman, S. W. *Motivation and productivity.* New York: American Management Association, 1963.

Grice, G. R., and Davis, J. D. Effect of irrelevant thirst motivation on a response learned with food reward. *Journal of Experimental Psychology,* 1957, **53,** 347–52.

Harlow, H. F. Comments on Professor Brown's paper. In, *Current theory and research in motivation.* Lincoln: University of Nebraska Press, 1953, pp. 22–23.

Herzberg, F., Mausner, B., and Snyderman, B. *The motivation to work.* (2nd ed.) New York: Wiley, 1959.

Holland, J. G., and Skinner, B. F. *The analysis of behavior.* New York: McGraw-Hill, 1961.

Kelleher, R. T., and Gollub, L. R. A review of positive conditioned reinforcement. *Journal of the Experimental Analysis of Behavior,* 1962, **5,** 543–97.

Selekman, B. M. Living with collective bargaining. *Harvard Business Review,* 1941, **22,** 21–23.

Skinner, B. F. *Science and human behavior.* New York: Macmillan, 1953.

Verplanck, W. S., and Hayes, J. R. Eating and drinking as a function of maintenance schedule. *Journal of Comparative and Physiological Psychology,* 1953, **46,** 327–33.

Vroom, V. H. *Work and motivation.* New York: Wiley, 1964.

Wike, E. L., and Barrientos, G. Secondary reinforcement and multiple drive reduction. *Journal of Comparative and Physiological Psychology,* 1958, **51,** 640–43.

Wolfe, J. B. Effectiveness of token-rewards for chimpanzees. *Comparative Psychology Monographs,* 1936, **12,** No. 60, 1–72.

Money as a Motivator: Some Research Insights
David C. McClelland

For nearly half a century, industrial psychologists have been demonstrating that money isn't nearly so potent a motivating force as theory and common sense suggest it ought to be. Elton Mayo's 1922 study of work output in a Philadelphia textile mill set the tone of what was to follow. Management had found that incentive payment schemes had not succeeded in increasing work or decreasing turnover in a department where the jobs were particularly monotonous and fatiguing. Mayo found, on the other hand, that allowing the men to schedule the work for themselves brought dramatic increases in productivity. Where money incentives hadn't proven effective, psychic rewards worked.[1]

From *The McKinsey Quarterly,* Fall, 1967. Reprinted by permission of McKinsey & Company, Inc., and the author.

Over and over again, later students[2] of industrial psychology emphasized the same point: Money isn't everything. Its meaning is in the eye of the beholder. It functions only as a symbol representing more important psychological factors in the work situation.

Why, then, in spite of all the evidence, do people still take money so seriously as a motivator? In the first place, money obviously is very important. Work, unless it is volunteer or "play," involves a contract between two parties "guaranteed" by the payment of money. The pay may symbolize the psychological realities of the contract imperfectly—which may be all the psychologists are saying. The employee may think he is working for it, and the manager may think he is using it to get the employee to work, but both are only partly right. To understand the situation better, particularly if we wish to manage motivation or behavior, we must penetrate beyond the money itself and consider what it really represents to employer and employee.

MONEY MISCONCEPTIONS

But it is not just man's tendency to confuse symbols with realities that leads him to talk as if money were an end in itself. There are at least three other reasons why he does so. In the first place, no idea is more deeply entrenched in contemporary American psychology than the notion that in the end all learning is based on a few simple material rewards. I suspect practically all top managers today learned in Psychology I that there are so-called primary material rewards, such as food and water, and that all other rewards are "secondary," getting their "motivating value" from learned associations with the primaries. Money obviously falls into the secondary category.

This notion involves some major misconceptions, and there is not good reason why it should continue to shape the thinking of men who are interested in managing motivation. But it has persisted because of its appealing simplicity, and because the alternatives to it are hard to formulate so neatly.

Let me, however, illustrate one of these alternative approaches by a quick analogy. Think of what goes on in a man's mind as if it were a computer printout of a lot of miscellaneous material. In commonsense terms, a lot of thoughts buzz through a man's head during any given time. As anyone who has tried to do content analysis of computer printouts knows, the periods or other punctuation marks are of key importance. That is, if you are to search and simplify what is otherwise a bewildering mass of material, it is first necessary to break it up into units within which co-occurrences can be noted.

In real life, rewards or incentives are like punctuation marks. They break up sequences or call attention to them. In psychological terms, they are attention-getting, affect-producing mechanisms, rather than substitutes for something else. As such they are of tremendous importance in producing organization or order in thought and action. Note, however, that they are only one possible type of attention-getting mechanism. Bright lights and colors, changes in rest periods, reorganization of work flow—all sorts of things—can also get attention.

In short, rather than being some kind of substitute for simpler material rewards, money is more sensibly regarded as *one of a class* of attention-getters. And, like other members of its class, it can lose its attention-getting power with repetition.[3]

A second reason why managers go on thinking that money is a prime motivator is that most of them are highly achievement-oriented; in the psychologist's terms, they are "high in *n* Ach." We know that such men attach special significance to money rewards. They are strong believers in steeply increasing financial rewards for greater accomplishment. Because they themselves are particularly interested in some concrete measure that will sensitively reflect how well they have done, it is easy and natural for them to mistake this idea for a related one—namely, that the more money you offer someone the harder he will work.

Obviously, believing in more pay for more work is simply not the same as saying that more pay will lead *to* more work. But the fallacy in this reasoning is not only logical by psychological, for other experimental evidence shows that even men who score high in *n* Ach are not themselves spurred to greater efforts by money incentives. While they attribute greater importance to money as a motivator, it doesn't motivate *them* to work harder.

The apparent explanation: They seek financial reward, not for its own sake, but because it tells them how well they are doing. As Saul Gellerman has pointed out, the incentive value of top executive salaries must lie primarily in their "merit badge" quality, since high taxes result in rather minor differences in take-home pay at this level of compensation. So managers believe money is important in motivating others because they mistakenly think it motivates themselves. Actually, while it *is* more important to them as a measure of accomplishment, it doesn't really motivate them. And it doesn't motivate others either, except indirectly—as workers and others are ready to point out whenever they are asked.

Finally, the third reason why managers keep coming back to money as a way of motivating people is because at the practical level it is the one thing they can manipulate rather easily. After all, it is part of their job to motivate the people working for them, to get more work out of people, or at the very least to make sure that people aren't loafing. The higher their achievement motivation, the more they will want to show an improvement in the quality or quantity of the work done by their people. They may listen patiently to the psychologists and sociologists who seek to convince them that money isn't important for its own sake, but then what can they do to change those other psychological factors which are supposedly more important? Payment plans are real and manipulable. Plans for dealing with psychological factors often seem nebulous.

What, then, does all this add up to? Are we left with the conclusion that the nature of incentive plans makes no difference at all? Hardly. It is one thing to say that psychological factors will modify how incentive plans work; it is quite another to conclude that variations in incentive plans do not make any difference.

What we need is a change in orientation. The problem is managing motivation—not managing work, but managing the *desire* of men to work. This means seeing incentive plans as a particular means of achieving specific objectives within the larger framework of the work situation.

THE WORK VARIABLES

It has recently been shown[4] that a work situation involves four sets of variables which must be accurately diagnosed before a "prescription" can be written for improvement:

1   The motives and needs of the persons working at the task.
2   The motivational requirements of the task they have to perform.
3   The motives (or strengths and limitations) of the manager.
4   The organizational climate.

Once a manager knows where he stands on these variables in a particular work situation, he is in a position to do various things. For example, if he finds that most of his workers are strongly achievement-oriented, while the tasks to be performed are assembly-line work that doesn't satisfy this motivation, he has an obvious mismatch. To bring the interests of the people into line with the motivational requirements of the job, he can get a different type of worker or change the nature of the task.

Our focus here, however, is narrower: Given different settings on these four types of variables, how can management use payment plans to help motivate men? Obviously, there can be no simple sovereign payment system that will work best for all people under all conditions. But we can give illustrations.

Variations in the Motives of Workers

Whether workers or managers are high or low in achievement motivation makes a real difference in the effectiveness of financial incentives. Several studies have shown that offering additional financial rewards for doing a task does not make strongly achievement-oriented people work harder or better.[5] A group of aggressive, achievement-minded salesmen would certainly be angry if their extra efforts were not recognized with a much greater financial reward; yet offering them bonuses is not what produces the extra effort. This may seem like a psychological distinction without a difference, but the interpretation of the meaning of the bonus plan genuinely affects performance, as a later example will show.

People with relatively low achievement motivation, on the other hand, *will* work harder for increased financial rewards. It is not the task itself that interests them, however, nor does the money they get by doing it interest them primarily as a measure of accomplishment. Rather, it has other values for them.

Two consequences flow from this simple fact. First, if there is any way to get the reward without doing the work, they will naturally tend to look for it. This means that managers who rely primarily on money to activate people who are low in achievement motivation will have a much harder job of policing the work situation than they would if the work satisfied certain other motivational needs. This conclusion will hardly come as news to managers who have been struggling with employee incentive plans over the past generation.

The second implication is that such employees will have to want something that the money can buy. Obviously, there are lots of important things that money *can't* buy: tolerable working conditions, friendship, and job security, to name a few. As a number of studies have shown, even the material possessions that most middle-class managers assume everyone wants, such as a home of one's own, are in fact not wanted by many of the people he is trying to motivate. It follows that if a manager must deal largely in financial incentives for these people, he will have to give some thought to creating psychological wants that money will satisfy—such as more education for children, a happier retirement, and more exciting (and expensive) vacation, etc.

But money can also have other values for people who are most strongly motivated by needs for social approval and solidarity with others in the work group. One study found, somewhat to the experimenters' surprise, that girls who scored high in *n* Affiliation actually worked harder for money prizes than girls who scored low on this factor, whereas there had been no difference between the two types of girls when the extra incentives were not offered.[6] Evidently the money helped to create a general expectancy on the girls' part that they should work hard to please the experimenters. The moral again is simple: For a working force that scores high on this factor, incentive plans and payments should be framed in terms of working together for the common good, not—as achievement-oriented managers nearly always assume—of working for one's own gain.

Finally, another study showed that college students who scored high in *n* Power spend more money on prestige supplies expensive liquor, college insignia, powerful motorcycles or cars, etc.—in other words, on things which will make them feel or seem big, strong, powerful and respected.[7] If a manager finds his staff scores high in *n* Power, then he ought to administer his financial incentives in different ways, perhaps even presenting some of them in the form of prestige supplies—such as a trip to Europe or a new Cadillac—for especially outstanding performance.

One simple lesson to be learned from all these studies is that the motivational characteristics of the staff make a lot of difference. Even with the cost of incentives held constant, their form and meaning have to be shaped to fit the needs of the people they are designed to influence.

Variations in the Motivational Requirements of Tasks

Researchers have suggested some simple measuring devices for the motivational requirements of different tasks.[8] For instance, the job of an assembly-line worker has more "affiliation" than "achievement" elements, because workers must interact with each other. Successful task accomplishment depends on the cooperation of co-workers, stable working relationships over time, etc. If this is so, how can incentive plans help? Actually they are more likely to hinder, because most incentive plans are based on the assumption that all tasks primarily involve achievement. And in fact such plans usually make less than 10 percent of the people into "ratebusters," while they make the rest of the work force angry because the extra incentives reinforce behavior which is in direct opposition to the affiliation requirements of the task.[9] Such "gung-ho" achievers often disrupt normal working patterns and lower average productivity over the long run.

Even at the sales level this can be true. While, generally speaking, successful salesmen are strongly achievement and power-oriented and low in affiliation needs, at least one sales situation has been identified in which the very best salesmen scored only moderately high in achievement orientation, quite a bit higher in affiliation orientation than most salesmen, and lower in power orientation.[10] These particular salesmen were involved in a task which, in the researchers' words, required "a much greater emphasis on coordinating the efforts of the sales and service function, and on building long-term close customer relationships involving a high degree of trust, than on entrepreneurial selling." Here an incentive plan based on sales volume alone could easily attract the wrong men (those too high in *n* Ach) into sales, or influence existing salesmen to neglect the long-term consumer relationships that experience shows to be necessary for success in this job. Money payments have to fit not only the characteristics of the people in a work force, but also the nature of the jobs they have to perform.

Variations in the Motives of Managers

As we have seen unless the manager understands his own motives, he may project them onto others. It is all too easy for a manager, in making plans for other people, to assume that they are like himself. But if he knows what *he* wants, he may be able to avoid falling into the trap. He may, for example, even be able to see when his own motivations are leading him to propose new ideas that have little chance of success. I have sometimes wondered how many personnel managers think up new incentive plans in order to convince *their* superiors that they are high achievers, deserving of a special bonus. Actually, a personnel man ought to be specially rewarded for picking and keeping outstanding men, but such day-to-day performance may be less promptly noticeable and rewardable than the installation of a brand-new incentive plan. Here again, the pay system may tend to distort the personnel job by treating and rewarding it as a straightforward achievement proposition.

Beyond such considerations, a manager must understand himself well enough to know what he can or should do in a given organizational situation. Thus he may discover that, while his staff is heavily affiliation-oriented and therefore wants and needs many signs of approval and friendship, he himself is rather aloof, priding himself that he got where he is today by not wasting time with "the boys." This kind of self-understanding should help him create the kind of climate that will make the incentive system work under a given set of conditions.

Variations in Climate

Two researchers, G. H. Litwin and R. A. Stringer, have identified some nine different dimensions on which organizational climates can vary.[11] They hypothesize that each of these variables has different effects on the motivations of people working in the organization. For example, a high degree of *structure* (rules, regulations, going through channels), reflecting an emphasis on power and control, should reduce affiliation and achievement needs among its employees, but at the same time make them more power-oriented. Similarly, a high degree of risk or challenge in the tasks to be performed should arouse achievement motivation but have little or no effect on workers' affiliation or power needs.

Consider how these climatic factors may operate when the incentive system is held constant. In one study[12] four outstanding sales offices were contrasted with four average sales offices, not only in terms of climate differences as perceived by the salesmen, but also in terms of actual observations of how managers interacted with their men during the day.

The incentive system in all offices was the same and men in the outstanding and the average offices were equally satisfied with it. Yet other climate variables apparently made for very different performance averages. The outstanding offices, as perceived by their salesmen, had more structure, evoked more identity and loyalty, and were warmer and friendlier. The salesmen from these outstanding offices also felt that higher standards were being set and that they were more often rewarded by the manager for their efforts than criticized for nonperformance. Their views were substantiated by observation of managers in the two types of offices. Those in the outstanding offices gave almost twice as much praise and encouragement as the managers from the average offices. To quote from the study,

" . . . the outstanding manager makes it a habit to compliment a man sincerely on a job well done; a personal thank-you is always given over the phone and in person. He might also drop the man a note of congratulation and thanks for a successful sale. He also typically thanks the customer in the same manner and makes a real effort to visit the new installation with the salesman and compliment the salesman's efforts before the customer. In contrast, the average manager's attitude is that "these men are on very large commissions and that's what makes them hustle. They know they can go out on any day of the week and get a raise just by selling another piece of equipment. Oh, I *might* buy them a drink, but it's money that motivates these guys."[13]

Once again we see that nonfinancial, situational factors are important, but with a difference. Furthermore, we have a nice illustration of how too exclusive a concern for money can distract a manager's attention from other psychological variables that he ought to be taking into account.

INCENTIVE PLAN VARIABLES

But it is no use repeating that everything depends on the way financial plans are perceived. If variations in the incentive plan really matter, we should be able to discover just what difference they make by investigating them while holding situational variables constant. Until such specific studies have been made, we cannot generalize very confidently about the important variables in the incentive plan itself. But on the basis of some theory and laboratory research it may be permissible to speculate about three of these variables: the probability of success (winning the incentive award), as perceived by participants in the plan; the size of the incentive offered; and the nature of the response-reward relationship.

Probability of Success

Experimental evidence indicates that moderate probabilities of winning an incentive reward produce better performance than either very low or very high probabilities.[14] In general, one researcher has shown, a person who has one chance in two of getting a reward will work harder than if he has a lower or higher probability of getting it, regardless of the strength of his achievement motivation or the size of the money incentive.[15] A study of my own confirmed the fact that students will work harder when the odds are lower than three chances out of four.[16] The generalization seems likely to hold for financial incentive plans, though the optimum probability for winning a special reward obviously would need to be worked out for each particular situation. John W. Atkinson's estimate that it is somewhere around the one-chance-in-two level is not a bad place to start.[17]

We know two further facts about this phenomenon. First, strongly achievement-oriented individuals work best under odds as slim as one in three, or even longer.[18] Thus, an incentive plan for a strongly achievement-oriented sales force should obviously offer a different set of odds from a plan designed for a group of clerical workers who score low in *n* Ach.

Second, we know that the perceived probability of success changes with experience. This is probably why achievement-oriented people work better under somewhat longer odds than the average person. They know from past experience that they tend to be more successful than the average person in tasks they undertake. Therefore, what to the outside observer is a one-in-three chance of winning for an average worker is correctly perceived by the high achiever as a one-in-two chance for him.

Many of the difficulties that incentive plans get into flow from the fact that experience changes the perceived probability of success. Suppose a salesman or a worker exposed to a new incentive plan works extra hard and gets a special bonus. Then what does he do in the next time period? If he notices that a lot of other people have made it, and if he makes it again, he may fear that management will raise the normal standard. Management, on its side, may wonder how it can keep the perceived probability of success at the optimal level without raising standards as individuals get better at their jobs. Most managers are unhappy if incentive plans stop working after a while. Yet, theory suggests that, because experience changes perceived probability of success, plans would have to be changed regularly in order to keep expectancies of winning at an optimal level for producing performance.

Size of Incentive

Offered $2.50 for the best performance, a group of college students solved more arithmetic problems than when they were offered only $1.25—regardless, again, of their level of achievement, motivation, or the odds under which they were attempting to win the prize.[19] Obviously, then, size of reward makes a difference.

Just as obviously, "size" is a relative matter—relative, that is, to one's own starting point and to what other people are getting. Five hundred dollars is much more of an incentive to a $5,000 wage earner than to a $50,000 executive. Almost certainly, the increment in money necessary to create a "just noticeable incentive" is some kind of constant fraction of the base. But, again, this function has yet to be determined for real-life situations. It would probably be easier to work out in a personnel recruiting context, where the incentive effect of additional pay is more obvious than that of incentives offered for increased output in a given work setting.

Many authors have recently turned their attantion to how large a man perceives an incentive to be, in comparison not with his own starting level but rather with what others like him are getting.[20] Here, oddly enough, the yardstick seems to be more absolute than relative. That is, for a man earning $50,000, $500 may not seem like much of an incentive relative to his own past earnings, but it could become an important incentive if it puts him clearly ahead of another man whom he sees as a competitor.

One other finding relates to the size of incentives. In a couple of studies, managers receiving middle-level compensation scored higher in n Ach than either lower- or higher-paid managers.[21] The data are hard to interpret with any certainty but they are suggestive. One can infer that the managers with relatively low compensation (here, less than $20,000 a year) are those in the 35 to 50 age range who just haven't "made it." They are less successful, less achievement-oriented, and less rewarded. But why should the higher-paid managers (here, $25,000 a year and up) also be lower in achievement motivation? Older men, who may also get higher salaries, tend to become less achievement-oriented, but in this study age was controlled. Do the findings mean, then, that high financial rewards may lower motivation to achieve? Or do they mean that while high achievement motivation is necessary to get to the top, other motives are necessary for performing really well once one has gotten there?

Interestingly enough, the same pattern has been found in society: The middle-class people "on the way up" score highest in n Ach, whereas those from lower- and upper-class backgrounds are less achievement-oriented.[22] This might mean that very large financial rewards tend to decrease achievement motivation, perhaps not because they satisfy so many needs in the traditional sense but because they lead people to get interested in other things. At any rate, the possibility that very large rewards decrease motivation is intriguing and would seem to deserve further investigation.

The Response-Reward Relationship

Even in seniority systems where a man gets more pay as he grows older, the tacit assumption is that, with greater experience on the job, he is presumably doing the job better, even though it would be impractical to try to measure exactly how.

This suggests the first variable in the incentive situation: how specifically the desired response is defined. If a person doesn't know what he is supposed to do to earn the reward, he will obviously be less able to do it. So, in general, the supposition is that the more clearly specified the behavior, the greater the incentive value of the reward.

In some jobs—selling, for example—desired performance is relatively easy to define, while in others, such as the job of a personnel manager, it is quite difficult. In any case, it seems probable that successful incentive plans involve goals worked out as specifically as possible in advance, between superior and subordinate, so that the subordinate will know whether he is achieving his goals.

Two types of errors are commonly made in specifying the response for which the reward is offered. First, the manager may assume that the task primarily involves work output and may specify the expected responses in those terms, whereas a careful job analysis would show that other factors are important to success. A case in point is the sales offices mentioned previously, where too much emphasis on selling interfered with service functions and actually lowered performance.

Second, the manager may believe he is rewarding better performance from his staff, when in fact he is primarily rewarding other kinds of behavior, such as being loyal to him or "not rocking the boat." A comparative study of two large business organizations in Mexico provides an interesting illustration.[23] In Company A, where rewards were clearly given for better performance, men with high achievement motivation got significantly more raises over a three-year period. However, in Company P, where men were highly regarded if they were loyal to the boss and stayed in line, men who scored high in n Power were more often promoted. Company A was growing much more rapidly than Company P. Yet the president of Company P declared that he was interested in better performance for his top executives and couldn't understand why his company was not growing faster. He did not realize, though his subordinates did, that he was actually dispensing financial rewards primarily for loyalty to himself.

Another important characteristic of the response is whether it is expected from a group or from individuals. Should incentives be prorated on the basis of group performance, as in profit-sharing plans, or given for individual performance alone? No easy generalization is yet possible, though everyone agrees that each work situation should be carefully analyzed to see which type of performance it is most appropriate to reward in a given case. For example, where the staff is strongly affiliation-oriented and the job requires lots of interpersonal cooperation, some kind of group incentive plan would obviously be more effective than one rewarding individual excellence.

Still another important variable is the delay between the response and the reward. How often should bonus reviews be held—monthly, semiannually, or annually? Most studies with lower animals in simple learning situations suggest that the shorter the delay, the greater the incentive value of the reward. Applying this principle to the design of an industrial incentive plan could lead to "atomizing" expected improved responses so that a person could accumulate "points" every time he showed a better response, the points to be totaled and cashed in for money at regular intervals. The difficulty of measuring performance in a given work situation will almost certainly decide how often and how immediately rewards can be given. Generally speaking, such variations in timing are probably less important than the other variables mentioned, since most adults, and certainly most managers, are able to work for rewards deferred at least a month, and often a year or even longer.

In summary, then, money is one tool among many for managing motivation. It is a treacherous tool because it is deceptively concrete, tempting many managers to neglect variables in the work situation and climate that really affect productivity. In the near future, there will be less and less excuse for neglecting these variables, as the behavioral sciences begin to define them and explain to management how they can be manipulated just as one might change a financial compensation plan.

Incentive plans will continue to play an important role in the overall management framework. But the effective manager will also need to diagnose the needs of his staff, the motivational requirements of their jobs, his own motives, and the climate of the present organizational setup. Then he can rationally plan how to improve productivity by improving the climate; by developing certain motives in key people; by making a better match between the needs of the people and the needs of the job; or, finally, by specifically gearing incentive plans to the organizational situation.

REFERENCES

1 Cf. S. W. Gellerman, *Motivation and Productivity*, New York: American Management Association, 1963.

2 Cf. R. Likert, "A Motivational Approach to a Modified Theory of Organization and Management" in *Modern Organization Theory*, M. Haire, ed., New York: Wiley, 1959; F. Herzberg, B. Mausner, and B. Snyderman, *The Motivation to Work*, 2d ed., New York: Wiley, 1959; W. F. Whyte, *Money and Motivation*, New York: Harper, 1955; D. McGregor, *The Human Side of Enterprise*, New York: McGraw-Hill, 1960. For review of these studies see *Motivation and Productivity*, op. cit.

3 See J. Kagan, "On the Need for Relativism," *American Psychologist*, 1967, pp. 22, 131–142.

4 G. H. Litwin and R. A. Stringer, *Motivation and Organization Climate*, Cambridge: Harvard, 1967.

5 J. W. Atkinson and W. R. Reitman, "Performance as a Function of Motive Strength," *Journal of Abnormal and Social Psychology*, 1956, pp. 53, 361–366; J. W. Atkinson, ed., *Motives in Fantasy, Action and Society*, Princeton, N.J.: D. Van Nostrand, 1958; C. P. Smith, "The Influence of Testing Conditions on Need for Achievement Scores and Their Relationship to Performance Scores," in *A Theory of Achievement Motivation*, J. W. Atkinson and N. T. Feather, eds., New York: Wiley, 1966, pp. 277–297.

6 *Journal of Abnormal and Social Psychology,* op. cit.

7 D. G. Winter, "Power Motivation in Thought and Action," Unpublished Ph.D. thesis, Harvard University, 1967.

8 *Motivation and Organization Climate,* op. cit.

9 *Money and Motivation,* op. cit.

10 G. H. Litwin and J. A. Timmons, *Motivation and Organization Climate: A Study of Outstanding and Average Sales Offices,* Boston: Behavioral Sciences Center, 1966.

11 *Motivation and Organization Climate,* op. cit.

12 *Motivation and Organization Climate: A Study of Outstanding and Average Sales Offices,* op. cit.

13 Ibid., p. 13.

14 *Motives in Fantasy, Action and Society,* op. cit.; *A Theory of Achievement Motivation,* op. cit.

15 *Motives in Fantasy, Action and Society,* p. 196.

16 D. C. McClelland, *The Achieving Society,* Princeton, N.J.: Van Nostrand, 1961.

17 *Motives in Fantasy, Action and Society,* op. cit.

18 Ibid.; see also *The Achieving Society,* op. cit.

19 *Motives in Fantasy, Action and Society,* p. 293.

20 See R. L. Opsahl and M. D. Dunnette, "The Role of Financial Compensation in Industrial Motivation," *Psychological Bulletin,* 1966, pp. 66. 94–118.

21 See *The Achieving Society,* op. cit., p. 269.

22 B. C. Rosen, "Race, Ethnicity, and the Achievement Syndrome," *American Sociological Review,* 1959, pp. 24, 47–60.

23 J. D. W. Andrews, "The Achievement Motive in Two Types of Organizations," *Journal of Personality and Social Psychology,* June 1967.

Using Pay to Motivate Job Performance
Edward E. Lawler, III

The research evidence . . . clearly indicates that under certain conditions pay can be used to motivate good performance. The required conditions are deceptively simple . . . in the sense that establishing the conditions is easier said than done. Theory and research suggest that for a pay plan to motivate people, it must (1) create a belief among employees that good performance will lead to high pay, (2) contribute to the importance of pay, (3) minimize the perceived negative consequences of performing well, and (4) create conditions such that positive outcomes other than pay will be seen to be related to good performance. In this section, we shall consider some of the problems an organization confronts when it tries to set up a pay system that will satisfy these four conditions. . . .

TYING PAY TO PERFORMANCE

One obvious means of creating the perception that pay is tied to performance is actually to relate pay closely to job performance and to make the relationship as visible as possible. Several studies have attempted to determine the degree to which this is done in organizations and have come up with some unexpected results. Their evidence indicates that pay is not very closely related to performance in many organizations that claim to have merit increase salary systems. Lawler and Porter (1966) show that pay is related to job level, seniority, and other non-performance factors. Svetlik, Prien, and Barrett (1964) show that there is a negative relationship between amount of salary and performance as evaluated by superiors. Lawler (1964) shows that managers' pay is relatively unrelated to superiors' performance evaluations. Meyer, Kay, and French (1965) show that managers' raises are not closely related to what occurs in their performance appraisal sessions.

Studies by Haire, Ghiselli, and Gordon (1967) and by Brenner and Lockwood (1965) also indicate that at the managerial level, pay is not always related to performance. The evidence in both these studies consists of salary history data; they point up some interesting tendencies. Haire et al., for example, have established that the raises managers get from one year to another often show no correlation with each other. If the companies were tying pay to performance, the lack of correlation would mean that a manager's performance in one year was quite different from his performance in another year. This assumption simply does not fit with what is known about performance: A manager who is a good performer one year is very likely to be a good performer the next. Thus, we must conclude that the companies studied were not tying pay to performance. Apparently, pay raises were distributed on a random basis, or the criteria for awarding raises were frequently changed. As a result, recent raises were often not related to past raises or to performance.

Overall, therefore, the studies suggest that many business organizations do not do a very good job of tying pay to performance. This conclusion is rather surprising in light of many companies' very frequent claims that their pay systems are based on merit. It is particularly surprising that pay does not seem to be related to performance at the managerial level. Here there are no unions to contend with, and one would think that if organizations were effectively relating pay to performance for any group of employees, it would be at the managerial level. Admittedly this conclusion is based on sketchy evidence, and future research may prove it to be wrong. It may be, for instance, that pay is indirectly tied to performance and that the tie is obscured by promotion policies. All the studies reviewed here looked at the relationship between pay and performance within one management level. Even though there is no relationship between pay and performance within a level, there may actually be a relationship if the better performing managers are promoted and because of this receive higher pay. There is little evidence, however, to suggest that this is true.

Failure to tie pay closely to performance in many companies could mean that pay is not motivating job performance. In order to pay to motivate performance, it must appear to be related to performance; and employees are not likely to believe that pay is related to performance if it actually is not. Lawler (1967a) has shown that in one instance where pay was not related to performance, managers were aware of this fact and, consequently were not motivated by pay. This study also showed that in a group of organizations where measurements indicated that pay was only marginally tied to performance, managers had a fairly high belief that pay was related to performance. Thus, the data suggest that, given some positive indicators, employees are willing to believe that pay is based upon performance. Often, however, the positive indicators are missing, and as a result, pay does not motivate the employees to perform effectively.

METHODS OF RELATING PAY TO PERFORMANCE

There are virtually as many methods of relating pay to performance as there are organizations, and at times it seems that every organization is in the process of changing its approach. The R.I.A. (1965) study found, for example, that one out of every three companies has "recently" changed its method of paying salesmen. Campbell, Dunnette, Lawler, and Weick (1970) report that their survey of company personnel practices showed widespread dissatisfaction with current pay systems. Such dissatisfaction is hardly surprising in light of the previously reported finding that pay is not closely related to performance in many companies. It is doubtful, however, that the problems and the dissatisfaction can be corrected simply by changing the mechanics of the plan already in use. Many plans seem to fail not because they are mechanically defective, but because they were ineffectually introduced, there is a lack of trust between superiors and subordinates, or the quality of supervision is too low. No plan can succeed in the face of low trust and poor supervision, no matter how valid it may be from the point of view of mechanics.

Still, some types of plans clearly are more capable than others of creating the four conditions mentioned at the beginning of the [section]. Some plans certainly do a better job of relating pay to performance than others, and some are better able to minimize the perceived negative consequences of good performance and to maximize the perceived positive consequences. One of the reasons pay often is not actually related to performance is that many organizations simply do not have pay plans that are correctly set up in order to accomplish this. Often this comes about because the particular conditions in the organization itself may not have been taken into account when the plan was developed. No plan is applica-

Table 1   A classification of pay-incentive plans

	Performance measure	Reward offered	
		Salary increase	Cash bonus
Individual plans	Productivity Cost effectiveness Superiors' rating	Merit rating plan	Sales commission Piece rate
Group plans	Productivity Cost effectiveness Superiors' rating		Group incentive
Organizationwide plans	Productivity Cost effectiveness Profit	Productivity Bargaining	Kaiser, Scanlon Profit sharing (e.g., American Motors)

ble to all situations. In a sense, one may say that a pay plan should be custom tailored. Companies often try to follow the latest fads and fashion in salary administration, not recognizing that some plans simply do not fit their situation (Dunnette & Bass, 1963). Let us stress again, however, that mechanical faults are by no means the only reason that pay plans fail to relate pay to performance. Many of those which fail are not only well designed mechanically but also appropriate to the situation where they are used.

In looking at the mechanics of various types of pay programs, we shall group them together according to the way they differ on three dimensions. First, pay plans distribute rewards on different bases: individual, group, or organizationwide. Second, they measure performance differently: The measures typically vary from admittedly subjective (i. e., based on superiors' judgments or ratings) to somewhat objective (i. e., based on costs, sales, or profits). Third, plans differ in what they offer as rewards for successful performance: salary increases, bonuses, piece rates, or—in rare cases—fringe benefits. Table 1 presents a breakdown of the various plans, following this classification system. This classification yields some eighteen different types of incentive plans. A more detailed classification system would, of course, yield more. The table shows where the better-known plans fit in. It also shows a number of plans that are seldom used, and thus do not have a commonly known name. For example, companies do not typically base salary increases to individuals on the cost effectiveness of their work group. This does not mean that such a plan is a bad approach to distributing pay; it just means that it is not used very often.

EVALUATING THE DIFFERENT APPROACHES TO MERIT-BASED PAY

It is possible to make some general statements about the success of the different merit pay plans. We shall evaluate the plans in terms of how capable they have proved to be in establishing three of the conditions that are necessary if pay is to motivate performance. Such an evaluation must, of course, reflect actual experience with the different approaches in a number of situations. Here we are ignoring for the moment the effect of situational factors on the effectiveness of the plans in order to develop general ratings of the plans.

Table 2 lists the different types of incentive plans and provides a general effectiveness rating for each plan on three separate criteria. First, each plan is evaluated in terms of how effective it is in creating the perception that pay is tied to performance. In general, this indicates the degree to which the approach actually ties pay closely to performance, chronologically speaking, and the degree to which employees believe that higher pay will follow good performance. Second, each plan is evaluated in terms of how well it minimizes the perceived negative consequences of good performance. This criterion refers to the extent to which the approach eliminates situations where social ostracism and other negative consequences become associated with good performance. Third, each plan is evaluated in terms of whether it contributes to the perception that important rewards other than pay (e. g., recognition and acceptance) stem from good performance. The ratings range from $+3$ to -3, with $+3$ indicating that the plan has generally worked very well in terms of the criterion, while -3 indicates that the plan has not worked well. A 0 rating indicates that the plan has generally been neutral or average.

A number of trends appear in the ratings presented in Table 2. Looking just

Table 2 Ratings of Various Pay-Incentive Plans

	Type of plan	Performance measure	Tie pay to performance	Minimize negative side effects	Tie other rewards to performance
Salary reward	Individual plan	Productivity	+2	0	0
		Cost effectiveness	+1	0	0
		Superiors' rating	+1	0	+1
	Group	Productivity	+1	0	+1
		Cost effectiveness	+1	0	+1
		Superiors' rating	+1	0	+1
	Organizationwide	Productivity	+1	0	+1
		Cost effectiveness	+1	0	+1
		Profits	0	0	+1
Bonus	Individual plan	Productivity	+3	−2	0
		Cost effectiveness	+2	−1	0
		Superiors' rating	+2	−1	+1
	Group	Productivity	+2	0	+1
		Cost effectiveness	+2	0	+1
		Superiors' rating	+2	0	+1
	Organizationwide	Productivity	+2	0	+1
		Cost effectiveness	+2	0	+1
		Profit	+1	0	+1

at the criterion of tying pay to performance, we see that individual plans tend to be rated highest, while group plans are rated next, and organizationwide plans are rated lowest. This reflects the fact that in group plans to some extent and in organizationwide plans to a great extent, an individual's pay is not directly a function of his *own* behavior. The pay of an individual in these situations is influenced by the behavior of others with whom he works and also, if the payment is based on profits, by external market conditions.

Bonus plans are generally rated higher than pay raise and salary increase plans. Under bonus plans, a person's pay may vary sharply from year to year in accordance with his most recent performance. This does not usually happen with salary increase programs, since organizations seldom cut anyone's salary; as a result, pay under the salary increase plan reflects not recent performance but performance over a number of years. Consequently, pay is not seen to be closely related to present behavior. Bonuses, on the other hand, typically depend on recent behavior, so that if someone performs poorly, it will show up immediately in his pay. Thus, a person under the bonus plan cannot coast for a year and still be highly paid, as he can be under the typical salary merit pay program.

Finally, note that approaches which use objective measures of performance are rated higher than those which use subjective measures. In general, objective measures enjoy higher credibility; that is, employees will often grant the validity of an objective measure, such as sales or units produced, when they will not accept a superior's rating. Thus, when pay is tied to objective measures, it is usually clear to employees that pay is determined by their performance. Objective measures such as sales volume and units produced are also often publicly measurable, and when pay is tied to them, the relationship is often much more visible than when it is tied to a subjective, nonverifiable measure, such as a superior's rating. Overall, then, the suggestion is that individually based bonus plans which rely on objective measures produce the strongest perceived connection between pay and performance.

The ratings with respect to the ability of pay programs to minimize the perceived negative consequences of good performance reveal that most plans are regarded as neutral. That is, they neither contribute to the appearance of negative consequences nor help to eliminate any which might be present. The individual bonus plans receive a negative rating on this criterion, however. This negative rating reflects the fact that piece rate plans often lead to situations in which social rejection, firing, and running out of work are perceived by individuals to result from good performance. Under a piece rate system, the perceived negative consequences of good performance may cancel out the positive motivational force that piece rate plans typically generate by tying pay closely to performance.

With respect to the final criterion for pay plans, tying nonpay rewards to performance, the ratings are generally higher for group and organizationwide plans than for individual plans. Under group and organizationwide plans, it is generally to the advantage of everyone for an individual to work effectively. Thus, good performance is much more likely to be seen to result in esteem, respect, and social acceptance, than it is under individual plans. In short, if a person feels he can benefit from another's good performance, he is much more likely to encourage his fellow worker to perform well than if he will not benefit, and might even be harmed.

It should be clear from this short review that not one pay plan presents a panacea for a company's job motivation problems. Unfortunately, no one type of pay program is strong in all areas. Thus, no organization probably ever will be satisfied with its approach, since it will have problems associated with it. It is therefore not surprising to find that companies are usually dissatisfied with their pay programs and are constantly considering changing them. Still, the situation is not completely hopeless. Clearly, some approaches are generally better than others. We know, for example, that many of the approaches not mentioned in the table, such as stock option plans, across-the-board raises, and seniority increases, have no real effect on the performance motivation of most employees. In addition, the evidence indicates that bonus-type plans are generally superior wage increase plans and that individually based plans are generally superior to group and organizationwide plans. This suggests that one widely applicable model for an incentive plan might take the following form.

Each person's pay would be divided into three components. One part would be for the job the employee is doing, and everyone who holds a similar job would get the same amount. A second part of the pay package would be determined by seniority and cost-of-living factors; everyone in the company would get this, and the amount would be automatically adjusted each year. The third part of the package, however, would not be automatic; it would be individualized so that the amount paid would be based upon each person's performance during the immediately preceding period. The poor performer in the organization should find that this part of his or her pay package is minimal, while the good performer should find that this part of his or her pay is at least as great as the other two parts combined. This would not be a raise, however, since it could vary from year to year, depending on the individual's performance during the last performance period. Salary increases or raises would come only with changes in responsibility, cost of living, or seniority. The merit portion of the pay package would be highly variable, so that if a person's performance fell off, his or her pay would also be decreased by a cut in the size of the merit pay. The purpose of this kind of system is, of course, to make a large proportion of an individual's pay depend upon performance during the current period. Thus; performance is chronologically closely tied to large changes in pay.

The really difficult problem in any merit pay system, including this one, is how to measure performance. A valid measure of performance must meet several requirements. Not only must it be valid from the point of view of top management, but it must lead to promotion and pay decisions that are accepted by people throughout the organization: Supervisors, subordinates, and peers must all accept the results of the system. Without this wide acceptance, pay raises will not be seen to reflect merit. Employees gain much of their knowledge about how pay systems operate by watching what happens to other people in the organization. If people whom they feel are doing good work get raises, then they accept the fact that a merit pay system exists. On the other hand, if workers they do not respect get raises, their belief in the system breaks down. Obviously the more the appraisal system yields decisions that are congruent with employee consensus about performance, the more the employees will believe that a merit system exists. The performance measure should also be such that employees feel that their contributions to the organization show up in it very directly. They must feel that they have control over it, rather than feeling that it reflects so many other things that what they do has little weight. . . .Finally, the performance measure or measures should be influenced by all the behaviors that are important for the job holder to perform. People perform those behaviors that are measured, and thus it is important that the measure be sufficiently inclusive.

The performance appraisal systems that are actually used by organizations range all the way from superiors' subjective judgments to the complicated "objective" accounting-based systems that are used to measure managers' effectiveness. The problems with the simple, subjective, superiors' judgments are obvious—the subordinates often see them as arbitrary, based upon inadequate information, and simply unfair. The more objective systems are appealing in many ways. Where they can be installed, they are the best, but even they often fail to reflect individual efforts. Stock option plans are a good example. With these plans, pay is tied to the price of the stock on the market, and this presumably motivates managers to work so that the price of the stock will go up. The problem with this approach is that for most managers the connection between their effort and the price of the stock is very weak.

Plans that base bonuses or pay increases on profit centers or on the effectiveness of certain parts of the business may work, but all too often much of the profitability of one part of the organization is controlled more by outside than by inside forces. Another problem with this kind of system is illustrated by the fate of most piece rate incentive plans used at the worker level. They give the false illusion that objective, highly measurable rates can be "scientifically" set and that trust between superiors and subordinates is not necessary, since the system is objective. Experience has shown that effective piece rate systems simply cannot be established where foremen and workers do not trust each other and have a participative relationship. No completely "objective" system has ever been designed, nor will one ever be. Unexpected contingencies will always come up and have to be worked out between superiors and subordinates. Such events can be successfully resolved only when trust based upon mutual influence exists. Where poor relationships exist, workers strive to get rates set low and then they restrict their production, because they do not believe that good performance will in fact lead to higher pay in the long run.

Thus the answer in many organizations must rest in a reasonable combination of the simple, superior-based rating system and a system which uses more objective measures. First, we must accept the fact that no system can ever be 100 percent objective and that subjective judgments will always be important. Second, we must realize that the key to general acceptance of the decisions that the appraisal system yields lies in having as broad as possible participation in the system.

What would such a system look like? It would be based upon superior-subordinate appraisal sessions where subordinates feel that they have a real opportunity to influence their boss. Obviously, such a system cannot operate, nor can any other for that matter, unless superior-subordinate relations are such that mutual influence is possible. In the first appraisal session the superior and subordinate would jointly decide on three things. First, they would decide on the objectives the subordinate should try to achieve during the ensuing time period. This period might last from three months to several years, depending on the level of the job. Second, they would decide on how the subordinate's progress toward these objectives will be measured. Objective measures might be used as well as subjective ratings by peers and others. Third, they would decide what level of reward the subordinate should receive if he accomplishes his objectives. A second meeting would be held at the end of the specified time period in order for the superior and subordinate to jointly assess the progress of the subordinate and decide upon any pay actions. Finally, a few weeks later the whole process would begin again with another objectives-setting session. The advantages of this kind of system extend far beyond pay administration. It can create a situation where superiors and subordinates jointly become much more certain of what the subordinate's actual job duties and responsibilities are. Some recent studies suggest that there is often greater than 70 percent disagreement between superior and subordinate about what constitutes the subordinate's job, so agreement on his score would not be an insignificant step forward. The fact that the subordinate has a chance to set goals and that he commits himself to a certain level of performance may have an impact on his motivation that is independent of rewards like pay. There is evidence that when people commit themselves to challenging goals, needs like esteem and self-realization can come into play and motivate them to achieve the goals. This system also offers the subordinate a chance to become involved in important decisions about his own future and thereby encourages a kind of give and take that seldom exists between superiors and subordinates.

Despite the fact that it is possible to state some general conclusions about the effectiveness of different pay plans, perhaps the most important conclusion arising from the discussion so far is that it is vital to fit the pay plan to the organization. What might be a wonderful plan for one organization may for a whole series of reasons be a bad plan for another. Thus, although it is tempting to say that X approach is always best, it is wiser to turn now to a consideration of the factors that determine which kind of plan is likely to be best in a given situation.

FACTORS INFLUENCING THE EFFECTIVENESS
OF DIFFERENT PAY PLANS

In selecting a plan for a particular organization, what situational factors must be considered? . . . One factor that must be considered when an organization is deciding what type of pay plan to use is the degree of cooperation that is needed among the individuals who are under the plan. When the jobs involved are basically independent from one another, it is perfectly reasonable to use an individual-based plan. Independent jobs are quite common: examples are outside sales jobs and certain kinds of production jobs. In these jobs, employees contribute relatively independently to the effectiveness of the total group or organization, and thus it is appropriate to place them on an incentive scheme that motivates them to perform at their maximum and to pay little attention to cooperative activities.

As organizations become more complex, however, more and more jobs demand that work be done either successively (i. e., work is a function of the joint effort of all employees) (Ghiselli & Brown, 1955). With successive jobs and especially with coordinate jobs, it is doubtful that individual incentive plans are appropriate. For one thing, on these jobs it is often difficult to measure the contribution of a given individual, and therefore difficult to reward individuals differentially. The organization is almost forced to reward on the basis of group performance. Another problem with individual plans is that they typically do not reward cooperation, since it is difficult to measure and to visibly relate to pay. Cooperation is essential on successive and coordinate jobs, and it is vital that the pay plan reward it. Thus, the strong suggestion is that group and organizationwide plans may be best in situations where jobs are coordinate or successive.

A related issue has to do with the degree to which appropriate inclusive subgoals or criteria can be created for individuals. An example was cited earlier of an individual pay plan that motivated salesmen to sell but did not motivate them to carry out other necessary job activities such as stocking shelves. The problem was that pay was tied to the most obvious and most measurable goal in the job, and some of the less measurable activities were overlooked and unrewarded. This situation occurs frequently; for many jobs, it is quite difficult to establish criteria that are both measurable quantitatively and inclusive of all the important job behaviors. The solution to the problem with the salesmen was to establish a group incentive plan. Indeed, inclusive criteria may often be possible at the group and organizational level but not at the individual level. It is quite easy to think of jobs for which a criterion like productivity might not be inclusive enough when individuals are looked at, but might be inclusive enough when a number of jobs or employees are grouped together. The point, of course, is that in choosing an incentive plan, an organization must consider whether the performance measures that are related to pay include all the important job activities. One thing is certain: If an employee is not evaluated in terms of an activity, he will not be motivated to perform it.

The point has often been made that, wherever possible, objective performance measures should be used. There are, however, many situations where objective measures do not exist for individual or even group performance. One way of dealing with such situations is to measure performance on the basis of larger and larger groups until some objective measures can be found. Another approach is to measure performance on the individual or small group level and to use admittedly subjective measures. This is possible in some situations but not in others. The key factor in determining whether this approach is feasible is the degree of superior-subordinate trust. The more subjective the measure, the higher the degree of trust needed, because without high trust there is little chance that the subordinate will believe that his pay is really fairly based upon performance. Figure 1 illustrates the relationship between trust and the objectivity of the performance criteria. Note that it indicates that, even with the most objective system, some trust is still required if the individual is going to believe in the system. It also shows that unless a high degree of trust exists, pay plans based on subjective criteria have little chance of success.

One further issue must be considered when an organization is installing a pay plan: will the individuals under the plan actually be able to control the criteria on which they will be evaluated? All too often the criteria are unrelated to the individual worker's efforts. A good example of this is the American Motors Corporation profit-sharing plan: The individual worker is not in a position to influence the profits of the company, yet this is a criterion upon which part of his pay is based. If a pay system is going to motivate employees, the criteria must be such that the employees can directly influence them. The criteria must, in short, be within the employees' control. This point, of course, argues for the use of individual criteria where possible, since they best reflect an individual's efforts.

Pay systems may also be results or process-oriented; that is, they may reward employees chiefly for results (e. g. actual production) or for the way the task or job is carried out. There are usually problems with any system that rewards process only, just as there are problems with systems that reward results only. Perhaps the ultimate example of what can happen in the process-oriented system can be seen in the large bureaucracies that grow up in many civil service and other large organizations. In these bureaucracies people seem motivated to follow

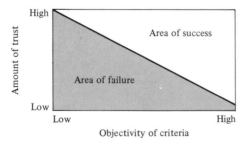

Figure 1 Relationship of trust and the objectivity of performance criteria to success of the program.

the rules, and not to accomplish the objectives for which the organization was established. On the other hand, a salesman may be motivated only by a short-term desire to maximize results. His behavior may lead to a sale, but it may be such that his organization never makes another sale to that buyer. A pay system must be designed to reward both process and results. This may be difficult in many situations; process is particularly difficult to measure objectively, and thus subjective measures may have to be used. As has already been pointed out, subjective measures can only be used effectively where a high degree of trust exists.

SHOULD PAY BE USED TO MOTIVATE?

Although we have not said so explicitly, it is clear that there are many situations in which pay should not be used to motivate job performance. In many jobs, it is impossible to develop adequate criteria for relating pay to performance. There may be no objective measures of performance, so that very subjective measures are needed but cannot be used because of the low level of trust between superiors and subordinates. On the other hand, the problem may be that objective measures are available but the level of trust is not even sufficient to allow their use. As was illustrated in Figure 1, there are situations where it simply may not be wise to measure performance for the purpose of relating it to pay. As has already been pointed out, it may be possible to measure some but not all of the relevant aspects of performance. A number of new problems can be created if pay is tied only to those aspects of performance that are measurable: The measurable aspects may receive all the employee's attention, while the others are neglected. In this situation it may well be better not to try to use pay to motivate performance.

Often, profit-sharing plans are used where individual performance measures are not appropriate, and the organization desires to use pay to motivate performance. There is some doubt whether this is worthwhile in large organizations. The larger the organization, the less likely it is that a companywide profit-sharing or cost effectiveness plan will work. The reason for this is simple: The larger the organization, the less influence any one individual has over companywide results, and the less an individual feels that his pay is related to performance. Thus, where individual based pay plans are not possible, it is not always advisable to use an organizationwide plan. It may in fact be better to have no incentive pay plan at all. Often when organizationwide plans are installed in large organizations, they produce no extra motivation but do produce quite a few extra costs for the company: thus, the suggestion that the cost effectiveness of each plan should be considered.

Finally, motivating people with financial rewards is not a piker's game. Large amounts of money must be given to the good performers if employees are to place a high value on good performance and the raises to which it leads. A company must be willing and able to give certain employees very large raises and/or bonuses if pay is to motivate performance. If a company cannot afford to do this or is not willing to, it should probably forget about using pay to motivate performance. Even if they are willing to spend large amounts of money it may be that pay is not important to the employees and because of this not a possible source of motivation. In this case some other reward may be more appropriate. For example, in one factory that employed large numbers of unmarried women, time off the job was more important than money so when the women were told they could go home after a certain amount of work was done productivity increased dramatically. Several earlier attempts to use pay to motivate high productivity had failed.

In summary, serious thought should be given to *not* using pay as an incentive in organizations where:

1   The trust level is low.
2   Individual performance is difficult to measure.
3   Performance must be measured subjectively.
4   Inclusive measures of performance cannot be developed.
5   Large pay rewards cannot be given to the best performers.

PAY SECRECY

Secrecy about pay rates seems to be an accepted practice in organizations, regardless of whether they use individual or group plans, bonus or salary increases, objective or subjective performance measures. Secrecy seems to be particularly prevalent with respect to management pay (Lawler, in press). Some research suggests that one of the effects of secrecy may be to reduce the ability of pay to motivate (Lawler, 1965; Lawler, 1967b). . . . The argument that has been presented against secrecy is that it makes accurate social comparisons impossible (Festinger, 1954). Secrecy thus makes it difficult to conclusively and visibly establish that pay is tied to performance. Further, it is argued that because social comparisons are difficult, employees often get incorrect feedback about their own performance.

One of the findings that has consistently appeared in the research on pay secrecy is that managers tend to have incorrect information about the pay of other managers in the organization. Specifically, there is a general tendency for them to overestimate the pay of managers around them. For example, in one organization the average raise given was 6 percent, yet the managers believed that it was 8 percent, and the larger their raise was, the larger they believed other people's raises were (Lawler, in press). This had the effect of wiping out much of the motivational force of the differential reward system that was actually operating in the company. Almost regardless of how well the individual manager was performing, he felt that he was getting less than the average raise. This problem was particularly severe among the high performers, since they believed that they were doing well yet receiving a minimal reward. They did not believe that pay was in fact based upon merit. This was ironical, since their pay *did* reflect their performance. What actually existed did not matter as far as the motivation of the managers was concerned; they responded to what they thought existed. Thus, even though pay was tied to performance, these managers were not motivated because they could not see the connection.

There is another way in which pay secrecy may affect motivation. Several studies have shown that accurate feedback about quality of work is a strong stimulus to good performance (Vroom, 1964). People work better when they know how well they are doing in relation to some meaningful standard. For a manager, pay is one of the most meaningful pieces of feedback information. High pay means good performance. Low pay is a signal that he is not doing well and had better improve. The research shows that when managers do not really know what other managers earn, they cannot correctly evaluate their own pay and the feedback implications of it for their own performance. Since they tend to overestimate the pay of subordinates and peers and since they overestimate the raises others get, the majority of them consider their pay low; in effect, they receive negative feedback. Moreover, although this feedback suggests that they should change their work behavior, it does not tell them what type of change to make. When managers are not doing their jobs well, negative feedback is undoubtedly what they need. But it is doubtful that it is what managers who are working effectively need.

Note that one recommendation that appears in the discussion of factors affecting the importance of pay as well as in the discussion of factors affecting the belief that pay depends upon performance is that pay information should be more public. Unless this condition exists, pay is not likely to motivate performance, because it will be seen neither as an important satisfier of higher-order needs nor as something that is obtainable from good performance. Making pay informantion public will not itself establish the belief that pay is based upon merit or ensure that people will get accurate performance feedback. All it can do is clarify those situations where pay actually *is* based upon merit but where it is not obvious because relative salaries are not accurately known. This point is apparent in some unpublished data collected by the author. An organization was studied that had a merit-based plan and pay secrecy. At the beginning of the study, the data collected showed that the employees saw only a moderate relationship between pay and performance. Data collected after the company became more open about pay showed a significant increase in the employees' perceptions of the degree to which pay and performance were related. The crucial factor in making this change to openness successful was that pay was actually tied to performance. Making pay rates public where pay is not tied to performance will only serve to emphasize more dramatically that it is not, thereby further reducing the power of pay to motivate.

REFERENCES

Brenner, M. H., & Lockwood, H. C. Salary as a predictor of salary: A 20-year study. *Journal of Applied Psychology,* 1965, **49,** 295–298.

Campbell, J. P., Dunnette, M. D., Lawler, E. E., & Weick, K. E. *Managerial behavior, performance, and effectiveness.* New York: McGraw-Hill, 1970.

Dunnette, M. D., & Bass, B. M. Behavioral scientists and personnel management. *Industrial Relations,* 1963, **2,** 115–130.

Festinger, L. A theory of social comparison processes. *Human Relations,* 1954, **7,** 117–140.

Ghiselli, E. E., & Brown, C. W. *Personnel and industrial psychology.* New York: McGraw-Hill, 1955.

Haire, M., Ghiselli, E. E., & Gordon, M. E. A psychological study of pay. *Journal of Applied Psychology Monograph,* 1967, **51**(4), (Whole No. 636).

Lawler, E. E. *Manager's job performance and their attitides toward their pay.* Unpublished doctoral dissertation, University of California, Berkeley, 1964.

Lawler, E. E. Managers' perceptions of their subordinates' pay and of their superiors' pay. *Personnel Psychology,* 1965, **18,** 413–422.

Lawler, E. E. The multitrait-multirater approach to measuring managerial job performance. *Journal of Applied Psychology,* 1967, **51,** 369–381. (a)

Lawler, E. E. Secrecy about management compensation: Are there hidden costs? *Organizational Behavior and Human Performance,* 1967, **2,** 182–189. (b)

Lawler, E. E. Secrecy and the need to know. In R. House, M. Dunnette, and H. Tosi (Eds.) *Readings in managerial motivation and compensation,* in press.

Lawler, E. E., & Porter, L. W. Predicting managers' pay and their satisfaction with their pay. *Personnel Psychology,* 1966, **19,** 363–373.

Meyer, H. H., Kay, E., & French, J. R. P. Split roles in performance appraisal. *Harvard Business Review,* 1965, **43**(1), 123–129.

R.I.A. *Sales compensation practices, an RIA survey.* New York: Research Institute of America, File No. 32, 1965.

Svetlik, B., Prien, E., & Barrett, G. Relationships between job difficulty, employee's attitudes toward his job, and supervisory ratings of the employee effectiveness. *Journal of Applied Psychology,* 1964, **48,** 320–324.

Vroom, V. H. *Work and motivation.* New York: Wiley, 1964.

QUESTIONS FOR DISCUSSION

1 How would you design a program to increase the motivational levels of employees without using additional money? What factors would you think most important and how would you use such factors in your program design?

2 What role does money play in each of the five major motivational models discussed in the beginning of this book?

3 Why might you expect pay and promotional opportunities to have different motivational effects on blue- and white-collar employees?

4 Under what circumstances might money be a stronger influence on the decision to participate than on the decision to produce?

5 Opsahl and Dunnette list several functions served by money. How could managers use this list in an attempt to increase the output of their subordinates?

6 What are some advantages and disadvantages of group incentive plans?

7 Differentiate between extrinsic rewards and intrinsic rewards. Which type do you feel would generally be a stronger motivating force? Why?

Part Four

Motivation Theory in Perspective

Chapter 16

Work and Motivation: An Evaluative Summary

The concept of the organization has long symbolized the efficient, effective, and rational allocation of resources for task accomplishment. As such, many attempts have been made by managers and researchers to define the optimal balance of financial, physical, and human resources as they help determine the growth and development of business, governmental, and educational institutions. The present volume has focused on the human aspects associated with such concerns. Specifically, we have reviewed in a systematic fashion the current level of knowledge concerning motivational processes as they affect work behavior.

Before attempting to summarize the current status of motivation theory and research, however, we should review briefly what we know about the nature of work itself. After all, if one objective of an increased knowledge of motivational processes is to improve both work attitudes and work performance, then we must be aware of the functions served by work activities in a modern society.

THE MEANING OF WORK

Work is important in the lives of individuals for several reasons. First, there is the notion of reciprocity, or exchange. Whether we are talking about a corporate executive, an assembly-line worker, or a Red Cross volunteer, each worker receives some form of reward in exchange for his or her services. These rewards

551

may be primarily extrinsic, such as money, or they may be purely intrinsic, such as the personal satisfaction that comes from providing the service. In either case, a worker has certain personal expectations concerning the type and amount of reward he or she should receive for services rendered. The extent to which such expectations are met would presumably affect in large measure the inclination of the worker to continue at the current level of performance and, indeed, might even ultimately affect the decision of whether to remain with the organization.

Second, work generally serves several social functions. The workplace provides opportunities for meeting new people and developing friendships. In fact, many employees appear to spend more time interacting with their fellow employees than they do with their own families!

Third, a person's job is often a source of status, or rank, in society at large. For example, a carpenter who is trained in a specific craft is generally considered to be on a higher social plane than an unskilled ditchdigger. And a bank president would generally be accorded higher status than the carpenter. A point not to be overlooked here is the fact that work, or more precisely what one does at work, often transcends the boundaries of the work organization. The bank president in our example can have status in the *community* because of his position within the organization. Thus, work can be simultaneously a source of social differentiation as well as a source of social integration.

Fourth, and an aspect of work of special concern to the study of motivation, is the personal meaning that work has for the individual. From a psychological standpoint, it can be an important source of identity, self-esteem, and self-actualization. It can provide a sense of fulfillment by giving an employee a sense of purpose and by clarifying his value to society. Conversely, however, it can also be a source of frustration, boredom, and feelings of meaninglessness, depending on the characteristics of the individual and on the nature of the task. People tend to evaluate themselves according to what they have been able to accomplish. If they see their job as hampering the achievement of their full potential, it often becomes difficult for them to maintain a sense of purpose at work. Such feelings can then lead to a reduced level of job involvement, decreased job satisfaction, and a lowered desire to perform. Hence, the nature of the job—and the meaning it has for the employee—can have a profound impact on employee attitudes and work behavior.

As our society has increased in both complexity and affluence, so too have the problems, associated with such developments. Alcoholism and drug abuse at work are on the rise, as are problems of turnover and absenteeism. Moreover, by several indications, worker productivity appears to be declining in many areas. Managers have often tried to explain away such problems by reverting to the old scientific management, or Theory X, assumptions about human nature—namely, that people are basically lazy and have little desire to perform well on a job. However, a more realistic explanation for such problems may be found by looking at the type of work most employees are asked to perform.

Consider, for example, the case of the younger workers just entering the job market. With higher educational levels, as well as greater expectations concerning their work, many young workers have shown a strong aversion toward many of the more traditional (and well-paying) jobs at both the blue- and the white-collar levels. However, based on the available data (for example, Yankelovich, 1972), these same workers are largely in agreement with the notion that one should "work hard" on a job. How are these two points reconciled? Perhaps the answer lies in the nature of the tasks. That is, rather than simply rebelling against the traditional (hard) work ethic, many younger workers appear to be demanding greater substance in the *nature* of their job activities. In this sense, it is a qualitative revolt, not a quantitative one. What they object to, it seems, is being placed on jobs which are essentially devoid of intrinsic worth.

Other examples could be cited (minority-group workers, women employees, even corporate executives). In all cases, a common denominator appears to be a reduced level of employee motivation to perform his or her job or even to remain with the organization. If we are to understand more clearly the nature and extent of such work-related problems and, better still, if we are to be able to find appropriate solutions to these problems, we must begin by understanding the very basic role played by motivation as it affects job behavior.

IMPORTANCE OF MOTIVATION IN WORK BEHAVIOR

Review of Major Variables

Perhaps the most striking aspect of the study of work motivation is the all-encompassing nature of the topic itself. Consider again our definition of motivation: that which energizes, directs, and sustains behavior. Following such a definition, it becomes readily apparent how many divergent factors can affect in some way the desire of an employee to perform. In Chapter 1, a conceptual framework, or model, was proposed (after Porter & Miles, 1974) to assist us in organizing these factors for detailed study and analysis throughout this book (see Exhibit 3 in Chapter 1).

By way of review, the model suggested that variables affecting motivation can be found on three levels in organizational settings. First, some variables were unique to the individual himself (such as attitudes, interests, specific needs). Second, other variables arose from the nature of the job (such as degree of control over the particular job, level of responsibility, and so forth). Third, still other variables were found in the larger work situation, or organizational environment. Factors falling into this third category would include such things as peer group relations, supervisory practices, systemwide rewards, and organizational climate. In addition, it was emphasized in the model that a systems perspective was necessary. That is, instead of viewing these variables as three static lists of items, consideration had to be given to how they affected one another and changed over time in response to circumstances. The individual was thus seen as potentially being in a constant state of flux vis-à-vis his motivational level, based on the nature, strength, and interactive effects of these three groups of variables.

Let us consider briefly how some of the more important findings reviewed in this book relate to this conceptual framework, beginning with those variables unique to the individual himself. Only highlights of the major findings will be mentioned here. An analysis of the data presented throughout this volume reveals that several *individual* characteristics can represent a significant influence on employee performance. For instance, there is fairly consistent evidence that individuals who have higher needs for achievement generally perform better than those who have lower needs (as shown, for example, in Cummin, 1967). Moreover, other evidence (see, for example, Porter & Steers, 1973) indicates that individuals who have strong negative attitudes toward an organization are less inclined to continue their involvement in organizational activities. Locke and his associates (Locke, Cartledge, & Knerr, 1970) present laboratory evidence indicating that personal aspiration level on a task (the level of performance for which an individual is actually trying) can be an accurate predictor of subsequent performance. Finally, investigations by Adams (1965) and others found that *perceived* inequity in an organizational exchange situation was closely associated with changes (up or down) in performance levels. While many other examples could be cited, these kinds of findings generally support the proposition that personal characteristics unique to an individual can have an important impact on his or her work behavior.

A similar pattern emerges when we consider *job-related* characteristics. Evidence presented by Lawler (1969), Hulin, (1971), Steers and Porter (1974), and others indicates that variations in the nature of the task itself can influence performance and satisfaction. For example, several studies found that "enriching" an employee's job by allowing him more variety, autonomy, and responsibility tended to result in somewhat improved performance. However, these findings were not overly strong. Much stronger evidence concerning the impact of job- or task-related variables emerges when we simultaneously consider the role of individual differences in such a relationship. That is, when variations across individuals are also taken into account, the evidence indicates that certain task attributes are strongly related to performance only for specific "types" of people, such as, say, high need achievers. For other persons, such attributes appear to have greatly diminished effects (Carroll & Tosi, 1970; Hackman & Lawler, 1971; Hulin, 1971; Steers, 1975; Vroom, 1960). In other words, it appears that not everyone wants *to the same degree* to have an "enriched" job, nor does everyone necessarily perform better when assigned to one. Recognition must be given, therefore, to the background characteristics of the individual employees when considering job design changes.

Finally, let us review *work environment* effects on motivation and performance. A great deal of the discussion in this book has been devoted to such factors. For example, Campbell et al. (1970) reviewed much of the research on environmental impact and noted the importance of such variables as group influences, leadership styles, and systemwide reward structures in the determination of employee performance. Again, however, we must consider the interactive dynamics between such factors and other individuals and job-related factors. Thus, it is possible that high group cohesion (a work environment characteristic) may be a much more potent influence on behavior for a person with a high need for affiliation (an individual characteristic) than for a person with a low need for affiliation. Persons with high needs for achievement may be less influenced by the degree of group cohesion and more interested in potential economic rewards. Moreover, a job that lacks "enrichment" (a job-related characteristic) may be eased somewhat by a supervisor who shows a good deal of consideration toward his subordinates (another work environment characteristic).

The important point, then, is that when we consider the variables involved in work motivation we must take a strong, integrative approach. We must study *relationships* among variables rather than focus on one specific topic. Only then can we achieve a greater understanding of the complexities of the motivational process.

Review of Major Theories

A central purpose of any theory is to organize in a meaningful fashion the major sets of variables associated with the topic under study. In fact, one test of the usefulness of a theory, or model, is the degree to which it can account for a wide diversity of variables while simultaneously integrating them into a cohesive—and succinct—unifying framework. Such a theory of work motivation would ideally account for variables from the three major areas discussed above (individual, job, and work environment), as well as consider the implications of interactive effects among these three areas.

Five major theories of work motivation have been discussed here. Rather than present a case for a "favorite" theory, we will review several of the major characteristics and contributions of each of the five and allow the reader to make the final judgment as to which one makes the most sense to him. In any event, the decision as to which theory "works best" must ultimately be a personal one, based on the specific needs and desires of the individual.

The theories of Maslow and of McClelland and Atkinson, while not entirely ignoring job-related and work environment variables, are primarily individual theories of motivation. Strong emphasis is placed on the characteristics of the individual, and both models represent highly developed statements concerning the role played by personal need strengths in the determination of work behavior. While the influences of the job and work environment are seldom discussed, it is easy to see how such factors could play a major role in these models. For example, for employees with a strong need for self-actualization, providing a work environment which would promote fulfillment of this need should increase their propensity to remain and participate actively in organizational activities. A similar argument could be advanced for creating an achievement-oriented work environment under the McClelland-Atkinson model for individuals with a high need for achievement. Even so, although a good deal of speculation is possible concerning how such job and environmental variables might affect personal need satisfaction and performance, it should be recognized that such considerations are dealt with only lightly in these models. Certainly room is left for additional theoretical development and research.

In contrast to the two major "need" theories, which concentrated primarily on personal issues, Herzberg chose to focus his model on the nature of the tasks that individuals are called upon to perform. Herzberg advanced the argument that although work environment factors (he uses the term "job context") may be important, a much more influential factor in determining motivational levels is whether an employee has a job which allows for recognition, advancement, and achievement. Based on this notion, he held that the key to increased job performance and satisfaction lies in enriching jobs so that they provide opportunities for challenge and growth.

An important contribution of this two-factor theory becomes clear when we put the theory in historical perspective. Before Herzberg's initial efforts in the late 1950s, most managers and researchers were concentrating either on the individual himself (as in the case of Maslow and of McClelland & Atkinson) or on the work environment (supervisory relations, pay systems, group influences) as potential sources of motivation. Herzberg made a sound argument for paying greater attention to the more intrinsic aspects of the job itself. As with the need theories, however, Herzberg has largely ignored the interrelationships between the major sets of motivational variables, although many are implicit in his model.

Several other theories have, however, dealt more explicitly with relationships among these sets of variables. Locke (see Chapter 13), for example, has proposed a theory of task motivation which focuses primarily on the interaction between task characteristics and personal aspiration levels. Moreover, Adams's theory of inequity centers around the relationship between individual characteristics (attitudes toward inputs and outcomes, tolerance for feelings of inequity, and so on) and work environment characteristics (especially systemwide reward practices). Both Locke and Adams are very clear in their emphasis on interactive effects among the relevant variables and both view motivational force as a fairly volatile concept.

Finally, let us examine expectancy/valence theory in the light of our conceptual model. To begin with, this theory is very specific in dealing with the role of individual differences. Not only does it deal with the concept of perceived equitable rewards but it also points to the necessity of recognizing variations in individual need strengths (as do the two previous needs theories). The model acknowledges that not everyone values the same rewards equally; people attach different valences to perceived outcomes. Moreover, the model emphasizes that individuals have differing beliefs, or expectancies, that certain actions on their part will ultimately lead to desired rewards.

Expectancy/valence theory also encompasses job-related variables by pointing to how such variables can affect future expectancies and by arguing that job attributes may at times serve as sources of intrinsically valued rewards. The more sophisticated versions of the model have also included the notion of role clarity;

that is, performance can often be improved by clarifying exactly what the job entails. Finally, expectancy/valence theory focuses fairly explicitly on several work environment influences on performance, particularly those relating to reward structures. Throughout, this model stresses the necessity of analyzing relationships among variables as a prerequisite to an understanding of the motivational *process*.

In summary, each of the theories reviewed here has made important contributions to the study of work motivation. When these theories and the research associated with them are jointly considered, it becomes clear that our understanding of the motivational process has progressed greatly since the time of Frederick Taylor and scientific management. No longer do we view motivation solely as a function of money. We have also made significant progress since the time of the human relations movement in that we no longer assume that a satisfied worker is necessarily a productive one. We live today in a complex society where employees have come to expect more from their jobs in the way of both extrinsic *and intrinsic* rewards. What we need are models of motivation capable of dealing effectively with this increased complexity. It is hoped that future research can assist us here in pointing to new directions for satisfying both managerial demands for greater productivity and employee needs for increasingly meaningful work. In this sense, improved knowledge about motivational processes is requisite not only for management but also for the employees themselves if all members are to contribute more effectively to the goals of the organization and simultaneously receive greater personal satisfaction.

IMPLICATIONS FOR MANAGEMENT

As we have found, the level of understanding concerning work motivation has increased considerably in the past two decades. However, when we survey current practice in this area we soon discover that there is a sizable discrepancy in a number of organizations between such practice and many of the more advanced theories of motivation. Why does such a discrepancy exist? There are several possible explanations.

First, many managers still hold conservative beliefs about how much employees really want to contribute on a job (Miles, Porter, & Craft, 1966). They still tend to view motivation as largely a "carrot-and-stick" process, despite the fact that current research has demonstrated that employees by and large want active involvement in organizational activities.

Second, owing primarily to increased automation and machine-paced technology, some managers apparently feel that motivation is no longer a critical issue, since production control is often largely out of the employee's hands. Such a position ignores, however, the impact that turnover, absenteeism, strikes, output restrictions, and the like have on productivity, even with machine-paced technology. And, of course, the potential effects of motivation levels on performance are greatly increased as we move toward a more service-oriented economy.

Third, considering the attitudes of some labor union leaders, we find that a few such leaders apparently still feel that increasing motivational and performance levels might ultimately lead to fewer jobs. Such attitudes in the past have led to the strengthening of the status quo insofar as potential changes in the performance environment were concerned.

It is our contention that such reasoning is somewhat superficial and is, to a large extent, unfounded. The creation of a stimulating, productive, and satisfying work environment can be beneficial for both management and workers if honest concern is shown for all parties involved. If everyone is to derive some benefit from such an environment, however, the problems of the *employee* must be clearly recognized and taken into account. The pivotal role in this process belongs to managers because of their influence in determining the characteristics of the performance environment. If improvements are to be made, management must take the first step. Assuming such an orientation, several implications for managerial practices can be drawn from the material presented here. While this list does not pretend to be all-inclusive, we do feel that it points to several of the more important conclusions to be drawn:

1 Perhaps one of the most important lessons to be learned from the data reviewed here is that, if managers truly want to improve performance and work attitudes, they must take an active role in *managing* motivational processes at work. Managing motivation is conscious, intentional behavior; it is not something that just happens. Any organization desiring to improve attitudes or work behavior must therefore accept responsibility for active involvement and participation if such changes are to be successful.

2 Any attempt by managers to improve the motivational levels of their subordinates should be prefaced by a self-examination on the part of the managers themselves. Are they aware of their major strengths *and* their major limitations? Do they have a clear notion of their own wants, desires, and expectations from their jobs? Are their perceptions of themselves consistent with the perceptions others have of them? In short, before managers attempt to deal with others, they should have a clear picture of their own role in the organizational milieu.

3 The importance of recognizing individual differences across employees has been pointed to time and again throughout the studies reviewed here. Managers should increase their sensitivity to variations in employees' needs, abilities, and traits. Similarly, they should recognize that different employees have different preferences (valences) for the rewards available for good performance. Research has shown, for example, that money as a reward is much more important to some than to others. A greater awareness of such variations allows managers to utilize most efficiently the diversity of talents among their subordinates and, within policy limitations, to reward good performance with those things most desirable to the employees.

4 Somewhat relatedly, it is important that employees see a clear relation between successful performance on their part and the receipt of their desired rewards. It therefore becomes incumbent upon management to be able to identi-

fy superior performers and reward them accordingly. When this is done, employee expectations generally increase, and this in turn tends to lead to greater effort
toward goal attainment. Such an implication raises questions about the use of
non-merit-based compensation systems and of seniority as a major factor in
promotions. Where rewards are not based upon performance, we would expect
motivational levels to be markedly reduced.

5   A further factor to consider is the nature of the tasks which employees
are asked to perform. Questions should be raised by management concerning the
feasibility of providing employees with jobs that offer greater challenge, diversity,
and opportunities for personal need satisfaction. Managers might begin by putting themselves in the place of their subordinates and asking themselves what
they would get out of doing such a job. Similarly, questions should be raised as to
whether employees understand exactly what is expected of them. Research has
shown that increasing role clarity on a job generally increases the likelihood of
improving task performance.

6   In a broader sense, managers could give increased attention to the quality of the overall work environment. How are group dynamics affecting performance? Are the current styles of leadership effective, or would other styles be
preferable? In short, is the "climate" within the work group such that it would
facilitate task accomplishment or do obvious barriers exist that can be remedied?

7   In many cases greater efforts could be made to assess worker attitudes on
a continual basis. In the past, attitude surveys have received little attention outside of personnel departments, or sometimes they have been used as a tool of last
resort when managers have noted a decline in performance. Perhaps a more
effective strategy would be to monitor job attitudes periodically and to use such
information as a motivational barometer to identify potential trouble spots. It is
time for managers to become intelligent consumers of behavioral data so that
they can act more from a position of knowledge and understanding than from
one of uncertainty or ignorance.

8   Finally, if employee motivational levels—and consequently performance—are to be increased, it becomes especially important to involve the employees themselves in a cooperative venture aimed at improving output, for after
all they too have a stake in what happens to the organization. Thus, one key
factor in motivating employees is to allow them to participate more fully in the
processes aimed at attaining organizational effectiveness. Without employee cooperation and support, a great deal of managerial energy can be wasted.

In summary, it is our belief that theories of motivation, as with research in
the behavioral sciences in general, are useful for practicing managers and employees, and are not solely for academicians. Their value lies primarily in their
capacity to sensitize managers and researchers to specific factors and processes
that can have an important bearing on the behavior of people at work. In this
sense, theories and research data in the area of motivation are one more tool
available to managers—and to employees—in the performance of their jobs.

REFERENCES

Adams, J. S. Inequity in social exchange. In L. Berkowitz (ed.) *Advances in experimental social psychology.* Vol. 2. New York: Academic, 1965.

Campbell, J. P., Dunnette, M. D., Lawler, E. E., & Weick, K. E. *Managerial behavior, performance and effectiveness.* New York: McGraw-Hill, 1970.

Carroll, S. J., & Tosi, H. J. Goal characteristics and personality factors in management-by-objectives programs. *Administrative Science Quarterly,* 1970, **15,** 295–305.

Cummin, P. C. TAT correlates of executive performance. *Journal of Applied Psychology,* 1967, **51,** 78–81.

Hackman, J. R., & Lawler E. E., III. Employee reactions to job characteristics. *Journal of Applied Psychology,* 1971, **55,** 259–286.

Hulin, C. L. Individual differences and job enrichment—The case against general treatments. In J. R. Maher (ed.) *New perspectives in job enrichment.* New York: Van Nostrand Reinhold, 1971.

Lawler, E. E., III. Job design and employee motivation. *Personnel Psychology,* 1969, **22,** 426–435.

Locke, E. A., Cartledge, N., & Knerr, C. S. Studies of the relationship between satisfaction, goal-setting, and performance. *Organizational Behavior and Human Performance,* 1970, **5,** 135–158.

Miles, R. E., Porter, L. W., & Craft, J. A. Leadership attitudes among public health officials. *American Journal of Public Health,* 1966, **56,** 1990–2005.

Porter, L. W., & Miles, R. E. Motivation and management. In J. W. McGuire (ed.) *Contemporary management: Issues and viewpoints.* Englewood Cliffs, N.J.: Prentice-Hall, 1974.

Porter, L. W., & Steers, R. M. Organizational, work, and personal factors in employee turnover and absenteeism. *Psychological Bulletin,* 1973, **80,** 151–176.

Steers, R. M. Task-goal attributes, n achievement, and supervisory performance. *Organizational Behavior and Human Performance,* 1975, in press.

Steers, R. M., & Porter, L. W. The role of task-goal attributes in employee performance. *Psychological Bulletin,* 1974, **81,** 434–452.

Vroom, V. H. *Some personality determinants of the effects of participation.* Englewood Cliffs, N.J.: Prentice-Hall, 1960.

Yankelovich, D. *The changing values on campus: Political and personal attitudes on campus.* New York: Washington Square, 1972.

Name Index

Name Index

Adam, E. E., 474, 476, 491, 502
Adams, J. S., 135–136, 138, 142, 145, 149, 153,
     155–167, 169, 173–175, 488, 490, 499, 502, 554,
     556, 559
Adler, A., 36
Albright, L. E., 295
Alderfer, C. P., 32, 39–42, 44–45, 398
Aldis, O., 475, 491–494, 502
Allen, J., 177
Allport, F. H., 263, 275, 315, 317, 325–326, 391, 394
Allport, G. W., 11, 26, 77, 85, 185, 189
Alper, T. G., 420, 424
Altman, I., 346, 358
Alutto, J. A., 257
Anderson, B., 156, 176
Anderson, D., 177
Anderson, L. R., 202, 208, 352–353, 356
Anderson, S., 325–327
Andrews, F. M., 311, 313
Andrews, I. R., 156–163, 169, 171, 176, 516
Andrews, J., 52, 57, 61, 78, 85, 311, 314, 534
Appley, M. H., 9, 26, 41, 45, 49
Argyle, M., 292, 325–326
Argyris, C., 39, 41, 45, 299, 419–421, 423–424
Arnold, M. B., 465–466, 471
Arrowood, A. J., 156–158, 172, 176
Arvey, R., 278, 288–289
Asch, S. E., 316–317, 319, 326
Ashby, E., 496, 502
Atchison, T. J., 279, 292
Athelstan, G. T., 295
Atkinson, J. W., 6, 8–9, 14, 21, 23, 26, 48–52, 54,
     60–61, 69, 72, 74, 85–86, 88, 185, 187–189,
     393, 466, 470–471, 533, 555–556
Atkinson, R. C., 8, 11, 26
Ayllon, T., 494, 502
Azrin, N. H., 494, 502

Back, K., 320, 326
Backman, C. W., 350, 359

Baer, D. M., 494, 502
Baldamus, W., 427, 436
Bales, R. F., 342–343
Ballachey, E. L., 341, 344
Bamforth, K. W., 272, 275
Banas, P., 278, 288–289
Bandura, A., 69, 80, 85, 354, 356, 476, 478, 482–484,
     486–488, 492, 494, 498–499, 502
Banta, T. J., 349, 356
Barnard, C., 441, 449
Barrett, G., 535, 548
Barrett, R. S., 238
Barrientos, G., 519, 522
Barry, J., 107, 112–113, 123, 133
Bartlett, C. J., 300, 304, 306–307
Bass, B. M., 169, 176, 275, 350, 359, 484, 491, 502,
     514, 516, 537, 548
Bassett, G. A., 292
Batten, J. D., 443, 449
Bauer, R. A., 77, 85
Baumgartel, H., 112, 114, 123, 134, 274–275, 292
Bavelas, A., 349, 351, 356
Beck, A. C., 443, 449
Behling, O., 89, 477, 502
Bem, D. J., 500, 502
Bendix, R., 18, 26
Benedict, R., 78, 85
Bennis, W. G., 348, 352, 357, 359
Berberich, J. P., 494, 503
Berelson, B., 6, 26, 69, 73, 76, 78, 81, 85
Berggen, P., 404
Bergman, J. T., 165, 177
Berkowitz, L., 174, 176, 346, 356, 357
Berlew, D. E., 500, 503
Berlew, E. E., 310, 313
Berniger, J., 293
Berry, P., 326–327
Berscheid, E., 174, 176
Biggane, J. F., 424
Biglan, A., 183, 208–218, 445, 450

Subject Index

Subject Index

Abilities, 181, 246–247
Absenteeism, 276–292
  age and, 284
  compared to turnover, 291–292
  family considerations, 287
  future research needs, 292–293
  inequity and, 149
  job characteristics and, 282–284
  job enrichment and, 406, 409
  met expectations and, 291–292
  organization size and, 280
  organizational characteristics and, 280
  pay considerations in, 280
  personality and, 283, 286
  satisfaction and, 276–279
  supervision and, 282
  tenure and, 283
  vocational interests and, 283
  work group influences, 282
  (See also Turnover)
Achievement motivation theory, 47–86
  basic principles, 51–52
  executive performance and, 62–67
  measurement in, 53, 64–65
  motive acquisition, 67–86
  personality and, 48
Achievement-oriented leadership, 390
Action, regulation of, 465–466
Action-outcome associations (see Expectancies)
Action plans, 458–460
Advancement (see Promotion)
Aesthetic needs, 32
Affective anticipations, 470
Affective experiences, 69
Affective orientations, 185
Age:
  conformity and, 320
  equity and, 142, 145

  withdrawal and, 283
Aggression, 63
Alienation, 433
Anomie, 433
Anxiety:
  and behavior, 80
  change and, 103
  cohesiveness and, 320
  money and, 520
Aspiration level (see Level of aspiration)
Assemblyline technology:
  effects of, 396–397
  job redesign and, 404–416
  multiple balances of, 408
Assessment centers, 5
Associative networks, 69
Associative responses, 325
Attachment to organizations, 255–292
  exchange and, 256
  met expectations model, 287–291
  withdrawal and, 276–292
Attitudes:
  and behavior, 221–254
  continuous monitoring of, 559
  favorable, 260
  goal-setting and, 448
  job enrichment and, 406, 414
  and motivation, 22, 181–183
  (See also Job satisfaction)
Authoritarian personality, 56
Authority:
  leadership and, 341, 352
  of supervision, 19
Autokinetic effect, 318
Automation, effects of, 272–273
Autonomy, 19, 413, 432
  change and, 306
  and withdrawal, 282